SCHRIFTEN zur öffentlichen Verwaltung und öffentlichen Wirtschaft

Hrsg. von
Prof. Dr. Dr. h.c. mult. Peter Eichhorn und Prof. Dr. Dr. h.c. Peter Friedrich

Band 202

Prof. Dr. Xiao Feng und Dipl.-Vw. Alina M. Popescu

Infrastrukturprobleme bei Bevölkerungsrückgang

BWV • BERLINER WISSENSCHAFTS-VERLAG

Bibliografische Information der Deutschen Nationalbibliothek

Die Deutsche Nationalbibliothek verzeichnet diese Publikation in der Deutschen Nationalbibliografie; detaillierte bibliografische Daten sind im Internet über http://dnb.d-nb.de abrufbar.

ISBN 978-3-8305-1381-0

Vorwort

Mit diesem Sammelband möchten Freunde, Kollegen und Schüler Prof. Dr. Dr. h.c. Peter Friedrich zum Anlass seiner Emeritierung für seine Förderung und Leistungen im Dienst der Finanz- und Regionalwissenschaft danken. In zahlreichen Publikationen gelang es Prof. Friedrich, sich erfolgreich mit den verschiedensten Problemen der wirtschaftswissenschaftlichen Forschung auseinander zu setzen. Nicht zuletzt hervorzuheben sind seine Beiträge zur Verwaltungsökonomie.

Der Inhalt dieses Bandes beschäftigt sich mit dem in unserer Zeit brisanten Problem des demographischen Wandels. Die Auswirkungen der gesellschaftlichen Überalterung sind bereits heute zu spüren, werden jedoch zukünftig gravierende Einschnitte in die ökonomischen, sozialen und politischen Strukturen in Deutschland erfordern. Dieser Prozess ist jedoch für die meisten entwickelten Industrieländer kennzeichnend.

Mit der Auswahl und Zusammenstellung der Beiträge dieses Bandes wird die Absicht verfolgt, ein möglichst breites Spektrum der aktuellen wirtschaftspolitischen Diskussion zum Bevölkerungsrückgang wissenschaftlich zu erörtern. Die Probleme des öffentlichen Sektors stehen dabei im Mittelpunkt. Unter anderem beschäftigen sich die Autoren im Kontext des demographischen Wandels mit den daraus resultierenden veränderten Bedürfnissen hinsichtlich der Infrastruktur, des Gesundheitswesens und des Arbeitsmarktes. Ferner wird auf die Finanzierungs- und Anpassungsprobleme kommunaler und regionaler Gebietskörperschaften und ihrer Unternehmen hingewiesen.

Der Dank an dieser Stelle gilt den Autorinnen und Autoren der Beiträge sowie den Herausgebern der Schriften zur öffentlichen Verwaltung und der öffentlichen Wirtschaft sowie dem Berliner Wissenschafts-Verlag und der Tongji Universität Shanghai für die Unterstützung der Publikation. Für die redaktionelle Hilfe ist besonders Herrn Dipl.-Vw. Florian W. Bartholomae, Frau Dipl.-Ing. Radoslava Nikolova, Frau Dipl.-Oec. Qian Yang und Frau Helena Sevov zu danken.

Shanghai und München, August 2007

Prof. Dr. Xiao Feng und Dipl.-Vw. Alina M. Popescu

Inhaltsverzeichnis

Erstes Kapitel

Infrastrukturprobleme bei Bevölkerungsrückgang

A. General Considerations on Infrastructure: Essence of the Term, Role of the State, Impacts of Population Decline and Aging

Walter Buhr

I. Infrastructure Provision under a Changing Population Structure

Infrastructure is frequently understood as the sum of public capital stocks, as material infrastructure. Having defined this type of infrastructure and described its outputs, we shall point out in contrast the outstanding relevance of the supplementary constituting influences of the institutional rules and constraints, i.e., institutional infrastructure, and of the workforce and its qualifications, i.e., personal infrastructure, on these capital stocks and outputs. While the competence of the state (communities, Federal States, Federal Government (Bund)) for the creation and maintenance of institutional infrastructure is generally accepted, the role of the state in shaping material and personal infrastructure remains controversial. With respect to material infrastructure, for a long time state production of goods and services has been justified by people's need for future provision of basic necessities for life. Future reforms of this approach endangered by numerous types of government failure in all fields of infrastructure will extensively be discussed. With regard to the impacts of population decline on the requirements for material infrastructure provision, we shall look at the projections of population shrinkage and ageing which will result in a complex picture of future spatial population developments in Germany. On this basis we shall turn to the production of infrastructure outputs depending on the size and structure of population. General aspects of investigation, on the one hand, will concern the problems of estimating and adjusting to material infrastructure needs modified by population changes, particularly in small areas. Special aspects of analysis, on the other hand, will bring up some problems of selected categories of material infrastructure, i.e., housing, health care, and transport. These problems mainly refer to important aspects of institutional infrastructure which is interrelated to personal infrastructure. Concluding remarks sum up essential points of the paper.

II. On the Term “Infrastructure”

1. Defining Material Infrastructure

a) Qualities of Material Infrastructure

Modern language usage identifies infrastructure with material infrastructure meaning an enumeration of public capital stocks such as roads, ports, hospitals, schools, sewerage systems etc. in most cases produced and operated by the state (Frey 1978, p. 201; on the development of the term cf. Schatz 1996). This approach towards a definition of infrastructure is considered to be unsatisfactory on account of the following reasons.

It will be shown that Jochimsen’s (1966) classification of infrastructure in material, personal and institutional infrastructure forms a solid and rewarding basis for the discussion of infrastructure problems. This approach has the advantage of being systematically comprehensive and is in clear contrast to today’s isolated investigations of numerous aspects often preferentially performed by the scientific community. The role of the state in infrastructure provision must be evaluated in a much differentiated way.

Let us turn to the definition of material infrastructure in more detail. Assuming the preferences of the population, the levels of technology, the institutional rules, the level of development and the geographical particularities of a nation as given, material infrastructure is essentially characterized by two distinguishing qualities. The **first trait** refers to the essential prerequisites of human life. Those wants of economic agents (Douglas 1998) originating from physical and social requirements of human beings are satisfied by infrastructure outputs (goods and services) which have been produced by the use of the pertaining immobile, non-circulating capital stocks fixed to the ground, called material infrastructure. For example, the need of drinking water is met by the corresponding supply of water collected, say, in a reservoir which, as a capital good, is a specific type of material infrastructure. A material infrastructure output results from the interplay of its corresponding supply and demand depending on physical or social wants. The supply side is determined by the production functions, finance situation, and organizational structures (including regulations of ownership) of infrastructure producers such as industrial enterprises and administrative units. Representing technical characteristics of production, the production functions relate infrastructure outputs to the factors of production, which are the given quantities of land involved, the labor force employed and the capital stocks utilized (material infrastructure). They are changed by investment. Other cases are given with respect to the direct utilization of capital stocks over time as supplied infrastructure outputs, e.g., in the case of roads. These capital stocks are the capital outputs of preceding production processes. The main problems of production related to material infrastructure such as cost reduction, price formation or network design will not be discussed in the present context (cf., e.g., Bobzin 2006).

With respect to the different requirements of human life to be satisfied by material infrastructure outputs we may set up the following overview in Table 1. It collects important hints, but is not considered as complete.

want	infrastructure output (good or service)	pertinent capital stock (material infrastructure)
physical requirements		
water	drinking water, water for industrial uses, irrigation water, water for generating hydro-electric power	reservoirs, canals, pipes, waterways, irrigation facilities
warmth	gas, oil, electricity, coal, nuclear energy	drilling platforms, pipelines, generation plants, coal mines
light	electricity, gas	generation plants, drilling plants, circuits, pipelines
health	medical care, refuse collection, waste water disposal	hospitals, dumps, sewerage systems
protection against nature, shelter	accommodation, working places, flood protection	houses, buildings, plants, levees
social requirements		
security	legislation (laws), judiciary, stability of the value of money, protection against crimes, outward defense, military goods	public buildings, police stations, military installations
information	usage of telephones, radios, mobile phones, television, Internet, newspapers	telecommunication facilities, post offices, newspaper production works
education	child care, lectures, research, lending out books	kindergartens, schools, universities, research institutions, libraries
mobility	usage of roads by cars, buses, trucks usage of tracks by trains, usage of airports by airplanes usage of ports by ships	roads, highways tracks, train stations airports ports
environmental protection	clean air and water	air purification filters, waterworks

Tab. 1: Material infrastructure to satisfy requirements of human life

This overview has been developed essentially from the viewpoint of households, taking firms and other economic agents to be institutional offspring that evolved during the intensified process of division of labor so that their infrastructure demand is not neglected.

The fundamental importance of the indicated infrastructure goods and services and the pertinent material infrastructure becomes perfectly clear in a spectacular

situation of even temporary emergency such as the substantial contamination of water or the break-down of an electricity supply system.
We should also notice that material infrastructure facilities are usually highly complementary to each other. A good example is housing in relation to public utility networks (e.g., water and energy supply equipment).
The **second** distinguishing **quality** of material infrastructure is the non-availability of infrastructure goods and services to the individual household or firm for production and cost reasons, i.e., economic necessities of mass production. The usually high fixed costs of facilities require the (often joint) production of large volumes of outputs (fixed costs degression). Since the fixed costs are very different comparing various capital stocks, material infrastructure provision takes place under the conditions of different market structures (above all (natural) monopolies (e.g., electricity supply), however, also competition (e.g., housing construction)). We are aware that, at a low level of development, there may be relatively simple and small substitute facilities to satisfy basic infrastructure needs such as household-oriented electricity generators or sewage disposal arrangements.

b) Implications of the Term

The obligation of society, the responsibility of the government, to guarantee the supply of infrastructure goods and services to the individual economic agents of a nation, that is to build up an economy's material infrastructure, results from the second quality of material infrastructure.
The mentioned qualities of material infrastructure, reflected on the background of the given restrictions of analysis, are sufficient to delimit infrastructure goods or services. Here are two examples. Although bread may still our hunger, it is not an infrastructure good, since the inputs for bread production are easily procurable; everybody today is able to bake bread himself (second criterion not fulfilled). Also a car is not an infrastructure good because it belongs into the category of mobile or circulating capital goods which are excluded. Moreover, it cannot fulfill a social need, unless lanes, streets or roads exist. Driving a car implies the demand for road utilization (first criterion not fulfilled).
In a dual view, the satisfaction of the physical and social requirements of human life by material infrastructure outputs corresponds to the creation of the functions of material infrastructure stimulating and supporting economic growth. These functions help to mobilize the economic agents' potentialities and to safeguard the opening and the development of the activities of households, firms and markets. For example, roads enabling mobility of travelers (social requirement) serve economic agents to access specific locations (function of roads) (Buhr 2003, pp.

14 ff.) with the consequence of reduced or increased disparities among regions due to the rate of mobility people are prepared to accept. Reductions of material infrastructure capacities may have contrary effects.

State production of infrastructure goods and services and state ownership of material infrastructure are not stringently necessary characteristics of material infrastructure, as, for example, private schools, private hospitals and private railroads already indicate. If state influences within the institutional framework such as measures of public control are considered necessary, they refer to the economic behavior of producers, not to the infrastructure production process itself. In our context, the term "public capital" and its pretended relevance (Aschauer 1989; Esfahani, Ramirez 2003) have no importance.

Material infrastructure takes on different configurations: point infrastructure (e.g., airports), point-network infrastructure (e.g., electricity supply) and network infrastructure (e.g., roads). These forms may refer to different spatial levels: nation, area, region, community or lot. The capital goods as stocks located in space constitute the spatial order of a nation.

Thus we may define material infrastructure as those immobile, non-circulating capital goods that essentially contribute to the production of infrastructure goods and services needed to satisfy basic physical and social requirements of economic agents and unavailable to the individual economic agents (households, firms etc.) for production and cost reasons so that mass production is economically cogent; the fulfillment of these requirements implies the activation of the functions of material infrastructure.

2. Supplementary Personal and Institutional Infrastructure

a) Definitions

The emphasis on material infrastructure during these days has led to a separation of the important supplementary role of personal and institutional infrastructure, the different aspects of which are usually discussed in specific isolated contexts.

Personal infrastructure (human capital) covers the number (and the structure) and the relevant properties of the working population (e.g., general and special education, qualifications in different functions). That is, we have to consider population as a stock variable and the labor participation rate. Both are changed over time by the birth rate, death rate and migration (quantitative aspect of personal infrastructure). We must also be concerned with the characteristics of the working population (qualitative aspect of personal infrastructure).

Institutional infrastructure comprises all customary and established formal rules and informal constraints (conventions, norms of behavior) of the society as well

as the procedures of enforcement to guarantee and to implement these rules by the state. Codified rules are represented by the legal order which is based on the legal constitution of a nation (the German constitution being the Grundgesetz). From these fundamental principles the economic constitution (Wirtschaftsverfassung) of the country emerges as the sum of economically relevant laws, the legally determined main issues of the economic order (Wirtschaftsordnung) which is also constituted by commonly used economic practices.
Personal and institutional infrastructures also have specific mobilizing and safeguarding functions which are not discussed here.
While the role of the state in creating material and personal infrastructures is controversial, the leading competence of the state for shaping institutional infrastructure is beyond this discussion.

b) Connections

Another outstanding characteristic of infrastructure are the complementarities of its material, personal and institutional aspects. In discussing this issue, we must distinguish two levels of analysis. At the national level the interaction of all three categories of infrastructure constitute the preconditions of economic growth in a market economy. This is Jochimsen's approach (1966) of modifying the assumptions and results of Eucken's (1955; 1965) path breaking work on the economic order. Here institutional infrastructure, the economic order (critical criterion for a market economy: share of net investment in net domestic product), determines the market solutions of the growth problem, assuming the absence of growth barriers on the side of personal infrastructure. The location decisions of investment (critical criterion: long-run social or private profit) link the market results of the economic order to the spatial order of a market economy (critical criterion: distance) which displays material infrastructure facilities.
At the disaggregate, i.e., sector and region or community, level we may start from the demand for and supply of material infrastructure outputs. Personal infrastructure includes the employed workforce producing infrastructure supplies. Institutional infrastructure may refer to the demand for material infrastructure goods and services and, on the supply side, to the objective functions of producers, to the spheres of finance, organization (e.g., ownership solution), and investment in material infrastructure. Also personal infrastructure may be substantially influenced by institutional infrastructure, e.g., by population policy or education policy. The three categories of infrastructure obtain different weights according, for example, to the type of capital stock considered or to its state of existence (facilities under construction, unchanged, in the process of enlargement). A good example is an existing hospital (material infrastructure): The necessary

standards of health care outputs are dominantly guaranteed by the personnel including doctors, nurses etc. (personal infrastructure) working, associated by a given technical equipment, according to certain rules (medical knowledge; remuneration, insurance and payment rules as parts of institutional infrastructure).
Starting from personal infrastructure, specifically from actual employment in the private and public sectors of an economy, this employment may be taken as the result of the labor markets. In these markets the supplies of and the demands for labor are confronted. The supply side is determined by the working population (Clark et al. 1978; Grünheid, Höhn 1999; Börsch-Supan 2002; Johnson 2002) and the demand side by the labor requirements specific for the private sector and the public sector. The organization of the labor markets, the labor demand of the public sector and the volume and qualifications of the workforce (dependent, among other factors, also on education policies) are subject to the pertinent regulations of institutional infrastructure which are not discussed further here (cf., e.g., Franz 2003, pp. 17ff., 102f., 235ff).
Many practical problems of infrastructure provision arise because of neglecting the necessary interrelationships of material, personal and institutional infrastructure at the disaggregate level.

III. The State as Guarantor for the Future Provision of Basic Necessities for Life

1. Public Provision of Infrastructure

a) Future Provision of Basic Necessities for Life

The problems to be pursued now refer to the general regulatory and penetrating conditions of the economic system for the necessary adjustment of infrastructure, essential material and institutional infrastructure, to population shrinkage and ageing under way in Germany.
The public administrative supply of mainly material infrastructure, as one of the major state tasks, is called the future provision of basic necessities for life (Daseinsvorsorge) by Forsthoff (1973, pp. 368 ff., 410 f., 567ff.), a representative of public law, not an economist. This interpretation can be found in the German Constitution (Grundgesetz), especially Art. 87. The competition rules of the EC-Treaty of 2002 speak about "services of general economic interest" (Art. 86).
The role of the state in providing material infrastructure and its outputs must be questioned. First, throughout Europe consumers are dissatisfied, remarkably with the infrastructure goods and services offered by public production. Second, public activities have reached such dimensions that their output quality has often substantially suffered. Government failures in this respect have indeed become

regular. Third, there are alternatives to the exclusive public provision of infrastructure.

In more depth of argumentation, the people's confidence in well-meant effects of state activities obviously has historical reasons. This reliance on state operations dates back to times when Germany was made up of a substantial number of relatively small states governed by sovereign rulers who understood themselves, in the spirit of paternalistic protection, regimentation and care for subsistence, as benefactors of their subjects. The political background of the creation of state-owned enterprises (railroads, postal monopolies) at the end of the nineteenth century was a mixture of fiscal interests, religious objectives, protectionist group interests, and military considerations (Donges et al. 1993, p. 19). Moreover, there are a number of examples of how historical influences have determined the German federal economic order. An impact on the creation of this economic order can be related to the national-socialist economic policy of the Third Reich (1933-1945), as Ritschl (2005) demonstrates. All historical influences, especially concerning economically relevant activities of the state, must be reconsidered, many of them probably eliminated under economic aspects.

The capability of the state to secure the future provision of necessities for basic life requirements depends on the economic situation of the country. The sole reference to the implications of public finance in a federal state makes this point clear. If the German government nowadays withdraws from specific material infrastructure activities, the reasons are mostly of a financial nature (e.g., in the case of hospital privatization). This approach, dictated by the shortage of financial means, is unsatisfactory from a systematic economic viewpoint. Sound reasoning requires, in the sense of an overhaul of institutional infrastructure, the renaissance of Germany's economic order, the concept of the social market economy. In this context, Siebert (2005, Ch. 15) pleads, first, against the given level of support for the aim of social protection and equity, relying on distribution by government, and for rigorous stimulation of dynamic economic forces, originating from decentralized decisions, effort and initiative of the individual; second, against upholding collective interest and for favoring actively individual liberty; and third, against corporatist decision-making and for strengthening competition. An improvement of the institutional organization of market conditions will decisively help to tackle the general and infrastructure problems of a declining and ageing population (Klös, Kroker 2005).

As to the present economic situation of Germany, the central problems have been considerable lasting unemployment, especially of the unskilled, and, during the past ten years, slow growth resulting from the inflexibility of labor markets (rigidity of wages and wage structure mainly due to trade union power in nationwide collective bargaining), lack of investment at home (because of an exces-

sively complex, inadequate tax system, substantial non-wage employment costs, high direct investment abroad) and deficiency of consumer demand (due to the insecurity of consumers as to their employment and income opportunities in the future) and aggravated by the relatively fast ageing of the German population.
Other major consequences have been permanent budget deficits leading to a steadily increasing public debt and a social insurance system being in crisis. The ensuing effects of lacking adjustability of the German economy were made worse by outside shocks (Sinn 2005a). For example, the German re-unification which has turned out to be a failure in economic terms was predominantly understood as a problem of an adequate material infrastructure, neglecting the other two important fields of infrastructure. Eastern EU enlargement which brought new low-wage competition may be identified as an essential problem of personal infrastructure. And intensified globalization can be taken as a problem of an institutional infrastructure that is everywhere accepted.
The problems of present reforms are so numerous that only a few examples can be given. Among the general problems of the political sphere – particularly in the realm of personal infrastructure – is the omnipresent lack of economic reasoning leading to the corresponding waste of resources, time and human energy. Accordingly, many politicians do not understand the functioning of a market economy; those, who do, do not dare to explain to the people how a market economy works (Sinn 2005b). Politicians at least push away the insight that the market system strengthened by the effects of personal liberty thrives on change, inspiring new technologies, products, and profit opportunities, whereas democracy pursuing the objective of security as a consequence of social justice resists change. Political action creates powerful constituencies with a stake in the status quo (Samuelson 2005). Practical economic policy, nowadays in essence distribution policy, either reacts, in a superficial way without any concept, to problems urgently to be solved or creates laws at first sight in a rather simple and plausible form, but then complicated by exceptions and special rules in the sense of equity until any clearness will have gone lost.
Correspondingly, on the side of the population, there is increasing demand for the caring hand of the state. Getting alarmed at any change, e.g., inherent in market operations, as is typical for most older people, the citizen is considered a charge by the state. Germans also suffer from "equalities", an envy complex which generally renders wealth suspect and egoistical motives suspicious. So "...envy under the cover of demands for social justice penetrates the public debate" (Sinn 2005b).

b) Government Failures

In Germany government failures are a never ending story, concerning the state as an entrepreneur as well as an institution responsible for economic policy, public finance and budgetary policy (as a starting point in the literature cf. Jänicke 1987). The following examples make it clear that it needs careful analysis in each given case to separate the influences of the different fields of infrastructure. Related to material infrastructure, for instance, there are deficiencies in accountancy and all types of calculations (e.g., concerning actual project costs that turn out to be much higher than estimated costs); there is a lack of reports on the state of capital stocks (e.g., security of public buildings), on necessities of repair and re-investment. Projects without economic justification become realized (e.g., projects without future demand or dubious show projects). No assistance to objects, but to users should be the general rule of support, e.g., for low-cost housing since otherwise persons not in need of inexpensive accommodation will be supported (Engels et al. 1984, p.7).

As to personal infrastructure, for instance, politicians undertake experiments on cost reductions without any change of the underlying outdated institutional structures (e.g., in health care rewarding doctors who offer little care to their patients). Leaving aside the neglect of very serious problems, e.g., the reduction in the number of births in Germany since the 1970's, badly defined reforms have occurred which take a relatively long time to come properly into existence. The background for these circumstances is the permanent creation of new problems due to the fact that, contrary to superior knowledge, measures inadequate with respect to the causes of the problems are taken (cf., e.g., Eckey, Kosfeld 2005). One consequence is over regulation of, e.g., the activities of privatized, former public utilities. People, particularly firms, and public administration must often deal with an excess of regulations and laws. In many cases their basic intentions have been lost. As a result we observe all sorts of injustices (cf., e.g., German tax laws leading to the creation of a substantial underground economy) so that a reduction of bureaucracy as a perverse development of institutional infrastructure is urgently required. Government departments should work as service units to satisfy citizens' demand for adequate and solid infrastructure outputs rather than employ officials competent for certain subjects. The "responsibility" for mismanagement is often without any substance, since its ex-post investigative control usually ends up in a political or administrative blame-game. The education and qualification demands of civil servants and other employees in public administration must be raised.

Concerning institutional infrastructure two problems will be addressed as examples. On the one hand, there is no clear delimitation of the political tasks of the area public bodies (Federal Government, Federal States, communities) and correspondingly no solid distribution of financial means among these bodies in Germany. Mixed finance in the federal system and compound liability of the federal government for the states seduces the Federal States to initiate expenditures, particularly on material infrastructure, that they otherwise would not have made. On the other hand, it is an incredible fact that no savings have been accumulated in the past to cover future payments of civil servants' pensions. This is a "very special kind" of reference to the state guarantee of public provision of future basic necessities for its former employees.

In summary, these remarks should suffice to justify doubts about the capabilities of reform with respect to material, personal, and institutional infrastructure within the German political and administrative system. It can often hardly be evaluated what the critical points concerning system reform in detail mean to infrastructure provision. However, the spectrum of government failures and inefficiencies describes the framework within which we have to adjust material, institutional, and also personal infrastructure to the anticipated changes in population structure.

What answer in general terms can be given to the existence of government failures in the field of infrastructure? Following the insight that the high state share in national product is incompatible with the given economic order of a market economy, the general answer must be to reduce the scope of state activities here particularly in the fields of material and institutional infrastructure and to increase the efficiency of infrastructure provision. The advancement of efficiency must be the major aim of future reforms. Generally, there is indication that the strategy of improved efficiency is best suited to overcome a shock such as a birth rate reduction (Buhr 1987).

2. Suggested Reforms of Infrastructure Provision

a) Objective of Equity

The subsequently given issues of analysis and political action must be pursued in greater detail, each approach of reform being individually evaluated in a careful way.

As indicated above, an important and urgent task will be the far-reaching abandonment of the imprecise, equivocal and ill-founded objective of social justice in order to abolish the negative growth effects of distribution and redistribution policy. Two aspects are worth mentioning. First, recently the present German Minister of Finance Steinbrück published his theoretical guidelines of an activating state. His main point is: "...the most important task of the state (is) to enable every citizen to lead a self-determined life, to develop his capabilities and to fortify his existence by the exercise of his own faculties" (Steinbrück 2006). The mindful reader will discover a model of shaping the living conditions of the members of society. It seems to be acceptable, if this approach would solely be restricted to the implementation of the aim of equalizing opportunities for all economic agents (Rawls 1972, pp. 60 ff., 90ff.), e.g., to satisfy people's basic requirements such as their demand for education. However, in a wider context, we may also be afraid to be confronted with an invitation of the state to lobbying (e.g., of the health care industry) which implies reinforced stimuli to distribution policy of various forms, thus most probably again worsening the budget situation. The state must rather strengthen individual liberty in order to support the sphere of production (Barbier 2006). Second, the defense of public economic activity is weakest if deficit-prone public enterprises in the realm of material infrastructure are justified on the ground of price policies according to social aspects (Friedrich 1987, pp. 18 ff.). Social and structural-political obligations make the firms' adjustment to market conditions very difficult so that redistribution by means of price policy presupposes monopolistic market positions for the public enterprises. Thus, this type of social policy is expensive in terms of inefficiency (Donges et al. 1993, pp. 21 f.).

b) Economic Reasoning

Another approach to fight against government failures is a stronger emphasis on thinking in economic terms. In principle, it is absolutely intolerable that amateurs in economics have any say in economic decision-making. There is no hospital in the world where operations are performed by medical laymen. If the state supply of basic necessities for life is justified in public law by infrastructure provision needs of the population (Forsthoff 1973, p. 410), this argument may be satisfactory from a formal viewpoint, but it has no sufficient material content, i.e., no solid economic basis. The decisive disadvantage of tax finance of material infrastructure (roads, education, public buildings) is that there are no prices for the usage of the facilities, leaving aside the exceptions where road pricing was installed. As a consequence, people feel that the usage of these infrastructure capital stocks is free, explaining the practical difficulties of introducing road pricing schemes. A rigorous position in our general context was formulated by Tinbergen (1962, pp. 132 f.). He suggests that the decision on the public or private provision of material infrastructure should be subject to cost-benefit analysis. This means that the state officials as competitors, e.g., in project construction, must demonstrate the economic superiority of their proposal as compared to private solutions in order to be successful as to project realization – an approach implying a substantial reduction of the sovereign rights and power monopoly of the state. Even more rigorous is the strict and direct application of the principle of relativeness in the context of the policy of privatization and state holdings as formulated by the Federal Minister of Finance in 1990. Accordingly, it is not the task of the state to act as entrepreneur and to accumulate property to the disadvantage of the private economic agents in the spirit of the social market economy characterized by private initiative and private property (Donges et al. 1993, pp. 17 f.).

c) Deregulation

Let us assume that it is correct to divide the tasks of the state into two groups, those being superfluous today so that they can be eliminated immediately and those being superfluous soon (Milbradt 2005, p. 433). Then we take a short cut in suggesting the concentration of state activities on rationalizing and consolidating institutional infrastructure, especially the body of laws and other rules, and its pertinent public administration (Eichhorn, Friedrich 1976; Friedrich 1977) in order to reduce bureaucracy (Sachverständigenrat "Schlanker Staat" 1998). In a dual view, this aim indicates simultaneously to mobilize and strengthen private initiative acting within the framework of institutional infrastructure. In this sense, more specifically it is necessary to define guidelines for delineating the private and the government sector (Niskanen 1992). It is advisable to delimit carefully the elements of institutional infrastructure. For example, the term "commonweal economy" (Gemeinwirtschaft) has different meanings, one being non-governmental enterprises serving the fulfillment of public aims or tasks (Thiemeyer 1970, p. 22). Since the theory of the commonweal economy was taken to have the function of an ideology (von Weizsäcker 1987, p. 89) and thus being not convincing, it shall be dropped in this context. However, an important fact here is to improve qualitatively the production of genuine public goods such as legislation and judiciary, administration of the community, in particular internal national security, safeguard of the value of money, and outward defense. They are all related to the social requirement of security, a basic aim of society.
First steps of redirecting and reorganizing state activities have been subsumed under the heading of deregulation. This term refers to a broad scope of objectives ranging from an increase of competition in regulated product markets (Siebert 2005, Ch. 8) to privatization, from a reduction of bureaucracy to an introduction of market prices instead of regulated public prices. For details compare the two reports of the German Deregulation Commission (Deregulierungskommission 1990; 1991) which deal with transportation and electricity supply as far as material infrastructure is concerned. It should be clear – though frequently ignored –

that the state is and must be liable for public property; there can be no exceptions referring to deregulation (e.g., safety of public baths). Good examples of deregulation are given by important German infrastructure sectors such as telecommunications, electricity, railroads, and housing. In telecommunication, energy and railway industry problems of deregulation were tackled or are planned to be solved by vertical separation of private or public network provision from mostly private operation (cf. Rothengatter 1990; for the reform of railways in the United Kingdom cf. Quinet, Vickerman 2004, pp. 309 ff.; with respect to access regulation for the natural gas sector cf. von Hirschhausen 2006). Whether there will be sufficient investment into network quality mainly depends on the conditions of demand, i.e., on the type of access prices (freely set or regulated prices, prices linear or non-linear in relation to the amount of network access demanded, prices dependent on quality of service) (Buehler et al. 2004). Since new firms entered the market in telecommunications, it is now possible to select the supplier individually for every telephone call. Concerning decisions on the rededication of land for housing construction it should be required that all political objectives must be evaluated in a specific context. Even if the protection of the environment is an important aim in densely populated areas, it should not have absolute priority in view of the also existentially relevant objective of providing adequate accommodation of all citizens.

d) Regulatory Responsibility

Existing and new public activities or projects are or will be undertaken by the state, if the principle of production responsibility (Erfüllungsverantwortung) is pursued. In order to introduce private initiatives and influences, the state must increasingly concentrate on the principle of regulatory responsibility (Gewährleistungsverantwortung). Instead of public production the emphasis should lie on private production under public control (as an element of institutional infrastructure) of varying degrees in the fields of material and personal infrastructure (Bundesministerium für Verkehr, Bau- und Wohnungswesen (BVBW), Bundesamt für Bauwesen und Raumordnung (BBR) 2005, p. 13). The necessity of control of economic agents – by other agents, by the state, also by themselves – generally arises from the complex processes of the division of labor in view of the deficiencies of human thinking and action. The insight into this simple statement is missing; there is no culture of control due to the following reasons: (a) Cooperation in the sphere of labor and other interactions (e.g., city traffic) is more of an exception than the rule so that mistakes, errors and their expensive consequences are taken for granted. Also the institution of control within a group may be taken to have a frustrating and thus negative output effect. (b) Control is often neglected due to a lack of financial means (e.g., for control procedures of food chemistry). (c) There is considerable resistance to control measures due to objections against restrictions or excessively felt restrictions of individual freedom or against supervision, opposition to presumably or really absurd regulations of bureaucracy, and serious doubt in the integrity of the controllers. Economically, control can only be justified if the costs of a control measure are smaller than the pertinent benefits. This would be the case in publicly controlling the quality of drinking water supplied by a private waterworks.

e) Privatization

For the future, it turns out to be most necessary to reduce state entrepreneurial activities and to activate much more intensively private production initiatives. Private entrepreneurship is an outstanding expression of mobilizing the potentialities of private economic agents which constitutes the basic function of infrastructure – regarding privatization the reference is institutional infrastructure.

Before privatization came up as a key element in structural reform programs in the early 1980s (on the different forms of and criteria for privatization cf. Hofmann 1998), many countries had chosen nationalization over regulation as the instrument for control of monopoly power in the network industries (principal German state holdings in energy and water provision, transportation and banking). Important examples of "natural" monopolies can be found among network monopolies such as public utilities. These monopolies are given if one supplier, respectively, is able to satisfy market demand for a particular good at fewer costs than several producers. The fixed costs associated with a phone or power line network are considerable in comparison to lower variable costs, the result being substantially decreasing average costs as a function of the number of end users. Thus large utilities may undercut their smaller competitors until they remain the sole providers (Knieps 2001, pp. 24 ff.). Price formation – and subsequently investment (Friedrich 1969) – is the central issue of state-owned enterprises in a market economy, since they must not only pursue economic objectives, but also political goals and restrictions. Assuming also that the first objective of the firm is welfare improvement rather than profit maximization, the marginal cost principle of price formation emerges clearly as the focal point of the theory of public enterprise (Friedrich 1978; Bös 1981). Its practical relevance remains controversial (Gesellschaft für öffentliche Wirtschaft und Gemeinwirtschaft 1978; Bös 1986, pp. 410 f.).

In the last decades public enterprises in many cases suffered from severe performance problems such as poor service delivery and lackluster growth, acting according to poorly defined, conflicting objectives and under damaging political interference. Attempts at reforming state-owned enterprises often did not bring the desired results. Thus it became evident that radical structural change in the forms of privatization (Donges et al. 1993, pp. 25 ff.) was required, "... with the public's role mainly restricted to that of regulation which seeks to ensure a fair policy development and recognition of social and other policy goals" (Kessides 2005, p. 20). In the meantime we have enough empirical experience to derive basic "lessons" from privatization. Among them is support for the proposition that privately owned firms are more efficient and more profitable than comparable state-owned enterprises (Gonzalez-Paramo, Hernandez De Cos 2005; Megginson et al. 2005, pp. 9 f.). This statement in favor of private firms may be due to cost reductions as a consequence of more efficient management, improvements of output quality at constant output prices or strict avoidance of losses since public subsidies or inexpensive public capital are no longer available (Löbbe 1986, p. 24). However, it is difficult to reach an unequivocal verdict about the effects of privatization (Kessides 2005, pp. 21 ff.) because of the different starting conditions for the individual privatization projects and the actual performance of each privatized enterprise. Regarding the starting conditions, three points must be raised: (a) the institutional framework within which the state sell-off takes place (e.g., the most convincing results have been achieved where privatization has been accomplished in a competitive environment) (North 1992, Bishop, Kay 1992; Bortolotti 2005); (b) the implementation of a solid economic concept of privatization without deficiencies and contradictions (e.g., the network provider must accept a regulated access tariff independent of network usage intensity, thus not being interested in the maintenance of network quality) (Knorr, Eichinger 2002; Kuhlmann 2004a; Ströbele 2004; Kuhlmann 2004b); (c) the existence of an enterprise staff sufficiently qualified and experienced in organizing the transformation of economic activities from governmental to private control (e.g., at its start the privatization of the German telecommunication industry suffered from serious management mistakes). Substantial problems may be encountered in cases, which represent the partial or total privatization of public goods production (e.g., private operation of a prison; establishment of a private army); here the extent of privatization is a matter of the characteristics of each case. Finally, there are cases in which privatization will be rejected. For example: In Germany the provision of drinking water is characterized by low efficiency (CESifo Group Munich 2005). Supervision and ownership of the network as a natural monopoly is recommended to remain in the hands of the communities or the state, since private owners have little incentives to maintain the network at an optimal state so that waste and losses of water as well as dangers to health can be avoided. By property rights and holdings the state representatives influence the operations of water supply, typified by provision security and quality, by regional monopolists. The monopolistic market structure originates from water being a very heterogeneous product. In order to increase the efficiency of provision, mergers of water suppliers and partnerships of privately owned enterprises are suggested.

f) Regulation

The establishment of a regulatory system is the key to utility privatization (Blankart, Faber 1982; Quinet, Vickerman 2004, Ch. 9; Siebert 2005, Ch. 8). Since only the range of regulation to be restricted is of interest here, the following discussion will solely concentrate on some basic problems of regulation (also Knieps 2001, pp. 79 ff.). First, public regulation may refer to the control of prices, qualities and quantities sold of goods, of rates of return on capital as well as of market entry or exit of competitors. The consequences become realized in distorted price structures, internal cross-subsidization of products and increased capital input in the sense of the Averch-Johnson effect (Averch, Johnson 1962). Implementing the control of the mentioned magnitudes, processes and consequences creates information problems stemming from incomplete and asymmetrically distributed information. Second, while privatization implies the elimination of state influence, regulation means the return of public interference in private activities. Here, the problem may easily be overregulation as it exists, e.g., in the German telecommunications industry. At present there is sufficient network competition in this field so that regulation of market power has become obsolete and general competition law should apply (Knieps 2005). In setting up regulations it would pay to act and to adjust slowly and carefully to changing circumstances. The application of rules of thumb may be useful, for instance, a rule dealing with the relationship of output price and profit variations in the case of a monopoly (Buhr, Christiaans 2001). Third, there is little empirical knowledge on the dynamic aspects of regulation. Over time it represents a process of continuous actions and reactions of the regulated enterprise and the regulation agency, in which no party may dispose of complete information on the future behavior of the other participant. Correspondingly, decisions based on conjectures about the future behavior of the other side will be affected by mistakes. Thus, regulation is a self-correcting process of reciprocal answers with successive information analysis. On the theoretical implications of regulation dynamics see Bobzin (2002).

g) Public Private Partnerships

Looking at the installation of new infrastructure projects, privatization of existing facilities corresponds to the operator model of material infrastructure provision. According to this build-own-operate approach a private enterprise takes care of the planning, finance, construction and operation of the project. Public or own revenues reimburse the operator (example: municipal facilities of sewage disposal). No state participation characterizes the consortium model as was applied to the construction of the Channel tunnel between France and England. If we abstractly reduce the impact of private agents, we may turn to public private partnerships in project realization, i.e., the switch in the fulfillment of public tasks to private enterprises in the context of partnership collaboration, maintaining certain defined state influences. This form of cooperation is pursued, e.g., by about a quarter of German communities when erecting public buildings such as schools, town-halls, physical training and entertainment facilities. The other communities lack the necessary experience to found the relevant partnerships, so that intensified propagation of this form of cooperation is desirable. The incorporation of private agents results in an increase of operational efficiency (cost reduction, improvement of output quality), the mobilization of additional capital and the acceleration in the completion of infrastructure projects. The confrontation of the public and private spheres also creates tensions, e.g., originating from budget laws. The dedication of public expenditures to a particular year finds little understanding in the circles of private agents; however, exceptions may be possible. Moreover, expert knowledge in legal, financial and economic details is required on both sides. The starting point of public private partnerships was private financing of infrastructure investments, the advantage of which over public funding may be given including tax effects in private financial calculations (Willms 1998, pp. 13 ff.). According to the build-own-transfer approach and the build-own-operate-transfer approach the planning, finance and construction of infrastructure projects occur under private administration. The transfer of the project into public hands takes place either immediately or after a certain time span, respectively. The private partner is either a leasing corporation (leasing model) or a fund (fund model), the planning being ex ante performed by the state in these models (both models can be found in highway construction). The main difference between these two models is the method of financing: the leasing corporation uses bank credits, whereas the fund mainly reverts to deposits of private economic agents. In the similar license model the license-taker acquires a building permit without becoming the proprietor of the ground. From the start of the project operations the state pays a remuneration agreed upon. At the end of license duration the object will be transferred to the state. Cooperation models solely refer to the interaction of the state, the communities and the private economy in the sphere of project finance (example: dump clearance and renewal).

h) Political System

In view of the inefficiencies of the present political system, we should also consider reforms of the existing structure of democracy, particularly related to personal and institutional infrastructure. This is a wide field so that only one suggestion may suffice: the prohibition of the immediate re-election of politicians. Before his election the future member of parliament must inform the public on his professional education. He has to be suspended from his current job, with the firm obligation to return to this job after his time of mandate. It will last five years at a maximum. The politician's re-election will only be possible after a considerable time will have elapsed. This model refers to the social duties of every individual that takes his political liberties serious. The applicant of political office will make the experience that his compulsion to populism and popularity will be greatly reduced. His service will approach an honorary activity in which he will be rewarded by the pertinent prestige. The political parties must recruit competent candidates in order to educate them according to their objectives. Thus, in the long run, the parties will represent a larger segment of the population as before by the permanent rotation of their representatives in office.
The kinds and extent of existing government failures and the progress of reforms, above all in the fields of institutional and personal infrastructure, will decisively determine the future impacts of the changing population structure on producing outputs related to material infrastructure.

IV. Impacts of Population Shrinkage and Ageing on Infrastructure Provision

1. Population Decline and Ageing in Germany

Subsequently, a sketch of the expected population development in Germany for the time 2000-2050 will be given. This rough outline is justified by the intentions of this paper and the estimation problems of national and regional population projections (as introductions cf. Schwarz 1969; Mälich 1973). Think, e.g., about the determinants of future death rates, among them the unknown consequences of obesity or of a pandemic.
Future national population (and work force) development in Germany is characterized by insufficient reproduction, a low total fertility rate (= average number of births per woman), and ageing, an increasing old dependents ratio (= number

of persons older than 65 years in relation to the number of persons aged 15 to 64 years). Positive net migration, i.e., there will be more arrivals than departures, will not suffice to cover the growing birth deficit (= difference between the number of deaths and births). Probably between 2010 and 2020 the increase of German population will be reversed so that it will begin to shrink (Birg 2000; Sinn 2005c, pp. 55 ff.). With reference to the age structure it was calculated that the number of young people below 20 years of age will be reduced, that the number of persons aged 20 to 59 years will be augmented until 2020 and then decrease, and that the older people of 60 years and more will increase in number at least until 2030. In all German States the older population group is already larger than the younger group. In 2050 the relationship will be two to one (Sommer 2005, pp. 101 ff.). Due to international immigration society will be more differentiated with regard to origin and cultural background (heterogenization of population). And the average number of people per household will be falling (individualization of population).

The low fertility rate in Germany which is an outstanding issue of personal infrastructure is mainly explained by society's lack of support for women in the solution of their problems of matching their roles as housewife and mother with their professional aspirations. The deficiencies must be understood as a bundle: lack of maternal infrastructure and care (day-nurseries, kindergartens, all-day schooling), lack of sufficient financial support such as child allowance, and lack of part-time working arrangements.

"More and more regions in West Germany are being hit by ... (population) decline. Advancing from the East, a "shrinkage wedge" is moving across major areas of eastern North Rhine-Westphalia into southern Lower Saxony, northern Hesse, and northern Bavaria. And the decline of population in East Germany has amplified" (Müller, Siedentop 2004, p. 16), also under the influence of East-West migration. This wedge will be embraced by a semi-circle of areas marked by stable to increasing population in West Germany ranging from Kiel via Hamburg, the Ruhr district (north and west of Düsseldorf), Wiesbaden/Mainz, Stuttgart to Munich (BVBW, BBR 2005, pp. 6 f.).

In the built-up regions growing and shrinking communities will exist side by side. Soon in the West and about fifteen years later in the East core cities of urbanized regions will lose population to a varying degree; there will be population increases in eastern agglomeration areas up to 2020. While the population loss of the city of Berlin will be substantial, the cities of Dresden, Leipzig and Erfurt will experience rather modest population shrinkages. At about 2020 the trend toward suburbanization will weaken in the West without sustained reurbanization, as this process is already under way in the East. The core cities and urbanized environs will be supported by the intake of immigrants from abroad. Rural

areas will generally shrink, more so in the East than in the West (Müller, Siedentop 2004; Röhl 2005, pp. 331 ff.).
Ageing of population happens everywhere, in the West and the East, in the cities and the rural areas, with different dynamics. This process will develop stronger and quicker in the East than in the West, in the periphery and the countryside more vigorous than in the core cities (BVBW, BBR 2005, p. 8).
Future population distribution at the disaggregate level will be determined by a number of changing factors such as economic development, institutional arrangements, provision of material and personal infrastructure, proximity to cities and quality of housing environment (Bode 2002; Franz 2004; Gans, Schmitz-Veltin 2005).
In all, we depicted a complex picture of population development in Germany for the future.

2. Population-dependent Provision of Infrastructure Goods and Services

a) General Aspects: Estimation of and Adjustment to Modified Material Infrastructure Needs

The influence of population on infrastructure draws our attention to the determinants of material and personal infrastructure provision (on planning cf. Klaus 1984), population being one of the main determinants of infrastructure. Accordingly, the spatial population distribution, among other factors, determines the spatial order of material infrastructure facilities. Thus we shall look at the population-dependent production of material infrastructure goods and services (cf. Table 2). Observe that, in this context, the consideration of the subsequent effects of material infrastructure facilities on population distribution is usually neglected (an exception is von Rohr 1981).
The material infrastructure category of housing takes a central place in Table 2 because (1) it refers to the physical requirement of shelter for human life; (2) houses or apartments are directly connected to other infrastructure categories, e.g., to water and energy networks; (3) the places of accommodation are the locations of population and thus the reference points for trips to workplaces, infrastructure supplies such as schooling and services of the tertiary sector.
Most of the given infrastructure fields are specific with regard to the age groups indicated. The shifting of the age structure, e.g., in favor of the elderly and in disfavor of the young people leads to increasing demand for infrastructure goods and services for the older generation (e.g., in the health care sector or in old aged care) and to decreasing demand for youth-related infrastructure outputs. In order to capture the dependencies of infrastructure provision on population variables,

mostly constant usage factors, e.g., per capita quantities or values, or constant relationships are applied, e.g., number of pupils per school class, number of classes per elementary school or pupil-teacher relationships. On the problems connected with these proportionality factors (Müller, Siebert 1977). The question of how to determine the future size of an infrastructure capacity in view of a continuously shrinking local population without having to readjust the capacity with substantial costs from time to time in the future is of particular interest here. Additional estimation problems arise from given excess capacities of indivisible large units, the consideration of peak demand, of age, wear and tear of equipment, the rededication of facilities due to the realization of other applications, the restructuring of service areas of facilities to comply with minimum sizes of population or minimum standards of provision and the measures of eliminating usage barriers such as kindergarten fees (Markus 1978). Finally, let us also have in mind that population decline can be an opportunity to think about the renewal and modernization of capital stocks and to plan improved output qualities.

infrastructural provision of population	main material infra-structure category	age of population	spatial reference
accommodation, drinking water supply systems, sewage disposal systems, energy supply facilities, IT-connections	housing and related material infrastructure categories	young, middle aged, old	city, urbanized area
hospitals (obstetrics, child care etc.), homes for aged people, day-care homes, cemeteries, leisure time homes for the youth, physical training grounds, facilities for the treatment of youth delinquency, public baths, recreation facilities	health care	young, middle aged, old	city, urbanized area
day-nurseries, kindergartens, children playgrounds, primary and secondary schools, special schools, colleges, universities, facilities for workplace assistance and retraining courses	Education	young, middle aged	city, urbanized area, state
Roads, highways	Transport	young, middle aged, old	city, urbanized area, state

Tab. 2: Population-dependent material infrastructure

Some of these problems may be coped with or mitigated by adjustment strategies (on difficulties and opportunities cf. also Robinson 1982, pp. 277 ff.). Here we must observe that we have no experience and knowledge in the management of a changing population structure and its consequences for material infrastructure provision. Table 3 indicates the most important alternative policy options of infrastructure adjustment, their characteristics, and the possible changes of service areas. This table is taken, in a slightly changed form (BVBW, BBR 2005, p. 31).

policy option	Characteristic	service area	example
increase of accessibility	improvement of transport to increase carrier usage	larger, same	demand-oriented transport supply
reduction	proportional reduction of supply according to population decline	same, smaller	reduced bus network
decentralization	separation into smaller efficient units (high network costs)	smaller	several biological sewerage treatment plants instead of one big treatment unit
centralization (with accessibility strategy)	merger of underutilized units with complementary improvement of accessibility	larger	merger of different schools with the introduction of a school bus system
Temporarily mobile approaches	provision at limited time available	same	mobile library
restructuring, substitution	purpose reached by new method of problem solution	depends on case	reorganization and consolidation of medical tasks of several regional hospitals

Tab. 3: Policy options of infrastructure adjustment

The change of service areas of different infrastructure facilities may make it necessary to improve the coordination of communal construction zoning so that decentralized planning of infrastructure provision in space will be created without gaps (for a detailed analysis cf. Bloch 1982, pp. 41 ff.) and to redefine the central place system of German regional economic policy (Jost 1974, pp. 75 ff.; BVBW, BBR 2005, pp. 56 ff.).

Even if the adjustment measures will successfully be realized, population deconcentration of settlement areas will lead to considerable increases of tied-up infrastructure capital per resident, ultimately augmenting average provision costs of existing systems. Thus, infrastructure charges and prices must rise because of reduced infrastructure demand (Koziol 2004, pp. 80).

The discussion and implementation of adjusting infrastructure provision to shrinking and ageing population in reality must concentrate on selected adjustment strategies for specific infrastructure projects in relatively small areas, as correctly suggested by BVBW, BBR 2005. The main reasons lie in the problems of projecting regional population developments, correspondingly planning and realizing the adjustments of regional infrastructure capacities. The background will be set up by the extent and diversification of actual government failures.

b) Special Aspects: Discussion of Selected Material Infrastructure Categories

Since it would be impossible to investigate thoroughly the impacts of spatial population changes on the related infrastructure provision, we shall subsequently concentrate on some important aspects of selected material infrastructure categories: housing, health care, and transport, being decisively influenced by institutional infrastructure.

ba) Housing

Regarding public housing policy as an element of institutional infrastructure in Germany, supporting measures exist on the demand side of the housing markets such as housing transfers for rent payment (Wohngeld) for low-income receivers and tax rebates to stimulate the formation of residential property of economic agents. On the supply side, policy measures are low-cost housing construction and, related or separated tax relief of the construction of dwelling units for rent, public subsidies and credits, and municipal facilitation of developing new ground for construction (Jenkis 1991, pp. 98 ff.).

Until about 2015 a lack of living space in West Germany, particularly in agglomerations and urbanized areas, is expected to occur since the supply of accommodation units may be reduced more than demand. It will remain relatively stable due to increases in the number of households, in the space requirement per resident, in the number of immigrants from abroad and other German areas (migrating old aged people). The shrinkage of supply will be determined by private investors' distrust in the growth of housing demand, intensified rent control (price cap on rents, protection of tenants against notices of the landlords), rationing of construction land by municipalities (there is no market for this type of land!), environmental and social policy restrictions, the only opposing force being relatively high rates of accelerated depreciation and immediate depreciation for housing maintenance. The market results will be the unpredictability of the scarcity of dwelling units and the distortion of competition in the housing markets (Pfeiffer 2002, 2005).

From 2010 the demand for larger dwelling units will decrease since the couples in those age groups originating from times of reduced fertility rates will only start to establish their families and to accumulate property. About five years later, for reasons of future population development, the construction of multiple dwelling units will be reduced, investment in units for rent will become even less attractive, rehabilitated apartments and houses cannot be leased anymore, the prices of one-family houses will fall. Maintenance and consolidation of dwelling units will be the main topics of housing. From 2020 vacant housing units will be possible (Röhl 2005, pp. 335 f.).

The above mentioned developments projected to occur in the West from 2015 onwards are already a fact in the East. Millions of dwelling units in concrete buildings assembled out of prefabricated elements (Plattenbauten), and even bigger settlements of this type, are vacant. According to the program "City Reconstruction East" (Stadtumbau Ost) destruction of these excess supplies is the solution of the problem. The alternative idea of rent reduction in order to increase housing demand again has not been realized. Due to their market power the housing associations and co-operative societies which possess the unoccupied dwelling units may pursue their demolition strategy, as they are only interested in keeping up the rent level. The advantage of this strategy must be substantial, also considering the state subsidies received, since at the start of the program the associations and societies forgot about the material infrastructure beneath the buildings (e.g., pipelines for water, sewage, and gas). Part of the costs of restructuring the networks is now also covered by municipalities and consumers.

Regarding the housing-political consequences of long-term population development, the Federal Office for Construction and Spatial Order (Bundesamt für Bauwesen und Raumordnung – BBR) discusses two outlines of housing market outcomes (on the development of German housing markets in the past and in the presence cf. Börsch-Supan 2000 and Bundesamt für Bauwesen und Raumordnung (BBR) 2004b). The main objective of the scenario "urbanity" is less rededication of open space so that the growth of the settlement area must be reduced. Thus the correction of market results by housing-political instruments is supposed to lead to equal housing provision, state participation in the increasing value of residential property, lot recycling, modernization and restructuring of living space and condensation of residential areas. By contrast, the scenario "market" has the main objective of the effectiveness of consumer sovereignty within the boundaries of a given spatial order. This means the freedom to construct in zoned areas and the competition of municipalities for residents. There are free markets of land for construction. Deregulation is not considered in view of the presently given interventions into the German housing markets. This study (cf. BBR 2004a) is important since the development of the regional housing markets in its relationship to political decision-making cannot be reliably predicted.

As already indicated, urban shrinkage and redevelopment confront housing-related material infrastructure outputs, particularly as supplied by network utilities, with technical challenges (the following statements mainly refer to Koziol 2004, pp. 71 ff., 81 ff.). The urgent problem is underutilization of existing infrastructure capacities due to falling consumption of network outputs so that efficient operation without disturbances, cost-effectiveness and some times also the existence of the installations are endangered. In the drinking water network, reduced consumption results in longer water retention times and may lead to a greater risk of bacterial contamination. As to sewage and waste water disposal, lower flow rates cause sediment deposition in oversized sewers so that it is necessary to flush sewers frequently, if not odor problems and problems of pipeline corrosion are to occur (cf. also Herz 1999). In district heating networks, falling consumption leads to a rise in heat transport losses and to the creation of plant overcapacities; it may even bring about the collapse of the steam works. The necessary adjustments of material infrastructure give rise to substantial cost increases which can only be kept in limits by the realization of a number of policy recommendations. For example, city reconstruction and network adjustment should be coordinated so that new infrastructure equipment can be planned according to realistic dimensions; also decentralized solutions should be possible if they will have a long-term advantage.

bb) Health Care

The German health system as another element of institutional infrastructure includes two markets: (a) the market of health services in which the physician (or any health service provider in a hospital) medically attends his patient and gets paid by the patient's health insurance, the doctor being a member of the associations of statuary health insurance physicians; and (b) the insurance market in which the patient chooses an insurance company which is able to comply with his medical requirements at an acceptable premium. This system is characterized by several misplaced incentives. The patient, e.g., determines his demand for medical services without knowing about the involved costs. Moreover, hospital planning of the Federal States is not only oriented at health policy objectives, but also considers regional policy aims such as equity goals. One possibility to overcome these deficiencies would be to organize a health system according to the principles of competition. The implementation of incentives to induce physicians to be interested in cost-effective service of their patients is one of the necessary steps. The introduction of a remuneration according to diagnosis related groups (DRGs), using diagnosis-specific prices, could be helpful. Basically, there is a strong need for starting a process of competition as to the quality and the costs of medical services among physicians (cf. Siebert 2001, pp. 154 ff.; Donges et al. 2002 on these statements).

If we assume specific ratios of inhabitants to physicians for the various medical services, then population shrinkage with an old aged bias has two effects. There will come forth a general reduction of the demand for these services, while population ageing will increase the demand for old age specific treatments of consultant doctors against arteriosclerosis, osteoporosis, cancer, consequences of strokes and back problems (Kruse 2002). Also the services of general practitioners will be in higher demand. Then rural areas and population-losing suburban areas will particularly be characterized by a shortage of medical services due to the lack of medical applicants of the coming generation and to the unattractive conditions of opening up their practices (material infrastructure). On the basis of support from health insurers and associations of physicians new institutional arrangements may solve the problems. Examples for such organizational steps are the reinforced cooperation among physicians, including those in hospitals, and the foundation of health houses in suitable central places including medical staff of different disciplines (Rosenbrock, Gerlinger 2004, pp. 106 ff.; BVBW, BBR 2005, pp. 43 ff.).

With reference to hospital planning in the German State of Nordrhein-Westfalen (Ministerium für Frauen, Jugend, Familie und Gesundheit des Landes Nordrhein-Westfalen 2001), we may refer to recent efforts for the region Siegen (County of Siegen-Wittgenstein) that has six hospitals. The County Assembly (Kreistag) in collaboration with hospital representatives have the legal obligation to project the future development of the demands for hospital services and to change periodically the existing hospital planning for the region. The attraction of additional medical services to the region, the formation of specific treatment centers in the different hospitals and the reduction of the number of beds in the hospitals to a diverging extent according to the principle of cost-effectiveness and to the loss of regional population have been among the objectives pursued. The future demand for beds to be planned is estimated by the quotient of the arithmetic product of the number of regional inhabitants, the frequency of sickness and the length of stay in the hospitals divided by the product of the degree of bed utilization and the days per year. The record of the adjusted planning as a consensus proposal had to be agreed upon by the hospital administrations, the associations of health insurances and the regional political institutions and then to be send to the state ministry of health for approval (cf. DRK-Kinderklinik Siegen GmbH et al. 2002), in order to be integrated into state hospital planning after possible corrections were made.

The projection of the future demand for hospital beds may become obsolete by 2009 when the DRG-price system (Breyer et al. 2005, pp. 422 ff.) will be completely established as a major step in changing health care institutions, thus guaranteeing uniform prices for medical services, on the level of the German federal states. It is not unrealistic to expect that the effects of population shrinkage on the demand for beds will worsen. On the one hand, the German DRG-price system is also so complex, with a substantial number of parameters, that its implications can hardly be grasped fully. For instance, the reimbursement to a hospital for an admission in a specific DRG is given by the arithmetic product of the DRG weight (obtained from hospital cost data by charges and using cost-charge ratios) and the (federal) state basic DRG-price. The reduction of the given basic price (on its calculation cf. Rochell, Roeder 2000, pp. 2 ff.; Bundesministerium für Gesundheit und Soziale Sicherung 2005) for political reasons ceteris paribus may force a hospital to eliminate the DRG service in question and the related number of beds, assuming constant service costs. On the other hand, experiences in the United States with the DRG system fifteen years after its start indicate that it reduced the duration of stays in hospitals, shifted the necessary services from the hospitals to nursing-homes and increased the number of out-patient instead of in-patient operations. Above all, the expected cost reducing effect of the introduction of the DRG system and the increased competition among the hospitals that was assumed in view of augmented DRG-prices did not occur (Rochell, Roeder 2000, p. 16; L.S. Dafny 2005).

bc) Transport

Population shrinkage, particularly in rural and suburban areas, changes the spatial network of service providers (e.g., retail firms, lawyers) and material infrastructure producers (e.g., physicians, kindergartens, primary, secondary and vocational schools). An expansion of service areas leads to additional transport costs and augmented output costs due to the widening gap between the actual reduced and optimal sizes of the production units which may grow because of technical progress. Accessibility of infrastructure facilities thus is of high importance in residential location decisions. If the service areas of central places are enlarged, the accessibility of infrastructure facilities in the surrounding areas and the suitability as residential places is deteriorated, resulting in a pressure of emigration so that the initial population shrinkage is made worse (Feichtinger 1977, p. 420; Clark et al. 1978, pp. 947 f.).

A similar conclusion, however, with a positive final effect, emerges if urban residents' expenditures for transportation and for housing are substitutional interrelated, assuming that households choose their housing locations and transportation modes so as to maximize their utility. Employees working in core cities have an option between high housing costs and low transportation costs when living in the cities and between lower housing costs and higher transportation costs when residing in the suburbs. If the suburbanized areas lose population with the consequence of falling housing demands and rents, it pays for residents located in the urban rim to stay or to move even further out into rurally dominated urban sprawl. In doing so, they stabilize the initially existing spatial population pattern.

Both examples for interdependencies of population and economic variables show the difficulty of deriving final valid results on the effects of spatial population changes on the pertinent usage of transport infrastructure. Nevertheless, Aberle et al. (2004), as a council of advisers, indicate the following main tendencies of effects on passenger transport which partly aim in the same direction and partly are opposed to each other.

- In the long run we shall experience a reduction in the volume of passenger transport due to the decline of total population and of the number of persons in the mobile age groups.
- On the basis of deconcentrated settlement patterns, the volumes of transport will occur in dispersed forms as to space and time, the consequence being increased trip lengths; thus it will be more difficult to satisfy transport demand by public short-distance rail transport.
- Traffic growth in suburbanized areas results not only from the general population increases, but also from the increased number of high income and mobile households.
- Because of age, household and location related influences (e.g., increased motorization of the elderly, augmented number of one-person-households and of households residing in the periphery) the individual motorization will grow while the demand for public short-distance transport will be reduced (e.g., by the decrease of the number of pupils to be transported).
- The expected increase of dispersed traffic demand will make it necessary to adjust the street networks and their characteristics in urbanized regions (reduction of congestion, improved possibilities of traffic through cities). A more than proportional reduction of transport demand in rural and old industrialized areas, in the large residential settlement areas of the East and in structurally weak areas of West Germany may enable downsizing of road capacities, improved facilities of parking and cuts in maintenance expenditures.

Finally, the advisers give a number of recommendations on how to cope with these future developments in the field of regional passenger transport, e.g., the improved integration of transport and spatial development planning (cf. also Bundesministerium für Verkehr, Bau- und Wohnungswesen (BVBW) 2005; Lehmbrock 2005, pp. 68 ff., 97 ff.) and the assistance to the development and implementation of differentiated services in public short-distance transport. Moreover, the advisers assemble a list of neglected aspects and deficiencies in actual regional transport planning, the binding force of which remains a problem of personal and institutional infrastructure.

There is a number of additional issues in transport planning as an aspect of institutional infrastructure that may affect the relationships between the variations of spatial population structure and regional infrastructure provision. Without further detailed analysis these effects cannot be evaluated. The main topics and their important aspects are

- choice of transport modes (private automobile versus transit (rail, bus, tramways)
  - financial and organizational measures to activate public short-distance transport (Koziol 2004, p. 75; BVBW, BBR 2005, pp. 51 ff.; Lehmbrock et al. 2005, pp. 135 ff.) and improved integration of public and private transport,
  - pricing in a multi-modal transportation network (Yang, Meng, Hau 2004; Schöb 2005),
- highway construction and usage
  - designing and capacitating rail and/or road transport (Thomas 1996),
  - road pricing for private automobiles as confronted with a tax solution, e.g., increase of gasoline tax,
  - private road construction (cf. discussion of public private partnerships),
- railway usage
  - closure of railway connections: basic discord between the viewpoint of economics stressing accessibility in space and the viewpoint of business administration pointing out profit orientation of production,
  - separation of network provision and operation as discussed above.

V. Concluding Remarks

The actual problems in the field of material infrastructure seem to be of limited size. Certainly, there are many physical, technical, and economic difficulties of provision in practice such as the consideration of investment periods taken too short to cope with the problems of operating, maintaining, refinancing, modifying and finally removing facilities. However, these problems can be handled, especially since we are able to dispose of high standard planning approaches and techniques and sufficient implementation experiences. The influences to be criticized of institutional and personal infrastructure on material infrastructure output generation are more serious. In this context we must realize that the quantitative aspects (volume of employed workforce) and qualitative aspects (qualifications of workforce resulting from education) of personal infrastructure are determined by the pertinent facets of institutional infrastructure. Thus, institutional infrastructure in an aggregate and disaggregate view is a major problem area in infrastructure provision of an economy. This point has been demonstrated for Germany by reference to selected government failures. At the national and regional level, deficiencies of institutional infrastructure result in occupational and industrial abstinence as well as education-economic inefficiency. Both factors lead to extensive present consumption of social services or, in other words, a lack of investment disastrous for a market economy. The consequences are high national debt, substantial unemployment, and low economic growth (Klös, Kroker 2005, p. 396). With respect to material infrastructure, it is more important for future reforms of institutional rules and constraints to establish solid solutions of the underlying economic problems than to find compromises among diverging interests in the sense of a consensus democracy.

What explains the precarious situation of institutional infrastructure? The answer focuses on the circumstances of personal infrastructure so that the interrelation between personal and institutional infrastructure becomes apparent. The main crux in the role of infrastructure is the state and variation of personal infrastructure. Population change, here shrinkage and ageing, is one issue; the other is the qualification of politicians and administrative personnel. In the public sphere, administrative reform, adaptation of service law and education are some of the relevant catchwords. Compared to other nations, Germany has been unable for decades to mobilize the educational potential of her people, especially in favor of the fields of economics, engineering, and natural sciences (Schnuer 1986, Weiß 2003, The Economist 2005), to the advantage of the present population and especially to the economic future of our children.

Since there is hardly any field of infrastructure that must not be improved with respect to economic efficiency, we have inherited a weak starting position from past decision-making from which to adjust the provision of material infrastructure to future population changes. The core of this problem is formed by the issues of spatial population projections, questions of determining future infrastructure demand and of adjusting infrastructure output production. In view of our modest experience and knowledge with the management of population decline and its consequences, we should concentrate on relatively small service areas for specific infrastructure goods and services such as those related to the discussed categories housing, health care and transport. The future results will be problems of unsatisfied demand of the population, on the one hand, and excess capacities of facilities, on the other hand. There will be opportunities of modernization and redevelopment, the introduction of technical progress, but also additional financial burdens in the form of additional infrastructure output costs. The ranges of these phenomena will largely depend on the effectiveness of a population-oriented policy (Klös, Kroker 2005, pp. 400 ff.).

References

Aberle, G. et al., Demographische Veränderungen – Konsequenzen für Verkehrsinfrastrukturen und Verkehrsangebote, Papier des Wissenschaftlichen Beirats beim Bundesminister für Verkehr, Bau- und Wohnungswesen, in: Raumordnung und (Bundes-)Verkehrswegeplanung im 21. Jahrhundert, Informationen zur Raumentwicklung, ed. by Bundesamt für Bauwesen und Raumordnung – BBR, Anhang 1, Heft 6, 2004, pp. 401-417.

Aschauer, D.A., Is public expenditure productive? in: Journal of Monetary Economics, Vol. 23, 1989, pp. 177-200.

Averch, H. and *L.L. Johnson*, Behavior of the Firm under Regulatory Constraint, in: The American Economic Review, Vol. 52, 1962, pp. 1052-1069.

Barbier, H.-D., Art. Schrankwärter, in: Frankfurter Allgemeine Zeitung, 20. Jan. 2006.

Birg, H., Perspektiven der demographischen Entwicklung Deutschlands an der Schwelle zum 21. Jahrhundert, in: Prosperität in einer alternden Gesellschaft, ed. by Frankfurter Institut and Stiftung Marktwirtschaft und Politik, Bad Homburg, 2000, pp. 25-81.

Bishop, M.R. and *J. Kay*, Privatization in Western Economies, in: Privatization, Symposium in Honor of Herbert Giersch, ed. by H. Siebert, Tübingen 1992, pp. 193-209.

Blankart, C.B. and *M. Faber* (eds.), Regulierung öffentlicher Unternehmen, Königstein/Ts. 1982.

Bloch, A., Tendenzen der Bevölkerungsentwicklung und Infrastrukturversorgung unter Berücksichtigung der Ziele für die Entwicklung der Siedlungsstruktur gem. LEP I/II, Schriftenreihe Landes- und Stadtentwicklungsforschung des Landes Nordrhein-Westfalen 4.020, Dortmund 1982.

Bobzin, G., Dynamische Modelle zur Theorie der Regulierung, Wiesbaden 2002.

Bobzin, H., Principles of Network Economics, Lecture Notes in Economics and Mathematical Systems 561, Berlin and Heidelberg 2006.

Bode, E., Aktive und passive Sanierung im Wachstumsprozess ostdeutscher Regionen, in: Die Weltwirtschaft, No. 4, 2002, pp. 362-382.

Bortolotti, B., Political Institutions and Privatization Policy, in: CESifo DICE Report, No. 3, 2005, pp. 12-18.

Börsch-Supan, A., Die Entwicklung der Wohnungsmärkte seit dem Zweiten Weltkrieg im internationalen Vergleich, in: Die unternehmerische Wohnungswirtschaft: Emanzipation einer Branche, Der Strukturwandel der deutschen Wohnungswirtschaft seit dem ausgehenden 19. Jahrhundert, ed. by V. Eichener, H. van Emmerich and D. Petzina, Frankfurt/M., 2000, pp. 22-37.

Börsch-Supan, A., Kann die Finanz- und Sozialpolitik die Auswirkungen der Bevölkerungsalterung auf den Arbeitsmarkt lindern? in: Finanzpolitik und Arbeitsmärkte, ed. by B. Genser, N.F., Bd. 289, Berlin 2002, pp. 9-44.

Bös, D., Economic Theory of Public Enterprise, Lecture Notes in Economics and Mathematical Systems 188, Berlin, Heidelberg and New York 1981.

Bös, D., Public Enterprise Economics, Theory and Application, Amsterdam, New York and Oxford 1986.

Breyer, F., P. Zweifel and *M. Kifmann*, Gesundheitsökonomik, 5th Ed., Berlin and Heidelberg 2005.

Buehler, S., A. Schmutzler and *M.-A. Benz*, Infrastructure quality in deregulated industries: is there an under investment problem? in: International Journal of Industrial Organization, Vol. 22, 2004, pp. 253-267.

Buhr, W., Efficiency versus Equity in Regional Economic Growth, in: Fiscal Decentralization, ed. by P. Friedrich and P. van Rompuy, Baden-Baden 1987, pp. 217-230.

Buhr, W. and *T. Christiaans*, Economic Decisions by Aproved Principles, Rules of Thumb as Behavioral Guidelines, in: Advances in Behavioral Economics, Essays in Honor of Horst Todt, ed. by F. Bolle and M. Carlberg, Heidelberg and New York 2001. pp. 25-38.

Buhr, W., What is infrastructure? Discussion Paper No. 107-03, Department of Economics, School of Economic Disciplines, Siegen 2003.

Bundesamt für Bauwesen und Raumordnung – BBR (ed.), Wohnungspolitische Konsequenzen der langfristigen demographischen Entwicklung, Forschungen Heft 117, Bonn 2004a.

Bundesamt für Bauwesen und Raumordnung – BBR (ed.), Wohnungsmärkte in Deutschland, Ergebnisse der regionalisierten Wohnungsmarktbeobachtung des Bundesamtes für Bauwesen und Raumordnung, Berichte 18, Bonn 2004b.

Bundesministerium für Gesundheit und Soziale Sicherung, Verordnung zur Bestimmung vorläufiger Landes-Basisfallwerte im Fallpauschalensystem für Krankenhäuser für das Jahr 2005 (Fallpauschalenverordnung 2005 – KFPV 2005), Berlin 2005.

Bundesministerium für Verkehr, Bau- und Wohnungswesen – BVBW and Bundesamt für Bauwesen und Raumordnung – BBR (eds.), Öffentliche Daseinsvorsorge und demographischer Wandel, Erprobung

von Anpassungs- und Entwicklungsstrategien in Modellvorhaben der Raumordnung, Berlin, Bonn 2005.
Bundesministerium für Verkehr, Bau- und Wohnungswesen – BVBW (ed.), Nachhaltige Raum- und Verkehrsplanung, Beispiele und Handlungsempfehlungen, Direkt: Verbesserung der Verkehrsverhältnisse in den Gemeinden, 60, Wirtschaftsverlag NW, Verlag für neue Wissenschaft, Bonn 2005.
CESifo Group Munich, Deutsche Trinkwasserversorgung: Mehr Effizienz, Pressemitteilung zur Studie von M. Egerer vom 20.12.2005.
Clark, R., J. Kreps and *J. Spengler*, Economics of Ageing: A Survey, in: Journal of Economic Literature, Vol. 16, 1978, pp. 919-962.
Dafny, L.S., How Do Hospitals Respond to Price Changes? in: The American Economic Review, Vol. 95, 2005, pp. 1525-1547.
Deregulierungskommission, Marktöffnung und Wettbewerb, Erster Bericht, Bonn 1990, Zweiter Bericht, Bonn 1991.
Donges, J.B. et al., Privatisierung auch im Westen, Schriftenreihe des Frankfurter Instituts für Wirtschaftspolitische Forschung e.V. 26, Bad Homburg 1993.
Donges, J.B. et al., Mehr Eigenverantwortung und Wettbewerb im Gesundheitswesen, Stiftung Marktwirtschaft, Schriftenreihe 39, Berlin 2002.
Douglas, M. and *A. Wants*, The New Palgrave, in: The New Palgrave, A Dictionary of Economics, Vol. 4, ed. by J. Eatwell, M. Milgate and P. Newman, London 1998, pp. 872-874.
DRK-Kinderklinik Siegen gGmbH et al., Anträge zur Fortschreibung der Krankenhausplanung auf der Grundlage des gemeinsamen Strukturkonzeptes der Krankenhäuser der Region Siegen, Siegen 2002.
Eckey, H.-F. and *R. Kosfeld*, Regionaler Wirkungsgrad und räumliche Ausstrahlungseffekte der Investitionsförderung, in: Jahrbuch für Regionalwissenschaft, Nr. 25, 2005, pp. 149-173.
Eichhorn, P. and *P. Friedrich*, Verwaltungsökonomie I, Methodologie und Management der öffentlichen Verwaltung, Baden-Baden 1976.
Engels, W. et al., Mehr Markt in der Wohnungswirtschaft, Schriftenreihe des Frankfurter Instituts für wirtschaftspolitische Forschung e.V. 7, Bad Homburg 1984.
Esfahani, H.S. and *M.T. Ramirez*, Institutions, infrastructure and economic growth, in: Journal of Development Economics, Vol. 70, 2003, pp. 443-477.
Eucken, W., Grundsätze der Wirtschaftspolitik, 2nd Ed., Tübingen 1955.
Eucken, W., Die Grundlagen der Nationalökonomie, 8th Ed., Berlin 1965.
Feichtinger, G., Ursachen und Konsequenzen des Geburtenrückgangs, in: Soziale Probleme der modernen Industriegesellschaft, 1. Halbband, Schriften des Vereins für Socialpolitik, ed. by B. Külp and H.-D. Haas, N.F., Bd. 92/I, Berlin 1977, pp. 393-434.
Forsthoff, E., Lehrbuch des Verwaltungsrechts, Bd. 1: Allgemeiner Teil, 10th Ed., München 1973.
Franz, P., Schrumpfende Städte – schrumpfende Wirtschaft? Der Fall Ostdeutschland, in: Deutsche Zeitschrift für Kommunalwissenschaften, 43. Jg, 2004, pp. 33-50.
Franz, W., Arbeitsmarktökonomik, 5th. Ed., Berlin, Heidelberg and New York 2003.
Frey, R.L., Art. Infrastruktur, in: Handwörterbuch der Wirtschaftswissenschaft, ed. by W. Albers et al. 4. Bd., Stuttgart et al. 1978, pp. 200-215.
Friedrich, P., Volkswirtschaftliche Investitionskriterien für Gemeindeunternehmen, Tübingen 1969.
Friedrich, P., Strukturpolitische Auswirkungen von Standortentscheidungen öffentlicher Verwaltungen, in: Funktionalreform in Nordrhein-Westfalen, ed by Deutsches Institut für Urbanistik, Berlin 1977, pp. 113-141.
Friedrich, P., Ausrichtung der Preisbildung öffentlicher Unternehmen am Grenzkostenpreisprinzip bei differierenden Marktformen, in: Kosten und Preise öffentlicher Unternehmen, Eine Diskussion im wissenschaftlichen Beirat der Gesellschaft für öffentliche Wirtschaft und Gemeinwirtschaft, Schriftenreihe der Gesellschaft für öffentliche Wirtschaft und Gemeinwirtschaft e.V., ed. by Gesellschaft für öffentliche Wirtschaft und Gemeinwirtschaft e.V., Heft 16, Berlin 1978, pp. 90-129.
Friedrich, P., Ordnungspolitische Rahmenbedingungen und öffentliche Unternehmenstätigkeit, in: Öffentliche Unternehmen und ökonomische Theorie, ed. by T. Thiemeyer, Baden-Baden 1987, pp. 15-51.
Gans, P. and *A. Schmitz-Veltin*, Bevölkerungsentwicklung in ländlichen Gemeinden: Szenarien zu kleinräumigen Auswirkungen des demographischen Wandels, in: Auswirkungen der demographischen Alterung und der Bevölkerungsschrumpfung auf Wirtschaft, Staat und Gesellschaft, ed. by H. Birg, Münster 2005, pp. 111-129.
Gesellschaft für öffentliche Wirtschaft und Gemeinwirtschaft e.V. (ed.), Kosten und Preise öffentlicher Unternehmen, Schriftenreihe Heft 16, Berlin 1978.
Gonzalez-Paramo, J.M. and *P. Hernandez De Cos*, The Impact of Public Ownership and Competition on Productivity, in: Kyklos, Vol. 58, 2005, pp. 495-517.

Grünheid, E. and *C. Höhn* (eds.), Demographische Alterung und Wirtschaftswachstum, Seminar des Bundesinstituts für Bevölkerungsforschung 1998 in Bingen, Opladen 1999.
Herz, R., Der Zustand von Abwasserkanälen und Versorgungsleitungen, in: Umbau, Über die Zukunft des Baubestandes, ed. by U. Hassler, N. Kohler and W. Wang, Tübingen and Berlin 1999, pp.133-139.
Hirschhausen, C. von, Reform der Erdgaswirtschaft in der EU und in Deutschland: Wieviel Regulierung braucht der Wettbewerb? in: Perspektiven der Wirtschaftspolitik, Nr. 7, 2006, pp. 89-103.
Hofmann, H., Privatisierung, in: Leitfaden zur Modernisierung von Behörden, ed. by Sachverständigenrat „Schlanker Staat", Bonn 1998, pp. 121-136.
Jänicke, M., Staatsversagen, Die Ohnmacht der Politik in der Industriegesellschaft, 2nd Ed., München 1987.
Jenkis, H.W. (ed.), Kompendium der Wohnungswirtschaft, München and Wien 1991.
Jochimsen, R., Theorie der Infrastruktur, Grundlagen der marktwirtschaftlichen Entwicklung, Tübingen 1966.
Johnson, P., The Impact of Ageing: The Supply of Labor and Human Capital, in: Economic Policy for Aging Societies, ed. by H. Siebert, Berlin et al., 2002, pp. 111-125.
Jost, P., Bevölkerungsimplosion in der Bundesrepublik Deutschland, in: Struktur, Heft 4, 1974, pp. 73-79.
Kessides, I.N., The Challenge of Infrastructure Privatisation, in: CESifo DICE Report, No. 3, 2005, pp. 19-25.
Klaus, J. (ed.), Entscheidungshilfen für die Infrastrukturplanung, Neuere Entwicklungen auf dem Gebiet der Analyse und Bewertung öffentlicher Projekte, Baden-Baden 1984.
Klös, H.-P. and *R. Kroker*, Perspektive 2050: Ordnungsökonomische Weichenstellungen und wirtschaftspolitischer Handlungsbedarf, in: Perspektive 2050, Ökonomik des demographischen Wandels, ed. by Institut der deutschen Wirtschaft Köln, 2nd. Ed., Köln 2005, pp. 391-415.
Knieps, G., Wettbewerbsökonomie, Regulierungstheorie, Industrieökonomie, Wettbewerbspolitik, Berlin, Heidelberg and New York 2001.
Knieps, G., Art. Gegen das Virus der Überregulierung in der EU, in: Frankfurter Allgemeine Zeitung, 21.Juni 2005.
Knorr, A., and *A. Eichinger*, Die Bahnreform in Großbritannien – eine kritische Würdigung, in: List Forum für Wirtschafts- und Finanzpolitik, 28 Jg., 2002, pp. 370-390.
Koziol, M., Folgen des demographischen Wandels für die kommunale Infrastruktur, in: Deutsche Zeitschrift für Kommunalwissenschaften, 43. Jg., 2004, pp. 69-83.
Kruse, A., Demografische Umgestaltung der Gesundheitsversorgung, in: Antworten auf die demografische Herausforderung, ed. by Hanns-Seidel-Stiftung e.V., Sonderheft 2 der Politischen Studien, 53 Jg., 2002, pp. 135-154.
Kuhlmann, A., Die Elektrizitätskrise in Kalifornien – oder: Wie riskant ist die Liberalisierung von Netzsektoren? in: List Forum für Wirtschafts- und Finanzpolitik, 30. Jg., 2004a, pp. 49-68.
Kuhlmann, A., Replik auf den Kommentar von Wolfgang Ströbele, in: List Forum für Wirtschafts- und Finanzpolitik, 30 Jg., 2004b, S. 194-195.
Lehmbrock, M. et al., Verkehrssystem und Raumstruktur, Neue Rahmenbedingungen für Effizienz und Nachhaltigkeit, Difu-Beiträge zur Stadtforschung 40, Berlin 2005.
Löbbe, K., Privatisierung öffentlicher Dienstleistungen und öffentlicher Unternehmen – Möglichkeiten und Widerstände, in: Den Strukturwandel gestalten? – Optionen für Wirtschaft und Politik, ed. by Kreditanstalt für Wiederaufbau, Frankfurt/M 1986. pp. 19-27.
Mälich, W., Analyse und Prognose räumlicher Bevölkerungsverteilungen und ihrer Veränderungen, Berlin 1973.
Markus, G., Infrastrukturelle Folgen abnehmender Einwohnerzahlen, in: Zur Bedeutung rückläufiger Einwohnerzahlen für die Planung, Veröffentlichungen der Akademie für Raumforschung und Landesplanung, Forschungs- und Sitzungsberichte 122, ed. by K. Schwarz, Hannover 1978, pp. 229-246
Megginson, W.L., Netter, J.M. and *C.S. Chahyadi*, Size and Impact of Privatisation – A Survey of Empirical Studies, in: CESifo DICE Report, No. 3, 2005, pp. 3-11.
Milbradt, G., Erfordernisse und Grenzen staatlicher Risikoübernahme in der Marktwirtschaft, in: Perspektiven der Wirtschaftspolitik, Heft 6, Nr. 4, 2005, pp. 433-448.
Ministerium für Frauen, Jugend, Familie und Gesundheit des Landes Nordrhein-Westfalen (ed.), Krankenhausplan 2001 des Landes Nordrhein-Westfalen, Düsseldorf 2001.
Müller, B, and *S. Siedentop*, Wachstum und Schrumpfung in Deutschland – Trends, Perspektiven und Hausforderungen für die räumliche Planung und Entwicklung, in: Deutsche Zeitschrift für Kommunalwissenschaften, 43. Jg., 2004, pp. 14-32.
Müller, J.H. and *W.D. Siebert*, Das Problem der Richtwerte in Programmen und Plänen der Raumordnung und Landesplanung, in: Das Problem der Richtwerte in Programmen und Plänen der Raumordnung

und Landesplanung, ed. by Akademie für Raumforschung und Landesplanung, Hannover 1977, pp. 23-52.

Niskanen, W.A., Guidelines for Delineating the Private and the Government Sector, in: Privatization, Symposium in Honor of Herbert Giersch, ed. by H. Siebert, Tübingen 1992, pp. 217-225.

North, D.C., Privatization, Incentives and Economic Performance, in: Privatization, Symposium in Honor of Herbert Giersch, ed. by H. Siebert, Tübingen 1992, S. 3-16.

Pfeiffer, U., Artikel in Frankfurter Allgemeine Zeitung, I: Droht in den kommenden Jahren abermals Wohnungsnot? (4. Jan. 2002), II: Der verschärfte Mieterschutz hat einen hohen Preis (11. Jan. 2002), III: In expandierenden Städten wird Wohnungsnot programmiert (18. Jan. 2002).

Pfeiffer, U., Art. Ein absurdes Theater um Subventionen, in: Frankfurter Allgemeine Zeitung, 22. Juli 2005.

Quinet, E. and *R. Vickerman*, Principles of Transport Economics, Cheltenham 2004.

Rawls, J., A Theory of Justice, London, Oxford and New York 1972.

Ritschl, A., Der späte Fluch des Dritten Reichs: Pfadabhängigkeiten in der Entstehung der bundesdeutschen Wirtschaftsordnung, in: Perspektiven der Wirtschaftspolitik, Heft 6, 2005, pp. 151-170.

Robinson, I.M., Urban Growth in Canada: Implications of Recent Changes in Certain Demographic Characteristics for Urban and Regional Planning and Policy, in: Planning und Regional Stagnation, ed. by W. Buhr and P. Friedrich, Baden-Baden 1982, pp. 245-293.

Rochell, B. and *N. Roeder*, Starthilfe DRGs, Aktueller Stand und Perspektiven der Einführung eines DRG-Systems in Deutschland und die notwendige Vorbereitung des Krankenhauses, Das Krankenhaus, Media Sonderheft: Starthilfe DRGs 2000, pp. 1-24.

Röhl, K.-H., Räumliche Entwicklung, in: Perspektive 2050, Ökonomik des demographischen Wandels, ed. by Institut der deutschen Wirtschaft Köln, 2nd. Ed., Köln 2005, pp. 321-344.

Rohr, H.-G. von, Bevölkerungsentwicklung und Infrastrukturversorgung in den 80er Jahren, Konsequenzen für die Siedlungsstruktur und die zentralörtliche Infrastruktur in Nordrhein-Westfalen, Schriftenreihe Landes- und Stadtentwicklungsforschung des Landes Nordrhein-Westfalen 1027, Dortmund 1981.

Rosenbrock, R. and *T. Gerlinger*, Gesundheitspolitik, Eine systematische Einführung, Bern et al. 2004.

Rothengatter, W., Deregulation and the Problem of Capacity/Price Planning for the Transport and Communication Infrastructure, in: Infrastructure and the Space-Economy, Essays in Honor of Rolf Funck, ed. by K. Peschel, Berlin et al. 1990, pp. 227-253.

Sachverständigenrat „Schlanker Staat" (ed.), Leitfaden zur Modernisierung von Behörden, Bonn 1998.

Samuelson, R.J., Capitalism vs. Democracy, in: Newsweek, 03. Oct. 2005, S. 47.

Schatz, K.-W., Zur Entwicklung des Begriffs Infrastruktur, in: Wettbewerb und Infrastruktur in Post- und Telekommunikationsmärkten, ed. by H. Berger, Beiheft 19 der Zeitschrift für öffentliche und gemeinwirtschaftliche Unternehmen, Baden-Baden 1996, pp. 122-136.

Schnuer, G., Die deutsche Bildungskatastrophe, 20 Jahre nach Picht -Lehren und Lernen in Deutschland, Herford 1986.

Schöb, R., Not Optimal, But Effective: The Multi-Mode Ticket for Reducing Urban Traffic Congestion in Medium-Sized Towns, in: CESifo Report, No. 3, 2005, pp. 28-33.

Schwarz, K., Analyse der räumlichen Bevölkerungsbewegung, Hannover 1969.

Siebert, H., Der Kobra-Effekt, Wie man Irrwege der Wirtschaftspolitik vermeidet, Stuttgart and München 2001.

Siebert, H., The German Economy Beyond the Social Market, Princeton 2005.

Sinn, H.-W., The Five Shocks: Why Germany is Lagging Behind, in: The Ifo Viewpoints 2005, No. 67, Ifo Institute for Economic Research, München 2005a.

Sinn, H.-W., The Envy Tax, in: The Ifo Viewpoints 2005, No. 69, Ifo Institute for Economic Research, München 2005b.

Sinn, H.W., Das demographische Defizit, Die Fakten, die Folgen, die Ursachen und die Politikimplikationen, in: Auswirkungen der demographischen Alterung und der Bevölkerungsschrumpfung auf Wirtschaft, ed. by H. Birg, Münster 2005c, pp. 53-90.

Sommer, B., Die Bevölkerungsentwicklung in den Bundesländern bis zum Jahr 2050, in: Auswirkungen der demographischen Alterung und der Bevölkerungsschrumpfung auf Wirtschaft, Staat und Gesellschaft, ed. by H. Birg, Münster 2005, pp. 91-109.

Steinbrück, P., Art. Lobbyisten in die Produktion! in: Frankfurter Allgemeine Zeitung, 12. Jan. 2006.

Ströbele, W., Energie, Strom und Netze – Warum ereignen sich Blackouts? Kurzkommentar zum Aufsatz von Andreas Kuhlmann, in: List Forum für Wirtschafts- und Finanzpolitik, 30. Jg., 2004, pp. 185-193.

The Economist, The brains business, September 10, 2005.

Thiemeyer, T., Grundsätze einer Theorie der Gemeinwirtschaft, Schriftenreihe Gemeinwirtschaft 3, Bank für Gemeinwirtschaft AG, Frankfurt/M. 1970.

Thomas, U., Dichtung und Wahrheit in der Verkehrspolitik, Renaissance der Schiene – flüssiger Verkehr auf der Straße? Bonn 1996.

Tinbergen, J., Shaping the World Economy, Suggestions for an International Economic Policy, The Twentieth Century Fund, New York 1962.

Weiß, R., Reformagenda: Wege zu mehr Qualität, in: Bildungs-Benchmarking Deutschland, Was macht ein effizientes Bildungssystem aus? ed. by H.-P. Klös and R. Weiß, Köln 2003, pp. 383-425.

Weizsäcker, C.C von, Öffentliche Bindung – Deregulierung – Privatisierung, in: Öffentliche Unternehmen und ökonomische Theorie, ed. by T. Thiemeyer, Baden-Baden 1987, pp. 89-94.

Willms, M., Private Finanzierung von Infrastrukturinvestitionen, Theoretische und empirische Grundlagen, Baden-Baden 1998.

Yang, H., *Q. Meng* and *T.D. Han*, Optimal integrated pricing in a bi-modal transportation network, in: Urban and Regional Transportation Modeling, Essays in Honor of David Boyce, ed. by D.-H. Lee, Cheltenham 2004, pp. 134-156.

B. Raumstrukturelle Effekte des Bevölkerungsrückgangs

Xiao Feng und *Qian Yang*

I. Problemstellung

Die Wechselbeziehung zwischen dem Wirtschaftswachstum und der Bevölkerungsentwicklung zählt zu einem der am häufigsten diskutierten Probleme der Wirtschaftswissenschaften (Ehrlich, Lui 1997). Es war spätestens seit Malthus bekannt, dass der Bevölkerungszuwachs von der Einkommensseite determiniert wird (Malthus 1798). Die Bevölkerungsentwicklung Europas in den letzten 200 Jahren zeigt allerdings, dass die Geburtenrate und die Einwohnerzahl trotz dem wachsenden Einkommen je Einwohner langsamer oder gar in die Gegenrichtung laufen (Wrigley 1969; Coale, Watkins 1986; Livi-Bacci 1997, Rosenzweig, Stark 1997; Maddison 2001). Es liegt also anstatt des malthusianischen Regimes das post-malthusianische Regime bzw. das so genannte moderne Wachstumsregime vor (Dyson, Murphy 1985; Galor, Weil 2000).
Als endogene Größen sind bislang die Einwohnerzahl, die Fertilität und die Kindererziehung im Zusammenhang mit dem technischen Fortschritt und dem Wirtschaftswachstum umfänglich untersucht worden (Lack 1954; Cody 1966; Becker, Barro 1988; Kremer 1993; Lee 1997; Galor, Weil 2000). Auch bei raumwirtschaftlichen Forschungen ist die Bevölkerung stets ein nicht unbedeutendes Thema (Casetti 1971; Ijiri, Simon 1977; Fujita u.a. 1999; McCann 2001). So lässt sich die Formation der Zentrum-Peripherie-Struktur hinsichtlich einer zunehmenden Bevölkerungszahl im Rahmen der positiven Ökonomik erklären (Fujita u.a. 1999; Fujita, Thisse 2002). Demgemäß entstehen Siedlungsgebiete, kleinere und größere Zentren im Zuge des Bevölkerungszuwachses. Wie wird aber die Raumstruktur angepasst, wenn das moderne Wachstumsregime vorherrscht und die Einwohnerzahl fällt?
Um diese Frage zu beantworten, beschäftigen wir uns in dem vorliegenden Beitrag mit den nachstehenden Problemstellungen:

- Wie lassen sich bedeutende Einflussfaktoren der Raumstrukturformation mittels eines analytischen Modells herauskristallisieren?
- Geschieht die Raumstrukturanpassung an einen Bevölkerungsrückgang spiegelbildlich zu jener infolge eines Bevölkerungszuwachses?
- Wenn die Raumstrukturanpassung im Falle des Bevölkerungszuwachses bzw. -rückgangs zwar gegenläufig, jedoch nicht spiegelbildlich erfolgt, was ist der Grund dafür?

II. Ein Raumstrukturmodell

1. Raumbeschreibung

Wir unterstellen einen Wirtschaftsraum mit mehreren städtischen Zentren r, r=1,2,... Um die Zentren herum existiert ein Umland r=0. Die Einwohner in den Zentren und im Umland teilen sich in zwei Gruppen, die jeweils aus den Erwerbspersonen L_r und den älteren bzw. nichterwerbstätigen Einwohnern N_r bestehen. Die Summe der erwerbstätigen Personen beträgt $L=\sum_{r\geq 0} L_r$. Hiervon nehmen die im Umland beschäftigten Personen L_0 einen Anteil von μ ein. Für die älteren bzw. nichterwerbstätigen Personen gilt $N=\sum_{r\geq 0} N_r$. Die Relation $\eta=N/L$ ist gegeben.

Um die Extension des Wirtschaftsraumes zu beachten, wird der Transportentfernung $\delta_{rr'}$ jeweils zwischen zwei beliebigen Orten r bzw. r′ Rechnung getragen. Die räumliche Dimension der Zentren wird nicht expliziert. Stattdessen ist die Lagerente heranzuziehen.

In den Zentren werden Güter q_i, i=1,2,...,n, produziert. Die Produktionsfunktion eines Gutes q vom Cobb–Douglas–Typ lautet:

$$q = A_r \cdot L_r^{\alpha} \cdot M_r^{1-\alpha}, \quad r > 0, \tag{1}$$

wobei:

- das Produktivitätsniveau $A_r \geq 1$ je nach der Infrastrukturbedingung und der Kapitalintensität der Produktionsausstattung in den jeweiligen Zentren unterschiedlich sein kann und eine bestimmte Höhe von Fixkosten $F_r \geq 0$ impliziert,
- die Arbeitsleistung L_r zum lokalen Preis w_r vor Ort bezogen wird und
- M_r die in den Produktionsprozess eingesetzten Produkte $m_i \in q_i$ umfasst:

$$M_r = (\sum_{i=1}^{n} m_i^{(\sigma-1)/\sigma})^{\sigma/(\sigma-1)}. \tag{2}$$

Die Zusammensetzung des Input M_r entspricht der CES–Technologie mit einer Substitutionselastizität $\sigma>1$ und impliziert Skalenerträge der Produktvielfalt à la Dixit–Stiglitz (1977).

Da $m_1, m_2, \ldots, m_n$ möglicherweise in verschiedenen Zentren hergestellt werden, notieren wir den ab-Werk-Preis eines im Zentrum r herstellt Gutes mit p_r, den Lieferpreis an einem anderen Ort r′ mit $p_r^{r'}$. Die Transportkosten werden nach von Thünen (1826) und Samuelson (1952) mittels der Eisbergapproximation zum Ausdruck gebracht:

$$p_r^{r'} : p_r = t(\delta_{rr'}) \geq 1. \tag{3}$$

Die Gleichungen von (1) bis (3) treffen auf alle im Zentrum r ansässigen Firmen zu.

Im Umland findet die Agrarproduktion statt, dessen Erzeugnis q_0 wir als ein homogenes Konsumgut vereinfachen. In die Agrarproduktion wird die Arbeit L_0 eingesetzt:

$$q_O = L_O, \quad (4)$$

wobei das Produktivitätsniveau auf 1 normiert wird. Ferner wird angenommen, dass die Fixkosten der Agrarproduktion approximativ gleich 0 sind. Die Transportkosten können vernachlässigt werden, da überall um die Zentren die Agrarproduktion angesiedelt ist. Der Agrarproduktpreis und der Arbeitslohn im Umland dienen als Numéraire.

Ein Haushalt konsumiert Agrarprodukte $m_0 \in q_0$, die in verschiedenen Zentren produzierten Güter $m_i \in q_i$, i=1,..., n und nimmt zudem Wohnfläche G in Anspruch. Seine Nutzenfunktion vom Cobb–Douglas–Typ lautet:

$$U = m_O^{\beta_O} \cdot M^{\beta_M} \cdot G^{\beta_G}. \quad (5)$$

Für das à la Dixit-Stiglitz abzubildende Güterbündel M wird der Einfachheit halber dieselbe Substitutionselastizität wie in der Gleichung (2) unterstellt. Der Aufwand für die Wohnfläche G spiegelt die Landrente R in einem Zentrum oder im Umland wider. Die durchschnittliche Lagerente im Umland wird auf 1 normiert. Ferner gehen wir davon aus, dass die Ausgaben zur Instandhaltung der gewerblichen wie auch zum Wohnzweck genutzten Flächen durch die Einnahmen entsprechend der Lagerente gedeckt werden.[1]

Ein Einwohner bezieht entweder ein Arbeits- oder ein Transfereinkommen. Das Arbeitseinkommen wird mit dem Satz τ besteuert. Mit den Steuereinnahmen werden die Transferzahlungen finanziert.

2. Unternehmensverhalten

Wir betrachten ein gewinnstrebendes Unternehmen in einem Zentrum r. Für die kostenminimale Inputkombination in der Gleichung (2) gilt:[2]

$$m_i / m_j = (p^r_{r'j} / p^r_{r'i})^{\sigma}, \quad (6)$$

wobei der Fußindex r′ den Produktionsstandort der Inputleistungen m_i bzw. m_j angibt. Nach den Gleichungen (2) und (6) kann jeder einzelne Input m_r, i=1,..., n als eine Funktion des Inputbündels M_r gefasst werden:

$$m_i = (P^r_M / p^r_{r'i})^{\sigma} \cdot M_r. \quad (7)$$

Der Inputpreisindex P^r_M ist der Definition $\sum_{i=1}^{n} m_i \cdot p^r_{r'i} = P^r_M \cdot M_r$ gemäß zu ermitteln:

$$P^r_M = (\sum_{i=1}^{n} p^{r\,1-\sigma}_{r'i})^{1/(1-\sigma)}. \quad (8)$$

1 Die Approximation stützt sich auf das Herry Geoge Theorem. Siehe dazu z.B. Whitaker, J.K., 1998.

2 Die nachstehenden Rechenschritte sind in den wirtschaftsgeographischen Forschungen sehr gebräuchlich und werden nicht im Einzelnen erläutert.

Im nächsten Schritt werden die Produktionskosten $C_r = F_r + w_r \cdot L_r + P_M^r \cdot M_r$ unter der gegebenen Produktionstechnologie (1) minimiert. Daraus ergeben sich die optimalen Faktorinputs L und M in Bezug auf den Output q:

$$L_r = [\alpha/(1-\alpha)]^{1-\alpha} \cdot (P_M^r / w_r)^{1-\alpha} \cdot q\,, \quad M_r = [(1-\alpha)/\alpha]^{\alpha} \cdot (w_r / P_M^r)^{\alpha} \cdot q\,. \tag{9}$$

Dementsprechend lautet die Kostenfunktion:

$$C_r = F_r + c_r \cdot q\,, \qquad c_r = A_r^{-1} \cdot (w_r/\alpha)^{\alpha} \cdot [P_M^r/(1-\alpha)]^{1-\alpha}\,, \tag{10}$$

wobei die Grenzkosten unter c_r dargestellt werden.

Die Maximierung des Unternehmensgewinns $\pi = p_r \cdot q - C_r$ führt zu:

$$p_r = [\sigma/(\sigma-1)] \cdot c_r\,, \tag{11}$$

$$\pi = [c_r/(\sigma-1)] \cdot q - F_r\,. \tag{12}$$

Sei der Markt frei zugänglich, so können wir zur Festlegung des Output q vom Grenzfall der monopolistischen Konkurrenz $\pi=0$ Gebrauch machen:

$$q = [(\sigma-1)/c_r] \cdot F_r\,. \tag{13}$$

Für den Umsatz und die variablen Produktionskosten gelten:

$$p_r \cdot q = \sigma \cdot F_r\,, \tag{14}$$

$$c_r \cdot q = (\sigma-1) \cdot F_r \tag{15}$$

Die Arbeitskosten und die anderen Beschaffungsausgaben betragen jeweils:

$$w_r \cdot L_r = \alpha \cdot c_r \cdot q = \alpha \cdot (\sigma-1) \cdot F_r\,, \tag{16}$$

$$P_M^r \cdot M_r = (1-\alpha) \cdot c_r \cdot q = (1-\alpha) \cdot (\sigma-1) \cdot F_r\,, \tag{17}$$

$$p_{r'i}^r \cdot m_i = (1-\alpha) \cdot (\sigma-1) \cdot (P_M^r / p_{r'i}^r)^{\sigma-1} \cdot F_r \quad . \tag{18}$$

Aus den Lösungen von (16) bis (18) resultieren die Einsatzmengen der einzelnen Produktionsfaktoren.

Zur Veranschaulichung der Agrarproduktion genügt die Gleichung (4). Am Markt des Agrarproduktes herrscht annahmengemäß vollständige Konkurrenz.

3. Haushaltsverhalten

Wir betrachten zunächst das Nettoeinkommen:

- der in den Zentren erwerbstätigen Einwohner Y_r^L, $r>0$,
- der im Umland/Agrarbereich beschäftigten Einwohner Y_O^L und
- aller nichterwerbstätigen Einwohner Y_r^N bzw. Y_O^N.

Den vorangegangenen Darstellungen zufolge bezieht eine erwerbstätige Person in einem Zentrum r das Einkommen w_r. Das Nettoeinkommen nach dem Steuerabzug $\tau \cdot w_r$ ist:

$$Y_r^L = (1-\tau) \cdot w_r\,, \qquad r>0\,. \tag{19}$$

Da der Arbeitslohn im Umland Numéraire ist, beträgt das Nettoeinkommen einer im Agrarbereich beschäftigten Person:

$$Y_O^L = 1-\tau\,. \tag{20}$$

Ein älterer/nichterwerbstätiger Einwohner erhält überall ein gleiches Transfereinkommen, das mit der Einkommensteuer $\tau \cdot (L_O + \sum_{r>0} w_r \cdot L_r)$ gegenfinanziert wird:

$$Y_r^N = Y_O^N = \tau \cdot (L_O + \sum_{r'>0} w_{r'} \cdot L_{r'}) / N . \tag{21}$$

Bei den in den Gleichungen von (19) bis (21) gegebenen Einkommen und bei gegebenem Preisverhältnis können die Anteile der Konsumausgaben eines städtischen Einwohners direkt aus seiner Nutzenfunktion (5) abgeleitet werden:

$$m_O = \beta_O \cdot Y_r , \tag{22}$$

$$P_M^r \cdot M_r = \beta_M \cdot Y_r , \tag{23}$$

$$p_{r'i}^r \cdot m_i = (P_M^r / p_{r'i}^r)^{\sigma-1} \cdot \beta_M \cdot Y_r , \tag{24}$$

$$R_r \cdot G_r = \beta_G \cdot Y_r , \tag{25}$$

wobei der Konsum einzelner Güter m_i und der Preisindex P_M^r analog (7) bzw. (8) zu berechnen sind. Aus den Gleichungen (5), (22), (23) und (24) folgt die indirekte Nutzenfunktion:

$$U_r = \beta_O^{\beta_O} \cdot (\beta_M / P_M^r)^{\beta_M} \cdot (\beta_R / R_r)^{\beta_R} \cdot Y_r . \tag{26}$$

Die Konsumausgaben und die indirekte Nutzenfunktion eines Einwohners im Umland ergeben sich aus demselben Rechenverfahren:

$$m_O = \beta_O \cdot Y_O , \tag{27}$$

$$P_M^O \cdot M_O = \beta_M \cdot Y_O , \tag{28}$$

$$p_{r'i}^O \cdot m_i = (P_M^O / p_{r'i}^O)^{\sigma-1} \cdot \beta_M \cdot Y_O , \tag{29}$$

$$G_O = \beta_G \cdot Y_O , \tag{30}$$

$$U_O = \beta_O^{\beta_O} \cdot (\beta_M / P_M^O)^{\beta_M} \cdot \beta_R^{\beta_R} \cdot Y_O . \tag{31}$$

Bezüglich der Wahl des Wohnsitzes wird vereinfachend angenommen, dass diese Aktion per se keine zusätzlichen Kosten verursacht. So orientiert sich ein erwerbstätiger Einwohner an dem jeweils im Zentrum und im Umland erreichbaren Nutzen (26) bzw. (31):

$$\frac{U_r^L}{U_O^L} = \frac{Y_r^L / (P_M^{r\,\beta_M} \cdot R_r^{\beta_r})}{Y_O^L / P_M^{O\beta_M}} = \frac{P_M^{O\beta_M}}{P_M^{r\,\beta_M} \cdot R_r^{\beta_r}} \cdot w_r , \tag{32}$$

wobei das Produkt $P_M^{r\,\beta_M} \cdot R_r^{\beta_r}$ den Lebensunterhaltungskostenindex im Zentrum r und der Term $P_M^{O\beta_M}$ der Lebensunterhaltungskostenindex im Umland zeigt. Ähnliches gilt für die Wohnsitzentscheidung einer nichterwerbstätigen Person:

$$\frac{U_r^N}{U_O^N} = \frac{Y_r^N / (P_M^{r\,\beta_M} \cdot R_r^{\beta_r})}{Y_O^N / P_M^{O\beta_M}} = \frac{P_M^{O\beta_M}}{P_M^{r\,\beta_M} \cdot R_r^{\beta_r}} . \tag{33}$$

Den Gleichungen (32) und (33) zufolge ist ein Zentrum umso attraktiver, je höher der Arbeitslohn w_r dort ist und je niedriger der Lebensunterhaltungskostenindex ausfällt, vice versa.

Der Lebensunterhaltungskostenindex beinhaltet den Konsumpreisindex P_M^r. Der letztere involviert die Lieferpreise einzelner Konsumgüter:

$$P_M^r = (\sum_{i=1}^n p_{r'i}^{r\;1-\sigma})^{1/(1-\sigma)} = \{\sum_{i=1}^n [t(\delta_{rr'}) \cdot p_{r'i}]^{1-\sigma}\}^{1/(1-\sigma)} . \tag{34}$$

Die Gleichung (34) besagt, dass ein Zentrum umso wahrscheinlicher als Wohnort gewählt wird, je mehr Konsumgüter vor Ort hergestellt und angeboten werden, d.h. t=1, und je kürzere Transportwege zwischen dem Wohnort und anderen Zentren liegen, vice versa.

Um pekuniäre Skaleneffekte hervorzuheben, nehmen wir einen Sonderfall an, in dem alle Konsumgüter in einem Zentrum produziert werden und die ab–Werk–Preise aller Konsumgüter gleich sind. Dementsprechend sieht der Konsumpreisindex wie folgt aus:

$$P_M^r = \{\sum_{i=1}^n [t(\delta_{rr}) \cdot p_{ri}]^{1-\sigma}\}^{1/(1-\sigma)} = (\sum_{i=1}^n p_{ri}^{1-\sigma})^{1/(1-\sigma)} = p_r / n^{1/(\sigma-1)} . \qquad (35)$$

Da der Konsumpreisindex $\mathrm{P}_\mathrm{M}^\mathrm{r}$ mit dem Auswahlspektrum der Konsumgüter n in einer reziproken Beziehung steht, steigt die Attraktivität des Zentrums mit der Vielfalt der dort produzierten und angebotenen Konsumgüter.

Zur Eruierung der Bestimmungsfaktoren des Güterpreises p_r greifen wir auf die Gleichungen (11) und (10) zurück. Danach hängt der ab–Werk–Preis eines Gutes u.a. von dessen Grenzproduktionskosten c_r ab, und die Grenzkosten hängen wieder vom Inputpreisindex $\mathrm{P}_\mathrm{M}^\mathrm{r}$ ab. Der Inputpreisindex fällt mit der Produktvielfalt. In Anbetracht der Einkommenseffekte der Produktvielfalt auf der Nachfrageseite und der Skalenerträge der Produktvielfalt auf der Angebotsseite, die zu den sinkenden Güterpreisen führen, können wir die nachstehende Aussage treffen:

Ein Zentrum zieht die Einwohner umso stärker an, je höher die Rangordnung des Zentrums – im Sinne von Christaller (1933) – ist.

4. Gleichgewicht

Um zumindest ein temporäres Raumgleichgewicht zu identifizieren, betrachten wir zuerst das Wanderverhalten. Ein Einwohner entscheidet sich je nach der Nutzenrelation (32) bzw. (33) entweder für ein Zentrum oder für das Umland. Ein Gleichgewicht liegt vor, wenn die nachstehende Situation eintritt:

$$1 = U_r^L / U_O^L = [P_M^{O\,\beta_M} / (P_M^{r\,\beta_M} \cdot R_r^{\beta_r})] \cdot w_r \quad \text{bzw.} \quad w_r = R_r^{\beta_r} \cdot (P_M^r / P_M^O)^{\beta_M} \qquad (32')$$

$$1 = U_r^N / U_O^N = P_M^{O\,\beta_M} / (P_M^{r\,\beta_M} \cdot R_r^{\beta_r}) \quad \text{bzw.} \quad R_r = (P_M^O / P_M^r)^{\beta_M / \beta_R} . \qquad (33')$$

Die Bedingung (33′) gilt für die älteren bzw. nichterwerbstätigen Einwohner. Da die Einwohner in dieser Kategorie dasselbe Transfereinkommen erhalten, muss der Lebensunterhaltungskostenindex in allen Zentren und im Umland gleich sein. Wie aus der Gleichung (8) zu entnehmen ist, setzt sich der Konsumpreisindex $\mathrm{P}_\mathrm{M}^\mathrm{r}$ bzw. $\mathrm{P}_\mathrm{M}^\mathrm{O}$ aus den Lieferpreisen von Gütern zusammen, die möglicherweise in verschiedenen Zentren erzeugt werden. Die Lieferpreise steigen, wenn die im Absatzvorgang anfallenden Transportkosten zunehmen. Die Lagerente R_r enthüllt den Standortvorteil eines Zentrums dem Umland gegenüber dank seiner Zentralität und besseren Verkehrsinfrastrukturbedingung. Denn, je mehr Güter vor Ort produziert werden bzw. je besser das betrachtete Zentrum an die anderen Produktionsstandorte angebunden ist – z.B. in Hinsicht auf den Verkehrsknotenpunkt des Marknetzes nach Lösch (1939) – umso weniger bedeutend sind die Transportkosten.

Die Lagerente reflektiert nicht nur den Standortvorteil in Anbetracht der Transportkosten, sondern auch die standortabhängigen Grenzproduktionskosten c_r, die der Gleichung (11) zufolge mit dem ab- Werk-Preis p_r positiv korreliert sind. Die Grenzproduktionskosten schlagen sich somit im Konsumpreisindex nieder. Da die Grenzkosten laut der Gleichung (10) im standortabhängigen Produktivitätsniveau $\overline{A}_r$ fallen und mit dem standortabhängigen Inputpreisindex P_M^r steigen, offenbart die Lagerente R_r den Standortvorteil angesichts der Agglomeration im betrachteten Zentrum und der Kapitalintensität der dortigen Produktion, welche die Produktivität $\overline{A}_r$ anderer Faktoren, wie Arbeit und Zwischenprodukte, tendenziell erhöht.

Wenn die Lebensunterhaltungskostenindexe in den Zentren und dem Umland gleich sind, dann ist der Lohnsatz überall derselbe $w_r = R_r^{\beta_r} \cdot P_M^{r\,\beta_M} / P_M^{O\beta_M} = 1$.

Liegt ein Raumgleichgewicht vor, so ist die Zahl der erwerbstätigen Einwohner in jedem Zentrum gemäß der Gleichung (16) zu errechnen. Da wir trotz der Güterheterogenität die gleiche Produktionstechnologie aller in demselben Zentrum ansässigen Unternehmen unterstellen, lässt sich der aus der Gleichung (16) gefolgerte Arbeitseinsatz als die gesamte Beschäftigungszahl in diesem Zentrum interpretieren:

$$L_r = \alpha \cdot (\sigma - 1) \cdot F_r . \tag{36}$$

Die obigen Fixkosten F_r wachsen mit der Zahl der Ansiedlungsunternehmen.

Die erwerbstätigen Einwohner in allen Zentren werden in der Gleichung (37) summiert:

$$\sum_{r>0} L_r = \alpha \cdot (\sigma - 1) \cdot \sum_{r>0} F_r , \tag{37}$$

wobei die Anzahl r der Zentren u.a. von den nicht landwirtschaftlichen Erwerbspersonen $\sum_{r>0} L_r$ abhängt.

Während wir die Arbeitsbeschäftigung in den Zentren auf der Produktionsseite bestimmt haben, ist die Arbeitsbeschäftigung im Agrarbereich nachfrageseitig zu ermitteln. Laut der Gleichungen (22) und (27) gilt:

$$q_O = \beta_O \cdot (Y_O^L \cdot L_O + \sum_{r>0} Y_r^L \cdot L_r + Y^N \cdot N) . \tag{38}$$

Das Nettoeinkommen der erwerbstätigen Personen beträgt überall $1-\tau$. Das Transfereinkommen Y^N ist in der Gleichung (21) gegeben. Danach wird die Agrarproduktnachfrage expliziert:

$$q_O = \beta_O \cdot [(1-\tau) \cdot \sum_{r\geq 0} L_r + \tau \cdot \sum_{r\geq 0} L_r] = \beta_O \cdot \sum_{r\geq 0} L_r = \beta_O \cdot L \tag{39}$$

Um q_O zu erzeugen, wird der Produktionsfunktion (4) zufolge die Arbeit L_O eingesetzt:

$$q_O = L_O = \beta_O \cdot L = \mu \cdot L . \tag{40}$$

Der Elastizitätsparameter β_O der Nutzenfunktion (5) gibt den für das Agrarprodukt q_O ausgegebenen Einkommensanteil an. Dieser stimmt mit dem Anteil der im Agrarbereich beschäftigten Arbeitskräfte μ überein. Aus den Gleichungen (37) und (40) ergibt sich die gesamte Arbeitsbeschäftigung:

$$L = L_O + \sum\nolimits_{r>0} L_r = [\alpha \cdot (\sigma - 1)/(1 - \beta_O)] \cdot \sum\nolimits_r F_r . \tag{41}$$

Ferner ziehen wir das Gütermarktgleichgewicht in Betracht. Das Angebot und die Nachfrage am Agrarproduktmarkt entsprechen den Darstellungen in den Gleichungen (4) bzw. (40) und (39). Das Angebot anderer Konsumgüter und Zwischenprodukte wird mittels der Gleichung (13) veranschaulicht. Die Nachfrage nach den in den verschiedenen Zentren produzierten Gütern setzt sich aus den Gleichungen (18), (24) und (29) zusammen. Bei der Suche nach einer Gleichgewichtslösung handelt es sich im Grunde um die Frage, ob ein Preisvektor $[p_r]$ bzw. eine Preismatrix $[p_r^{r'}] = [t(\delta_{rr'})] \cdot [p_r]$, mit deren/dessen Hilfe das Güterangebot und die Güternachfrage ausgeglichen werden, zu finden ist. Da für Güter $q_1, q_2, \ldots q_m$ n×Gleichgewichtsbedingungen gelten müssen und die n×Gleichgewichtsbedingungen n-mal zu berechnende Güterpreise enthalten, können wir ohne weiteres feststellen, dass der gesuchte Preisvektor bzw. die gesuchte Preismatrix existiert.

5. Raumstruktur und deren Determinanten

Um herauszukristallisieren, wie viele Zentren im Raumgleichgewicht existieren können und welche Determinanten dafür relevant sind, nehmen wir einen simplen Fall an, in dem alle Zentren symmetrisch sind und die Fixproduktionskosten überall in der gleichen Höhe liegen, d.h. $F_1 = F_2 = \ldots = F_r = F$.

Aus der Gleichung (5) folgt:

$$r = \frac{1 - \beta_O}{\alpha} \cdot \frac{1}{\sigma - 1} \cdot \frac{L}{F} . \tag{42}$$

Folglich determinieren die nachstehenden Einflussfaktoren die Zahl der Zentren:

- der für das Agrarprodukt ausgegebene Einkommensanteil β_O (entspricht dem Anteil der Einwohner im Umland),
- die Outputelastizität α der Arbeit im Produktionsprozess der Zentren,
- die Substitutionselastizität σ der sowohl konsumierbaren als auch produktiv verwertbaren Erzeugnisse $m_1, m_2, \ldots, m_n$,
- die den Kapitalstock der städtischen Produktion implizierenden Fixkosten F und,
- die gesamten Erwerbspersonen bzw. das Erwerbspersonenpotential L.

Denn:

- je expansiver die Produktion im Umland ist, desto restriktiver ist der Beschäftigungsengpass in den Zentren und desto geringer wird die Zahl der Zentren,
- je outputelastischer die Arbeit ist, desto arbeitsintensiver wird die Produktion in einzelnen Zentren ausfallen, beim gegebenen Erwerbspersonenpotential hält sich die Zahl der Zentren in Grenzen,
- je größer das Güterangebotsspektrum der Zentren ist, desto stärker wirken die Skaleneffekte der Produktvielfalt auf die Vor- und Rückwärtsverkopplungen (Hirschman 1958.), diese führen zur Agglomeration und zur Reduzierung der Zahl der Zentren,
- je höher die Fixkosten in den Zentren sind, desto signifikanter sind die lock-in-Effekte, infolgedessen konzentriert sich die Produktion auf wenige große Zentren,
- je größer das Erwerbspersonenpotential ist, desto mehr Zentren bilden sich aus dem nahe liegenden Grunde heraus.

Die obigen Erläuterungen lassen sich anhand der unteren Zahlenbeispiele demonstrieren:

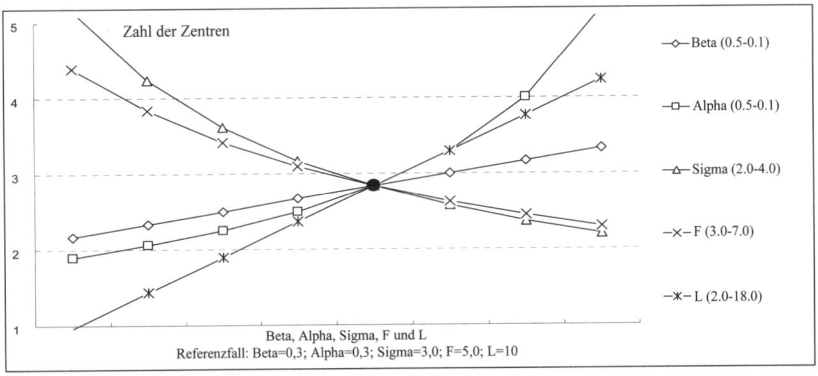

Abb. 1: Zahl der Zentren und deren Einflussfaktoren

III. Einfluss des Bevölkerungsrückgangs auf die Raumstruktur

1. Folgerungen aus dem analytischen Raumstrukturmodell

Nachdem wir die raumstrukturellen Einflussfaktoren analysiert haben, lassen sich Effekte des Bevölkerungsrückgangs auf die Raumstruktur eruieren. In Anlehnung an die Lösung (42) ist zu prognostizieren, dass die Zahl der Zentren infolge des Bevölkerungsrückgangs tendenziell zurückgeht. Weil die Zentren normalerweise nicht symmetrisch und räumlich ungleichmäßig verteilt sind, können wir aus der vorangegangenen Untersuchung folgern, dass jene Zentren, deren:

- Produktion weniger kapitalintensiv ausgestattet ist und die für die sich in den Fixkosten F_r niederschlagenden lock-in-Effekte nicht erheblich sind,
- Produktivitätsniveau $\overline{A}_r$ vergleichsweise niedriger ist, der Outputumfang relativ kleiner ist und Skalenerträge der Produktvielfalt unzureichend sind,
- räumliche Lage mit hohen Transportkosten $t(\delta_{rr'})$ verbunden ist, insbesondere vom Bevölkerungsrückgang betroffen sind.

Die Argumente für die obige Aussage werden anschließend erläutert:

- Gemäß der Gleichung (36) haben die hohen Fixkosten bzw. deren lock-in-Effekte unmittelbar eine große Beschäftigungs- bzw. Einwohnerzahl zur Folge.
- Laut der Gleichung (10) bewirkt ein niedrigeres Produktivitätsniveau c.p. die höheren Grenzproduktionskosten c_r, sodass der Outputumfang q eines Zentrums r, wie in der Gleichung (13) ausgewiesen, und die Skalenerträge der dortigen Produktion rückläufig sind. Daraufhin legen die Konsum- bzw. Inputpreise p_r in der Formel (14) zu. Der Preisindex P_r^M steigt in Einklang mit der Lösung (8). Der Funktion (26) entsprechend fällt der Nutzen U_r. Sofern die Bedingung (32′) bzw. (33′) nicht erfüllt werden, wandern die Einwohner aus.
- Wenn der Preisindex P_r^M im betroffenen Zentrum – inklusive der von der Verkehrsbedingung abhängenden Transportkosten – wegen der eingeschränkten Marktzugangsmöglichkeit zunimmt, dann steigt die Zahl der Auswanderer nochmals.

2. Numerische Rechenbeispiele

Um die raumstrukturellen Effekte des Bevölkerungsrückgangs anschaulich zu machen, greifen wir auf numerische Rechenbeispiele zurück. Der Ausgang der Rechenbeispiele ist ein Wirtschaftsraum mit zwei Zentren und einem gemeinsamen Umland. Die Ausgangsdaten dafür sind in der Tabelle 1 gegeben:

	$\overline{A}_r$	α	β_O	β_M	$t(\delta_{rO})$	σ	τ	η	F	L
Zentrum 1	1,2	0,3	0,3	0,5	1	3	0,15	0,15	7	4,2
Zentrum 2	1,1				2				3	1,8

Tab. 1: Ausgangsdaten der numerischen Raumstrukturrechenbeispiele

In der Abbildung 2 wird ein proportionaler Rückgang der erwerbstätigen wie auch nichterwerbstätigen Einwohner in den Zentren und dem Umland geschildert:

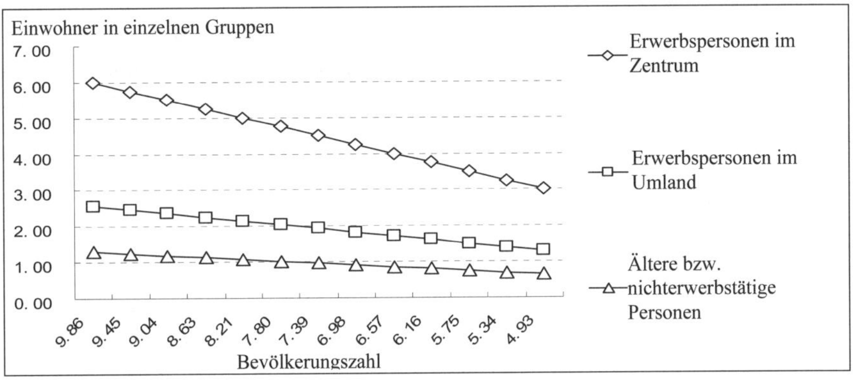

Abb. 2: Bevölkerungsrückgang in einem proportionalen Falle

Da die Zahl der Erwerbspersonen zurückgeht, sinkt die Produktion sowohl in den Zentren insgesamt, als auch im Umland. Die betrachtete Wirtschaft schrumpft.

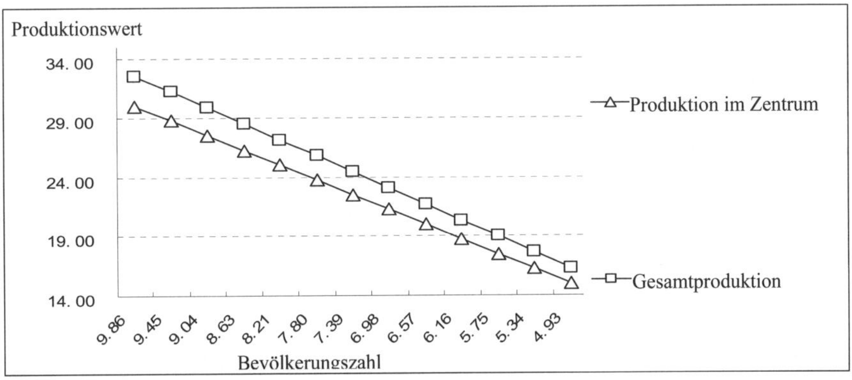

Abb. 3: Produktionsschrumpfung infolge des Bevölkerungsrückgangs

Die Produktion in den Zentren, die eine gewisse Infrastruktur und Kapitalausstattung voraussetzt, kann langfristig nur erhalten werden, wenn die Fixkosten finanzierbar bleiben. Jedoch ist dies bei der Produktionsschrumpfung nicht der Fall. Die mit Verlust produzierenden Unternehmen müssen entweder geschlossen oder umgesiedelt werden. Für die Umsiedlung gibt es zwei Alternativen: Entweder wird die Produktion des kleinen Zentrums 2 in das große Zentrum 1 verlagert oder die Umsiedlung läuft in die Gegenrichtung.

Infolge der Umsiedlung werden zusätzliche Investitionen zwecks der Infrastrukturanpassung und Kapitalaufstockung getätigt. Weil das große Zentrum umfangreicher mit der Infrastruktur und dem Kapitalstock ausgestattet ist, bewirkt die

Umsiedlung vom kleinen Zentrum zu dem großen Zentrum geringere Anpassungskosten. D.h., der Bevölkerungsrückgang hat zur Folge, dass sich die Produktion im großen Zentrum konzentriert und das kleine Zentrum allmählich verschwindet. Die Investition der Raumstrukturanpassung im großen Zentrum ist auf der linken Seite der Abbildung 4 dargestellt.

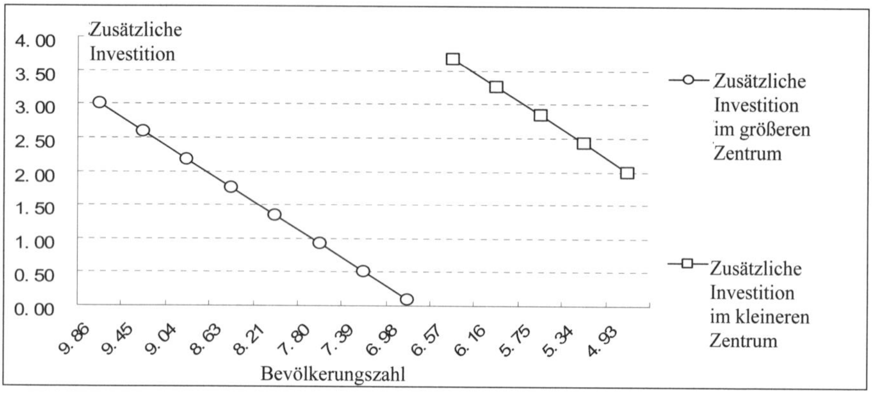

Abb. 4: Zusätzliche Investitionen bei der Raumanpassung infolge des Bevölkerungsrückgangs

Neben den geringeren Raumanpassungskosten sind die Vorteile der Produktionsverlagerung vom kleinen Zentrum zu dem großen Zentrum noch in Relationen:

- der Grenzproduktionskosten jeweils im großen bzw. kleinen Zentrum,
- des Güterangebotsumfangs und der Produktvielfalt,
- der Güterpreise bzw. Preisindexe sowie
- der Lebensunterhaltungskostenindexe

zu sehen. Die in der Tabelle 2 aufgezeigten Rechenergebnisse verdeutlichen, dass die auf dem großen Zentrum basierende Raumanpassung sowohl aus Sicht der Konsumenten als auch aus Sicht der Produzenten eine bessere Alternative ist.

	Grenzkosten	Angebotsumfang	Produktvielfalt	Güterpreis	Preisindex	Preisindex im Umland	Lebensunterhaltungskosten
	Großes Zentrum : Kleines Zentrum						
Indikatorverhältnisse	0,76	1,32	1,07	0,79	0,76	0,38	0,54

Tab. 2: Vergleich der Umsiedlungslösung mit dem großen bzw. kleinen Zentrum

Die obige Darstellung trifft auf einen mäßigen Bevölkerungsrückgang zu. Falls die Einwohnerzahl sehr stark fällt, sodass die Fixkosten im großen Zentrum trotz der Ansiedlung zuvor im kleinen Zentrum ansässiger Unternehmen nicht tragbar sind, so siedeln die Unternehmen vom großen Zentrum zum kleinen Zentrum um, weil sie nur dort ohne Verlust produzieren können. Die rechte Kurve in der Abbildung 4 zeigt diesen Fall.

Anschließend stellen wir ein weiteres Szenario vor, in dem der Bevölkerungsrückgang zusätzlich mit einem steigenden Anteil älterer/nichterwerbstätiger Einwohner einhergeht. Im Vergleich mit der Situation zuvor sinkt die Zahl der Erwerbspersonen nun schneller. Dies hat zur Folge, dass die Produktionsreduktion im betrachteten Wirtschaftsraum noch signifikanter wird. Ferner geht die Raumstrukturanpassung mittels der Produktionsverlagerung zu dem größeren Zentrum schon vorzeitig zur auf dem kleineren Zentrum beruhenden Anpassungslösung über.

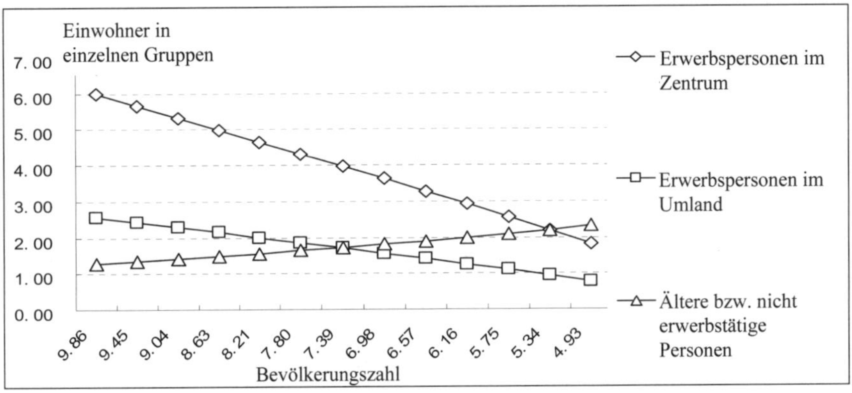

Abb. 5: Bevölkerungsrückgang mit einem zunehmenden Anteil älterer Einwohner

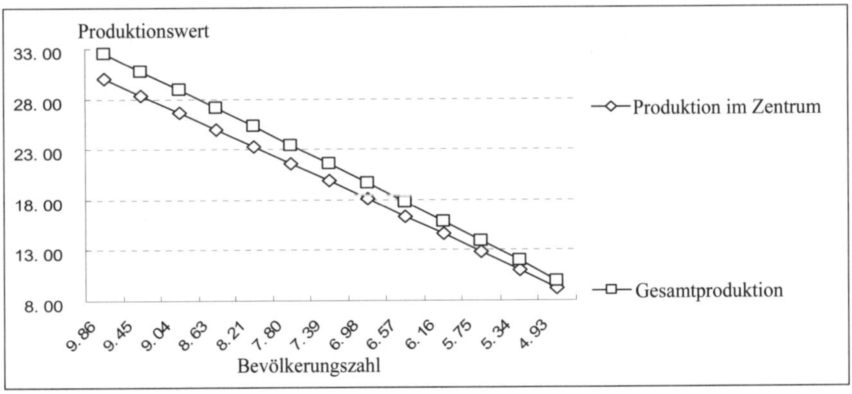

Abb. 6: Produktionsreduktion infolge des Bevölkerungsrückgangs mit einem zunehmenden Anteil älterer Einwohner

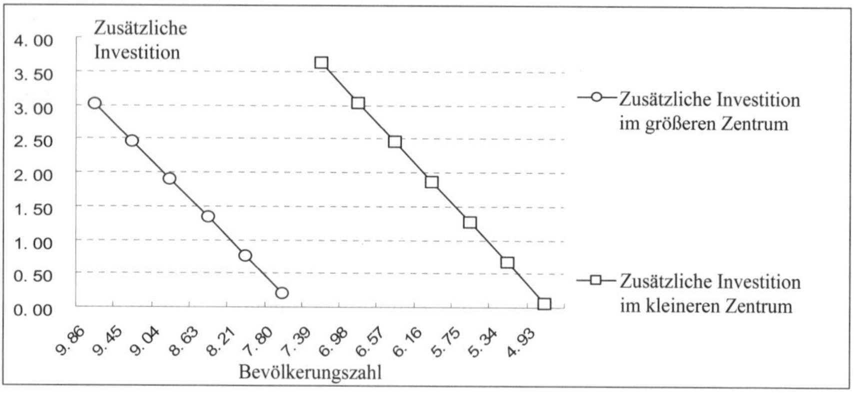

Abb. 7: Raumanpassungskonsequenz des Bevölkerungsrückgangs mit einem zunehmenden Anteil älterer Einwohner

IV. Schlussbemerkung

Die Raumstrukturbildung und -anpassung hängen mit der Bevölkerungsentwicklung eng zusammen. Während der Bevölkerungszuwachs, sofern das technologische Niveau nicht rückläufig ist, zur zunehmenden Agglomeration und Entstehung neuer Zentren führt, resultiert aus dem Bevölkerungsrückgang eine tendenziell sinkende Zahl von Zentren.

Die Raumstrukturanpassung an den Bevölkerungsrückgang erfolgt allerdings nicht spiegelbildlich zu jener an eine steigende Bevölkerungszahl. Erwartungsgemäß schrumpfen die kleinen Zentren zuerst, da Firmen und Einwohner von den kleinen Zentren in die großen Zentren umziehen. Insofern können die großen Zentren trotz der insgesamt zurückgehenden Einwohnerzahl noch wachsen. Verantwortlich für die Raumstrukturanpassung auf diese Art und Weise sind in erster Linie:

- Agglomerationsvorteile und
- Raumanpassungskosten.

Die Entstehung der Zentren ist bekanntlich eine Konsequenz der Agglomeration aufgrund steigender Skalenerträge und Einkommenseffekte der Produktvielfalt, welche umso bedeutsamer sind, je charakteristischere Vor- und Rückwärtsverkopplungen in den betrachteten Zentren existieren. Bei der Raumstrukturanpassung an den Bevölkerungsrückgang verringern sich solche Vorteile in einem schrumpfenden großen Zentrum signifikanter als die in einem schrumpfenden kleinen Zentrum. Deshalb bleiben die großen Zentren erhalten, oder sie wachsen sogar, da die aus den kleinen Zentren ausgewanderten Firmen und Einwohner hinzukommen.

Von der Raumstrukturanpassung rühren Anpassungskosten her. Weil die großen Zentren in Hinsicht auf deren Infrastrukturbedingung, den dort bereits gebildeten Kapitalbestand und somit die Fähigkeit, weitere Firmen wie auch Einwohner aufzunehmen, den kleinen Zentren überlegen sind, verursacht eine sich auf die großen Zentren stützende Anpassung geringere Anpassungskosten als die Raumstrukturanpassung durch Erhaltung der kleinen Zentren.
Wenn aber die Bevölkerungszahl so rapide zurückgeht, dass die mit dem Infrastrukturausbau und der Kapitalaufstockung in den großen Zentren einhergehenden Anpassungskosten vom dortigen Produktionssektor nicht mehr tragbar sind, dann werden die großen Zentren aufgegeben. Die zuvor in den großen Zentren ansässigen Firmen und Einwohner wandeln sich in die kleinen Zentren um.
Fällt die Bevölkerungszahl noch drastischer, dann lassen sich die kleinen Zentren langfristig nicht mehr erhalten.

Literaturverzeichnis

Becker, G.S. und *R.J. Barro*, A Reformulation of the Economic Theory of Fertility, in: Quarterly Journal of Economics, Vol. 103, 1988, S. 1-25.

Casetti, E., Equilibrium population partitions between urban and agricultural occupations, in: Geographical Analysis, Vol. 12, 1971, S. 47-54.

Christaller, W., Die zentralen Orte in Süddeutschland, Jena 1933.

Coale A.J. und *S.C. Watkins* (Hrsg.), The Decline of Fertility in Europe, Princeton/N.J. 1986.

Cody, M.L., A General Theory of Clutch Size, in: Evolution, Vol. 20, 1966, S. 174-184.

Dixt, A.K. und *J.E. Stiglitz*, Monopolistic Competition and Optimum Product Diversity, in: American Economic Review, Vol. 67, 1977, S. 297-308.

Dyson, T. und *M. Murphy*, The Onset of Fertility Transition, in: Population and Development Review, Vol. 11, 1985, S. 399-440.

Ehrlich, I. und *F. Lui*, The Problem of Population and Growth: A Review of the Literature from Malthus to Contemporary Models of Endogenous Population and Endogenous Growth, in: Journal of Economic Dynamics and Control, Vol. 21, 1997, S. 205-242.

Fujita, M., P. Krugman und *A.J. Venables*, The Spatial Economy, Cambridge/Mass. 1999.

Fujita, M. und *J.-F. Thisse*, Economics of Agglomeration, Cities, Industrial Location and Regional Growth, Cambridge 2002.

Galor, O. und *D.N. Weil*, Population, Technology and Growth: From Malthusian Stagnation to the Demographic Transition and Beyond, in: The American Economic Review, Vol. 90, 2000, S. 806-828.

Hirschman, A.O., The Strategy of Economic Development, New Haven 1958.

Ijiri, Y. und *H. Simon*, Skew Distribution and the Sizes of Business Firms, Amsterdam 1977.

Kremer, M., Population Growth and Technological Change: One B.C. to 1990, in: Quarterly Journal of Economics, Vol. 108, 1993, S. 681-716.

Lack, D., The Natural Regulation of Animal Numbers, Oxford 1954.

Lee, R.D., Population Dynamics: Equilibrium, Disequilibrium, and Consequences of Fluctuations, in: Handbook of Population and Family Economics, hrsg. von M. Rosenzweig und O. Stark, Vol. 1B., Amsterdam 1997, S. 1063-1115.

Livi-Bacci, M. A Concise History of World Population, Oxford 1997.

Lösch, A., Die räumliche Ordnung der Wirtschaft, Jena 1939.

Malthus, Th.R., An Essay on the Principle of Population, London 1798.

Maddison, A., The World Economy. Paris 2001.

McCann, Ph., Urban and regional economics, Oxford 2001.

Rosenzweig, M. und *O. Stark* (Hrsg.), Handbook of Population and Family Economics, Amsterdam 1997.

Samuelson, P.A., The transfer problem and transport costs: The terms of trade when impediments absent, in: Economic Journal, Vol. 62, 1952, S. 278-304.
Thünen, J.H. v., Der Isolierte Staat in Beziehung auf Landschaft und Nationalökonomie, Stuttgart 1826.
Whitaker, J.K., Henry George oh the location of economic activity, in: Industry, Space and Competition, hrsg. von M Bellet und C. L'Harmet, Cheltenham 1998, S. 174-184.
Wrigley, E.A., Population and History, New York 1969.

C. Demographischer Wandel als Herausforderung für kommunale Unternehmen in Deutschland

Peter Eichhorn

I. Kommunale Wirtschaft heute

1. Betätigungsgebiete

Kommunale Wirtschaft als Zusammenfassung kommunaler Unternehmen lässt sich schon lange nicht mehr mit den vier Säulen Versorgungswirtschaft, Verkehrswirtschaft, Wohnungswirtschaft und Sparkassenwesen erfassen. Abgesehen davon, dass sich diese Betätigungsgebiete stark differenzierten, kamen neue unternehmerische Aktivitäten hinzu. Was die Differenzierung anbelangt, entstanden in der Versorgungswirtschaft kommunale Unternehmen für die Strom-, Gas-, Fernwärme- und Wasserversorgung, Abwasser- und Abfallentsorgung mit Beteiligungsgesellschaften für Consulting, Projektentwicklung, Kundenberatung und Verbrauchsabrechnung. Zum öffentlichen Personennahverkehr mit Bahnen und Bussen gesellten sich Parkhäuser, Werkstätten, Hafenbetriebe und Flughäfen. Die Wohnungswirtschaft gliederte sich in Unternehmen für Bau, Vermietung, Betreuung und Finanzierung. Von den Sparkassen wurden Beteiligungen an Venture Capital-Gesellschaften, Technologie-Gründerzentren, Finanzierungsberatungs- sowie Grundstückserschließungsunternehmen eingegangen.

Zu diesen oftmals in Beteiligungs- und Konzernstrukturen gegliederten vier Hauptbetätigungsgebieten gesellten sich in den vergangenen Jahrzehnten zahlreiche weitere kommunale Unternehmen in den diversen Rechtsformen Eigenbetrieb, GmbH, AG, Anstalt öffentlichen Rechts, Stiftung privaten oder öffentlichen Rechts und Zweckverband. Sie entstanden teils durch Ausgliederung von Aufgaben aus der Ämterverwaltung in Form der Umwandlung von Bruttobetrieben in Nettobetriebe, teils durch Aufspaltungen, Beteiligungen und Neugründungen (Eichhorn 1997, S. 97 f.). Heute finden sich kommunale Unternehmen in den Bereichen Bildung, Kultur, Erholung, Sport, Gesundheit, Altenbetreuung, Ausstellungswesen, Tourismusförderung, Wirtschaftsförderung – kommunalrechtlich ausgedrückt in wirtschaftlichen und nichtwirtschaftlichen Betätigungsgebieten.

In vielen Städten ist die Kommune nicht mehr alleinige Trägerin bzw. Anteilseignerin, sondern nur Mitgesellschafterin neben einem oder mehreren anderen öffentlichen oder privaten Partnern. Vielerorts zeigt sich, dass die kommunalen samt den gemischtöffentlichen und gemischwirtschaftlichen Unternehmen mehr Arbeitnehmer beschäftigen als die kommunale (Ämter-) Verwaltung (Eichhorn 2005, S. 217 ff.).

2. Regimewechsel

Die Entwicklung der kommunalen Unternehmen lässt sich durch zwei Phänomene kennzeichnen. Erstens: Aus ehemaligen in die kommunale Selbstverwaltung eingebetteten örtlichen Monopolbetrieben wurden Gemeindegebietsgrenzen überschreitende Unternehmen im Wettbewerb. Zweitens: Die immer selbstständiger agierenden kommunalen Unternehmen übernehmen das privatwirtschaftliche Paradigma der Kundenorientierung bei gleichzeitiger Kommerzialisierung. Der Regimewechsel ist evident: Von der Politik zum Markt bzw. anders formuliert: von der kollektiven Bedarfslenkung zur Ausrichtung auf die kaufkräftige Nachfrage (Bluhm 1999, S. 143 ff.).

Dieser Anpassungsprozess bei kommunalen Unternehmen hat dazu geführt, dass trotz des öffentlichen Auftrags und der daraus resultierenden Sachzieldominanz, kommunale Unternehmen mit gewerblichen Privatunternehmen gleichgestellt wurden. Exemplarisch steht dafür das Streichen von Steuerprivilegien. Von Seiten kommunaler Unternehmen wird kritisiert, dass sie angeblich gleich behandelt werden, tatsächlich aber durch das strenge Subsidiaritätsprinzip privaten Unternehmen Vorrang eingeräumt wird. Nachteile erwachsen kommunalen Unternehmen auch, wenn ihnen Quersubventionierungen zum Beispiel zwischen Geschäftssparten untersagt oder öffentliche Ausschreibungen auferlegt werden (Eichhorn 1989, S. 19 f.).

3. Neue Arrangements

Die wirtschaftspolitische Wettbewerbsdoktrin der Europäischen Union zieht wirtschaftliche und sog. nichtwirtschaftliche Branchen in ihren Bann. Selbst städtische Schulen, Freizeitstätten, Krankenhäuser und Altenheime werden „marktfühliger" und nutzen Angebote im Markt. Stichworte dazu lauten für die gesamte kommunale Wirtschaft, zum Teil auch für die Kommunalverwaltung, Make or Buy, Insourcing, Outsourcing und Contracting Out. Man setzt verstärkt Marketing ein, sucht Finanzierer und Förderer (Sponsoren, Stifter, Freunde, Helfer) und wendet das betriebswirtschaftliche Instrumentarium im Innern an. Einzug halten Fragen der Führungsphilosophie, Organisationskultur und der Leistungsanreize. Zum Einsatz kommen Budgetierung, Controlling, Lean Management, Qualitätssicherung und kaufmännische Rechnungslegung (Bleyer 2004, S. 160 ff.).

Das einzelne kommunale Unternehmen baut einerseits ein Netzwerk auf der Beschaffungs- und Absatzseite auf, andererseits ist der kommunale Träger darum bemüht, seine Unternehmen zu koordinieren und zu konsolidieren, etwa in Form eines gemeinsamen Jahresabschlusses.

Zusammenfassend lassen sich gegenwärtig folgende Trends in der kommunalen Wirtschaft registrieren: Es findet eine Entpolitisierung statt, zugleich eine Entflechtung bzw. Dezentralisierung, die von Teil- und Vollprivatisierungen begleitet wird. In den kommunalen Unternehmen intensiviert sich die Ökonomisierung, die zwar auch die (z.B. sozial-, verkehrs- und umweltpolitischen) Sachziele erfasst, aber mehr und mehr die Formalziele (Rentabilität, Liquidität und Sekurität) präferiert. Die Frage stellt sich, wie die weitere Entwicklung angesichts des demographischen Wandels aussehen wird (Eichhorn 2005, S. 192).

II. Daseinsvorsorge und Demographie

1. Daseinsvorsorgeziele

Der von Ernst Forsthoff geprägte Begriff der Daseinsvorsorge wird im europasprachlichen Kontext mit Dienstleistungen von allgemeinem wirtschaftlichen Interesse, manchmal auch mit gemeinwohlorientierten oder gemeinwirtschaftlichen Leistungen oder öffentlichen Dienstleistungen gleichgesetzt (Forsthoff 1976, S. 204 ff.). Stets sucht man damit Leistungen für eine zukunftssichernde Versorgung der Bevölkerung mit existenziellen Gütern zu erfassen. Ihre Art, Menge und Güte sind nicht exakt zu bestimmen, sondern hängen von gesellschaftlichen und wirtschaftlichen Bedingungen und Einstellungen sowie von Raum und Zeit ab. Hierzulande und heutzutage spielen neben rein physischen Bedürfnissen auch kulturelle Bedürfnisse eine Rolle, die es zu decken gilt. Im Wesentlichen handelt es sich um für Bürger und Unternehmen zugängliche, preisgünstige, sichere, dauerhafte und insgesamt für die Allgemeinheit nutzenstiftende Leistungen. Herkömmlicherweise zählen dazu netzgebundene Leistungen, aber auch andere infrastrukturell bedeutsame Leistungen etwa im Bereich Bildung, Gesundheit und Soziales.
In wirtschaftlichen Wechsellagen können manche kommunalen Leistungen dringend benötigt oder entbehrlich werden. Die Wohnungswirtschaft steht dafür beispielhaft. Nach dem 2. Weltkrieg sorgten städtische Wohnungsämter und Wohnungsgesellschaften für Wohnraum; inzwischen schafft der Wohnungsmarkt weitgehend einen Ausgleich zwischen Nachfrage und Angebot, wurde die gemeinnützige Wohnungswirtschaft aufgegeben und trat an die Stelle objektgeförderter Wohnungsunternehmen die Subjektförderung durch Wohngeld (Eichhorn, Merk 2006, S. 30).

2. Nachfragewandel

Allen Anzeichen nach wird die Zukunft der Daseinsvorsorge in Deutschland von zwei gravierenden Entwicklungen beeinflusst: Die Bevölkerung schrumpft und die Alterung nimmt zu. Da sich die Leistungsangebote kommunaler Unternehmen weniger an einzelne, womöglich sogar von den demographischen Entwicklungen weniger betroffene Zielgruppen wenden, sondern an die Allgemeinheit richten, sind einschneidende Änderungen bei kommunalen Unternehmen unvermeidbar. An einem Beispiel sei dies erklärt: Die Bahnen und Busse eines kommunalen Verkehrsunternehmens dienen sowohl den Fahrgästen als auch dem Individual- und Werkverkehr, die großes Interesse an einem funktionstüchtigen ÖPNV haben. So gesehen sind Fahrgäste sowie PKW-Fahrer und Firmen (direkt und indirekt) Kunden des kommunalen Verkehrsunternehmens!

Mit welchem Nachfragewandel muss wo gerechnet werden? Es ist offensichtlich, dass der Bevölkerungsrückgang nicht überall im gleichen Ausmaß stattfindet; ebenso verhält es sich mit der Alterung. Tendenziell legen die Großstädte mit ihrem Umland an Einwohnern samt Jugendlichen zu, während kleinere Gemeinden nicht zuletzt infolge geringer Ausbildungs- und Einkommenschancen Bevölkerungsabnahme und Überalterung zu gewärtigen haben (o.V. 2006, S. 11). Unter dieser Annahme werden sich kommunale Unternehmen in der Großstadt behaupten, wogegen die Kleinstadt- bzw. Landflucht in den kleinen Gemeinden zu folgenden Änderungen führen dürfte: Vorhandene Netzkapazitäten und weitere Infrastrukturleistungen werden immer weniger genutzt und sind entweder relativ teuer zu reduzieren oder man geht in die Offensive und sucht durch attraktive Ansiedlungen eine prosperierende Situation zu erhalten oder zu schaffen. Einzelnen Gemeinden mag letzteres gelingen, nicht aber der Mehrzahl. Da die älteren und dann gewöhnlich nicht berufstätigen Menschen mehr gesundheitliche, kulturelle und soziale Daseinsvorsorgeleistungen nachfragen, ergeben sich Verlagerungen, die freilich nur partiell von den verkleinerten kommunalen Unternehmen wahrgenommen werden können.

Kleine kommunale Unternehmen haben mittel- bis langfristig kaum eine Chance zu bestehen. Selbst mit diversifizierten Produkten wird die Nachfrage sinken und es liegt nahe, sich verstärkt zu interkommunalen Unternehmen zusammenzuschließen oder mit benachbarten kommunalen Unternehmen zu kooperieren. Betriebswirtschaftliche Synergieeffekte lassen allerdings erwarten, dass in den meisten Fällen entweder aus kleinen kommunalen Unternehmen Außenstellen bzw. Tochtergesellschaften von größeren kommunalen Unternehmen werden oder gemischtwirtschaftliche Unternehmen entstehen. Eine vollständige Privatisierung ist schwer vorstellbar, denn es wird kaum Investoren in Gemeinden mit schrumpfender und alternder Bevölkerung geben für die Übernahme eines defizitären Krankenhauses, Theaters, Altenheims oder anderer stationärer Einrichtungen (Isbruch 1990, S. 119 ff.; Mühlenkamp 1999, S. 58 ff.). Im Übrigen eröffnen mobile Dienste Substitutionsmöglichkeiten, die aber traditionellerweise weniger von Seiten kommunaler Unternehmen, sondern von Freiberuflern, Wohlfahrtsverbänden und neuerdings auch von Privatfirmen angeboten werden.

3. Neue Angebotsstrukturen

Über kurz oder lang findet bei kommunalen Unternehmen eine Art Maßstabsvergrößerung statt. Große kommunale Unternehmen werden weiter wachsen und zwar durch zentripetale und zentrifugale Kräfte. Das heißt, sie identifizieren sich mit ihrer zentralörtlichen Funktion und übernehmen einerseits in ihrer Region mittelgroße und kleine kommunale Unternehmen, andererseits entfalten sie sich zu Konzernen mit räumlich verteilten Absatzmärkten. Diese Entwicklung ist im Gange und dürfte sich in den nächsten Jahrzehnten fortsetzen. Es wird sich zumindest bei leitungsgebundenen kommunalen Unternehmen private Investoren bzw. Unternehmen als Mitgesellschafter einfinden und sich Ketten auch über nationale Grenzen hinaus bilden.

Die immer offensiver sich gestaltende Geschäftspolitik vieler kommunaler Unternehmen ruft zwei Konsequenzen hervor: Es wird die Regulierungsintensität weiter zunehmen und ebenso die Wettbewerbsintensität zwischen rein kommunalen, gemischtwirtschaftlichen und rein privaten Unternehmen. Die Frage, wer Eigentümer des Unternehmens ist, tritt in den Hintergrund. Die Funktionstüchtigkeit des Anbieters wird bei Bewerbungen um den Leistungsauftrag ausschlaggebend sein. Der immer wieder aufkommende Streit zwischen Kommunen und Privaten um Privilegien bzw. Ungleichbehandlung endet vorerst nicht; im Gegenteil: er dürfte sich mit der Tendenz zur Kommerzialisierung auch der öffentlichen Dienstleistungen noch steigern (Gottschalk 1999, S. 170 ff.).

Angenommen, eine Daseinsvorsorgeaufgabe lässt sich künftig politisch eindeutig festlegen und man strebt eine wirtschaftliche (d.h. kostengünstige), effiziente (d.h. zweckmäßige) und effektive (d.h. zielführende) Aufgabenerfüllung an. Dann müssten für die sich bewerbenden Aufgabenerfüller wirklich gleiche Wettbewerbschancen gelten (Schmidt 2001, S. 94 f.). Es melden sich Zweifel, ob dies möglich ist. Unternehmen im Eigentum einer Stadt unterscheiden sich von privaten Anbietern durch mehrere „essentials“: Kommunale Unternehmen bleiben trotz aller Entwicklungen stakeholder-orientiert; sie mausern sich nicht zum Shareholder-Ansatz. Insolvenzrisiken fallen de facto wegen der großen Gebietskörperschaft und ihrer Verantwortung für öffentliche Aufgaben wesentlich kleiner aus als bei haftungssummenbegrenzten Privatunternehmen. Die institutionellen und personellen Interdependenzen zwischen politischem Prinzipal und unternehmerischen Agenten sind eng und „do ut des"-geprägt, legen also weniger Wert auf eine strikte Trennung zwischen privatwirtschaftlicher Aufgabenwahrnehmung einerseits und städtischer und sonst wie behördlicher Aufgabenüberwachung andererseits. Vielleicht gelingt eines Tages eine formale Gleichstellung. Materiell wird sie nie erreicht werden, weshalb es auch in Zukunft politische, wirtschaftliche, rechtliche und gerichtliche Auseinandersetzungen geben dürfte.

III. Demographie und Management

1. Governance Watch

Das durch Übernahme kleiner und mittelgroßer kommunaler Unternehmen und durch Beteiligung privater Investoren hervorgerufene Wachstum kommunaler und gemischtwirtschaftlicher Unternehmen nimmt weiter zu (Raupp 2006, S. 19). Sitz dieser Großunternehmen ist die Großstadt. Von dort aus werden die Umlandgebiete und die entfernt liegenden Regionen verstärkt kommerziell gesteuert. Für die kommunale Selbstverwaltung (besser: Selbstgestaltung) bedeutet dies, auf der Hut zu sein, denn die Entscheidungen selbst mit Bezug auf die örtlichen Lebensverhältnisse treffen häufig Vorstände fernab.

Die Betonung erwerbswirtschaftlichen Handelns führt dazu, dass dieser Prozess vornehmlich die marktnahen öffentlichen Dienstleistungen erfasst. Marktferne öffentliche Dienstleistungen wie auf öffentliche Zuschüsse angewiesene städtische Galerien, Musikschulen, Orchester, Theater, Museen, Sportstätten, Freizeiteinrichtungen, Jugend- und Altenheime sowie Sozialdienste und -einrichtungen werden den Kommunen vor Ort verbleiben, soweit sie überhaupt erhalten werden können.

Die Diskussion über Governance Watch gewinnt auch in Kommunen an Fahrt. Die Kommunalpolitik wird im Hinblick auf ihre Legitimation hinterfragt. Es mehren sich die Anzeichen, dass die Politisierung aller Lebensbereiche ihren Höhepunkt überschritten hat. Die Kommunalpolitik wandelt sich, weil durch den Abzug kommunaler Wirtschaftsunternehmen und durch die Verlagerung kommunaler Selbstgestaltung auf zu subventionierende Kultur-, Gesundheits- und Sozialunternehmen künftig deren Förderung und Finanzierung im Vordergrund stehen (Fröhlke 2003, S. 28 ff.). Aufgabe der Kommunalpolitik wird es sein, mehr Anreize zu schaffen und weniger über kommunalpolitische Vorgaben, Auflagen, Einflussnahmen usw. zu beschließen. Was die erwerbswirtschaftlichen kommunalen Unternehmen anbelangt, ist vorstellbar, dass sich die Kommunen auf ihre Gewährleistungsfunktion zurückziehen.

Die Kunst, ein kommunales Unternehmen zu führen und zu überwachen, wird angesichts des Bevölkerungsrückgangs und der Überalterung nicht einfacher, eher schwieriger. Auf Gewinnerzielung bedachte kommunale Unternehmen haben dem Markt und Wettbewerb Tribut zu zollen und dabei den öffentlichen Auftrag wahrzunehmen. Die Beratung und Betreuung der Kunden wird aufwendiger sein, denn aller Erfahrung nach sind wenige und ältere Kunden anspruchsvoller. Der öffentliche Auftrag unterscheidet diese kommunalen Unternehmen zwar von selbstbestimmten, rein kommerziell tätigen Unternehmen der privaten Wirtschaft, aber der Unterschied ist nicht essentieller, sondern nur gradueller Natur. In jedem Fall muss die öffentliche Aufgabenerfüllung von den kommunalen Gebietskörperschaften als Aufgabenträger entgolten werden. Die entgeltliche Entsorgung von Haushaltsmüll durch private Unternehmen steht seit langem dafür exemplarisch. Wie hoch der Abgeltungspreis ist, hängt von der Marktform und der Marktstellung der Leistungsanbieter ab. Tendenziell dürften mehr und mehr Angebotsoligopole vorherrschen. Die Kommunen als Aufgabenträger besitzen Marktmacht, sei es durch Informationsvorsprünge, die ihnen durch andere Gemeinden zuteil werden, sei es als solventer Auftraggeber gegenüber eigenen oder fremden Unternehmen.

Die primär bedarfswirtschaftlich ausgerichteten kommunalen Kultur-, Gesundheits- und Sozialunternehmen dürften der Entwicklung der kommunalen Versorgungsunternehmen folgen. Bei diesen dominierten früher auch Bedarfsdeckungsziele, die sich durch Marktöffnung und Wettbewerbsverhalten in Rentabilitätsziele verwandelten. Dieser Zielsetzungswandel lässt sich inzwischen auch bei kommunalen Sparkassen, Wohnungsunternehmen, Krankenhäusern und vereinzelt im öffentlichen Personennahverkehr feststellen. Die frühere Sachzielsteuerung könnte über eine betonte Ökonomisierung nach und nach zur Kommerzialisierung denaturieren (Blume 2000, S. 66 ff.). Sie beginnt mit markt-konformen Angeboten (z.B. via Studiengebühren, Selbstbeteiligung, Eintrittsgeldern, Preisdifferenzierung), bemüht sich um die kaufkräftige Nachfrage (statt Bedarfslagen zu lenken) und vergleicht den Markterfolg mit dem Finanzergebnis anderer Unternehmen (o.V. 2004, S. 75 f.).

Behält man die Zweiteilung in formal- und sachzieldominant geführten Unternehmen für kommunale Dienstleistungen bei, verlagern sich die strategischen und operativen Entscheidungen bei ersteren auf Dachgesellschaften und geraten die Kommunen in die Rolle des „Zwischenhändlers" zwischen Anbieter und Letztverbraucher. Bei den Sachziele präferierenden Unternehmen werden die Kommunen auf die Strategien und Strukturen über Leistungs- und Finanzierungsvereinbarungen einwirken, während die operativen Maßnahmen den Unternehmen zuwachsen. Vom Standpunkt der Entrepreneurship ist dies zu begrüßen, weil durch diese (Teil-) Verselbständigung dezentraler Kompetenz und Verantwortung der Weg geebnet wird.

3. Transparenzgebot

Weniger und ältere Kunden sowie wenige und größere kommunale und private Unternehmen führen dazu, dass sich die Beziehungen zwischen nachfragenden Bürgern und Unternehmen auf der einen Seite und den öffentliche Dienstleistungen anbietenden Unternehmen auf der anderen Seite zugunsten Letzterer entwickeln dürften. Denn die Anbieter können Synergieeffekte (Bündelung von Aufgaben und Optimierung von Betriebsgrößen) nutzen, während die Kunden auf die Angebote angewiesen sind (Riess 2004, S. 13 f.). Die Nachfrager werden umso stärker den Infrastrukturangeboten ausgeliefert sein, desto mehr Kaufkraftschwäche und Bedürftigkeit vorherrschen. Um nicht übervorteilt zu werden, sollten die Interdependenzen zwischen öffentlichen Auftraggebern, öffentlichen oder privaten Auftragerfüllern sowie den Aufgabenadressaten offen gelegt werden. Sowohl die Prinzipale als auch die Agenten haben Informationspflichten über Leistungen und Tarife zu genügen, die den Kunden Vergleiche mit den Bedingungen andernorts erlauben. Erkennen die Kunden samt der Allgemeinheit Konditionendefizite, können sie auf die Prinzipale einwirken, weniger hingegen auf die Agenten, die ja als Erfüllungsgehilfen tätig sind.

Überhaupt wären die kommunalen Dienstleistungen prädestiniert, eine Bresche in die Intransparenz auf den regulierten Märkten zu schlagen. Ein Beispiel: Es würde nicht schaden – im Gegenteil nützen und die Effizienz steigern helfen –, wenn gesetzlich Versicherte über die ihnen zuteil werdenden ärztlichen Leistungen sowie über die Kosten und deren Erstattungen informiert würden (Schuhen 2002, S. 174). Genauso instruktiv und verbessernd wäre es, über die Ziel- und Leistungsvereinbarungen zwischen Kommune und Dienstleistungsherstellern und zwischen diesen und den Leistungsabnehmern aufgeklärt zu werden.

Die kommunalen Unternehmen könnten und sollten im Falle zurückgehender politischer Ingerenz und wachsender Vermarktung und Öffentlichkeitsarbeit ihre Berichterstattung signifikant erweitern. Die bislang eher bescheidenen Geschäftsberichte lehnen sich an die handelsrechtlichen Erfordernisse an und geizen mit Auskünften sowohl über kulturelle, soziale, gesundheitliche, ökologische und andere kommunalpolitische Ziele als auch über Zielerreichung, Innovationen, Qualitäten, Arbeits- und Lieferbedingungen, Beschwerden usw. Erst so würde die Allgemeinheit den Wert von Daseinsvorsorge dezidiert wahrnehmen.

Literaturverzeichnis

Bleyer, M., Verwaltungsreformen im öffentlichen Haushaltswesen durch Public Governance, Berlin 2004.

Bluhm, K., Zwischen Markt und Politik, Opladen 1999.

Blume, H. H., Sparkassen im Spannungsfeld zwischen öffentlichem Auftrag und kreditwirtschaftlichem Wettbewerb, Baden-Baden 2000.

Eichhorn, P., Synergieeffekte des kommunalen Querverbunds, in: Der kommunale Querverbund aus Sicht von Theorie und Praxis, hrsg. von R. Schauer, Baden-Baden 1989, S. 17-29.

Eichhorn, P., Ausgliederung als Instrument zur Flexibilisierung kommunaler Aufgabenerfüllung, in: Privatisierung kommunaler Aufgaben, hrsg. von W. Fettig und L. Späth, Baden-Baden 1997, S. 96-102.

Eichhorn, P., Das Prinzip Wirtschaftlichkeit, 3. Aufl., Wiesbaden 2005.

Eichhorn, P. und *J. Merk*, Von der Objekt- zur Subjektfinanzierung in der Gesundheitswirtschaft, in: Liberalisierung im Gesundheitswesen, hrsg. von G. E. Braun und F. Schulz-Nieswandt, Baden-Baden 2006, S. 27-46.

Forsthoff, E., Rechtsstaat im Wandel – verfassungsrechtliche Abhandlungen, 2. Aufl., München 1976.

Fröhlke, D., Aufbruch – von der Kommunalen Selbstverwaltung zu Kommunalen Selbstgestaltung, Kronach 2003.

Gottschalk, W., Kommunale Unternehmen zwischen öffentlichem Auftrag und Wettbewerb, in: Stand und Perspektiven der Öffentlichen Betriebswirtschaftslehre, hrsg. von D. Bräunig und D. Greiling, Berlin 1999, S. 167-174.

Isbruch, H., Privatisierung – ein Ausweg aus der finanziellen Krise des Theaters?, Bremen 1990.

Meinen, J., Konzernrecht im kommunalen Bereich, Berlin 2005.

Mühlenkamp, H., Eine ökonomische Analyse ausgewählter institutioneller Arrangements zur Erfüllung öffentlicher Aufgaben, Baden-Baden 1999.

o.V., Nachgefragt: Was bedeutet Corporate Governance?, in: Akademie, 49. Jg., 2004, Heft 3, S. 75-76.

o.V., Wie schließen Sie die demographische Lücke?, in: Süddeutsche Zeitung, Nr. 5, 7./8. Jan. 2006, S. 11.

Raupp, J., Siemens und die Megatrends, in: Süddeutsche Zeitung, Nr. 24, 30. Jan. 2006, S. 19.

Riess, B., Ist Corporate Social Responsibility messbar?, in: Forum, 1. Jg., 2004, Heft 3, S. 13-14.

Schmidt, H.-J., Betriebswirtschaftslehre und Verwaltungsmanagement, 5. Aufl., Heidelberg 2001.

Schuhen, A., Nonprofit Governance in der freien Wohlfahrtspflege, Baden-Baden 2002.

Zweites Kapitel

Finanzierungsprobleme bei Bevölkerungsrückgang

A. Der demographische Wandel als politische Herausforderung – Das Beispiel des Freistaats Sachsen

Georg Milbradt

I. Schrumpfung und Alterung in Sachsen

Der demographische Wandel ist ein säkularer Prozess, der bereits vor mehr als 100 Jahren begann. Der Geburtsjahrgang 1880 war der letzte, der sich vollständig reproduziert hat; alle nachfolgenden Jahrgänge hatten weniger Kinder, als zwecks Erhaltung einer stationären Bevölkerung nötig gewesen wären (Wahl 2003, S. 3). Dieser zunächst schleichende Prozess hat sich in den vergangenen Jahrzehnten immer mehr beschleunigt. Der Sterbeüberschuss betrug in der Bundesrepublik zwischen 1970 und 1990 1,5 Millionen; von 1991 bis 2001 bereits knapp 935.000. In Westdeutschland ist der Schrumpfungsprozess lange Zeit durch die Zuwanderung sowie die deutliche Zunahme der Lebenserwartung kaschiert worden. In Ostdeutschland und insbesondere in Sachsen dagegen ist die Schrumpfung schon seit langem nicht zu übersehen. 1950 lebten in Sachsen 5,7 Millionen Menschen, Anfang 1990 waren es 4,9 Millionen, Ende 2004 waren es nur noch knapp 4,3 Millionen. Für 2020 wird ein weiterer Rückgang auf 3,7 bis 3,8 Millionen prognostiziert (Statistisches Landesamt 2004a, S. 6).

In diesen Zahlen steckt zunächst die massive Abwanderung aus der DDR-Zeit bzw. die Arbeitsmigration nach der Wende. Zweitens schlägt hier der Geburtenrückgang zu Buche: Sachsen hat seit 1967 eine negative Geburtenbilanz, auch während der 1980er Jahre, als die DDR insgesamt einen leichten Geburtenüberschuss zu verzeichnen hatte. Nach der Wende brach die Geburtenzahl dramatisch auf 3 Geburten je 1000 Einwohner ein; mittlerweile nähert sie sich wieder dem Niveau der alten Bundesländer an (2004: 7,7 Geburten je 1000 Einwohner, zum Vergleich Baden-Württemberg: 9,0 je 1000). Mit tendenziell rückläufiger Abwanderung wird immer deutlicher sichtbar, dass das Geburtendefizit die Hauptursache der Schrumpfung ist.

Diese Schrumpfung geht einher mit einem Alterungsprozess. Der Altersdurchschnitt wird bis 2020 um fünf auf etwa 49 Jahre steigen. Dann wird jeder dritte Sachse 65 Jahre und älter sein (Statistisches Landesamt 2004a, S. 7).

Beide demographischen Effekte, Schrumpfung und Alterung, haben Auswirkungen auf sämtliche Bereiche von Politik, Wirtschaft und Gesellschaft. Im Folgenden sollen die wichtigsten Probleme skizziert werden.
Die ersten Auswirkungen des Schrumpfungsprozesses waren am Wohnungsmarkt und im Bildungswesen zu spüren. Das Eduard-Pestel-Institut für Systemforschung in Hannover prognostizierte 1996, dass 2010 in Ostdeutschland eine Million Wohnungen leer stehen werden (DSL Bank 1996). Diese Studie stieß damals bei den Verantwortlichen auf große Empörung und wurde als abwegig bezeichnet. In Wirklichkeit hat sie das Ausmaß des Leerstandes sogar noch unterschätzt. Dem Mikrozensus 1998 zufolge standen in Ostdeutschland bereits 960.000 Wohnungen oder 13,2% des Wohnungsbestandes leer. Der Mikrozensus 2002 ermittelte 1,2 Millionen leer stehende Wohnungen oder rund 16% des Bestandes, davon in Sachsen knapp 415.000 Wohnungen oder 17,5% des sächsischen Bestandes – trotz begonnener Abrissprogramme!
Ein ähnlicher Frühindikator des demographischen Wandels waren die Schülerzahlen. Da die Geburtenzahl sich nach der Wende halbierte, verzeichneten die Grundschulen Ende der 1990er Jahre eine Halbierung ihrer Schülerzahl. Mittlerweile ist der Rückgang der Schülerzahl auch in den Mittelschulen und Gymnasien angekommen. Insgesamt mussten bisher mehr als 800 Schulen geschlossen werden. Im vergangenen Sommer hat das Kultusministerium bei weiteren Schulen keine neuen Eingangsklassen genehmigt, weil die Zahl der Schüler für eine zweizügige Mittelschule oder ein dreizügiges Gymnasium nicht ausreicht.
In den nächsten drei bis vier Jahren wird sich die Halbierung der Schülerzahl auch bei den Ausbildungsbetrieben, Berufsschulen und Hochschulen bemerkbar machen. Gegen Ende dieses Jahrzehnts dürfte die Zahl der Berufsaustritte über der der Berufseintritte liegen. Bei unverändertem effektivem Renteneintrittsalter wird sich die Zahl der Berufsaustritte bis 2010 verdoppeln, während die Zahl der Berufsanfänger abnimmt. Ähnliches gilt für die Hochschulen: die Gruppe der 18- bis 25-Jährigen halbiert sich bis 2020. Insgesamt wird das Erwerbspersonenpotenzial stärker schrumpfen als die Gesamtbevölkerung, um rund 25% oder knapp 800.000 (Statistisches Landesamt 2004a, S. 7).
Eine erste Folge dieser Entwicklung spürt die sächsische Wirtschaft schon jetzt: den Mangel an Hochqualifizierten oder, ökonomisch gesprochen, die Verknappung des Faktors Humankapital. Trotz hoher Arbeitslosigkeit haben zahlreiche Unternehmen Probleme, Facharbeiter, Ingenieure und Wissenschaftler zu rekrutieren, um altersbedingte Abgänge zu kompensieren oder gar zu expandieren. Selbst mit überdurchschnittlichen Löhnen sind Abgewanderte oft nicht mehr zurück zu gewinnen. Bereits für dieses Jahr hat das Ifo Dresden ein Unterangebot

an hochqualifizierten Arbeitnehmern prognostiziert, für 2020 je nach Szenario eine Lücke zwischen 40.000 und 74.000 (Thum u.a. 2004, S. 26ff.).
Die Schrumpfung des Erwerbspersonenpotenzials wird sich auf die Arbeitslosigkeit qualifikationsspezifisch allerdings sehr verschieden auswirken. Während sich bei den Hochqualifizierten der Engpass bereits abzeichnet, dürfte bei den Erwerbsfähigen ohne Berufsabschluss die Arbeitslosigkeit nicht nennenswert sinken. Bei den mittleren Qualifikationen dürfte sich ab Mitte des nächsten Jahrzehnts ebenfalls eine Angebotslücke ergeben.
Doch auch bei Vollbeschäftigung kann der vollständige Abbau der Arbeitslosigkeit die Schrumpfung des Erwerbspersonenpotenzials nicht annähernd kompensieren.[1] Das Arbeitsvolumen der sächsischen Wirtschaft wird deshalb sinken. Sofern nicht eine deutliche Zunahme der Produktivität[2] bzw. eine höhere Erwerbsneigung oder erfolgreiche Einwanderung in den Arbeitsmarkt den Rückgang auffängt, wird die Wertschöpfung der sächsischen Wirtschaft rückläufig sein.
Die Verschiebung der Altersstruktur dürfte ferner einhergehen mit Gefahren für das sächsische Innovationssystem, denn mit zunehmendem Altersdurchschnitt steigt der Abstand der Belegschaften von ihrer ursprünglichen Ausbildung. Es kommt zu einer Akkumulation an Erfahrungswissen, zugleich aber fehlt es an Nachwuchs, dessen Kenntnisse auf dem neuesten Stand sind. Es wird zunehmend schwieriger werden, optimal altersgemischte Belegschaften zu bilden.
Nach Prognosen des IW Köln dürfte der Altersstruktureffekt ferner zur Folge haben, dass die Zahl der Existenzgründungen bis 2050 doppelt so stark zurückgeht wie die Gesamtbevölkerung, also im Bundesdurchschnitt um rund ein Drittel, sofern sich an den altersspezifischen Gründungsquoten nichts ändert (IW Köln 2004, S. 178). In Sachsen dürfte der Rückgang noch stärker ausfallen, da der Altersdurchschnitt deutlich über dem Bundesdurchschnitt liegt und die gründungsrelevanten Altersgruppen schon bis 2020 stärker schrumpfen werden als im Bundesdurchschnitt. Hinzu kommt, dass Unternehmensnachfolgeregelungen zunehmend problematisch werden. Damit sind zahlreiche Arbeitsplätze bedroht. Nicht zuletzt ist zu befürchten, dass die Alterung eine geringere berufliche und regionale Mobilität zur Folge hat und sich dadurch die fiktionale Arbeitslosigkeit erhöht (Thum u.a. 2004, S. 39).

1 Im Februar 2006 waren rund 428.000 Sachsen arbeitslos gemeldet, etwa 40.000 weitere befanden sich in Maßnahmen der Bundesagentur für Arbeit (ohne Optionskommunen). Es bleibt also eine Lücke von mehr als 300.000.

2 Es gibt keine überzeugenden Hinweise darauf, dass die Alterung einen produktivitätsdämpfenden Effekt haben könnte (Börsch-Supan u.a. 2005). In vielen Fällen lassen sich Produktivitätsunterschiede zwischen Alten und Jungen nicht nachweisen. Die Frage ist, ob es möglich ist, auch mit deutlich älteren Belegschaften höhere Produktivitätszuwächse zu erzielen bzw. ob die Kapitalproduktivität weiter gesteigert werden kann.

Auch der Haushalt des Freistaates ist betroffen. Nach Seitz (2004, S. 25ff.) werden die Einnahmen im sächsischen Haushalt von (2002) 14,6 Milliarden Euro bis 2020 demographieinduziert um rund 1,8 Milliarden Euro zurückgehen. Hinzu kommt, dass die Transferzahlungen aus dem Solidaritätspakt und weitere Ost-Transfers abgeschmolzen werden, so dass das Budget des Freistaates um weitere 3,7 Milliarden Euro sinkt. Unter der Annahme eines Realwachstums von 1% p.a. wird sich der Haushalt 2020 auf etwa 11,1 Milliarden Euro belaufen, der Rückgang beträgt rund 24%. Die Pro-Kopf-Einnahmen des Jahres 2020 werden real ca. 12% unter dem Niveau des Jahres 2002 liegen und damit leicht unterproportional zum Bevölkerungsrückgang von rund 14% zurückgehen.

III. Strategien im Umgang mit Schrumpfung und Alterung

Während sich der Bevölkerungsrückgang auf der Einnahmenseite des Haushalts automatisch bemerkbar macht, gibt es auf der Ausgabenseite keinen Konsolidierungsautomatismus. Insbesondere sieht sich der Fiskus dem Problem der Kostenremanenzen gegenüber: ceteris paribus steigen bei einer schrumpfenden Bevölkerung die Ausgaben pro Kopf. Die Leistungen der Daseinsvorsorge lassen sich aber nicht unbegrenzt skalieren: Man kann nicht die Zahl der Lehrer proportional zum Rückgang der Schülerzahl halbieren, bei gleich bleibender Anzahl der Schulen und Klassen, denn dann ist eine individuelle Förderung der Schüler nach Neigung und Begabung nicht mehr zu leisten. Solche kritischen Mindestgrößen, unterhalb derer ein Angebot nicht mehr sinnvoll aufrechtzuerhalten ist, existieren für alle staatlichen Dienstleistungen. In Frage kommen also zwei Konsolidierungsstrategien: erstens die Skalierung relativ zum Nachfragerückgang, zweitens bei Erreichen subkritischer Größen die Einsparung staatlicher Dienstleistungen. Erstere Strategie wendet der Freistaat Sachsen bereits im Schulwesen an, allerdings modifiziert durch einen unterproportionalen Abbau. Während die Zahl der Schüler um etwa 50% zurückging, wurde die Zahl der Lehrerstellen (gemessen in Vollzeitäquivalenten) nur um 30% reduziert – betriebsbedingte Kündigungen gab es dabei nicht. Dies wurde einerseits erreicht durch eine verringerte Wochenarbeitszeit, andererseits durch die Zusammenlegung von Schulen. Im Gegenzug mussten Kostenremanenzen in Kauf genommen werden: Von 1996 bis 2002 ging die Schülerzahl an allgemein bildenden Schulen um 29% zurück, die Ausgaben je Schüler stiegen aber um knapp 35%.[3] Das verlangt nach Umschichtungen im Haushalt.

3 Ähnliches gilt für alle ostdeutschen Flächenländer. Nach Kempkes und Seitz (2004, S. 19ff.) gingen die laufenden Ausgaben von Ländern und Gemeinden im Schulbereich zwischen 1995 und 2001 um 10,7% zurück, die Zahl der Schüler jedoch um 21,2%, so dass die laufenden Ausgaben je Schüler um 13,3 Prozent stiegen.

Eine ähnliche Strategie der unterproportionalen Angebotsreduzierung wird beim Stadtumbau zur Anwendung kommen müssen. Ein proportionaler Abriss von etwa 16% des Wohnungsbestandes würde die öffentlichen Haushalte – nicht nur des Freistaats, auch des Bundes, der über das Programm „Stadtumbau Ost“ an der Finanzierung beteiligt ist – weit überfordern. Ein gewisser Leerstand wird deshalb mit allen stadtplanerischen und ökonomischen Konsequenzen als unvermeidlich hingenommen werden müssen. Der von der sächsischen Staatsregierung angestrebte Abriss von 250.000 Wohnungen bis 2010 ist immer noch eine gewaltige Aufgabe für Bund, Land, Kommunen und Hauseigentümer, insbesondere da der jährliche Abgang aus dem Bestand heute bei brutto 13.000 und netto (abzüglich der Zugänge durch Neubauten und Sanierungen) weniger als 5.000 liegt (Statistisches Landesamt 2005).

Zu den fiskalischen Kosten kommen hier die politischen: Der Abbruch von Infra-Struktur wird von den Bürgern immer als Verlust empfunden und mit großer Vehemenz bekämpft. Der Abriss eines Wohnblocks, der seinen Bewohnern eine gute Heimat war, oder die Schließung einer Schule lösen Emotionen aus, denen mit rationaler Argumentation nur sehr schwer beizukommen ist. Die Erfahrungen in Sachsen haben aber gezeigt, dass es möglich ist. Die Politik braucht den Mut zu Klarheit und Wahrheit: Sie muss sich selbst verteilungspolitisch vom Wachstumsparadigma verabschieden und anschließend die Bürger davon überzeugen, dass es keine quantitativen Zuwächse zu verteilen gibt. Positive Veränderungen werden künftig immer nur qualitativer Art sein können.

Das ist auch die Prämisse der Stadtumbaustrategie, die sich nicht auf den Abriss beschränkt, sondern auch die Aufwertung von Quartieren einschließt. Diese Strategie wird in der Debatte oft als alternativlos dargestellt, verbunden mit dem Ruf nach Subventionen. Sie wird insbesondere von den kommunalen und genossenschaftlichen Wohnungsbauunternehmen, die Hauptnutznießer der staatlichen Fördermittel sind, unterstützt und forciert.[4]

Aus volkswirtschaftlicher Perspektive bietet sich allerdings noch eine andere Lösung an. Als Alternative zum Abriss schlägt Dascher 2005 vor, auf den Nachfrageeinbruch am Wohnungsmarkt mittels Mengenanpassung durch sinkende Mieten insbesondere für nichtsanierten Wohnraum zu reagieren. Der Umzug in größere Wohnungen werde dann für viele weniger zahlungskräftige Haushalte attraktiv, Einpendler würden sich eine Zweitwohnung am Arbeitsort leisten, kleine Wohnungen würden zu größeren zusammengelegt, wodurch der Leerstand sinke. Es sei zu erwarten, dass um 20% fallende Mieten einen Zuwachs der Flächen-

---

4 Mit Erfolg: Die durchschnittliche Leerstandsquote bei den kommunalen Wohnungsgesellschaften und den Wohnungsgenossenschaften sank nach Angaben des GdW Bundesverband (GdW 2005, S. 13) deutscher Wohnungs- und Immobilienunternehmen von durchschnittlich 16,0% im Jahr 2003 auf 14,9% Ende 2004. Für das Jahr 2005 rechnet der Verband aufgrund weiterer Abrisse mit einem Rückgang auf 14,0%.

nachfrage von 8% auslösen und der Leerstand damit fast halbiert würde (Dascher 2005, S. 5).

Dies ist ordnungs- und sozialpolitisch ohne Zweifel der bessere Weg. Ordnungspolitisch, weil diese Lösung lehrbuchmäßig marktkonform ist: ein Überangebot hat auf anderen Märkten auch sinkende Preise zur Folge. Sozialpolitisch, weil die Höhe der Mieten neben dem Einkommen einer der bestimmenden Faktoren für die Kaufkraft ist; bei sinkenden Mieten würde der Einkommensabstand zwischen Ost- und Westdeutschland nicht so sehr ins Gewicht fallen.

Die Vermieter begegnen dem Vorschlag einer deutlichen Mietpreissenkung mit dem Hinweis auf die Gefahr von Insolvenzen weiterer kommunaler und genossenschaftlicher Wohnungsbauunternehmen, was Schwierigkeiten für die bürgenden Kommunen, staatlichen Bürgschaftsbanken etc. nach sich ziehen würde.

Vor allem aber löst eine Preissenkung die Leerstandsproblematik aus drei Gründen nicht: Erstens nimmt die Bevölkerung weiter ab, d.h. ohne weitere Abrisse nimmt der Leerstand zu. Bevölkerungsrückgänge von regional 15 bis 40% spiegeln sich zwar nicht proportional in der Zahl der Haushalte wider, da der Trend zur Vereinzelung und zu größerem Flächenverbrauch geht. Sie bedeuten aber, dass die Nachfrage in den am stärksten betroffenen Regionen gegenüber heute weiter sinken wird, selbst wenn sich der Flächenverbrauch je Haushalt deutlich erhöht.

Zweitens spielt beim Bevölkerungsrückgang immer stärker das Geburtendefizit die Hauptrolle, nicht die Arbeitsmigration nach Westdeutschland. Die Überlegung, abgewanderte Ostdeutsche mittels niedriger Mieten wieder zurück nach Ostdeutschland zu locken, ist zwar auch mit Blick auf den sich abzeichnenden Mangel an Fachkräften reizvoll. Aber gerade in den am stärksten von Schrumpfung und Leerstand betroffenen Städten und Regionen würde es wenig nützen, weil es dort an geeigneten Arbeitsplätzen fehlt.

Drittens kann man den Wohnungsmarkt nicht isoliert von anderen Infrastrukturen betrachten. Eine schrumpfende Bevölkerung hat Nachfrageausfälle etwa bei Wasser und Abwasser oder Elektrizität zur Folge, die auch von größeren Wohnungen nicht vollständig kompensiert werden. An den Kostenremanenzeffekten der Versorgungsinfrastruktur würde eine Vergrößerung der Wohnfläche pro Kopf folglich wenig ändern. Die Mietpreissenkung würde lediglich steigende Mietnebenkosten nach sich ziehen. Dies würde den vermeintlich wohlfahrtssteigernden Effekt einer Preisanpassung am Ende konterkarieren.

Dennoch ist die Überlegung nicht völlig von der Hand zu weisen. Eine Senkung der Mietpreise könnte Teil einer Strategie für den Umgang mit Leerstand sein. Insbesondere in Anbetracht der Tatsache, dass Ostdeutschland in den nächsten Jahrzehnten mit dem Phänomen der Altersarmut infolge unsteter Erwerbsbiographien nach der Wende und mutmaßlich weiterer Absenkungen des Rentenniveaus umgehen muss.

Eine solche Strategie der Mietpreissenkung setzt allerdings voraus, dass die kommunalen Wohnungsbauunternehmen auch ohne Abriss von ihren Altschulden aus DDR-Zeiten befreit und die dem Abriss gewidmeten Stadtumbaumittel entsprechend in die Entschuldung umgeschichtet werden. Ferner macht sie den Abriss nicht überflüssig, sondern flankiert ihn. Beide Instrumente müssen in ihrer Gewichtung jeweils entsprechend den lokalen Bedürfnissen angepasst werden. Hier wie an vielen anderen Stellen erweist sich eine größere Flexibilität als Schlüssel zur Anpassung an den demographischen Wandel.

Flexibilität ist auch entscheidend beim anstehenden Verwaltungsumbau. Der Konsolidierungsbedarf bis 2020 beläuft sich auf ca. 25.000 Stellen (Vollzeitäquivalente). (Seitz 2004, S. 33) Mit einer proportionalen Verkleinerung der Verwaltung ist es dabei nicht getan. Vielmehr sind grundlegende Veränderungen des Verwaltungsaufbaus und der Verwaltungsorganisation erforderlich. Die Details der bereits in Angriff genommenen sächsischen Verwaltungs- und Funktionalreform sind noch in der Diskussion (Zu den Varianten vgl. Expertenkommission 2005). Klar ist aber bereits jetzt: Sie läuft auf größere Einheiten, weniger Ebenen und eine geringere Präsenz in der Fläche hinaus. Die physische Entfernung zwischen Verwaltung und Bürgern nimmt damit absehbar zu. Das ist ein gerne vorgebrachtes, aber keineswegs triftiges Argument gegen die Verschlankung der Verwaltung. Vielmehr stellt sich hier die Frage, mit welchen neuen Methoden die Distanz überwunden werden kann.

Hier wird ohne Zweifel E-Government, also der elektronische Zugang zu Dienstleistungen der Verwaltung, eine zentrale Rolle spielen. Entsprechende Angebote werden auf allen staatlichen Ebenen bereits entwickelt, auch ist in Sachsen zumindest auf staatlicher Seite sowohl bei den Kommunen als auch beim Freistaat die erforderliche Infrastruktur vorhanden. Problematisch dürfte nur sein, den Zugang für alle Bürger technisch zu gewährleisten. Denkbar wäre, analog zu Bankautomaten internetgestützte Verwaltungsterminals in Gemeinden ohne eigene Verwaltung zu installieren, oder einen rollenden Verwaltungsservice einzurichten, der die Gemeinden regelmäßig anfährt – nicht anders, als es Fleischer und Bäcker im ländlichen Raum schon tun.

IV. Neues Selbstverständnis von Politik und Verwaltung

Kreative organisatorische Lösungen sind nur eine Seite des demographieinduzierten Verwaltungsumbaus. Die andere Seite ist das Selbstverständnis von Politik und Verwaltung. Bisher wird der Staat überwiegend als Umverteilungsinstanz betrachtet. Die Bürger tragen an den Staat die Forderung heran, Gerechtigkeit herzustellen im Sinne materieller Gleichverteilung und Gleichversorgung. Ein großer Teil staatlicher Aktivitäten diente bisher dazu, dieses Gerechtigkeitsempfinden zu befriedigen.

Der demographische Wandel macht die Fortsetzung dieser Politik unmöglich. Während die Mittel der öffentlichen Haushalte knapper werden und die Ausgaben pro Kopf steigen, nehmen die regionalen Disparitäten zu und damit auch die Ungleichheiten, die zu beseitigen bisher die erste Aufgabe der Politik war. Anders ausgedrückt: Das Gefälle zwischen den einander anzugleichenden Niveaus wird größer und damit auch der Aufwand für die „Planierungsarbeiten". Diese Entwicklung macht eine grundsätzliche Aufgabenkritik unausweichlich. Wenn Umverteilung nicht mehr die hauptsächliche Aufgabe von Politik und Verwaltung ist, stellt sich die Frage: Welches sind dann die Kernaufgaben des Staates?

Mit der Beantwortung dieser Fragen vollzieht der Staat mit einiger Verspätung eine Entwicklung nach, welche in der Wirtschaft bereits stattgefunden hat. Die in den 1980er Jahren favorisierten Mischkonzerne haben sich als schwer steuerbar und wenig effizient erwiesen. Deshalb sahen sich in den 1990er Jahren viele Unternehmen mit ganz ähnlichen Fragen nach der Kernkompetenz konfrontiert wie heute der Staat. Die Antwort war einerseits die Aufspaltung von Unternehmen, andererseits die Vergabe von Geschäftsprozessen an andere Anbieter, etwa die Auslagerung der IT von Banken an externe Firmen. Was zum Kerngeschäft zählte, wurde neu definiert.

Ähnliche Tendenzen gab es bisher auch im öffentlichen Dienst. Alle staatlichen Ebenen haben wegen knapper öffentlicher Haushalte staatliche Unternehmen privatisiert – angefangen bei Post und Telekom bis hin zu kommunalen Versorgern wie dem öffentlichen Nahverkehr, Müllentsorgung, Stadtwerken oder Krankenhäusern. Deren Privatisierung hat allerdings weniger mit Steuerungs- oder Effizienzgesichtspunkten zu tun als vielmehr mit Haushaltsnotlagen, die Anlass gaben, staatliches „Tafelsilber" zwecks Deckung von Defiziten zu verkaufen.[5] Auch steckt hinter diesen Verkäufen in der Regel nicht die Erkenntnis, dass der Markt viele Dienstleistungen effizienter und kostengünstiger bereitstellt als der Staat. Deswegen kann man hier nur in den seltensten Fällen von einer konsequent verfolgten Strategie sprechen.

Aus der Summe der Privatisierungen ergibt sich ein Trend weg vom allgegenwärtigen Versorgungsstaat. Weniger klar ist, wohin der Trend geht. Dafür fehlt es diesem Veränderungsprozess an einem Ziel und geeigneten Orientierungsmarken. Die Frage nach den Kernkompetenzen des Staates bleibt im Zusammenhang mit den Privatisierungen meist unbeantwortet.

5 Das aktuellste Beispiel dafür ist die Stadt Dresden, die ihre Wohnungsbaugesellschaft an die amerikanische Beteiligungsgesellschaft Fortress verkauft hat, um mit den Erlösen ihre Schulden zu tilgen.

Die Antwort auf diese Frage ergibt sich aus den Folgen, die der demographische Wandel für Wirtschaft und Gesellschaft hat. Eines der ernstesten Probleme ist die sich verschlechternde Humankapitalausstattung mit allen ihren Folgen für Wertschöpfung, Wachstum und Innovation. Eine zentrale Aufgabe des Staates wird es künftig sein, für dieses Problem Lösungen zu finden.[6] Vorschläge dafür liegen auf dem Tisch (Thum u.a. 2004, S. 41ff.). Zum einen ist das Erwerbspersonenpotenzial besser auszuschöpfen. In Sachsen sind nur etwa 45% der 55- bis 64-Jährigen erwerbstätig, bei den 60- bis 65-Jährigen sogar nur knapp 28%. (Statistisches Landesamt 2004b) Weniger Spielraum gibt es bei der Frauenerwerbsquote: sie liegt in Sachsen mit 73,4% nahe an der Männererwerbsquote von 79,9%. Doch auch diese Arbeitskräftereserve gilt es zu mobilisieren.
Weiterhin kommt in Betracht, das Arbeitsvolumen durch höhere Wochen- und Lebensarbeitszeiten zu vergrößern. Da die Wochenarbeitszeit mit durchschnittlich 39,6 Stunden aber schon deutlich höher liegt als in den westdeutschen Ländern, ist der Spielraum hier nicht sehr groß. Eine Erhöhung des effektiven Rentenzugangsalters[7] dagegen erschließt eine zusätzliche Arbeitskräftereserve von rund 14.000 Personen allein bei den Hochqualifizierten (Thum u.a. 2004, S. 77). Doch ist hier nicht allein der Staat gefragt, auch die Unternehmen müssen durch eine andere Personalpolitik und insbesondere bessere Weiterbildung im Sinne von lebenslangem Lernen etwas gegen die Humankapitalknappheit tun. Auch ist die bessere Vereinbarkeit von Familie und Beruf nicht allein eine Frage des Betreuungsangebots und finanzieller Hilfen für Familien, sondern auch einer flexiblen Arbeitsorganisation und familienfreundlichen Personalpolitik.
Nicht zuletzt muss die Zahl der Schulabbrecher bzw. der Erwerbsfähigen mit geringer Qualifikation deutlich gesenkt werden – insbesondere da die Arbeitsnachfrage nach Arbeitnehmern mit geringer Qualifikation weiter zurückgehen wird (Hummel, Reinberg 2003, S. 1ff.), während der Anteil Studierender an den Abiturienten steigen muss. Hier ist ganz klar die Bildungspolitik gefordert, die Qualität der Schulbildung zu verbessern.
Aus diesen Überlegungen leitet sich als künftige Kernaufgabe des Staates ab, die Humankapitalressourcen besser als bisher zu erschließen, die relevanten Akteure besser als bisher zu aktivieren und ihre Aktivitäten zu koordinieren. Die Humankapitalbildung wird zur tragenden Säule der Wirtschaftspolitik, von ihr wird maßgeblich abhängen, ob sich Schrumpfung und Alterung dämpfend auf das Wirtschaftswachstum auswirken oder ob neue Wachstumsimpulse gesetzt werden können. Zugang zu Bildung zu gewährleisten wird eine der wichtigsten Aufgaben des Staates sein.

---

6 Das mag angesichts des gegenwärtig großen Überangebots an Arbeit nicht intuitiv verständlich sein, ist aber mit Blick auf das nächste Jahrzehnt nicht zu vernachlässigen. Vgl. Anmerkung 1.

7 D.h. Steigerung der Erwerbsquote der 60 bis 65-Jährigen auf das Niveau der 55- bis Unter-60-Jährigen.

In diesem Zusammenhang fällt stets das Stichwort vom lebenslangen Lernen. Dahinter steckt ein neuer bildungspolitischer Ansatz, der Bildungsangebote vom Kindergarten bis hin zum Seniorenstudium vorsieht. Die Herausforderung ist aber nicht nur eine inhaltlicher Art für die etablierte Bildungspolitik im engeren Sinne, sondern liegt quer zu allen Politikfeldern. Bisher fällt Bildung in die Zuständigkeit von einem halben Dutzend Ressorts[8], von denen jedes seine sehr eigene Sicht auf den Bildungsprozess hat und entsprechend andere Prioritäten setzt. Ein integriertes Management des lebenslangen Lernens ist mit einer solchen Struktur nur schwer machbar. Zu prüfen wäre, inwieweit ein Bildungsministerium im Sinne eines Humankapitalministeriums realisierbar wäre, mit umfassenden Zuständigkeiten für alle Bereiche von Bildung, Forschung und Technologie.

An dieser Überlegung zeigt sich auch, dass die Konzentration auf die Kernkompetenzen des Staates nicht nur etwas mit dem Umfang staatlicher Aufgaben zu tun hat, sondern auch mit der Zuweisung bzw. Zusammenfassung von Zuständigkeiten. Der demographische Wandel hat Auswirkungen auf sämtliche politische Bereiche, er ist eine Querschnittsaufgabe. Diese wird die Politik kaum wirksam lösen können, wenn sie sich auf isolierte Reaktionen nach dem etablierten Ressortprinzip verlässt. Hier ist eine Querschnittspolitik gefragt, die sich zum einen durch stärkere Integration bisher über verschiedene Ressorts verstreuter Politikfelder auszeichnet und zum anderen durch eine viel stärkere Koordination und zentrale Steuerung, gewissermaßen ein zentrales Demographiemanagement.

Neben einer Humankapitalbildungspolitik lassen sich zwei weitere Kernkompetenzen des Staates identifizieren. Das ist zum einen die Infrastrukturpolitik. Darunter ist nicht allein Verkehrswegeplanung, Städtebau oder ländliche Entwicklung zu verstehen. Vielmehr geht es darum, für alle wirtschaftlichen und sozialen Infrastrukturen neue Konzepte und Modelle zu entwickeln, die unter den jeweiligen, regional unterschiedlichen demographischen und fiskalischen Bedingungen optimal sind. Das betrifft gleichermaßen das Angebot an und den Zugang zu Wohnungen, Öffentlichem Personennahverkehr, Ver- und Entsorgung, aber auch Bildung, Kultur und Gesundheit.

Alle diese Infrastrukturen sind je nach demographischer Entwicklung sehr verschieden betroffen und verlangen deshalb nach flexiblen, situationsangepassten Lösungen. So wäre es vorstellbar, in dünn besiedelten Gegenden Mittel vom Öffentlichen Personennahverkehr zu Taxiunternehmen umzuschichten, beispielsweise um eine wirtschaftliche Schülerbeförderung sicherzustellen. Ganz ähnlich stellt sich bei kulturellen Angeboten die Frage, wie man sie entweder zu den Nutzern bringt oder umgekehrt die Nutzer zu den Einrichtungen.

8 Das Finanzministerium ist das einzige Ressort, das inhaltlich nichts mit Bildung zu tun hat.

Hier wird die Staatsregierung viel stärker als bisher beratend und steuernd auf die kommunalen Gebietskörperschaften einwirken müssen. Die Debatte um die Neugestaltung des Schulnetzes hat gezeigt, dass die Eigeninteressen der Gemeinden oft den Blick darauf verstellen, dass die Zusammenarbeit mit anderen Gemeinden Vorteile bringt. Auf solche Kooperationen wird es allerdings zunehmend ankommen, wenn den Bürgern weiterhin eine qualitativ hochwertige, wenn auch weniger verdichtete Infrastruktur angeboten werden soll. Zu diesem Zweck wird die Landesregierung Anreize entwickeln müssen, die Kooperation belohnen und den anstehenden Strukturwandel beschleunigen.

Eine weitere Aufgabe der Landesregierung wird es sein, einen gesetzlichen Rahmen zu schaffen, innerhalb dessen die Akteure auf lokaler und regionaler Ebene flexibel agieren können. Angesichts zunehmender Disparitäten – Dresden und Leipzig werden weiter Einwohner gewinnen, Hoyerswerda wird bis 2020 noch einmal fast 40% verlieren – kann man den unterschiedlichen Bedingungen nicht mehr mit einheitlichen Grundsätzen der Stadtplanung oder einheitlichen baurechtlichen Normen begegnen.

Die Gewährleistung des Zugangs zu Infrastruktur ist noch in einem anderen Sinn zu verstehen: Künftig müssen alle Infrastrukturen altengerecht gestaltet sein.[9] Dabei geht es nicht allein um Barrierefreiheit. Sondern es geht auch darum, das Zusammenleben der weniger werdenden Jungen und der zunehmenden Zahl der Älteren neu zu organisieren. So können generationsübergreifende Wohn- und Begegnungsangebote Bestandteil der demographiegerechten Gestaltung unserer Städte sein, etwa Mehrgenerationenhäuser oder Altenheime mit angeschlossenem Kindergarten. Solche Strukturen ermöglichen neue Formen und Institutionen des sozialen Zusammenhalts, etwa Familienpatenschaften und „Leihomas“ (Bosch-Stiftung, S. 26). Eine altengerechte Infrastruktur ist zudem meist automatisch eine kinderfreundliche Infrastruktur. Es kommt also darauf an, familien- und seniorenpolitische Konzepte in enger Abstimmung zu entwickeln und umzusetzen.

Damit ist das dritte Kompetenzfeld benannt: die Familien- oder besser Bevölkerungspolitik. Der demographische Wandel ist kein unabänderliches Schicksal, keine Naturgewalt, in das sich die Politik nur noch mittels einer intelligenten Anpassungsstrategie ergeben kann. Zwar lässt sich der Schrumpfungstrend kurz- und mittelfristig kaum stoppen. Eine langfristig angelegte Politik – über mindestens fünf, besser zehn Legislaturperioden – sollte aber dazu in der Lage sein.

Bevölkerungspolitik kann durchaus zu höheren Geburtenraten führen, wie das französische Beispiel zeigt: Frankreich verzeichnete 2004 bei einer Bevölkerung

9 Insbesondere im Hinblick auf alte Menschen mit Behinderungen. Deren Zahl war bisher vergleichsweise klein, weil im „Dritten Reich“ mehr als 200.000 Menschen mit Behinderungen ermordet worden waren. Zugleich gab es aufgrund der Millionen von Menschen, die Judenvernichtung und Krieg zum Opfer fielen, in den vergangenen Jahrzehnten deutlich weniger alte Menschen, als ohne diese Ereignisse der Fall gewesen wäre, und damit auch weniger alte Menschen mit Behinderungen.

von 62 Millionen rund 800.000 Geburten (Geburtenüberschuss: rund 280.000), also etwa 13 Geburten je 1000 Einwohner.[10] In Sachsen wurden bei einer Bevölkerung von 4,3 Mio. rund 33.000 Kinder geboren (Sterbeüberschuss: rund 15.200), das waren weniger als 8 Geburten je 1000 Einwohner. Lägen die Geburten auf französischem Niveau, wären knapp 56.000 Kinder geboren worden, gleichbedeutend mit einem Zuwachs von rund 7.600 Einwohnern.

Die bevölkerungspolitische Herausforderung besteht nun darin, dass sich kein eindeutiger Parameter bestimmen lässt, dessen Veränderung eine Zunahme der Geburtenhäufigkeit nach sich zieht. Vielmehr zeigt sich bei einer Betrachtung auf Kreisebene, dass sowohl die Geburtenhäufigkeit als auch die Korrelation von Geburtenhäufigkeit und Faktoren wie Erwerbstätigkeit, Sozialhilfequote oder Wirtschaftswachstum sehr unterschiedlich ausfällt (Dorbritz 2004, S. 29ff.). Es bedarf folglich je nach Situation eines Bündels abgestimmter Maßnahmen, mit denen die lokalen und regionalen Bedingungen so gestaltet werden, dass mindestens der überwiegend vorhandene Kinderwunsch nach zwei Kindern realisiert wird. Diese Maßnahmen umfassen eine familienfreundliche Gestaltung des Wohnungsangebots und der Umgebung, verschiedenste inner- wie außerbetriebliche Hilfen zur besseren Vereinbarung von Familie und Beruf, sowie auf Familien zugeschnittene Gesundheits- und Beratungsangebote. Das ist vorrangig eine Aufgabe der Gemeinden. Doch auch hier wird die Landesregierung viel stärker als bisher beratend und steuernd tätig werden und den Gemeinden Lösungswege für ihre Probleme aufzeigen müssen.

Auf Landes- und Bundesebene kann auch über diese praktischen Hilfen hinaus bevölkerungspolitisch etwas getan werden. Hier ist nicht in erster Linie an die zahlreichen monetären und sonstigen Transfers an die Familien zu denken, sondern an die Verankerung des Prinzips der Generationengerechtigkeit im Grundgesetz und den Landesverfassungen. Der Gesetzgeber muss sich verpflichten, nicht zu Lasten künftiger Generationen zu entscheiden, wie es bisher – Stichworte: umlagenfinanziertes Rentensystem und Verschuldung – geschieht.[11] Insbesondere ist hier an ein Verschuldungsverbot zu denken, das anders als jetzt nicht umgangen werden kann.

Zudem muss es offenbar positive Anreize geben, die Interessen der Familien im politischen Prozess stärker als bisher zu berücksichtigen, da es anders als in Frankreich keinen tragfähigen familienpolitischen Konsens zwischen den Partei-

---

10 Der vorläufigen Zählung für 2005 zufolge stieg die Zahl der Geburten sogar auf mehr als 807.000 (INSEE 2006).

11 Das Grundgesetz (Art 20a GG) sowie alle Landesverfassungen kennen bereits das Gebot der ökologischen Generationengerechtigkeit, also der Erhaltung der Umwelt im Interesse künftiger Generationen. Dieses Gebot wäre auf einen umfassenden Begriff von Generationengerechtigkeit auszuweiten. Dieses Staatsziel müsste allerdings mit einer Ewigkeitsgarantie versehen werden, da die jetzt Lebenden den noch nicht Wahlberechtigten und noch Ungeborenen gegenüber immer in der Mehrheit sind und bei Verteilungskonflikten das Staatsziel Generationengerechtigkeit wieder abschaffen könnten.

en gibt. Auch die heute lebenden Kinder sowie die noch Ungeborenen sind (potenziell) Bürger dieses Landes und haben Interessen, die im politischen Prozess aber nicht vertreten werden. Familienpolitik ist deshalb bisher Teil des sozialpolitischen Reparaturbetriebs statt eines echten politischen Anliegens. Ein – allerdings verfassungsrechtlich umstrittenes – Mittel, daran etwas zu ändern, wäre die Einführung eines Familienwahlrechts, das den Eltern für jedes Kind eine zusätzliche Stimme gibt.[12]

Aus diesen beiden Prämissen für die Bevölkerungspolitik ergäbe sich in Verbindung mit lokalen bzw. regionalen Netzwerken (wie sie mit den „Lokalen Bündnissen für Familie“ seit einigen Jahren entstehen) ein Umfeld, das insgesamt mehr Mut zu Kindern und insbesondere zur Großfamilie machen dürfte, als das bisher der Fall ist. Die Familienpolitik würde verstetigt und potenziellen Eltern eine verlässliche Perspektive gegeben. Diese bevölkerungspolitisch inspirierte Umgestaltung der politischen Landschaft würde sich auf die demographische Entwicklung zwar erst langfristig und in kleinen Schritten auswirken, aber ohne eine bevölkerungspolitische Gegenstrategie würde die Entwicklung in eine unaufhaltsame und politisch auf die Dauer nicht mehr beherrschbare Abwärtsspirale münden.

V. Fazit und Ausblick

Der Freistaat Sachsen steht aufgrund des demographischen Wandels vor tief greifenden Veränderungen. Diese Veränderungen gehen weit über jenes Maß hinaus, das die allgemeine Lage der öffentlichen Haushalte erwarten lässt. Zwar hätte sich die Abwanderung von per Saldo rund 200.000 Sachsen seit 1990 auch ohne zusätzlichen Geburtenrückgang bemerkbar gemacht. In den von Abwanderung stark betroffenen Gemeinden hätten sich die Probleme des Stadtumbaus, der Schulnetzplanung und des Fachkräftemangels trotzdem gestellt. Der zusätzliche Geburtenrückgang und die dadurch verursachte Alterung aber betreffen das ganze Land und werden die bestehenden Probleme in absehbarer Zeit deutlich verschärfen.

Die Auseinandersetzung mit diesen Problemen zeitigt zwei zentrale Einsichten. Erstens ist es nicht länger möglich, sie mittels der bestehenden Instrumentarien einer auf Zuwachs programmierten Gesellschaft zu lösen, die sich beispielsweise den „Luxus“ leisten kann, wertvolle Humanressourcen zu verschwenden, indem sie Menschen vom Arbeitsmarkt ausschließt, und die in Infrastrukturen investiert, ohne die künftige Nachfrage zu berücksichtigen. Es gilt, unter den Bedingungen einer schrumpfenden Bevölkerung – die im Idealfalle nicht zugleich wirtschaftli-

12 Vgl. den interfraktionellen Antrag Deutscher Bundestag 2003c.

che Schrumpfung bedeutet –, für das Zusammenleben der Generationen und ihre Versorgung mit Leistungen der Daseinsfürsorge neue Strukturen und Formen zu finden. Das gesellschaftspolitische Wachstumsparadigma des „Es wird immer besser“ muss von einem Schrumpfungsparadigma abgelöst werden.
Dieser Paradigmenwechsel ist die zentrale politische Herausforderung: gelingt er, dann sollte die Entwicklung neuer Instrumente und Strukturen möglich, wenn auch nicht gerade unproblematisch sein. Gelingt er nicht oder dauert der Bewusstseinswandel zu lange, hat die Politik kaum eine Chance, die Probleme in den Griff zu bekommen.
An zweiter Stelle steht die Erkenntnis, dass sich die Gegenstrategien nicht allein auf (betriebswirtschaftlich gesprochen) Change Management, also auf kontinuierliche Anpassung an die Umstände, beschränken dürfen. Flankierend muss ein Turnaround Management etabliert werden, mit dem der Abwärtstrend zumindest langfristig gestoppt, wenn nicht sogar umgekehrt wird. In diesem Sinne müssen Politik und Verwaltung, aber auch die Unternehmen und gesellschaftliche Gruppen für den demographischen Wandel sowohl Bewältigungs- als auch Überwindungsstrategien entwickeln.
Im Freistaat Sachsen ist dieser Prozess bereits eingeleitet. Mit dem Sächsischen Demographiegipfel in Dresden hat die Staatsregierung im März 2004 begonnen, sich auf die anstehenden Veränderungen vorzubereiten. Eine interministerielle Arbeitsgruppe analysiert die Betroffenheit der Ressorts und entwickelt Vorschläge für eine Neuausrichtung von Politik und Verwaltung. Eine Expertenkommission wird der Staatsregierung im Herbst Empfehlungen für das weitere Vorgehen geben, im parlamentarischen Raum ist eine Enquetekommission des Landtags tätig. In der Oberlausitz und im Westerzgebirge hat das Innenministerium zwei Modellprojekte initiiert, die erproben sollen, mit welchen Mitteln lokal und regional am besten auf den demographischen Wandel reagiert werden kann. Viele Kommunen verfügen mittlerweile über Stadtentwicklungskonzepte, mit denen auf die Veränderung der Wohnungsnachfrage und die Alterung langfristig reagiert werden soll. Die Industrie- und Handelskammern bemühen sich darum, Aus- und Weiterbildung mit Blick auf den Fachkräftemangel zu verbessern.
Diese Schritte in die richtige Richtung werden zum Ziel führen, wenn es gelingt, diese Aktivitäten zu koordinieren und auf Landesebene in ein umfassendes Demographiemanagement einzubinden.

Literaturverzeichnis

Dorbritz, J., Demographische Entwicklung im Freistaat Sachsen. Analyse und Strategie zur Familien und Bevölkerungspolitik. Gutachten für die Sächsische Staatskanzlei, Wiesbaden 2004.

DSL-Bank (Hrsg.), Zwischen Sanierung und Abriss. Plattenbauten in den neuen Bundesländern, erstellt vom Eduard-Pestel-Institut für Systemforschung in Hannover, Bonn 1996.

IW Köln (Hrsg.), Perspektive 2050. Ökonomik des demographischen Wandels, Köln 2004.
Kempkes, G. und *H. Seitz*, Auswirkungen des demographischen Wandels auf die Bildungsausgaben – Eine empirische Analyse der Ausgaben im Schulbereich auf der Länder- und Gemeindeebene, Wiesbaden 2004.
Deutscher Bundestag, Mehr Demokratie wagen durch ein Wahlrecht von Geburt an, Drucksache 15/1544 vom 11. September 2003.
Müller, J.H. und *W.D. Siebert*, Das Problem der Richtwerte in Programmen und Plänen der Raumordnung und Landesplanung, in: Das Problem der Richtwerte in Programmen und Plänen der Raumordnung und Landesplanung, hrsg. von Akademie für Raumforschung und Landesplanung, Hannover 1977, S. 23-52.
Müller, B., Demographische Entwicklung im Freistaat Sachsen. Analyse und Strategien zur Raumentwicklungs- und Raumplanungspolitik. Gutachten im Auftrag der Sächsischen Staatskanzlei, Dresden 2004.
Robert-Bosch-Stiftung (Hrsg.), Starke Familie. Bericht der Kommission „Familie und Demographischer Wandel“, Stuttgart 2005.
Sächsische Aufbaubank (Hrsg.), Wohnungsbaumonitorring 2004/2005, Dresden 2005.
Sächsisches Staatsministerium des Inneren (Hrsg.), Expertenkommission Verwaltungsreform. Vorschläge zur Neuordnung der Verwaltung im Freistaat Sachen. Bautzen 2005.
Seitz, H., Demographischer Wandel in Sachsen. Teilprojekt: Analyse der Auswirkungen des Bevölkerungsrückgangs auf die Ausgaben und Einnahmen des Freistaates Sachsen und seiner Kommunen, Frankfurt/Oder 2004.
Statistisches Landesamt des Freistaates Sachsen, Demographischer Wandel in Sachsen, Kamenz 2004.
Statistisches Landesamt des Freistaates Sachsen, Statistischer Bericht FII 2 – j 04, Kamenz 2005.
Thum, M. u.a., Demographische Entwicklung im Freistaat Sachsen – Analyse und Strategien zum Bevölkerungsrückgang auf dem Arbeitsmarkt. Gutachten im Auftrag der Sächsischen Staatskanzlei, Dresden 2004.

Internetquellen

Börsch-Supan, A., I. Düzgün und *M. Weiss*, Altern und Produktivität: Zum Stand der Forschung, Mannheim 2005, 10. März 2006, abrufbar unter: http://www.mea.uni-mannheim.de/mea_neu/pages/files/nopage_pubs/eav29m3ka608x80a_73-2005.pdf
Dascher, K. (2005), Der Stadtumbau in Ostdeutschland, Ein Abriss in zehn Abschnitten. Frankfurt/Oder, 10. März 2006, abrufbar unter: http://viadrina.euv-frankfurt-o.de/~dascher/Der_Stadtumbau_in_Ostdeutschland_web.pdf
GdW (2005), Wohnungswirtschaftliche Daten und Trends 2005/06. Zahlen und Analysen aus der Jahresstatistik des GdW, hrsg. vom GdW Bundesverband deutscher Wohnungs- und Immobilienunternehmen e.V. Berlin 2005. Kurzfassung, 10. März 2006, abrufbar unter: http://www.gdw.de/db/publ.nsf/536188C7BEAF5C3AC12570A00050F326/$file/GdW-Daten-und-Trends-2005-Inhalt-Kurzfassung.pdf?OpenElement
INSEE (Institut Nationale de la Statistique et des Études Économiques), France in Facts and Figures. Population: Birth and Fertility, 2006, 10. März 2006, abrufbar unter: http://www.insee.fr/en/ffc/pop_age3c.htm
Reinberg, A. und *M. Hummel*, Steuert Deutschland langfristig auf einen Fachkräftemangel zu?, IAB Kurzbericht Nr 9 vom 7.7.2003, Nürnberg 2003, 10. März 2006, abrufbar unter: http://doku.iab.de/kurzber/2003/kb0903.pdf
Statistisches Landesamt des Freistaates Sachsen, Bildungsstatistik, 10. März 2006, abrufbar unter: http://www.statistik.sachsen.de/appsl1/Bildung/index2.html?allgemein/insgesamt/start.html.
Statistisches Bundesamt (1996), Pressemitteilung v. 12.12.1996: Ergebnisse der Gebäude- und Wohnungszählung 1995 in den neuen Ländern und Berlin-Ost, abrufbar unter: http://www.destatis.de/presse/deutsch/pm1996/p3430162.htm
Statistisches Landesamt des Freistaates Sachsen (2004b), Erwerbstätigenquote, Erwerbslosenquote und Erwerbsquote in Sachsen im März 2004 nach Altersgruppen, 10. März 2006, abrufbar unter: http://www.statistik.sachsen.de/21/02_05/02_05_04_tabelle.asp
Wahl, S., Geburtenverhalten in Deutschland und anderen ausgewählten Ländern, 10. März 2006, abrufbar unter: http://www.iwg-bonn.de/uploads/tx_smartextendedcontent/GeburtenverhaltenD_EU.pdf

B. Strukturelle Reform der überörtlichen Sozialhilfe

Chang Woon Nam und *Rüdiger Parsche*

I. Einführung

Deutschlandweit nehmen die Ausgaben für überörtliche Sozialhilfeleistungen seit Jahren zu. Speziell die Eingliederungshilfe, die als größter Bestandteil der so genannten überörtlichen Sozialhilfe behinderte Menschen unterstützt und fördert, verzeichnet in den letzten Jahren Steigerungsraten von bis zu 7%.[1] Nahezu alle überörtlichen Träger, Landeswohlfahrtsverbände (LWV), Bezirke oder das Land selbst sind daher gezwungen, ihre Finanzmittel in diesem Bereich aufzustocken (Friedrich, u.a. 2004). Personen, die nicht nur vorübergehend körperlich, geistig oder seelisch wesentlich behindert sind, sowie Personen, die von einer derartigen Behinderung bedroht sind, erhalten nach dem Bundessozialhilfegesetz (BSHG) Eingliederungshilfe. Die Behinderung muss gleichzeitig die Hilfe in einer Anstalt, einem Heim oder einer gleichartigen Einrichtung notwendig machen. Zur Hilfe zählt auch, den behinderten Menschen durch Aus- und Fortbildung die Ausübung eines angemessenen Berufes oder einer sonstigen Tätigkeit zu ermöglichen. Die Eingliederungshilfe setzt auf die aktive Beteiligung des Betroffenen. Der Empfänger der Hilfe muss nach seinen Kräften mitwirken, um ihn selbst soweit wie möglich zu befähigen, unabhängig von der Hilfe zu leben. Eingliederungshilfe erhält nicht, wer sich selbst helfen kann oder die erforderliche Hilfe von anderen Sozialleistungsträgen oder von Angehörigen erhält.

Werden die Sozialhilfeleistungen über eine Umlage finanziert, wie es beispielsweise in Bayern der Fall ist, muss der Umlagesatz angehoben werden, womit die jeweiligen Mitgliedskörperschaften Landkreise bzw. kreisfreie Städte erneut belastet sind. Im Falle der Landkreise schlägt diese Steigerung über die Kreisumlage durch auf die kreisangehörigen Gemeinden. Die ohnehin schon angespannte Finanzlage der kommunalen Körperschaften wird zudem dadurch noch zusätzlich verschärft, dass die Bevölkerungszahl zurückgeht und der Anteil der Aktiven schrumpft. An dieser Kettenreaktion setzt die im Folgenden dargelegte Kritik an und begründet die Notwendigkeit einer strukturellen Reform der überörtlichen Sozialhilfe unter der Berücksichtigung des Konnexitäts- und des Subsidiaritätsprinzips bei der Aufgaben- sowie Einnahmenverteilung in einem föderalistischen Staat.

---

1 Die Entlastungen, die die Einführung der Pflegeversicherung für die Sozialhilfeträger mit sich gebracht hat, sind inzwischen durch die Entwicklung in der Eingliederungshilfe längst aufgezehrt.

II. Verteilung der Aufgaben- und Einnahmenkompetenzen nach dem Kongruenz-, dem Konnexitäts- und dem Subsidiaritätsprinzip

Im Zusammenhang mit der Frage, in wessen Kompetenzbereich welche Arten von Entscheidungen zur Bekämpfung von finanzpolitisch relevanten Marktversagen in einem föderalistischen Staat wie Deutschland fallen sollen, empfiehlt die traditionelle Theorie des Föderalismus, stabilitäts- und distributionspolitische Kompetenzen auf der Zentralebene anzusiedeln (Oates 1972; Musgrave, 1980; Oates 1999). Im Gegensatz dazu sollen allokationspolitische Kompetenzen und Finanzierungslasten nach verschiedenen Zuordnungsprinzipien auf unterschiedlichen Gebietskörperschaftsebenen verteilt werden (Grossekettler 1985; Grossekettler 2002).

Als das erste der drei wichtigen Konzepte föderaler Staatssysteme „stellt das Kongruenzprinzip (das sich eigentlich am Vorbild idealtypischer Beschaffungsgenossenschaften orientiert) eine Verteilungsregel von Allokationskompetenzen dar, nach der die Gebietskörperschaften sowohl über die Gesetzgebungs- als auch Verwaltungskompetenzen verfügen sollen, die mit den von ihnen jeweils zu verantwortenden Leistungen verbunden sind, und nach der die Finanzierung im Sinn einer möglichst guten Realisation des (fiskalischen) Äquivalenzprinzips (zwischen Nutzern und Zahlern der Leistungen) bei der Aufgabenverteilung stets mit bedacht werden soll" (Grossekettler 2002, S. 57).

Mit anderen Worten verlangt das Kongruenzprinzip, dass der räumliche Wirkungsbereich (Nutzenstreuungsbereich) eines öffentlichen Gutes mit dem lokalen Zuständigkeitsbereich der betreffenden Bereitstellungsorganisation zusammenfällt. Ist der Nutzenstreuungsbereich größer als der Zuständigkeitsbereich, gelangen Personen außerhalb dieses Territoriums in den Nutzen des Gutes, ohne an den Kosten beteiligt zu sein (spill-outs). Ist der Nutzenstreuungsbereich aber kleiner als der Zuständigkeitsbereich, sind Personen trotzdem an der Finanzierung beteiligt, obwohl sie keinen Nutzen empfangen können (spill-ins). Diese spill-overs sollten dann mit entsprechenden Finanzzuweisungen korrigiert werden, damit Produktionsfaktoren nicht abwandern.

Das Konnexitätsprinzip sichert die einheitliche Rechtsanwendung im föderalen Staat indem es z.B. dem Bund zum Preis der zumindest teilweisen Kostentragung die Möglichkeit einräumt, den Ländern Verwaltungsangelegenheiten in Form von **Auftragsverwaltung** zu übertragen, ohne dass er selbst als **Bundesverwaltung** und damit zentralistisches Organ in Aktion treten müsste. Andererseits schützt es die Länder gegenüber dem Bund und damit die Funktionsfähigkeit des **Föderalismus**, aber auch die Kommunen gegenüber den Ländern vor übermäßiger finanzieller Belastung durch übertragene Aufgaben, die nach dem **Subsidiaritätsprinzip** auf der niedrigsten geeigneten Ebene wahrgenommen werden sollen. Dieses Prinzip formuliert also die Identität von Vollzugs- und Finanzierungszuständigkeit bei der Erfüllung einer öffentlichen Aufgabe. Es gilt insbesondere für die ökonomisch effiziente Verteilung der Finanzierungskompetenz. Die Einheit von Aufgabenkompetenz und Ausgabenverantwortung ermöglicht eine Rückkopplung zwischen der Veranlassung öffentlicher Aufgaben und deren Deckung, womit ein entsprechender Anreiz zu kostenbewusstem Verhalten und verantwortungsvollem Umgang mit den zur Verfügung stehenden Finanzmitteln geschaffen wird (Grossekettler 1985; Trapp 1997; Grossekettler 2002; Klein 2003; Hennecke 2003; Friedrich u.a. 2004).

Somit ist das Konnexitätsprinzip auch eine wichtige Säule der ebenfalls im Grundgesetz garantierten **kommunalen Selbstverwaltung** (Art. 28 GG), denn die von **Bund** und **Ländern** den Städten, **Gemeinden** und **(Land-)Kreisen** zugewiesenen öffentlichen Aufgaben können die Kommunen finanziell so stark belasten, dass damit faktisch die kommunale Selbstverwaltung unterbunden würde. Nach dem Konnexitätsprinzip aber muss der auftragende Gesetzgeber als Verursacher (Verursacherprinzip) für den finanziellen Ausgleich der von ihm aufgetragenen Aufgaben sorgen (striktes Konnexitätsprinzip, so in den Ländern **Baden-Württemberg**, **Sachsen**, **Sachsen-Anhalt**, **Schleswig-Holstein** und **Thüringen**), zumindest aber Bestimmungen zur Kostendeckung treffen. Trotzdem wird von Seiten der Kommunen immer noch kritisiert, dass sie gegenüber Bund und Ländern nicht vom Konnexitätsprinzip vor übermäßiger finanzieller Belastung durch übertragene Aufgaben geschützt werden (Ausnahme z.B. NRW, Änderung der Landesverfassung (Art.78) und Konnexitätsausführungsgesetz v. 22. Juni 2004).

Im Freistaat Bayern wurde das Konnexitätsprinzip der Gemeinden gegenüber dem Land nach Volksentscheid mit Wirkung zum 1. Januar 2004 in der Verfassung (Artikel 83 Abs. 3 und 7) verankert. Mit dieser Ausgleichsregelung wird sichergestellt, dass sich das Land nicht auf Kosten der Kommunen finanziell entlasten kann. Zudem sind die Kommunen davor geschützt, dass ihnen vom Land neue kommunale Aufgaben auferlegt werden, ohne die dafür notwendigen Finanzmittel zu erhalten. Die Kostenregelung kann darin bestehen, dass den Kommunen die notwendigen Finanzmittel aus dem Landeshaushalt zur Verfügung gestellt werden oder dass eine neue Einnahmequelle eröffnet wird. Auch die Entlastung von einer bestehenden Aufgabe ist als Ausgleichsregelung möglich.

Subsidiarität beschreibt eine Gesellschaftsauffassung, die die Eigenständigkeit und Eigenverantwortung kleinerer Sozialgebilde betont und staatlichen Zentralismus und Kollektivismus ausdrücklich ablehnt. Es ist ein der katholischen Sozialphilosophie entnommenes Prinzip, das eine Zuständigkeitsordnung der Gesellschaft formuliert, wonach staatliche oder gesellschaftliche, übergeordnete Stellen nur aushilfsweise, eben subsidiär eingreifen sollen. Aufgaben, die von einer Kommune erfüllt werden können, sollen nicht von höherer Stelle oder vom

Staat übernommen und zentral gesteuert werden, sondern im Gegenteil soll der Staat die nötigen Voraussetzungen für eine bürgernahe Umsetzung schaffen (Schmidt-Jortzig, Schink 1982; Döring, Stahl 1999; Nam u.a. 2001). Im Zusammenhang mit der Sozialhilfe bedeutet dies, dass zuvorderst die Kommunen gefordert sind, da diese als niedrigste Ebene dem Bürger am nächsten stehen. So sollen also im Interesse einer bürgernahen, überschaubaren und flexiblen Verwaltung Aufgaben, die noch im örtlichen Bereich wahrgenommen werden können, auch nachgeordneten Verbänden vorbehalten sein.

III. Finanzielle Belastungen überörtlicher Sozialhilfeträger

Die überörtlichen Träger der Sozialhilfe in Deutschland unterscheiden sich je nach Bundesland u.a. bereits in der bloßen Namensgebung. Während in Bayern die Bezirke als überörtliche Träger fungieren, ist es beispielsweise in Hessen ein so genannter Landeswohlfahrtsverband oder im Rheinland ein Landschaftsverband. Diese Verbände übernehmen für ein Bundesland bzw. einen Teil eines Bundeslandes die ihnen nach BSHG und dem jeweiligen landesspezifischen Ausführungsgesetz zugeschriebenen Aufgaben. Hauptaufgabe ist insbesondere die verwaltungsmäßige Abwicklung der Eingliederungshilfe für körperlich, geistig oder seelisch behinderte Menschen.

Einige Verbände, wie beispielsweise in Bayern, Hessen oder Nordrhein-Westfalen, werden dabei von ihren Mitgliedskörperschaften, den Landkreisen und kreisfreien Städten über eine Umlage finanziert. Die Umlage deckt die nicht durch eigene Einnahmen finanzierten Ausgaben ab. Der überörtliche Träger stellt sich quasi als ein sozialer, kommunaler Zweckverband dar, der für seine Mitglieder Aufgaben im Bereich der überörtlichen Sozialhilfe wahrnimmt. Die Mitgliedschaft ist in der Regel verpflichtend.

Seit Jahren haben die überörtlichen Sozialhilfeträger deutschlandweit mit steigenden Fallzahlen in der Eingliederungshilfe zu kämpfen. Gründe dafür sind im Wesentlichen die demographische Entwicklung als auch die verbesserte medizinische Versorgung. Auch behinderte Menschen werden zunehmend älter und bedürfen somit länger der Hilfe. Hinzu kommt, dass das momentane Durchschnittsalter der Heimbewohner noch unter dem Durchschnitt der Gesamtbevölkerung liegt. Es verlassen also in den kommenden Jahren weniger Menschen die Wohnheime, als junge behinderte Menschen hinzukommen. Mit dem Anstieg der Fallzahlen steigen parallel die Ausgaben und damit die Finanzierungslast (Friedrich u.a. 2004).

IV. Reformüberlegungen

1. Suche nach anreizkompatiblen Strukturen

Vor dem Hintergrund der steigenden finanziellen Belastungen überörtlicher Sozialhilfeleistungen stellt sich die Frage, wie dennoch die Kosten in den Griff zu bekommen sind. Insbesondere interessieren Wege, die durch mehr Effizienz in der Leistungsbereitstellung und anreizkompatible Strukturen Einsparpotentiale generieren können.[2] Die Formulierung konkreter Optionsvorschläge in der Verteilung der Aufgaben und Kostenträgerschaft der überörtlichen Sozialhilfe (Eingliederungshilfe) stützt sich dabei auf die beiden finanzwissenschaftlichen Prinzipien Konnexität und Subsidiarität. Die Anforderungen des Subsidiaritätsprinzips in Verbindung mit dem Konnexitätsprinzip schaffen für die ökonomisch effiziente Zuordnung der mit einer Aufgabe verbundenen Entscheidungs-, Durchführungs- und Finanzierungskompetenz auf die verschiedenen föderalen Ebenen die notwendigen Voraussetzungen für mehr Wirtschaftlichkeit und Effektivität.

Der folgenden Diskussion zugrunde liegt ein überörtlicher Sozialhilfeträger, der sich mittels einer Umlage über alle im Einzugsgebiet liegenden Landkreise und kreisfreien Städte finanziert und im Gegenzug dazu für diese Körperschaften die Aufgaben der überörtlichen Sozialhilfe übernimmt. Die Mitgliedskörperschaften fungieren selbst als örtliche Träger der Sozialhilfe und kümmern sich im Bereich der Eingliederungshilfe um die ambulanten Hilfemaßnahmen. Abstrakt formuliert heißt das, Entscheidungs- und Durchführungskompetenz liegen beim höheren Kommunalverband, die Finanzierungskompetenz aber liegt bei den ihn tragenden Gebietskörperschaften. Aufgabenwahrnehmung und Finanzverantwortung fallen demnach auseinander – das finanzwissenschaftlich geforderte Konnexitätsprinzip ist in seiner strikten Form nicht realisiert: Der Entscheider für die Ausgaben hat die durch ihn verursachten finanziellen Auswirkungen nicht in direkter Weise zu tragen. Damit fehlen aber dem überörtlichen Sozialhilfeträger die notwendigen Rückkopplungseffekte für effizientes und budgetverantwortliches Handeln.

Für eine einzelne Körperschaft wird darüber hinaus in keiner Weise transparent, für wie viele und wie schwere Eingliederungshilfefälle sie überhaupt zahlt. Sie überweist lediglich über die Umlage einen pauschalen Betrag nach ihrer Steuerkraft. Je nach Haushaltslage erhöht der überörtliche Sozialhilfeträger den Umlagesatz, um die nicht durch eigene Einnahmen gedeckten Ausgaben zu finanzieren. Für den Letztfinanzier, kreisfreie Stadt bzw. Landkreis, bestehen nur unzureichende Möglichkeiten der Kontrolle bzw. Steuerung im Einzelfall.

---

2 Von einer Diskussion der Leistungsstandards sei hier abgesehen.

Schließlich zeigt die unterstellte Aufgabenverteilung eine Differenzierung nach der Hilfeart stationär, teilstationär bzw. ambulant. Die örtlichen Sozialhilfeträger, Städte und Kreise, sind dabei für die ambulante Versorgung von Menschen mit Behinderung zuständig, die im Regelfall kostengünstiger ist als eine Heimunterbringung. Die Kommunen jedoch haben im angenommenen System keinen Anreiz, diese Betreuungsform zu forcieren, weil sie die Kosten dafür aus ihrem eigenen Sozialhaushalt bestreiten müssen und daher eine stationäre, teurere Unterbringung vorziehen. Diese höheren Kosten tragen sie dann nur indirekt und, aus ihrer individuellen Sicht, nur zu einem geringeren Teil über die Umlage.
Als letztes Moment der Beschreibung der fingierten Verteilung von Aufgaben und der Kostenträgerschaft soll die Tatsache Erwähnung finden, dass seitens der Gebietskörperschaften kreisfreie Städte und Landkreise quasi eine verpflichtende Mitgliedschaft gegenüber dem höheren Sozialverband besteht. Die Körperschaften sind gezwungen, die Aufgaben der überörtlichen Sozialhilfe und deren Durchführung dem überörtlichen Träger zu übertragen und diesen über eine Umlage zu finanzieren. Der überörtliche Sozialhilfeträger nimmt damit eine Monopolstellung ein und steht zu keiner anderen Einrichtung in Konkurrenz. Daraus lässt sich die Vermutung ableiten, dass dieser Verband strukturell bedingt keine besonderen Anreize zu effizientem Handeln und keine besondere Motivation zur Entwicklung günstigerer Versorgungs- und Betreuungsformen hat.

2. Alternative Strukturen überörtlicher Sozialhilfesysteme

Auf der Grundlage der Ausführungen zum Subsidiaritäts- und Konnexitätsprinzip wird für die Eingliederungshilfe eine Verlagerung der Aufgaben der überörtlichen Sozialhilfe vom überörtlichen sozialen Kommunalverband auf die Kommunen selbst vorgeschlagen. Damit wäre eine Zusammenführung von Entscheidungs- und Finanzierungskompetenz erreicht und explizit der notwendige Anreiz zu budgetverantwortlichem Handeln in der Struktur des Systems verankert. Des Weiteren würden alle Hilfearten in der Eingliederungshilfe, stationär, teilstationär bzw. ambulant, aus einer Hand geleistet, d.h. es wäre sichergestellt, dass pro Hilfefall jeweils nur die angemessene und kostengünstigste Versorgung geleistet wird. Die Möglichkeit des Verschiebens von hilfebedürftigen behinderten Menschen aus Kostenaspekten würde von vornherein strukturbedingt entfallen.
In der konkreten Umsetzung – gedacht ist hier an den LWV im Freistaat Sachsen – müsste die Verlagerung von Aufgaben jedoch in differenzierter Form und in Stufen stattfinden (Abbildung 1). Differenziert in der Weise, dass sich nicht alle Aufgaben dazu eignen, dezentral von den örtlichen Trägern der Sozialhilfe ausgeführt zu werden. Planerische und koordinierende Aufgaben in der Eingliederungshilfe können naturgemäß effizienter von zentraler Stelle aus übernommen

werden und sollten daher im Gegensatz zu den operativen Aufgaben beim LWV verbleiben. Dazu gehören u.a. der Um- und Aufbau der Infrastruktur, der bundeslandweit und bundeslandeinheitlich geplant und koordiniert werden sollte, die fachlich kompetente Vertretung in diversen Kommissionen, aber auch die Entgeltverhandlung mit den Leistungserbringern, den Trägern der Einrichtungen. Letztere spielen in Bezug auf die tatsächlich anfallenden Hilfekosten eine entscheidende Rolle: Verhandlungsgeschick und -stärke sind eine wesentliche Voraussetzung, um zweckmäßige und wirtschaftliche Vereinbarungen zu erreichen. Dies kann am besten von einer zentralen Stelle aus sichergestellt werden.

Die angesprochene Verlagerung sollte in Stufen erfolgen. Der entscheidende Vorteil dabei ist, die betroffenen Parteien können mit jedem Schritt in die Aufgabe hineinwachsen und hinzulernen. Sie hätten im Zweifel auch die Möglichkeit, falls sie mit einer Aufgabe unvorhergesehenerweise gänzlich überfordert wären, im Verlagerungsprozess wieder einen Schritt zurückzugehen. Angedacht ist eine Verlagerung gestaffelt nach dem Alter der Personen in drei Stufen. In der ersten Stufe sollten alle Aufgaben, die bisher schon dem örtlichen Träger per Delegation[3] zur Durchführung übertragen waren, sowie Hilfen für Kinder bis zum schulpflichtigen Alter per Ausführungsgesetz übergehen. Im zweiten Schritt sollten dann alle teil- und vollstationären Leistungen, die Kinder und Jugendliche im schulpflichtigen Alter bis zur Vollendung des 18. Lebensjahres benötigen, auf die örtlichen Träger übertragen werden. Abschließend würden in der dritten Stufe alle Hilfen für Erwachsene im Alter vom 18. bis zur Vollendung des 65. Lebensjahres übergehen. Die Zuordnung der einzelnen Hilfeempfänger auf die Gebietskörperschaften würde nach dem Prinzip des gewöhnlichen Aufenthaltsorts erfolgen.

Die diskutierte Verlagerung würde wie erwähnt dazu führen, die Entscheidungs- und Finanzierungskompetenz auf der Ebene der Kommunen (Landkreise und kreisfreie Städte) zusammenzuführen. Die Durchführungskompetenz der Aufgaben bleibt dabei explizit außen vor. Denn es soll den Gebietskörperschaften ausdrücklich die Wahl gelassen werden, von wem sie die Aufgabe ausführen lassen. Sie können dabei zwischen einer Selbstdurchführung oder einer Durchführung durch Dritte im Auftragsverhältnis optieren. Beispielsweise kann nach wie vor der bestehende höhere Kommunalverband die Versorgung der Hilfebedürftigen eines Landkreises oder einer kreisfreien Stadt übernehmen, wenn der Landkreis bzw. die Stadt dies für die beste Alternative hält. Die verwaltungsmäßige Versorgung könnte aber auch im Auftrag an eine große kreisfreie Stadt bzw. einen finanzstarken Landkreis vergeben werden.

---

3 Der überörtliche Sozialhilfeträger hat in der Regel die Möglichkeit, Aufgaben zur bloßen Durchführung an die örtlichen Träger zu delegieren. An der Verteilung der sachlichen Zuständigkeit ändert dies grundsätzlich nichts. Die vom örtlichen Sozialhilfeträger aufgewendeten Entgelte werden dabei in der Regel vom überörtlichen Träger selbst verhandelt und den Kommunen erstattet.

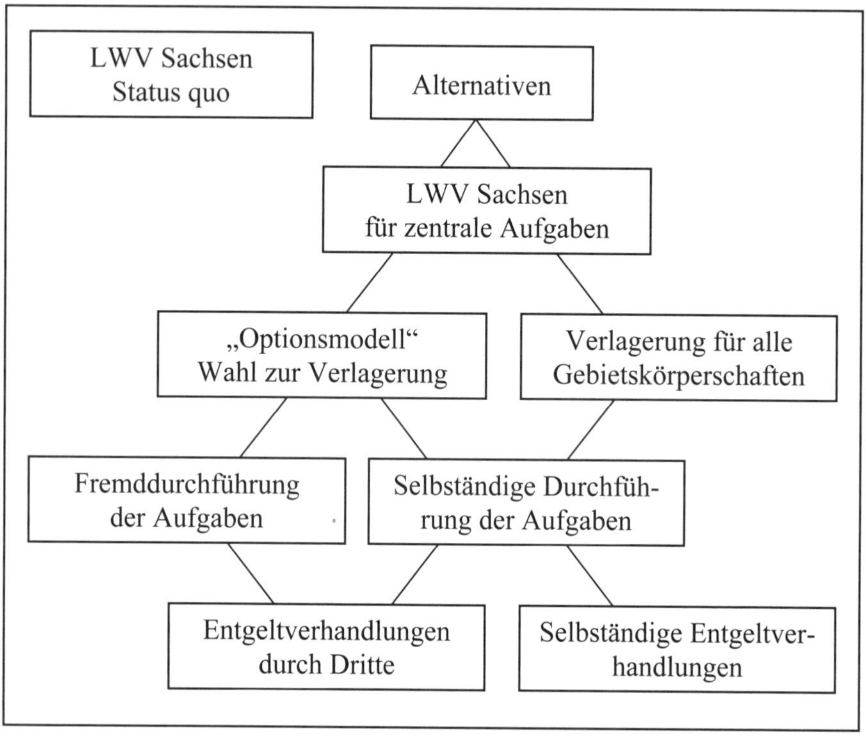

Quelle: Friedrich, Hammerschick, Hartmann, Parsche 2004.

Abb. 1: Alternativen zur Verteilung der Aufgaben der überörtlichen Sozialhilfeleistungen am Beispiel des Freistaates Sachsen

So wird sich der höhere kommunale Sozialverband plötzlich in einem gewissen Wettbewerb mit den Landkreisen und kreisfreien Städten wieder finden und fungiert dann als so genannte Functional Overlapping Competing Jurisdiction (FOCJ).[4] In Deutschland lassen sich FOCJ zwischen Kommunen, z.B. über Zweckverbände, die landesgesetzlich gegründet werden, errichten. In diesem Kontext wird aus einem verpflichtenden Zweckverband ein Verband, der sich um Mitglieder bemühen muss. Seine Marktstellung als Monopolist ist dahin. Er muss sich als Dienstleister seinen Kunden, den Gebietskörperschaften, anbieten, d.h. er muss durch seine Arbeitsergebnisse beweisen, dass er durch seine Erfahrung und sein Know-how der Konkurrenz, beispielsweise anderen Städten oder Landkreisen überlegen ist, will er weiterhin am Markt bestehen. Es entsteht dadurch ein

4 FOCJ ist eine Körperschaft, die gemäß der zu erfüllenden Funktion zu anderen öffentlichen oder privaten Institutionen, die derartige Leistungen ebenfalls anbieten, im Wettbewerb steht. Der Wettbewerb existiert innerhalb eines gleichen Zuständigkeitsgebietes, so dass sie sich überlappen (Frey, Eichenberger 1996, 1999; Frey 1997).

nicht unerheblicher Druck und Anreiz, die anstehenden Aufgaben möglichst kostengünstig zu bewältigen (Friedrich 2002; De Spindler 2003).

3. Berücksichtigung der Finanzierungsaspekte

Neben den inhaltlichen Aspekten gilt es, die finanzielle Seite der Verlagerung von Sozialhilfeaufgaben auf die Kommunen zu betrachten. Zum einen muss die Frage geklärt werden, wie die örtlichen Sozialhilfeträger ihre konkreten Hilfefälle finanzieren und zum anderen, mit welchen Mitteln der örtliche Sozialhilfeträger selbst ausgestattet sein muss, um diese Hilfeleistungen bezahlen zu können.
Die Finanzierung der Hilfefälle könnte nach dem bereits erwähnten Zuordnungsprinzip des gewöhnlichen Aufenthalts (gA) durchgeführt werden. Bei dieser Variante finanziert jeder Landkreis und jede kreisfreie Stadt diejenigen Hilfeempfänger, die dem Ursprung nach aus dieser Gebietskörperschaft stammen. Jede Kommune sollte für ihre eigenen Hilfeempfänger Verantwortung tragen. Die Finanzierung nach dem gewöhnlichen Aufenthalt hat den Vorteil der erhöhten Transparenz, insbesondere aus der Sicht der finanzierenden Gebietskörperschaft. Den kommunalen Gebietskörperschaften wird, anders als bei einer anonymisierten Umlage, bewusst, wie viele Menschen aus ihrer Gesellschaft betreut werden müssen. Damit werden steigende Belastungen aufgrund steigender Fallzahlen auch direkt beim Letztfinanzier deutlich. Bis zur tatsächlichen Umsetzung einer Strukturreform bzw. in der Übergangsphase könnte durch die Einführung einer so genannten Kostenträgerquote[5] bereits ein gewisses Maß an Transparenz und Anreizpotentialen geschaffen werden (Friedrich u.a. 2004).
Bei der möglichen Realisierung des beschriebenen Optionsmodells zum unterstellten Fallbeispiel würde die von den Mitgliedskörperschaften zu bedienende Umlage bis auf eine kleine Restumlage zur Finanzierung des für die Wahrnehmung zentraler Aufgaben verbliebenen sozialen Zweckverbandes wegfallen, d.h. den Landkreisen und kreisfreien Städten verblieben nun diese Mittel zur Finanzierung der ihnen übertragenen Aufgaben (Abbildung 2). Geht man nun nach

5 Als alternative Form zur Umlagefinanzierung käme die Einführung einer so genannten Kostenträgerquote für die Landkreise und kreisfreien Städte in Betracht. Dies bedeutet, dass die eigentlichen Kosten der Hilfegewährung pro Fall zu einem gewissen Anteil von der Gebietskörperschaft übernommen werden, aus der der Hilfeempfänger nach seinem gewöhnlichen Aufenthalt (vor Aufnahme in eine Einrichtung) stammt. Der Rest wird weiterhin gemeinschaftlich über die Umlage finanziert. So könnten sich beispielsweise die Gebietskörperschaften zu 50% direkt an den Fallkosten beteiligen, und die restlichen 50% werden weiter über die Umlage abgedeckt. Diese Aufteilung könnte in Stufen eingeführt werden. Eine solche Kostenträgerquote ermöglicht den Landkreisen und kreisfreien Städten einen Einblick in die tatsächlichen Kosten der Hilfegewährung, während beim jetzigen System der reinen Umlagefinanzierung keine Transparenz gegeben ist, wohin die Gelder der Umlagezahler tatsächlich fließen. Außerdem schafft eine solche Kostenträgerquote einen entsprechenden Anreiz für die örtlichen Sozialhilfeträger, sich bei kostengünstigeren (ambulanten) Versorgungsformen für die Hilfeempfänger zu engagieren, statt sie in teuren Einrichtungen unterzubringen.

gA-Fällen vor, so werden sich normalerweise Verschiebungen hinsichtlich der Finanzierungssituation gegenüber dem Status quo ergeben: Landkreise bzw. kreisfreie Städte, die von der Umlagefinanzierung profitiert haben, werden nun zusätzliche Mittel für ihre gA-Fälle aufbringen müssen. Diese Verteilung der finanziellen Belastungen könnte man nun als eine Art natürliche Verteilung ansehen, d.h. die Gebietskörperschaften müssten dann mit den ihnen zur Verfügung stehenden Mitteln die ihnen obliegenden Aufgaben bewältigen, zu denen dann die Hilfeleistungen im Rahmen der Hilfe in besonderen Lebenslagen zählen.[6]
Kommt es aufgrund einer Ungleichverteilung der Anzahl sowie der Schwere der Eingliederungshilfefälle zu größeren unterschiedlichen Belastungen unter den einzelnen Landkreisen und kreisfreien Städten, so bestünde die Möglichkeit, diese Unterschiede, sofern sie tatsächlich statistisch signifikant sein sollten, über eine zusätzliche Komponente im Kommunalfinanzausgleich abzufedern. So könnten die Belastungen, die einem Landkreis bzw. einer kreisfreien Stadt durch die veränderte Zuständigkeitsverteilung entstehen, über einen zusätzlichen Nebenansatz (Abbildung 3), einen so genannten Soziallastennebenansatz, ausgeglichen werden.[7] Wünschenswert wäre ein Ausgleich der Anzahl als auch der Schwere der Fälle. Es wäre im Einzelfall zu prüfen, ob das dafür notwendige Datenmaterial bereits vorliegt oder aber erst in der gewünschten Qualität generiert werden müsste. Das Material müsste genau aufschlüsseln, wie viele Hilfeempfänger aus einer Gebietskörperschaft welche Hilfe erhalten.[8]

6 Auftretende unterschiedliche Belastungen durch die übernommenen Sozialhilfeausgaben werden dadurch freilich nicht explizit berücksichtigt. Hier gäbe es also keinen Ausgleich zwischen finanzstärkeren und finanzschwächeren Gebietskörperschaften, teuren und billigen sowie vielen und wenigen Fällen. Die Gebietskörperschaften erhielten ausschließlich Mittel über die bestehenden kommunalen Finanzausgleiche je nach Finanzkraft und Bedarf zugewiesen.

7 Ein zusätzlicher Nebenansatz wird nach Meinung der Autoren erst in der dritten Phase einer stärkeren Aufgabenverlagerung notwendig. Dieser Soziallastennebenansatz sollte dann aber neben den jetzigen überörtlichen Sozialhilfeausgaben auch die örtlichen Sozialhilfeausgaben berücksichtigen. Was die Indikatoren für die örtliche Sozialhilfe betrifft, so könnte hier bereits auf Erfahrungen aus anderen Bundesländern, wie z.B. Nordrhein-Westfalen (vgl. Parsche, Steinherr 1995) oder Rheinland-Pfalz (vgl. Parsche, Steinherr 1998) zurückgegriffen werden.

8 Allerdings wird von zu komplexen Nebenansätzen abgeraten.

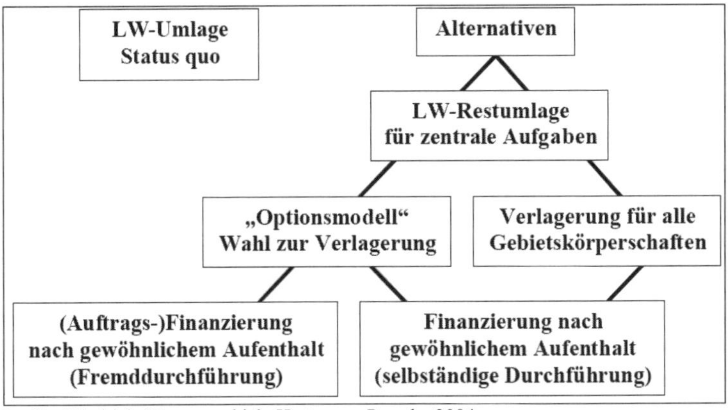

Quelle: Friedrich, Hammerschick, Hartmann, Parsche 2004.

Abb. 2: Alternativen zur Finanzierung der Aufgaben der überörtlichen Sozialhilfeleistungen im Freistaat Sachsen

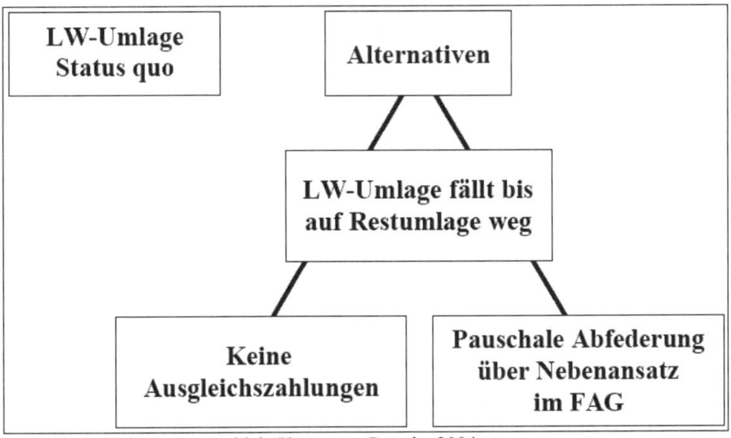

Quelle: Friedrich, Hammerschick, Hartmann, Parsche 2004.

Abb. 3: Alternativen zur Finanzierung der Gebietskörperschaften zur Durchführung von überörtlichen Sozialhilfeleistungen in Sachsen

V. Zusammenfassung

Das Auseinanderfallen von Aufgabenwahrnehmung und Finanzierungsverantwortung in der organisatorischen Struktur einiger überörtlicher Sozialhilfeträger in Deutschland bedingt, dass für eine sparsame Mittelverwendung ungenügende zielkonforme Anreize verankert sind. Hinzu kommt die fehlende Transparenz gerade für die im Umlagesystem finanzierenden Landkreise und kreisfreien Städte. Für eine einzelne Gebietskörperschaft wird nicht transparent, wie viele und

wie schwere Fälle nach dem gewöhnlichen Aufenthalt eigentlich in ihre Zuständigkeit fallen. Durch diese fehlende Transparenz kann darüber hinaus auch keine effektive Finanzkontrolle von Seiten des Letztfinanzieres stattfinden, der von Natur aus ein erhöhtes Interesse daran haben müsste.
Darüber hinaus besteht tendenziell aufgrund der Verteilung der Aufgaben und Kostenträgerschaft das Problem, dass insbesondere die örtlichen Sozialhilfeträger einen Anreiz haben, Hilfefälle zum überörtlichen Träger abzuschieben. Durch die geteilten Zuständigkeiten (stationär-überörtlich, ambulant-örtlich) haben die Landkreise und kreisfreien Städte einen Vorteil daraus, einen Hilfeempfänger von der ambulanten Betreuung in eine stationäre Einrichtung zu bringen, um selbst Kosten zu sparen. Insgesamt ist eine stationäre Unterbringung in der Regel teurer – dies trifft die einzelne Gebietskörperschaft über die Umlage aber nur zu einem geringen Teil.
Eine nach dem Subsidiaritätsprinzip vorgenommene Aufgabenverlagerung bietet dagegen entscheidende Vorteile in den Punkten Finanzierung und Steuerung. Durch das in der unterstellten Fallkonstellation mit Hilfe des vorgeschlagenen Optionsmodells realisierte Konnexitätsprinzip befinden sich Aufgabenwahrnehmung und Ausgabenverantwortung sowie Finanzierung in einer Hand, so dass zum einen strukturelle Anreize für die beteiligten Parteien zum kostenbewussten Umgang mit den zur Verfügung stehenden Finanzmitteln gegeben sind und zum anderen eine effektive Finanzkontrolle möglich ist. Des Weiteren wird für den Letztfinanzier transparent, für wie viele und welche Fälle er bezahlen muss, was wiederum eine funktionierende Einzelfallsteuerung zur Folge hat. Dadurch, dass die Verpflichtung wegfällt, die überörtliche Sozialhilfe von einem höheren Sozialverband ausführen zu lassen, entsteht darüber hinaus in der Leistungsbereitstellung ein gewisses Maß an Wettbewerb. In der Summe werden von der Umsetzung der geschilderten strukturellen Reformen erhebliche Effizienzgewinne und Einsparpotentiale erwartet, was insbesondere im Hinblick auf die gestiegenen und noch steigenden Fallzahlen – auch im Zusammenhang mit der schrumpfenden und zudem alternden Bevölkerung – eine notwendige Voraussetzung für die Konsolidierung der Finanzen im Bereich der Eingliederungshilfe ist.[9]

9 An dieser Stelle nicht angesprochen wurden die Standards in der Leistungsgewährung. Neben den finanzwissenschaftlichen Aspekten der Aufgabenverteilung und der Finanzverantwortung sind auch diese kostenwirksamen Vorgaben kritisch zu diskutieren und womöglich auf ein angemessenes Maß zu senken. Dies verlangt freilich erheblichen politischen Mut, könnte allerdings auch ein beachtliches Einsparpotential generieren.

Literaturverzeichnis

De Spindler, J., FOCJ – Ein Konzept zur Neuordnung der Zusammenarbeit öffentlichrechtlicher Gebietskörperschaften, Bern 2003.

Döring, T. und *D. Stahl,* Räumliche Aspekte der föderalen Aufgabenverteilung, der Finanzverfassung und Subventionspolitik in der Bundesrepublik Deutschland, Hannover 1999.

Frey, B. S., Ein neuer Föderalismus für Europa: Die Idee der FOCJ in Beiträge zur Ordnungstheorie und Ordnungspolitik, Tübingen 1997.

Frey, B.S. und *R. Eichenberger*, FOCJ: Competitive Government for Europe, in: International Review of Law and Economics, Vol. 16, 1996, S. 315-327.

Frey, B.S. und *R. Eichenberger*, The New Democratic Federalism for Europe, Functional Overlapping and Competing Jurisdictions, Cheltenham 1999.

Friedrich, P., Functional, Overlapping, Competing, Jurisdictions-FOCJ – An Instrument of Regional Competition, in: Urban Regions: Governing Interacting Economic, Housing, and Transport Systems Development, hrsg. von J. van Dijk, P. Elhorst, J. Oosterhaven und E. Wever, Nederlandse Geografische Studies, Nr. 303, Utrecht 2002, S. 237-263.

Friedrich, P., J. Gwiazda und *Ch.W. Nam*, Strengthening Municipal Fiscal Autonomy through Intergovernmental Transfers, in: Urban Dynamics and Growth, hrsg. von R. Capello und P. Nijkamp, Amsterdam u.a. 2004, S. 691-728.

Friedrich, P., J. Hammerschick, H. Hartmann und *R. Parsche*, Überörtliche Sozialhilfe im Freistaat Sachsen und Alternativen zur gegenwärtigen Verteilung von Aufgaben und Kostenträgerschaft für überörtliche Sozialhilfeleistungen, ifo Forschungsberichte, Nr. 21, München 2004.

Grossekettler, H., Options- und Grenzkostenpreise für Kollektivgüter unterschiedlicher Art und Ordnung, Ein Beitrag zu den Bereitstellungs- und Finanzierungsregeln für öffentliche Leistungen, in: Finanzarchiv, Vol. 43, 1985, S. 211-260.

Grossekettler, H., Die österreichische Finanzverfassung vor dem Hintergrund des internationalen Standortwettbewerbs, in: Kompendium der österreichischen Finanzpolitik, hrsg. von E. Theurl, H. Winner und R. Sausgruber, Wien 2002, S. 32-89.

Hennecke, H.-G., Darf der Bund bestellen, wenn er bezahlt, oder soll der Bund bezahlen müssen, wenn er bestellen darf, in: Landkreistag, Vol. 73, 2003, S. 137-148.

Klein, O., Das verfassungsrechtliche Konnexitätsprinzip, Kommunalwissenschaftliches Institut der Universität Potsdam, Potsdam 2003.

Musgrave, R. A. und *P. B. Musgrave*, Public Finance in Theory and Practice, 3. Aufl., New York u.a. 1980.

Nam, Ch. W., R. Parsche, und *M. Steinherr*, The Principles of Parallel Development of State and Municipalities as Useful Benchmarks for the Determination of Intergovernmental Grants in Germany, in: European Planning Studies, Vol. 9, 2001, S. 525-537.

Oates, W. E., Fiscal Federalism, New York 1972.

Oates, W. E., An Essay on Fiscal Federalism, in: Journal of Economic Literature, Vol. 37, 1999, S. 1120-1149.

Parsche, R. und *M. Steinherr*, Der kommunale Finanzausgleich des Landes Nordrhein-Westfalen, ifo Studien zur Finanzpolitik, Nr. 59, München 1995.

Parsche, R. und *M. Steinherr*, Der Ausgleich zwischen Finanzbedarf und Finanzkraft im kommunalen Finanzausgleich des Landes Rheinland-Pfalz, ifo Studien zur Finanzpolitik, Nr. 66, München 1998.

Schmidt-Jortzig, E. und *A. Schink*, Subsidiaritätsprinzip und Kommunalordnung, Schriftenreihe des Freiherr-vom-Stein-Institutes, Band 2, Köln 1982.

Trapp, G., Das Veranlassungsprinzip in der Finanzverfassung der Bundesrepublik Deutschland, Berlin 2003.

C. Finanzierungsinstrumente für öffentliche Infrastrukturinvestitionen in Zeiten des demographischen Umbruchs – Public Private Partnership am Beispiel Toll Collect

Sylvia Kreiß

I. Einleitung

Die ökonomischen Konsequenzen einer im Durchschnitt immer älter werdenden Bevölkerung gehören zu den zentralen wirtschafts- und finanzpolitischen Herausforderungen der nächsten Jahre. Bei den offensichtlichen Problemfeldern, wie dem des Alterssicherungssystems, hat es schon erste Anpassungsmaßnahmen gegeben (Deutsche Bundesbank 2004, S. 15). Darüber hinausgehend wird der demographische Wandel aber noch eine Reihe weiterer Probleme für die öffentliche Hand aufwerfen. Laut Schätzungen wird der Gesamtlastquotient – das ist die Zahl der nicht erwerbsfähigen Personen[1] in Relation zu den Personen im erwerbsfähigen Alter, von gegenwärtigen 82% bis zum Jahre 2050 auf 112% ansteigen (Statistisches Bundesamt 2003). Das Arbeitskräfteangebot geht zurück, die Steuereinnahmen sinken.

Gleichzeitig steigt der Bedarf an öffentlichen Investitionen (Reichenbach 2002, S. 112ff.). Vor allem in den Bereichen Krankenhäuser, Altenheime, Pflegeeinrichtungen und Friedhöfe dürften die Investitionserfordernisse deutlich zunehmen. Zudem hat sich der Staat aufgrund finanzieller Engpässe in den letzten Jahren deutlich mit Investitionen zurückgehalten. So sanken die Infrastrukturinvestitionen des Staates während der letzten zehn Jahre sogar nominal um 37,6% (Institut der Deutschen Wirtschaft 2005, S. 23).[2] In der wissenschaftlichen Literatur mehren sich derweil die Analysen, die von positiven direkten und indirekten Impulsen von Infrastrukturinvestitionen auf die langfristige Produktivität privatwirtschaftlicher Investitionen sprechen (Aschauer 1989, S. 177ff.; Aschauer 1998).[3] Für den Bereich der öffentlichen Investitionen lässt sich daher ein erheblicher Nachholbedarf vermuten.

Die sich öffnende Schere zwischen dem Bedarf an Infrastrukturinvestitionen einerseits und finanziellen Handlungsmöglichkeiten der öffentlichen Hand andererseits führt zu vermehrten Diskussionen über den Einsatz von öffentlich-

---

1 Hier definiert als Jugendliche unter 20 Jahren und ältere Mitbürger über 60 Jahren.

2 Von 34,4 Mrd. € 1994 auf 25,0 Mrd. € in 2004.

3 Die erste diesbezügliche Untersuchung in den USA stammt von Aschauer, der für die USA eine signifikant positive Wirkung von Infrastrukturkapital im engeren Sinne (Straßen, Schienen, Flughäfen, Strom- und Gasversorgung) auf die Faktorproduktivität des privaten Sektors feststellte.

privaten Kooperationen, sogenannten Public Private Partnerships (PPPs). Interessanterweise wird diese Finanzierungsform derzeit sowohl von Jüngern des schlanken Staates als auch von Anhängern stärkerer wirtschaftlicher Staatstätigkeit propagiert.[4] So könnten PPPs eine dritte Antwort auf die Frage sein, ob die Errichtung und Bereitstellung von Infrastruktureinrichtungen und gemeinwirtschaftlichen Unternehmen vom Staat oder vom Privatsektor wahrgenommen werden soll.

Es stellen sich folgende Fragen:

- Was sind Public Private Partnerships?
- Welche finanziellen Vorteile erhoffen sich die jeweiligen Akteure?
- Welche Schwierigkeiten können auftreten?
- Welche Erfahrungen wurden bislang damit gemacht?
- Wodurch kamen bei bekannten PPPs, z.B. Toll Collect, die Probleme zustande und wie kann man ihnen begegnen?

II. Der Begriff Public Private Partnership

Der Begriff des Public Private Partnership wurde in den 40er Jahren in den USA geprägt. Private Unternehmer und Stadtverwaltungen hatten sich zusammengeschlossen, um die Infrastruktur einiger Städte zur verbessern und somit Vorteile sowohl für die Einwohner als auch für die Geschäftsleute zu erzielen (Belina 2001; Jacobs 2000). Als allgemeine Definition bietet Oberender an:

„Public Private Partnership ist eine Form der Interaktion zwischen handelnden Akteuren der öffentlichen Hand und privaten Investoren mit dem Fokus auf die Verfolgung komplementärer Ziele und der Realisierung von Synergiepotenzialen. Die Partnerschaft ist prozessorientiert, wobei die Identität und Verantwortlichkeit für das eigene Handeln intakt bleiben." (Oberender, Rudolf 2004, S. 493f.)

Wichtig ist hierbei vor allem der Fokus auf komplementäre Ziele. Eine reine Vergabe bestimmter Leistungsbereiche der öffentlichen Hand an private Auftragnehmer kann nicht als PPP verstanden werden (Budäus, Grüning 1997, S.48 ff.). So stellt z.B. die Beauftragung einer Putzfirma zur Reinigung des Landratsamtes kein Public Private Partnership dar. Die Putzfirma muss hier nur ihren Vertrag erfüllen und wird demnach bezahlt. Sie hat kein originäres Interesse an einem sauberen Landratsamt.

Als weiterer wichtiger Punkt wäre die Risikoteilung zu nennen. Bei PPP-Projekten geht regelmäßig ein Teil des Risikos von der öffentlichen Hand auf

4 Erstere erwarten v.a. Effizienzgewinne durch privates Management, letztere betonen die Wichtigkeit der **Bereitstellung** von Gütern zur Daseinsvorsorge durch die öffentliche Hand; die tatsächliche Produktion dieser Güter kann dann auch durch Private erfolgen.

den Privaten über. Hintergedanke ist hierbei, dass das Risiko jeweils von demjenigen getragen werden sollte, der es am besten beeinflussen kann.
Merkmale von PPPs (Budäus, Grüning 1997, S.48 ff.; Europäische Kommission, Generaldirektion 2003; Europäische Kommission 2004):

- Zusammenarbeit von mindestens einem öffentlichen und privaten Partner
- Die Zusammenarbeit bezieht sich auf ein abgegrenztes Aufgabenfeld
- Die Partner bringen in die PPPs eigene Ressourcen ein, die je nach Formalisierungsgrad der PPP unterschiedlich verbindlich und mit unterschiedlicher Dauer für das Projekt gebündelt werden
- Die Partner haben i.d.R. unterschiedliche Ziele, die aber komplementär sein müssen
- Die partnerschaftlichen Ziele lassen sich durch eine Ressourceneinbringung der Partner besser erreichen, als ohne eine entsprechende Kooperation.
- Die Zusammenarbeit vollzieht sich auf einer durch Verträge geregelten formalen Grundlage
- Es findet eine Risikoteilung zwischen öffentlichem und privaten Partner statt
- Der vom PPP erwirtschaftete Nutzen muss für den einzelnen Partner so sein, dass für ihn ein Anreiz besteht, weiter in der Partnerschaft zu bleiben.

Vorteile/Nachteile aus Sicht der jeweiligen Akteure

Die Vorteile bei der öffentlichen Hand werden im Allgemeinen in den finanziellen Einsparmöglichkeiten gesehen. Hier wird auch gerne die ausbleibende budgetäre Belastung durch Investitionen ins Feld geführt.
Dies ist aus finanzwirtschaftlicher Sicht nicht schlüssig. Die Investitionssumme muss auf jeden Fall aufgewandt werden, sei es durch den privaten oder durch den öffentlichen Partner. Bringt der private Investor, wie in den meisten Fällen bei PPP, die Investitionsmittel auf, so will er dafür vom öffentlichen Partner kompensiert werden. Die öffentliche Hand muss die Kapitalkosten nur nicht einmalig, sondern in Form von Leasingraten, Mieten oder Gewinnbeteiligungen an den privaten Investor überweisen. Hierbei treten zwei Nachteile auf:
Die Bundesrepublik Deutschland und ihre Gebietskörperschaften werden derzeit mit den weltweit besten Ratings bewertet.[5] Das Ausfallrisiko eines Kredites an Bund oder Gebietskörperschaften ist minimal. Daher ist eine Finanzierung durch die öffentliche Hand häufig wesentlich günstiger als die Finanzierung über einen privaten Investor. Dieser muss Kreditzinsen entsprechend der Bonität seiner Firma zahlen. Diese Finanzierungskosten für das jeweilige Projekt gibt er dann an die öffentliche Hand über höhere Leasingraten oder Gewinnbeteiligungen weiter. Das heißt, durch die private Finanzierung der Investitionssumme entsteht dem

5 AAA sowohl bei Moody's Ratings als auch bei Standard and Poor's Ratings.

Staat meistens ein finanzieller Nachteil, es sei denn andere Kosteneinsparungen kompensieren die höheren Finanzierungskosten (Kirchhoff, Müller-Godefrey 1994, S. 38 ff.; Plaßmann 2004, S.40 f.).

Der zweite Nachteil ist budgetrechtlicher Natur. Eine staatliche Ausgabe zählt nur dann als öffentliche Investition, wenn ein Träger des öffentlichen Rechts sowohl Auftraggeber als auch Eigentümer des Objekts wird. Bringt der private Investor die Mittel auf, so wird dieser auch Eigentümer des Objekts. Die Ausgaben der öffentlichen Hand für Mieten oder Leasingraten gelten dann als öffentlicher Konsum (Beirat für Wirtschafts- und Sozialfragen 1998, S. 21). Nun wird die mögliche Kreditaufnahme der öffentlichen Hand aber durch Artikel 115 Grundgesetz auf die Höhe der Investitionen beschränkt (Art. 115 GG 2005). Das heißt, durch die Betreibung von Public Private Partnerships schränkt die öffentliche Hand, ihren eigenen finanziellen Spielraum deutlich ein. Je nach Vertragsgestaltung müssen sämtliche Kosten aus solchen Projekten einschließlich Kapitalkosten aus den laufenden Einnahmen finanziert werden. So führen Leasingverträge ohne Eigentumsübergangsregelung bei Gemeinden zu Mietzahlungen und konsumtiven Ausgaben, die im Verwaltungshaushalt veranschlagt werden (Kirchhoff, Müller-Godefrey 1994, S.50). Handelt es sich jedoch um einen Mietkaufvertrag mit Risikoübernahme seitens der Gemeinde, dann erfolgt eine Berücksichtigung als Investition im Vermögenshaushalt (Kirchhoff, Müller-Godefrey 1994, S.50). Allerdings geht im ersteren Falle bei den Gemeinden die Leasingrate voll in die Gebührenkalkulation der Gemeinden ein, so dass zusätzliche Einnahmen im Verwaltungshaushalt entstehen. Im zweiten Fall handelt es sich um Investitionen, die im Rahmen der Kreditaufnahmebegrenzungen finanziert werden können (z.B. § 72 der Gemeindeordnung in Nordrhein-Westfalen). Diese Schwierigkeiten bilden zum heutigen Zeitpunkt bei den geringen PPP-Volumina in Deutschland keine große Einschränkung. Doch wird v.a. von der FDP eine Übernahme des englischen Modells, wonach sämtliche öffentliche Investitionen durch PPPs vorgenommen werden müssen, falls keine zwingenden Gründe dagegen sprechen, angestrebt. Dies käme bei geltendem Grundgesetz einer beträchtlichen Reduzierung der Staatsneuverschuldung gleich.

Zusammenfassend lässt sich also sagen, dass auf der Finanzierungsseite durch das Eingehen von Public Private Partnerships öfters negative Effekte für die öffentliche Hand auftreten.

Auf der anderen Seite stehen die Effizienzgewinne durch private Bereitstellung. Es ist weitgehend unstrittig, dass sich durch privates Management eine verbesserte Wirtschaftlichkeit und höhere Effizienz der Bereitstellung ergeben. Bei der Investitionsentscheidung kommt es über eine Ausschreibung zu intensiven Wettbewerb zwischen den möglichen privaten Anbietern. Dadurch erreicht man, dass derjenige, der am kostengünstigsten anbieten kann auch wirklich zum Zuge kommt. Anders als bei Bereitstellung über die Verwaltung kann man dadurch davon ausgehen, dass jeweils spezialisierte Fachleute das Management des Projekts übernehmen. Bei den Schätzungen der Einsparung durch Public Private Partnerships kommt die Literatur zu unterschiedlichen Ergebnissen. Doch geht man davon aus, dass die Effizienzgewinne durch private Bereitstellung trotz höherer Finanzierungskosten zu deutlich geringerer Gesamtbelastung der öffentlichen Haushalte führen. Manche Veröffentlichen sprechen von bis zu 30% Kosteneinsparungen bei PPP-Beispielen aus dem kommunalen Bereich in Deutschland und Österreich (Beirat für Wirtschafts- und Sozialfragen 1998, S. 35, Europäische Kommission Generaldirektion Regionalpolitik 2004). Allerdings fallen diese Einsparungen bei Vorliegen effizienter staatlicher und kommunaler Verwaltungen gering aus. Zu beachten ist auch die doppelte Ausschreibungspflicht zum Auffinden eines privaten Partners und wegen des überwiegenden Verbots der Inhousegeschäfte mit dem PPP für die Aufgabenübertragung an das PPP. Das bedeutet, dass eine weitere Ausschreibung für die vom PPP zu erbringende Leistung erfolgen muss. Diese Ausschreibung kann durchaus ein anderer Anbieter gewinnen, wodurch das PPP seinen Gründungszweck nicht erreicht (Europäische Kommission 2004; Cox 2005; Radwan 2006).

Ein großer Vorteil des Public Private Partnerships gegenüber herkömmlicher Auftragsvergabe an private Betreiber liegt in der Teilrisikoübernahme durch die privaten Investoren. Diese übernehmen das Risiko der rechtseitigen, vollständigen und vertragsgemäßen Erfüllung der von ihnen zu verantwortenden Leistungen. Allerdings muss betont werden, dass die Identifikation der möglichen Risiken sowie ihre vertragliche Zuweisung auf die Partner eine intensive Risikoanalyse sowie eine detaillierte Vertragsgestaltung nötig macht. Verwaltungsmitarbeiter sind zum gegenwärtigen Zeitpunkt wohl nur unzureichend in der Lage, wasserdichte Verträge über die Risikoteilung zu entwerfen und gegenüber ihren Vertragspartnern durchzusetzen. Als in Großbritannien Anfang der 80er Jahre die Durchführung von Infrastrukturprojekten über Public Private Partnership als Regelfall eingeführt wurde (Beirat für Wirtschafts- und Sozialfragen 1998, S. 38),[6] traten auch genau hier die größten Probleme auf. Die Verwaltungen waren nicht aus dem Stand in der Lage, Auftragsvergabe, Vertragsgestaltung und Risikomanagement effizient zu gestalten. Die Regierung reagierte mit der Schaffung von Musterverträgen, in denen eine standardisierte Risikoaufteilung, Finanzierungsstruktur und ein Muster der Projektspezifikation vorgegeben waren (Beirat für Wirtschafts- und Sozialfragen 1998, S. 53). Über die Jahre scheint sich nun in Großbritannien das nötige Fachwissen in den Verwaltungen herausgebildet zu haben. Die Gestaltung der Infrastruktur in so weitgehenden Bereichen wie der

6 Investitionen dürfen in Großbritannien nur dann über das Budget finanziert werden, wenn sachliche oder finanzielle Gründe zwingend gegen eine Durchführung auf Basis von PPP sprechen.

Trinkwasserversorgung, Krankenhäusern, Schulen und Gefängnissen scheint problemloser über PPP zu funktionieren (Fawkner 2004, S. 82 f., Europäische Kommission, Generaldirektion Regionalpolitik 2004). Berichte wirtschaftlicher Schwierigkeiten wie die Finanzierung des channel tunnels (Europäische Kommission, Generaldirektion Regionalpolitik 2004, S.119; Schüler 2006) über Public Private Partnership bleiben die Ausnahme.

Ein weiterer Vorteil der PPPs besteht darin, dass sämtliche Kosten für eine bestimmte Leistung über die gesamte Projektlaufzeit erfasst und transparent gemacht wird (Positionspapier des Wissenschaftlichen Beirats der Gesellschaft für öffentliche Wirtschaft 2004, S. 2). Dies ist bei Finanzierung über das Budget nicht üblich. Die Erstinvestitionskosten werden den Entscheidungsträgern vorgelegt, die Folgekosten werden nur selten veranschlagt. Dabei sind im Durchschnitt die Folgekosten (Personal und laufende Sachausgaben) fünfmal so hoch wie die ursprünglichen Kosten für die Infrastrukturinvestition (Beirat für Wirtschafts- und Sozialfragen 1998, S. 22). So kann durch eine stärkere Einbeziehung von PPPs die Transparenz für die Entscheidungsträger deutlich erhöht werden.

III. Toll Collect

Toll Collect ist eines der in der Öffentlichkeit am breitesten diskutierten Public Private Partnerships. Dennoch sind dazu fast keine verlässlichen Daten veröffentlicht worden. Von den Ausschreibungsdetails über die Vertragsgestaltung zu den späteren Nachverhandlungen wurde von allen Beteiligten Verschwiegenheitspflicht vereinbart, selbst Mitgliedern des Bundestages wurde der Einblick verwehrt. So ist die Datenlage mager, teilweise stützen sich die nachfolgenden Ausführungen auf vom Verkehrsministerium weder bestätigte noch dementierte Journalistenrecherchen, teilweise auf öffentliche Verlautbarungen der beteiligten Unternehmen. Wo möglich, wurde auf die Gesetzestexte und Bundestagsanfragen zu Toll Collect und auf die veröffentlichten Daten des Bundeskartellamtes zurückgegriffen.

Seit 1995 wurde die Einführung einer streckenbezogenen LKW-Maut im Bundestag diskutiert.[7] Das Mautsystem und dessen technische Infrastruktur sollten durch ein privates Unternehmen finanziert, installiert und betrieben werden. Im Januar 2000 begann das Vergabeverfahren als Verhandlungsverfahren mit vorgeschaltetem Teilnahmewettbewerb. Am 15. August 2001 beschloss das Bundes-

---

7 1995 kündigte der damalige Bundesverkehrsminister Matthias Wissmann (CDU) die Einführung einer solchen Abgabe an. Auch seine Nachfolger sprachen sich für eine solche Maut aus. Im September 1999 setzte Franz Müntefering, damals Bundesverkehrsminister, eine Regierungskommission „Verkehrsinfrastrukturfinanzierung“ ein, nach ihrem Leiter Wilhelm Pällmann auch Pällmann-Kommission genannt.

kabinett die Einführung einer LKW-Maut auf deutschen Autobahnen, am 12. April 2002 trat das Gesetz zur Einführung von streckenbezogenen Gebühren für die Benutzung von Bundesautobahnen mit schweren Nutzfahrzeugen in Kraft.[8] Darin ist eindeutig festgelegt, dass das Bundesamt für Güterverkehr sowohl die Errichtung als auch den Betrieb eines Systems zur Mauterhebung an einen Privaten übertragen kann. Alternativ wird ein reines Betreibermodell ermöglicht (ABMG § 4 Abs. 2). In § 6 wird festgelegt, dass das private Unternehmen für Beschaffung, Anbringung, Unterhaltung und Entfernung der erforderlichen Ausstattung zur Mauterhebung verantwortlich ist. Die Kontrolle für die Einhaltung der Mautpflicht wird in § 7 Abs. 1 dem Bundesamt für Güterverkehr übertragen, wobei dieses sie wiederum auf ein privates Unternehmen übertragen kann.

Die Ausschreibung zur LKW-Maut wurde von der Arbeitsgemeinschaft Beratergruppe verfasst. Die Kölner Inter Traffic GmbH (eine Tochter des TÜV Rheinland) und das Beratungsunternehmen Price Waterhouse Coopers waren dabei für die IT Technik zuständig. Laut einem vom Verkehrsministerium weder bestätigten noch dementierten Bericht des Norddeutschen Rundfunks entstanden für diese externe Beratertätigkeit Honorarkosten in Höhe von 15,6 Mio. Euro (NDR Online 03. 2004, http://www.ndr.de/ndr/wirtschaft/meldung).

Nur der erste, allgemeine Teil der Ausschreibung war öffentlich, teilnehmende Unternehmen bekamen dann weitere Unterlagen übermittelt. Nach Ablauf der Einsendefrist im Februar 2000, hatten sechs Unternehmensgruppen einen Antrag auf Teilnahme an dem Verfahren gestellt. Fünf der Konsortien wurden aufgefordert, ein Angebot abzugeben. Diese fünf Bewerber bekamen unter Verschwiegenheitsverpflichtung vertrauliche Unterlagen mit den Ausschreibungsdetails, die bis heute nicht veröffentlicht wurden. Nur drei dieser potentiellen Anbieter reichten ein fristgerechtes Angebot ein.[9] Den Zuschlag erhielt die Bietergemeinschaft ETC (Electronic Toll Collect) aus Berlin, an der Daimler Chrysler Financial Services und die Deutsche Telekom AG mit jeweils 45%, und die französische Firma Cofiroute S.A. mit 10% beteiligt sind (Toll Collect, http://www.toll-collect.de /unternehmen). Während der Verhandlungsphase mit den drei Bietergemeinschaften war es zu mehreren Schwierigkeiten gekommen, die ausgeschlossenen Unternehmen hatten teils mit Erfolg vor dem Bundeskartellamt oder vor dem Vergabesenat beim Oberlandesgericht in Düsseldorf Beschwerde eingelegt. Letztlich konnte die Vergabekammer des Bundeskartellamts keine vergabe-

8 Gesetz zur Einführung von streckenbezogenen Gebühren für die Nutzung von Bundesautobahnen mit schweren Nutzfahrzeugen, BGBL 1, Nr. 23, S.1234.

9 Neben der erfolgreichen ETC.de waren dies die Bietergemeinschaft AGES Maut System GmbH & Co KG aus Düsseldorf, bestehend aus der damaligen Mannesmann AG, der Aral AG, der euroShell Deutschland Gmbh und dreier weiterer kleinerer Unternehmen; der dritte Bieter war die schweizerische Fela Management AG.

rechtswidrige Ungleichbehandlung der Angebote feststellen, obwohl das Bundeskartellamt ausdrücklich auf die Problematik hinwies, dass der Bund selbst an einem mittelbar beteiligten Unternehmen von ETC, nämlich der Telekom AG wesentlich beteiligt ist (Bundeskartellamt, http://www.bundeskartellamt.de).
Wie oben geschildert, ist einer der Hauptvorteile des PPP, dass der jeweils effizienteste Anbieter den Zuschlag erhält. Im Falle von Toll Collect sind hier gewisse Zweifel angebracht. So werden dem Verkehrsministerium in der Öffentlichkeit die unterschiedlichsten Motive unterstellt, z.B. den Börsenkurs der Telecom stützen zu wollen, über den Wunsch ein Anwendungsfeld für das Satellitenprojekt Galileo zu finden bis hin zu dem Ziel, einen Innovationsschub in Deutschland auszulösen. Unglücklicherweise hat das Verkehrsministerium selbst diese Zweifel genährt, indem es öffentlich einem satellitengestützten System den Vorzug gab, mit der Begründung, die erstmalige Realisierung eines solchen Systems könne in Deutschland auch auf anderen Feldern der Informationstechnologie einen Innovationsschub auslösen (Bundesministerium für Verkehr 2004).
Dadurch entsteht der Eindruck, dass möglicherweise ein teureres System bevorzugt wurde. Der vom Ministerium erwartete Zusatznutzen für Deutschland kann aber von diesem in keiner Weise ermittelt werden. Es könnte sich also um eine verdeckte Subventionierung gehandelt haben, die dem Geiste des Public Private Partnership eklatant widerspricht.

Der Vertrag

Am 20. September 2002, zwei Tage vor der Bundestagswahl, kam es zur Vertragsunterzeichnung zwischen Bundesverkehrsministerium und Toll Collect in der schweizerischen Stadt Zug. Der Vertrag umfasste 17.000 Seiten und wurde auch vor den Mitgliedern des Deutschen Bundestages geheim gehalten. Die Frage der Haftung und Risikoaufteilung war deshalb unklar und Inhalt zahlreicher Spekulationen in Politik und Medien. Als Starttermin wurde der 31. August 2003 vereinbart. Heute ist bekannt, dass im Vertrag drei Zwischenschritte vereinbart worden sind. Bis Ende Mai 2003 sollte das System stehen, bis Mitte Juni 2003 sollte dessen Funktion überprüft sein und bis Mitte August 2003 sollte dann der Probebetrieb laufen (Freenet.de 01.12.2005, http://lexikon.freenet.de).
Zum festgesetzten Starttermin konnte die Erfassung der Mautgebühren nicht beginnen, da Probleme beim Aufbau des Systems bestanden. Nach Aussage des Bundesverkehrsministeriums versicherte Toll Collect entgegen allen Bedenken des Bundesamtes für Güterverkehr, das mit der Überwachung der Vertragseinhaltung betraut war, bis zum 30. Juli wiederholt, dass ein vertragsgemäßer Start des Systems am 31. August gesichert sei (Deutscher Bundestag 2003b). Auch ein neuer Termin, zwei Monate später, konnte nicht eingehalten werden. Das Bundesverkehrsministerium sprach von sechsundachtzig bekannten Fehlern im

Mautsystem (Financial Times Deutschland 2003). Auf Druck des Verkehrsministeriums gab Daimler Chrysler seinen Widerstand gegen die Vertragsveröffentlichung auf. Der Vertrag wurde den Mitgliedern des Verkehrsausschusses im Bundestag zugänglich gemacht. Der Gebührenausfall wurde von der Bundesregierung auf 163 Millionen Euro pro Monat beziffert (Deutscher Bundestag 2003b). Dies scheint im Nachhinein sogar noch vorsichtig kalkuliert. In den letzten Monaten lagen die tatsächlichen Einnahmen bei etwa 240 Millionen Euro pro Monat (Wikipedia 01.12.2005, http://de.wikipedia.org). Im Dezember scheiterten Nachverhandlungen mit Toll Collect. Diese wollten keinen neuen Einführungstermin nennen und auch keinen Schadensersatz zahlen. Am 18. Dezember 2003 beschloss der Haushaltsausschuss des Deutschen Bundestages, den Vertrag mit Toll Collect (den sie nicht kannten) zu kündigen, falls bis zum 31. Dezember kein verbindlicher Termin zur Einführung der LKW-Maut genannt werden sollte und Toll Collect nicht bereit sei, die entstandenen Einnahmeausfälle des Bundes zu begleichen. Offensichtlich hatte es zu diesem Zeitpunkt schon Gespräche mit weiteren Anbietern gegeben. In einer Bundestagsanfrage wurde um Bestätigung eines Zeitungsberichtes gebeten, der über ein Angebot des Mautbetreibers Autostrade berichtet, das eine volle Risikoübernahme für die termingerechte Mauteinführung Mitte 2004 mit einschließt, also anbot, ab Juli 2004 monatlich 156 Millionen Euro pro Monat an die Bundesregierung zu überweisen, falls das Mautsystem noch nicht operationsfähig sein sollte (Deutscher Bundestag 2003c). Diesen Frageteil überging die Bundesregierung in ihrer Antwort (Deutscher Bundestag 2004).

Dann verlängerte der damalige Verkehrsminister Stolpe aber überraschend die Verhandlungsfrist und verschob den Kündigungstermin auf Ende Januar. Am 27. Januar 2004 bot Toll Collect an, das System in zwei Stufen ab Dezember 2004 und dann Dezember 2005 einzuführen. Die maximale Höchsthaftung für den Fall weiterer Verzögerung sollte auf 500 Millionen Euro festgeschrieben werden.

Am 17.02.2004 gab Verkehrsminister Stolpe die Kündigung des Vertrages bekannt. Das Mautsystem sollte neu ausgeschrieben, die alte Maut-Vignette zwei Monate später als Interimslösung wieder eingeführt werden. Am 29.02.2004 gab der Bundeskanzler Schröder die Einigung mit den Anteilseignern von Toll Collect bekannt. Das Mautsystem sollte mit eingeschränkter Funktionalität am 01.01.2005, mit voller Funktionalität am 01.01.2006 eingeführt werden.

Der reguläre Betrieb der LKW-Maut begann also nicht wie vertraglich vereinbart 11 Monate nach Vertragsunterzeichnung, sondern 39 Monate danach. Selbst bei größtem Wohlwollen gegenüber dem Unternehmen Toll Collect erscheint es sehr unwahrscheinlich, dass sie im Monat 10 noch immer – wie öffentlich zugesichert

– an eine Einführung im Monat 11 geglaubt haben und nicht wussten, dass sie noch 29 Monate brauchen würden.
Die seit Dezember 2003 fällige Vertragsstrafe ist Presseberichten zufolge wesentlich geringer, als der ursprünglich in der (geheimen) Ausschreibung vorgesehene Betrag.[10] Leider ist dies von der Autorin nicht nachzuprüfen, da die FDP in mehreren Kleinen Anfragen damit scheiterte, Antwort auf die Frage der „Vertragsstrafenbewehrung" zu bekommen (Deutscher Bundestag 2003b; 2003d). Unstrittig zwischen Toll Collect und dem Verkehrsministerium ist offensichtlich, dass Toll Collect ab dem vierten Monat, in dem das System nicht regulär läuft, also vom 1. Dezember 2003 an eine tägliche Vertragsstrafe von 25.000 € (das entspricht einer monatlichen Zahlung von 7,5 Millionen €) zu zahlen hat. Diese Summe verdoppelt sich ab dem siebten Monat, also vom 1. März 2004 an auf 500.000 € pro Tag.
Außerdem ist unstrittig, dass das Verkehrsministerium bei anhaltender Vertragsverletzung über eine Kündigungsoption verfügt, die erstmals am 15.12.2003 greift. Umstritten ist dagegen, ob Toll Collect unter bestimmten Bedingungen für die monatlichen Mautausfälle schadensersatzpflichtig gemacht werden kann. Der Bund müsste dann Toll Collect eine vorsätzliche Verzögerung oder Täuschungen nachweisen. In diese Richtung deuten Aussagen von Stolpe, sein Ministerium sei vom Konsortium über die Funktionsfähigkeit des Mautsystems falsch informiert worden. Solche Vorwürfe weist Toll Collect aber zurück. Nun soll ein Schiedsgericht, bestehend aus je einem von Toll Collect und der Regierung benannten Vertreter sowie einem Dritten die strittigen Fragen klären.

IV. Toll Collect als typisches Public Private Partnership?

Toll Collect erfüllt die formalen Kriterien für ein Public Private Partnership gut. Es arbeiten ein öffentlicher und ein privater Partner zusammen, das Aufgabenfeld ist abgegrenzt, jeder der Partner bringt eigene Ressourcen ein (der Bund die Autobahnen, auf denen die Maut erhoben werden soll, Toll Collect die Technik und den Überwachungsapparat).
Wie sieht es mit der Zielkomplementrarität der beiden Partner aus? Offensichtlich wollen beide ein funktionierendes System, denn sonst werden für Toll Collect Vertragsstrafen fällig. Aber sind sie tatsächlich an einer möglichst schnellen, fehlerfreien und vollständigen Erfassung aller LKWs interessiert? Dafür müssten sie entweder Altruisten sein, oder aber an den Einnahmen beteiligt werden. Dies ist aber so nicht der Fall. Toll Collect bekommt für den Aufbau der LKW-Maut

10 Es muss hier darauf hingewiesen werden, dass diese nachträgliche Reduktion der Haftungssumme nicht aktenkundig ist. Sowohl Ausschreibung als auch Vertragsinhalt sind nicht in vollständiger Form an die Öffentlichkeit gekommen.

und das Betreiben über 12 Jahre ein jährliches Entgelt von 650 Millionen Euro (Toll Collect 01.12.2003, www.toll-collect.de /unternehmen). Toll Collect hat also kein originäres Interesse daran, die LKW-Maut möglichst lukrativ zu machen, da es an den Gewinnen nicht beteiligt wird.
Für die Risikoteilung gilt ähnliches. Die (offensichtlich) vereinbarten Vertragsstrafen sind zwar auf den ersten Blick nicht niedrig, doch wenn man den Kapitalwert des Auftrages berechnet, erhält man bei einer Zinsannahme von 8% knapp 4,5 Milliarden Euro,[11] allerdings ohne die Kosten in Abzug zu bringen. Eine monatliche Vertragsstrafe von 7,5 Millionen Euro nimmt sich dagegen eher klein aus – ein halbes Promille des Auftragswertes . Im Vergleich dazu beziffert sich das Risiko einer verspäteten Einführung für den Bund auf monatlich 156 Millionen Euro. Das Risiko wurde also großteils nicht von demjenigen Partner getragen, der es einschätzen und beeinflussen konnte, sondern vom Verkehrsministerium, das realistisch betrachtet keinerlei Ahnung hatte, welcher zeitliche Spielraum für die Einführung eines satellitengestützten Mautsystems nötig ist. Hier wurden die Regeln für ein erfolgreiches PPP deutlich verletzt. Natürlich handelt es sich hierbei um Spekulation, doch ist es durchaus denkbar, dass bei einer fairen Bestimmung einer Vertragsstrafe, z.B. 100 Millionen Euro monatlich, vom Bieterkonsortium Toll Collect deutlich gemacht worden wäre, dass der anvisierte Termin nicht einhaltbar ist. Möglicherweise wäre dann ein anderes Konsortium mit einfacherer Technik zum Zuge gekommen, oder die Bundesregierung hätte zumindest ihren unglaublichen Fehler vermeiden können, die LKW-Vignette vorzeitig abzuschaffen.
Wie oben schon berichtet, treten bei der erstmaligen Einführung von PPPs häufig Probleme bei der Vertragsgestaltung auf. Eine stringente und zwingende Zuordnung der Rechte und Pflichten ist Voraussetzung für eine reibungslose Zusammenarbeit. Bei 17.000 Seiten Vertragswerk scheint vordergründig jeder denkbare Umstand festgelegt worden zu sein, doch zeigen die momentanen Gerichtsstreitigkeiten, dass es offenbar doch noch großen Interpretationsspielraum gibt. Probleme bei der Vertragsgestaltung von PPPs können sicher bei Standardprojekten, wie den Bau von Schulen oder Autobahnabschnitten über Musterverträge aus dem Raum geschafft werden, doch dürfte dies bei Großprojekten wie eben dem der LKW-Maut schwierig sein.
Inzwischen wurde nach den Verzögerungen das Projekt jedoch technisch und laufend kommerziell zufriedenstellend gestartet (Toll Collect 2006).

---

11 Daimler Chrysler rechnet nach seinem betriebsinternen Capital Asset Pricing Modell derzeit mit einem weighted average cost of capital von 8%. Hier wird angenommen, dass dies auch für die Telekom und Cofiroute gilt, wobei die Telekom durch höhere Durchschittsbetas etwas über acht Prozent liegen müsste.

V. Zusammenfassung:

Toll Collect ist eines der größten Public Private Partnerships, das in Deutschland je in Angriff genommen wurde. Gleichzeitig ist es einer der größten wirtschaftlichen Fehlschläge für die damalige Bundesregierung. Es wurden mehrere grobe Fehler begangen:

- Das Risiko wurde nicht von dem Partner übernommen, der es einschätzen und beeinflussen kann
- Das private Unternehmen hat keinen großen Anreiz im Sinne der Bundesregierung eine möglichst schnelle und umfassende Erhebung der Maut anzustreben. Die Ziele sind nicht komplementär.
- Bei der Ausschreibung kam möglicherweise nicht das günstigste Unternehmen zum Zuge. Die Bundesregierung musste hohe Einnahmeausfälle hinnehmen, möglicherweise in der Annahme, dadurch irgendwie mehr den Standort Deutschland zu stützen, als bei Vergabe an Siemens oder Mannesmann. Subventionen sollten aber offen und transparent stattfinden und dürfen keinesfalls in PPP-Vergaben versteckt werden.

Toll Collect hat das Image der Finanzierung von Infrastrukturinvestitionen über Public Private Partnerships beeinträchtigt. Es wurde grobe handwerkliche Fehler gemacht. Es hat sich gezeigt, dass bei PPPs die Vertragsgestaltung anders gehandhabt werden muss, als bei reinen Vergaben. Der Fokus muss auf Zielkomplementarität und auf Risikoteilung liegen. Nur so kann ein für beide Seiten zufrieden stellendes Ergebnis erzielt werden.

Literaturverzeichnis

Aschauer, D.A., Is public expenditure productive? in: Journal of Monetary Economics, Vol. 23, 1989, S. 177-200.

Beirat für Wirtschafts- und Sozialfragen, Innovative Kooperationen für eine leistungsfähige Infrastruktur, Nr. 75, 1998.

Budäus, D. und G. Grüning, Public Private Partnership – Konzeption und Probleme eines Instruments zur Verwaltungsreform aus der Sicht der Public Choice-Theorie, in: Public Private Partnership, Neue Formen öffentlicher Aufgabenerfüllung, hrsg. von D. Budäus und Peter Eichhorn, Schriftenreihe der Gesellschaft für öffentliche Wirtschaft, Heft 41, Baden-Baden 1997, S. 25-66.

Belina, P. (Hrsg.), Stadt gestalten durch public private partnership, Bonn 2001.

Cox, H., Strukturwandel in der öffentlichen Wirtschaft unter dem Einfluss von Marktintegration und europäischer Wettbewerbsordnung. Zum Paradigmenwechsel in Theorie und Praxis der öffentlichen Wirtschaft, Schriften zur öffentlichen Verwaltung und öffentlichen Wirtschaft, Band 200, Berlin 2005, S. 213-248.

Bundesministerium für Verkehr, Bau- und Wohnungswesen (Hrsg.), Fakten zur LKW-Maut, Presseerklärung 2004.

Deutsche Bundesbank, Demographische Belastungen für Wachstum und Wohlstand in Deutschland, in: Monatsberichte, Dezember 2004.

Deutscher Bundestag, Verschobene Einführung der LKW-Maut, Kleine Anfrage der FDP, 27.07.2003, Bundestagsdrucksache, BT 15/1465, 2003a.

Deutscher Bundestag, Verschobene Einführung der LKW-Maut, Antwort der Bundesregierung auf die Kleine Anfrage der FDP, 25.08.2003, Bundestagsdrucksache, BT 15/1489, 2003b.

Deutscher Bundestag, Verzögerte Einführung der LKW-Maut sowie Prüfung von Angeboten anderer Mautbetreiber, Kleine Anfrage der FDP, 19.12.2003, Bundestagsdrucksache, BT 15/2280, 2003c.

Deutscher Bundestag, Verzögerte Einführung der LKW-Maut sowie Prüfung von Angeboten anderer Mautbetreiber, Antwort auf die Kleine Anfrage der FDP, 08.01.2004, Bundestagsdrucksache, BT 15/2313. 2004.

Europäische Kommission, Grünbuch zu öffentlich-privaten Partnerschaften und den gemeinschaftlichen Rechtsvorschriften für öffentliche Aufträge und Konzession, KOM (2004) 327 end vom 30 April 2004.

Europäische Kommission, Generaldirektion, Regionpolitik, Guidelines for Successful PPP, Brüssel 2003.

Europäische Kommission, Generaldirektion, Regionpolitik, Resource Book on PPP Case Studies, Brussel 2004.

Fawkner, J., PPP im Vereinigten Königsreich: Positive und negative Erfahrungen. Das Problem hoher Risiken für die öffentliche Hand, in: Public Private Partnership: Formen, Risiken, Chancen, hrsg. von Gesellschaft für öffentliche Wirtschaft, Beiträge zur öffentlichen Wirtschaft, Heft 21, Berlin 2004, S. 76-86.

Gabler Wirtschaftslexikon, Public Private Partnership, 16. Aufl., Wiesbaden 2004.

Gesetz zur Einführung von streckenbezogenen Gebühren für die Nutzung von Bundesautobahnen mit schweren Nutzfahrzeugen, BGBL 1, Nr. 23.

Grundgesetz für die Bundesrepublik Deutschland vom 23. Mai 1994 mit Änderungen bis zum 17. August 2005 (Art. 115 GG).

Institut der Deutschen Wirtschaft, Deutschland in Zahlen 2004, Köln 2005.

Jacobs, B., Strategy and Partnership in Cities and Regions, London 2000.

Oberender, P. und *T. Rudolf*, Public Private Partnership, in: Wirtschaftswissenschaftliches Studium, Heft 8, 2004, S. 493-494.

Plaßmann, R., Das angekündigte Grünbuch der EU-Kommission zu Public Private Partnership, in: Public Private Partnership: Formen-Risiken-Chancen, hrsg. von Gesellschaft für öffentliche Wirtschaft, Beiträge zur öffentlichen Wirtschaft, Heft 21, Berlin 2004, S. 39-51.

*Radwan, A.,*Die Auswirkungen des EU-Wettbewerbsrechts im Bereich der Daseinsvorsorge, in: Öffentliche Dienstleistungen für die Bürger,Wege zu Effizienz, Qualität und günstigen Preisen, hrsg. Von Gesellschaft für öffentliche Wirtschaft, Beiträge zur öffentlichen Wirtschaft, Heft 23, Berlin 2006, S. 80-88.

Reichenbach, M., Der kommunale Investitionsbedarf in Deutschland. Eine Schätzung für die Jahre 2000 bis 2009, in: Deutsches Institut für Urbanistik, Beiträge zur Stadtforschung, Bd. 35, Berlin 2002, S. 112ff.

Recker, E., Bedarf und Finanzierung kommunaler Verkehrsinfrastruktur, in: Zeitschrift für Kommunalfinanzen, 54. Jg., 2004, S. 34-37.

Schüler, A., Is there a light at the End of the Eurotunnel ?, Journal of Finance Case Research, Vol. 8, 2006 (in print).

Statistisches Bundesamt (Hrsg.), Bevölkerungsentwicklung bis zum Jahr 2050, Wiesbaden 2003.

Wissenschaftlichen Beirat der Gesellschaft für öffentliche Wirtschaft Public Private Partnership, Positionspapier, Berlin 2004.

Internetquellen

Bundeskartellamt, Bundeskartellamt weist Nachprüfungsantrag im Vergabeverfahren „LKW-MAUT" zurück, abrufbar unter: http://www.bundeskartellamt.de

NDR Online, URL Stand, März 2004, abrufbar unter: http://www.ndr.de/ndr/wirtschaft/meldung

Toll Collect, Informationen zum Unternehmen, abrufbar unter: http://www.toll-collect.de/ unternehmen

Toll Collect, Informationen zum Unternehmen, abrufbar unter: http://www.toll-collect.de/ unternehmen

Vergabeverfahren zur LKW-Maut in Deutschland, abrufbar unter: http://lexikon.freenet.de

Wikipedia, LKW-Maut in Deutschland, Stand 01.12.2005, abrufbar unter: http://de.wikipedia.org

Toll Collect, Show Case German Toll Collect, Stand 2006, abrufbar unter: http//www.sczm.t-systems.de/.../t-systems.de/en/37544/blobBinary/TollCollect_Status-Operativer-Wirkbetrieb-ps.pdf

Drittes Kapitel

Anpassung der Verkehrsinfrastruktur, des Wohnungswesens und des Veranstaltungswesens

A. Anpassungsstrategien kommunaler Infrastrukturbetriebe an gesunkene Bevölkerungszahlen

Helmut Brede

I. Einleitung

Wenn sich auch die Abwanderung aus den neuen Bundesländern etwas abgeschwächt hat (o. V. 2005b, S. 1), so sind die Auswirkungen des bereits eingetretenen Bevölkerungsschwunds noch immer besorgniserregend. Zahlen vermitteln nur ein unzulängliches Bild, dennoch seien ein paar statistische Daten genannt. Nach Aussagen der Bundesregierung im Mai 2005 standen drei Jahre zuvor in den neuen Bundesländern 1,1 Mio. Wohnungen leer. Das waren 14,4 Prozent des gesamten Wohnungsbestandes (o.V. 2005a, Antwort zu Frage 1). Was das bedeutet, kann man sich vorstellen, wenn man z.B. aus Wittenberge erfährt, dass ein Drittel der Einwohner die Stadt verlassen hat und in einigen Stadtteilen die Hälfte aller Häuser leer steht (Lembke 2005, S. 8).

Der Bevölkerungsschwund führt überall zu Herausforderungen, für die betroffenen Menschen, für die Politik und nicht zuletzt für die Kommunalwirtschaft. Im Weiteren sollen nur die **kommunalwirtschaftlichen** Herausforderungen betrachtet werden, genauer: die Möglichkeiten und Grenzen der Infrastrukturbetriebe, den Herausforderungen zu begegnen.

Die Probleme der Infrastrukturbetriebe angesichts des Bevölkerungsschwunds haben sich zum Glück entschärft, als die Bundesregierung im Jahre 2001 das Programm Stadtumbau Ost verkündete und sich die Landesregierungen mit eigenen Programmen anschlossen. Allein das Programm des Bundes verfügt über genügend Mittel, um ein Drittel des Bestands an leer stehenden Wohnungen abzureißen (o.V. 2005a, Antwort zu Frage 2). Weitere Mittel sollen helfen, die verbleibenden Wohnungsbestände aufzuwerten sowie das Wohnungsumfeld und den „öffentlichen Raum“ zu erhalten und zu verbessern (o.V. 2005a, Antwort zu Frage 3). Beim Stadtumbauprogramm Ost wird erfreulicherweise auch die Infrastruktur gebührend beachtet. Dazu schreibt die Bundesregierung: „Auf kommunaler Ebene ergibt sich aus der Zuständigkeitsverteilung zum Beispiel, dass grundsätzlich die Gemeinde ... entscheidet, in welchem Verhältnis sie die vom

Land bereitgestellten Aufwertungsmittel für die einzelnen ... Aufwertungstatbestände einsetzt. Deshalb obliegt es in erster Linie der Gemeinde zu entscheiden, inwieweit sie die Aufwertungsmittel für die Anpassung der technischen Infrastruktur verwendet." (o.V. 2005a, S. 3)

Der Breite des Themas wegen beschränken wir uns darauf, **Anpassungsstrategien** in der Kommunalwirtschaft zu erörtern, und konzentrieren uns auf einige wenige Betriebstypen: auf Versorgungs- und Entsorgungsbetriebe, Nahverkehrsbetriebe und Sparkassen. Sie haben nicht nur auf den Bevölkerungsschwund selbst, sondern auch auf kommunalpolitische Maßnahmen zu reagieren, die zur Abhilfe getroffen wurden. Die Betriebe sehen sich also einem Umfeld gegenüber, das zunächst als Faktum zu akzeptieren ist, aber keinen Versuch ausschließt, zukunftsgerichtet gestaltenden Einfluss zu nehmen.

Um die später zu entwickelnden Thesen zuzuspitzen, wählen wir als Hintergrund einen besonders ernsten Fall, ein fiktives Beispiel: Das **Ausgangsszenario** bildet danach eine Großstadt, die Problemzonen in Gestalt von Plattenbau-Siedlungen und Stadtteilen mit großem Bestand an älteren Mietshäusern aufweist. In den letzten fünfzehn Jahren sind der Stadt zwanzig Prozent – in manchen Stadtteilen (Plattenbau-Siedlungen) vierzig bis sechzig Prozent – der Bevölkerung verlorengegangen. Für die Modellstadt wird ferner angenommen, dass sie von dem Programm Stadtumbau Ost profitiert. Sie hat begonnen, ihre Plattenbau-Siedlungen umzubauen, indem obere Stockwerke abgetragen, Wohnungen durch Zusammenlegen vergrößert, Balkone und Laubengänge angebracht, Aufzüge eingebaut und lange Gebäude durch Herausnahmen von Teilen „aufgelockert" werden. Auf eine Politik der Siedlungsverdichtung oder „Konzentration" (Hannemann 2004, S. 98) durch Umsiedlung verbliebener Bewohner in den Stadtkern und des Abrisses sämtlicher Plattenbauten am Rande soll die Stadt bewusst verzichtet haben. Der nun eingeleitete Umbau muss noch über die nächsten fünf Jahre fortgesetzt werden.

Was bedeutet dieses Szenario für die Infrastrukturbetriebe? Welche Problemlösungen bieten sich an?

II. Folgen des Bevölkerungsschwunds für Infrastrukturbetriebe

Für das Szenario liegt es auf der Hand, dass der Bevölkerungsrückgang verminderte Nachfrage nach sich zieht. Mit der Zahl der Haushalte nahm nicht nur der Verbrauch an Strom, Gas, Wasser und Fernwärme ab, sondern verminderte sich auch die Menge an Abfall und Abwasser. Auch die Fahrgastzahlen im Öffentlichen Personennahverkehr sind zurückgegangen. Außerdem es gibt in der betreffenden Gegend weniger Nachfrage nach Leistungen der Städtischen Sparkasse. Das alles bewirkt eine Verschlechterung der Ertragslage der betroffenen Infra-

strukturbetriebe. Hinzu kommt eine verschlechterte Kostensituation, die allerdings bei den einzelnen Betriebstypen verschieden ausfällt. Die verschlechterte Kostensituation hat folgende Gründe:
Verminderte Nachfrage bei fortbestehendem Anspruch auf Infrastrukturleistungen der verbliebenen Bevölkerungsteile führt zu Fixkosten (Cronauge 2005, S. 13),[1] die nun bei gesunkenen Erträgen zu decken sind. Hinzu kommen Kosten des Rückbaus und hohe Belastungen durch Ausbuchung der Restbuchwerte dort (Verband kommunaler Unternehmen 2005, S. 2), wo es gelingt, die nicht mehr benötigten Kapazitäten zu beseitigen (Meigen 2005, S. 14). Das Ausbuchen von Restbuchwerten stillgelegter Anlagen ist in den neuen Bundesländern besonders schmerzlich, weil die Infrastruktur durchweg ein noch recht geringes Durchschnittsalter hat und dementsprechend hoher Abschreibungsbedarf besteht (Herdt 2005, S. 9).
Für die einzelnen Betriebstypen ergibt sich folgende Situation:
Der **Versorgungs- und Entsorgungsbetrieb** muss feststellen, dass in der Problem-Gegend einzelne Gebäude gänzlich aufgegeben sind, in anderen Gebäuden ein Teil der Wohnungen leer steht, während sich in manchen Gebäuden an der ursprünglichen Nutzung nichts geändert hat. Diese Struktur einer teilweise entvölkerten städtischen Region ist für den Versorgungs- und Entsorgungsbetrieb problematisch, weil nach wie vor das Leitungsnetz für die Gas-, Wasser und Stromversorgung ganz oder teilweise zu unterhalten ist, weil es nach wie vor der Einrichtungen zur Abfallentsorgung und der Abwasserbeseitigung bedarf und weil an einen Abbau der Fernwärmeversorgung, d.h. eine Umstellung auf dezentrale Heizanlagen, nur auf mittlere Frist zu denken ist. Eine Verminderung der Größe von Abfalldeponien, Müllverbrennungs- und Kläranlagen kommt gar auf absehbare Zeit – das heißt über einen Zeitraum von Jahrzehnten – nicht in Frage. Nur die Häufigkeit, mit der in einem bestimmten Zeitraum Hausmüll abgeholt wird, lässt sich kurzfristig reduzieren und damit die Kapazität des Wagenparks samt Personal zurücknehmen. Kapazitätsabbau könnte auch durch enge Kooperation mit anderen, benachbarten Entsorgungsbetrieben erzielt werden. Am günstigsten ist es noch, wenn ganze Teilbereiche des Gas-, Wasser- oder Stromnetzes einfach stillgelegt werden können. Dann entstehen nur noch Kosten des Zählerausbaus.
Die Betriebe der Wasserversorgung leiden noch unter einem besonderen Problem: Sinkt der Wasserverbrauch und nimmt dadurch die Fließgeschwindigkeit des Frischwassers ab, entstehen gesundheitliche Gefahren (Müller 2005, S. 5; Herdt 2005, S. 11). Dem kann durch häufiges Spülen der Rohrleitungen, durch Verringerung des Leitungsquerschnitts oder durch netzverkürzende Leitungsumlegung begegnet werden – was allerdings die Kosten noch einmal an-

1 In der Wasserwirtschaft betragen die Fixkosten 80%.

steigen lässt. Es ist jedoch darauf hinzuweisen, dass die Dimensionierung der Frischwasserleitungen von den Erfordernissen einer eventuellen Brandbekämpfung bestimmt wird (Herdt 2005, S. 8). Das bedeutet, der Rückgang der Bevölkerungsdichte erlaubt nicht in jedem Fall, mit geringer dimensionierten Leitungsrohren auszukommen. Für die Stadtentwässerung gilt Ähnliches: Hier droht infolge der reduzierten Fließgeschwindigkeit stärkeres Verschlammen der Kanalisation (Burger 2005, S. 8). Es bildet sich Schwefelwasserstoff, so dass es aus den Gullys nach faulen Eiern stinkt (Einhaus 2005, S. 3f.). Auch in diesem Fall hilft häufigeres Spülen, was wiederum zu höheren Kosten führt. Selbst in den Fernwärmeleitungen macht sich der geringe Durchsatz störend bemerkbar. Dort „staut sich der Dampf, so dass er bereits hier kondensiert, und den Kunden kalt wird, weil zu wenig Wärme ankommt." (Einhaus 2005, S. 3f.)

Verschärft wird die Lage durch das Auftreten von „Leere-Inseln". Sehen wir einmal von Plattenbau-Siedlungen ab und betrachten anders strukturierte Stadtteile mit starker Entvölkerung, so verödet ja nicht der ganze Straßenzug, sondern es treten leerstehende Gebäude neben noch genutzten auf. Es ist vor allem diese „zahnlückenartige" Struktur verödender Städte oder Stadtteile, die kaum einfache Problemlösungen auf dem Gebiet der Versorgung und Entsorgung zulässt.

Für **Betriebe des Öffentlichen Nahverkehrs** gilt Ähnliches, jedoch in gemilderter Form. Auch sie können das Leistungsangebot vermindern. Das bedeutet in ihrem Fall, Strecken stillzulegen, Verkehrszeiten einzuschränken, Fahrpläne auszudünnen und sich ggf. vom Schienen- auf den Omnibusverkehr umzustellen. Das erlaubt vor allem, den Fahrzeugpark und die Werkstätten zu verkleinern. Aber ansonsten bleiben viele Fixkosten erhalten. Sofern nicht ganze Strecken stillgelegt werden, müssen noch immer die vorhandenen Haltestellen, ggf. auch Schienen und Oberleitungen gepflegt werden.

Den leichtesten Stand haben **Sparkassen** mit ihrem Filialnetz. Sie können bei Bevölkerungsschwund ohne größere Schwierigkeiten Fixkosten abbauen, indem sie in nachfrageschwächeren Stadtteilen Filialen schließen – eine Politik, die ebenfalls seit langem gang und gäbe ist. Einzig der damit notwendig werdende Personalabbau schafft Probleme. Erst über einen gewissen Zeitraum hinweg lässt sich der Personalbestand der geringer gewordenen Betriebsgröße anpassen.

Die Existenz der kommunalen Betriebe steht auf dem Spiel. Resignierte man und ließe die betreffenden Infrastruktureinrichtungen verkommen, wäre der damit verbundene Niedergang der Leistungsqualität in besseren Zeiten kaum noch zu korrigieren. Deshalb gibt es nur eine Alternative, nämlich geeignete Anpassungsstrategien zu entwickeln, bei denen allerdings die Betriebe selbst, ihre Träger und alle politischen Kräfte gefordert sind.

III. Diskussion verschiedener Problemlösungen

1. Preis- und Gebührenerhöhung

Für einen Versorgungs-, Entsorgungs-, Verkehrsbetrieb oder die Städtische Sparkasse liegt das Bestreben am nächsten, die Preise bzw. Gebühren in den betreffenden Gebieten so weit zu erhöhen, dass sie die Ausfälle aufgrund der verschlechterten Ertrags-/Kostensituation ausgleichen. Ob sich eine solche Maßnahme tatsächlich, rechtlich und politisch durchsetzen ließe, bleibe dahingestellt. Hier ist nur ein ökonomischer Effekt beachtlich, nämlich die Tatsache, dass die verbliebene Bevölkerung auch noch gedrängt würde, die Gegend zu verlassen. Doch immer noch blieben einzelne Bevölkerungsteile in der Gegend zurück, Menschen, die Anspruch auf die Versorgung mit Infrastrukturleistungen hätten. Ob die Infrastrukturbetriebe nach der Preis-/Gebührenerhöhung besser dastünden als zuvor, ist daher nicht ausgemacht.

Allein schon diese Ungewissheit sollte ausreichen, um in Preis- und Gebührenerhöhungen keine probate Anpassungsstrategie zu sehen. Hinzu kommt noch, dass Preis- und Gebührenerhöhungen geeignet wären, Vertreibung zu bewirken. Das könnte erst recht nicht hingenommen werden. Vertreibung darf kein Mittel oder Ergebnis kommunalpolitischen Handelns sein, auch nicht, wenn die Akteure – in diesem Falle die Infrastrukturbetriebe – nur Instrumente der Kommunalpolitik wären.

Nebenbei – an dieser Stelle wird deutlich, dass es seitens der Infrastrukturbetriebe abwegig wäre, gar auf irgendeinen behördlich verfügten Zwang zur Umsiedlung verbleibender Bevölkerungsteile zu hoffen. Zwänge dieser Art sind in unserem Gemeinwesen zum Glück nicht möglich.

2. Verminderung des Leistungsangebots

Einige Möglichkeiten zur Verminderung des Leistungsangebots wurden schon weiter oben im Zusammenhang mit den Folgen des Bevölkerungsschwunds genannt, so insbesondere die verzögerte Abfuhr von Hausmüll, die „Ausdünnung“ von Fahrplänen und die Schließung von Sparkassenfilialen. In der Beurteilung kommt ein ähnliches Ergebnis wie bei Preis- und Gebührenerhöhungen heraus: Führen die Maßnahmen weiterer Abwanderung der Bevölkerung aus den problematischen Stadtteilen, sind sie nicht zu befürworten – was freilich nicht ausschließt, dass solche Maßnahmen aus eng betriebsbezogenen Zielen oftmals ergriffen werden.

Befriedigender – weil sie das Gemeinwohl beachten – sind Maßnahmen, die die Bevölkerung in den betroffenen Stadtteilen halten, indem ihnen die Infrastrukturleistungen im bisherigen Umfang und zu angemessenen (gewohnten) Preisen oder Gebühren geboten werden. Wenn gleichzeitig die Ertrags-/Kostensituation der Infrastrukturbetriebe ins Gleichgewicht gebracht werden soll, so geht dies für den Betrieb allerdings nur über grundlegende technische Veränderungen.
Hier sind Ideen gefragt. Einige seien kurz angedeutet. Ob sie wirklich etwas taugen, d.h. die genannten Ziele erfüllen, müsste im einzelnen und unter Würdigung der örtlichen Gegebenheiten geprüft werden:
Bei der **Energieversorgung** liegt es nahe, von zentralen zu dezentralen Versorgungseinrichtungen überzugehen. Das heißt also etwa weg von der Fernwärmeversorgung und hin zur Kraft-Wärme-Kopplung in Blockheizkraftwerken. Damit lassen sich überflüssige, kostspielige Leitungen einsparen. Auch wird eine bessere Anpassung an den tatsächlichen Energiebedarf möglich. Allerdings verlangt die Umstellung den Einsatz erheblicher Investitionsmittel. Inwieweit dafür die schon erwähnten Stadtumbauprogramme aufkommen könnten, müsste geprüft werden.
Bei der **Abfallentsorgung** wäre es denkbar, den Ausfall von Abfuhrterminen, d.h. zum Beispiel den Übergang vom wöchentlichen zum vierzehntägigen Turnus, dadurch zu kompensieren, dass an zentralen Plätzen Sammelstellen für Hausmüll eingerichtet werden, der, in Säcken verpackt, anzuliefern wäre. Es ließen sich offene Lastwagen einsetzen, und es brauchte nicht mehr jedes Haus angefahren zu werden. Dies ergäbe sicherlich für die Stadtreinigung eine beachtliche Kostenersparnis.
Für die **Stadtentwässerung** käme in Frage, in dem Problemgebiet die Trennung zwischen Schmutzwasser- und Regenwasserkanälen aufzuheben und einen der beiden Bereiche stillzulegen. Auf diese Weise könnte in dem verbleibenden System mit der höheren Durchlaufmenge die nötige Fließgeschwindigkeit erreicht werden. Die Sorge, wegen der größeren zu reinigenden Abwassermengen könnten die vorhandenen Kläranlagen nicht mehr ausreichen, wären unbegründet. Sie mussten ja schon vor dem Bevölkerungsschwund auf größere Abwassermengen ausgelegt worden sein und somit immer noch über eine genügende Kapazität verfügen.
Bei der **Frischwasserversorgung** sind keine Möglichkeiten zur Änderung der Prozesstechnik zu sehen.
Für den **Öffentlichen Personennahverkehr** bietet sich in den von starkem Wegzug betroffenen Stadtgebieten an, die Einschränkung des aufwendigen Schienen- und Omnibusbetriebs – oder gar Streckenstilllegung – durch das Angebot wett-

zumachen, die Dienste von Taxiunternehmen in Anspruch zu nehmen. Selbstverständlich müssten vergleichbare Preise wie im Schienen- oder Omnibusverkehr gelten. Dadurch würden vor allem Leerkosten vermieden. Im konkreten Fall hinge es allerdings von Vergleichsrechnungen ab, ob die Zuschüsse zu Taxifahrten über oder unter den Einsparungen der öffentlichen Verkehrsbetriebe lägen. Da bereits Erfahrungen aus der Zusammenarbeit von öffentlichem Nahverkehr und Taxigewerbe existieren – etwa bei der Bewältigung spärlichen Verkehrsaufkommens in Randbezirken oder zur Nachtzeit –, sollte es leicht sein, im konkreten Fall über diese Idee zu befinden.

Weiter oben war im Zusammenhang mit Bevölkerungsschwund nur von der **Schließung** von **Sparkassenfilialen** in problematischen Stadtgebieten die Rede. Wie aber wäre es, wenn die Sparkassen auf die völlige Schließung verzichteten, die Dienste einer Filiale reduzierten und zum Ausgleich die Nutzung des Direct Banking förderten? Auch diese Idee ist nicht neu, könnte aber noch stärker genutzt werden. **Reduktion** der Dienste einer Filiale bedeutete z.B., neben Automaten zur Abwicklung von Ein- und Auszahlungen nur noch Ansprechpartner vorzuhalten, die den mit Automaten nicht vertrauten Kunden helfen. Ansonsten, insbesondere hinsichtlich der seltener auftretenden Wertpapiergeschäfte könnte den Kunden zugemutet werden, sich an die Sparkassenzentrale in der Innenstadt zu wenden. **Förderung** des Direct Banking könnte z.B. zweierlei beinhalten, einmal die Abhaltung von Kursen für Kundenkreise, die Direct Banking nicht nutzen, und zum anderen die Bereitstellung von Internetanschlüssen in der Filiale, damit den Kunden dort geeignete Terminals zur Verfügung stünden. Die Chancen zu Kosteneinsparungen durch Änderung der Prozesstechnik auf diesem Felde sind sicherlich noch nicht ausgereizt.

4. Finanzielle Anreize

Finanzielle Anreize zum Verbleib der noch nicht abgewanderten Bevölkerungsteile in den problematischen Stadtteilen können von verschiedener Seite und für verschiedene Zwecke geboten werden. Aus welchen Quellen die dafür eingesetzten Mittel stammen, spielt hier keine Rolle. Entscheidend ist für unser Thema allein, welche Anreize den Infrastrukturbetrieben helfen, ihre Aufgaben trotz des Bevölkerungsschwunds zu erfüllen. Unter diesem Blickwinkel werden nicht betrachtet finanzielle Beihilfen der Kommune beim Abriss, dem Modernisieren oder dem Konservieren von Gebäuden. Es interessiert auch nicht, inwieweit die Infrastrukturbetriebe selbst finanziell unterstützt werden – etwa bei der Ablösung eines Fernwärmesystems durch Blockheizkraftwerke. Wir gehen einfach davon aus, dass die Mittel für derartige Projekte zur Verfügung stehen. Somit können wir uns auf die Frage konzentrieren, welche (eigenen) Strategien Infrastrukturbetriebe nutzen können, um bei den Leistungsnehmern Anreize zum Verbleib in den verödendenden Gegenden auszulösen. Wie sie die Mittel für finanzielle Anreize gegenüber ihren Kunden aufbringen, bleibe wiederum ausgeklammert, geht es im Augenblick nur darum, die instrumentellen Anreizmöglichkeiten zu betrachten.

Die schwächere Kapazitätsauslastung führt zu höheren Leerkosten und damit zu höheren Kosten pro Leistungseinheit. Eine erste und sehr wichtige Möglichkeit, die restlichen Bewohner zum Verbleib in den problematischen Stadtteilen zu bewegen, könnte für Infrastrukturbetriebe im Verzicht bestehen, diese Kostensteigerungen in Gestalt von Preis- und Gebührenerhöhungen auf die Bürger abzuwälzen. Weitere branchenspezifische Anreizmöglichkeiten kommen noch hinzu. **Versorgungsbetriebe** könnten die erwähnte Ablösung der Fernwärme selbst in die Hand nehmen und den Gebäudebesitzern finanzielle Prämien für die Installation von Blockheizkraftwerken anbieten. In Frage käme außerdem, den Haushalten finanzielle Hilfe bei der Modernisierung ihrer Geräteausstattung (Elektro-, Gasherde usw.) zu leisten. **Entsorgungsbetriebe** könnten den Bürgern die oben genannte Änderung in der Prozesstechnik (z.B. in jeder zweiten Woche Verbringen des Hausmülls in Säcken zu Sammelstellen) durch Gebührenermäßigung schmackhaft machen. Für die **Nahverkehrsbetriebe**, die von der Zusammenarbeit mit Taxiunternehmen Gebrauch machen wollten, wäre die Subventionierung von Taxifahrten anzuraten, mehr noch: Die Subventionierung stünde eigentlich außer Frage; denn ohne Preise, die sich ungefähr auf dem Niveau der Fahrpreise im Öffentlichen Personennahverkehr bewegten, hätte die Idee überhaupt keine Realisierungschancen. Und für die **Sparkassen** gilt prinzipiell Gleiches: Auch sie müssten ihren Kunden in den problematischen Stadtteilen finanzielle Vorteile bieten – etwa in Gestalt von kostenlosen Kursen zur Nutzung des Internet oder niedrigeren Gebühren bei Direct Banking –, damit sie bei der Umstellung auf neue Prozesstechniken mitspielten. Denn es sei noch einmal daran erinnert: Es geht letztlich darum, die restlichen Bewohner in den gefährdeten Stadtteilen zu halten, und dazu müssten sie das Verbleiben in der angestammten Wohngegend trotz aller Veränderungen reizvoller als den Wegzug empfinden.

Unsere Erörterung stand bislang unter dem Bestreben, mit finanziellen Anreizen, die von Infrastrukturbetrieben ausgehen, den weiteren Bevölkerungsschwund zu verhindern. Denkbar wäre aber außerdem der Versuch, mit finanziellen Anreizen Menschen – und Gewerbebetriebe! – zum Zuzug in die bevölkerungsschwachen Stadtteile zu bewegen. Dazu kämen alle eben genannten Maßnahmen in Frage – nur mit einer noch stärkeren Ausprägung. Die Preise und Gebühren für Infrastrukturleistungen dürften sich nicht einfach auf dem bisherigen Niveau bewegen, sondern müssten unter dem liegen, was in den nichtproblematischen Stadtteilen gilt – vorausgesetzt eine solche Differenzierung wäre möglich.

Natürlich müsste, wie bei jeder Subventionierung, sorgfältig auf mögliche Fehlsteuerung geachtet werden. So wäre es zum Beispiel fatal, wenn das Füllhorn finanzieller Gaben unterschiedslos über **alle** verbleibenden Bewohner eines problematischen Stadtteils ausgeleert würde. Dann würden auch die Modernisierungs- oder Umzugsunwilligen davon profitieren, und der „Stadtumbau", der zu einer attraktiven Stadtlandschaft führen soll, würde gehemmt. Auch bloße Mitnahmeeffekte sollten verhindert werden. Würden zum Beispiel Internet-Kurse der Sparkasse nur von Jugendlichen besucht, die den Kenntniserwerb zu anderen Zwecken, nicht aber zur Anwendung im Direct Banking nutzen wollten, zahlten sich die Bemühungen der Sparkasse nicht aus. Das bedeutet auch hier, dass die Vor- und Nachteile dieser Strategie im Einzelnen genau abgewogen werden müssten.
Ein Nachtrag: Wenn schon von finanziellen Anreizen die Rede ist, könnte die Idee aufkommen, besonders hohe Preise und Gebühren für Infrastrukturleistungen zum Vertreiben der restlichen Bewohner einzusetzen. Es sei nicht untersucht, ob die Maßnahme zulässig und moralisch vertretbar wäre. Sondern es geht nur darum, ob sie aus enger betriebswirtschaftlicher Sicht Sinn hätte. Aus Berichten über Slums in anderen Weltgegenden wissen wir von Bewohnern, die unter keinen Umständen bereit sind, ihre Behausungen in den verödenden Stadtvierteln zu verlassen. Immer noch finden sich in heruntergekommenen Häusern einzelne Bewohner, die sich nicht von Verfall und Verlust aller Infrastrukturleistungen vertreiben lassen. Deshalb ist auch hierzulande nicht zu sehen, wie ein solches Problem bewältigt werden könnte. Im Übrigen wäre zu einer auf Freiwilligkeit begründeten Umsiedlungs- und Vertreibungsstrategie langer Atem nötig. Denn das ist klar, auch die letzten Bewohner hätten noch Anspruch auf die Grundversorgung mit Infrastrukturleistungen. Könnten sich die Infrastrukturbetriebe die Aufrechterhaltung ihrer Dienste in einem weitgehend entvölkerten Stadtgebiet über längere Zeit – ohne Subventionierung – leisten? Bestimmt nicht. Schon von daher ist die Idee untauglich.

5. Beteiligung an kommunalen Infrastruktur-Entscheidungen

An sich ist es selbstverständlich, dass die städtischen Infrastrukturbetriebe an kommunalpolitischen Entscheidungen, die sie betreffen, beteiligt werden. Aber es müsste von den Betrieben im Zusammenhang mit den gesunkenen Bevölkerungszahlen mehr denn je als strategisches Ziel begriffen werden, größtmöglichen Einfluss auf die Infrastrukturentscheidungen zu nehmen. Es liegt zum Beispiel im Interesse der Infrastrukturbetriebe, viele zusammenhängende Gebäudekomplexe freizubekommen „Verdichtung" zu verfolgen, die seitens der Kommune vor allem mit Umzugsbeihilfen zu fördern ist. Damit sich die Kommune diese Politik zu eigen macht, ergibt sich für die Infrastrukturbetriebe in verstärktem Maße die Pflicht, mit den maßgeblichen Politikern und Planern in Stadt und Land engen Kontakt zu pflegen, den wichtigen Ausschüssen der Vertretungskörperschaft zur Beratung zur Verfügung zu stehen, außerdem die Presse mit guter Überzeugungsarbeit auf ihre Seite zu ziehen und schließlich mit „**einer** Zunge zu sprechen".

IV. Schlussbemerkungen

Eine Reihe von Maßnahmen wurde erwogen und geprüft, die für Infrastrukturbetriebe in Frage kommen, um Ertragsausfällen und Kostensteigerungen bei gesunkenen Bevölkerungszahlen zu begegnen. Die meisten denkbaren Strategien erweisen sich als tauglich. Bei genauer Betrachtung erkennt man sogar, dass sie, soweit tauglich, auch miteinander vereinbar sind. Mehr noch: Es wäre den Infrastrukturbetrieben – die finanziellen Möglichkeiten vorausgesetzt – zu empfehlen, die Strategien miteinander zu kombinieren. Für die Energieversorger heißt das zum Beispiel, nicht nur die Umstellung auf moderne Heiz- und Stromgewinnungstechniken zu betreiben (Stichwort: Blockheizkraftwerke), sondern auch die Modernisierung der Geräteausstattung ihrer Kunden zu fördern, die Öffentlichkeitsarbeit (i. w. S.) zu intensivieren und durch Subventionierung für anreizkompatible Preispolitik zu sorgen.

Das untersuchte Problem ist Teil eines größeren Ganzen. Das wird auch schon daran erkennbar, dass nur die Strategien einiger weniger Infrastrukturbetriebe in einer städtischen Modellregion behandelt wurden. Damit wurden insofern verhältnismäßig einfache Modellbedingungen zugrunde gelegt, als in einer Stadt ausgesprochene Infrastrukturbetriebe existieren, in ländlichen Gemeinden aber nicht unbedingt. In der Stadt können Infrastrukturbetriebe die Kommunalpolitik und sich gegenseitig bei der Interessenverfolgung unterstützen, aber auf dem Lande – weil ausgesprochene, selbständig geführte Infrastrukturbetriebe fehlen – nicht. Das heißt, Impulse, um die Abwanderung zu hemmen, fallen in ländlichen Regionen schwächer aus. Oder gibt es doch ausgleichende Faktoren?

Wie auch immer, wenigstens in einer Stadt sind die Infrastrukturbetriebe nicht darauf angewiesen, den sinkenden Bevölkerungszahlen tatenlos gegenüber zu stehen. Unterstellt, es fehlt nicht an der Finanzierbarkeit (was seit dem Programm Stadtumbau Ost angenommen werden darf), stehen Strategien zur Verfügung, die den Infrastrukturbetrieben das Überleben sichern helfen. Es ist gut, dies zu wissen; denn wie bald schon müssen sich nicht nur die neuen Bundesländer mit dem Bevölkerungsschwund befassen, sondern auch der Westen der Bundesrepublik (Hannemann 2004, S. 72; Cronauge 2005, S. 13). Am meisten beruhigt die in der Untersuchung zutage tretende Erkenntnis, dass auch in diesem Fall die Krise eine große Chance zur Modernisierung und Erneuerung eröffnet. Zum Beispiel zeigt sich schon heute, dass die meisten der ehemaligen Plattenbau-Siedlungen ein Bild guter Wohnqualität bieten.

Zum Schluss soll aber doch noch die Frage aufgeworfen werden, welche Folgen aufträten, wenn die so angenehme Prämisse der Finanzierbarkeit aller Strategien entfällt. Immerhin ist damit zu rechnen, dass die Umbauprogramme auslaufen oder gekürzt werden, ehe die Stadtsanierungen abgeschlossen sind. Was bedeutete dies für die Strategien der Infrastrukturbetriebe? In diesem Fall heißt die einzige – realistische – Möglichkeit, den Prozess des Schwindens geduldig und unter Ausschöpfen aller Chancen der Effizienzsteigerung zu begleiten. Es muss solche Potentiale noch geben. Das legt z.B. die Beobachtung nahe, dass noch verhältnismäßig selten Kooperationen von Infrastrukturbetrieben über die kommunalen Grenzen hinweg existieren. Dabei sollte noch einmal betont werden, was auch immer geschieht, ob die Finanzierung der Infrastrukturbetriebe durch Beihilfen gesichert ist oder nicht, die Infrastruktur muss intakt bleiben, auch wenn die Bevölkerungsdichte immer weiter schwindet. Die technischen Bedingungen (Netzgebundenheit) und die rechtlichen Pflichten (Daseinsvorsorge) zwingen dazu. Notfalls müsste das Überleben durch immer höhere Verschuldung erkauft werden. Die Infrastrukturbetriebe hätten keine andere Wahl.

Literaturverzeichnis

Burger, R., Alles schmeckt nach Abschied, in: Frankfurter Allgemeine Zeitung, 1. Sep. 2005, S. 8.

Cronauge, U., Die Folgen des Wegzugs. Infrastrukturprobleme beim Umbau schrumpfender Städte, in: Zeitschrift für kommunale Wirtschaft, 8. Jan. 2005. S.13.

Einhaus, G., Menschen machen sich auf und davon. Ver- und Entsorger fordern Fördermittel für die technische Infrastruktur, in: Zeitung für kommunale Wirtschaft, 4. Juni 2005, S. 3-4.

Hannemann, C., Marginalisierte Städte Probleme: Differenzierungen und Chancen ostdeutscher Kleinstädte im Schrumpfungsprozess, Berlin 2004.

Herdt, H., Fallbeispiel Magdeburg. Anpassung der Ver- und Entsorgungsinfrastruktur im Rahmen des Stadtumbau Ost. Vortrag auf der AGFW-/VKU-/DST-Konferenz „Infrastrukturaufgaben bei der Ver- und Entsorgung unter der Bedingungen des Stadtumbau Ost“, Leipzig 2005.

Lemke, J., Leben hinter der Tristesse-Kulisse, in: Frankfurter Allgemeine Zeitung, 25. Aug. 2005, S. 8.

Meigen, M., Fernwärmeversorgung und Stadtumbau Ost: Praxisbeispiele aus Leipzig. Diskussionsbeitrag auf der ENTERTEC, Leipzig 2005.

Müller, C. P., Platten zu Mustervillen, in: Frankfurter Allgemeine Zeitung, 1. Okt. 2005, S. 5.

o.V., Antwort der Bundesregierung auf die Kleine Anfrage der Abgeordneten Henry Nitzsche u. a., Belange der städtischen Ver- und Entsorgungsinfrastruktur beim Stadtumbau Ost, Drucksache 15/5379, vom 20. Mai 2005a.

o.V., Weniger Menschen verlassen den Osten, in: Frankfurter Allgemeine Zeitung, 29. Sep. 2005b, S. 1.

Verband kommunaler Unternehmen, Rückbau und Anpassung der kommunalen Versorgungs- und Entsorgungsinfrastruktur aufgrund des Stadtumbaus erfordern eine gezielte öffentliche Förderung, Stellungnahme, Berlin 2005.

B. An Account of a Road Network Design Method: Expressway Spacing, System Configuration and Economic Evaluation

David Boyce

I. The Road Network Design Problem and Its Background

In the decade following the worldwide economic depression of the 1930s and the ensuing world war, prosperity returned to America; in contrast, in Germany and the remainder of Europe, as well as much of Asia, the struggle for survival occupied many people. Post-war prosperity in America provided sufficient income for many urban families to pursue their dreams of home ownership, often to shelter expanding families resulting from the post-war "baby boom." Acquiring their first new car in many years, or possibly their first car ever, was also a priority for such households. Housing construction in suburban areas adjacent to large central cities, together with generous terms on mortgages for war veterans and middle income households, provided new opportunities to purchase single-family homes. The suburban location of such housing, as well as new employment opportunities on the edges of cities, made commuting by car increasingly necessary. Although these trends began only in 1945, the future shape, form and extent of American cities were changing rapidly, trends that would continue for the next 25 years until metropolitan expansion slowed in the 1970s.

Before and during the war, exploratory studies were initiated to determine the scope and extent of an American system of interregional, limited-access highways. Following his inauguration as President in 1953, Dwight Eisenhower set in motion further studies leading to the authorization and design of the National System of Interstate and Defense Highways to link 90% of American cities with populations of 50,000 or more with 41,000 miles of freeways at an initially estimated cost of $25 billion; see Weiner (1997, p. 31). Envisaged and promoted as an interregional system, Eisenhower was reportedly opposed to building highways through congested cities, but the agreed-upon system did include urban radials and beltways that promised entirely new freedom of movement to urban dwellers; cf. Garrison and Levinson (2005, pp. 183 ff.).

The new field of urban transportation planning was confronted with these and related challenges as it emerged in the early 1950s. Origin-destination surveys were initiated in many urban areas during the late 1940s, and led to the creation of a more ambitious "urban transportation study" for the Detroit area in 1953. More comprehensive than the earlier data collection and analysis efforts, the Detroit Metropolitan Area Traffic Study set out to prepare and evaluate long-range highway plans for the Detroit area. Given this mandate, Director J. Douglas Carroll, Jr., and the young staff he assembled, embarked upon the development and application of novel methods, which appear highly ambitious even today, especially if one realizes useable digital computers did not yet exist. Just two years later, Carroll was persuaded to move with a portion of his staff to Chicago in order to repeat and amplify upon this undertaking. The plan and recommendations for the Detroit area were issued in 1956, followed by the Chicago plan six years later in 1962; both plans were published in detailed reports replete with colored charts and maps. Soon the three-volume Chicago Area Transportation Study (CATS) report became known worldwide as the premier example of how to undertake such a study; cf. Creighton (1970).

Although I was privileged to know Dr. Carroll and several staff members personally, as well as to witness firsthand the growth and transformation of the Chicago area during the late 1950s, today I wonder what vision they held for its future as they set about creating a plan for roads and transit for 1980. In reading the record created at the time, however, two points are clear. First, Dr. Carroll and his staff envisaged their task as a highly scientific endeavor. Whatever they believed personally about the desirability of future forms of urban density, travel, and transportation facilities, they approached their task in a scientifically rigorous and objective manner. Second, they clearly sought an optimal solution to the planning task confronting them. In particular with regard to investment in roads, they wanted to devise a plan that would be best in terms of minimizing the total cost of road investment, plus users' travel time, operating costs and accident costs. Whether they believed intuitively that the city of the future would be best served by a dense grid of expressways is unknown. That they set out to discover the answer to such a question is remarkable.

To perform this task, they needed to solve two daunting problems. The first problem was to forecast the amount of personal travel that would occur on a typical weekday in 1980 by road and transit, given one of the alternative plans under consideration. To this end, they devised a sequence of forecasting methods, and used the IBM 704, the first main frame computer available for civilian use, to apply them as early as 1958. In devising their methods, they evidently overlooked a theoretical model of travel demand and route choice proposed by three young economists at the University of Chicago only a few years earlier; see Beckmann et al. (1956).

The second problem was road system design: what should be the extent and layout of the system of expressways and arterial roads to serve the existing pattern of urban activities of the late 1950s and the prospective expansion that would occur by 1980. In response to this problem, they derived an expressway spacing formula, identified practical principles of expressway system design, and applied both to design alternative system plans that substantially augmented the system of existing and committed expressways and tollways on which agreement had been reached prior to the Study.

One should pause at this point and attempt to imagine the problem they faced. Travel in America's large urban areas was rapidly shifting from public transit to cars. New limited access highways offered freedom from congested street systems. What should be the density and layout of this new type of facility, especially in inner cities where large areas of 19th century housing and manufacturing facilities were being considered for demolition?

In all, five main alternatives were created, analyzed and evaluated, and in 1962 a refined plan was recommended to the governmental agencies sponsoring the Study. Nearly in parallel, a second study employing the same methodology was completed for the Pittsburgh region. Staff members from CATS were in much demand for their expertise and experience, and some pursued separate opportunities in the New York region and upstate New York metropolitan areas. Others remained in Chicago to continue the studies begun in 1955.

Now 50 years have passed since those pioneering transportation studies of the 1950s and the Chicago Area Study in particular. Travel forecasting methods that originated at CATS and similar studies of the day are now routinely applied throughout the developed and developing world, as embodied in several software systems designed for modern personal computers and engineering workstations. Research has greatly deepened our understanding of the scientific basis for these methods, mathematically as well as in economic and social terms. In the interim the seminal contribution of Beckmann and his co-authors, which provides the theoretical framework for forecasting travel on congested road networks, has become more fully appreciated.

I would like to report that similar gains have been made in understanding and solving the road system design problem. In fact, quite the opposite is the case. Apart from a few academic studies of this vexing problem, e.g., Vaughn (1987), little has been accomplished since the pioneering efforts at CATS. Moreover, the attempts to devise and apply a design method, the expressway spacing formula, has been forgotten nearly completely. It is not mentioned at all in current textbooks on the subject of urban transportation planning. And what of the landmark road plan for the Chicago area for 1980? Did it successfully guide future investments in expressways and arterial roads during the next 20 years, and beyond? Unfortunately, it did not; not one of its core recommendations was implemented. On the positive side, the proposed rapid transit system was implemented successfully, and continues to serve the region well.

Over four decades after the completion of the 1980 Plan for the Chicago area, why is it appropriate to inquire about the reasons that this effort failed to yield useful policy directions? In addition to drawing attention to this pioneering study from an historical perspective, I seek to offer guidance to future studies, perhaps not in America or Europe where much system development has already occurred, but rather in emerging urban regions in Asia, which are now rapidly acquiring automobile-based urban transportation systems. For both reasons it seems pertinent to ask whether a technical failure of the methods devised and applied occurred, whether insufficient weight was given to some factors, or perhaps other factors were not considered at all? Or was the task of building a roadway system for the region simply so overwhelming and disruptive that money and political will were lacking beyond the original pre-CATS system? In this account, I primarily seek to answer the question of whether a technical failure occurred.

The plan of the paper is the following. First, the general context of the transportation planning problem is described, including population, employment, land in urban use, and travel characteristics in 1956 and forecast for 1980. Second, the expressway spacing formula is introduced, and its properties examined. Third, the application of the method to the Chicago area is considered, and the alternative plans presented. Finally, the economic analysis performed on the alternatives is examined for the insights it revealed. The paper concludes with a discussion of the lessons learned from this review and possible implications for the future.

As noted, the purpose of this examination is to try to learn from these pioneering efforts in our field, and certainly not to offer criticism of well-intentioned, hard-working planners and engineers from an earlier period. Those investigators, working under the most arduous circumstances from today's perspective, performed amazing feats in a remarkably short period of time. As the principal actors are either no longer with us, or perhaps not inclined to engage in discussion about this remote period, the best I can offer is an interpretation of the written record they left us at the time.

II. Demographic and Economic Setting of the Chicago Area Study

One reason for the initiation of the Chicago Area Transportation Study in 1955 was the rapid growth in population, employment and land development being experienced in the post-war era. Seven indicators of the anticipated growth from the Study's 1956 Base Year to the 1980 Design Year, shown in Table 1 for the 1,237 square-mile Study Area, indicate the extent of this growth. Population and employment were forecast to increase by 50% and vehicle travel by 90%. Only travel by public transit was expected to remain constant during this period of rapid growth in vehicle ownership.

Indicator Variable Chicago Study Area	Base Year 1956	Design Year 1980	Percent Increase
Population (1,000s)	5,170	7,802	50.9
Employment (1,000s)	2,549	3,874	52.0
Developed Land (square miles)	563	1,083	92.1
Registered Vehicles (1,000s)	1,597	3,046	90.7
Daily Person Trips (1,000s)	10,212	18,081	77.1
Daily Vehicle Trips (1,000s)	6,534	12,604	92.9
Daily Public Transit Trips (1,000s)	2,452	2,481	1.2

Source: CATS (1960, pp. 13, 31, 47, 69, 76)

Tab. 1: Demographic, Economic and Travel Indicators for 1956 and 1980

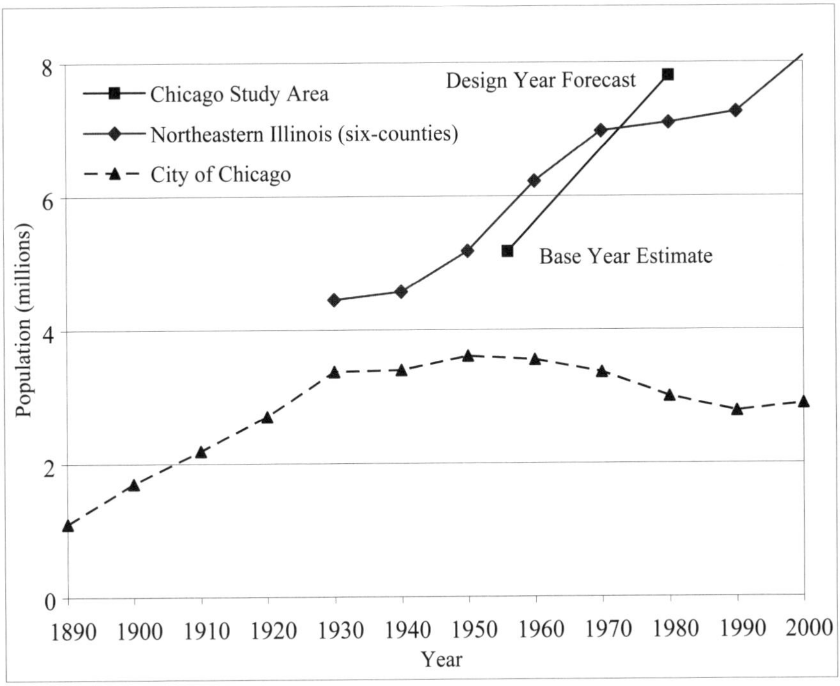

Source: CATS (1960, p. 112); US Census of Population

Fig. 1: Population of City of Chicago and Northeastern Illinois

In fact, the 1980 population forecast for the Study Area was substantially greater than what occurred. Although population did grow substantially during the 1950s and 1960s, it leveled off in the early 1970s as birth rates fell throughout the United States and rural to urban migration into the largest urban areas tapered off. This outcome may be seen clearly in Figure 1. As a result of these unanticipated changes, the 1980 population forecast for the Chicago Study Area was substantially in error, even higher than the six-county Northeastern Illinois region, a geographic area over three times larger than the Study Area.

In contrast, the densely populated City of Chicago, with a land area of 212 square miles, lost population from 1950 onwards. Only in 2000 did Chicago experience a modest population increase of 4%, while the six-county area grew by more than 11%. (Comparable totals for the Chicago Study Area have not been compiled since the initial Study ended in 1962.) Hence, the planners at CATS were actually facing a situation of a declining central city, initially surrounded by a rapidly growing hinterland, whose growth substantially slowed during the last decade of the planning period. In the following sections, their response to these unanticipated trends will become clear.

III. Expressway Spacing Formula

The principal description of the expressway spacing formula is found in Creighton, Hoch, Schneider and Joseph (1960), and was incorporated into the Final Report, Volume III, as an Appendix; cf. CATS (1962, pp. 121 ff.). The description of the application of the method is found in CATS (1962, pp. 39 ff.). Preliminary results were reported by Creighton and Schneider (1958) and Joseph (1959). The description offered below is based on these sources.

The expressway spacing formula was derived for an idealized situation, likely suggested by the grid of local and arterial streets prevalent in the City of Chicago and its inner suburbs. The basic idea was to determine the spacing of expressways in a road network consisting of arterial and local streets as well as expressways. The derivation of the method assumes: a) user travel costs are decreasing functions of travel speeds on the three types of facilities; b) construction costs are proportional to facility length, and therefore to facility spacing; and c) travel on a higher type facility is preferred to travel on a lower type facility.

Using the authors' notation, the problem is formulated as follows: minimize the sum of construction and user travel costs for the three types of facilities defined on a square grid of length *S*. The construction cost per grid cell of length *S* is:

$$C_1 = 2S^2\left(\frac{C_X}{x}+\frac{C_Y}{y}+\frac{C_Z}{z}\right)$$

where C_X, C_Y, C_Z are the annualized construction costs per unit distance of local and arterial streets and expressways, respectively; and *x*, *y*, *z* are the intervals between each type of roadway.

For example, if *x* is 1/8th mile for local streets, *y* is 1 mile for arterial streets and *z* is 4 miles for expressways, this assumption corresponds to a grid of facilities per square mile of 16 miles of local streets, 2 miles of arterial streets and 0.5 miles of expressways, if it is assumed that when higher level facilities overlap with lower level ones, both are included. Double-counting of construction costs of two coinciding streets seems reasonable, and can be considered in determining the construction costs per mile. Local street spacing of 1/8th mile is standard for the City of Chicago; major arterials are generally spaced at 1 mile intervals, although 1/2 mile spacing is also found in densely developed areas. (Results are expressed here in miles, since the figures and tables taken from the references use that traditional unit of measure; 1 mile = 1.6 kilometers, or 1 kilometer = 0.6 miles.)

To derive the equation for C_1, note that C_X / x is the construction cost for a one-mile wide corridor (\$/mile/miles = \$/mile^2). Adding these corridor costs for the three facility types yields the total cost for a one-mile wide corridor in \$/mile^2. Multiplying by S miles determines the cost for a one-mile wide corridor of length S. Multiplying again by S miles adjusts the cost of the corridor from a width of one mile to a width of S miles. Doubling this result adds the cost of facilities in the orthogonal direction.

The total cost of travel time per grid cell of length S is:

$$C_2 = NK\left[\sum_{i=1}^{r-1}\left(\frac{L_i}{v_X}\right)F_i + \sum_{i=r}^{s-1}\left(\frac{2A}{v_X}+\frac{L_i-2A}{v_Y}\right)F_i + \sum_{i=s}^{t}\left(\frac{2A}{v_X}+\frac{2B}{v_Y}+\frac{L_i-2A-2B}{v_Z}\right)F_i\right]$$

where N = the number of trips/day originating or terminating in the analysis area;

K = (value of time/hr) · (number of days/yr)/Present Worth Factor (30 years, 5%);

= \$1.43/hr·340 days/yr/0.065 ≈ \$7,500 (1960 dollars)

L_i = the average trip length for interval i of the trip length distribution, $i = 1,\ldots t$;

F_i = the proportion of trips occurring in interval i, $i = 1,\ldots t$;

v_X, v_Y, v_Z = the average travel speeds on facility types x, y and z;

A = the average distance traveled in moving from facility type x to type y;

B = average distance traveled in moving from facility type y to type z.

To see that C_2 is the total user cost of travel, we begin with the expression in the square bracket. L_i is the distance traveled in interval i, i = 1 to r-1, which is the upper limit of travel on local streets (x). As v_X is the speed of travel on local streets, the ratio L_i / v_X is the travel time on local streets in interval i. Multiplying by F_i and summing from 1 to r-1 gives the total time traveled on local streets through interval r-1. If travel terminates at a distance less than interval r-1, the calculation is complete. If not, A represents the total time on local streets at the outset of travel, and $2A / v_X$ is the total travel time on local streets at the outset and completion of travel.

The distance traveled beyond local streets in interval i, $i = r$ to s-1 is (L_i – $2A$). Dividing by the arterial speed v_Y gives the arterial travel time in interval i. Multiplying the sum of travel time by the trip frequency yields the total travel time on arterials. A similar explanation accounts for the third summation from $i = s$ to t.

The entire travel time determined by the terms in the brackets is multiplied by the number of trips N and K, which is the product of the value of time, the number of days per year, and the inverse of a present worth factor to convert this annual total value of time to a 30 year period. The result is the total value of time over 30 years for the specified facility speeds and spacing of facilities.

Clearly, a very considerable amount of effort was expended to determine the values of A and B, as described by Hoch (1959). Approximate values of A and B obtained for the facility spacing assumptions were: $A = 0.2y$, and $B = 0.2(y + z)$. Note these approximations depend on the facility spacing assumptions. Figure 2 shows representative findings of this analysis. The over-the-road travel distance by facility type is given on the y-axis for an assumed airline travel distance on the x-axis. The over-the-road distance is segmented by local and arterial streets and expressways, as determined by their assumed spacings. No scale is shown because the results are generalized from calculations for specific cases. An experimental method was employed in an effort to confirm these results.

Herein lies an apparent shortcoming of the method. Values of A and B derived for optimizing the facility spacings are functions of those spacings. Moreover, these formulas are approximations of more complex expressions, and further complicated by the use of both airline and over-the-road distances. Although an iterative solution process sought to take account of the interdependence of spacing and values of A and B, it is unclear whether it was successful.

Differentiating $C(y,z)=C_1(y,z)+C_2(y,z)$ with respect to y and z, while holding the spacing of local streets fixed at $x = 1/8^{th}$ mile, the authors obtained the following equations for y and z:

$$y=\left[\frac{5\cdot C_Y}{K\cdot D\cdot\left(P_R\cdot V_{XY}+P_S\cdot V_{XYZ}\right)}\right]^{1/2};\quad z=\left[\frac{5\cdot C_Z}{K\cdot D\cdot\left(P_S\cdot V_{YZ}\right)}\right]^{1/2}$$

where $P_R = \sum_{i=1}^{s-1} F_i$ = total trip frequency of trips using local and arterial streets, $P_S = \sum_{i=s}^{t} F_i$ = total trip frequency of trips using local and arterial streets and expressways, $D = N/S^2$ is the density of trip originations or terminations, the number of trips divided by the area of a square with a side of length S, and

$$V_{XY}=\frac{v_Y-v_X}{v_X\cdot v_Y};\; V_{YZ}=\frac{v_Z-v_Y}{v_Y\cdot v_Z};\; V_{XYZ}=\frac{v_Y\cdot v_Z+v_X\cdot v_Z-2\cdot v_X\cdot v_Y}{v_X\cdot v_Y\cdot v_Z}$$

For speeds of 12 mph, 20 mph and 50 mph for local and arterial streets and expressways, these values are: $V_{XY}=0.033$; $V_{YZ}=0.030$; $V_{XYZ}=0.093$.

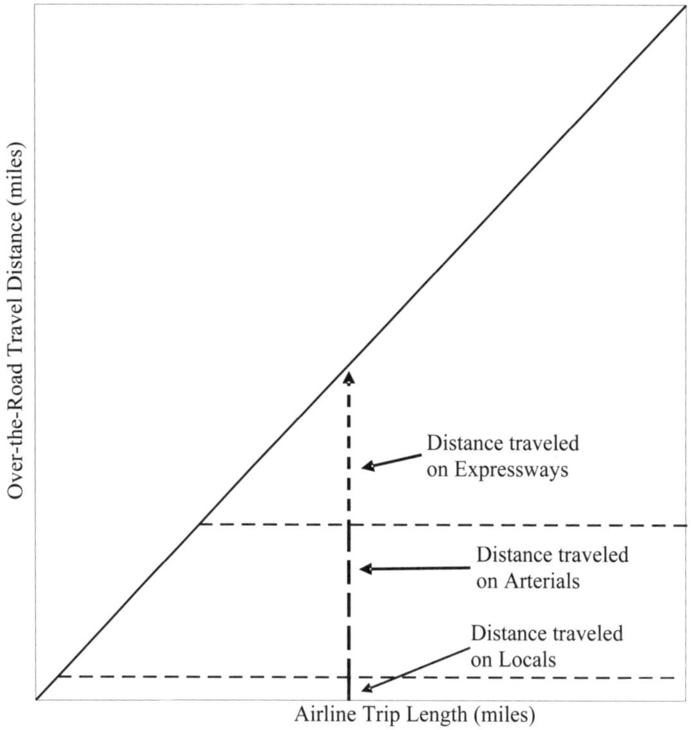

Source: based on Creighton et al (1960, p. 14)

Fig. 2: Use of Local and Arterial Streets and Expressways by Trips of Various Airline Lengths

After solving these equations for the minimum values for the trip length frequency distribution observed in the 1956 home interview survey, the authors also developed a simplified graphical method, which they stated confirmed the spacing formula results. Two examples of their findings are reproduced here. The assumptions for the two examples are given in Table 2. In this case, local streets and arterials streets were grouped into one category, called non-expressways.

Given values	Example 1	Example 2
Expressway cost per mile (1960 $)	$8,000,000	$4,000,000
Trip density, destinations/sq. mile	20,000	6,200
Expressway speed	50 mph	50 mph
Non-expressway speed	12 mph	20 mph

Source: Creighton et al. (1960, Table 4, p. 19) he trip length frequency distribution is for the entire Chicago Study Area, with a mean of 4.3 miles.

Tab. 2: Values Used in Graphically Estimating the Minimum-Cost Spacing

The findings for the graphical formula are shown in Figures 3a and 3b. According to the authors, these results show a minimum-cost spacing for expressways of 3 miles for Example 1 and 6 to 7 miles for Example 2. The figures are plotted at a similar scale to those in the published paper. From the tables on which these figures are based in Creighton et al. (1960, p. 20), one may observe that the total costs for Example 1 are very similar in the range of 2 to 4 miles; for Example 2, the results are highly similar in a range of 2 to 10 miles. Hence, the method and the cost estimates did not succeed in identifying a sharp minimum for either case. Although the expressway and arterial street spacing formulas were derived based on an idealized grid, their first application to the Chicago area network was actually for a radial configuration. The radial layout may have seemed more appropriate, since the existing and committed system of expressways and tollways had consisted of radials and rings. Moreover, several major arterials leading into the center of Chicago are radial routes following along long-established wagon roads and Native American trails. When the region was surveyed during the 1840s, a one-mile grid land surveying system was utilized, which resulted in arterial roads and streets at one-mile intervals.

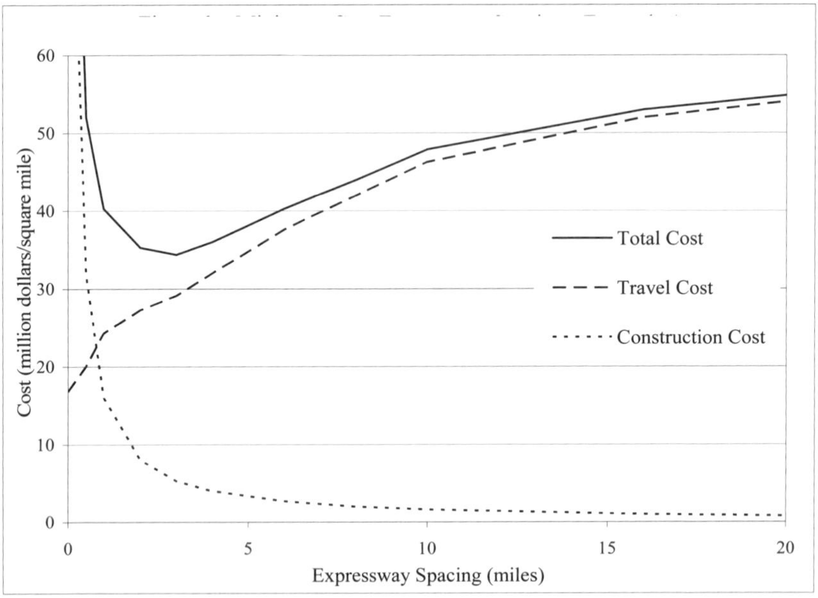

Source: Creighton et al (1960, Tab. 5, p. 20)

Fig. 3a: Minimum Cost Expressway Spacing – Example 1

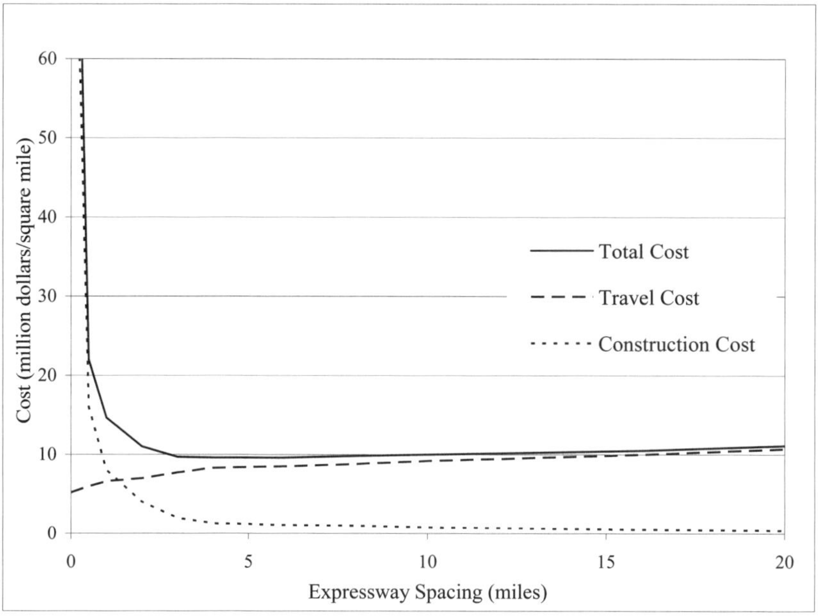

Source: Creighton et al (1960, Table 6, p. 20)

Fig. 3b: Minimum Cost Expressway Spacing – Example 2

As documented by Joseph (1959) and Creighton et al. (1960), extensive studies were made of the spacing of radial expressways for the 1956 base year, and for the 1980 design year, based on the expressway spacing formula. Table 3 shows the results of the optimal expressway spacing calculations in relation to trip destination densities and distances from the center of the region, on the assumption of a radial pattern. The resulting layout is depicted in Figure 4.

Ring	Distance to CBD (miles)	Area (square miles)	Trip Destinations (square miles)		Optimal Spacing (miles)	
			1956	1980	1956	1980
0	0.0	1.2	134.0	152.0	1.2	1.3
1	1.5	12.4	40.7	47.2	2.1	2.2
2	3.5	26.1	24.8	28.7	2.8	2.7
3	5.5	41.2	22.0	25.3	3.0	2.8
4	8.5	85.0	17.0	19.6	3.7	2.9
5	12.5	129.2	8.6	13.4	6.5	4.0
6	16.0	293.7	3.5	9.0	8.3	6.3
7	24.0	647.7	1.1	6.2	12.1	6.9

Sources: Creighton et al. (1960, Tab. 9, 11, 13, 14, pp. 29. ff.); Joseph (1959, Tab. 1, p.13)

Tab. 3: Expressway Spacing Requirements for 1956 and 1980

Source: Creighton et al (1960, Fig. 16, p. 32)
Each rectangle is about 35 miles by 50 miles.

Fig. 4: Minimum Cost System – 1956

Source: Joseph (1959, Fig. 2, p. 12)

Fig. 5: Optimum System – 1980

The description of Figure 4 by Creighton et al. (1960) states that "the pattern of circumferential and radial expressways suggested," by the analysis in Table 3 and elsewhere, "has been applied without any adjustment to a map of the Chicago Study Area." Using 11 expressways, as suggested by the spacing analysis, would result in spacing of 33 degrees; however, the accompanying map shows 10 radials with a spacing of 36 degrees, for half of a circle, of course. The radial expressways match up fairly well with the six radial expressways on the existing and committed plan, with the exception of the committed expressway extending directly south from the city center. The circumferential expressways also had some relation to the committed system: the outermost ring fairly closely corresponds to the Tri-State Tollway; and the innermost ring mirrors connections among the radial expressways.

Creighton et al. did not present their preliminary thinking concerning the layout of the 1980 expressway system. However, Joseph (1959) presented a map of the "1980 optimum expressway system" that gives some insights into the emerging direction of thinking. In commenting on the optimal spacings, as shown in Table 2, Joseph (1959, p. 13) stated: "Note that the spacings vary little from rings 2 through 4, and then diverge after ring 4. This suggests a grid-type expressway system to ring 4 and a radial system for rings 5 through 7. (Figure 6, below) shows a graphical interpretation of the 1980 spacing results. An average of 16 radials for a complete circle provides optimum spacing for rings 5 through 7."

In summary, the attempt to devise an expressway spacing formula appears to have been suggestive, but did not yield a clear answer. The reasons are unclear and perhaps irretrievable. The grid-based formula was difficult to solve, and did not yield a definite answer. Evidently, no radial-ring formula derivation was attempted. Intuition and judgment gradually replaced mathematical analysis in the further development of the conceptual plan.

Why did the expressway planners shift from the radial and ring layout, which seemed to fit the existing and committed system so well, to a grid and radial pattern? An indication of their thinking is found in CATS (1962, pp. 36 f.), **Principles of System Planning:**

"The ring and radial pattern provides an even distribution of facilities against demands. That is, it provides more roadways and capacity near the center, yet progressively less as distance outward is increased. Since densities decline as traffic moves outward from the central area, the roadways are seen to thin out where traffic requirements will be lower. On the other hand, the radial system does provide roadways aimed at the center of town where it will be desirable and even necessary to encourage transit usage. Feeding cars to the center can build up heavy parking and street capacity problems and so work to inhibit a densely developed central business district. Densely developed centers can exist only if a sufficient number of customers and workers can be delivered each day in a satisfactory manner.

The grid system overcomes the problem of too much central focus. But it does not appear to serve (excepting by the possibility of differential numbers of lanes) the variety of trip densities of the region. It is simple and regular, making the intersection design easy and the user orientation very satisfactory.

A combination of grid and radials would meet the requirement of increasing service where there are higher travel demands. But it presents intersection problems of virtually impossible scale. It would be prohibitively expensive to try to design and build six-legged intersections.

A plan for the Chicago area would appear to be best constructed if it could have some blend of the attributes of the grid with those of the ring and radial system. To a large extent, the region is heavily committed to the radial system .... On the other hand, the underlying arterial system is a strong influence for a gridded network of expressways. The need to meet distributed traffic demands without encouraging further concentrations of flow also argues for a grid-like design. Making a compromise between the two would require ingenious design, but represents the direction that seems most likely to meet the traffic needs and, form a network viewpoint, sensible design."

Figure 5 shows "a graphical interpretation of the 1980 spacing results" presented in Joseph (1959). Although the figure was presented as a concept, it clearly represented the direction of expressway planning by the Chicago Area Study, as described in the next section.

IV. Economic Evaluation of the Alternative Expressway Plans

The following description of the evaluation of the roadway plan for the Chicago Area Study is based mainly on Haikalis (1962). Haikalis and Joseph (1961) presented their evaluation method somewhat earlier, but the final results are reported in the 1962 publication. The other principal source is CATS (1962), in which the detailed roadway plans and their economic analysis are presented.

The Chicago Area Study prepared, tested, evaluated and presented six expressway plans, designated A, B, K, I, J and L-3. Two variants of plans I and J were also developed, which represented an attempt to define an intermediate level of expressway design, dubbed "junior expressways." The latter are not considered in this review. Figure 6 shows Plan A, the existing and committed system at the outset of the Chicago Area Study. Plan B, shown in Figure 7, added two north-south expressways, which were under discussion at the outset of the Study, including the location of a major undecided connection among the radial expressways; cf. CATS (1962, p. 57). Figure 8 shows the 1980 expressway spacing requirements based on the optimal spacing formula, together with the existing and committed system. Plan K, in Figure 9, is the preliminary balanced plan based on the expressway spacing. According to Haikalis (1962, p. 33), "Plan K is the first try at the optimal plan." Plan I, an intermediate plan with more mileage than Plan K, is shown in Figure 10. Figure 11 shows the maximum mileage of any plan considered. Finally Plan L-3, Figure 12, emerged as the "optimal plan." The recommended expressway plan is shown in Figure 13, where the solid lines indicate the committed system, the heavy dashed lines are the first stage improvements, and the lighter dashed lines are the second stage improvements. Note the width of the lines in Figs. 6, 7, 9-12 indicates the daily volumes forecast for 1980.

The economic evaluation of alternative plans by CATS was based on three user attributes: the cost (value) of users' travel time, vehicle operating cost and vehicle accident cost. The first and third attributes decrease as speed increases. Vehicle operating cost has a well-known U-shaped relationship with speed: operating costs are higher at lower congested speeds and at higher speeds in freely flowing traffic than at speeds of 35-40 mph. Because the cost of travel time dominates the other two costs, the total cost is decreasing with speed.

The travel forecasting procedure devised by CATS considered the 24-hour weekday as a single period. That is, travel for all purposes during the 24 hours was assigned to the road network during one period. The daily road capacities during those 24-hours were based on the percentage of daily volume occurring in the highest one-hour period, 11%; actually, the 30th highest hourly flow over a year was used, the established practice at the time. To account for the fact that 60% of the flow occurred in the peak direction, the percentage was adjusted to 13.2%. Hence, daily capacity was set equal to the hourly capacity divided by 0.132.

In reality, of course, traffic is not distributed uniformly over the 24-hour day. To account for this fact, a procedure was developed for reducing the estimated total travel delay according to the empirically observed relation between the hourly rank of the traffic flow and the proportion of daily traffic during that hour, as described in Haikalis and Joseph (1961) and Haikalis (1962). (Note: in my experience, this procedure is unique, and has not been applied in subsequent studies.) Using this rank-size relationship, "the integration of each hour's expected delay over that hour's fraction of the daily flow provided a weighted average daily delay," as stated by Haikalis (1962, p. 17). Moreover, the delay formula was modified to values reported in a table in Haikalis and Joseph (1961, Table 2, p. 48). A similar procedure was followed for arterials; in this case the delay per link was estimated, rather than the delay per vehicle-mile.

Using these functions for travel time, and presumably similar functions for accidents and vehicle operating costs, estimates of travel costs were made for the six alternative plans, as shown in Table 4 and Figures 14-16. The alternative plans in the table and figures are arrayed in order of increasing capital cost. The first four row entries in Table 4, and plotted in Figure 14, show the extent of the expressway and arterial systems, and their associated cost of completion. The additional expressway mileage proposed, and its cost, is seen to be very substantial, as compared with the existing and committed system of Plan A. The next four entries, and Figure 15, show the predicted use of these systems in 1980 in vehicle-miles and vehicle-hours of travel. Figure 15 shows a substantial shift of vehicle-miles of travel from the arterial system to expressways, as well as a 10% reduction in total travel time. Total vehicle-miles of travel remain nearly equal across the six alternatives. Finally, the last four entries, and Figure 16, show the forecast weekday travel costs of users in terms of the costs of travel time, vehicle operation and accidents for 1980. The reduction in total costs from Plan A to Plan L-3 is about 10%, although operating costs increase slightly.

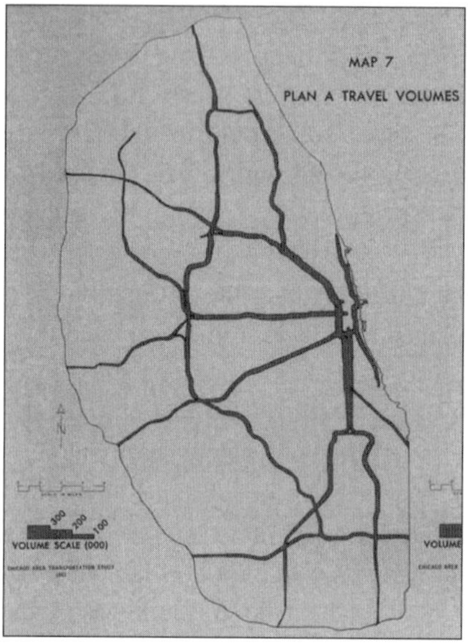

Fig. 6: Travel Volumes on Plan A, the Existing & Committed Expressway Plan

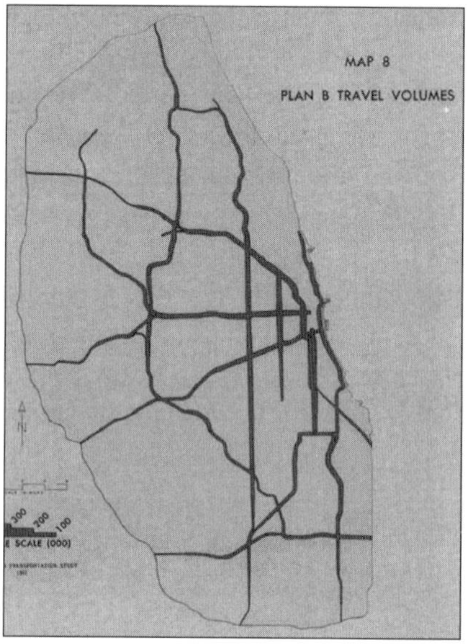

Fig. 7: Travel Volumes on Plan B, with the Addition of Two North-South Routes

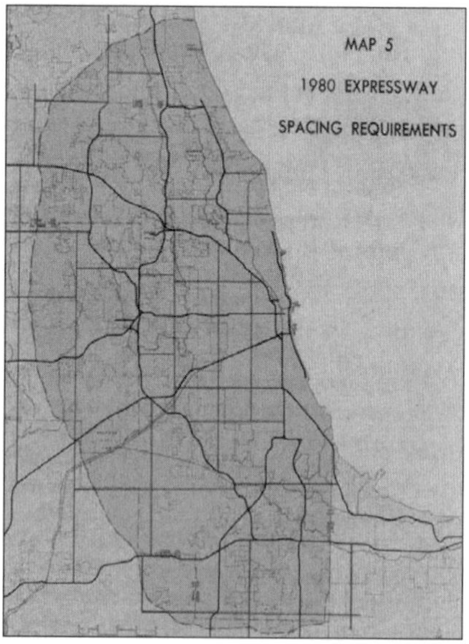

Fig. 8: New Facilities Recommended by Optimal Spacing Requirements

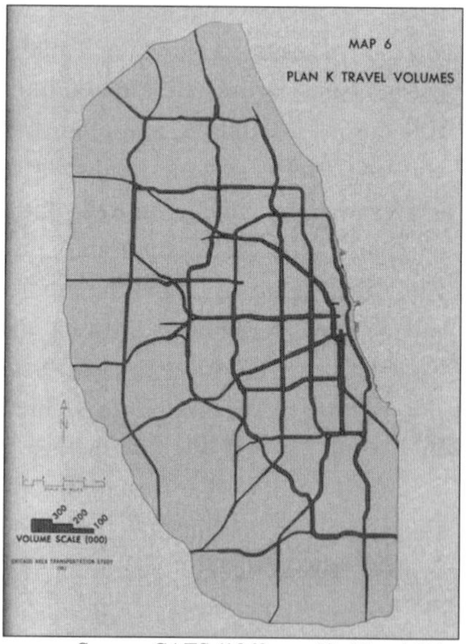

Source: CATS (1962, pp. 53, 55 and 57)

Fig. 9: Travel Volumes for Plan K Based on Optimal Spacing Requirements

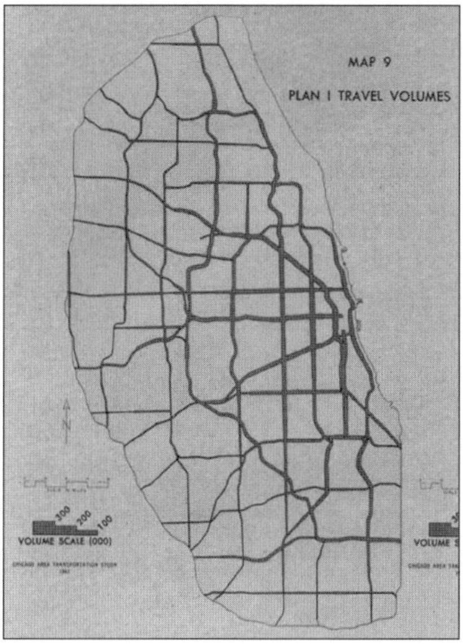

Fig. 10: Travel Volumes on Plan I with More Facilities than Plan K

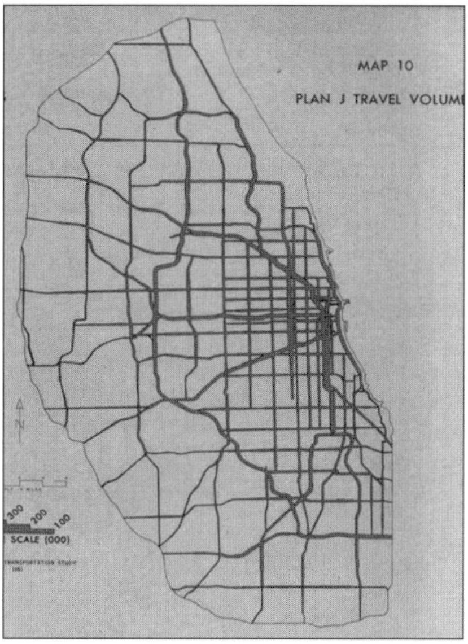

Fig. 11: Travel Volumes on Plan J with Maximum Length of Expressways

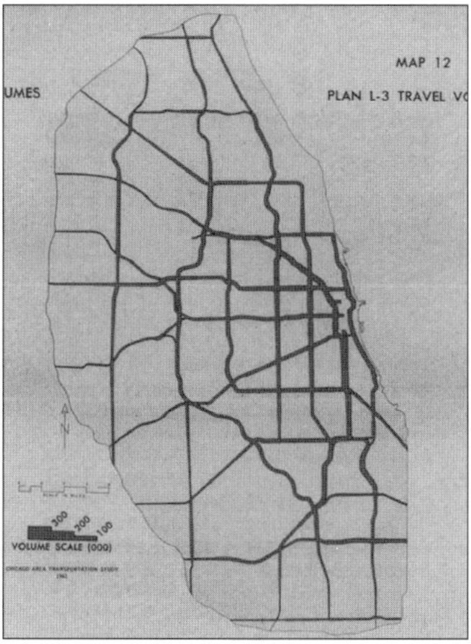

Fig. 12: Travel Volumes on the L-3 Recommended Expressway Plan

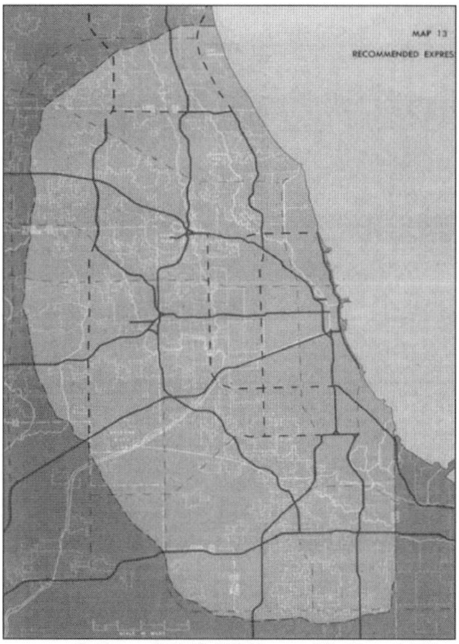

Source: CATS (1962, pp. 58, 61 and 64)

Fig.13: Recommended Plan (committed, first stage and second stage)

Plan Characteristics – 1980	Alternative Plan					
	A	B	K	L-3	I	J
Miles of proposed facilities						
Expressways	288	327	466	520	681	968
Arterials	2830	2830	2830	2823	2589	2247
Cost of completion to 1980 (M $)	907	1274	1797	2007	2392	3180
Weekday vehicle-miles travel (M)						
Expressways	22.9	25.2	33.3	34.4	35.1	41.6
Arterials	45.0	42.0	34.4	33.1	31.5	24.2
Total	67.9	67.1	67.7	67.6	66.6	65.8
Weekday vehicle-hours travel (M)	2.24	2.28	2.05	1.99	1.94	1.99
Weekday travel costs (M $)						
Travel time cost	3.63	3.38	3.07	2.99	3.03	2.98
Operating cost	1.87	1.85	1.91	1.91	1.82	1.75
Accident cost	0.68	0.61	0.51	0.48	0.49	0.47
Total costs	6.18	5.84	5.49	5.38	5.34	5.20

Sources: CATS (1962, Table 11, p. 62); Haikalis (1962, Tables 8 and 9, p. 40)

Tab. 4: Characteristics of Alternative Plans for 1980 for the Chicago Area

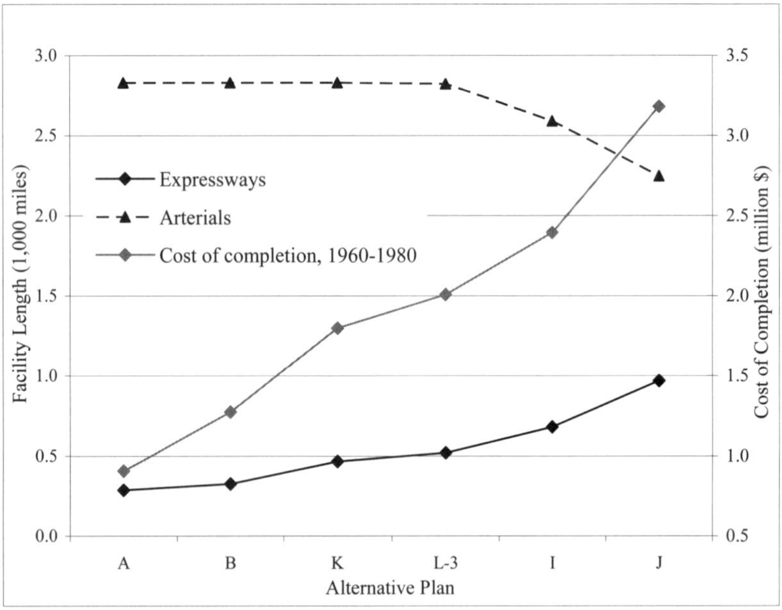

Source: Table 4

Fig. 14: Extent and Cost of the Alternative Plans

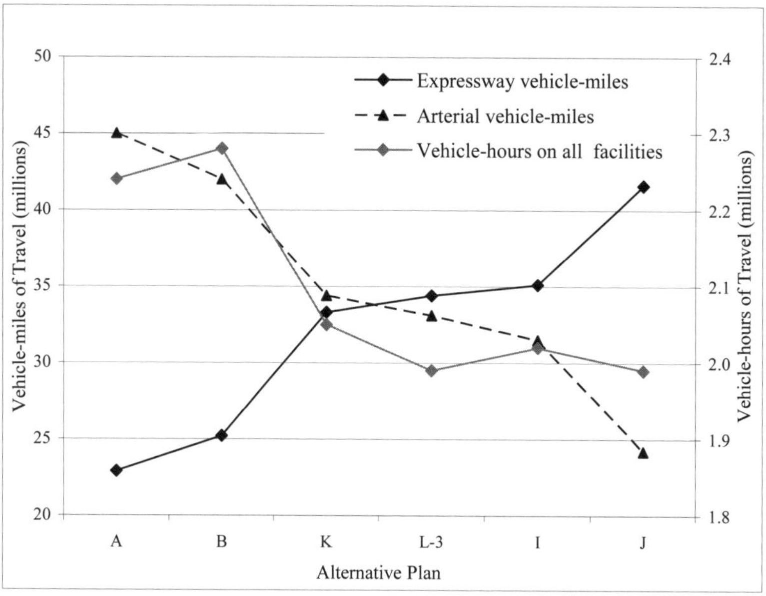

Source: Table 4

Fig. 15: Use of Roadways in the Alternative Plans

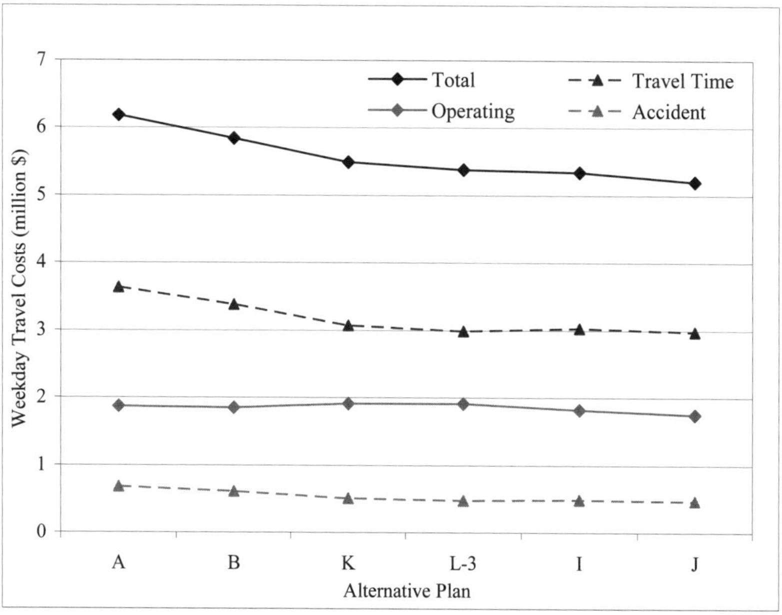

Source: Table 4

Fig. 16: Weekday Travel Costs of Alternative Plans

From the estimates of travel time, vehicle operations and accident costs, and the estimated cost of each alternative plan, an economic evaluation was conducted by Haikalis and Joseph (1961) and Haikalis (1962, pp. 40 f.). An interpretation of their analysis is offered in Table 5 in rows 1-5, 9 and 11. Some details are slightly different in the table because the plans involving junior expressways are excluded. The marginal rates of return, shown in line 11, support the basic recommendation of the Study, namely that the expressway system should be expanded to the level of Plan L-3, but not beyond. Plans B, K and L-3 have marginal rates of return in excess of 10%, the level adopted as necessary for a recommendation. Plans I and J fail this test. The relationship between the system costs in excess of Plan A, the existing and committed plan, and the annual savings in travel costs is shown in Figure 17. The slopes of the line segments in the figure correspond to the marginal rates of return on the investment. (One should note that the use of the marginal rate of return concept is not standard in that the plans are not hierarchical; that is, higher cost plans do not consist of added elements to lower cost plans. However, the plans are increasing in both costs and cost savings.)

The presentation of the economic evaluation by Haikalis (1962) and in CATS (1962, pp. 62 f.) does not consider the annual cost of the operation and routine maintenance of the roadway system. Such costs are substantial and incurred annually. In addition, expressways have a finite life, and must be extensively reconstructed after 25 to 35 years of service, as has been repeatedly observed in the Chicago area since the early 1980s. In order to explore hypothetically the effect of the operation and routine maintenance costs on the analysis of Haikalis (1962), I assumed annual operating and routine maintenance costs to be 15% of the construction costs required to complete each plan. One basis for this value is the estimate of these costs ($15 billion for 1996-2020, or $600 million per year) in the CATS (1998) plan for 2020; those operating and routine maintenance costs in 1995 dollars were discounted to 1960 by the GDP price deflator ratio of 4.37 (source: http://research.stlouisfed.org/fred2/data/GDPDEF.txt), resulting in an annual cost in 1960 dollars of $136 million for the existing and committed plan, or a rate of 15% per year. (To yield a more conservative estimate, an additional cost of $5.8 billion for Illinois Tollway operating costs and debt service was omitted from the calculation.) The estimate is intended only as an illustration of the effect on the analysis of omitting a significant ongoing cost.

System Completion Cost and Annual Savings in 1980 (M $)	Alternative Plan					
	A	B	K	L-3	I	J
1. Total cost of system completion, 1960 – 1980	907	1274	1797	2007	2392	3180
2. Total cost of completion over plan A	0	367	890	1100	1485	2273
3. Marginal cost of completion over preceding plan	0	367	523	210	385	788
4. Annual users travel cost: weekday cost x 340 days/yr	2098	1983	1864	1827	1813	1765
5. Annual user cost savings over plan A	0	115	234	272	285	333
6. Operation/maintenance costs: 15% of cost of completion	136	191	270	301	359	477
7. Operation/maintenance costs over plan A	0	55	134	165	223	341
8. Net savings: user costs less operations/maint costs: 5 – 7	0	60	101	107	62	-8
9. Cost savings over each preceding plan, by CATS	0	115	119	37	14	48
10. Net cost savings over each preceding plan, as amended	0	60	40	6	-44	-71
11. Marginal rate of return on total cost savings (%): 5/3	--	31.5	22.7	17.8	3.5	6.0
12. Marginal rate of return on net cost savings (%): 10/3	--	16.5	7.7	2.8	-11.5	-9.0

Source: Haikalis (1962, Table 10, p. 41) and calculations of the author

Tab. 5: System and User Costs, Operation/Maintenance and Rate of Return

The annual cost of operations and routine maintenance was deducted from the annual travel cost savings to obtain a *net* annual savings for each plan over Plan A, and the marginal rate of return was re-computed. The results of this analysis are shown in rows 6-8, 10 and 12. The net annual cost savings are also shown in Figure 19. The result of this analysis shows that only Plan B has a marginal rate of return in excess of 10%. Hence the omission or overestimate of cost savings as small as 15% substantially alters the conclusion of the Study.

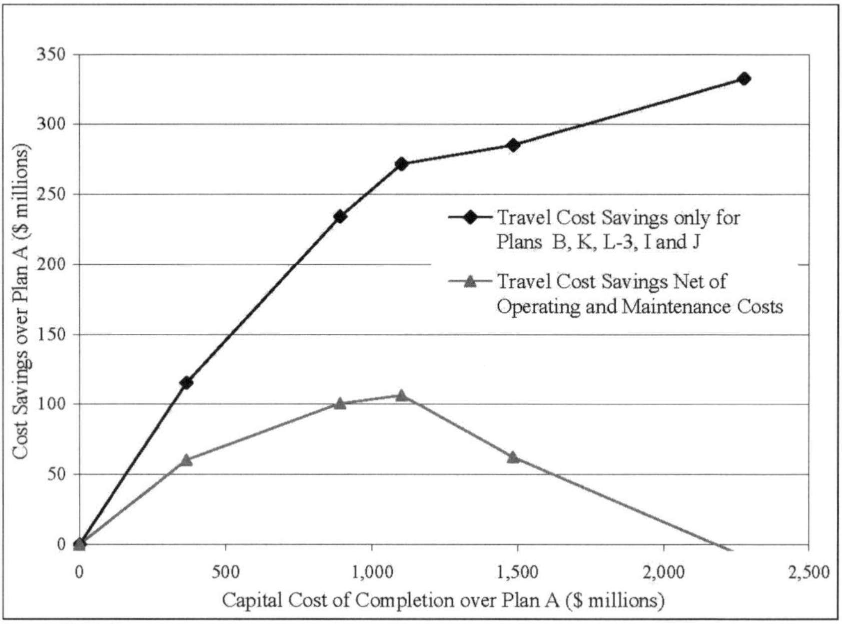

Source: Table 5

Fig. 17: Marginal Rate of Return of Alternative Plans

V. Discussion

To place the discussion of the impact of the1980 CATS Plan in an historical context, I first review very briefly the reaction and decisions in response to the plan. Aspects of this subject have been treated in more depth by Scheff (1977) and Petersen (2006) for the Chicago Crosstown Expressway, and by various authors for the United States as a whole; for a recent overview, see Garrison and Levinson (2006, Ch. 14).

The first large-scale project to be advanced to the location and preliminary design stage following the release of the 1980 Plan in 1962 was the Interstate Highway circumferential between the Edens and Dan Ryan Expressways, which became known as the Crosstown Expressway, or I-494. The construction of this facility was funded under the Interstate Highway Act. It is described in CATS (1962, p. 53) as "a committed facility whose location has not yet been determined."

Studies to determine the location and design of this 22 mile, eight-lane facility initially estimated to cost $300 to 500 million dollars were concluded in late 1965 by the Transportation Advisory Group (1965). By that time construction of urban freeways was beginning to be severely questioned, not only in Chicago but in most large American cities. Such protests were later described as the “freeway revolts,” which in some cases resulted in demonstrations of various levels of severity, leading in a few cases to civil unrest. In Chicago, in order to facilitate the design of an expressway passing through older, fully developed neighborhoods, a consortium of leading architectural and civil engineering firms was engaged. After years of studies, discussions and political wrangling, an agreement was reached to delete the Crosstown Expressway from the Plan, and allocate the funding for its construction to other road improvements, and including in an unprecedented manner, to transit improvements.

Following this agreement, no further expressway construction was undertaken until after 1980. During that decade, agreement was reached to construct a north-south tollway near the western periphery of the 1980 Plan Study Area as a part of the Illinois Tollway system, extending I-290 southward to I-55, and known today as I-355. Even this proposal met with severe criticism, in part because its construction required the taking of land belonging to a well-established and locally renowned arboretum. The facility was opened to traffic about 1990. The general locations of the proposed Crosstown Expressway and the constructed north-south tollway, I-355, are shown on Figure 18.

The above account places the intention of the Chicago Area Study to devise an optimal expressway plan in the bright light of history, now 44 years since completion of the 1980 Plan. Although the reasons for the failure of the plan are diverse and certainly related to political factors, they appear to reveal that in some fundamental manner the basic approach to the expressway system design was flawed. One objective of this paper is to identify the source of this fundamental error. Careful scrutiny of the written record has yielded some hints, but nothing so far that may be regarded as a “smoking gun,” to invoke an American expression for overwhelming incriminating evidence. Rather, we are left with some circumstances that appear questionable. Allow me to try to enumerate them.

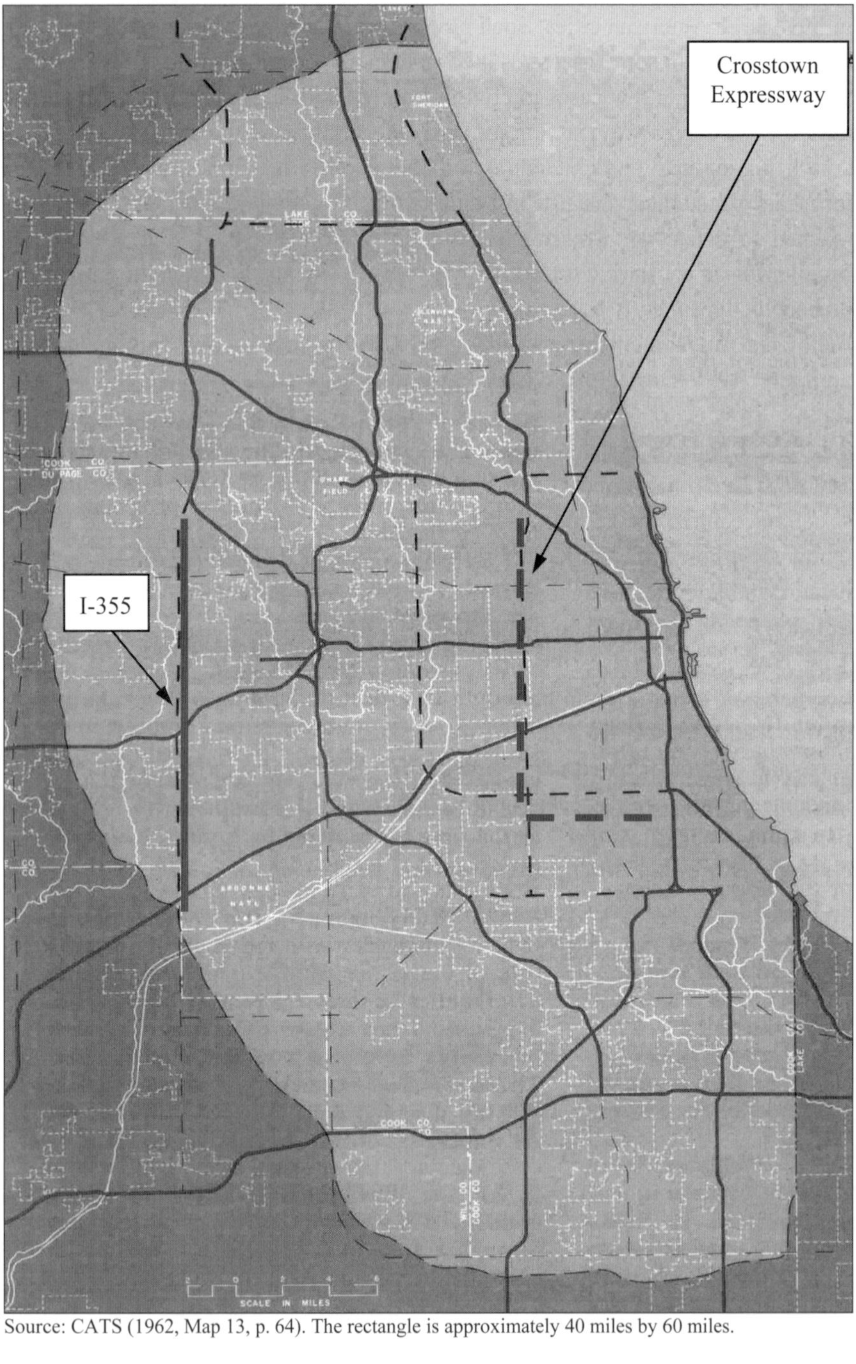

Source: CATS (1962, Map 13, p. 64). The rectangle is approximately 40 miles by 60 miles.

Fig. 18: Recommended Expressway Plan for the Chicago Study Area

1. The Expressway Spacing Formula

The spacing formula, reviewed in Section 2, is itself open to question and was not verified here, despite the lengthy documentation created at the time. One specific problem about the solution of the formula was identified here, namely that coefficients required for the solution of the optimal spacing depend upon those spacings themselves. In other words, the values of those coefficients are endogenous to the solution. Short of a fresh attempt to solve the formula using modern methods of computation, I am unable to conclude whether the formula and the conclusions drawn from it are correct. In the end, what is clear is that the conclusions offered were based on a much simpler analysis of costs, which lack a convincingly sharp minimum. The dilemma of re-solving the spacing formula, or a similar formulation today, raises the question of whether anyone wishes to know the answer. I return to this matter in my closing remarks in Section 5.

2. The Desire for a Grid Expressway System

The CATS Final Report is quite emphatic in arguing for a grid system of expressways, as contrasted with a radial and ring layout. As an indication of this emphasis, a lengthy section of the thinking of the Plan's authors was quoted at the end of Section 2. In reviewing the alternative plans, I am struck by the emphasis on the grid solution, as each successive alternative adds more density to the grid. Other than Plan A, no radial and ring plan was tested, suggesting the radial-ring solution was effectively excluded **a priori**.

Moreover, in the early note by Joseph (1959), we find evidence of an intuitive jump to a grid system, as illustrated by Figure 5, without strong evidence of its plausibility or desirability. One necessarily wonders whether the radial-ring system, shown in Figure 4, was prematurely dismissed in deference to the foregone conclusion that the only viable solution was a grid of expressways. Creighton (1970, p. 234) reiterates this view: "The best solution to this dilemma … is a warped grid, which is adapted to each local situation."

3. The Economic Evaluation

Next, I come to the economic evaluation, which was carefully documented with reasonable thoroughness. As noted in Section 3, the analysis contained some unexpected, positive insights. In particular, the estimates of travel delays on the expressway and arterial network did take account of the variations in volumes and delays over the 24-hour day, even though they were based on a single traffic assignment with capacities based on peak-hour conditions.

Despite the detail of the documentation, unanswered questions remain. First, why was the delay functions actually used to compute travel times scaled down from the values determined by the analysis, which resulted in a substantial reduction of the principal benefit of the expressway-intensive plans? Were there alterations in the analysis that were not described?

Second, why was such emphasis placed on travel time, vehicle operation and accident savings to the exclusion of all other costs? One excluded cost, annual operations and routine maintenance, has been used to illustrate the importance of these omitted costs in altering the conclusion. Other costs were not mentioned, such as the costs of land acquisition, neighborhood disruption and the loss of the real estate tax base. Neighborhood disruption was a primary reason for the freeway revolts of the late 1960s, and was readily observable in the Chicago area by 1960. Without carefully rereading the Final Report, I cannot be sure that there is no mention of these costs. But it is clear they were not given equal consideration with user cost savings.

Several years following the completion of the 1980 Plan, other variables came to the forefront. Among these were air quality concerns, which led to a mandated, atmospheric emissions conformity analysis since the early 1990s. Following the first OPEC oil embargo in 1973, just 11 years after the completion of the 1980 plan, conservation of fuel became important, a concern that continues to this day. Finally, although the 1980 plan did have a transit component, the emphasis was clearly on planning of the roadway system. To raise these concerns, and others such as equitable treatment of classes of the population, now known as environmental justice, is clearly unfair to the pioneering authors of this study, who did have a vision of the future far beyond their experience. Unfortunately, it was a vision that did not correspond to the reality of either 1980 or the present.

4. What Might Have Been Achieved?

With the advantage of 20-20 hindsight, the most powerful tool of analysis of all, one wonders whether events might have turned out very differently. Three thoughts come quickly to mind. From today's perspective, perhaps the most glaring omission of the expressway system serving the City of Chicago and its adjacent suburbs is the intermediate ring road connection, which the Crosstown Expressway was intended to provide. As the CATS's planners had foreseen, without this facility many vehicles must travel through Chicago's central area, even though their destinations are elsewhere. By completing this one facility, very substantial benefits would surely have accrued to users. Moreover, the leading elected official of that time, Mayor Richard J. Daley, did support the construction of the Crosstown Expressway.

Suppose in the 1980 Plan, CATS had made one of its primary objectives the testing of alternative designs for that yet to be located facility, in an effort to assure its viability. For example, they might have examined the costs and benefits of alternative numbers of lanes, rather than simply recommending an eight-lane facility. Perhaps a case could have been developed that was so compelling that the Crosstown Expressway's construction would have been assured, even in the anti-expressway construction climate of the period. At the same time, analyses might have concluded that other proposals embraced in alternatives based on the expressway spacing formula, such as the Western Avenue Expressway just three miles to the east, were not worthwhile.

As another example of possibly misplaced priorities, one wonders whether more attention ought to have been paid to testing proposals for expressways beyond the Tri-State Tollway, which was part of the committed system under construction. This suggestion is problematic because the CATS Study Area extended only about 10 miles beyond that ring road, so proposed outlying facilities could not be fully tested. Nevertheless, the fact that the only limited access facility constructed since the 1980 plan, I-355, is a circumferential tollway lying six miles further west, and which is now being extended further south and southeast after years of heated and contentious debate and lawsuits (Petersen, 2004). Had more emphasis been placed on locating and evaluating such outlying facilities, their construction might have proceeded in a more logical and consensus-based manner. Of course, the answers to these speculative musings cannot be known, any more than one can know what might have resulted if subsequent advances in travel forecasting methods had been available to the Chicago Area Study.

Finally, as noted in Section II, the population forecasts for the Study Area were very substantially higher than the actual population of 1980, and probably even today. Moreover, the population of the City of Chicago declined throughout the second half of the 20th Century. Much of the emphasis of the Chicago Area Study was devoted to improving the expressway system of a growing city, whereas in fact its population actually declined. What might have been done to anticipate better this result?

The risks associated with basic forecasts are fundamental to all types of planning. A way to reduce the risk is to prepare a range of forecasts, and conduct analyses and evaluations for a few points within this range, such as high, low and middle scenarios. Had such scenario analyses been performed, they might well have demonstrated the importance of a few key facilities, such as the Crosstown, and the marginal returns on increasing the density of the expressway grid. Again, we cannot answer what might have resulted from such "what if" conjectures. Risk analysis is a highly developed analytical tool. Yet, it is hardly ever applied in transportation planning.

VI. A Perspective on the Future

So why bother to read these dusty reports and puzzle over whether they are correct or not? The decisions concerning expressway construction of the past 40 years in the Chicago area are not going to change, and neither are past decisions in other major metropolitan areas of North America and Europe. Yet, other parts of the world are experiencing today what large North American cities experienced in the post-WW II period. Presently in China and India, large-scale programs of tollway construction are underway. In Beijing several ring roads have been constructed; when traffic congestion does not abate, construction of another ring road is proposed.

Moreover, automobile ownership is increasing in Asia at a rapid rate. Eastern Europe and Russia confront a similar phenomenon. No one asks, it seems, whether there is an alternative to a program of large-scale road construction and automobile use, like was first experienced in major American cities over 50 years ago. One small metropolitan country, Singapore, seems to have found an alternative pathway to a modern urban transportation system; unfortunately, its experience is often dismissed as irrelevant. (For further details and insights, see Sharp (2005) and www.lta.gov.sg.)

Based on a limited amount of personal experience in these places, I believe there are opportunities to learn from our past American and European experiences with urban transportation development, and to apply this knowledge to the planning of these emerging modern metropolises in developing countries. To paraphrase the philosopher, George Santayana, "Are those who fail to learn from history condemned to repeat it?"

References

Beckmann, M., C. B. McGuire and *C. B. Winsten*, Studies in the Economics of Transportation, New Haven 1956.

Chicago Area Transportation Study, Final Report, Survey Findings, Volume I, Chicago 1959.

Chicago Area Transportation Study, Final Report, Data Projections, Volume II, Chicago 1960.

Chicago Area Transportation Study, Final Report, Transportation Plan, Volume III, Chicago 1962.

Chicago Area Transportation Study, 2020 Regional Transportation Plan, Chicago 1998.

Creighton, R. L., Urban Transportation Planning, Urbana and Illinois 1970.

Creighton, R. L. and *M.*, The Optimal Spacing of Arterials and Expressways, in: C.A.T.S. Research News, 2 (16), Chicago Area Transportation Study, Chicago 1958, pp. 10-16.

Creighton, R. L., I. Hoch, M. Schneider and *H. Joseph*, Estimating Efficient Spacing for Arterials and Expressways, in: Bulletin 253, Highway Research Board, Washington, DC 1960. pp. 1-43.

Garrison, W. L. and *D. M. Levinson*, The Transportation Experience, New York 2006.

Haikalis, G., Economic Analysis of Roadway Improvements, Report 36, 500, Chicago Area Transportation Study, Chicago 1962.

Haikalis, G. and *H. Joseph*, Economic Evaluations of Traffic Networks, in: Bulletin 306, Highway Research Board, Washington, DC 1962, pp. 39-63.

Hoch, I., Some Formulas for Average Trip Length in a Network, in: C.A.T.S. Research News, 3 (3), Chicago Area Transportation Study, Chicago 1959, pp. 4-12.

Joseph, H., Preliminary Optimum Spacing Applications, in: C.A.T.S. Research News, 3 (5), Chicago Area Transportation Study, Chicago 1959, pp. 9-16.

Petersen, E. J., Regional Transportation Planning and Politics in Northeastern Illinois, Ph.D. Dissertation, Sociology, Northwestern University, Evanston and Illinois 2004.

Petersen, E. J., The Chicago Crosstown Expressway: Machine Politics, Grassroots Opposition and Federal Intervention, unpublished working paper 2006.

Scheff, H., Fighting the Chicago Crosstown, Appendix B, The End of the Road, A Citizen's Guide to Transportation Problemsolving, Washington, DC 1977.

Sharp, I., The Journey, Singapore's Land Transport Story, SNP Editions, Singapore 2005.

Transportation Advisory Group, The Proposed Chicago Crosstown Expressway, Chicago City Planning Commission, Chicago 1965.

Vaughn, R., Urban Spatial Traffic Patterns, London 1987.

Weiner, E., Urban Transportation Planning in the United States, 5th. Ed., DOT-T-97-24, US Department of Transportation, Washington, DC 1997.

C. Die alternde und schrumpfende Bevölkerung – ein städtebauliches Problem

Helmut Jenkis

Die Theorie der Bevölkerungswissenschaft ist für lange Zeit durch den englischen Ökonomen Thomas Robert Malthus (1766-1834) und durch das von ihm entwickelte Bevölkerungsgesetz maßgeblich beeinflusst worden:
Malthus (1798) hat in seinem „Essay on the Principle of Population as it Effects the Future Improvement of Society" und später unter dem Titel „An Essay on the Principle of Population or a View of its Past and Present Effects on Human Happines" (1903) eine **pessimistische Bevölkerungstheorie** begründet, da sich die Bevölkerung in geometrischer Reihe (1, 2, 4, 8, 16, usw.), hingegen der Nahrungsspielraum nur in arithmetischer Reihe (1, 2, 3, 4, 5, usw.) entwickelt. Diese unterschiedlichen Entwicklungsreihen führen zu einer Überbevölkerung und zu einer **Verelendung der Bevölkerung**; es ist eine aus dem biologischen Gesetz der Fortpflanzung abzuleitende unabwendbare Naturnotwendigkeit. Dem Bevölkerungsgesetz liegt auch das Gesetz vom abnehmenden Bodenertrag zu Grunde. Diese pessimistische Theorie wurde durch die Entwicklung im letzten Jahrhundert nicht bestätigt, da der Nahrungsspielraum überproportional wuchs und zugleich der Bevölkerungszuwachs zurückging. Der **Neo-Malthusianismus** geht von der These aus, dass die Welt auf Grund einer absoluten Überbevölkerung einer Katastrophe entgegengehe.
Im Gegensatz hierzu stehen die hochentwickelten Industrieländer vor dem Problem der schrumpfenden und der alternden Bevölkerung. Dieses gilt auch und gerade für Deutschland.

I. Die demographischen Vorausberechnungen bis 2050

Das deutsche demographische Problem besteht darin, dass einerseits die Bevölkerung schrumpft und sie andererseits altert. Die sich hieraus ergebenden sozialen und sozialpolitischen Probleme – Sozialversicherung, Gesundheitswesen, Arbeitsmarkt, Finanzpolitik, Integration der Zuwanderer usw. – belasten nicht nur die gegenwärtige, sondern auch und vor allem die künftigen Generationen. Die in Deutschland lange vernachlässigte Demographie ist in das Zentrum von Politik und Wissenschaft gerückt.

1. Die zu niedrige Geburtenrate

Während des 20. Jahrhunderts wurde die Malthusianische pessimistische Bevölkerungstheorie nicht bestätigt, denn in den meisten Industrieländern ist die Geburtenrate zurückgegangen:[1]

	1990	1991	1992	1993	1994	1995	1996	1997	1998	1999	2000
Europäische Union (15 Staaten)	1,57	1,53	1,51	I,47	1,44	1,42	1,44	1,45	1,45	1,45	1,48
Belgien	1,62	1,66	1,65	1,61	1,56	1,55	1,55	1,55	1,53	1,61	1.66
Dänemark	1,67	1,68	1,76	1,75	1,81	1,80	1,75	1,75	1,72	1,73	1,77
Deutschland	1,45	1,33	1,30	1,28	1,24	1,25	1,32	1,37	1,36	1,36	1,38
Finnland	1,78	1,79	1,85	1,81	1,85	1,81	1,76	1,75	1,70	1,74	1,73
Frankreich	1,78	1,77	1,73	1,65	1,66	1,70	1,72	1,71	1,75	1,79	1,88
Griechenland	1,39	1,38	1,38	1,34	1,35	1,32	1,30	1,31	1,29	1,28	1,29
Irland	2,11	2,08	1,99	1,90	1,85	1,84	1,89	1,92	1,93	1,88	1,89
Italien	1,33	1,31	1,31	1,25	1,21	1,18	1,20	1,22	1,19	1,23	1,24
Luxemburg	1,61	1,60	1,64	1,70	1,72	1,69	1,76	1,71	1,38	1,73	1,80
Niederlande	1,62	1,61	L,59	1,57	1,57	1,53	1,53	1,56	1,63	1,65	1,72
Österreich	1,45	1,49	1,49	1,48	1,44	1,40	1,42	1,37	1,34	1,32	1,34
Portugal	1,57	1,57	1,54	1,52	1,44	1,40	1,43	1,46	1,46	1,49	1,52
Schweden	2,13	2,11	2,09	1,99	1,88	1,73	1,60	1,52	1,50	1,50	1,54
Spanien	136	1,33	1,32	1,27	1,21	1,18	1,17	1,19	1,15	1,20	1,23
Vereinigtes Königreich	1,83	1,81	1,79	1,75	1,74	1,71	1,72	1,72	1,71	1,68	1,64
Island	2,30	2,18	2,21	2,22	2,14	2,08	2,12	2,04	2,05	1,99	2,10
Japan	1,54	1,53	1,50	1,46	1,50	1,42	1,44	1,44	k.A.	1,40	1,41
Norwegen	1,93	L,92	1,88	1,86	1,87	1,87	1,89	1,86	1,81	1,84	1,85
Schweiz	1,59	1,60	1,58	1,51	1,49	1,48	1,50	1,51	1,46	1,48	1,50
USA	2,08	2,07	2,07	2,05	2,04	2,02	2,04	2,06	k.A.	2,05	2,06

Quellen: Eurostat, Datenbank New Cronos; Statistisches Bundesamt 2003

Tab. 1: Zusammengefasste Geburtenziffer in ausgewählten Staaten

In der EU (15 Staaten) ging die Geburtenrate von 1,57 (1990) bis 2000 auf 1,48 Kinder zurück, in Deutschland im gleichen Zeitraum von 1,45 auf 1,38 Kinder (inzwischen liegt sie bei 1,36). Um in Deutschland die Bevölkerung zu stabilisieren, müssten 2,1 Kinder je gebärfähiger Frau geboren werden, die Geburtenrate mit knapp 1,4 Kindern liegt unterhalb der Reproduktionsrate. Bemerkenswert ist, dass sowohl Frankreich (2000: 1,88 Kinder) als auch die USA (2000: 2,06 Kinder) höhere Geburtenraten als Deutschland haben, dagegen liegt Japan mit 1,41 Kindern nahezu auf dem deutschen Niveau.
Die zu **niedrige deutsche Geburtenrate** führt zu einem **Echo-Effekt** (Gräf, Schattenberg 2006, S. 3 f.). Selbst ein rascher Anstieg der Geburtenrate auf das Reproduktionsniveau – was nicht wahrscheinlich ist – kann die seit den 70er Jah-

1 Statistisches Bundesamt 2003, S. 13. Die folgenden statistischen Übersichten sind aus dieser Veröffentlichung des Statistischen Bundesamtes entnommen, die Seitenangabe erfolgt im Text.

ren eingetretene Entwicklung nicht umkehren, sondern bestenfalls auf längere Sicht dämpfen. Auf Grund der nicht-geborenen Kinder sind auch weniger potentielle Mütter vorhanden; in den alten Bundesländern halbierte sich die Zahl der Mütter von 1,04 Mio. im Jahre 1965 auf 577.000 bis 2004. Nach der mittleren Variante sinkt die Anzahl der Frauen im gebärfähigen Alter von 20 Mio. auf gut 14 Mio. im Jahr 2050.

2. Annahmen zur Entwicklung der Lebenserwartung

Auf Grund der Fortschritte im Gesundheitswesen, der Hygiene, der Ernährung, der Wohnsituation, der Arbeitsbedingungen sowie des gestiegenen materiellen Wohlstandes nahm das **Sterblichkeitsniveau** in den letzten hundert Jahren spürbar ab:

Die Säuglings- und Kindersterblichkeit ging bei 1.000 lebendgeborenen Kindern von 200 vor 100 Jahren auf 21 vor 30 Jahren zurück und beträgt heute nur noch 4. Auch die Sterblichkeit älterer Menschen sank erheblich. Noch 1970/72 erlebten nur 39% aller Männer und aller Frauen das 75. Lebensjahr, heute werden jeder zweite Mann und 7 von 10 Frauen 75 Jahre alt.

Die **durchschnittliche Lebenserwartung** zeigt, wie viele Lebensjahre ein neu geborenes Kind zu erwarten hat. Seit Anfang des 20. Jahrhunderts hat sich die Lebenserwartung um rund 30 Jahre erhöht: Ein 1910 geborener Junge hatte im Durchschnitt 47 und ein Mädchen 51 Lebensjahre vor sich, die in den Jahren 1998 bis 2000 geborenen Jungen und Mädchen erwarten dagegen 75 bzw. 81 Lebensjahre.

Ein 60-jähriger Mann kann heute damit rechnen, dass er noch 19 Jahre lebt, eine 60-jährige Frau mit 23 Jahren. Vor hundert Jahren waren es 13 bzw. 14 Jahre. Das durchschnittliche Rentenbezugsalter betrug im früheren Bundesgebiet 1965 knapp 11 Jahre, 2001 aber über 16 Jahre. Der Anstieg der Lebenserwartung der älteren Menschen hat nicht nur erhebliche finanzielle Auswirkungen auf die Altersversorgung, sondern auch auf die wohnungsmäßige Unterbringung.

Ein **internationaler Vergleich** zeigt, dass die Lebenserwartung Unterschiede aufweist (Statistisches Bundesamt 2003, S. 17).

Im Vergleich zur durchschnittlichen Lebenserwartung in den 15 EU-Staaten ist die deutsche niedriger, bei den Jungen 0,5 und bei den Mädchen 0,6 Jahre. Bemerkenswert ist, dass die Lebenserwartung in den USA sogar niedriger als die deutsche ist, dagegen weist Japan eine höhere aus. Hinsichtlich der Entwicklung der Lebenserwartung in Deutschland bis zum Jahr 2050 geht das Statistische Bundesamt von drei Varianten aus: L1 (Lebenserwartung l), L2 und L3, d.h. dass die Steigerung niedrig, mittel oder hoch ist. Bei der mittleren Variante steigt die

Lebenserwartung (bei Geburt) bis 2050 bei den Männern um 6,3 und bei den Frauen um 5,8 Jahre.

	Lebenserwartung eines Neugeborenen, 2001		Abweichungen gegenüber Deutschland	
	Jungen	Mädchen	Jungen	Mädchen
Europäische Union* (15 Staaten)	75,3	81,4	0,5	0,6
Belgien*	74,6	80,8	-0,2	0,0
Dänemark	74,3	79,0	-0,5	-1,8
Deutschland*	74,8	80,8	0,0	0,0
Finnland	74,6	81,5	-0,2	0,7
Frankreich	75,5	83,0	0,7	2,2
Griechenland	75,4	80,7	0,6	-0,1
Irland	73,0	78,5	-1,8	-2,3
Italien	76,7	82,9	1,9	2,1
Luxemburg*	74,9	81,3	0,1	0,5
Niederlande	75,5	80,6	0,9	-0,2
Österreich*	75,4	81,2	0,6	0,4
Portugal	73,5	80,3	-1,3	-0,5
Schweden	77,5	82,1	2,7	1,3
Spanien	75,6	82,9	0,8	2,1
Vereinigtes Königreich	75,7	80,4	0,9	-0,4
Island*	78,0	81,4	3,2	0,6
Norwegen*	76,0	81,4	1,2	0,6
Vereinigte Staaten	74,4	80,0	-0,4	-0,8
Japan	77,6	84,2	2,8	3,4

Quelle: Eurostat, Datenbank New Cronos; Statistisches Bundesamt 2003; (* Stand 2000)

Tab. 2: Lebenserwartung bei Geburt in ausgewählten Staaten

3. Annahmen zum Wanderungsgewinn

Für die künftige demographische Entwicklung sind die Wanderungen über die Grenzen Deutschlands – die **Außenwanderungen** – bedeutsam, da diese nicht nur die Bevölkerungszahl, sondern auch die Altersstruktur beeinflussen. Dabei ist der Wanderungssaldo – die Differenz zwischen den Zu- und Fortzügen – ausschlaggebend. Im Unterschied zur Geburtenhäufigkeit und Lebenserwartung lässt sich der künftige Wanderungssaldo nicht aus der früheren Entwicklung ableiten, denn das Wanderungspotential hängt von der politischen, ökonomischen und der sozialen Lage in den Herkunftsländern sowie der deutschen Migrationpolitik ab.
Das Statistische Bundesamt ist von drei Annahmen ausgegangen (Statistisches Bundesamt 2003, S. 23):

Annahme	Jährlicher Wanderungssaldo		Kumulierter Wanderungsgewinn bis 2050
	Deutsche	Ausländer	
W1	Schrittweiser Abbau von 800,000 bis zum Nullniveau	100,000	5,660,000
W2	im Jahr 2040	200,000	10,400,000
W3		200,000 ab 2011: 300,000	14,460,000

Tab. 3: Annahmen zur künftigen Entwicklung der Außenwanderungen

Bei den Vorausberechnungen der Bevölkerungsentwicklung wird in der Regel von der mittleren Variante ausgegangen, d.h., dass jährlich netto 200.000 Personen (bzw. 14,46 Mio. bis 2050) zuwandern. Für die Geschlechts- und Altersstruktur wird von den empirischen Werten der Jahre 1999 bis 2001 ausgegangen, das bedeutet, dass ein **Verjüngungseffekt** eintritt, da die zuziehenden Personen jünger als die fortziehenden sind.
Die auf dem zu niedrigen Niveau verharrende Geburtenrate (die vielleicht sogar noch weiter sinken wird) und die steigende Lebenserwartung belasten das gesamte Sozialsystem, dagegen ist die Zuwanderung positiv, denn sie führt zu einer Verjüngung der Gesamtbevölkerung. Diesem positiven Effekt steht die bisher nur zum Teil gelungene Integration der Zuwanderer – insbesondere aus fremden Kulturkreisen – als Negativum gegenüber, das vornehmlich die Kommunen und die Wohnungswirtschaft belastet.

4. Die Entwicklung der Bevölkerungszahl

Langfristig war die deutsche Bevölkerungsentwicklung positiv: Seit 1950 nahm die Bevölkerung – trotz der Rückgänge in den 70er und 80er Jahren – um 14 Mio. oder rund 20% auf 82 Mio. zu. Alle Varianten der 10. koordinierten Bevölkerungsvorausberechnung zeigen, dass sich dieser Trend in Zukunft ändert und langfristig in Richtung Schrumpfung der Bevölkerung weist. Lediglich bei sehr hoher Zuwanderung und gleichzeitig sehr hoher Zunahme der Lebenserwartung wird die Bevölkerungszahl 2050 fast so hoch sein wie heute (Statistisches Bundesamt 2003, S. 26).
Eine Bevölkerung schrumpft, wenn die Zahl der Sterbefälle die der Geburtsfälle übersteigt und das Geburtendefizit nicht durch die Zuwanderung kompensiert wird. In Deutschland wurde erstmalig 1972 der Geburtenüberschuss durch einen Sterbeüberschuss abgelöst, da sowohl die Zahl der Geburten als auch die der Zuwanderung von Ausländern auf Grund des Anwerbestopps von Arbeitskräften zurückging.

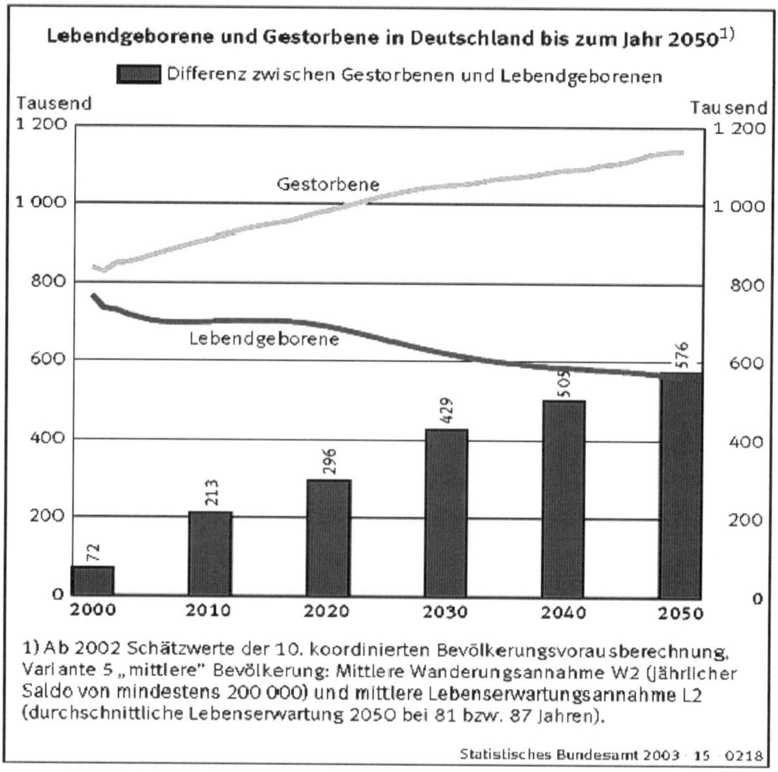

Abb. 1: Lebendgeborene und Gestorbene in Deutschland bis zum Jahr 2050

Die Schere zwischen der Zahl der Neugeborenen und der Gestorbenen wird sich bis 2050 immer stärker öffnen, das **„Geburtendefizit"** wird von 72.000 (2000) bis 2050 auf 576.000 steigen. Bei einer konstanten Geburtenhäufigkeit kann das aktuelle Niveau der Geburten nur dann erhalten werden, wenn jede folgende Müttergeneration zumindest nicht kleiner ist als die vorherige, was bei einer Geburtenhäufigkeit von knapp 1,4 Kindern auf Grund des **Echo-Effekt**es nicht gegeben ist: „Die heutigen etwa 30-jährigen Frauen werden bis zum Ende ihres geburtsfähigen Alters (49 Jahre) weit weniger Kinder zur Welt bringen, als es für den zahlenmäßigen Ersatz ihrer Generation erforderlich wäre (das **Bestandserhaltungsniveau** liegt bei 2,1 Kinder pro Frau). Die jetzt geborenen Mädchenjahrgänge sind also kleiner als die ihrer Mütter. Sind diese Mädchen einmal erwachsen und haben ebenfalls durchschnittlich 1,4 Kinder, wird die Kinderzahl weiter sinken, weil dann auch weniger potentielle Mütter leben." (Statistisches Bundesamt 2003, S. 28)

Es ist realistisch anzunehmen, dass die Geburtenhäufigkeit nicht wesentlich steigen wird, folglich wird die Bevölkerungszahl – gemindert durch die Zuwanderung – bis zum Jahre 2050 zurückgehen (Statistisches Bundesamt 2003, S. 26).

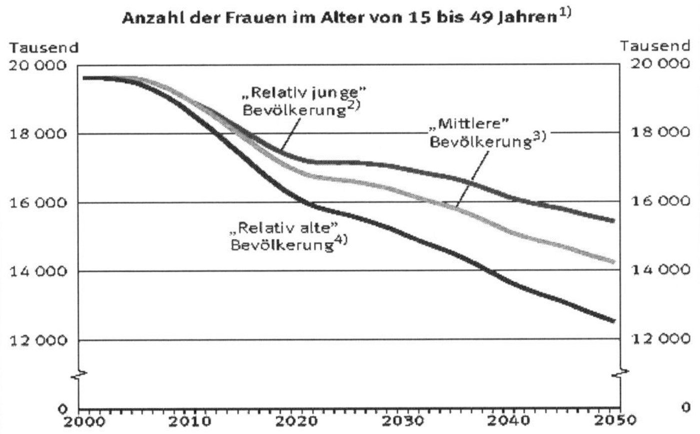

1) Ab 2002 Schätzwerte der 10. koordinierten Bevölkerungsvorausberechnung. - 2) Variante 3: Hohe Wanderungsannahme W1 (jährlicher Saldo von mindestens 300 000) und niedrige Lebenserwartungsannahme L1 (durchschnittliche Lebenserwartung 2050 bei 79 bzw. 86 Jahren). - 3) Variante 5: Mittlere Wanderungsannahme W2 (jährlicher Saldo von mindestens 200 000) und mittlere Lebenserwartungsannahme L2 (durchschnittliche Lebenserwartung 2050 bei 81 bzw. 87 Jahren). - 4) Variante 7: Niedrige Wanderungsannahme W1 (jährlicher Saldo von mindestens 100 000) und hohe Lebenserwartungsannahme L1 (durchschnittliche Lebenserwartung 2050 bei 83 bzw. 88 Jahren).

Statistisches Bundesamt 2003 15 0219

Abb. 2: Anzahl der Frauen im Alter von 15 bis 49 Jahren

Für die Entwicklung der **Bevölkerungszahl bis 2050** hat das Statistische Bundesamt **mehrere Varianten** errechnet:

- Die **höchste Variante** liegt dann vor, wenn eine hohe Zuwanderung und zugleich eine hohe Lebenserwartung angenommen werden (Variante 9). Unter diesen Annahmen dürfte sich die Bevölkerungsanzahl gegenüber dem Ist-Zustand nur geringfügig verändern.
- Bei der **höheren Variante** (Variante 6) dürfte sich die Bevölkerungszahl auf 80 Mio. belaufen.
- Die **mittlere Variante** (Variante 5) ergibt für 2050 noch 75 Mio. Einwohner.
- Bei niedrigerer Zuwanderung (Variante 4) sinkt die Bevölkerung auf 68,5 Mio. Einwohner.
- Die **niedrigste Variante**: „Bei einem ausgeglichenen Wanderungssaldo und einer im Vergleich zu heute unveränderten Lebenserwartung werden 2050 etwa 45 Mio. leben." (Statistisches Bundesamt 2003, S. 28)

Die Entwicklung der Bevölkerungszahl hängt von zwei Faktoren ab: Einmal von der Geburtenhäufigkeit und zum anderen von der Zuwanderung. Da die **Zahl der Geburten** relativ konstant ist und kaum damit gerechnet werden kann, dass kurzfristig ein „Babyboom" ausbricht, kommt der **Netto-Zuwanderung** eine besondere Bedeutung zu, d.h. je mehr Einwanderer aufgenommen werden, desto größer ist die Chance, die Gesamtbevölkerung sowie den Altersaufbau zu beeinflussen. Diesem positiven Effekt stehen die Integrationsprobleme als Negativen gegenüber. Auf Grund der bisherigen Erfahrungen wird man wahrscheinlich eine relativ restriktive Zuwanderungspolitik verfolgen, so dass bis 2050 die Bevölkerung zurückgehen wird. Es dürfte realistisch sein, die **mittlere Variante** anzunehmen, d.h. dass 2050 etwa 75 Mio. Einwohner in Deutschland leben werden. Andere Schätzungen gehen davon aus, dass die Bevölkerungszahl zwischen 70 und 75 Mio. liegen wird, dieses dürften realistische Vorausberechnungen sein.

5. Der Altersaufbau der Bevölkerung[2]

Der derzeitige Altersaufbau hat sowohl einen großen Einfluss auf die künftige Bevölkerungszahl als auch die Alterung (Statistisches Bundesamt 2003, S. 31). Auf Grund der zu niedrigen Geburtenrate nimmt der Anteil der Kinder bzw. Jugendlichen bis 20 Jahren von 30,4% (1950) über 20,9% (2001) bis zum Jahr 2050 auf nur noch 16,1% ab. Die Gruppe der 20- bis 59-jährigen – die aktive Bevölkerung – geht von 55% (1950 bzw. 2001) bis 2050 auf 47,2% relativ moderat zurück. Bemerkenswert ist der **prozentuale Anstieg der 60 Jahre und älteren Einwohner**, insbesondere der über 80 Jahre. Der Anteil der 60 Jahre und älteren Einwohner steigt von 14,6% (1950) innerhalb von 100 Jahren auf 36,7% und der 80-jährigen im gleichen Zeitraum von 1,0% auf 12,1%. Die zunehmende Lebenserwartung führt dazu, dass die Zahl der 80-jährigen und älteren von gegenwärtig 3,2 Mio. Personen bis 2050 auf 9,1 Mio. (Variante 5) ansteigen wird; wenn die Lebenserwartung noch stärker ansteigen sollte (Variante 8), dann erhöht sich diese auf 9,9 Mio. Personen oder 13%.
Diese **Verschiebungen im Altersaufbau** belasten nicht nur das gesamte Sozialsystem – Renten- und Krankenleistungen –, sondern auch die wohnungsmäßige Versorgung der Alten und deren physische sowie psychische Betreuung. Die Betreuung der alten Menschen wird zu einer zentralen Zukunftsaufgabe der Wohnungswirtschaft.
Auf Grund des Alterungsprozesses verschiebt sich das **mittlere Alter**: 2001 lag es bei 40,6 Jahre, 2050 werden dagegen 50% der Bevölkerung älter als 48 sein.

2 Vgl. Schimany 2003, S. 237 ff.

	Insgesamt am Jahresende	Davon im Alter von ... bis ... Jahren			
		Unter 20	20 – 59	60 und älter	
				insgesamt	80 und älter
	Millionen	in%			
1950	69,3	30,4	55,0	14,6	1,0
1970	78,1	30,0	50,1	19,1	2,0
1990	79,8	21,7	57,9	20,4	3,8
2001	82,4	20,9	55,0	24,1	3,9
2010	83,1	18,7	55,7	25,6	5,0
2030	81,2	17,1	48,5	34,4	7,3
2050	75,1	16,1	47,2	36,7	12,0

Tab. 4: Altersaufbau der Bevölkerung Deutschlands[3]

6. Der Altenquotient

Als Altenquotient wird das Verhältnis der Bevölkerung im Rentenalter (Gruppe der potentiellen Empfänger von Leistungen der Rentenversicherung) zur Bevölkerung im Erwerbsalter definiert. Das gegenwärtige durchschnittliche Rentenzugangsalter beträgt 60 Jahre, das Erwerbsalter mit 20 bis 59 Jahren abgegrenzt, d.h., der Altenquotient gibt die Relation der Rentnergruppe zu der Erwerbsgruppe an.

Der Altenquotient hat sich in den letzten Jahren erhöht: 1995 betrug er 37, d.h. 100 Personen im Erwerbsalter (20-59 Lebensjahre) standen 37 im Rentenalter gegenüber; 1999 betrug er 41 und 2001 44. Bis zum Jahr 2030 wird der Altenquotient (Variante 5) auf 71 und bis 2050 auf 76 steigen.

Wenn das **Renteneintrittsalter** von gegenwärtig 60 auf 65 Jahre erhöht wird, dann sinkt der Altenquotient von 27,5 (2001) auf 47,3 im Jahr 2030 und auf 54,5 im Jahr 2050 (bei 60 Jahren 77,8). Die gegenwärtige Diskussion über die schrittweise Erhöhung des Renteneintrittsalters auf 67 Jahre würde dazu führen, dass der Altenquotient 2050 auf 47,4 sinkt. Die Erhöhung des Renteneintrittsalters hat einen deutlich größeren Effekt als unterschiedliche Annahmen zur Lebenserwartung und zur Zuwanderung. Das bedeutet, dass die Zuwanderung die Alterung der Gesamtbevölkerung für einige Jahre dämpft, sie stellt aber keine langfristige Lösung dar.

Die gegenwärtige und insbesondere die künftige Erwerbsgeneration wird als die **Sandwich-Generation** bezeichnet: Sie ist „eingeklemmt" zwischen der Versorgung der Alten und der eigenen Altersversorgung, da auf Grund des Echo-Effektes zu wenig Kinder geboren werden. Die Zuwanderung kann nur temporär die Bevölkerung verjüngen und die Sandwich-Generation entlasten. Im Übrigen

3 Ab dem Jahr 2010 Schätzwerte der 10. koordinierten Bevölkerungsvorausberechnung (Variante 5 „mittlere" Bevölkerung): Mittlere Wanderungsannahme W2 (jährlicher Saldo 200.000 Personen) und mittlere Lebenserwartungsannahme L2 (durchschnittliche Lebenserwartung 2050 bei 81 bzw. 87 Jahren).

führen die bisherigen Erfahrungen zu der Vermutung, dass die zweite Generation der Zuwanderer eine geringere Kinderzahl haben wird als in ihren Ursprungsländern, so dass kein dauerhafter Effekt eintritt.

7. Der Altersaufbau der Bevölkerung von 1910 bis 2050

Das Statistische Bundesamt hat die Bevölkerungsentwicklung durch die Bevölkerungspyramiden dargestellt, die die dramatischen Veränderungen bis zum Jahr 2050 optisch verdeutlich (Statistisches Bundesamt 2003, S. 30).

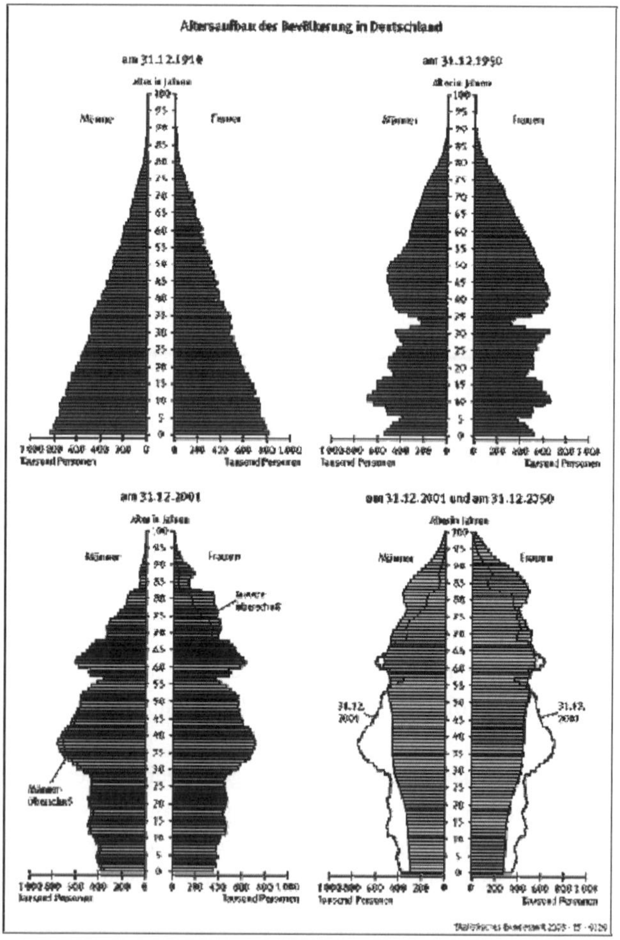

Abb. 3: Altersaufbau der Bevölkerung in Deutschland

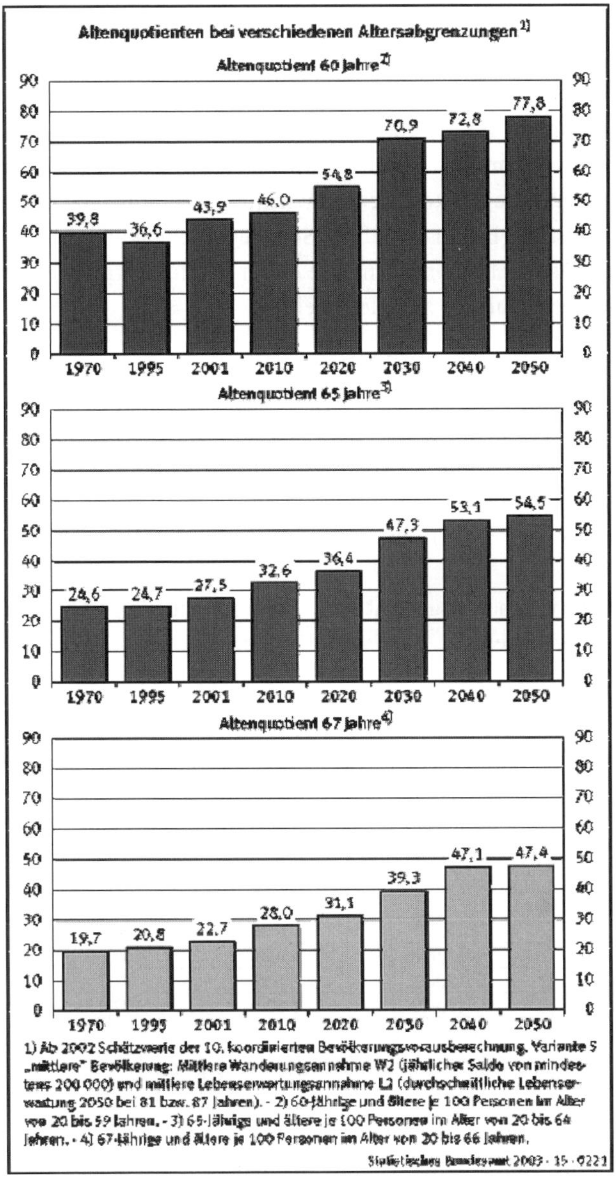

Abb. 4: Altenquotienten bei verschiedenen Altersabgrenzungen

II. Die demographischen Auswirkungen auf die Städte und die Wohnungswirtschaft

In der Wissenschaft, in der Politik und nicht zuletzt in der Öffentlichkeit werden die demographischen Auswirkungen auf das gesamte Sozialsystem lebhaft und kontrovers diskutiert. Im Vordergrund der Diskussionen stehen das Renten- und das Gesundheitssystem, das Renteneintrittsalter usw., die das Steuersystem, die Subventionen und die Einkommensentwicklung beeinflussen. Dagegen werden die demographischen Einflüsse auf die Stadtentwicklung und die Wohnungswirtschaft vernachlässigt. Bei einer Analyse dieser Einflussfaktoren ist zwischen den beiden Teilen Deutschlands zu unterscheiden.

1. Wohnungswirtschaftliche Daten

Das Bundesministerium für Verkehr, Bau- und Wohnungswesen hat 2005 in der Broschüre „Wohnen und Bauen Zahlen" (Bundesministerium für Verkehr, Bau- und Wohnungswesen 2005) umfassende wohnungswirtschaftliche Daten veröffentlicht.
Der Wohnungsbestand insgesamt und die individuelle Wohnraumversorgung sind seit 1990 gestiegen.

Jahr	Wohnungen		Wohnfläche (qm)	
	insgesamt	Je 1,000 Einwohner	Je WE	Je Einwohner
1) Deutschland				
1990	33,856,321	425	81,9	34,8
1995	35,954,317	439	83,6	36,7
2000	38,383,645	467	84,6	39,5
2004	39,362,909	477	85,6	40,8
2) Darunter neue Länder:				
1990	7,016,977	438	64,4	28,2
1995	7,055,908	456	69,7	31,8
2000	7,652,868	506	71,2	36,0
2004	7,710,942	524	72,4	37,9

Tab. 5: Wohnungsbestand und individuelle Versorgung

In Gesamtdeutschland ist seit 1990 nicht nur der Wohnungsbestand gewachsen, sondern auch die individuelle Wohnraumversorgung hat sich – allerdings unterschiedlich in beiden Teilen Deutschlands – verbessert:
In Westdeutschland hat die **Zahl der Wohnungseinheiten** von 1990 bis 2004 nur um 52 Einheiten je 1.000 Einwohner, in den neuen Bundesländern hingegen um 86 Einheiten zugenommen. Diese unterschiedliche Entwicklung ist zum Teil auf die Neubautätigkeit, im Wesentlichen auf die Abwanderung der Bevölkerung

aus den neuen Bundesländern zurückzuführen. Auch die **Fläche je Wohnung** hat sich unterschiedlich entwickelt: In Westdeutschland nahm die Wohnungsgröße 1990 bis 2004 lediglich um 3,7 qm ab, in Ostdeutschland aber um 8,0 qm zu. Es liegt eine Nachholprozess vor, da in der ehemaligen DDR die Fläche der neu gebauten Wohnungen nur rund 60 qm betrug.
Im ersten **Armuts- und Reichtumsbericht** hat das Bundesministerium für Arbeit und Sozialordnung festgestellt:[4] „Die Wohnungsversorgung in Deutschland hat sich in den letzten Jahrzehnten stetig verbessert und nach der Überwindung der zwischenzeitlichen Wohnungsmarktengpässe in den Jahren 1989 bis 1993 einen Stand erreicht, bei dem breite Schichten der **Bevölkerung gut bis sehr gut mit Wohnraum versorgt** sind".
Mit Beginn der Industrialisierung und Verstädterung – etwa ab 1850 bzw. ab 1870/71 – entstand die Wohnungsfrage als quantitatives und qualitatives Problem, das insbesondere nach dem Ersten und dem Zweiten Weltkrieg intensive rechtliche Interventionen und staatliche Förderungen erforderte. Nach 150 bzw. 125 Jahren kann die Wohnungsnotlage im Jahr 2000 als gelöst angesehen werden. Der Wohnungsmangel wurde durch den **strukturellen Wohnungsleerstand** abgelöst, der zuerst in den neuen Bundesländern auftrat und sich zunehmend auch in Westdeutschland abzeichnet. Dieses hat zum Stadtumbau Ost geführt.

2. Die Fehleinschätzung des ostdeutschen Wohnungsmarktes

Nach der Wiedervereinigung gingen die Politiker und die meisten Fachleute davon aus, dass in den neuen Bundesländern ein Wohnungsdefizit bestehe. Der **„Lehmann-Grube-Bericht"** (Pfeifer u.a. 2000, S. 89) stellte feste: „Am Wohnungsmarkt in Ostdeutschland müssen noch über lange Zeit Anpassungen bewältigt werden, bis eine befriedigende Versorgung und ein Ausgleich von Angebot und Nachfrage erreicht wird. Nach der Vereinigung **herrschte schwerer Wohnungsmangel**, die Nachfrage überstieg das Angebot deutlich. Es gab zu wenig bewohnbare Wohnungen. ... Große Teile des Althausbestandes standen leer (in 1990 standen 420.000 Wohnungen leer, überwiegend Altbauten) und waren verfallen oder wiesen erhebliche Mängel auf."[5] Unausgesprochen ging man davon aus, dass die Plattenbauten langfristig nicht bewohnbar sein würden.
Auf Grund dieser Bewertung des ostdeutschen Wohnungsmarktes hat die Politik mit einer **breiten Platte von Fördermaßnahmen** reagiert: Die Stadtsanierung stand an erster Stelle, dann die Förderung des sozialen Wohnungsbaus sowie die

4 Bundesministerium für Arbeit und Sozialordnung, Lebenslagen in Deutschland – Der erste Armuts- und Reichtumsbericht der Bundesregierung, Berichts-Band, o.O., o.J. (Bonn, wahrscheinlich 2001), S. 159.
5 Pfeifer u.a. 2000, S. 10.

Programme zur Eigentumsbildung, der Bund und die Länder förderten verschiedene Programme der Modernisierung des Wohnungsbestandes. Von besonderer Wirkung war das **Fördergebietsgesetz** vom 24. Juni 1991(mehrfach geändert), das neben den regulären Abschreibungen von 2% p.a. Sonderabschreibungen von 50% in fünf Jahren zuließ, d.h. 60% in fünf Jahren. „Die Märkte haben der Politik mit einem Investitionsboom geantwortet, der deutlich ausgeprägter war als der große Wohnungsbauboom zu Anfang der siebziger Jahre in Westdeutschland" (Pfeifer u.a. 2000, S. 11). Dieser steuerinduzierte Wohnungsbauboom hat maßgeblich zu den Leerständen und damit verbundenen Problemen beigetragen. Allerdings ist bereits Mitte der 90er auf die Gefahr der Leerstände und die Notwendigkeit des Abrisses - euphemistisch „Rückbau" genannt – hingewiesen worden. Unter der Leitung von Prof. Dr. Lothar Hübl (Universitäten Hannover) wurde im Auftrag der Deutschen Siedlungs- und Landesrentenbank das Gutachten „Zwischen Sanierung und Abriss" Mitte 1996 erstellt (Deutsche Siedlungs- und Landesrentenbank 1995). Im Resümee heißt es: „Den Unternehmen der Wohnungswirtschaft ist zu **empfehlen**, bereits heute (1995/56) ein langfristiges Konzept zu entwickeln, welches die zu erwartenden Überhänge berücksichtigt. Bei den für den Rückbau ausgewählten Beständen sollte nicht mehr saniert oder modernisiert werden, sondern es sind nur noch die unmittelbar notwendigen Instandhaltungsmaßnahmen durchzuführen. ... Bei der künftigen Vergabe von Bundes- und Landesmitteln an die Wohnungsunternehmen sollte ein **langfristiges Rückbau- und Erhaltungskonzept** verlangt werden, um zu verhindern, dass in nächster Zukunft öffentliche Mittel in demnächst leerstehende Bestände investiert werden." (Deutsche Siedlungs- und Landesrentenbank 1995, S. 99)
Diese konkreten Empfehlungen Mitte der 90er Jahre wurden weder von der Wohnungswirtschaft noch von der Politik beachtet. Das hatte zur Folge, dass öffentliche Mittel zur Sanierung und Modernisierung des maroden DDR-Wohnungsbestandes eingesetzt wurden, die wenige Jahre später wegen des Leerstandes unter erneutem Einsatz von öffentlichen Geldern abgerissen werden mussten.

3. Die innerdeutschen Wanderungen

Der zweite und entscheidende Grund für die Wohnungsleerstände sind die innerdeutschen Wanderungen, wobei zwischen der Stadt-Umland-Wanderung und der Ost-West-Wanderung zu unterscheiden ist.
Die **Stadt-Umland-Wanderung** hat es in Westdeutschland seit den 50er Jahren gegeben. Diese Wanderung setzte ein, als die Einkommensverhältnisse und das Bausparen es zuließen, die Mietwohnungen gegen das Eigenheim einzutauschen. Preiswerte Eigenheimgrundstück waren vornehmlich im Umland der Großstädte

zu finden. Die Wohnwünsche führten zur Stadt-Umland-Wanderung. Dieses wird an den beiden Stadtstaaten Hamburg und Bremen besonders deutlich und gilt nicht für Berlin; das Umland wird als „Speckgürtel“ bezeichnet. Ähnliche Tendenzen waren in der ehemaligen DDR nur begrenzt vorhanden, da es keine systematische Eigenheimförderung gab. Allerdings wurden an den Stadträndern große Wohnkomplexe als Plattenbauten errichtet, die jetzt teilweise abgerissen werden müssen.

Gravierender war und ist die **Ost-West-Binnenwanderung**, die mit der Wiedervereinigung einsetzte und die maßgebliche städtebauliche und wohnungswirtschaftliche Probleme verursacht:

Der Mauerbau erfolgte am 13. August 1961, weil Hunderttausende die DDR verließen und in die Bundesrepublik flüchteten. Die DDR stand vor dem Ausbluten und vor dem ökonomischen Kollaps. Mit dem Mauerfall am 9. November 1989 wurde das Tor zum Westen geöffnet und es setzte wiederum eine **Ost-West-Wanderung** ein. Von der Maueröffnung bis zum 15. Januar 1990 wurden bereits 42.500, bis zum 11. Februar 1990 74.421 Übersiedler registriert. Da es die „Wilde Zeit“ der Flucht aus der noch bestehenden DDR war, gibt es keine exakten Zahlen; die Zahl der Übersiedler wird bis Ende 1991 auf rund 200.000 geschätzt. Die Wanderungen von Ost- nach Westdeutschland (und umgekehrt) wurden ab 1991 erfasst, so dass hierüber genaue Daten vorliegen (Grobecker u.a. 2005, S. 1261 ff.).

Zeitraum	Zuzüge aus früheren Bundesgebieten			Fortzüge in das frühere Bundesgebiet			Wanderungssaldo		
	In den neun Länder	nach Berlin	zusammen	aus den neuen Ländern	aus Berlin	zusammen	Für die neuen Länder	Für Berlin	zusammen
Insgesamt									
1991 bis 1999*	807714	256470	1064184	1343059	236776	1579835	-535345	+19694	-515651
2000	92216	43301	135517	168167	36116	204283	-75951	+7185	-68766
2001	94414	44334	138615	191979	38223	230202	-97565	+6111	-91454
2002	95876	43536	139412	176703	39465	220239	-80827	-4071	-84898
2003	97035	40482	137517	155387	39829	195216	-58352	+653	-57699
2004	94677	38672	133349	146352	39526	185878	-51675	-854	-52529
1991 bis 2004	1281932	466795	1748594	2181647	429935	2615653	-899715	+28718	-870997
Männlich									
1991 bis 1999*	471118	153097	624215	664357	126650	791007	-193239	+26447	-166792
2000	48098	22927	71025	84010	18841	102851	-35912	+4086	-31826
2001	49050	23061	72111	96095	19714	115809	-47045	+3347	-43698
2002	49878	22772	70230	87921	20352	110693	-38043	-2420	-40463
2003	50786	21128	71914	76814	20540	97354	-26028	+588	-25440
2004	49661	20048	69709	73104	20408	93512	-23443	-360	-23803
1991 bis 2004	718591	263033	979204	1082301	226505	1311226	-363710	+31688	-332022

Weiblich									
1991 bis 1999*	336596	103373	439969	678702	110126	788828	-342106	-6753	-348859
2000	44118	20374	64492	84157	17275	101432	-40039	+3099	-36940
2001	45364	21273	66637	95884	18509	114393	-50520	+2764	-47756
2002	45998	20764	65111	88782	19113	109546	-42784	-1651	-44435
2003	46249	19354	65603	78573	19289	97862	-32224	+65	-32259
2004	45016	18624	63640	73248	19118	92366	-28232	-494	-28726
1991 bis 2004	563341	203762	765452	1099346	203430	1304427	-536005	-2970	-538975

Quelle: Grobecker u.a. 2005, S. 1264
* Einschl. der Wanderungen von und nach Berlin-Ost

Tab. 6: Wanderungen zwischen dem früheren Bundesgebiet (ohne Berlin-West) und den neuen Ländern

Von 1991 bis Ende 2004 sind 870.000 aus den neuen Bundesländern abgewandert, unter Berücksichtigung der „wilden Übersiedler" vom 9. November 1989 bis Ende 1991 dürfte es sich um rund 1 Mio. handeln. Es ist nicht nur Quantität, sondern auch und vor allem die Altersstruktur, d.h. die Qualität der innerdeutschen Wanderungen, von Bedeutung: Von den 146.400 Personen, die im Jahr 2004 die neuen Länder verließen, waren 54% zwischen 18 und 30 Jahre alt, 24% zwischen 30 und 50, 14% jünger als 18 und nur 8% älter als 50 Jahre. Der Anteil der 18- bis 30-jährigen ist in den letzten Jahren kontinuierlich angestiegen, dagegen ist der Anteil der Jugendlichen unter 18 Jahren zurückgegangen.
Die Zusammensetzung der **West-Ost-Wanderer** weicht von dem der Ost-West-Wanderer ab: 2004 migrierten 94.700 Personen vom Westen in den Osten, davon nur 43% zwischen 18 und 30 Jahre, aber 27% zwischen 30 und 50 und jeweils 18% unter 18 bzw. älter als 50. Nach Westdeutschland sind insbesondere junge Erwachsene gezogen, die entweder bereits eine gute Ausbildung hatten bzw. sich in der Ausbildung befanden, es ist die aktive Bevölkerung; dagegen gingen 27% der 30- bis 50-jährigen in die neuen Bundesländer. Man kann vermuten, dass es sich hierbei um qualifizierte Arbeitskräfte wie Manager, Techniker, Ärzte usw. handelte. Das Statistische Bundesamt stellt fest: „Darüber hinaus haben sich die Wanderungen in beiden Richtungen immer mehr auf die Gruppe der **jungen Erwachsenen** konzentriert, auch wenn dies in der West-Ost-Richtung weniger ausgeprägt ist." (Grobecker u.a. 2005, S. 1264).
Diese **differenzierten Wanderungsströme** haben zur Folge, dass die neuen Bundesländer nicht nur quantitativ sondern auch qualitativ „ausbluten", d.h., sie verlieren mittelfristig nicht nur die künftigen Väter und Mütter sondern auch kurzfristig ihr produktives Humankapital. Diese Tendenz führt zu einer Überalterung und zum Bevölkerungsschwund in den neuen Ländern, davon profitieren vornehmlich die strukturstarken Länder wie Baden-Württemberg und Bayern, aber auch Industriekerne wie Frankfurt-Mainz-Wiesbaden oder Köln-Düsseldorf

und Hamburg. Da nach der Wende die Geburtenrate in den neuen Ländern auf durchschnittlich 0,77 Kinder pro Frau zurückgegangen war, ist eine halbe Generation an Eltern ausgefallen; folglich werden spätestens 2015 die neuen Länder einen zweiten „demographischen Wendeschock" erleben.

4. Die demographischen Auswirkungen auf die Wohnungswirtschaft und die Stadtstrukturen in Ost und West

Die Auswirkungen der alternden und schrumpfenden Gesellschaft fallen geographisch unterschiedlich aus und betreffen zum einen die Wohnungswirtschaft und zum anderen die Stadtstrukturen. Da sich die demographischen Veränderungen insbesondere in den neuen Ländern vollziehen, soll in erster Linie hierauf eingegangen werden.[6]

a) Der Abriss leerstehender Wohnungen in Ostdeutschland

Wenn man die Entwicklung der Stadtstrukturen und die Beseitigung der Wohnungsleerstände dem Markt überlassen würde, dann wären staatliche Eingriffe – insbesondere der Einsatz öffentlicher Mittel – unzulässig. Dieses hätte aber zur Folge, dass der Anpassungsprozess sich nicht nur über Jahre und möglicherweise über Jahrzehnte hinzieht, sondern auch zu (negativen) **externen Effekten** führen würde, d.h., dass Slums entstehen und sich soziale Gettos bilden, die erhebliche gesellschaftliche Kosten – es sei nur auf die Jugendkriminalität verwiesen – verursachen. Bei einer Güterabwägung zwischen den externen (gesellschaftlichen) Kosten und dem Einsatz von Subventionsmitteln zur Beseitigung oder zumindest der Reduzierung dauerhaft leerstehender Wohnungen hat sich die Politik für eine partielle **finanzielle Unterstützung der Abrisse** entschieden, der euphemistisch Rückbau genannt wird. Zugleich benutzt man diese Chance, um den **Stadtumbau** – die qualitative Verbesserung der Stadtstrukturen – zu fördern. Aus den genannten demographischen Gründen vollziehen sich diese Prozesse in erster Linie in Ostdeutschland, es gibt aber Anzeichen, dass diese Instrumente in absehbarer Zeit auch in Westdeutschland eingesetzt werden müssen; die neuen Länder können als „Labor" für Gesamtdeutschland angesehen werden.

Im Lehmann-Grube-Bericht (S. 69 ff.) wurde darauf hingewiesen, dass sich ein Nebeneinander von Stadtbrache (Leerstand) und noch bewohnten Gebäuden ergibt, die zu einem „Umkippen" des sozialen Milieus und des Wohnumfeldes führen kann, das einen Verfall der Mieten verursacht. Um dieser Entwicklung ent-

6 Einen umfassenden Einblick in die unterschiedliche Struktur der einzelnen deutschen Regionen vermittelt Stefan Kröhnert u.a. 2006.

gegenzuwirken, sind Abrisse als Voraussetzung für eine städtebauliche Aufwertung durch den Stadtumbau unerlässlich. Die Lehmann-Grube-Kommission empfiehlt (S. 71 ff.): „Die Politik muss für ein **Abrissprogramm sofort Finanzmittel mobilisieren**, um Wohnungsabrisse auf Vorrat zu bewältigen und einen großen Pool von Recyclingflächen zu schaffen." Möglichst schnell sollten jährlich 30.000 bis 40.000 WE abgerissen werden, die Förderung sollte höchstens 140 DM je qm Wohnfläche betragen, die Kosten seien auf den Bund, die Länder und die Gemeinden zu verteilen.

Die Lehmann-Grube-Kommission ging 1999 von einem Leerstand von 1 Mio. Wohnungen aus, bis Herbst 2003 hatte er sich auf 1,3 Mio. WE erhöht. In dem am 15. August 2001 für die neuen Länder beschlossenen und am 1. Januar 2002 in Kraft getretenen **Programm „Stadtumbau Ost"** wurden 2,6 Mrd. Euro durch den Bund und die Länder bereitgestellt; mit diesem Betrag sollen bis 2009 rund 350.000 WE zurückgebaut (abgerissen) werden. Auf Grund der Altschuldenhilfeverordnung vom 15. Dezember 2000 können Wohnungsunternehmen, deren Wohnungsleerstand mindestens 15% beträgt, eine Entlastung nach dem Altschuldenhilfe-Gesetz erhalten (Gdw 2005, S. 143 ff.).

„**Ziel des Programms** ist, die Attraktivität der Städte und Gemeinden durch eine Stärkung insbesondere der Innenstädte, die **Reduzierung des Wohnungsleerstandes** und die **Aufwertung** der von der Schrumpfung betroffenen Stadtquartiere zu erhöhen." (Gdw 2005, S. 145)

Das Programm Stadtumbau Ost verfolgt ein doppeltes Ziel: Einmal soll der Wohnungsleerstand reduziert und zum anderen sollen die von der Abwanderung betroffenen Stadtquartiere aufgewertet werden. Diese staatlich beeinflusste und teilfinanzierte Anpassung des Wohnungsangebotes an den Bedarf ist nicht nur eine wohnungswirtschaftliche, sondern auch eine die Stadtstrukturen verändernde und damit eine gesamtgesellschaftliche Aufgabe, die nicht ausschließlich marktwirtschaftlich gelöst werden kann.

Auf Grund des Stadtumbauprogramms Ost konnte bis Ende 2004 bei den Kommunalen Wohnungsunternehmen und Wohnungsgenossenschaften der Leerstand von 16% auf 14,9% gesenkt werden; ohne die geförderten Abrisse wäre bis 2004 die Leerstandsquote auf 18,2% gestiegen. Von den bis 2009 geplanten 350.000 Abrissen wurden 87.000 kommunale und genossenschaftliche WE aus dem Markt genommen, für 2005 waren weitere 46.000 Rückbauten geplant. Trotz dieser Ergebnisse hat sich die Lage auf dem ostdeutschen Wohnungsmarkt nicht entspannt, denn es stehen über 1 Mio. WE leer. Wenn die Abwanderung nach dem Westen anhält, wird sich trotz der Rückbauten der Leerstand kaum reduzieren, vielleicht sogar leicht erhöhen.

Der Wohnungsleerstand als Folge der demographischen Veränderungen betrifft in erster Linie die neuen Bundesländer, er zeichnet sich aber auch in West-

Deutschland ab: Innerhalb der unternehmerischen Wohnungswirtschaft belief sich der Leerstand Ende 2004 in Ostdeutschland auf 363.551 WE, in West-Deutschland auf 115.505 WE, mit jeweils regionalen Unterschieden.
Beispiel für die **demographische Abwärtsentwicklung** ist das Saarland (Kröhnert et al. 2006, S. 15): In den 70er Jahren sind viele junge Menschen abgewandert, daher ist heute die Bevölkerung durchschnittlich gealtert, außerdem weist es die niedrigste Geburtenrate der westdeutschen Flächenländer auf. „Das Saarland macht damit vor, was auf ganz Deutschland zukommt: Ein sich stetig beschleunigender Bevölkerungsrückgang durch hohe Sterbefallüberschüsse.“ Das eigentliche **Krisenzentrum im Westen ist aber das Ruhrgebiet**: Der „Kohlenpott“ leidet unter seiner einseitigen Wirtschaftsstruktur, die Kohlesubventionen haben den Aufbau konkurrenzfähiger Industrien gehemmt oder verhindert. In den Städten bleiben häufig die sozial Schwachen zurück, vor allem Rentner, Arbeitslose und Zuwanderer.
Diese demographische Struktur beeinflusst nicht nur die Wirtschaftskraft und das Sozialsystem, sondern auch die Wohnungswirtschaft und die Städte. Aus diesem Grunde initiierte die Bundesregierung 2002 das **Forschungsprojekt „Stadtumbau West“**. Im Jahr 2005 hat die Bundesregierung die Pilotprojekte des Forschungsfeldes „Stadtumbau West“ in ein neues, dauerhaftes Programm übergeleitet, wofür vorerst 40 Mio. Euro bereitgestellt wurden. Spätestens ab 2010 ist das Stadtumbauprogramm Ost und das des Westens zu **einem Programm für Gesamtdeutschland** zusammenzuführen und die hierfür erforderlichen Mittel sind aufzustocken.
Der demographisch bedingte Wohnungsleerstand führt zu einer **neuen Stadtpolitik:** Nicht mehr – wie in den letzten hundert Jahren – die Stadterweiterung, sondern die Stadtschrumpfung – der **Stadtrückbau** – wird die Aufgabe der kommenden Jahrzehnte sein.

b) Der Stadtrückbau

Die alternde und schrumpfende Gesellschaft führt über den Wohnungsleerstand und deren Abriss zum Stadtrückbau: Geistig müssen die Politiker und die Stadtväter von der Idee des kontinuierlichen Bevölkerungs- und Wirtschaftswachstums sowie der Stadterweiterung Abschied nehmen. An die Stelle des Städtewachstums muss der Stadtrückbau treten, der einmal die technische und zum anderen die soziale Infrastruktur betrifft.
Voraussetzung für einen erfolgreichen Stadtrückbau ist, dass – von Ausnahmen abgesehen – die aus dem Bevölkerungsrückgang sich ergebenden Sachzwänge nicht nur diskutiert, sondern in reale Politik umgesetzt werden. Wenn zum Beispiel von 1991 bis 2004 die Bevölkerung in Görlitz um 24%, in Halle um 23%,

in Chemnitz um 21%, in Zwickau um 20% und in Leipzig um 11% zurückgegangen und dieser Schrumpfungsprozess noch nicht zum Stillstand gekommen ist,[7] dann ist das gesamte Förder- und Stadtentwicklungssystem zu überprüfen. Diese **Umsteuerung** ist aber deshalb problematisch, weil zum Beispiel Investitionsmittel von der EU, dem Bund und vom Land in Aussicht gestellt werden, die nur durch einen geringen städtischen Anteil ergänzt werden müssen. Da man diese „Geschenke" nicht verfallen lassen will, wird in die technische oder soziale Infrastruktur investiert, die bei reduzierter Bevölkerung in absehbarer Zeit nicht mehr benötigt wird. Hinzu kommt, dass in der Kameralistik nur die Investitions- nicht aber die Folgekosten berechnet werden.[8] Beispiel hierfür sind die Spaß- oder Wellenbäder: Die Baukosten werden von Dritten subventioniert, die sachlichen und persönlichen Unterhaltungskosten muss für die gesamte Nutzungsdauer die Kommune tragen. Bei sinkender Bevölkerungszahl und Realeinkommen nimmt die Benutzerzahl ab und steigt der kommunale Subventionsbedarf. An die Stelle der kurzfristigen fiskalischen Betrachtungsweise sollte die langfristige kaufmännische Kalkulation treten.

Der Wohnungsabriss – durch spektakuläre Sprengungen oder durch die Abrissbirne – steht im Bewusstsein der Öffentlichkeit. Dabei wird übersehen, dass der **Städterückbau** sowohl die unterirdische als auch die oberirdische Infrastruktur verändert.

Es gilt die **Faustregel**, dass etwa 60% der gesamten städtebaulichen Investitionen zum Teil unterirdisch und zum Teil oberirdisch erfolgt. Unter der Erdoberfläche befinden sich die Wasserversorgung und die Abwasserentsorgung, die Leitungen für Strom, Gas, Telefon, Fernwärme und in den Großstädten die U-Bahn; oberirdisch befinden sich die Kläranlagen, die Trinkwasseraufbereitung, die Gas- und Elektrizitätswerke, der öffentliche Personennahverkehr, die Mülldeponien usw. Zwischen den Anlagen der Daseinsvorsorge durch die öffentliche Hand (Kommune) und den Wohnungsbau besteht ein grundlegender Unterschied: Die wohnungswirtschaftlichen Investitionen, ihre laufende Instandhaltung und die Modernisierungen erfolgen privatwirtschaftlich, die kommunalen Infrastrukturanlagen werden durch die Gebietskörperschaften errichtet und unterhalten, d.h. durch die öffentliche Hand finanziert. Trotz dieser Unterschiede besteht ein technischer und ökonomischer Zusammenhang:

Wenn auf Grund der schrumpfenden Bevölkerung und der Abwanderung in den neuen Bundesländern Wohnungsleerstände durch den Abriss beseitigt werden, dann wirkt sich dieses auf die kommunale technische Infrastruktur aus: Sowohl die unter- als auch die oberirdischen Anlagen werden nicht mehr optimal genutzt,

---

7 Wenn in einigen Städten die Einwohnerzahl zugenommen hat, dann ist diese auf Eingemeindungen zurückzuführen, d.h., dass nur die ‚Stammbevölkerung' verglichen werden kann.

8 So zum Beispiel bilden die Gebietskörperschaften keine Pensionsrückstellungen.

so dass die fixen Kosten auf eine geringere Zahl von Haushalten umgelegt werden müssen. Dieses gilt für die Trinkwasseraufbereitung, die Entsorgung des Abwassers, die Stadtwerke, die öffentliche Personenbeförderung, die Müllentsorgung, die kommunalen Kindergärten, die Grund- und weiterführenden Schulen usw. Diese **unzureichende Auslastung der kommunalen technischen Infrastrukturanlagen** führt bei konstanten fixen Kosten zu einer Erhöhung der Gebühren und Beiträge bei den verbliebenen Bürgern. Eine andere Lösung besteht unter anderem darin, dass in die Abwasserkanäle teures Trinkwasser eingeleitet wird, um die Fließgeschwindigkeit zu erhöhen, um dadurch Verstopfungen zu vermeiden; die auf eine größere Bevölkerungszahl dimensionierten Mülldeponien oder Verbrennungsanlagen müssen von den restlichen Bürgern bezahlt werden; Buslinien werden ausgedünnt oder eingestellt, so dass sich die Versorgung verschlechtert; auf Grund der sinkenden Schülerzahl werden Schulen geschlossen und für die Fahrschüler sind Zubringerbusse einzusetzen usw. Diese Entwicklung ist in den neuen Bundesländern deshalb besonders problematisch, weil nach der Wende – in Erwartung eines wirtschaftlichen Aufschwunges – mit öffentlichen Mitteln zahlreiche neue größere Anlagen erstellt oder vorhandene erweitert und modernisiert wurden.

Der Stadtumbau Ost – tendenziell zeichnet sich diese Entwicklung auch für Westdeutschland ab – führt nicht nur zum Wohnungsabriss, sondern über diesen zu einer Reduzierung der Auslastung der kommunalen technischen Infrastrukturanlagen. Da eine technische Redimensionierung der Installationen, die häufig erst ein Jahrzehnt alt sind, zu teuer ist, werden die städtischen Leistungen der Daseinsvorsorge eingeschränkt und die konstanten fixen Kosten auf eine geringere Zahl von Haushalten und Bürgern verteilt, häufig handelt es sich um Rentnerhaushalte, deren Altersbezüge stagnieren oder real sogar sinken.

Die Redimensionierung der technischen Infrastruktur führt auch zur **Ausdünnung der sozialen Struktureinrichtungen**: Wenn auf Grund der Abwanderung die Bevölkerung und auf Grund der niedrigen Geburtenrate die Schülerzahlen sinken, dann werden Schulen geschlossen, was insbesondere für die weiterführenden Bildungseinrichtungen gilt; die Zahl der Ärzte, der Apotheken, der Bank- und Poststellen usw. nimmt ab. In den Klein- und Mittelstädten praktizieren nur noch Allgemeinmediziner, nicht aber Fachärzte mit spezialisierten medizinischen Geräten wie Strahlen- oder Chemotherapie, Herzkatheteruntersuchungen usw. Akute Fälle müssen mit dem Hubschrauber in Großklinken gebracht werden, obgleich gerade ältere Bürger derartige Untersuchungen benötigen. Gegenwärtig werden Kindergärten und Kindertagesstätten gefordert und gefördert, ab 2015/20 werden diese teilweise leer stehen und man wird Betreuungsplätze für Senioren brauchen. In Niedersachsen will man bereits einen Teil eines Schulhofes zur Erweiterung des Friedhofes benutzen.

III. Fazit

Die demographische Entwicklung war seit den 70er Jahren des letzten Jahrhunderts bekannt, aber die Politik hat diese wissenschaftlichen Erkenntnisse nicht zur Kenntnis genommen. Seit Beginn des neuen Jahrhunderts ist die alternde und schrumpfende Bevölkerung in das Zentrum der politischen Erörterung gerückt, verstärkt durch die **missglückte Integration der Migranten**; denn die Elternhäuser, die Schulen und die gesamte Gesellschaft haben in den letzten Jahrzehnten keine aktive Integrationspolitik betrieben. Diese Versäumnisse haben die Bildung von Gettos und Parallelgesellschaften in den Großstädten begünstigt, die gleichfalls ein wohnungswirtschaftliches und städtebauliches Problem darstellen. Im Vordergrund der wissenschaftlichen und politischen Diskussion steht die Sozialordnung, zum Beispiel das Gesundheits- und Rentensystem. Die aus der demographischen Entwicklung sich abzeichnenden **Konsequenzen für die Städte und Regionen** – verstärkt durch die Abwanderungen von Ost nach West – werden weitestgehend ausgeblendet.

Der Bielefelder Demograph Herwig Birg hat bereits 2000 auf den Zusammenhang zwischen der Bevölkerungsentwicklung und dem künftigen Bedarf an Wohnungen hingewiesen (Birg 2000). Es handelt sich um die demographischen Auswirkungen auf die Neubautätigkeit, weniger um die Konsequenzen für die Bestandpolitik. Da inzwischen die Neubaurate kontinuierlich gesunken ist und die Wohnungsleerstände insbesondere in den neuen Ländern eine besorgniserregende Höhe erreicht haben, soll durch den **Stadtumbau Ost** einmal der Leerstand reduziert und zum anderen die Stadtstrukturen revitalisiert werden (Bundestransferstelle Stadtumbau Ost 2006).

Mit dieser Entscheidung hat die Politik deutlich gemacht, dass **wohnungswirtschaftliche und städtebauliche Anpassung** unter veränderten demographischen Gegebenheiten **nicht dem Markt überlassen** werden kann, denn dieses würde nicht nur zu einem langfristigen Prozess, sondern zu negativen externen (geschäftlichen) Effekten der Ghettobildung und der Konzentration von Migranten in Parallelgesellschaften führen. Die in den meisten Konsumgüterbereichen erfolgreiche Preispolitik versagt, weil einmal der Mietpreissenkung durch die fixen Kosten – die Kapitalkosten und die Grundbesitzangaben – Grundbesitzabgaben – Grenzen gesetzt sind und weil zum anderen insbesondere durch die Abwanderung die physischen Bedarfsträger (Haushalte) fehlen.[9] Es ist eine gesamtgesellschaftliche Aufgabe, die nicht nur ökonomisch betrachtet und nicht kurzfristig gelöst werden kann.

9 Dieses gilt auch für andere Wirtschaftsbereiche: Auf Grund der niedrigen Geburtenrate wird die Zahl der Kinderärzte abnehmen, die Nachfrage nach Babyausstattungen, Schulbüchern, der Bedarf an Lehrern, Schulen usw. wird zurückgehen.

Das Stadtumbauprogramm Ost wird in erster Linie als ein wohnungswirtschaftliches Problem gesehen, d.h., dass die leerstehenden Wohnungen – häufig Plattenbauten – abgerissen werden müssen und die so freigemachten Grundstücke als Grünflächen, Kinderspielplätze usw. genutzt werden. Wenn eine entsprechende Umnutzung vorliegt, kann es sich um eine städtebauliche Aufwertung handeln; der Zusammenhang zwischen der wohnungswirtschaftlichen und städtebaulichen Zielsetzung wird deutlich. Der eigentliche **städtebauliche Aspekt** liegt aber darin, dass die gesamte **technische Infrastruktur redimensioniert** werden muss: Dieses gilt für die unter der Oberfläche befindlichen Versorgungs- und Entsorgungsleitungen wie Strom, Gas, Wasser, Abwasser, Fernwärme, Telefon usw. Aber auch oberirdisch werden Anpassungen notwendig: Der öffentliche Personennahverkehr, die Kindergärten, Schulen, die Bank- und Poststellen werden abnehmen, die Versorgung mit Ärzten, Apotheken, Einkaufsmöglichkeiten usw. werden ausgedünnt. Dieses führt zur kleinräumigen Abwanderung in die Mittel- oder Hauptzentren, so dass die ländlichen Regionen und Kleinstädte an Attraktivität verlieren. Es ist ein sich aufschaukelndes Problem.

Unter den spezifischen Bedingungen ist dieses Problem in den **neuen Bundesländern** aufgetreten. Es gibt erste Anzeichen, dass diese Probleme – regional unterschiedlich – sich auch in den **alten Bundesländern** abzeichnen. Aus diesem Grunde sind Pilotprojekte bereits in Westdeutschland durchgeführt worden. Speziell die Wohnungswirtschaft fordert, dass mit dem Auslaufen des Stadtumbauprogramms Ost im Jahre 2009 ein **gesamtdeutsches Stadtumbauprogramm** angeschlossen wird. Die Notwendigkeit ist erkannt, es ist aber fraglich, ob Bund, Länder und Gemeinden finanziell in der Lage und bereit sein werden, die hierfür erforderlichen öffentlichen Mittel bereitzustellen.

Der **Stadtumbau Ost** hat einen **Paradigmenwechsel** eingeleitet: Die Industrialisierung hat um 1850 bzw. um 1870/75 eingesetzt. Seitdem gab es ein Bevölkerungswachstum, neben der Auswanderung eine Binnenwanderung und Verstädterung. Der Wohnungs- und Städtebau war 150 bzw. 125 Jahre durch ständiges Wachstum gekennzeichnet, das durch den Ersten und insbesondere durch den Zweiten Weltkrieg noch verschärft wurde. Erstmalig werden die Expansionsprozesse durch die demographische Schrumpfung und Abwanderung abgelöst. Dieses muss zu einem Umdenken führen, um nicht neue Investitionen zu tätigen, die zu Investitionsruinen führen.

In der Mitte der 90er Jahre hat die öffentliche Hand großzügig steuerliche Präferenzen gewährt, um sowohl den Neubau als auch die Sanierung des desolaten Wohnungsbestandes in den neuen Bundesländern zu fördern, nunmehr werden zum Teil diese Wohnungen – wiederum mit öffentlicher Förderung – abgerissen. Es ist fraglich, ob man aus den Fehlern der Vergangenheit gelernt hat und erneut öffentliche Mittel verschwendet.

Literaturverzeichnis

Birg, H., Trends der Bevölkerungsentwicklung: Auswirkungen der Bevölkerungsschrumpfung, der Migration und der Alterung der Gesellschaft in Deutschland und Europa bis 2050, insbesondere im Hinblick auf den Bedarf an Wohnungen – Ein Gutachten im Auftrag des Verbandes deutscher Hypothekenbanken, Schriftenreihe des Verbandes deutscher Hypothekenbanken, Bd. 12, Frankfurt 2000.

Deutsche Siedlungs- und Landesrentenbank (Hrsg.), Zwischen Sanierung und Abriss – Plattenbauten in den neuen Bundesländern, bearbeitet von Prof. Dr. Lothar Hübl u. a., Leipzig 1995.

Bundesministerium für Arbeit und Sozialordnung, Lebenslagen in Deutschland – Der erste Armuts- und Reichtumsbericht der Bundesregierung, Berichts-Band, Bonn 2001.

Bundesministerium für Verkehr, Bau- und Wohnungswesen (Hrsg.), Wohnen und Bauen in Zahlen 2005, Berlin 2005.

Gräf, B. und *Schattenberg, M.*, Die demografische Herausforderung – Simulation mit einem überlappenden Generationsmodell, in: Deutsche Bank Research, Aktuelle Themen 343, Frankfurt 2006.

Bundestransferstelle Stadtumbau Ost (beim Institut für Regionalentwicklung und Strukturplanung (IRS) in Erkner), Stadtumbau Ost – Stand und Perspektiven, Erster Statusbericht der Bundestransferstelle im Auftrag des Bundesministeriums für Verkehr, Bau- und Stadtentwicklung und des Bundesamtes für Bauwesen und Raumordnung, Berlin 2006.

Bundesverband deutscher Wohnungs- und Immobilienunternehmen – GdW, Wohnungswirtschaftliche Daten und Trends 2005/2006, – Zahlen und Analysen aus der Jahresstatistik des GdW, Berlin 2005.

Grobecker, C., *Krack-Roberg, E.* und *Sommer, B.*, Bevölkerungsentwicklung 2004, in: Wirtschaft und Statistik, Heft 12, 2005, S. 1261-1272.

Kröhnert, S., *Medicus, F.* und *Klingholz, R.*, Die demografische Lage der Nation – Wie zukunftsfähig sind Deutschlands Regionen?, München 2006.

Pfeifer, U., *Simons, H.* und *Porsch, L.*, Wohnungswirtschaftlicher Strukturwandel in den neuen Bundesländern – Bericht der Kommission, erstattet im Auftrag des Bundesministeriums für Verkehr, Bau- und Wohnungswesen, o.O. 2000 („Lehmann-Grube-Berich").

Schimany, P., Die Alterung der Gesellschaft – Ursachen und Folgen des demographischen Umbruchs (Passauer Habil – Schrift), Frankfurt – New York 2003.

Statistisches Bundesamt, Bevölkerung Deutschlands bis 2050 – 10. koordinierte Bevölkerungsvorausberechnung (Presseexemplar), Wiesbaden 2003.

D. Die kommunale Energiewirtschaft unter Bedingungen der Liberalisierung und des Bevölkerungsrückgangs

Wolf Gottschalk

I. Einige Grundsachverhalte

Folgende Entwicklungen bilden die Basis für unsere Erörterungen:

- Bis zum Jahr 2040 geht der PROGNOS-Report von einem **Rückgang der deutschen Bevölkerung** auf 71 Mio. aus. Das entspreche einem jährlichen Bevölkerungsverlust in der Größe einer mittleren Großstadt von 250 000 Einwohnern (Eckerle, Oczipka 1998, S. 33 ff.).
- Die einzelnen **Länder**, Kreise und Gemeinden werden sehr **unterschiedlich** im Rahmen eines West-Ost-Gefälles und Süd-Nord-Gefälles betroffen sein.[1]
- **Ungleich** verteilt ist auch der **Anteil** der über 65-Jährigen sowie der wohlhabenden und der weniger wohlhabenden Alten. Letztere werden vor allem in Ostdeutschland lokalisiert (Grohmert u.a. 2006).
- Wesentliche **Gründe** (Grohmert u.a. 2006) für diesen Befund bilden die längere Lebenserwartung der Älteren, die zu geringe Kinderzahl und der Fortzug (Binnenwanderung) der betreffenden Jahrgänge, u.a. wegen ungleicher Verteilung der Zukunftsfähigkeit der Regionen in Deutschland (Arbeitsplätze, Lebensbedingungen, Freizeitangebote), sowie die nicht ausreichende und regional ungleich verteilte Zuwanderung.
- Bevor strategische Überlegungen in bezug auf diese Entwicklungen aufgezeigt werden, soll auf die strategischen Aspekte als Folge der seit **1998 gegebenen Veränderungen** des Energierechtsrahmens eingegangen werden, der alle kommunalen Energieversorger gleichermaßen betrifft.

II. Die neuen rechtlichen Bedingungen der kommunalen Energieversorgung

Die kommunalen EVU befanden sich bis 1998 in einem **eingependelten Zustand** der optimalen Energieversorgung unter den damals und heute geltenden rechtlichen Vorgaben einer sicheren, preisgünstigen und umweltfreundlichen Versorgung. Kritik erfuhr die bis dahin geltende Struktur der Energieversorgung in Deutschland (Verbund,- Regional- und Ortversorgung) bei Strom und Gas. Ferner wurde eine als unzureichend empfundene Energiepreisstruktur für die ein-

1 Vergleiche den Beitrag von Helmut Jenkis, S. 161 in diesem Band.

zelnen Kundengruppen und das Energiepreisniveau insgesamt als unzureichend empfunden.

In den Jahren 1998 und 2005 wurde das deutsche **Energierecht (EnWG)**, (BGBl. Teil I, S. 1970, 3621; Schulz 2006, S. 173 ff.) entscheidend **geändert**. Die Einführung des Wettbewerbs erfolgte im Netzbereich durch die Erzwingung der Durchleitung fremder Strom- und Gasmengen, die Trennung von Netzbetrieb und dem Vertrieb der Waren Strom und Gas sowie die scharfen Vorgaben und Kontrollen der Preisbildung für die Netznutzung. Der Zugang der Kunden zu anderen Stromanbietern, später auch zu anderen Gasanbietern, wurde ermöglicht.

Die **Fernwärmeversorgung** wird vom neuen EnWG nicht unmittelbar berührt, denn die Fernwärmeversorgung stand seit jeher im Wettbewerb mit der Gasversorgung und dem Heizöl. Indirekt ist sie aber insoweit betroffen, als die ortsnahe Kraft-Wärme-Kopplung vom neuen EnWG tangiert wird und es eines eigenen Gesetzes (KWK-G) (BGBl. Teil I, S. 286) bedurfte, um die Fernwärmeversorgung nicht als unrentabel vom Markt verschwinden zu lassen. Im Zusammenhang mit der demographischen Entwicklung kommt der Fernwärmeversorgung allerdings wieder eine besondere Bedeutung zu.

Seit dem Jahre 2005 stehen die kommunalen Energieversorger vor folgenden **wichtigen Problemen** und Sachverhalten:

- Sie haben nach wie vor den allgemeinen **Anschluss- und Versorgungszwang** und die Verpflichtung zu gewähren, die Versorgung preisgünstig, sicher und umweltverträglich zu gestalten. Sie verantworten einen grundlegenden Infrastrukturbereich mit allen Konsequenzen.
- Sie befinden sich nunmehr im **Wettbewerb um Kunden** und Absatz mit Verbund- und Regionalunternehmen und mit anderen kommunalen Unternehmen.
- Ab einer gewissen Größe werden sie zukünftig ihre Unternehmen **zerlegen** müssen in einen Netzbetrieb mit selbständigen Aufgaben und Rechten und in einen Restbetrieb, in dem Energieerzeugung bzw. -einkauf und Energievertrieb gebündelt sind (**Unbundling**). (Ohlms, 2005, S.183 ff.).
- Die **Netznutzungsentgelte** werden künftig von einer besonderen Behörde (Bundesnetzagentur BNetzA) (Schulz 2006, S. 174 ff.) methodisch festgelegt, kontrolliert und genehmigt. Die dazu notwenigen Verfahrensschritte und Datenaustausche mit der BNetzA sind höchst aufwendig und konfliktreich, vor allem, wenn die sog. Anreizregulierung, wie im Gesetz vorgesehen, eingeführt wird.
- **Höchst kompliziert** sind auch die Regelungen für den Netzzugang für Kunden und dritte Anbieter und die notwendigen Verfahren zur Aufrechterhaltung der jederzeitigen Versorgungssicherheit (sog. Strombilanzen und Bilanzausgleiche). Dabei kommt auch die neu geschaffene Strombörse (EEX,

European Energy Exchange, Leipzig, http://www.eex.de) ins Spiel, an der die für die Bilanzierung notwendigen Termin- und Spotmengen der Ware „Strom" gehandelt werden.

- Der Wettbewerbsdruck und die neuen Regulierungsvorschriften haben die **innere Struktur** der kommunalen Energieversorger deutlich verändert:
  Sie sind kunden- und **absatzorientierter** geworden.
  Sie sind **kostenbewusster** und -orientierter.
  Sie verstehen sich eher als **marktbewusste Unternehmen** als früher. Der gemeinwirtschaftliche Aspekt tritt in gleichem Maße zurück.
  Davon werden auch die **Führungskräfte** und Mitarbeiter hinsichtlich ihrer Ausbildung und der Anforderungen sowie ihres Verhaltens und Auftretens nach innen und nach außen berührt.
  Die **Haltung der kommunalen Energieversorgungsunternehmen gegenüber privaten Versorgern** wird offener und entspannter. Dies gilt auch für die kommunalen Eigentümer, die Gemeinden und Kreise.

Seit dem Jahre 1998 hat sich die Struktur der deutschen Versorgungswirtschaft also deutlich verändert:

- Aus acht Verbundunternehmen sind **vier** sehr starke **Verbundunternehmen** übrig geblieben.
- Die Zahl der **Regionalunternehmen** ist stark zurückgegangen. Die meisten Regionalunternehmen gingen in ihren Verbundmüttern auf.
- Die kommunalen Energieversorger blieben zahlenmäßig gleich, aber sie bekamen vielfach eine andere Eigentümerstruktur. Sie ist gekennzeichnet durch eine starke Beteiligung Dritter im Rahmen von PPP. Damit einher ging ein spürbarer Einflussverlust der kommunalen Eigentümerschaft mit allen damit verbundenen Nachteilen. Diese Entwicklung wurde erst 2002 durch einen Eingriff des Bundeskartellamts gestoppt (20%-Beteiligungsgrenze für vorliefernde Versorgungsunternehmen) (B8-40000-U-109/01).

Die tendenziell preissenkende Wirkung der Netzentgeltregulierung wird seit 2005 überkompensiert durch die weltweite **Preiserhöhung** der wichtigsten Energieträger Kohle, Öl und Gas, die für die Umwandlung in die Nutzenergien Strom und Fernwärme eingesetzt werden.

Netzzusammenbrüche aus unterschiedlichen Gründen[2] haben in der letzten Zeit zum Nachdenken über die Werthaltigkeit und damit die Bewertung von Energie-Netzen und der Relativität der Bedeutung von Netzentgelten geführt. Netzentgelte machen übrigens am gesamten Stromendpreis nicht mehr als 30% aus. Die anderen 70% sind Erzeugungskosten und öffentliche Abgaben.

Vor diesem Szenario erfolgen nun einige Bemerkungen zu den **Anpassungsstrategien** der kommunalen Energieversorgung unter den Bedingungen der demo-

2 Z.B. im Münsterland, in der Schweiz, in Italien.

graphischen Entwicklung und der Liberalisierungstendenzen in diesem Wirtschaftszweig.

III. Anpassungsstrategien der kommunalen Unternehmen aufgrund der Liberalisierung der Energieversorgung

Folgende Anpassungen werden erforderlich:

1. Investitionen

a) Netze

Erforderlich wird die Anpassung der Strom-, Gas- und Fernwärmenetze an die Kundennachfrage unter den besonderen Gegebenheiten der Aufrechterhaltung der jederzeitigen Versorgungssicherheit und Umweltverträglichkeit bei strikter Beachtung der Wirtschaftlichkeit.
Letztere wird überwacht durch die BNetzA, die die Kalkulationsmethoden verbindlich vorschreibt.
Zielkonflikte entstehen zwischen dem technisch Wünsch- und Machbaren einerseits und wirtschaftlich Zulässigem andererseits. Diese Konflikte werden sich erst vollständig auswirken, wenn die Anreizregulierung eingesetzt wird und greift.
Es kommt zu einem starken Rückbau der Netze in Kommunen und Kreisen mit deutlichem Bevölkerungsrückgang und dem Nachlassen der wirtschaftlichen Tätigkeiten, in Folge einer verstärkten Wärmedämmung der Gebäude sowie der Energieeinsparprogramme. In der neuen Ländern erfolgt der Rückbau der Fernwärmenetze, teilweise zugunsten der Gasversorgung, denn letztere ist wesentlich investitionskostenfreundlicher.

b) Erzeugungsanlagen

Kommunale Unternehmen investieren verstärkt in moderne Anlagen der Stromerzeugung i.d.R. auf der Basis der Kraft-Wärme-Kopplung, unterstützt durch das KWK-Gesetz.
Ebenso streben sie den Neubau von kommunalen Gemeinschaftskraftwerken (Trianel, Südweststrom GmbH, Rhein Energie) an. Steigende Strompreise machen diese Investitionen wirtschaftlich möglich. Zugleich eröffnen sie Alternativen zu Strombezügen von Verbundunternehmen.

Die Nutzung industrieller Abwärme und die Verbrennung heizwertreicher sortierter Reststoffe (Abfallbehandlung) bewirken weitere Investitionen.
Dazu führen auch die Beteiligung an Windkraftparks und größeren Solaranlagen sowie die Nutzung von Erdwärme.
Der Einsatz von Optimierungsverfahren und -einrichtungen zum bestmöglichen Einsatz von eigenerzeugtem und eingekauftem Strom erfordert ebenfalls Veränderungen der Anlagen.

2. Faktor Arbeit

Neue **Anforderungen an Führungskräfte** und Mitarbeiter resultieren.
Erwartet werden Führungskräfte, die unter strikter Beachtung des nach wie vor geltenden **gemeinwirtschaftlichen Auftrags** des Infrastrukturdienstleistens kommunale Energieversorgung:

- effizienz- und **kostenorientiert** arbeiten und das Unternehmen dahin gehend organisieren und führen; und
- dies auch **durchzusetzen** verstehen, z.B. gegenüber Anteilseignern und Arbeitnehmern;
- das **Stakeholder-Prinzip** dem Shareholder-Prinzip vorziehen und durchsetzen;
- flexibel auf **Marktänderungen** reagieren, sowohl auf der Kundenseite als auch auf der Lieferantenseite;
- die **Regulierungsprinzipien** und -mechanismen für einen natürlichen Monopolbereich (Energienetze) **akzeptieren** und sich darauf einrichten (BNetzA, BKartA, Min.Aufsicht);
- sich **Kooperationen** zu öffnen verstehen;
- das technisch Wünschbare vom **technisch-wirtschaftlich Machbaren** zu unterscheiden wissen und gleichwohl immer auf dem Stand des neuesten Niveaus bleiben;
- die **kommunalpolitischen Gegebenheiten** und Spielregeln ihrer Eigner kennen und respektieren ohne von ihnen abhängig zu sein oder zu werden.

Von den Mitarbeitern wird erwartet, dass sie sich auf das **unternehmerische Wirken** der kommunalen Energieversorgung einstellen. Das bedeutet:

- für Ingenieure: Sie müssen die **Netztechnik optimieren**, nicht maximieren. Sie haben den Ausbau der Steuerungstechnik zur Optimierung von Eigenerzeugung und Beschaffung (Strom) und des Gaseinsatzes im Rahmen der Bilanzmaßnahmen nach EnWG zu betreiben. Moderne Informationstechnologie ist von ihnen einzusetzen.

- für Betriebswirte: Eine betriebswirtschaftliche Steuerung streng nach **Kostengesichtspunkten** ist erforderlich. Kostenrechner, Controller, Bilanz- und Steuerfachleute werden gebraucht.
- Wenn der (frühere) Abnehmer zum Kunden wird, steigt die Bedeutung der Absatzwirtschaftler im Unternehmen. Marketing, Markt- und Meinungsforschung, Key Accounting, Einsatz von Werbe- und Absatzinstrumenten etc. sind gefragt.
- Wichtig ist die sehr enge Zusammenarbeit mit der **kommunalen Entwicklungsplanung** und Wohnungswirtschaft zur Optimierung der Ausbau- bzw. der Rückbauplanung im kommunalen Raum.

3. Innere Organisation

Für kommunale Energieversorger, die mehr als 100 000 Kunden versorgen (jeweils Strom und Gas) gilt: Sie müssen den bisherigen **Netzbetrieb** aus dem (Querverbund) Unternehmen heraustrennen (Unbundling).
Der **Netzbetrieb** wird ein **selbständiges Unternehmen** (wenn auch im Rahmen eines Konzernverbundes), es bekommt eine eigene Geschäftsführung, eine eigene Mannschaft und eigene Handlungsmöglichkeiten zum Betrieb des Netzes. Jeder, der das Netz nutzen will, wird gleich behandelt, auch das (bisherige) eigene Stadtwerk.
Dies bedeute die **Aufteilung** des bisher gemeinsamen Rechnungswesens, der gemeinsamen und gegenseitigen Informationen über die Kunden und deren Verhalten und Abnahmeeigenschaften.
Die innere Organisation muss sich auf das **Regulieren** einstellen: Erforderlich wird der Einsatz eines **Regulierungsbevollmächtigten** als Verbindungsglied zwischen der BNetzA und den regulierungsrelevanten Aktivitäten und Einrichtungen der Energieversorgung (zeitliche und inhaltliche Abstimmung und Prüfung der abzuliefernden Datenmengen für die BNetzA, Auseinandersetzung mit der BNetzA über deren Anforderungen etc. Ausrichtung der Aufbau- und Ablauforganisation an die Erfordernisse des Regulierungsverfahrens).
Die **Kostenrechnung** muss zum umfassenden Controlling-Instrument für die Zwecke der Unternehmenssteuerung und der Anforderungen der Regulierungsbehörde ausgebaut werden. Ferner erfolgt der Ausbau des Budgetierungswesens im Unternehmen. Man entwickelt ein Kosten- und effizienzorientiertes **Entlohnungssystem** für Mitarbeiter und Führung. Die Einführung eines (überbetrieblichen) Benchmarking-Systems wird notwendig.
Die Einführung entsprechender Software und des notwendigen Knowhows im Unternehmen muss bewerkstelligt werden.

4. Eigentümersteuerung: Kommune, PPP

Seit Anfang der 90er Jahre besteht eine Tendenz zur **Beteiligung Dritter** an kommunalen Energieversorgern. Damit einher geht ein Verlust des Einflusses der kommunalen Eigner auf die kommunalpolitisch erwünschte Steuerung des Unternehmens zugunsten einer Mitsteuerung durch den Partner.
Dies hat spürbaren Einfluss auf die **Unternehmensziele**, die operative Tätigkeit, die Besetzung der Führungspositionen, die personelle Struktur, das finanzwirtschaftliche Handeln usw.
Die geänderte Führungsstruktur beeinflusst ihrerseits die **Strategien** und Entwicklungen des Unternehmens.

5. Kunden: Änderung der Kundenbeziehungen und des Kundenverhaltens

Mit der Liberalisierung der Energiemärkte geht eine Änderung des Kundenverhaltens einher. **Industrie- und Gewerbekunden** tendieren zum Wechsel des Energielieferanten. Ihre Entscheidungsgröße ist der Energiepreis. Wichtig wird außerdem das kundenorientierte Dienstleistungsverhalten des Energieversorgers. Der Kunde muss umworben und mit Zusatzdienstleistungen um die reine Energielieferung bedient werden. Großkunden erwarten eine besondere Betreuung.
Haushaltskunden wechseln den Lieferanten weniger oft, sind aber empfindlich geworden gegenüber unangemessenem Auftreten des Energieversorgers und schalten dann immer häufiger die Verbraucherschutzorganisationen ein. Ein Beispiel bilden die Gas- und Strompreiserhöhungen der Jahre 2005/2006. Die Unternehmen reagieren vorsichtig bei Zahlungsprotesten und allgemeinem Kunden Unwillen.
Haushaltskunden haben registriert, dass Ver- und Entsorgung inzwischen zu einer spürbaren **„zweiten Miete“** geworden sind. In Regionen mit einer starken Überalterung und gleichzeitiger Verarmung kommt es zu besonders starken Kundenprotesten. Daher ist es Unternehmensstrategie, die Kunden richtig anzusprechen, sie einzubinden und ihnen Serviceleistungen anzubieten.

6. Lieferanten: ein neues Beziehungsgeflecht

Auch kommunale Energieversorger können sich seit dem Jahre 1998 ihren Energielieferanten aussuchen. Sie nutzen dies als Chance ihrerseits günstige Einkaufspreise zu erzielen und an ihre Kunden weiterzugeben und damit im Wettbewerb mit überregionalen Anbietern konkurrieren zu können, z.B. Yello. Als Folge resultieren die Kündigung teilweise sehr langfristiger Energielieferungsverträge, der Aufbau eines **Beziehungsgeflechts** mit anderen Lieferanten (Produzenten, Energiehändlern, Strombörsenhändlern), der Abbau teilweise sehr alter und vertrauter Geschäftsbeziehungen. Man begegnet sich zunehmend gleichrangiger und selbstbewusster.

Der Versuch der Verbundwirtschaft, diese Entwicklung durch starke Beteiligungen an kommunalen Energieversorgern zu unterlaufen, wurde 2002 durch das Bundeskartellamt dadurch unterbunden, dass es keine Beteiligung eines Vorlieferanten über 20% mehr zulässt (reine Finanzbeteiligung) (Beschluss des Bundeskartellamtes, 2002).

7. Andere Unternehmen: Kooperationen, Konkurrenzen

Durch die Liberalisierung hat sich auch das Verhältnis zu anderen Energieversorgungsunternehmen verändert. Der aufkommende Wettbewerb insbesondere um große Strom- und Gaskunden machte aus manchen früheren guten Nachbarn **scharfe Konkurrenten**. Gleiches gilt für Vorlieferanten und kommunale Unternehmen. Dies führt auch zu Schwierigkeiten im Rahmen des früher relativ unproblematischen Betriebsvergleichs/Benchmarking.

Andererseits gebietet die neue Marktsituation, z.B. beim Energieeinkauf, eine deutlich stärkere **Kooperationsbereitschaft** kommunaler Unternehmen. Beispiele sind die Gesellschaften Trianel, Südweststrom,[3] die beide eigene Gemeinschaftsgroßkraftwerke errichten mit dem Ziel, ihre kooperierenden Mitglieder hinsichtlich Stromeinkauf und -handel unabhängiger von den Verbundunternehmen zu stellen.

Im Zusammenhang mit der Ausgründung von Netzgesellschaften gibt es auch Entwicklungen zu größeren **Netzkooperationen** mit gemeinsamen Aufbau, Zusammenschluss und Betrieb von Strom und Gasnetzen.

IV. Das zusätzliche strategische Problem: Die Bewältigung der Auswirkungen der demographischen Entwicklungen

Vorbemerkung: Dieses Problem betrifft zurzeit nicht alle kommunalen Unternehmen, sondern vor allem diejenigen in den neuen Ländern und in einigen Gemeinden in den alten Bundesländern. Allerdings ist absehbar, dass auch dort in einigen Jahren Infrastrukturanpassungen notwendig sein werden.

---

3 Trianel European Trading GmbH, Aachen, Lombardstr.8, http://www.trianel.com, Südweststrom, Südwestdeutsche Stromhandels GmbH, Tübingen, Eisenhutstr. 8, http://www.suedweststrom.de.

- Die Unternehmen stehen dann verstärkt im **Spannungsfeld** von Wirtschaftlichkeit, Versorgungssicherheit und kommunaler Gesamtenwicklungsplanung (Stadtentwicklung) zur Bewältigung eines bisher nicht bekannten Schrumpfungsprozesses aller Funktionen und Institutionen.
- Der Bevölkerungsrückgang in den betroffenen Versorgungsgebieten führt zur **Unterauslastung** bestehender Ver- und natürlich auch Entsorgungsnetze. Wohnungsbauten werden zum Teil abgerissen, Straßen und Plätze zurückgebaut. Die darin befindlichen Ver- und Entsorgungsanlagen werden ausgebaut, mit Auswirkungen auf zentrale Anlagen, z.B. Heizwerke und Heizkraftwerke, Kanäle und Kläranlagen, Umspann- und Verteileranlagen, Druckstationen usw.
- Die Unterauslastung führt zunächst zu **verminderter Anlageneffizienz** und zu höheren Kosten je produzierte Einheit, denn die gegebenen Fixkosten verteilen sich auf weniger verkaufte Energieeinheiten.
- Vor allem in den neuen Ländern müssen **neue Anlagen zurückgebaut** werden bevor sie abgeschrieben worden sind. Im Zusammenhang mit dem Nachweis der Kosten im Rahmen der Regulierung der Netze durch die BnetzA besteht erheblicher Klärungsbedarf, wie diese Kosten geltend gemacht werden können. Die Behörde wird nicht mit dem Argument der „stranded investments" arbeiten können. Sollte dies doch der Fall sein, drohen gerichtliche Auseinandersetzungen.
- Der Rückbau erfolgt in der Regel vom Netzende aus. Der Rückbau erfordert erhebliche Finanzmittel, die teilweise nur durch **öffentliche Fördermaßnahmen** durchgeführt werden können (z.B. Stadtumbau-Ost-Mittel).[4] Der Umbau früherer Drei- und Vierleiternetze in moderne Zweileiternetzsysteme ist zu erwarten. Ferner wird die Umgestaltung der Versorgungsgebiete von dreischieinige auf zweischieinige Versorgung (Gas/Strom bzw. Fernwärme/Strom) erfolgen.
- Man rechnet in einigen Städten Ostdeutschlands mit **Anpassungs- und Umlegungskosten** (Koziol 2006)[5] für Energieversorgungsnetze Strom + Gas + Fernwärme mit einem groben Durchschnittswert von 450 Euro je Wohneinheit.

Dazu kommen noch die höheren Kosten für die Anpassungs- und Umlegungs-Arbeiten für Wasser und Abwasser in Höhe von 800.- Euro je Wohneinheit. Die **spezifischen Kosten** für die Anpassung von Gas-, Strom- und Fernwärmeversorgung, sowie Wasser und Abwasser werden auf 20 bis 25 Euro je qm Wohnfläche geschätzt.

---

4 Vergleiche den Beitrag von Helmut Jenkis, S. 161 in diesem Band.
5 Informationen aus dem Verband kommunaler Unternehmen, Köln 2006.

- Speziell im Betrieb der **Fernwärmeversorgung** wird mit erheblichen Veränderungen zu rechnen sein, z.B. der Ersatz zu groß dimensionierter Leitungen durch solche mit kleinerer Nennweite, das Zurückfahren komfortabler Netz-Strukturen, die Verringerung von Vorlauf- und Rücklauftemperaturen der Wärmemedien, die Anpassungen der Übergabearmaturen beim Verbraucher, die Errichtung von Provisorien zur Aufrechterhaltung der Versorgung übrig bleibender Kundeneinrichtungen, die Wiederherstellung früherer Zustände des Geländes und der Wege vor dem Fernwärmebau.
- Alle vorgenannten Maßnahmen haben schwerwiegende Auswirkungen auf die Planung und den Betrieb der **laufenden Energieversorgung**. Sie erfordern Klärungsprozesse mit der Energieaufsicht und der BNetzA. Sie sind der Öffentlichkeit und insbesondere den Kunden im Hinblick auf die notwendige Akzeptanz verständlich zu machen.
- Darüber hinaus muss für ihre **Finanzierung** gesorgt werden. Die Mittel aus der Städtebauförderung/Stadtumbau Ost werden in verschiedenen Fällen eher den Wohnungsbauunternehmen als den Ver- und Entsorgungsbetrieben ausgereicht. Dadurch kommt es zu Spannungen im Rahmen der kommunalen Gesamtentwicklungsplanung und -steuerung.
- Ohne weiteres einsichtig sind die **Probleme beim Rückbau** der Wasserversorgung und Abwasserentsorgung und -behandlung. Zuwenig verbleibende Kunden an einem gegebenen Netz bedeuten Verlangsamung der Durchflüsse und damit Gefahren für Verkeimungen beim Trinkwasser und Versumpfungen beim Abwasser. Bei gleich bleibenden Rohrdurchmessern muss dann ständig mit Trinkwasser gespült werden. Als Auswege bieten sich unter Umständen der Einzug von Rohren geringerer Querschnitte in bestehende Netze oder das Abschalten bestehender, also bereits investierter Klärwerksteile an. Nur so sind die hohen Kosten beim Rückbau von Wasser- und Abwasseranlagen zu erklären.

Literaturverzeichnis

Beschluss des Bundeskartellamtes vom 18.1. 2002 (B8-40000-U-109/01).

Eckerle, K. und *T. Oczipka*, Prognos – Gutachten 1998 für den Verband deutscher Rentenversicherungsträger – Auswirkungen ökonomischer und rechtlicher Rahmenbedingungen auf die gesetzliche Rentenversicherung in Deutschland, DRV/Schriften, Band 9, Basel 1998.

Grohmert, S., F. Medicus und *R. Klingholz*, Die demographische Lage der Nation – wie zukunftsfähig sind Deutschlands Regionen, Institut für Bevölkerung und Entwicklung Berlin, München 2006.

Koziol, M., Stadtumbau Ost – Anpassung der technischen Infrastruktur, Gutachten für den VKU, Köln 2006.

Ohlms, N., Notwendigkeit ausgewogener Zielkataloge für eine volkswirtschaftlich sinnvolle Regulierung der Netzgebundenen Energieversorgung, in: Öffentliche Dienstleistungen für die Bürger. Wege zur Effizienz, Qualität und günstigen Preisen, hrsg. von Gesellschaft für öffentliche Wirtschaft, Heft 23, Berlin 2005, S.183-190.

Schultz, K.-P., Regulierung am Beispiel der netzgebundenen Energieversorgung. Erste Erfahrungen der Bundesnetzagentur, in: Öffentliche Dienstleistungen für die Bürger, Wege zur Effizienz, Qualität und günstigen Preisen, Beiträge zur öffentlichen Wirtschaft, Beiträge zur öffentlichen Wirtschaft, hrsg. von Gesellschaft für öffentliche Wirtschaft, Heft 23, Berlin 2006, S. 173-182.

Zweites Gesetz zur Neuregelung des Energiewirtschaftsrechts, Energiewirtschaftsgesetz vom 7. Juli 2005. BGBl. Teil I.

E. Der Veranstaltungsmarkt im Wandel der Zeiten
Essay

Günter Valjak

Der Veranstaltungsmarkt ist einem ständigen Wandel ausgesetzt. Alleine in den letzten 25 Jahren haben sich das Kundenverhalten, die Kundenansprüche und wünsche mehrfach geändert, was in den Veranstaltungshäusern zu einem Wandel der Strukturen und Veranstaltungsprofile führte.

Zurückzuführen ist dies auf unterschiedliche Ursachen. Zum einem ist es der Wertewandel in der Gesellschaft. Wir sprechen heute von einer Freizeitgesellschaft, einer Spaßgesellschaft und einer Multioptionsgesellschaft, um nur einige Modeworte zu verwenden.

Es wird nicht mehr für eine Veranstaltung ein Raum gesucht, sondern man sucht eine „Location" für einen Event. Und je ausgefallener und ungewöhnlicher diese Location ist, desto größer ist der Anreiz, in einer neuen ungewöhnlichen Umgebung eine Veranstaltung durchzuführen.

Auch die Veranstaltungen selbst haben sich größtenteils diesem „Eventismus" angepasst. Wichtig ist das Happening, der besondere Reiz, der Kick und der dadurch entstehende Erinnerungseffekt. Qualität und Information kommen dabei häufig zu kurz. Dekoration ist wichtiger als der Inhalt! Leider!

Ein anderer zu beachtender Aspekt ist die zurzeit allgemeine negative Stimmung in der Bundesrepublik. Sie führt zu Angst vor noch schlechteren Zeiten sowohl innerhalb von Wirtschaftskreisen als auch in der Bevölkerung. Unternehmen halten sich größtenteils merklich zurück bei Planung ihrer Veranstaltungsaktivitäten. Entscheidungen werden meistens nur noch kurzfristig getroffen. Bisherige Traditionsveranstaltungen werden abgesagt, Jubiläen nur noch im kleinen Rahmen gefeiert. Auch werden Mitarbeiter weniger zu Fortbildungen geschickt, so dass die Weiterbildungsbranche ebenfalls rückläufig ist.

Der Endverbraucher hat weniger Geld für Kultur und Freizeit. Viele Personen, vor allem die über 50 jährigen, haben, bedingt durch Arbeitslosigkeit, Teilzeitarbeit und Rentenkürzungen erhebliche finanzielle Probleme, die sie automatisch an das eigene Heim binden. Das Grillen auf dem Balkon ist preisgünstiger als ein Besuch im Biergarten! Hinzu kommt bei diesem Personenkreis das zunehmende Bedürfnis nach Sicherheit, was ihn häufig von Großveranstaltungen fernhält.

Laut Aussage der Forscher gibt es zu jedem Trend auch einen Gegentrend. Diesen Part nimmt zur Zeit die Jugendkultur ein. Veranstalter oder Trendgastronomen, die sich auf das Geschäft mit der Jugend konzentrieren, haben zurzeit großen Zulauf bzw. hohe Zuwachsraten. Voraussetzung ist, das Angebot muss aktuell und trendy sein. Eine Musikgruppe, die heute 4000 Besucher zu ihren Konzerten lockt, kann bereits in 5 Monaten wieder absolut „out“ sein. Noch schneller geht es teilweise bei Diskotheken und Trendlokalen, deren Aktualität kann bereits nach zwei Besuchen vorbei sein. Wichtig für die jungen Leute ist der Neuheitseffekt, das besondere Angebot und die richtige Besucherzielgruppe. Von Veranstalterseite muss kurzfristig auf solche Trends reagiert werden! Hierbei sind die vielen neu gegründeten Eventagenturen wesentlich flexibler als traditionelle Veranstaltungsbetriebe!

Dieser Anstieg von Aktivitäten für die Jugend ist ein Phänomen, zumal es sich hier größtenteils um eine Zielgruppe handelt, die bisher noch erwerbslos ist bzw. in ihren Berufsanfängen steckt und entsprechend wenig Geld zum Ausgeben haben sollte.

Das sogenannte „Vorglühen“ mit preisgünstigen Getränken aus dem Supermarkt vor allen Veranstaltungsbesuchen ist deshalb eine weitverbreitete Erscheinungsform. Die Selbstversorgung mit Getränken aus dem eigenen Rucksack bei Straßenfesten und Open-Air-Veranstaltungen ist üblich und gleichzeitig Ärgernis für die Gastronomen, die größtenteils mit ihren Gastronomieumsätzen diese Veranstaltungen finanzieren müssen.

Eine weitere Tatsache ist die erschreckend hohe Verschuldungsrate vieler Jugendlicher bei den Kreditinstituten, weil sie den Verlockungen der Kontoüberziehungsmöglichkeiten nicht widerstehen können. Ein Boom, der gut ist für Gastronomie- und Veranstaltungsbranche! Ob dies auch für alle Jugendlichen gut ist, wird die Zukunft zeigen.

Eine andere Entwicklung belebt seit einigen Jahren die Veranstaltungsbranche. Es ist der kommunale Standortwettbewerb.

In den letzten Jahren führte der Standortwettbewerb zwischen den einzelnen Kommunen, zwischen Ober- und Mittelzentren oder sogar zwischen Kleinstädten und Dörfern zu einem quantitativen Anstieg von Veranstaltungen im Freizeitbereich. „Umsonst und draußen“ ist das große Schlagwort. Mit unterschiedlichen Aktivitäten, die allerdings hauptsächlich den Musik- und Unterhaltungsbereich betreffen, will man Besuchergruppen in die eigene Stadt oder Gemeinde locken. Damit die Kaufmannschaft auch davon profitiert, werden die Geschäfte an Sonn- und Feiertagen und in den Abendstunden geöffnet, z.B. beim „Moonlight-Shopping“, was mittlerweile ebenfalls von vielen Kommunen angeboten wird.

Ob dieser Personenkreis, der feiern möchte, dem Handel tatsächlich zusätzlichen Umsatz bringt, ist sehr zu bezweifeln. Eine ernst zu nehmende Untersuchung gibt es hierzu nicht.

Feststellbar ist, dass die um sich greifende „Umsonst und draußen – Mentalität“ der traditionell gewachsenen Veranstaltungsbranche sehr schadet. Warum soll man auch eine Musikveranstaltung in einer Halle, Diskothek oder einem Club besuchen, zusätzlich noch Eintritt zahlen, wenn man alles umsonst bei Stadt- und Straßenfesten haben kann? Bei der Osnabrücker Maiwoche traten im Jahr 2005 an 12 Tagen 130 Musikgruppen und Bands auf fünf verschiedenen Bühnen auf. Hinzu kamen noch 19 Musikangebote für Kinder. Unter den 130 Musikgruppen befanden sich 25, die im gleichen Jahr in der Stadthalle Osnabrück Konzerte gaben, für die Eintritt bezahlt werden musste.

Die bisher gemachten Aussagen zu Veränderungen im Veranstaltungsmarkt sind Feststellungen aus der Praxis und betreffen den Zeitraum der letzten zehn Jahre. Der Veranstaltungsmarkt insgesamt ist nicht rückläufig. Er ist quantitativ sogar gewachsen. Allerdings haben sich die Zielgruppen der Nutzer bei Veranstaltungen im Kultur- und Freizeitbereich geändert.

Nicht unerwähnt darf bleiben, dass es ebenfalls eine Wachstumsrate bei traditionellen Veranstaltungen im Messe- und Kongressbereich gibt. Laut einer Studie des Deutschen Kongressbüros (GCB) wuchs die Zahl der Veranstaltungen in Deutschland von 1999 bis 2002 um knapp 10% auf 1,3 Mio. und das Umsatzvolumen gar um 14% auf knapp 50 Mrd. Euro.

Mit dem Wandel innerhalb der Gesellschaft und mit jedem Generationenwechsel entstehen neue Ansprüche, die mit neuen Veranstaltungen und Veranstaltungsinhalten befriedigt werden müssen. Dies war schon immer so und wird sich auch in Zukunft nicht ändern.

Der sich abzeichnende Bevölkerungsrückgang wird meines Erachtens hierauf keinen großen Einfluss haben. Attraktive Veranstaltungen werden immer starken Zulauf haben.

Veranstaltungen, die nicht mehr dem Publikumsgeschmack entsprechen, werden vom Markt verschwinden. Dafür wird es Veranstaltungen für neue Zielgruppen und auch ganz neue Veranstaltungsformen geben. Der Veranstaltungsmarkt ist in Bewegung und spannenden Veränderungen ausgesetzt.

Solange die Menschheit wert auf Musik und Unterhaltung legt, solange die Menschen wissbegierig und neugierig sind und solange es Idole und Stars in der Musikszene gibt, wird es eine Veranstaltungsindustrie und Anbieter geben, die diese Ansprüche und Bedürfnisse befriedigen werden.

Der Rückblick in die Geschichte zeigt, dass es in allen Kulturen und zu allen Epochen Veranstaltungen, sogar Großveranstaltungen gab, die zu den damals niedrigen Bevölkerungszahlen gar nicht passten. Es ist teilweise beeindruckend, wie mit aus heutiger Sicht fehlenden Marketing-, Logistik- und Organisationsstrategien Veranstaltungen mit mehreren tausend Besuchern durchgeführt wurden. Deshalb möchte ich jetzt in einem geschichtlichen Rückblick zeigen, wie kreativ, unerschrocken und risikobereit Veranstalter waren.

Ich werde Ihnen Veranstaltungen vorstellen, die heute nicht mehr durchführbar wären und vor allem auf Grund der deutschen Versammlungsstättenverordnung und der vielen neuen EU-Richtlinien keine Chance auf Genehmigung hätten.
Mit Beginn der menschlichen Gemeinschaft gab es Feste und Zusammenkünfte – also Veranstaltungen. Leider gibt es keine Aufzeichnungen über Veranstaltungen in der Frühgeschichte der Menschheit. Wir können allerdings davon ausgehen, dass es Feste zu Ehren der Götter gab. Mit Sicherheit wurde der Abschluss einer erfolgreichen Jagd gefeiert. In vielen Kulturen waren Totenfeiern, Siegesfeiern und Sonnwendfeiern die ersten Veranstaltungen.
Es ist bekannt, dass bereits 4000 Jahre v. Chr. der altägyptische Mensch das Opet-Fest zu Ehren der Götterfamilie Amun, Mut und Chon feierte. Im Jahr 1462 v. Chr. ließ die ägyptische Pharaonin Hatschepsut auf 450 Steinblöcken Aufwand und Ablauf des Opet-Festes einmeißeln, um die Kunde dieses Festes den kommenden Generationen zu vermitteln. Dies ist eine der ersten uns bekannten und vor allem erhaltenen Aufzeichnungen über ein Fest, eine Großveranstaltung.
Den Beweis für ein gutes Veranstaltungskonzept, das in der Antike entwickelt wurde und heute noch zu den größten Events zählt, liefern die Olympischen Spiele. Wenn man den Überlieferungen glauben darf, versammelte man sich seit 776 v. Chr. alle vier Jahre in Olympia zum Wettkampf. Faszinierend, wenn man sich vor Augen hält, dass mehr als 1000 Jahre, von 776 v. Chr. bis 261 n. Chr., die Spiele kein einziges Mal ausfielen.
Es war eine die damalige Welt prägende Veranstaltung, die sogar Einfluss auf Krieg und Frieden hatte. Bewundernswert sind die Marketing- und Organisationsleistungen der damaligen Veranstalter. Alle kannten den Termin, und Teilnehmer und Besucher trafen sich pünktlich in Olympia!
1896 wurde dieses Fest wieder reaktiviert und ist seit dem ein Mega-Event und bedeutender wirtschaftlicher Faktor.
Mit den Veranstaltungen im Mittelalter und der Renaissance verhält es sich so ähnlich wie mit dem Bau der gotischen Kathedralen. Man wollte immer mehr! Kathedralen und Feste waren Spitzenprodukte der damaligen Zeit. Sie waren einmalig, gigantisch und voll neuer Ideen – aus heutiger Sicht allerdings nicht mehr finanzierbar. Es waren Produkte der damaligen Zeit, die von der Kirche und absolutistischen Fürsten und Königen bestimmt wurden. Ich möchte nur zwei Beispiele nennen, die den marketingtechnischen, organisatorischen, logistischen und finanziellen Aufwand verdeutlichen.
Zu einem Hoffest von Kaiser Friedrich Barbarossa kamen Pfingsten 1184 ca. 70.000 Ritter inklusive Begleitpersonen für mehrere Tage nach Mainz. Turniere, Sängerwettstreite, Festbankette und Treffen wurden durchgeführt. Der Personenkreis musste untergebracht und verpflegt werden. Die Veranstaltungen mussten geplant, koordiniert, kontrolliert und durchgeführt werden. Bei den unterschiedli-

chen Gesellschaftskreisen gab es Protokollfragen zu beachten. Es mussten Ordnung und Sicherheit gewährleistet sein. Wie wurden das Sanitärproblem und die Abfallbeseitigung gelöst? Wer war für die medizinische Versorgung zuständig? Offensichtlich hat aber alles geklappt.
Es gibt keine Berichte über große Unglücksfälle, es sind keine Seuchen ausgebrochen. Auch konnte Kaiser Friedrich Barbarossa seine Amtszeit unbeschadet fortsetzen. Eine wirklich meisterliche organisatorische Leistung!
Großer Berühmtheit und Beliebtheit erfreuten sich die Renaissance-Feste in der Toskana zwischen 1280 und 1520.
Pisa, Florenz, Siena und Arrezzo waren Schauplätze von unglaublichen Veranstaltungen. Pferderennen, Jagden auf Löwen, Leoparden und Büffel. Alles innerhalb der Stadtgrenzen, wobei es die Pferderennen heute noch in einigen Städten z.B. Siena gibt.
Einmal fand sogar die Paarung einer Stute mit mehreren Hengsten auf einer Piazza statt – vor 40.000 Frauen und Mädchen. Männer waren nicht zugelassen. Eine heute nicht mehr nachvollziehbare Veranstaltungsidee. Man stelle sich vor, wie bei den schlechten Wegstrecken und ohne öffentliche Verkehrsmittel 40.000 Frauen und Mädchen aktiviert und zum Veranstaltungsort transportiert wurden! Wer war für die Sicherheit und die Sanitätsprobleme zuständig? Diese Aufgaben wären in der heutigen Zeit fast nicht lösbar.
Die hier beschriebene Zeit wurde von der Medici-Dynastie geprägt, die Unsummen für die Gestaltung und Dekoration von Festen und mobilen Kunstwerken ausgab. Sie beschäftigte die namhaftesten Künstler der damaligen Zeit. Leonardo da Vinci und Michelangelo erfanden und schufen bewegliche Bilder, gestalteten Kunstwerke aus Wachs oder bemalten Kulissen, die bereits nach einigen Tagen wieder vernichtet wurden. Man suchte Hochgenuss durch eine absolut perfekte Inszenierung!
Aus heutiger Sicht waren es Events, echte Marketingevents, die mit großer Nachhaltigkeit kein Produkt, sondern das absolutistische Fürstentum vermarkten sollten.
Aus jeder Epoche und jedem Kulturkreis ließe sich über großartige Veranstaltungen und Großevents berichten.
Denken wir nur an die Krönungsfeierlichkeiten der Könige, Kaiser und Päpste. Teilweise gibt es hierfür bis ins Detail ausgearbeitete Protokolle und Ablaufregelungen.
Kaiser Karl V. ließ im Jahr 1356 in einer Goldenen Bulle nicht nur den zeremoniellen Ablauf festlegen, sondern er regelte auch die Sitzordnung und Bestuhlungsart. Es wurde bestimmt, dass der König sechs, die Kurfürsten eine Stufe höher als die übrigen Anwesenden zu sitzen hatten. Es wurde festgehalten, welche Würdenträger separate Tische erhalten, wer neben dem König sitzen durfte,

in welcher Entfernung sich die anderen Adeligen aufhalten mussten etc. Diese Richtlinien hatten sehr lange Gültigkeit.
Sogar der junge Goethe war beeindruckt und berichtete in seinem Werk Dichtung und Wahrheit über die Zeremonien des Krönungsmahles von Joseph II. im Frankfurter Römer am 03. April 1764. Aber gerade das Bestehen auf dieser starren protokollarischen Regelung führte bei den Krönungsfeierlichkeiten immer wieder zu Streit und tätlichen Auseinandersetzungen. Es mussten im Laufe der Geschichte einige Krönungsmahlzeiten abgesagt werden bzw. sie wurden an leeren Tischen durchgeführt.
Nicht gerade an leeren Tischen fand das Hambacher Fest in der Ruine des Hambacher Schlosses im Jahr 1832 statt. Zu dieser Protestfeier baute man im Innenhof der Schlossruine Tribünen und eine Festtafel für 16 x 160 Patrioten auf. Die Gemeinde Neustadt ließ den Weg zur Burgruine verbreitern.
Am 27. Mai um 08.00 Uhr setzte sich der Festzug, der auf dem Marktplatz in Neustadt Aufstellung genommen hatte, in Bewegung. Bereits um 09.00 Uhr war der ganze Berg mit einem Gewimmel von Menschen bedeckt.
Die Zahl der Festteilnehmer wurde auf 20 – 30.000 Menschen geschätzt. Der Andrang war so groß, dass sich die meisten Teilnehmer außerhalb der Ringmauer aufhalten mussten, da innerhalb der Umgrenzung kein Platz war. So hörten sie von dem Rednermarathon mit 16 Hauptrednern nichts. Außerhalb der Ruinen fanden im Laufe des Tages viele spontane und improvisierte Kundgebungen statt, was die Feier völlig unübersichtlich machte. Es ist offensichtlich, dass die Veranstalter im Vorfeld keine Vorstellung hatten, wie groß der Zulauf sein würde und wie man diese Veranstaltung organisieren musste. Entsprechend konnten die vielen Teilnehmer auch nicht mit Speisen und Getränken bedient werden, da lediglich die Versorgung für die Festtafel organisiert war.
Die Feier fand dann am Nachmittag ein schlichtes Ende. Die Helden waren müde, hungrig und durstig. Kein neuer Redner betrat die Bühne, und so strömte die Menge in kleinen Gruppen zurück nach Neustadt, wo abends einige private Ballvergnügungen gegeben wurden.
Das Hambacher Fest von 1832 weist einen hohen Rang in der Tradition nationaler und liberaler Bestrebungen in der Geschichte unseres Landes auf. Es ist daher unvergesslich, obgleich es organisatorisch und veranstaltungstechnisch gesehen ein Flop war.
Die Leistungen der Veranstaltungsorganisatoren der vergangenen Zeiten ist um so höher einzuschätzen, wenn man erfährt, wie das legendäre und heute sogar glorifizierte Woodstock Music and Art Festival tatsächlich ablief. Dies Musik-Festival gilt als musikalischer Höhepunkt der US-amerikanischen Hippiebewegung Flowerpower, und kann guten Gewissens als Vorläufer unserer heutigen Open Air-Musikveranstaltungen bezeichnet werden.

Eine Generation suchte hier ihr Paradies aus Kriegsverweigerung, Musikversöhnung und Gemeinschaftssexualität.
Die Veranstaltung fand offiziell vom 15. – 17. August 1969 statt, endete tatsächlich jedoch am 18. August. Ursprünglich war das Festival im Dorf Woodstock im Bundesstaat New York geplant, musste dann aber nach Protesten der Dorfbevölkerung auf ein 243 Hektar großes Gelände in White Lake bei Bethel, ebenfalls im Bundesstaat New York gelegen, ausweichen. Bethel liegt ca. 150 km von New York entfernt und besaß damals weniger als 4000 Einwohner.
Der Veranstalter rechnete mit 60.000 Besuchern. Tatsächlich machten sich rund 1 Mio. Menschen auf den Weg. Die Hälfte von ihnen blieb in verstopften Zugangswegen stecken. Über 400.000 erreichten jedoch das Festivalgelände.
Auf dem Festival traten 32 Bands und Solisten der Musikrichtungen Folk, Rock, Soul und Blues für insgesamt ca. 200.000 Dollar Gage auf. Das Ticket für alle drei Tage kostete 18 Dollar.
Das Festival selbst war für den Veranstalter ein finanzielles Desaster. Wegen des unerwartet hohen Besucherandranges war es schon bald nicht mehr möglich, Besucher ohne Ticket abzukassieren.
Die Absperrungen wurden niedergetreten, und nur ein Bruchteil der Besucher war im Besitz einer bezahlten Eintrittskarte. Auf den schlammigen Wiesen versanken Besucher und Pkw im Morast. Die Notdurft wurde wegen mangelnder Toilettenanlagen an Ort und Stelle verrichtet. Zusätzlich mussten alle Musiker sowie Verpflegung und medizinische Betreuung für die Besucher wegen der verstopften Zugangswege mit Hubschraubern eingeflogen werden.
Erst durch die nachträgliche Vermarktung des Festivals durch einen Film und ein Dreifachalbum stellte sich der kommerzielle Erfolg ein.
Blicken wir in der Geschichte zurück, so wären viele Veranstaltungen zu nennen, die heute noch bekannt und bedeutend sind. Einige haben die Welt verändert, wie der Westfälische Frieden zu Münster und Osnabrück, der nach dreijährigen Verhandlungen im Jahre 1648 abgeschlossen wurde oder der Wiener Kongress 1814 und 1815. Andere haben bedeutende weltwirtschaftliche Veränderungen eingeleitet, wie die Feierlichkeiten zur Eröffnung des Suezkanals 1869 oder die Weltausstellungen. Angefangen bei der ersten Weltausstellung in London im Jahr 1851, zu der bereits über 6 Mio. Besucher kamen. Zur Pariser Weltausstellung 1889, es ist die Ausstellung mit dem Eiffelturm, kamen 25 Mio. Besucher. Und 1900 – ebenfalls in Paris – konnten mehr als 50 Mio. Ausstellungsbesucher gezählt werden.
Leider muss auch darauf hingewiesen werden, dass Veranstaltungen häufig zur Verherrlichung von Macht und Stärke missbraucht wurden. Vor allem in totalitären Staaten, ganz gleich ob rechts oder links, wird und wurde die Macht des jeweiligen Regimes mit Paraden und Aufmärschen demonstriert.

In den freien und aufgeklärten Gesellschaften werden Veranstaltungen hauptsachlich zur Weiterbildung, zur Kommunikation, zu wirtschaftlichen Zwecken, als kulturelle Ereignisse oder zum Freizeitvergnügen genutzt.
Die Mehrzahl der Veranstaltungen sind allerdings nicht die Großveranstaltungen mit ihrer nationalen oder internationalen Bedeutung, sondern es ist die Vielzahl der kleineren Veranstaltungen von der Familienfeier über Konzerte, Seminare, Tagungen, Messen- und Ausstellungen, Sportveranstaltungen, Ballveranstaltungen, Volksfeste, Stadtfeste um nur einige Kategorien zu nennen.
Wie bereits erwähnt, nimmt die Zahl der Veranstaltungen zu. Allerdings werden viele Veranstaltungen nicht mehr in traditionellen Veranstaltungshäusern, Hotels und Messehallen durchgeführt, sondern es bieten sich überall Event-Locations an. Es sind alte, leer stehende Fabriken, Lager- und Verkaufsräume von Autohäusern oder anderen Wirtschaftsunternehmen, Kirchen, Diskotheken, Kinos, Schwimmbäder, Theater, Museen, Tiefgaragen, Flugplätze, Bahnhöfe, Sportstadien, Parkanlagen und Marktplätze. Es gibt fast keine Örtlichkeit, die heute nicht als Event-Location infrage kommt.
Es gibt einen Eventveranstalter im norddeutschen Raum, der wartet darauf, dass irgendwo in Deutschland ein Güterzug ausbrennt. Zu diesem ausgebrannten Güterzug, davon ist er überzeugt, werden tausende von Besuchern strömen, wenn er eine Fete im ausgebrannten Güterzug anbietet. „Schließlich", so seine Argumentation, „hat noch niemand eine Party in so einer ausgefallenen Location gefeiert."
Nach wie vor begeben sich Kommunen in den Wettbewerb, „wer hat die schönste und wer hat die größte Veranstaltungshalle". Heute sind es allerdings keine Hallen mehr, heute will man die größte Arena haben. 60.000 bis 100.000 Besucher sollen möglichst hinein passen. Und dies bei einem zu erwartenden Bevölkerungsrückgang. Auch ist der Anteil von Hallenveranstaltungen rückläufig, so dass der vorhandene „Veranstaltungskuchen" in kleinere Stücke aufgeteilt werden muss. Mit fast 500 großen Veranstaltungszentren sind die Deutschen bereits Weltmeister, und sollten sich alle Planungen realisieren, werden wir demnächst 520 bis 550 große Veranstaltungshallen und Arenen haben. Auf die Belastungen der öffentlichen Hand wird keine Rücksicht genommen. Es werden vordergründig private Investoren und Betreiber vorgeschickt. Nur wenn dieses Experiment schief geht – und damit ist in vielen Fällen zu rechnen – wird die Kommune einspringen müssen.
Wir sind bereits heute in der Situation, dass Städte und Gemeinden Großhallen bauen mussten, damit der örtliche Handball- , Eishockey- oder Basketballverein nach eigener sportlicher Qualifikation tatsächlich die Spielberechtigung für die erste Liga erhält.
Die Mehrzahl der Vereine ist allerdings nicht in der Lage, eine adäquate Miete für diese großen Hallen zu zahlen.

Ich kenne Beispiele, dass Vereine seit 2 bis 3 Jahren überhaupt keine Hallenmiete mehr zahlen. Dadurch erhöhen sich die Zuschüsse für die Hallenbetriebe, und der öffentliche Haushalt wird zusätzlich finanziell belastet.
Ich versuchte, Ihnen zu zeigen, dass in der Vergangenheit die Bevölkerungszahlen keinen großen Einfluss auf die Größe von Veranstaltungen hatten. Dies wird sich auch in der Zukunft so verhalten. Es gelten eigene Gesetze. Genusssucht, Verschwendungssucht, Eitelkeit, Machtpotential, Größenwahn, sind einige negativ besetzte Begriffe in der Veranstaltungsbranche. Spaß, Freude, Neugierde, Kommunikation, Lernen, Wohl fühlen sind positive Begriffe für das Veranstaltungswesen. Und der positive Aspekt überwiegt eindeutig. Es wäre ein trauriges Leben, wenn es Veranstaltungen und das damit verbundene gemeinsame Erleben und Kommunizieren – das Gemeinschaftsgefühl – nicht mehr gäbe.

Viertes Kapitel

Gesundheitswesen bei Bevölkerungsrückgang

A. Perspektiven der stationären Versorgung aufgrund demographischer Veränderungen

Günther E. Braun und *Jan Güssow*

I. Einführung

Statt heute 600 Millionen werden 2050 etwa 2 Milliarden Menschen auf der Erde leben, die älter als 65 Jahre sind (UN 2002). Es ist bekannt, dass sich die Bevölkerungsstruktur vor allem in Industrieländern verändert (Kessler 2006, S. 18ff.), da neben einer steigenden Lebenserwartung gleichzeitig auch immer weniger Kinder geboren werden (Dinkel 1989, S. 6ff.; Statistisches Bundesamt 2003a, S. 13ff.). Diese Entwicklung verlangt ein Umdenken in der Politik. Nachhaltige Reformen der Wirtschafts- und Sozialsysteme werden Reaktionen auf die demographische Entwicklung sein, da diese nicht nur gravierende Auswirkungen auf die umlagefinanzierte Rentenversicherung, den Arbeitsmarkt, das allgemeine Wirtschaftswachstum und das soziale Gefüge der Gesellschaft hat (Weizäcker 1996, S. 729ff.). Auch das Gesundheitswesen, für welches die umlagefinanzierte Gesetzliche Krankenversicherung (GKV) kennzeichnend ist, steht vor großen Herausforderungen. In der Bundesrepublik Deutschland waren 1999 88,5% der Bevölkerung gesetzlich versichert (Simon 2005, S. 96). Die Ausgaben der GKV beliefen sich im Jahr 2003 auf 136,2 Mrd. Euro, wobei die stationäre Versorgung mit 46,8 Mrd. Euro (ca. 34%) den größten Ausgabenanteil hatte. Die in der Enquete-Kommission „Demographischer Wandel" des Bundestags vorliegenden 13 Prognosen verschiedener Institute und Einzelautoren berechnen aufgrund der demographischen Entwicklung bis 2040 bzw. 2050 Beitragssätze zwischen 15 und über 30%. Diese Prognosen sind jedoch sehr abhängig von den zugrunde gelegten Annahmen über die zukünftige Entwicklung der Rahmenbedingungen. Es muss daher bei den Reformbemühungen darum gehen, das Gesundheitswesen zielgerichtet im Kontext der demographischen Herausforderungen und im gesellschaftlichen Diskurs so umzubilden, dass eine zweckmäßige, ausreichende, notwendige und wirtschaftliche Versorgung aller Bevölkerungsschichten auch in Zukunft gesichert ist. Dabei liegt inhaltlich und kostenmäßig ein besonderes Augenmerk auf dem stationären Sektor, dem sich dieser Beitrag widmet.

II. Einfluss des demographischen Wandels auf den stationären Sektor

Bevor Überlegungen hinsichtlich der demographiebedingten Effekte auf die stationäre Versorgung vorgenommen werden können, ist zu klären, wie die Krankheitserwartung in Anhängigkeit vom Alter variiert.

1. Altersstruktur- und Morbiditätseffekt

Grundsätzlich sind Aussagen über die Konsequenzen der demographischen Entwicklung auf die Nachfrage von Gesundheitsleistungen sehr schwierig, weil sehr unterschiedliche Effekte die demographiebedingten Auswirkungen auf die medizinische Versorgung bestimmen. Abbildung 1 zeigt einen vereinfachten Bezugsrahmen hierfür.

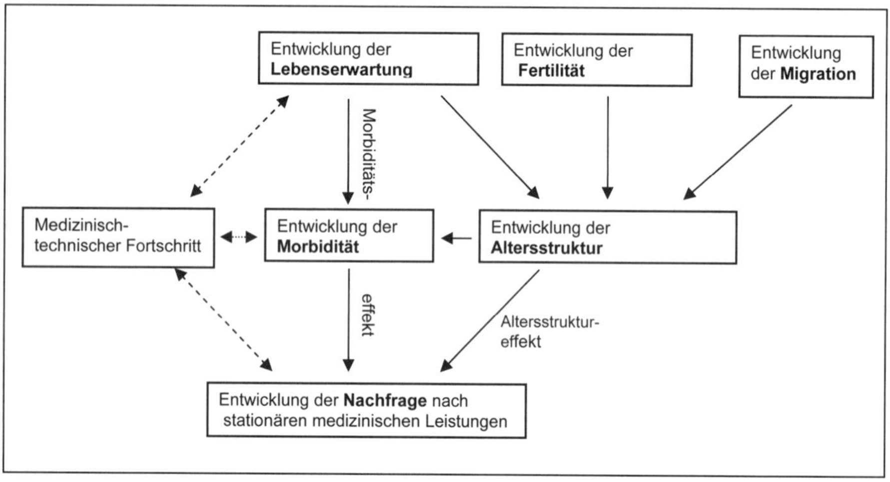

Abb. 1: Vereinfachter Bezugsrahmen des Einflusses der demographischen Entwicklung auf die Nachfrage nach medizinischen Leistungen

Der demographische Wandel wird auf Grund der steigenden Lebenserwartung und der relativ geringen Geburtenrate in Deutschland zu einer absoluten und relativen Zunahme der Bevölkerungszahlen in den höheren Altersklassen führen. Auch die Migration, welche dieser Entwicklung theoretisch entgegenwirken könnte, wird von ihren praktischen Auswirkungen auf die Altersstruktur der Gesamtbevölkerung von untergeordneter Bedeutung bleiben. Die daraus resultierende Altersstrukturveränderung wird allerdings mit einer zunehmenden durchschnittlichen Krankheitserwartung einhergehen. Wenn beispielsweise die Höhe der **Gesundheitsausgaben** den Indikator für die abgeleitete Nachfrage nach Gesundheitsleistungen darstellt, ist aus Abbildung 2 zu ersehen, dass die Gesundheitsnachfrage in Abhängigkeit des Alters, insbesondere im stationären Bereich, stark zunimmt.

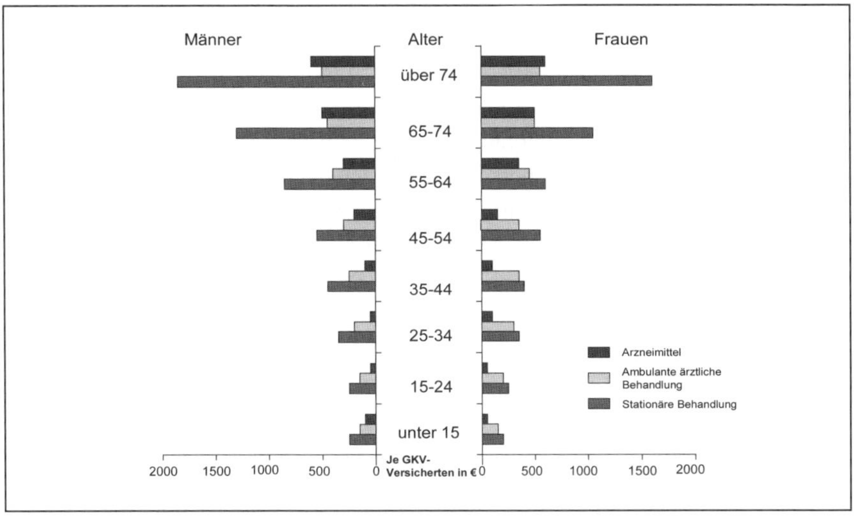

Quelle: Erbsland, Wille (1995), S. 661ff.

Abb. 2: Ausgewählte Ausgaben der gesetzlichen Krankenversicherung im Westen Deutschlands vor 1995

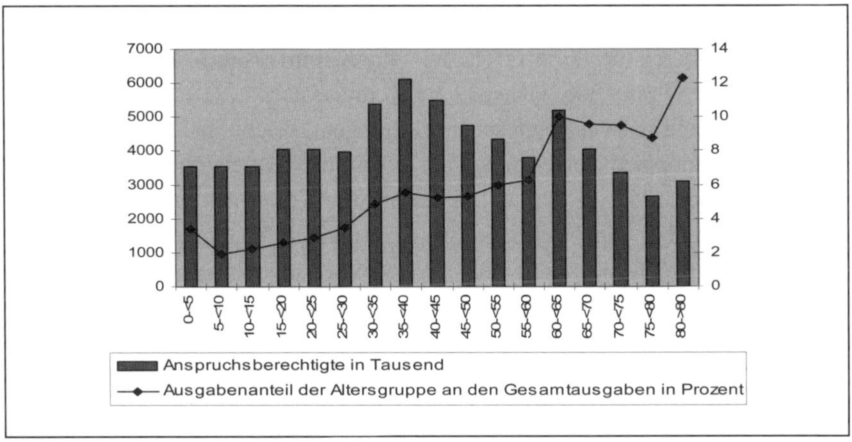

Quelle: in Anlehnung an Pimpertz 2005, S. 254

Abb. 3: Anteil der Ausgaben einzelner Altersgruppen an den Gesamtausgaben sowie die altersspezifischen Mitgliederzahlen in der GKV in 2001

Dieser Wirkungszusammenhang wird als **Altersstruktureffekt** bezeichnet. Die zahlenmäßig starken Jahrgänge zwischen 30 und 55 Jahren vereinen heute ein unterdurchschnittliches Krankheitsrisiko auf sich und erzeugen so Gesundheitsausgaben, welche unter dem Durchschnitt liegen. Die über 60-Jährigen verursachen dagegen 50,2 Prozent der Gesundheitsausgaben, obwohl jene Versichertengruppe lediglich 21,1 Prozent aller Versicherten repräsentiert (Pimpertz 2005, S. 254).

Wenn die geburtenstarken Jahrgänge der heute 30- bis 50-Jährigen das durchschnittliche Krankheitsrisiko überschreiten, erzeugen diese für die nächsten Jahre – nach den Daten von heute zu urteilen – eine stark zunehmende Nachfrage nach medizinischen Leistungen. Diese Nachfrage- bzw. Kostenzunahme, welche in 25 Jahren voraussichtlich ihren Höhepunkt erreicht haben wird, ist alleine darauf zurückzuführen, dass die absolute Zahl der Hochbetagten in den verschiedenen Altersklassen wächst.

Auf der anderen Seite ist angesichts einer steigenden Lebenserwartung zu fragen, ob das **Morbiditätsniveau**, d.h. die unterschiedliche Schadens- bzw. Krankheitserwartung generell zu- oder abnimmt (Pimpertz 2005, S. 251). Ausgehend von einem relativ hohen Niveau des Risikos nach der Geburt eines Menschen sinkt diese in Abhängigkeit vom Alter bis zum dritten Lebensjahr ab, um anschließend bis zum Lebensende kontinuierlich anzusteigen. Ab etwa dem 53. Lebensjahr liegt das Krankheitsrisiko über dem Durchschnitt aller Versicherten und nimmt stetig zu. Inwiefern die steigende Lebenserwartung die Morbidität der Bevölkerung verändert (Morbiditätseffekt) und folglich zu einer Korrektur der Nachfrage nach stationärer Versorgung führt, kann nicht eindeutig geklärt werden. Im Wesentlichen existieren hierfür zwei Thesen – die **Kompressions-** und die **Medikalisierungsthese** (Brand 2005). Gemäß der Kompressionsthese verschiebt sich die höhere Nachfrage nach medizinischen Leistungen, welche insbesondere für die letzten Lebensmonate kennzeichnend ist, in ein höheres Lebensalter (Fries 2000, S. 1584ff.; Fries 1989, S. 19ff.).[1] Die verlängerte Lebenszeit wird vornehmlich gesund verlebt. Für die Nachfrage nach Gesundheitsleistungen bedeutet dies, dass sie während der Lebenszeit mehr oder weniger unverändert bleibt, da sie nur über einen längeren Zeitraum verteilt wird. Prognosen, welche die Alterung mit Krankwerden gleichsetzen, wären demnach falsch (Häussler, Albrecht 2005). Im Gegensatz dazu erhöhen sich die Schadenserwartungen und damit auch die Gesundheitsausgaben nach der Medikalisierungsthese, da die altersspezifische Morbidität ansteigt (Verbrugge 1984, S. 474ff.; Hof 2001, S. 43).

Eine wesentliche Stellgröße ist hier der **medizinisch-technische Fortschritt**, der bewirkt, dass immer mehr Menschen mit unterschiedlichsten Leiden therapiert

1 Die Empirie zeigt, dass insbesondere kurz vor dem Tod die Gesundheitsausgaben besonders hoch sind (Felder u.a. 2000, S. 579ff.; Lubitz u.a. 1995, S. 999ff.).

werden können. Die zunehmende Alterung der Gesellschaft und der medizinisch-technische Fortschritt sind zwei sich gegenseitig verstärkende Entwicklungen (Breyer u.a. 2005, S. 524). Breyer, Zweifel und Kifmann nennen dieses Phänomen „Sisyphus-Syndrom“: Dadurch, dass der medizinisch-technische Fortschritt zur Verlängerung der Lebenszeit führt, bedingt er eine Erhöhung der Zahl derjenigen, die eine medizinische Versorgung überdurchschnittlich nachfragen (Breyer u.a. 2005, S. 525). Auch durch die Spezialisierung verschiedener Anbieter auf ältere Personenkreise als Zielgruppe schafft sich das Angebot mitunter eine zunehmende Nachfrage selber.

Dass auch die Prägvalenz von Stoffwechselerkrankungen, Herz-Kreislauf-Krankheiten, Krebs, Muskel- und Knochenkrankheiten, Demenz etc., d.h. chronischen Leiden allgemein mit dem Alter stark zusammenhängt, zeigt z.B. Güther (1998, S. 43) in einer Untersuchung von 12 ausgewählten **chronischen Krankheiten**. Ähnlich stellt der erste Altenbericht der Bundesregierung fest, „...dass die Zunahme der alten Alten eine Zunahme der Wahrscheinlichkeit (bedeutet), dass häufige Erkrankungen des Alters noch häufiger werden, dass bisher im Alter seltene Krankheiten eine Zunahme ihrer Häufigkeit erfahren, und dass vor allem aufgrund der zunehmenden Lebenserwartung, die mit einer Zunahme der Dauer chronischer Verläufe verbunden sein kann, bisher kaum beobachtete Erkrankungskonstellationen gefunden werden“ (Bundesregierung 1993, S. 105). Längsschnittanalysen durch Kohortenvergleiche zeigen dementsprechend,[2] dass sich die Ausgaben je Altersklasse im Zeitverlauf gegenüber dem ambulanten Bereich insbesondere im stationären Bereich versteilern: So lagen die Krankenhausausgaben der 70-jährigen Männer 1997 um 16% höher als zwei Jahre zuvor und in darüber liegenden Altersjahrgängen reichen sie, wenn auch nicht durchgängig, an 25% heran (Hof 2001, S. 61).

Auf der Makroebene treten beide Effekte, die Konstanz und Abnahme (Kompressionsthese) sowie die Zunahme der Morbidität (Medikalisierungsthese), gleichzeitig auf, sodass eine eindeutige Aussage, welcher Effekt überwiegt, auch mithilfe der Empirie nicht möglich ist (Breyer u.a. 2005 S. 530; Hof 2001, S. 108 f.; Ulrich 2003, S. 10). Wenn z.B. hinsichtlich des sozialen Milieus, in dem sich die Patienten befinden, differenziert wird, ist sowohl die Medikalisierungs- als auch die Kompressionsthese empirisch nachweisbar. Für Menschen der ärmeren Gesellschaftsschichten gilt die Medikalisierungsthese, dort stagniert sogar die Lebenserwartung, und für reichere Schichten trifft die Kompressionsthese zu (Deutscher Bundestag 2002, S. 399). Eine entsprechende Synthese beschreibt das **bimodale Konzept** von Kane (1988). Er prognostiziert, dass sich der Gesund-

2 Pohlmeier /Ulrich weisen zu Recht darauf hin, dass Querschnittsanalysen wenig aufschlussreich sind, da es zur Vermischung verschiedener Alterseffekte kommt und nicht zwischen Morbidität und Nachfrage nach medizinischen Leistungen unterschieden werden kann (Pohlmeier, Ulrich 1996, S. 49ff.).

heitszustand der nachkommenden Generation langfristig verbessert, gleichzeitig aber auch der Anteil behinderter, gesundheitlich beeinträchtigter und pflegebedürftiger Menschen zunehmen wird. Eine präzisere Aussage wird sich nicht treffen lassen, da sich nachfragedämpfende Effekte, aber auch nachfrageerhöhende Effekte, die beide durch staatliche (Fehl-)Steuerung initiiert (Periodeneffekte) oder biographische Hintergründe bestimmter Kohorten (z.B. Kriegsjahrgänge) ausgelöst sein können, nicht vollständig herausrechnen lassen (Pimpertz 2005, S. 253; Getzen 1992, S. 98ff.). Hof (2001, S. 49, 58, 62) zeigt allerdings, dass die Relevanz der Kompressionsthese für den stationären Bereich geringer ausfällt als für den ambulanten Bereich. Und selbst unabhängig von der Verifikation der Kompressions- oder die Medikalisierungsthese kann angenommen werden, dass der Altersstruktureffekt den Morbiditätseffekt mehr als kompensieren dürfte (Schulz u.a. 2000).

2. Eine Prognose auf Grundlage des Status quo

Nach den Vorausberechnungen der 10. koordinierten Bevölkerungsvorausschätzung (Statistisches Bundesamt 2003) steigt die Zahl der 65 bis 80-Jährigen um rund 15%, die Zahl der 80-Jährigen und Älteren um das 2,7-fache von 3,4 Mio. auf 9,1 Mio. Die Zunahme älterer Personen wird sich auch auf den stationären Sektor auswirken, weil ältere Personen um ein Vielfaches mehr an Krankenhausleistungen in Anspruch nehmen.
Da quantitative Aussagen über künftige Veränderungen im altersspezifischen Morbiditätsspektrum kaum möglich sind und auch die Wirkung des technischen Fortschritts auf die altersgruppenspezifische Erkrankungshäufigkeit und den Pflegebedarf nicht eindeutig ist, wird anhand von konstanten altersgruppen- und geschlechtsspezifischen Erkrankungshäufigkeiten und Verweildauern die demographisch bedingte Entwicklung der Krankenhausfallzahlen und des Krankenhaustagevolumens als **Status-quo-Betrachtung** berechnet.
Die 10. **koordinierte Bevölkerungsvorausberechnung** des Statistischen Bundesamtes (2003) stellt neun Szenarien zur Prognose der Bevölkerungsentwicklung von den Jahren 2002 bis 2050 auf. Alle neun Varianten gehen von einer Fertilitätsrate von 1,4 Kindern pro Frau bis zum Jahr 2050 aus. Variiert werden jedoch die Annahmen bzgl. der Zuwanderung und der Lebenserwartung. Auf Grundlage dieser Modelle ergibt sich eine Bevölkerungszahl in Höhe zwischen 67 Millionen und 81 Millionen Menschen. Gemäß dem 5. Szenario, welches als mittlere Variante von 200.000 Einwanderern und einer Lebenserwartung von 81,1 für Männer und 86,6 Jahren für Frauen ausgeht, wird sich die Einwohnerzahl von Deutschland im Jahr 2050 auf 75 Millionen reduziert haben. Dieser Variante wird die größte Plausibilität zugesprochen und auch die Ergebnisse ver-

schiedener anderer Prognosen zur zukünftigen demographischen Entwicklung in Deutschland weisen ähnliche Zahlen und eine geringe Varianz auf (Statistisches Bundesamt 2003a; Grohmann 2003, S. 449ff.; Deutscher Bundestag 2002, S. 60ff.; United Nations 2002; Schulz 1999), weshalb sich die weiteren Ausführungen auf dieses Szenario beziehen.

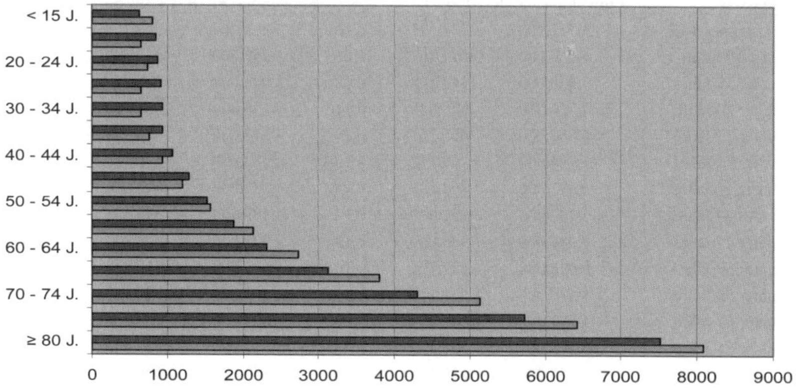

	≥ 80 J.	75 - 79 J.	70 - 74 J.	65 - 69 J.	60 - 64 J.	55 - 59 J.	50 - 54 J.	45 - 49 J.	40 - 44 J.	35 - 39 J.	30 - 34 J.	25 - 29 J.	20 - 24 J.	15 - 20 J.	< 15 J.
■ Frauen	7520	5719	4298	3128	2326	1877	1535	1290	1062	932	930	918	872	857	636
■ Männer	8093	6424	5124	3809	2740	2151	1565	1212	941	769	662	662	737	661	810

Quelle: BKK Bundesverband (2004)[3]

Abb. 4: Krankenhausbehandlungen von Frauen und Männern nach Alter in Deutschland 2003 (Tage je 1.000 Versicherte)

Legt man die Krankenhausfälle von 2003 zu Grunde, so lässt sich eine Verhältniszahl (VZ) zwischen der Bevölkerung 03 und den Krankenhausfällen (KH-Fälle) 03 ermitteln. Nach der Krankenhausdiagnosestatistik betrug die Zahl der vollstationär behandelten Patienten 2003 17,3 Mio. Fälle. Da es sich um **Fallzahlen** handelt, werden Patienten, die während eines Jahres mehrfach vollstationär behandelt wurden, oder die von einem Krankenhaus in andere Krankenhäuser verlegt wurden, mehrfach gezählt. Unter der Annahme, dass sich die für 2003 ermittelte Verhältniszahl auch auf das Jahr 2050 projizieren lässt, ergibt sich eine Fallzahlverringerung bei den Altersklassen 0 bis 70 Jahre (mit Ausnahme der 55 bis 60-Jährigen) und eine Fallzahlsteigerung bei den 70-Jährigen und Älteren. Der Anteil der Fallzahlen der 65-Jährigen und Älteren wird sich von 39% im Jah-

3 Es muss beachtet werden, dass nicht jeder Versicherte jedes Jahr zur stationären Behandlung im Krankenhaus ist. Im Jahr 2003 waren 11,3 Prozent der BKK-Versicherten von einem Krankenhausaufenthalt betroffen. Die dargestellten Krankenhaustage beziehen sich aber auf alle Versicherten und nicht nur auf die, die im Krankenhaus waren.

re 2003 auf ca. 56% im Jahre 2050 erhöhen. Insgesamt lässt sich ein Gesamtmengeneffekt von ca. 2,4 Mio. Fällen ermitteln (vgl. Tabelle 1). Hierbei nicht berücksichtigt wurde die geschlechterspezifische Verteilung der Krankenhausfälle. Im Jahre 2003 entfielen ca. 57% aller Krankenhausfälle der 65-Jährigen und Älteren auf Frauen.

Altersklassen	Einwohner 03	KH-Fälle 03	VZ	Einwohner 50	KH-Fälle 50	Veränderung
0 Jahre bis unter 5 Jahre	3.751.000	744.311	0,20	2.861.000	567.708	- 176.603
5 bis unter 10 Jahre	4.000.000	314.462	0,08	2.955.000	232.309	- 82.153
10 bis unter 15 Jahre	4.460.000	347.108	0,08	3.043.000	236.827	- 110.281
15 bis unter 20 Jahre	4.764.000	525.845	0,11	3.235.000	357.076	- 168.769
20 bis unter 25 Jahre	4.871.000	652.265	0,13	3.612.000	483.675	- 168.590
25 bis unter 30 Jahre	4.754.000	709.712	0,15	4.087.000	610.137	- 99.575
30 bis unter 35 Jahre	5.671.000	868.184	0,15	4.387.000	671.614	- 196.570
35 bis unter 40 Jahre	7.147.000	951.001	0,13	4.483.000	596.521	- 354.480
40 bis unter 45 Jahre	6.986.000	936.829	0,13	4.491.000	602.247	- 334.582
45 bis unter 50 Jahre	6.022.000	939.720	0,16	4.600.000	717.820	- 221.900
50 bis unter 55 Jahre	5.520.000	1.051.411	0,19	4.894.000	932.175	- 119.236
55 bis unter 60 Jahre	4.421.000	1.048.814	0,24	4.883.000	1.158.416	109.602
60 bis unter 65 Jahre	5.478.000	1.556.771	0,28	5.347.000	1.519.543	- 37.228
65 bis unter 70 Jahre	4.957.000	1.651.476	0,33	4.882.000	1.626.489	- 24.987
70 bis unter 75 Jahre	3.509.000	1.524.753	0,43	4.377.000	1.901.922	377.169
75 bis unter 80 Jahre	2.933.000	1.464.079	0,50	3.857.000	1.925.316	461.237
80 bis unter 85 Jahre	2.076.000	1.151.336	0,55	4.131.000	2.291.026	1.139.690
85 bis unter 90 Jahre	780.000	529.931	0,68	3.089.000	2.098.663	1.568.732
90 Jahre und älter	570.000	345.153	0,61	1.905.000	1.153.538	808.385
Total		**17.313.161**			**19.683.022**	**2.369.861**

VZ: Verhältniszahl – Durch sie wird das Verhältnis von Krankenhausfällen zu Einwohnerzahl dargestellt.
Quelle: Eigene Berechnungen auf Grundlage der 10. koordinierten Bevölkerungsvorausschätzung und des Statistischen Bundesamtes (2003)

Tab. 1: Prognose der Veränderung von Krankenhausfällen 2003-2050

Die Tabelle zeigt, dass insbesondere in den Altersklassen der über 70-Jährigen ein enormer Zuwachs an Krankenhausfällen um ca. 87% zu erwarten wäre. Da die Prognose allerdings auf der Bevölkerungsvorausschätzung des statistischen Bundesamtes beruht, die neben der Geburtenrate, der Migration und der jetzigen Bevölkerungsverteilung in den verschiedenen Altersgruppen als Determinanten des Altersstruktureffekts auch eine Schätzung der zukünftigen Lebenserwartung beinhaltet, entspricht die Prognose tendenziell eher der **Medikalisierungsthese**. Die momentan hohen Krankenhausfallzahlen der 70-Jährigen und Älteren werden in das Jahr 2050 und die dann hinzugewonnenen zusätzlichen Lebensjahre fortgeschrieben. Der Kompressionsthese zufolge würde die Verhältniszahl je Altersklasse entsprechend geringer ausfallen oder sich nach hinten verschieben, denn die Krankenhausfallzahlen bzw. -kosten vor dem Tode der Menschen verlagerten sich – so die Argumentation der Kompressionsthese – lediglich in höhe-

re Lebensjahre und die Kosten über den gesamten Lebenszyklus hinweg blieben weitgehend konstant.
Vergleicht man die Ergebnisse der Tabelle 1 mit einer Studie des Deutschen Instituts für Wirtschaftsforschung (DIW), welches im Jahre 2000 eine Prognoserechnung auf Grundlage der 9. koordinierten Bevölkerungsvorausschätzung durchführte, so lässt sich feststellen, dass die Schätzung von ca. 19,7 Mio. Fällen für 2050 sehr nahe bei der Schätzung des DIW von 19,3 Mio. Fälle liegt. Allerdings ist das DIW noch von einer Steigerung von 15,9 Mio. Fälle auf 19,3 Mio. Fälle, daher von 3,3 Mio. Fällen ausgegangen (vgl. Tabelle 2). Nachdem allerdings die Krankenhaus-Fälle schon 2003 sehr viel höher als noch 1998 lagen, wird für die verbleibenden 47 Jahre hier nur noch von einer Erhöhung um ca. 2,4 Mio. Fälle ausgegangen.

Altersklassen	**KH-Fälle 03**	**KH-Fälle DIW 98**	**Eigene Schätzung 50**	**DIW Schätzung 50**
0 bis unter 15 Jahre	1.405.881	1.430.000	1.036.844,36	830.000
15 bis unter 35 Jahre	2.756.006	3.030.000	2.122.502,124	1.790.000
35 bis unter 55 Jahre	3.878.961	3.410.000	2.848.763,37	2.470.000
55 bis unter 65 Jahre	2.605.585	2.620.000	2.677.959	2.460.000
65 bis unter 75 Jahre	3.176.229	2.610.000	3.528.410,853	3.550.000
75 Jahre und älter	3.490.499	2.840.000	7.468.542,134	8.150.000
	17.313.161	**15.940.000**	**19.683.021**	**19.250.000**

Quelle: Eigene Berechnungen, Statistisches Bundesamt (2003), DIW (2001)

Tab. 2: Vergleich mit dem Deutschen Institut für Wirtschaftsforschung

Auf der Grundlage der obigen Berechnungen lässt sich auch die Entwicklung der Pflegetage im Krankenhaus abschätzen. Auf Grund der Zunahme an älteren Menschen und der längeren Verweildauern je Krankenhausaufenthalt in dieser Bevölkerungsgruppe ist auch hier ein deutlicher Zuwachs an Pflegetagen zu vermuten, der nur teilweise durch die Abnahme der Bevölkerung in den jüngeren Altersklassen kompensiert werden kann. Insgesamt ergibt sich eine Zunahme der Pflegetage bis 2050 um 23% auf ca. 190 Mio. (vgl. Tabelle 3).
Eine Statistik über die Kosten je Fall und Altersklasse im akutstationären Bereich ist vom statistischen Bundesamt nicht verfügbar. Um dennoch einen Anhaltspunkt für die nach der Status-quo-Analyse zu prognostizierenden Mehrkosten zu berechnen, wurden in der folgenden Tabelle 4 die ermittelten Pflegetage in den Jahren 2003 und 2050 mit den durchschnittlichen Kosten je Pflegetag berechnet. Die so ermittelten Gesamtkosten 2003 stimmen ungefähr auch mit den Angaben des Statistischen Bundesamtes überein, welches 64,7 Mrd. Euro Gesamtgesundheitsausgaben für Krankenhäuser ermittelt (Statistisches Bundesamt 2003). Demzufolge würden die Kosten bis 2050 entsprechend um ca. 14 Mrd. Euro (23%) ansteigen. Zu einem ähnlichen Ergebnis gelangt man auch, wenn man die

Kosten 2002 nach ausgewählten Krankheiten und Altersgruppen im Krankenhaus auf die Altersstruktur von 2050 hochrechnet.

	KH Fälle 2003	**Verweil-dauer 2002**	**Pflegetage Gesamt 2003**	**KH Fälle 2050**	**Pflegetage 2050**	**Prozentuale Veränderung**
0 Jahre bis unter 5 Jahre	744.311	5,9	4.391.435	567.708	3.349.479	-24%
5 bis unter 10 Jahre	314.462	4,8	1.509.418	232.309	1.115.082	-26%
10 bis unter 15 Jahre	347.108	6,4	2.221.491	236.827	1.515.695	-32%
15 bis unter 20 Jahre	525.845	6,8	3.575.746	357.076	2.428.115	-32%
20 bis unter 25 Jahre	652.265	7	4.565.855	483.675	3.385.725	-26%
25 bis unter 30 Jahre	709.712	6,9	4.897.013	610.137	4.209.948	-14%
30 bis unter 35 Jahre	868.184	7,1	6.164.106	671.614	4.768.460	-23%
35 bis unter 40 Jahre	951.001	7,8	7.417.808	596.521	4.652.866	-37%
40 bis unter 45 Jahre	936.829	8,4	7.869.364	602.247	5.058.877	-36%
45 bis unter 50 Jahre	939.720	8,7	8.175.564	717.820	6.245.034	-24%
50 bis unter 55 Jahre	1.051.411	8,7	9.147.276	932.175	8.109.922	-11%
55 bis unter 60 Jahre	1.048.814	8,7	9.124.682	1.158.416	10.078.222	10%
60 bis unter 65 Jahre	1.556.771	9,1	14.166.616	1.519.543	13.827.838	-2%
65 bis unter 70 Jahre	1.651.476	9,7	16.019.317	1.626.489	15.776.943	-2%
70 bis unter 75 Jahre	1.524.753	10,5	16.009.907	1.901.922	19.970.180	25%
75 bis unter 80 Jahre	1.464.079	11,2	16.397.685	1.925.316	21.563.543	32%
80 bis unter 85 Jahre	1.151.336	11,7	13.470.631	2.291.026	26.804.999	99%
85 bis unter 90 Jahre	529.931	11,7	6.200.193	2.098.663	24.554.353	296%
90 Jahre und älter	345.153	11	3.796.683	1.153.538	12.688.914	234%
			155.120.788		**190.104.193**	**23%**

Quelle: Eigene Berechnungen, Statistisches Bundesamt (2003), Gesundheitsberichterstattung (2003), Deutsche Krankenhausgesellschaft (2005), S. 59

Tab. 3: Prognose der Veränderung von Pflegetagen im Krankenhaus 2003-2050

Obwohl die demographischen Entwicklungen anhand der einfachen Status-quo-Prognose einen zusätzlichen Bedarf an stationären Versorgungskapazitäten nahe legt, kann an dieser Stelle dennoch keine abschließende Aussage hinsichtlich der **Finanzierbarkeit** bzw. des Einflusses auf den Beitragssatz getroffen werden.[4]

---

4 Die Sachverständigen prognostizieren aufgrund der demographischen Entwicklung übereinstimmend einen Anstieg der Ausgaben und der Beitragssätze der GKV in den kommenden Jahrzehnten. Das Ausmaß dieses Anstiegs ist allerdings abhängig von der jeweils angewandten Methodik und den zugrunde gelegten Rahmendaten (z.B. medizinischer Fortschritt, Geburtenentwicklung, Erwerbsquoten, Zuwanderung, Morbidität). „So variiert der für das Jahr 2040 prognostizierte Beitragssatz in den zahlreichen Gutachten der letzten Jahre zwischen 15% und 30% (Übersicht in der Stellungnahme von Cassel). Ein aktuelles, auf Basis empirischen Datenmaterials der DKV und der PKV erarbeitetes und in der Anhörung präsentiertes Gutachten (Hof) kommt z.B. in seiner oberen Variante zu einem Beitragssatz von 17,2% für 2020 bzw. 26,1% für 2050. Der Beitragssatzanstieg ist Ergebnis eines jahresdurchschnittlichen GKV-Ausgabenanstiegs zwischen 1995 und 2050 in Höhe von 4,0%. Bemerkenswert ist, dass der Ausgabenanstieg in der Prognose sektorenspezifisch unterschiedlich ausfällt und für die ärztliche Behandlung (4,5%) und für Heil- und Hilfsmittel (4,4%) deutlich höher ist als für die im Durchschnitt liegende Krankenhausbehandlung." Deutsche Krankenhausgesellschaft 2001.

	Pflegetage 2003	Kosten 2003	Pflegetage 2050	Kosten 2050	Veränderung
0 Jahre bis unter 5 Jahre	4.391.435	1.765.356.870	3.349.479	1.349.840.037	-415.516.833
5 bis unter 10 Jahre	1.509.418	606.786.036	1.115.082	449.378.046	-157.407.990
10 bis unter 15 Jahre	2.221.491	893.039.382	1.515.695	610.825.085	-282.214.297
15 bis unter 20 Jahre	3.575.746	1.437.449.892	2.428.115	978.530.345	-458.919.547
20 bis unter 25 Jahre	4.565.855	1.835.473.710	3.385.725	1.364.447.175	-471.026.535
25 bis unter 30 Jahre	4.897.013	1.968.599.226	4.209.948	1.696.609.044	-271.990.182
30 bis unter 35 Jahre	6.164.106	2.477.970.612	4.768.460	1.921.689.380	-556.281.232
35 bis unter 40 Jahre	7.417.808	2.981.958.816	4.652.866	1.875.104.998	-1.106.853.818
40 bis unter 45 Jahre	7.869.364	3.163.484.328	5.058.877	2.038.727.431	-1.124.756.897
45 bis unter 50 Jahre	8.175.564	3.286.576.728	6.245.034	2.516.748.702	-769.828.026
50 bis unter 55 Jahre	9.147.276	3.677.204.952	8.109.922	3.268.298.566	-408.906.386
55 bis unter 60 Jahre	9.124.682	3.668.122.164	10.078.222	4.061.523.466	393.401.302
60 bis unter 65 Jahre	14.166.616	5.694.979.632	13.827.838	5.572.618.714	-122.360.918
65 bis unter 70 Jahre	16.019.317	6.439.765.434	15.776.943	6.358.108.029	-81.657.405
70 bis unter 75 Jahre	16.009.907	6.435.982.614	19.970.180	8.047.982.540	1.611.999.926
75 bis unter 80 Jahre	16.397.685	6.591.869.370	21.563.543	8.690.107.829	2.098.238.459
80 bis unter 85 Jahre	13.470.631	5.415.193.662	26.804.999	10.802.414.597	5.387.220.935
85 bis unter 90 Jahre	6.200.193	2.492.477.586	24.554.353	9.895.404.259	7.402.926.673
90 Jahre und älter	3.796.683	1.526.266.566	12.688.914	5.113.632.342	3.587.365.776
	155.120.788	**62.358.557.580**	**190.104.193**	**76.611.990.585**	**14.253.433.005**

Quelle: Eigene Berechnungen, Statistisches Bundesamt (2003), Gesundheitsberichterstattung (2003), Deutsche Krankenhausgesellschaft (2005), S. 59

Tab. 4: Prognose der Veränderung von Pflegetagen im Krankenhaus 2003-2050

Die schwierigste Prognose besteht dabei in der Schätzung des zukünftigen Produktivitätszuwachses. Im Jahre 1900 kamen 12,4 Erwerbsfähige (15-64 Jahre) auf eine alte Person (über 64 Jahre), 1950 waren es 6,9 und im Jahre 2000 waren es 4,1. Für das Jahr 2050 wird eine Zahl von 2 prognostiziert. Vor 100 Jahren war die Altersstruktur somit mehr als dreimal günstiger als heute und dennoch konnte das Sozialsystem aufgrund des Produktivitätszuwachses stetig ausgebaut werden. Die mittlere Variante der demographischen Prognose des statistischen Bundesamtes geht davon aus, dass im Jahre 2020 100 Personen 88 nicht erwerbstätige Personen (heute (2001) 82) gegenüberstehen und dass diese Zahl bis 2050 auf 112 Personen ansteigt. Hierdurch wächst die Belastung je Erwerbstätigem um ca. 27%. Demzufolge würde bereits ein verteilungsneutrales Produktivitätswachstum von 27% ausreichen, um diese Mehrbelastung auszugleichen. Neben der Produktivitätssteigerung spielt auch die Entwicklung der Arbeitslosigkeit, die Fertilitätsrate sowie die Zuwanderung eine gewichtige Rolle. Auf alle diese Faktoren kann die Politik grundsätzlich Einfluss nehmen, so dass die Auswirkungen der demographischen Entwicklungen auf den Beitragssatz bis 2050 kaum eine valide Aussagekraft haben können. Prognosen von vor 50 Jahren hätten ihrerseits trotz der relativ stabilen politischen Lage den „Pillenknick", die Immigration von 2,5 Millionen Aussiedlern aus Osteuropa sowie die Wiedervereinigung mit dem Einbruch der ostdeutschen Geburtenrate übersehen.

Auch die Prognose des Einfluss der demographischen Entwicklung auf die **Nachfrage** nach stationären Leistungen ist mit erheblichen Schwierigkeiten verbunden. So ist zu berücksichtigen, dass die demographischen Entwicklungen regional in Deutschland sehr unterschiedlich verlaufen (Schulz-Nieswandt, Kurscheid 2003, S. 41f.). Betrachtet man die Ergebnisse der Studie „Die demografische Lage der Nation" des Berlin-Instituts für Bevölkerung und Entwicklung 2006, so zeigt sich, dass in einigen ostdeutschen Ländern die Problematik des Kindermangels besonders virulent ist. Auch ist z.B. zwischen Vorpommern und dem Vogtland ein historisch einmaliges Missverhältnis zwischen Männern und Frauen entstanden. 63% aller Fortzügler seit 1991 waren dort weiblich. „In der für Partnersuche und Familiengründung wichtigen Altersklasse der 18 bis 29-Jährigen lebten 2004 in Ostdeutschland (einschließlich Berlin) je 100 Männer nur noch 90 Frauen." (Kröhnert u.a. 2006, S. 7). Seit der Wende haben ca.1,5 Mio. Menschen die neuen Bundesländer verlassen, so dass in den Ländern Thüringen, Sachsen, Sachsen-Anhalt und Mecklenburg-Vorpommern heute zwischen 8 und 12% weniger Menschen leben als zur Zeit der Wiedervereinigung. Für die einzelnen Regionen entfalten diese Abwanderungs- und Zuwanderungseffekte einen sehr viel größeren Einfluss auf den akutstationären Versorgungsbedarf als die demographische Entwicklung im Allgemeinen. Für die alten Bundesländer wurde von Lebok (2000, S. 373) mithilfe einer Simulationsberechnung ermittelt, dass nur ca. 25% der Zunahme der Krankenhausfälle im Zeitraum zwischen 1961 bis 1996 auf die demographische Entwicklung zurückgeführt werden kann. Diese Berechnung bestätigt auch die Ergebnisse von Dinkel und Görtler (1991, S. 22ff.).

III. Demographische Entwicklung im Lichte weiterer Aspekte mit Einfluss auf das Krankenhaus

Sowohl die benötigten stationären Kapazitäten als auch die Kostenentwicklung im stationären Bereich hängen von verschiedenen Einflussgrößen ab, wie der Entwicklung der Therapiemöglichkeiten, d.h. dem technischen Fortschritt, der Entwicklungen im Rahmen der Möglichkeiten des ambulanten Operierens und weiterer stationsersetzender Leistungen, aber auch der Entwicklungen von Art und Schwere verschiedener Erkrankungen sowie der allgemeinen Konstitution der Patienten und den Anreizwirkungen der Vergütungsstrukturen.

Berechnet man den Bettenbedarf nach der Hill-Burton-Formel (Simon 2005, S. 201f.), die sich aus der Einwohnerzahl, Verweildauer, Krankenhaushäufigkeit (Krankenhausaufnahmen je 1.000 Einwohner) und Bettennutzung (belegte Betten je 100 Betten) ableitet, so ergibt sich im Vergleich zur Bettenzahl des Jahres 2003 mit 542.000 Betten bei einer angenommenen durchschnittlichen Verweildauer von 8,9 Tagen (2003) und einem Auslastungsgrad von 85% ein zusätzlicher Bettenbedarf von ca. 23.000, mithin ein Anstieg auf 565.000 Betten. Betrachtet man die Verweildauer in Abhängigkeit der Altersklasse, so ergibt sich sogar ein zusätzlicher **Bettenbedarf** von 115.000, somit ein Anstieg auf 657.000 Betten. Dass eine solche, ebenfalls als Status-quo-Prognose zu bezeichnende Vorausschau allerdings zu kurz greifen muss, verdeutlicht schon ein Blick auf die im OECD-Vergleich nach wie vor sehr hohe durchschnittliche Verweildauer von Patienten in deutschen Krankenhäusern.

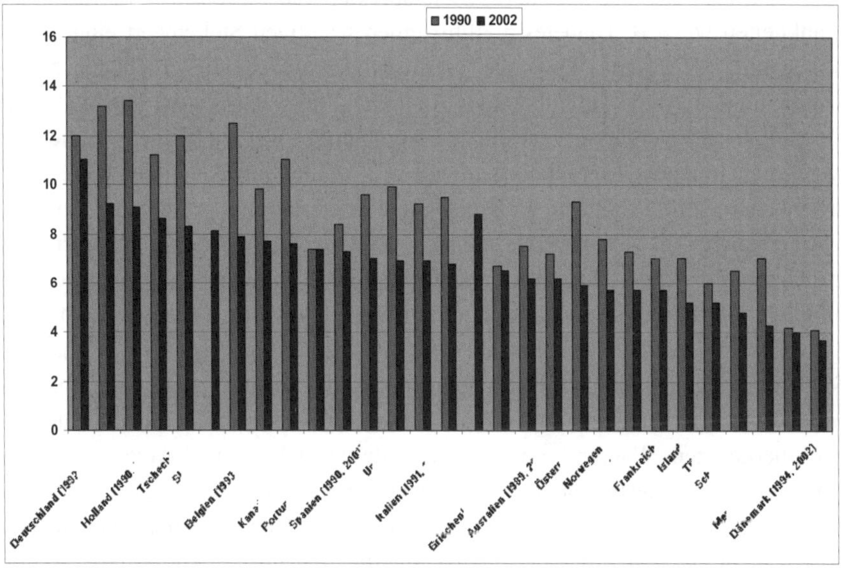

Quelle: Übersetzt aus OECD: Health at a Glance: OECD Indicators 2005, S. 57

Abb. 5: Durchschnittliche Verweildauern im Krankenhaus, 1990 und 2002

Könnte die Verweildauer in Deutschland, die im Jahre 2002 bei 9,1 Tage lag und mittlerweile schon bei unter 8 Tagen liegt, längerfristig auf das Niveau von Österreich (5,9 Tage, d.h. -35%) gesenkt werden, so ergäbe sich nach der Hill-Burton-Formel ein Bedarf von ca. 374.000 Betten im Jahre 2050, und damit – gemessen am Betten-Ist des Jahres 2003 – eine Überkapazität von ca. 168.000

Betten, sodass bis 2050 ca. 30% der Betten abgebaut werden könnten. Allerdings wären auch hier wiederum die demographische Entwicklung und die höheren Verweildauern in den oberen Altersklassen zu berücksichtigen.
Möglich wird die Verweildauerreduzierung durch den **technischen und medizinischen Fortschritt.**[5] Schon heute zeichnet sich ab, dass es in den nächsten 10 Jahren möglich sein wird, jegliche Daten (Sprache, Text, Bild) über das Internet zu übertragen, was zu erheblichen Zeitersparnissen führen dürfte. So prognostiziert Arthur Andersen (2000, S. 28) bereits für das Jahr 2015: „Die Telematik und Telemedizin haben sich auf breiter Front in Deutschland durchgesetzt. Information, Kommunikation und Beratung erfolgen vielfach zwischen Ärzten und Patienten online. (...) Das „vernetzte Krankenhaus" ist existent. Arztinformationssysteme (AIS), Radiologieinformationssysteme (RIS), Bildarchivierungs- und Kommunikationssysteme (PACS), Krankenhausinformationssysteme (KIS), Remote-Steuerungssysteme (RCS) sowie die elektronische Patientenakte (EPA) sind fest etabliert." Hinsichtlich des medizinischen Fortschritts werden insbesondere auch die Möglichkeiten der Gentherapie zur Bekämpfung von Zivilisationskrankheiten wie z.B. Diabetes mellitus einen wichtigen Stellenwert einnehmen. Sogenannte „High-Tech-Präparate" verursachen zwar häufig erhebliche Mehrkosten für die Arzneimitteltherapie (Andersen 2000, S. 43), die aber teilweise durch eine stark verkürzte Verweildauer kompensiert werden können. Schließlich werden auch neuere Therapieformen, wie z.B. minimalinvasive Therapien, einen erheblichen Einfluss auf die Notwendigkeit einer stationären Therapie bzw. die Verweildauern im Krankenhaus nehmen. Andererseits machen neue Verfahren zur Unterstützung der Diagnostik und Therapie Behandlungen teilweise auch erst möglich, die früher gar nicht durchgeführt werden konnten. Dies gilt z.B. für die Sensorik, insbesondere den Einsatz von Biosensoren an besonders gefährdeten Stellen innerhalb stationärer Einrichtungen. So sind auch Ferndiagnosen über das Internet realisierbar, wenn am Körper getragene Sensoren Routineuntersuchungen übernehmen. Während durch den Einsatz neuer Verfahren davon ausgegangen werden kann, dass sich die Verweildauer in den nächsten Jahren weiter reduzieren wird, lässt sich ein ähnlicher Effekt auf die Krankenhausfallzahlen undkosten nicht ableiten. Auch der Sachverständigenrat für die Konzertierte Aktion im Gesundheitswesen stellte schon 1995 im Zuge des medizinischen Fortschritts jene Technologien heraus, die zu bestehenden Anwendungen zusätzlich zum Einsatz kommen und neue Diagnose- und Therapiemöglichkeiten eröffnen, gleichzeitig aber zu Ausgabensteigerungen führen (SVR 1995, S. 40). Deshalb resümiert Lebok: „Während der Einsatz der Großgerätemedizin einen unbestreitbaren Beitrag zu Qualitätsverbesserung des stationären Leistungsangebots leistet,

5 Vgl. allerdings auch Punkt III 3.

führt die Expansion der Hochleistungsmedizin in Krankenhäusern auch zu Mengenausweitung und damit zu Kostensteigerung“ (Lebok 2000, S. 147f.).

2. Entwicklung von chronischen und Zivilisationskrankheiten

Prinzipiell bestimmt das Niveau der demographischen Transition den Verlauf der epidemiologischen Transition,[6] was schließlich zu bestimmten Nachfrageentwicklungen nach Gesundheitsleistungen führt. Wo in entwickelten Ländern vor hundert und mehr Jahren primär Infektionskrankheiten zu therapieren waren, sind infolge medizinischer und gesellschaftlicher Entwicklungen heute vor allem chronisch-degenerative Krankheiten zu behandeln. Neu ist, dass Anzeichen einer psychosozialen Transition existieren. Vor allem im Alter erhöht sich die Wahrscheinlichkeit psychischer Erkrankungen und demenzieller Leiden (Deutscher Bundestag 2002, S. 496). Die **Entwicklung der einzelnen Krankheitsbilder** ist daher in sehr unterschiedlichem Maße vom Alter und Geschlecht beeinflusst. So erkranken z.B. im Jugendalter Mädchen häufiger als Jungen an Krankheiten des Verdauungssystems, an Ernährungs- und Stoffwechselkrankheiten sowie an psychischen Krankheiten und Verhaltensstörungen. Diese Krankheiten und Störungen machten im Jahr 2003 34% der stationären Behandlungstage weiblicher Jugendlicher aus. Beinahe die Hälfte der stationären Krankenhausaufenthalte von Frauen unter 50 Jahre ist durch Komplikationen in der Schwangerschaft und bei der Entbindung sowie durch Erkrankungen der Harn- und Geschlechtsorgane bedingt. Ab dem 50. Lebensjahr ist die Anzahl der Krankenhaustage für die männlichen Versicherten höher als bei Frauen. Sie wurden im Jahr 2001 am häufigsten auf Grund einer chronischen ischämischen Herzkrankheit stationär behandelt. Der zweithäufigste Grund war eine psychische oder Verhaltensstörung durch Alkohol. Diese wenigen Beispiele verdeutlichen, dass der Bedarf an stationären Einrichtungen ganz wesentlich davon abhängig ist, welche Entwicklung z.B. psychisch bedingte Krankheiten in Zukunft nehmen werden.

Einen sehr wichtigen Stellenwert haben in diesem Zusammenhang insbesondere **chronische Krankheiten**. Obwohl heutzutage die Lebenserwartung um ein vielfaches höher ist, vertritt z.B. Bruker die These, dass „...der Gesundheitszustand der Menschen in den zivilisierten Völkern noch nie so schlecht war wie heute“ (Bruker 1991, S. 30). Auch existieren Anzeichen, dass die jungen Generationen

6 Ausgehend von einer hohen Mortalität und Fertilität sinkt die Sterblichkeit und Fruchtbarkeit im Laufe der wirtschaftlichen Entwicklung eines Landes. Dieser Zusammenhang zwischen demographischer und wirtschaftlicher Entwicklung wird als demographische Transition bezeichnet. Eine direkte Konsequenz dieser demographischen Transition ist die epidemiologische Transition. Die epidemiologische Transition meint den Übergang von Infektionskrankheiten, welche vor hundert und mehr Jahren primär zu therapieren waren, zu chronisch-degenerativen Krankheiten, die heute vor allem zu behandeln sind. Vgl. Fleßa 2001, S. 79-88.

zunehmend kränker sind als frühere. Beispielsweise leiden immer mehr Jugendliche an Adipositas, Essstörungen, kardiologischen Krankheiten, Stoffwechselerkrankungen und Diabetes mellitus. Manche Mediziner sehen daher erste Anzeichen, dass sich der Trend der steigenden Lebenserwartung abschwächt oder sogar umkehrt (Schwing 2005, S. 300f.). 1987 wurden die Kosten für ernährungsbedingte Zivilisationskrankheiten auf ca. 21 Mrd. Euro beziffert, 1993 waren es bereits mehr als 50 Mrd. (Bruker 1994). Nach der Krebsstatistik erlag 1900 jeder 30. Tote, 1920 jeder 15. Tote, 1950 jeder 6. Tote, 1960 jeder 5. Tote und 1984 bereits jeder 4. Tote dem Krebs.

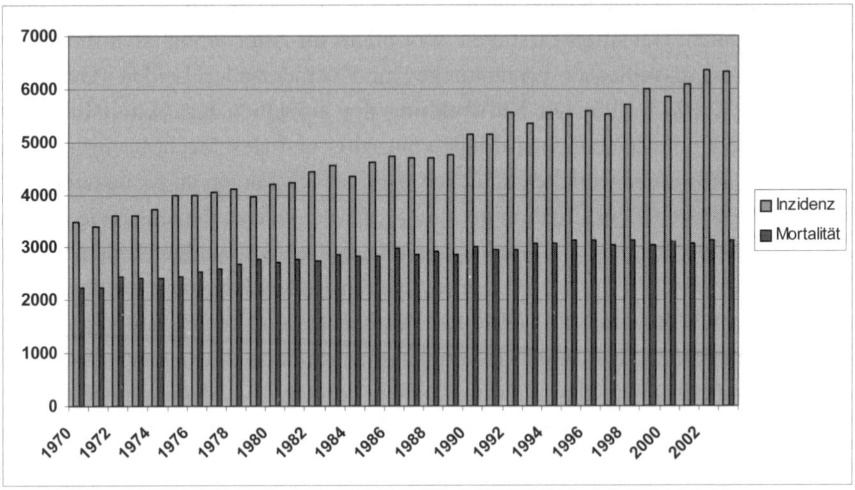

Quelle: Eigene Darstellung in Anlehnung an Krebsstatistik Saarland, abrufbar unter: http://www.krebsregister. saarland.de/datenbank/datenbank.html

Abb. 6: Inzidenz und Mortalität von bösartigen Krebserkrankungen im Saarland, 1970 – 2003, gemessen in Fällen pro Jahr

Ältere Menschen leiden dabei häufig nicht nur an den chronischen Krankheiten, von welchen sie in jüngeren Jahren befallen wurden, sondern zusätzlich auch noch an den chronischen Krankheiten, die typische „chronische Alterskrankheiten“ darstellen. Zu jenen gehören beispielsweise die Arthrose, das Altersdiabetes, die Herzinsuffizienz und die Demenz, an der in der Altersklasse der über-90-Jährigen alleine 40% leiden (Robert-Koch-Institut 2005).

3. Einzug von marktwirtschaftlichen Elementen in das Gesundheitswesen

Durch die Einführung **marktlicher Prinzipien** im Gesundheitswesen geraten Leistungserbringer zunehmend unter Druck, effiziente Strukturen aufzubauen und damit Kosten einzusparen. In diesem Zusammenhang lassen sich drei Haupttrends herausschälen:

- Die Zunahme privatwirtschaftlich geführter Krankenhäuser und Krankenhausketten.
- Die Einführung neuer pauschaler und damit preislicher Vergütungssysteme im stationären Sektor sowie
- die Zulassung neuer Versorgungsstrukturen mit weitreichenden Dispositionsspielräumen außerhalb der Rahmenbedingungen des Kollektivvertragrechts.

Die Anzahl der Krankenhäuser ist zwischen den Jahren 1991 und 2004 von 2.411 auf 2.166 und damit um rund 10% gesunken. Die Anzahl der Betten fiel im gleichen Zeitraum sogar um 20%. Deutliche Veränderungen sind auch in der Verteilung der Krankenhäuser auf öffentliche, freigemeinnützige und private Träger zu beobachten. Befanden sich im Jahr 1991 noch 46% der Krankenhäuser in öffentlicher **Trägerschaft**, so waren es im Jahr 2004 nur noch 36%. Der Anteil der privaten Krankenhausträger stieg im selben Zeitraum von 15 auf 26%. Der Anteil der freigemeinnützigen Krankenhäuser blieb mit 38% im Jahr 2004 gegenüber 39% im Jahr 1991 weitgehend konstant. Während daher die privaten Krankenhäuser von 1991 bis 2004 um 55% gestiegen sind, nahm die Zahl der öffentlichen Krankenhäuser um 29% ab. Die zunehmende Privatisierung im Krankenhaussektor wird sich bis 2050 weiter fortsetzen und den Druck auf öffentliche Krankenhäuser erhöhen, ihre Leistungen effizienter zu erbringen und sektorübergreifende Behandlungsabläufe zu schaffen, um einer drohenden Privatisierung zu entgehen. Insgesamt ist zu erwarten, dass der Wettbewerbsdruck dazu beitragen wird, die Konsequenzen aus der demographischen Entwicklung abzufedern.
Die Konvergenzphase zur **Einführung der G-DRGs** läuft 2009 endgültig aus. Dann wird ein fallpauschalierendes System das ehemalige Finanzierungssystem vollständig abgelöst haben. Fallpauschalen wirken wie prospektiv festgelegte Preise und orientieren sich nicht mehr an der Kostenstruktur des einzelnen Krankenhauses. Insbesondere Krankenhäuser mit einer ungünstigen Kostenstruktur werden dann vom Markt verschwinden, wenn sie es nicht geschafft haben, durch umfängliche Reorganisationsmaßnahmen und die Konzentration auf Kernkompetenzen effizientere Strukturen zu schaffen. Zudem soll auch die Vergütung der ambulanten Operationen in Zukunft über Fallpauschalen erfolgen. Die Weiterentwicklung des Vergütungssystems wird nicht nur einen erheblichen Einfluss auf die stationäre Leistungserbringung haben, sondern auch auf die Frage nehmen, auf welcher Behandlungsstufe eine Leistung zukünftig erbracht wird.

Schließlich zeigt die **Liberalisierung im Gesundheitswesen** die Auflockerung des herkömmlichen Rechtsrahmens in Richtung einer zunehmenden Patientensouveränität sowie verstärkter Entscheidungs- und Handlungsspielräume der Patienten, Leistungsbringer und Kostenträger auf der Mikro- und Mesoebene. Der benevolente Paternalismus der medizinischen Leistungserbringer rückt immer stärker in den Hintergrund, und die Informationsmündigkeit der Patienten und der Versicherten steigt (Braun, Schulz-Nieswandt 2005; Schulz-Nieswandt, Kurscheid 2004, S.114 ff.). Gleichzeitig wächst auf Seiten des Staates die Bereitschaft, Kompetenzen auf die verbandliche Ebene der Leistungserbringer und Kostenträger zu verlagern. Darüber hinaus nimmt der einzelwirtschaftliche Autonomiegrad der verschiedenen Leistungsanbieter und Kostenträger über die Jahre hinweg zu. Die traditionelle Vorgehensweise, wonach Leistungsanbieter und Kostenträger gehalten sind, „gemeinsam und einheitlich“ zu agieren, beginnt sich allmählich aufzulösen. Unterschiedliche und flexible Vertragslösungen zwischen den Anbietern untereinander und mit Krankenkassen werden weiter zunehmen. Das zeigt sich insbesondere an den immer wichtiger werdenden öffentlich-rechtlichen Handlungsalternativen integrierter Versorgungsstrukturen und den Medizinischen Versorgungszentren.

4. Konsequenzen für die Krankenhausplanung

Folgt man dem bimodalen Konzept von Kane kommt es in Zukunft nicht zu einer vollständigen Kompression von Gesundheitsleistungen im Alter, sondern die hinzugewonnen Lebensjahre führen im Sinne der Medikalisierungsthese – wie sie insbesondere auch durch Hof für den stationären Bereich bestätigt wurde (Hof 2001, S. 7) – zu einer zumindest teilweisen Zunahme des Bedarfs an Gesundheitsleistungen. Zusätzlich wird die veränderte Altersstruktur der Bevölkerung einen Einfluss auf die Nachfrage stationärer Leistungen entfalten. Es wurde auch gezeigt, dass verschiedene **Wechselwirkungen** zwischen dem zunehmenden Altersquotienten und anderen Einflüssen bestehen, welche sich bei der Nachfrage nach stationären Leistungen bemerkbar machen werden. So haben sich insbesondere die technischen Möglichkeiten, Krankheiten auch bei älteren Patienten zu diagnostizieren und zu therapieren, weiter fortentwickelt. Ebenso ist die Prävalenz von chronischen Krankheiten im Alter höher, die Multimorbidität von Patienten nimmt tendenziell zu. Schließlich muss davon ausgegangen werden, dass ältere Patienten in Zukunft einer Generation angehören, die mit den vielfältigen informationstechnologischen Medien vertraut ist. Ältere Menschen werden daher zunehmend die bestmögliche Therapie für sich einfordern, gleichzeitig ist aber eine frühere Entlassung, wie sie durch die G-DRGs anvisiert ist, häufig nicht

möglich. Es reicht somit nicht, die demographische Entwicklung isoliert von anderen Aspekten zu betrachten.
Für die Krankenhausplanung wird die Nachfrageseite bislang praktisch nicht berücksichtigt. Der Dualismus zweier **widersprüchlicher Systeme** ist jedoch längerfristig kaum aufrecht zu erhalten. Obwohl durch die Einführung eines leistungsorientierten preislich pauschalen Entgeltes das Angebot von stationären Leistungen stärker durch wettewerbliche Mechanismen gesteuert werden soll, behält sich der Gesetzgeber vor, über die Krankenhausplanung, Feststellungsbescheide und die Investitionsfinanzierung letztlich die planerisch notwendigen baulichen und apparativen Behandlungseinrichtungen sowie Vorhaltungen in Abhängigkeit von Versorgungsstufen regulativ zuzuweisen (SVR 2003, S. 653). Eine solche Kapazitätsplanung lässt dem einzelnen Krankenhaus nur einen sehr eingeschränkten Handlungsspielraum, um individuelle Kostenvorteile in breitem Maße zu erzielen und in Wettbewerbsvorteile umzusetzen. Es ist deutlich, dass der Gesetzgeber einen „regulierten Wettbewerb" anstrebt. Im Zuge der G-DRG-Einführung werden deshalb auch durch Sicherstellungszuschläge, Notfallversorgungsabschläge und Mindestmengenregelungen zentrale Steuerungsmöglichkeiten vorgesehen, deren Ausgestaltung eine **vollständige** Freisetzung wettbewerblicher Effekte und damit verbundene mögliche Versorgungsdefizite vorsorglich verhindern soll (Kostevoß 2005, S. 4). Insbesondere mit dem Sicherstellungszuschlag verfügen die Bundesländer über ein Instrument, mit dem die Funktion des DRG-Systems i.S. einer wettbewerblichen Selbststeuerung theoretisch komplett ausgehebelt werden könnte. Sollen die G-DRGs daher ihre Wirkung entfalten können, so wird zukünftig die zentrale Herausforderung in der **konkreten** Ausgestaltung dieser Regulative bestehen, ohne den Wettbewerb zu konterkarieren.
Eine verbreitete Methode zur Ermittlung des notwendigen stationären Kapazitätsumfangs ist die in Kapitel D.I dargestellte Hill-Burton-Formel, welche den **Bettenbedarf** auf Basis der Determinanten Krankenhaushäufigkeit, Verweildauer, Umfangs der zu versorgenden Bevölkerung und eines normativ vorgegebenen Auslastungsgrads bestimmt. Die Berechnung des Bettenbedarfs erfolgt für jedes Fachgebiet getrennt und kann sich auf verschiedene regionale Planungsgebiete beziehen. Der ermittelte Bettengesamtbedarf wird jedoch i.d.R. anschließend auf die bestehenden Standorte verteilt, ohne dass eine Analyse der räumlichen Verfügbarkeit unterhalb der Ebene der Krankenhausversorgungsbereiche durchgeführt wird (Kortevoß 2005, S. 52). Auch die tatsächliche Inanspruchnahme und differenzierte Nachfragekriterien werden kaum beachtet (Rüschmann u.a. 2000).
Im Kontext der demographischen Entwicklung ist zu fordern, dass **veränderte Nachfrageprofile** in Zukunft eine entsprechende Berücksichtigung bei der Krankenhausplanung finden. Das bedeutet formal vor allem an den Variablen „Krankenhaushäufigkeit" und „Verweildauer" prognostisch anzusetzen. Inhalt-

lich sind wesentliche Erkenntnisse zu berücksichtigen. So nimmt die Wahrscheinlichkeit des Auftretens einiger Krankheiten im Alter stark zu (z.B. Schlaganfall, Demenz, etc.), denen u.U. für ältere Menschen andere Behandlungspfade zu Grunde gelegt werden müssen als für jüngere. Auch sind ältere Bevölkerungsanteile weniger in der Lage, lange Strecken zu überwinden. Es ist offensichtlich, dass die reine Entfernung zur nächsten Behandlungseinrichtung aus Sicht des einzelnen Nutzers sehr unterschiedliche Zugangsbarrieren bedeuten kann. Um solche Faktoren zu integrieren, müssen zukünftig neue Wege in der Krankenhausplanung beschritten werden. Ebenso wird die Geriatrie im Rahmen der demographischen Entwicklungen weiter an Stellenwert gewinnen und mit ihr neben der inneren Medizin insbesondere Fachdisziplinen, wie die Orthopädie, Neurologie und Psychiatrie (Gerontopsychiatrie).
Im Lichte der demographischen Entwicklung auf der einen Seite und dem zunehmenden Wettbewerb mit der dadurch hervorgerufenen Ausdünnung einer flächendeckenden stationären Versorgung auf der anderen Seite muss die Versorgung älterer Menschen durch die besondere Berücksichtigung entsprechender räumlicher Kriterien gewährleistet bleiben. Eine ausschließlich normative Herangehensweise, die auf der Ausweisung von Verhältniszahlen beruht (z.B. Betten je 1000 Einwohner) und Kapazitäten für verwaltungstechnisch oder auch willkürlich abgegrenzte Regionen hochrechnet, ist dafür nicht ausreichend. Zieht sich der Gesetzgeber – wie heute schon durch die Aufgabe von Einzel- zugunsten von Rahmenplanungen teilweise beobachtbar – zunehmend aus der detaillierten Krankenhausplanung zurück, um den G-DRGs die wettbewerbliche Bedarfssteuerung zu übertragen und beschränkt er sich auf die Sicherstellung der Notfallversorgung, so sollte entsprechend auch der **geriatrischen Versorgung** ein besonderer Stellenwert beigemessen werden. Hierfür sollte z.B. bei der Schließung von Krankenhäusern die Aufrechterhaltung der Versorgung älterer Menschen bei einer Einzelfallprüfung durch gesonderte Prüfkriterien beurteilt werden, so dass eine geriatrische Grundversorgung erhalten bleibt. Für eine nachfrageorientierte Krankenhausplanung, in die auch sozio-demographische Unterschiede für die Modifizierung der Nachfrageprofile integriert werden, ist die Zusammenführung von unterschiedlichen Informationen eine grundlegende Voraussetzung. Dazu gehören z.B. Kenntnisse über den gegenwärtigen Status der stationären Versorgung, deren räumliche Struktur sowie Leistungsstruktur und die räumlichen Muster der Inanspruchnahme dieser Leistungen. Darüber hinaus wird es für die Aufrechterhaltung einer flächendeckenden Versorgung für ältere Menschen aufgrund der Entwicklung und Verbreitung **Integrierter Versorgungsstrukturen**, die zunehmend auch auf die Belange älterer Patienten ausgerichtet bzw. auf typische Alterskrankheiten (Demenz) spezialisiert sind und dadurch die stationäre Versorgung teilweise substituieren können, nicht mehr zielführend sein, die Notwen-

digkeit stationärer Kapazitäten gänzlich unabhängig von alternativen Versorgungsangeboten zu beurteilen.

IV. Ausblick: Integrierte Versorgungsstrukturen zur Versorgung einer alternden Gesellschaft

Deutlich verschieben wird sich die Inanspruchnahme bei den einzelnen Altersgruppen. Bei den unter 65-jährigen ist gemäß der Status-quo-Prognose mit einer wesentlichen Verringerung der Krankenhausfälle zu rechnen, während die der über 65-jährigen zunehmen werden. Insgesamt beträgt die Entlastung bei den unter 65-jährigen Patienten rund 2 Millionen Fälle, dagegen steigt die Fallzahl bei den über 65-jährigen und Älteren um 4,3 Millionen. Während der Anteil der 75-jährigen und Älteren an den Krankenhausfällen 1998 rund 18% betrug, wird sich deren Anteil bei 2050 damit auf über 38% erhöhen. Diese Alterung fällt bei den Krankenhauspatienten deutlich mehr ins Gewicht als in der Bevölkerung insgesamt und wird nicht ohne Auswirkungen auf die Krankenhausstrukturen sowohl in medizinischer als auch in pflegerischer Hinsicht bleiben können.

Die Zunahme an chronischen und altersspezifischen Krankheitsbildern stellt komplexe diagnostische und therapeutische Anforderungen an die zunehmend differenzierteren Behandlungsabläufe (Wandschneider, Rösener 2003, S. 4). Ziel der Gesundheitspolitik muss es deshalb sein, das Gesundheitssystem effizienter und nachfrageorientierter auszurichten (Stanowsky u.a. 2004, S. 1). Hierfür bieten sich neben **neuen kollektivvertraglichen Lösungen** (z.B. Medizinische Versorgungszentren) vor allem **individuelle Lösungen** an, die durch die Öffnung des Kollektivvertragsrechts für das selektive Kontrahieren nach §140 a-d SGB V vom Gesetzgeber ermöglicht wurden. Ziel Integrierter Versorgungsstrukturen ist die am inneren Zusammenhang orientierte (Re-)Integration medizinischer Leistungen. Sie bedeuten damit eine (Rück-)Besinnung auf die ganzheitliche Sichtweise der Leistungserbringung, die im Idealfall alle Etappen einer Patientenbehandlung über verschiedene Sektoren hinweg berücksichtigt. Dadurch steht die vertikale Perspektive der (gesamten) Wertschöpfungskette von Gesundheitsdienstleistungen im Mittelpunkt (Braun 2006, S. 1ff.; Braun, Güssow 2005, S. 65). Aber auch Vernetzungen, die innerhalb eines einzelnen Sektors greifen, wie z.B. unter niedergelassenen Ärzten, und die damit eine horizontale Perspektive von Integrationshandlungen bilden, dürfen nicht aus der Betrachtung ausgeschlossen werden (vgl. Abbildung 7).

Gerade der demographische Wandel fordert eine **zunehmende Vernetzung** der ambulanten, stationären und rehabilitativen Versorgung. Die steigende Zahl an alten Menschen mit mehr chronischen Leiden, somatischen und geriatrischen Multimorbiditäten, Pflegebedürftigkeit sowie Bedürfnissen nach sozialen Kontakten ist in besonderem Maße von den defizitären Verknüpfungen des Leistungsspektrums und der sektoralen Fragmentierung betroffen (Schulz-Nieswandt, Kurscheid 2003, S. 63). Die traditionelle Versorgung stößt an ihre Grenzen, weil sie im Alltag eines alten, kranken bzw. behinderten Menschen nicht so verläuft, dass medizinische Versorgung, Pflege, Alltagsbewältigung, Haushaltsführung, Teilhabe an der Gesellschaft usw. in einer integrierten Form erfolgen (Mrozynski 2001, S. 279). Fach- und Hausärzte, Sozialstationen, Alten- und Pflegeheime sowie Kommunen sollten in einer kooperativen und koordinierten Art und Weise zusammenwirken. Hierzu gehören insbesondere auch niedrigschwellige Hilfsangebote für Angehörige und Pflegende sowie Unterstützungsleistungen im Rahmen eines betreuten Wohnens (o.V. 2002). In diesem Zusammenhang müsste auch untersucht werden, ob die Trennung von Kranken- und Pflegekassen noch sinnvoll ist. Das tendenziell sinkende Angebot seitens der Leistungserbringung aufgrund des zunehmenden Wettbewerbs wirkt auf die Forderung nach einem Ausbau der integrierten Versorgung gerade für ältere Menschen noch verstärkend, weil diese im besonderen Maße von größeren räumlichen Distanzen betroffen sind (Braun, Güssow 2005, Andersen 2000, S. 47ff.).

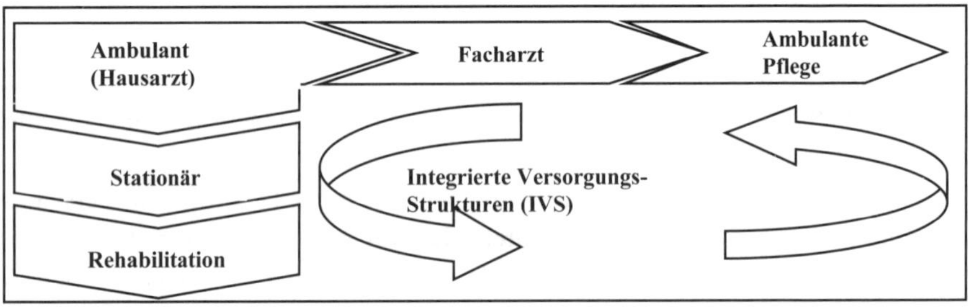

Quelle: Braun, Güssow (2006), S. 66

Abb. 7: Integrierte Versorgungsstrukturen im Gesundheitswesen

Einige **gute Ansätze** wurden bereits auf den Weg gebracht. Beispielhaft sei hier das Modellprojekt „IKARUS – Münchner Norden“ genannt, durch das die Unterstützung der unabhängigen Lebensführung älterer, behinderter oder kranker Menschen bzw. ihre Pflege und Rehabilitation durch einen pflegenden Angehörigen in ihrer häuslichen Umgebung gefördert wird. Hierbei wurde das Augenmerk in Zusammenarbeit mit technischen Fakultäten der Universität der Bundeswehr München insbesondere auf den Einsatz technischer Hilfsmittel und Maßnahmen zur Wohnungsanpassung, einschließlich neuer Informations- und Kommunikationstechnologien gerichtet.

Um die Qualität der Betreuung und Pflege von **Demenzkranken** zu verbessern,[7] haben sich auch in Bad Kreuznach 22 Institutionen, Organisationen, Behörden und Kostenträger zu einem „Netzwerk Demenz" zusammengeschlossen. Das Modellprojekt ist ein Beispiel für eine Integrierte Versorgung, in der Demenzkranke optimal über alle Leistungsbereiche hinweg betreut werden. Zu dem Netzwerk gehören u.a. zwei auf Bauen für Demenzkranke spezialisierte Architekten, mit denen zusammen eine Einheit „Betreutes Wohnen" und eine Tagesbetreuung von Demenzkranken betrieben wird. Zu den Dienstleistungen zählen u.a. ein Koordinierungs- und Informationsbüro mit Beratungstelefon, die Angehörigenbetreuung, gerontopsychiatrische Fortbildungsangebote, Wohnberatung, teil- und vollstationäre Versorgungsmöglichkeiten, eine Institutsambulanz, ein Ehrenamtlichenbüro sowie verschiedene Betreuungs- und Beaufsichtigungsangebote.

Schließlich sind auch **neue Dienstleister**, wie z.B. „Home Supply + Care" (http://www.hsc-online.de) entstanden, die das Krankenhaus bei der Fallplanung und dem Management gemeinsam festgelegter klinischer Pfade, beim Entlassungs- und Überleitungsmanagement, bei der Schulung des Klinikpersonals in den Bereichen Stoma-, Kontinenz- und Wundversorgung, bei der Patientenbetreuung und Angehörigeneinweisung, beim Aufbau von Stoma- und Kontinenzsprechstunden sowie der Definition von Qualitätsstandards für Klinik, Entlassung und Nachversorgung in Kooperation mit dem ärztlichen und pflegerischen Bereich unterstützen. Schließlich sind in jüngster Zeit im Bereich Palliativmedizin vielfältige neue Versorgungsstrukturen entwickelt worden, die eine bessere Koordination der Pflege unheilbar kranker Menschen in häuslicher Umgebung zum Ziel haben.[8]

Durch integrierte Versorgungsstrukturen kann der demographischen Entwicklung auch in **ländlichen Gebieten** begegnet werden, indem eine hinreichende medizinische Grundversorgung und ein Notfalldienst durch Vernetzung sichergestellt wird. Eine mögliche Form der institutionellen Organisiertheit können Kompetenzzentren darstellen, die vornehmlich in **dünn besiedelten Regionen** die Versorgung der dort meist älteren Menschen garantieren. Eine ähnliche Zielsetzung verfolgt beispielsweise das Projekt „Strukturinnovationen durch Integrierte Versorgung in den Neuen Bundesländern" (SIDIV) (http://www.sidiv.de). Zudem könnten mobile Operationseinheiten die Versorgung in der Peripherie sicherstellen (Ernst, Young 2005, S. 106f.). Weiterhin bieten sich virtuelle Konzepte als

7 Nach der Krankheitskostenrechnung des Statistischen Bundesamtes entfielen für das Jahr 2002 10% aller Krankheitskosten auf Psychische und Verhaltensstörungen (ca. 22 Mrd. Euro). Bezogen auf einzelne Diagnosen zeigt sich, dass dabei die Kosten für Demenz (ICD 10: F00-F03) mit 5,6 Mrd. Euro einen erheblichen Anteil ausmachen und Kosten für stationäre und teilstationäre Pflege mit 3,6 Mrd. Euro die größte Rolle spielen.

8 Vgl. z.B. http://www.hbh-kliniken.de/hbh- kliniken/artikel/download/Aktuelles/Akt_Aktuelle Themen/Aktuelles__IV_Palliativmedizin.pdf.

(Teil-)Lösung an, wie sie in ähnlicher Form bereits erprobt wurden (Pelikan, Nowak 1999). Armbanduhren, welche Vitalfunktionen des älteren Bürgers an den Hausarzt weiterleiten, sind beispielsweise eine präventive Maßnahme. Dabei ermöglichen neue Informationstechnologien Menschen mit chronischen Krankheiten eine bessere Betreuung.

Um die Versorgung ökonomisch sinnvoll anzubieten, stellt die **morbiditätsbasierte Vergütung** der Leistungserbringer vor allem vor dem Hintergrund des demographischen Wandels und seiner Effekte ein zwingendes Novum dar. Die Gesundheitspolitik muss hier transparente Vergütungsformen ermöglichen. Aufgrund der gebotenen integrierten Versorgungsform einer alternden Gesellschaft sind Komplexvergütungen praktikabel und anzustreben.

Allgemein besteht für vernetzte geriatrische Versorgungsmodelle nach wie vor noch ein großes **Evaluationsdefizit**. Da eine begleitende Versorgungsforschung auf methodisch ausreichendem Niveau fehlt, lässt sich bislang nicht sicher die Frage beantworten, welche Maßnahmen den Gesundheitszustand älterer Menschen nachhaltig verbessert, Pflegeeinweisungen verzögert und Kosten spart. Um aber den Herausforderungen des demographischen Wandels mit evidenzbasierten, alltagstauglichen und finanzierbaren Versorgungsformen begegnen zu können, ist eine begleitende Versorgungsforschung zukünftig essenziell.

Literaturverzeichnis

Andersen, A., Krankenhaus 2015: Wege aus dem Paragraphendschungel, Frankfurt a. M. 2000.

BKK Bundesverband, Gesundheitsreport 2004, Gesundheit und sozialer Wandel, Essen 2004.

Braun, G.E. und *F. Schulz-Nieswandt*, Einleitung: Die Liberalisierung im Gesundheitswesen – Philosophie des Sammelbandes und Einordnung der Beiträge, in: Liberalisierung im Gesundheitswesen, hrsg. von Braun, G.E. und Schulz-Nieswandt, F., Baden-Baden 2005, S. 9-18.

Braun, G. E. und *J. Güssow*, Integrierte Versorgungsstrukturen und Gesundheitsnetzwerke als innovative Ansätze im deutschen Gesundheitswesen, in: Liberalisierung im Gesundheitswesen: Einrichtungen des Gesundheitswesens zwischen Wettbewerb und Regulierung, hrsg. von Braun, G. E. und Schulz-Nieswandt, F., Baden-Baden 2005, S. 65-93.

Braun, G. E., Zukunftsaufgabe Vernetzung: Strategie und Management für Gesundheitsnetzwerke in Caritas-Strukturen, in: Krankendienst 1, 2006, S. 1-8.

Breyer, F., P. Zweife und *M. Kifmann*, Gesundheitsökonomik, 5. Aufl., Berlin und Heidelberg 2005.

Bruker, M.O., Unsere Nahrung unser Schicksal, 26. Aufl., Lahnstein 1994.

Bundesministerium für Familie, Senioren, Frauen und Jugend (Hrsg.), 1. Altenbericht der Bundesregierung, Bonn 1993.

Bundesministerium für Familie, Senioren, Frauen und Jugend (Hrsg.), 4. Altenbericht der Bundesregierung, Berlin 2004.

Deutsche Krankenhausgesellschaft, Zahlen Daten Fakten 2004/05, Düsseldorf 2005.

Deutscher Bundestag, Enquête-Kommission Demographischer Wandel: Herausforderungen unserer älter werdenden Gesellschaft an den Einzelnen und die Politik, Zur Sache 3, Berlin 2002.

Dinkel, R. H., Demographie, Band 1: Bevölkerungsdynamik, München 1989.

Dinkel, R. und *E. Görtler*, Demographische Ursachen der Entwicklung der Krankenhausfallzahlen, in: Arbeit und Sozialpolitik, Heft 1, 1991, S. 22-26.

Erbsland, M. und *E. Wille*, Bevölkerungsentwicklung und Finanzierung der Gesetzlichen Krankenversicherung, in: Zeitschrift für die gesamte Versicherungswissenschaft 84, Heft 4, 1995, S. 661-686.

Ernst & Young, Gesundheitsversorgung 2020, Frankfurt a. M. 2005.

Felder, S., M. Meier und *H. Schmitt*, Health care expenditure in the last months of life, in: Journal of Health Economics, Vol.19(5), 2000, S. 679-695.

Fleßa, S., Die epidemiologische Transition als Herausforderung für das Gesundheitswesen in Afrika, in: Gesundheitsökonomie und Qualitätsmanagement, 6 Jg., 2001, S. 79-88.

Fries, J. F., Compression of morbidity in the elderly, in: Vaccine 16, 2000, S. 1584-1589.

Getzen, T. E., Population Aging and the Growth of Health Expenditures, in: Journal of Gerontology. Social Sciences, 47, 1992, S. 98-104.

Grohmann, H., Die Alterung unserer Gesellschaft, in: Zeitschrift für Bevölkerungswissenschaft, 28. Jg., Heft 2-4, 2003, S. 443-462.

Güther, B., Morbidität und Krankheitskosten von Alten, in: Gesundheitswesen, Band 60, Stuttgart und New York 1998, S. 39-46.

Hof, B., Auswirkungen und Konsequenzen der demographischen Entwicklung für die gesetzliche Kranken- und Pflegeversicherung, Köln 2001.

Kane, R.C., Beyond Caring: the challenge to Geriatrics, in: Journal of American Geriatrics Society, Vol. 36(5), 1988, S. 467-472.

Kessler, M., Zu viele Menschen, zu wenige oder die falschen: Die Welt im demographischen Umbruch, in: Süddeutsche Zeitung, 04. Mai 2006, S. 18-19.

Kortevoß, A., Krankenhausplanung unter Bedingungen der German-Diagnosis Related Groups: Methodischer Beitrag zur Ausgestaltung ordnungspolitischer Handlungsoptionen der Bundesländer, Dissertation, LMU München: Fakultät für Geowissenschaften, München 2005.

Kröhnert, S., F. Mesicus und *R. Klingholz*, Die demografische Lage der Nation. Wie zukunftsfähig sind Deutschlands Regionen? Daten, Fakten, Analysen (Kurzfassung), Berlin-Institut für Bevölkerungsentwicklung, Berlin 2006.

Kühn, H., Demographischer Wandel und demographischer Schwindel. Zur Debatte um die gesetzliche Krankenversicherung, in: Blätter für deutsche und internationale Politik 6, 2004, S. 742-752.

Lebok, U., Die Auswirkungen der demographischen Entwicklung auf die Krankenhausverweildauer in Deutschland, Berlin 2000.

Lubitz, J. D., J. Beebe und *C. Baker*, Longevity and medicare expenditures, in: New England Journal of Medicine 332, 1995, S. 999-1003.

Mrozynski, P., Rehabilitationsleistungen – Integrierte Versorgung im gegliederten System, in: Die Sozialgerichtsbarkeit, 48 Jg., Nr. 6, 2001, S. 277-286.

OECD, OECD Indicators, Health at a Galance, Paris 2005.

Pimpertz, J., Soziale Sicherung, in: Institut der deutschen Wirtschaft Köln: Perspektive 2050, Ökonomik des demographischen Wandels, 2. aktualisierte Auflage, Kevelaer 2005, S. 239-264.

Pohlmeier, W. und *V. Ulrich*, Die Nachfrage nach medizinischen Leistungen im Lebenszyklus, in: Alter und Gesundheit, hrsg. von Oberender, P., Baden-Baden 1996, S. 49-81.

Robert Koch-Institut, Gesundheitsberichterstattung des Bundes: Gesundheit im Alter, Heft 10, Berlin 2005.

Rüschmann, H.-H., K. Schmolling, C. Krauss und *A. Roth*, Krankenhausplanung für Wettbewerbssysteme – Leistungssicherung statt Kapazitätsplanung, Berlin 2000.

Sachverständigenrat für die Konzertierte Aktion im Gesundheitswesen (SVR), Sondergutachten 1995: Gesundheitsversorgung und Krankenversicherung 2000. Mehr Ergebnisorientierung, mehr Qualität und mehr Wirtschaftlichkeit, Baden-Baden 1995.

Sachverständigenrat für die Konzertierte Aktion im Gesundheitswesen (SVR), Finanzierung, Nutzenorientierung und Qualität, Bonn 2003.

Schulz, E., Zur langfristigen Bevölkerungsentwicklung in Deutschland – Modellrechnungen bis 2050, in: Wochenbericht des DIW 42, 1999, S. 745-757.

Schulz-Nieswandt, F. und *C. Kurscheid*, Grundzüge der Alterssozialpolitik und der integrierten Versorgung, Köln 2003.

Schulz-Nieswandt, F. und *C. Kurscheid*, Integrationsversorgung. Eine Einführung für die gesundheitsökonomische, pflegewissenschaftliche und sozialpolitische Ausbildung, Münster u.a. 2004.

Schwing, C., Möglich, dass sich die Lebenserwartung wieder verkürzt, in: Krankenhaus Umschau 4, 2005, S. 300-301.

Simon, M., Das Gesundheitswesen in Deutschland. Eine Einführung in Struktur und Funktionsweise, Bern 2005.

Stanowsky, J., S. Schma und *R. Sandvoß*, Gesundheitsmarkt – ein Wachstumsmotor?, in: Economic Research Allianz Group, Working Paper Nr. 17, Economic Research Allianz Group Dresdner Bank 2004. o.O.

Statistisches Bundesamt (Hrsg.), Bevölkerung Deutschlands bis 2050 – 10. koordinierte Bevölkerungsvorausberechnung (Presseexemplar), Wiesbaden 2003a.

Statistisches Bundesamt (Hrsg.), Gesundheit – Ausgaben und Personal 2001, Wiesbaden 2003b.
Ulrich, V., Demographische Effekte auf Ausgaben und Beitragssatz der GKV, Diskussionspapier, Universität Bayreuth, Bayreuth 2003.
Verbrugge, L.M., Longer Life but Worsening Health?, in: The Milbank Quarterly, Vol. 62, 1984, S. 474-519.
Wandschneider, U. und *C. Rösener*, Entwicklungen des Gesundheitswesens in der Zukunft, Hamburg 2003.
Weizäcker, R. K. v., Distributive implications of an aging society, in: European Economic Review, Vol. 40, 1996, S. 729-746.

Internetquellen

Brand, H. (2005), Demografischer Wandel und Politikberatung im Gesundheitswesen, abrufbar unter: http://www.ibg-uni-bielefeld.de/downloads/ praesentation / 11brand.pdf
Deutsche Krankenhausgesellschaft (2001): Folgen der demographischen Entwicklung für das Gesundheitswesen, abrufbar unter:
http://www.dkgev.de/dkgev.php/cat/125/aid/127/title/Folgen+der+demographischen+Entwicklung+f%FCr+das+Gesundheitswesen.
Deutsches Institut für Wirtschaftsforschung (DIW) (2001): Wirtschaftliche Aspekte der Märkte für Gesundheitsleistungen, abrufbar unter:
http://www.diw.de/deutsch/produkte/ publikationen/gutachten/docs/diw_GesundheitsDL_200112.pdf
Häussler, B., und *M. Albrecht* (2005): Konsequenzen des demographischen Wandels für die Finanzierung der Gesundheitsausgaben, 3. Kongress zum Fortschritt im Gesundheitswesen von morgen, abrufbar unter: http://www.iges.de/e1281/e2696/e2713/e3044/programitem 3081/Haeussler_ger.pdf
o.V. (2002), Die Geriatrie ist das ideale Arbeitsfeld für eine Integrierte Versorgung in: Ärztezeitung online vom 18.04.2002, abrufbar unter: http://www.aerztezeitung.de
Pelikan, J. M. und *P. Nowak* (1999), Virtuelles Krankenhaus zu Hause, abrufbar unter: http://www.univie.ac.at/lbimgs/berichte/virhos.pdf
Schulz, E., H.-H. König und *R. Leid* (2000), Auswirkungen der demographischen Alterung auf den Versorgungsbedarf im Krankenhausbereich – Modellrechnung bis zum Jahre 2050, in: Wochenbericht des DIW Berlin 44/00, abrufbar unter:
http://www.diw.de/deutsch/produkte /publikationen/wochenberichte/ docs/00-44-1.html
United Nations (UN) (2002), World Population Ageing: 1950-2050, abrufbar unter: http://www.un. org/esa/population/publications/worldageing19502050/

B. Auswirkungen der demographischen Veränderungen auf die Gesundheitsversorgung in Deutschland

Günter Neubauer

I. Ausgangslage: Die demographische Entwicklung und die Sozialversicherung in Deutschland

Die demographische Entwicklung lässt sich für Deutschland für die nächsten 40 Jahre relativ gut vorhersagen. Als Eckpunkte sind heute schon bekannt, dass einerseits die Bevölkerung insgesamt um etwa 10 Mio. schrumpfen wird und andererseits, dass die Bevölkerung im Durchschnitt um 15 Jahre älter sein wird; statt heute 41 Jahre dann etwa 55 Jahre.[1] Hinter letzterer Entwicklung steht das sog. „double aging" was bedeutet, dass einerseits weniger Kinder geboren werden und andererseits die alten Menschen noch älter werden. Eine unbekannte Größe bei dieser Betrachtung ist die zu erwartende Bevölkerungswanderung. Zwar unterstellt man bei den meisten Schätzungen, dass Deutschland weiterhin eine positive Zuwanderungsbilanz haben wird, die in etwa bei 150.000 Menschen pro Jahr liegt, doch ist dies alles andere als gewiss.[2] Hier sind vor allem die Bedingungen in den wichtigen Zuwanderländern eine nicht abschätzbare Größe. Selbst wenn man bei der angegebenen Annahme bleibt, ändert sich an der demographischen Entwicklung nichts. Nur wenn es bei der Zuwanderung gravierende Abweichungen gäbe, könnten sich Veränderungen nach oben oder unten einstellen.

Damit ist Deutschland allerdings nicht alleine in Europa. Nahezu alle europäischen Länder sehen sich einer ähnlichen Entwicklung entgegen. In einigen Ländern ist der Alterungsprozess sogar noch schneller, so wie in Italien. In anderen Ländern verläuft der Prozess langsamer, hierzu zählt Frankreich. Gleichwohl stehen auch diese Länder vor ähnlichen Entwicklungen und Herausforderungen.

Die skizzierte demographische Entwicklung stellt eine massive Herausforderung an unser Sozialversicherungssystem dar. Da letzteres auf dem sog. Umlageverfahren aufbaut, ist das Verhältnis zwischen Beitragszahlern und Leistungsempfängern für das finanzielle Gleichgewicht entscheidend. Eindeutig und einfach lässt sich dies für das Alterssicherungssystem ableiten. Die Zahl der jeweiligen Erwerbstätigen macht die Summe der Beitragszahler aus, während die Zahl der nicht mehr Erwerbstätigen als Leistungsempfänger auftritt. Jede Veränderung in der Relation dieser beiden Gruppen zueinander führt zu Be- oder Entlastungen der jeweiligen Gruppe. Die geschilderte demographische Veränderung bedeutet

1 Zahlen entnommen aus der 10. koordinierten Bevölkerungsvorausberechnung des Statistischen Bundesamtes 2003.

2 Ebenda.

also, dass die Anzahl der Leistungsempfänger im Verhältnis zu der Anzahl der Beitragszahler sich zu ungunsten der Beitragszahler verändern wird. Die nachfolgende Abbildung gibt hierzu einen ersten Eindruck.

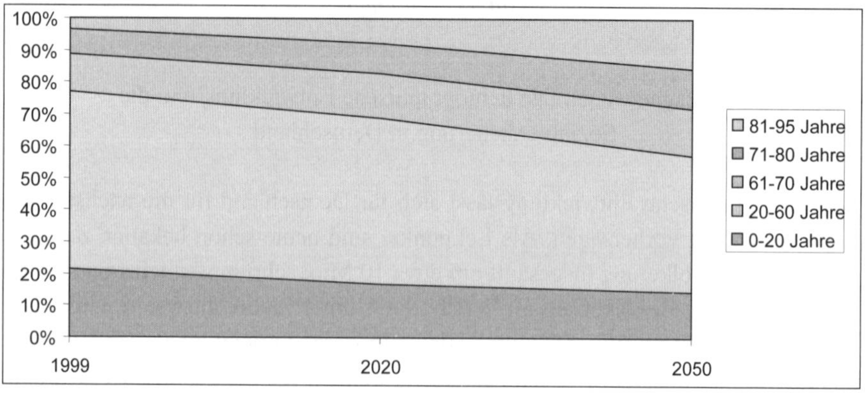

Quelle: 10. koordinierte Bevölkerungsvorausberechnung des Statistischen Bundesamtes 2003

Abb. 1: Anzahl der Erwerbstätigen (20-60 Jahre) zu den Leistungsempfängern der Sozialversicherung (60 Jahre und älter)

Die Abbildung 1 zeigt auf, dass die Zahl der Leistungsempfänger zunimmt, andererseits aber die Zahl der Kinder abnimmt, was bedeutet, dass die Belastung der Erwerbstätigen auf dieser Seite auch reduziert wird. Freilich ist die Reduktion der Kinderzahl eine Entlastungshypothek, die irgendwann auf die jeweilige Beitragsgruppe durchschlagen wird und somit der Schrumpfprozess der Bevölkerung weiterhin anhält.

Nicht ganz so einfach ist die Aussage zur Finanzierung im Bereich der Kranken- und Pflegeversicherung. In diesen beiden Leistungsbereichen zahlen alle Gesunden Beiträge und alle Kranken sind Leistungsempfänger. Insofern kann keine strenge Trennung nach Altersgruppen vorgenommen werden, wie es etwa im Bereich der Rentenversicherung möglich ist. Gleichwohl wissen wir, dass mit dem Alter das Krankheitsrisiko relativ streng korreliert ist, ebenso wie das Pflegerisiko. Von daher gilt der Zusammenhang, wenn auch weniger streng, wie in der Rentenversicherung. Eine älter werdende Bevölkerung braucht deutlich mehr Gesundheitsleistungen, vor allem, weil die ältere Bevölkerung häufiger den Arzt bzw. das Krankenhaus aufsuchen muss. Einen ersten Eindruck kann die nachstehende Abbildung 2 geben, die beschreibt, wie mit steigendem Alter die Gesundheitsausgaben zunehmen.

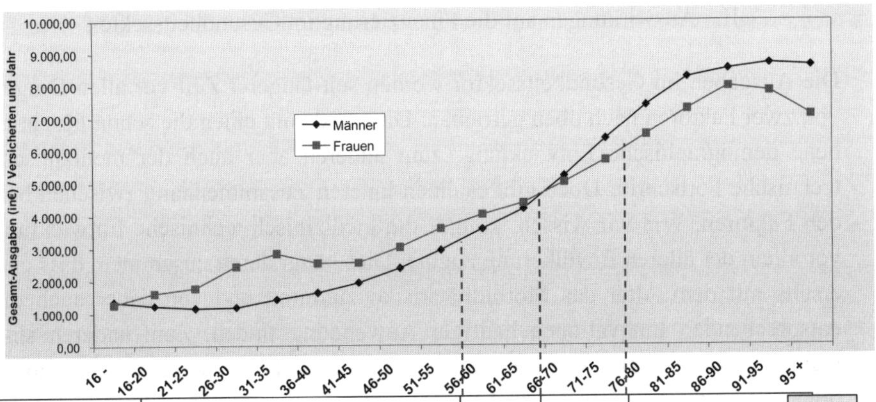

Bevölkerungszahl (Mio.)	45,75 (55,7%)	9,54 (11,6%)	6,40 (7,8%)	2,94 (3,6%)	82,16
Bevölkerungszahl (Mio.)	42,92 (52,3%)	11,37 (13,9%)	7,89 (9,6%)	6,25 (7,6%)	82,05
Bevölkerungszahl (Mio.)	31,41 (43,0%)	10,59 (14,5%)	9,2 (12,6%)	11,36 (15,6%)	73,00

Quelle: Verband der privaten Krankenversicherung 2003, 10. koordinierte Bevölkerungsvorausberechnung Statistisches Bundesamt 2003

Abb. 2: Demographieabhängigkeit und Gesundheitsausgaben

Die Abbildung 2 weist aus, dass ab dem 60. Lebensjahr die Ausgabenkurve deutlich steiler verläuft und im Bereich der etwa 90-jährigen bis 95-jährigen ihren Gipfelpunkt erreicht. Wenn auch die Zahlen der obigen Abbildung aus dem Bereich der privaten Krankenversicherung entnommen sind, so zeigen jedoch alle Statistiken der gesetzlichen Krankenversicherung in die gleiche Richtung. Wir haben unter diese Abbildung schon die Bevölkerungsentwicklung gesetzt. Während in der letzten Spalte noch einmal der Bevölkerungsrückgang um rund 10 Mio. Menschen bis 2050 ausgewiesen wird. Es ist ebenfalls der Abbildung 2 zu entnehmen, dass in der Altersgruppe der 80-jährigen und älteren die Bevölkerung um rund 10 Mio. zunehmen wird. Dies ist aber genau jene Bevölkerungsgruppe, die heute den höchsten Bedarf an Gesundheitsleistungen aufweist. Gleichzeitig wird die Bevölkerung unter 60 Jahren um rund 20 Mio. schrumpfen, wobei der Rückgang der Kinder in der Tabelle nicht ausgewiesen ist.
Diese wenigen Zahlen können bereits den Umfang des Problems, das auf die Sozialversicherungen in Deutschland zukommt, sichtbar machen. Im Weiteren konzentrieren wir unsere Ausführungen nur auf den Bereich der Gesetzlichen Krankenversicherung, die mit rund 145 Mrd. € nach der Gesetzlichen Rentenversicherung mit ca. 250 Mrd. € der zweitgrößte Sozialversicherungszweig ist (Statistischcs Bundesamt, Zahlen für das Jahr 2004).

II. Auswirkungen auf die Finanzierung im Gesundheitssektor

Die Ausgaben im Gesundheitssektor werden seit längerer Zeit vor allen Dingen von zwei Faktoren nach oben getrieben. Dies sind zum einen die schon beschriebene demographische Entwicklung, zum anderen aber auch der medizinisch-technische Fortschritt. Doch gibt es einen inneren Zusammenhang zwischen beiden Faktoren. Wie wir wissen, kommt die medizinisch-technische Entwicklung vor allem der älteren Bevölkerung zugute. Dies hängt damit zusammen, dass einerseits mit dem Alter das Morbiditätsrisiko zunimmt und von daher auch die entsprechenden Innovationen häufiger Anwendung finden. Zum anderen sind viele Krankheiten altersbedingt und werden dadurch von bestimmten Innovationen in erster Linie angesprochen. Ein einfaches Beispiel zu diesem Zusammenhang stellt die nachfolgende Abbildung 3 dar.

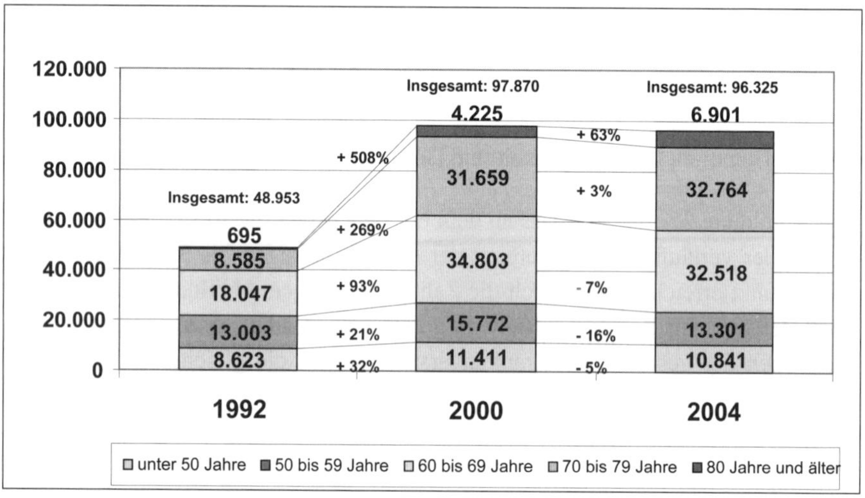

Quelle: Bruckenberger E. 2005

Abb. 3: Entwicklung der offenen Herzoperation nach Altersgruppen

Die Abbildung 3 macht sichtbar, dass vor allem in den Altersgruppen über 60 Jahren die Zahl der Operationen sprunghaft zugenommen hat. Am stärksten hat die Altergruppe der 80-jährigen und älteren von den Herzoperationen profitiert. Dies ist aber genau die Altergruppe, von der wir die größte Zunahme in den kommenden Jahrzehnten erwarten. Gleichzeitig sind die Menschen in höherem Alter in der Regel nicht mehr berufstätig, so dass die medizinischen Leistungen volkswirtschaftlich als Konsumleistungen einzustufen sind, da ihre Empfänger nicht mehr im Wirtschaftsprozess produktiv tätig sind. Dies bedeutet aber, dass für diese Leistungsausgaben andere, d.h. die Erwerbstätigen aufkommen müssen.

Von daher ist es auch nur logisch, dass Berechnungen der künftigen Ausgabenentwicklung für Gesundheitsleistungen und für die Entwicklung des Inlandsproduktes eine schnellere Ausgabenentwicklung für die Gesundheitsleistungen voraussagen als die Zunahme des Inlandsproduktes erwarten lässt. In Abbildung 4 haben wir diesen Zusammenhang wiedergegeben, der einerseits die Berechnung des Inlandsproduktes andererseits die Ausgaben für die Gesundheitsleistungen und zum dritten auch den Beitragssatz der gesetzlichen Krankenversicherung ausweist.

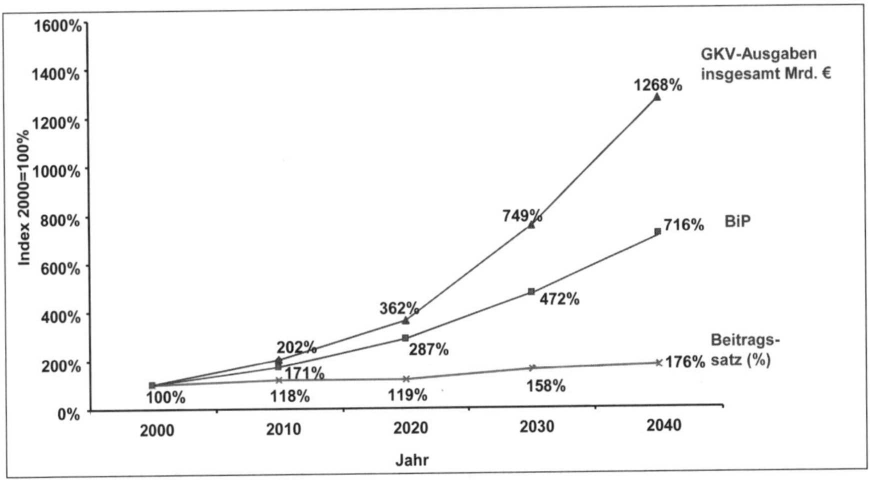

Quelle: Breyer F. und Ulrich V. 2000

Abb. 4: Prognose von Bedarf und Ressourcen bis 2040

Der Abbildung 4 ist zu entnehmen, dass die Gesundheitsausgaben bis 2040 um annähernd 80 Prozentpunkte schneller steigen werden als das Inlandsprodukt. Dies hat zur Folge, dass auch der Beitragssatz der gesetzlichen Krankenversicherung um etwa 80 Prozent ansteigen müsste. Dabei geht diese Prognose noch von einem relativ hohen Inlandsproduktzuwachs aus, so dass die Differenz und damit die Belastung des Beitragssatzes eher noch höher ausfallen dürfte. Der Anstieg der Gesundheitsausgaben, der oben beschrieben wird, geht jedoch nicht nur auf die demographische Veränderung der Bevölkerung zurück, sondern ist gepaart mit dem medizinischen Fortschritt. Aus diesem Grunde ist es hilfreich, den Effekt des medizinischen Fortschritts vom Effekt der demographischen Veränderung zu trennen. In der nachfolgenden Abbildung 5 haben wir eine derartige Betrachtung vorgenommen, in dem wir die Berechnungen von Ulrich und Breyer in eine Graphik umgesetzt haben (erschienen als „Gesundheitsausgaben, Alter und medizinischer Fortschritt: eine Regressionsanalyse" im Jahr 2000). Die Abbildung zeigt, dass ein großer Teil des Ausgabenzuwachses dem medizinischen Fortschritt zuzuordnen ist.

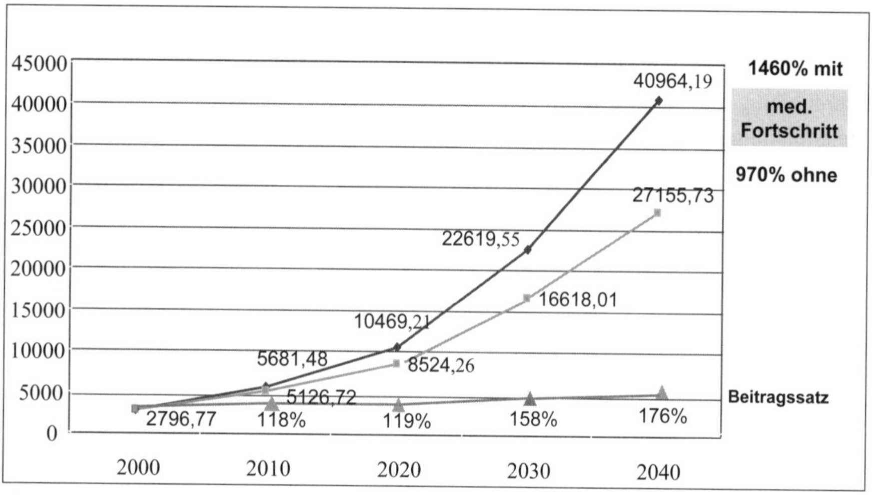

Quelle: Breyer F. und Ulrich V. 2000

Abb. 5: Entwicklung der GKV-Ausgaben je Mitglied mit und ohne medizinischen Fortschritt in €

Abbildung 5 sagt aus, dass die Ausgaben dennoch um rund 970 Prozent anwachsen würden, auch wenn die Demographie sich nicht verschieben würde. Von daher kann man wiederum erkennen, dass die Demographie zwar ein wichtiger, aber für die Ausgabenentwicklung nicht der wichtigste Faktor sein wird. Verbunden mit unserer obigen Aussage, in der wir dargestellt haben, dass der medizinische Fortschritt vor allen Dingen der älteren Bevölkerung zukommt, wird deutlich, dass es im Wesentlichen die Demographie ist, die diese Anwendungsexplosion des medizinischen Fortschritts auslöst.

Überträgt man nun diesen Anstieg der Ausgaben auf den Beitragssatz, so würde das bedeuten, dass der Beitragssatz in der gesetzlichen Krankenversicherung von heute 14 Prozent auf rund 26 Prozent ansteigen würde. Da dies nicht der einzige Beitragssatz der Sozialversicherung ist, der nach oben klettert, kommt man auf eine gesamte Sozialabgabenlast die bei 50 Prozent oder höher liegen dürfte. Eine solche Abgabenlast, die ja noch einmal um die Steuerquote zu erhöhen ist, kann schlichtweg der berufstätigen Generation nicht zugemutet werden. Aus diesem Grunde kann das Sozialleistungssystem in seiner heutigen Form nicht als zukunftsfähig bezeichnet werden.

Welche Lösungsmöglichkeiten für diese Problematik bestehen, werden wir im Weiteren ansprechen.

III. Auswirkung der demographischen Entwicklung auf die Gesundheitsversorgung

Neben der Finanzierung spielt auch die Veränderung in der Gesundheitsversorgung selbst eine große Rolle. Man kann sagen, dass die Veränderungen auf der Leistungsseite letztlich das Wichtigere für die Bürger sein werden. Gleichwohl sind Veränderungen auf der Leistungsseite stets unter dem Gesichtspunkt der Finanzierungskonsequenzen zu sehen. Im Folgenden wollen wir kurz zu den vier wichtigsten Versorgungsbereichen Stellung nehmen, nämlich: Zur allgemeinärztlichen Versorgung, zur fachärztlichen Versorgung, zur Arzneimittel- und zur Krankenhausversorgung.

1. Auswirkungen auf die allgemeinärztliche Versorgung

In Deutschland kann die praxisbasierte, ärztliche Versorgung in zwei Teilbereiche gegliedert werden. Zum einen ist dies die allgemeinärztliche Versorgung, die die Bevölkerung mit primären ärztlichen Leistungen zu versorgen hat, und zum anderen ist es die fachärztliche Versorgung, durch die spezielle Gesundheitsleistungen ambulant erbracht werden und so häufig eine teuere Krankenhausversorgung ersetzen.

Die allgemeinärztliche Versorgung dient vor allem der flächendeckenden bevölkerungsnahen medizinischen Versorgung. Diese Art der Versorgung wird durch eine Reduktion der Bevölkerung vor besondere Herausforderungen gestellt. Mit einer Reduktion der Bevölkerungsdichte wird gleichzeitig die wirtschaftliche Tragfähigkeit einer Arztpraxis in Frage gestellt. Ein Arzt braucht eine ganz bestimmte Bevölkerungsdichte und -anzahl, um genügend Patienten für eine betriebswirtschaftliche Führung seiner Praxis zu haben. Derzeit braucht ein Allgemeinarzt etwa 1.000 bis 1.500 Einwohner, um genügend Patienten zu finden, die ihm seine betriebswirtschaftlichen Kosten decken und ein angemessenes Einkommen erzielen lassen. Vermindert sich die Bevölkerungszahl, so wird automatisch das Einzugsgebiet einer Allgemeinarztpraxis ausgedehnt und damit die Wege der Patienten zum Arzt länger. Es kommt hinzu, dass immer mehr Allgemeinärzte es vorziehen in einer Gruppe tätig zu werden, weil so einerseits die betriebswirtschaftlichen Kosten leichter gedeckt werden können und zum anderen auch die Nachtdienste und Wochenenddienste weniger beeinträchtigend zu spüren sind. Würden sich nun drei Allgemeinärzte zusammenschließen, so wäre eine Bevölkerungszahl von 4.000 bis 5.000 Einwohner erforderlich, um die Praxis betriebswirtschaftlich führen zu können. Kommt ein Rückgang der Bevölkerung in der Fläche hinzu, führt dies dazu, dass Patienten in

Dörfern weniger schnell zu versorgen sind, da die Entfernungen zu den ärztlichen Schwerpunkt-Praxen entsprechend zunehmen.
Eine derartige Entwicklung kann teilweise dadurch gemindert werden, dass der Rettungsdienst kompensatorisch ausgebaut wird und die Kommunikationsmöglichkeiten durch Telefon, Internet und Telemedizin sich technisch verbessern. Gleichwohl kann man davon ausgehen, dass vor allen Dingen in den weniger attraktiven ländlichen Gebieten die patientennahe, ärztliche Versorgung spürbar – verglichen zu heute – zurückgehen dürfte.
Ein dritter Faktor schließlich kommt noch hinzu. Die zunehmende Finanznot der gesetzlichen Krankenversicherung bekommen die Ärzte in Form von gebremsten Einkommenszuwächsen zu spüren. Effekte dieser Art sind schon seit längerer Zeit im System zu beobachten. Werden nun die Einkommenszuwächse für Ärzte entsprechend gedämpft, so dürfte der Ärztemangel am ehesten in weniger attraktiven Regionen zu spüren sein. Ob hier eine Zuwanderung von Ärzten aus den europäischen Nachbarländern eine nachhaltige Erleichterung verschaffen kann, ist fraglich. Schließlich ist gerade in den ländlichen Gebieten die Sprachbarriere besonders schwer zu überwinden, ferner dürften auch für zuwandernde Ärzte diese wenig attraktiven Gebiete nur vorübergehend von größerem Interesse sein.

2. Die fachärztliche Versorgung

Die fachärztliche Versorgung zeichnet sich dadurch aus, dass der einzelne Facharzt ein deutlich größeres Einzugsgebiet an Bevölkerung braucht, da seine Spezialität nicht so häufig pro 1.000 Einwohner vorkommt als etwa die Allgemeinleiden, die vom Allgemeinarzt behandelt werden. So braucht ein Gastroenterologe die zehnfache Einwohnerzahl eines Allgemeinarztes. Daneben besteht auch für Fachärzte der allgemeine betriebswirtschaftliche Rationalisierungsdruck. Dies führt dazu, dass auch die Fachärzte sich mehr und mehr zu Gruppen zusammenzuschließen. Facharztzentren, bedeuten wiederum, dass die Flächenversorgung entsprechend ausgedünnt wird und die Wege der Bevölkerung zu den Facharztzentren zunehmen. Auf der anderen Seite ist dafür die Versorgung in einem Facharztzentrum hochwertiger als in der Einzelpraxis. Die apparative Ausstattung kann gemeinsam genutzt werden, ist dadurch früher amortisiert und schneller erneuert.
Facharztzentren der beschriebenen Art, die zugleich auch noch Zugang zu Krankenhausbetten haben, können in einem großen Umfang die kleinen ländlichen Krankenhäuser ersetzen. Letztere sind unter den sich abzeichnenden Kostendruck immer weniger in der Lage, in ihrer alten Form wirtschaftlich über die Runden zu kommen. Es ist Umstrukturierung angesagt. Werden diese kleinen

Krankenhäuser mit etwa 150 Betten in ein Facharztzentrum umgewandelt, in dem die niedergelassenen Fachärzte die apparative Ausstattung dieses Krankenhauses gemeinsam nutzen und ihre Patienten für kurzstationäre Eingriffe in den verbleibenden Krankenhausbetten unterbringen, so kann sich eine neue, betriebswirtschaftlich konkurrenzfähige Betriebsform entwickeln. In der nachfolgenden Abbildung 6 skizzieren wir den hier entwickelten Grundgedanken.

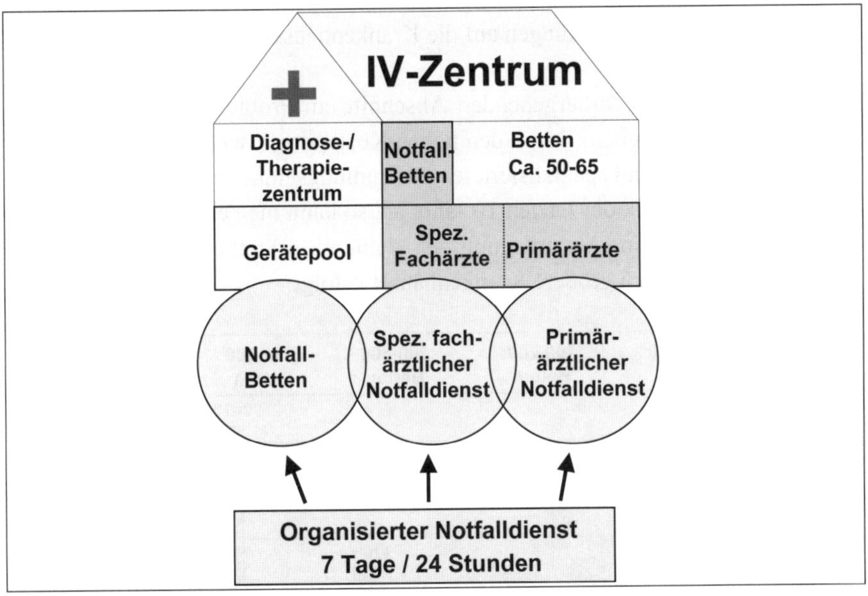

Quelle: Neubauer G. et al 2007

Abb. 6: Facharztzentren mit Krankenbettenversorgung

Die Umstrukturierung der Krankenhausversorgung im Verbund mit den niedergelassenen Fachärzten würde auch die sog. doppelte Facharztschiene in Deutschland in eine vernünftige Form überleiten. Heute behandeln Fachärzte sowohl in der Praxis als auch im Krankenhaus oft ganz ähnliche Krankheitsbilder. Diese Parallelität erfordert unnötige Kapazitätsvorhaltung. Sinnvoller ist es, wenn die Krankenhäuser sich auf die komplizierten Behandlungen konzentrieren und andererseits die leichteren Fälle den niedergelassenen Fachärzten überlassen. Da aber häufig Patienten zur Sicherheit noch ein oder zwei Tage in einem Krankenhausbett verbringen sollten, ist es erforderlich, dass auch den niedergelassenen Fachärzten Krankenbetten zur Verfügung stehen. Dies ist insbesondere für ältere Patienten immer wichtiger, da diese zur Erholung nach einem Eingriff in der Regel mehr Zeit brauchen und häufig zu Hause nicht entsprechend versorgt werden können.

Solche Facharztzentren mit Krankenbettenzugang können sehr viel patientennäher loziert sein, als Krankenhäuser, die ein größeres Einzugsgebiet brauchen. Von daher kann die fachärztliche bevölkerungsnahe Versorgung auf längere Sicht mit dem hier skizzierten Modell mutmaßlich besser erreicht werden als bei einer Fortführung der gegenwärtigen, aufwendigeren Struktur.

3. Auswirkungen auf die Krankenhausversorgung

Wir haben schon im vorhergehenden Abschnitt ein Problem der Krankenhausversorgung angesprochen: Durch den hohen Kostendruck werden Krankenhäuser zu immer größeren und spezialisierteren Behandlungseinheiten umorganisiert. Sieht man die Statistik der letzten 10 Jahre an, so kann man erkennen, dass schon seit geraumer Zeit eine Verdrängung der kleineren öffentlichen Krankenhäuser durch private und auch größere Krankenhäuser erfolgt.

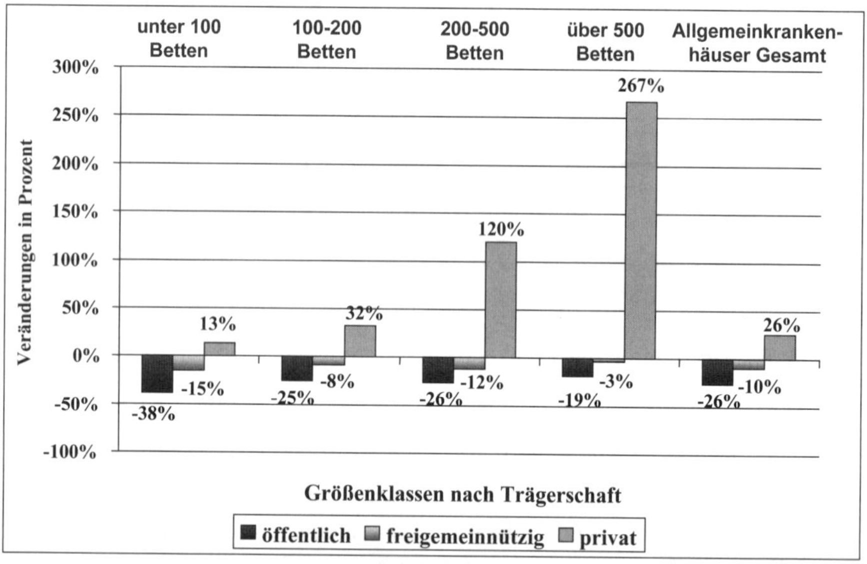

Quelle: Statistisches Bundesamt (Fachserie 12) 2005

Abb. 7: Umstrukturierung der Krankenhausversorgung (Gewinner und Verlierer) 1991-2003

Abbildung 7 lässt zwei Entwicklungstendenzen erkennen: Zum einen werden kleinere Krankenhäuser verdrängt und zum anderen ist offensichtlich, dass Krankenhäuser mit öffentlicher Trägerschaft besonders gefährdet sind. Beide Faktoren gehören aber zu dem gleichen Phänomen, nämlich dass das allgemeine Krankenhaus, das eine breite Grundversorgung in relativer Nähe zu seinen Patienten durchführt, immer weniger in der Lage ist, dies zu den betriebswirtschaftlich gebotenen niedrigen Kosten zu leisten. Hinzu kommt, dass aufgrund der hohen Mobilität der Bevölkerung, ein kleiner aber betriebswirtschaftlich entscheidender Teil der Patienten im Einzugsgebiet eines Krankenhauses es vorzieht, ein entfernteres aber höher spezialisiertes Krankenhaus aufzusuchen. Kommt es zu etwa fünf bis zehn Prozent Patientenabwanderung aus dem Einzugsgebiet eines kleinen Krankenhauses, beginnen bereits die betriebswirtschaftlichen Probleme. Krankenhäuser, die keine Auslastung von 80 Prozent und mehr ihrer vorgehaltenen Betten und des dazugehörigen Personals erreichen, können bereits ihre laufenden Betriebskosten nicht mehr abdecken. Verliert nun ein Krankenhaus die angesprochenen fünf bis zehn Prozent der Patienten, so wird es im Jahresdurchschnitt keine 80-prozentige Kapazitätsauslastung mehr erreichen können, da in der Regel im Sommer die Krankenhausbehandlungen zurückgehen und in den Frühjahrs- und Herbstmonaten einen Höhepunkt erreichen.

Betrachtet man nun die Entwicklung der kleinen Allgemein-Krankenhäuser mit bis zu 200 Betten und schreibt den Trend der letzen zehn Jahre fort, so kommt man zu dem Ergebnis, dass dieser Typ bald der Vergangenheit angehören wird.

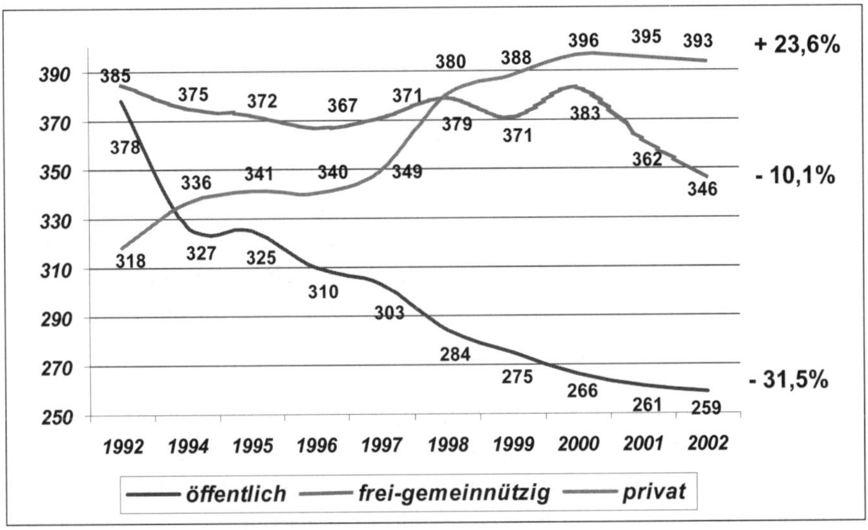

Quelle: Statistisches Bundesamt (Fachserie 12) 2005

Abb. 8: Entwicklungstrend der öffentlichen Allgemein-Krankenhäuser

Kommt es zu einem Rückzug bzw. einer Stilllegung der kleinen Krankenhäuser, besteht sowohl in der Versorgung als auch auf dem Arbeitsmarkt der jeweiligen Region eine empfindliche Lücke. Derzeit sind die Krankenhäuser gerade in we-

niger wirtschaftlich prosperierenden Gegenden häufig der wichtigste Arbeitgeber. Will man diese Lücke vermeiden oder möglichst reduzieren, so bietet es sich an, die im vorhergegangenen Abschnitt angesprochenen fachärztlichen Versorgungszentren einzurichten, die sowohl die fachärztliche ambulante Versorgung wie auch die kurzzeitige stationäre Versorgung bündeln und damit einen weitgehenden Ersatz für kleine Krankenhäuser bieten.
Langfristig wird sich die spezialisierte Krankenhausversorgung weitgehend in den Ballungsräumen konzentrieren, die ländliche Versorgung wird hingegen von hochwertiger und teurer stationärer Versorgung weitgehend entblößt sein. Die längeren Wege der Bevölkerung zu den Krankenhäusern wird zugleich eine neue Nachfrage nach Hotelkapazität schaffen, die sich in räumlicher Nähe zum jeweiligen spezialisierten Krankenhaus befindet. Solche Patientenhotels werden bereits in den Flächenstaaten Skandinaviens vorgehalten. Für Deutschland ist mit zunehmender Konzentration der Versorgung eine ähnliche Entwicklung zu erwarten. Der prognostizierte Bevölkerungsrückgang und die damit einhergehende Konzentration der verbleibenden Bevölkerung in den Ballungsräumen unterstützen diese Entwicklung.

4. Die Arzneimittelversorgung

Die Arzneimittelversorgung wird heute im wesentlichen durch die niedergelassenen Apotheken sichergestellt. In Deutschland sind derzeit etwa 20.000 Apotheken an der flächendeckenden Versorgung der Bevölkerung mit Arzneimitteln beteiligt. Da den Apotheken ein öffentlicher Auftrag zur Sicherstellung der Versorgung übertragen ist, haben sie einerseits die Pflicht, eine ständige Präsenz zu organisieren, d.h., dass sowohl nachts als auch an Wochenenden die Abgabe von Arzneimitteln stets ermöglicht sein muss. Als quasi Lohn für diese öffentliche Sicherstellung der Versorgung haben die Apotheken vom Staat feste Abgabenpreise zugebilligt erhalten. Das bedeutet aber auch, dass zwischen den Apotheken kein Preiswettbewerb bei verschreibungspflichtigen Medikamenten zulässig ist. Es kann lediglich einen Qualitäts- und Konditionen-Wettbewerb geben.
Wie lange der Ausschluss des Preiswettbewerbs noch durchzuhalten sein wird, ist jedoch aus heutiger Sicht fraglich. Bereits die Zulassung von Versandapotheken über das Internet führte zu einer Störung in diesem System. Internetapotheken, die aus dem Ausland deutsche Patienten versorgen, dürften nämlich Preise absenken, d.h., mit inländischen Apotheken indirekt in einen Preiswettbewerb eintreten. Nun ist die Marktdurchdringung durch Versandapotheken per Internet immer nur begrenzt möglich.

Die demographische Entwicklung führt im Arzneimittelbereich, ähnlich wie in anderen Versorgungsbereichen, zu einer zwiespältigen Entwicklung: einerseits steigt der Bedarf an Arzneimitteln mit zunehmendem Alter beträchtlich an. Dies verspricht einen erhöhten Bedarf und damit auch Umsatz für die Apotheken. Andererseits aber sinkt die Finanzkraft der Versicherten in dem Umfang wie die Zahl der Erwerbstätigen zurückgeht und die Zahl der Rentner und das sind vor allen Dingen die Mehrzahl der Patienten, ansteigt. Gerade diese Schere, die sich zwischen Bedarf und Finanzierung immer mehr öffnet, wird aber von den Leistungserbringern verstärkte Rationalisierungsbemühungen verlangen. Dies wird auch den Preiswettbewerb einschließen.

Neben dem Preiswettbewerb ist auch die Vertriebsstruktur der Apotheken heute noch wenig auf die Zukunft eingestellt. So sind die Mehrzahl der Apotheken immer noch selbständige Einzelbetriebe, die vor allen Dingen auf dem Land eine nicht unbedeutende gesellschaftliche wie wirtschaftliche Funktion inne haben. Für die Zukunft ist aber damit zu rechnen, dass Apotheken, die als Kettenbetriebe die Versorgung organisieren, über beträchtliche Rationalisierungsvorteile verfügen. Hierzu ist es freilich erforderlich, dass der Gesetzgeber das sog. Fremdbesitzverbot und Mehrbesitzverbot aufhebt. Ersteres meint, dass heute kein Nicht-Apotheker eine Apotheke betreiben darf, d.h. Kapitalgeber können keine Apotheke übernehmen und sie über einen angestellten Apotheker betreiben lassen. Das Mehrbesitzverbot wiederum schließt die Kettenbildung aus. Beide Verbote müssen aus heutiger Sicht als Rationalisierungshindernisse eingeschätzt werden. Längerfristig ist also damit zu rechnen, dass beide Verbote fallen oder zumindest weitgehend gelockert werden. Ein Ergebnis davon würde sein, dass viele der heutigen 20.000 Apotheken sich in Ketten wiederfinden würden und etwa 20 Prozent der Apotheken mutmaßlich zur Aufgabe gezwungen wären.

Es ist wiederum zu erwarten, dass vor allem die ländliche Versorgung darunter zu leiden hat. Die hohe Präsenz von Apotheken in den Klein- und Unterzentren dürfte dadurch mutmaßlich spürbar reduziert werden. Heute versorgt eine Apotheke nur noch etwa 2.000 bis 4.000 Einwohner. Bei einer entsprechenden Neuorganisation dürfte die Versorgung auf die doppelte Zahl von Bürgern angehoben werden, zu dem Preis, dass die Entfernung zur Apotheke steigen wird, die Abgabenpreise von Arzneimitteln aber entsprechend sinken. Die Politik wird auf längere Sicht keine andere Wahl haben, als diese möglichen Rationalisierungsreserven zu mobilisieren und anderenfalls den Patienten längere Wege zumuten.

Auch hier wird die Entwicklung dadurch in ihren negativen Auswirkungen begrenzt, dass durch die modernen Kommunikations- und Verkehrsmittel die Versorgungsnähe weniger beeinträchtigt wird als das aufgrund der größeren räumlichen Entfernung vermutet werden kann.

Die riesigen Probleme, vor der unsere Gesundheitspolitik steht, wie überhaupt unsere Sozialversicherungssysteme, zwingen die Politik einen langfristigen Reformprozess einzuläuten. Bei diesem Reformprozess, der schrittweise umgesetzt wird, weil sonst die älteren Wähler zu sehr verprellt werden würden, ist es wichtig, das langfristige Reformziel vor Augen zu haben. Es gilt die Schere zwischen wegbrechenden Einnahmen und weiter ansteigenden Ausgaben auf längere Sicht hin zu schließen oder zumindest auf ein erträgliches Maß zu konvergieren. Die Abbildung 9 zeigt diese Entwicklung auf und macht zugleich deutlich, was die wichtigsten Bestimmungsfaktoren sind.

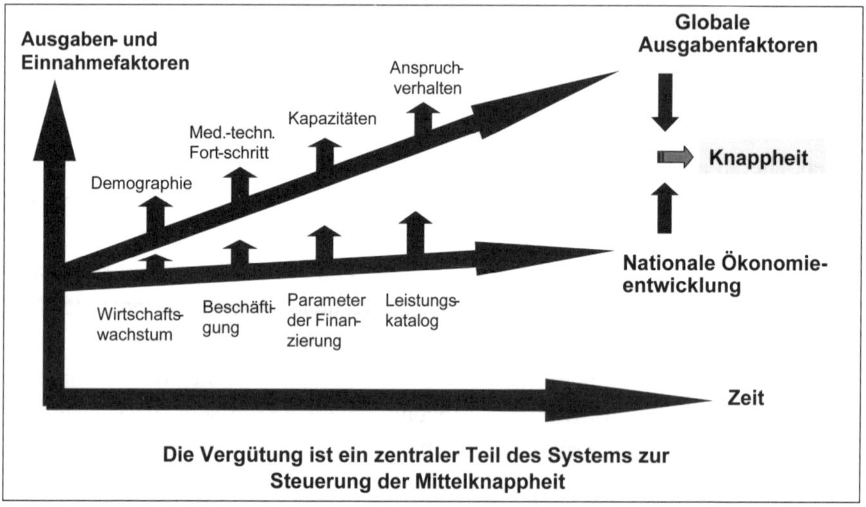

Quelle: Neubauer G. 2005

Abb. 9: Die Einnahmen- und Ausgabenschere in der Gesundheitsversorgung

Da die Faktoren, die den Bedarf bestimmen, weitgehend globalisiert sind, muss die deutsche Gesundheitspolitik vor allem die national beeinflussbaren Faktoren gestalten. Es bedarf keiner Erwähnung, dass vor allen Dingen ein höheres Wirtschaftswachstum zu einer nachhaltigen Erleichterung bei der Bewältigung der Probleme führen würde. Zugleich müssen die Beiträge der gesetzlichen Krankenversicherung stärker von den Arbeitskosten und der Konjunkturentwicklung abgekoppelt werden. Dies verlangt, dass die Versicherungspflichtigen aus ihrem Gesamteinkommen die Beiträge aufzubringen haben und andererseits die Arbeitgeber aus der Beitragspflicht zu entlassen sind. Letzteres ist erforderlich, um die unheilvolle Anbindung der Arbeitskosten an die Gesundheitsausgaben zu durchbrechen. Die diskutierte Gleichschaltung der Gesetzlichen Krankenversicherung (GKV) und der Privaten Krankenversicherungen (PKV) halten wir hingegen für keine wirkliche Lösung der Problematik. Wichtiger wird es hingegen sein, den Leistungskatalog, der gesetzlich vorgegeben ist, entsprechend zu reduzieren.

Gesundheitsversorgung, soweit sie gesetzlich vorgeschrieben ist, wird sich einerseits auf Großrisiken zu konzentrieren haben und andererseits die Versicherungspflichtigen an den kleineren Risiken direkt beteiligen müssen. Nur so ist ein fairer Risikoausgleich in der Bevölkerung zu erreichen, ohne dass die Eigenverantwortung erlahmt bzw. die fehlende Eigenverantwortung das Systems überfordert wird.

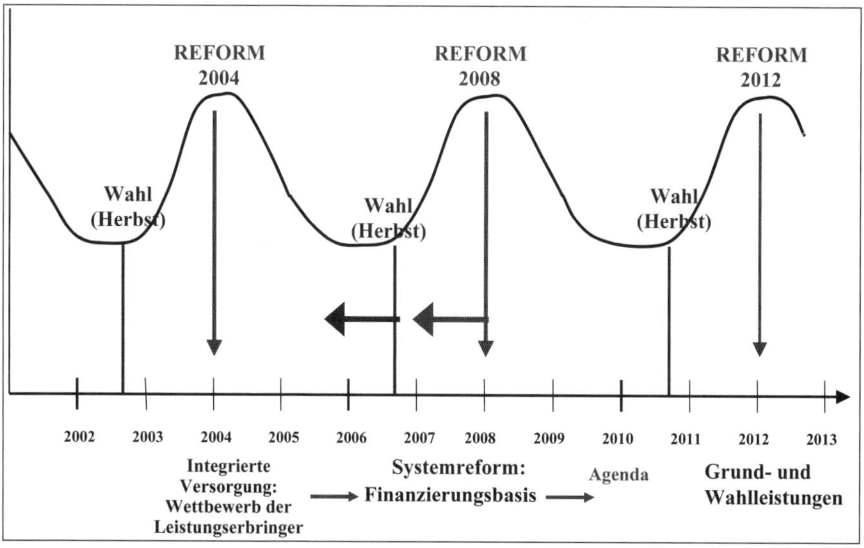

Quelle: Neubauer G. 2001

Abb. 10: Nach der Wahl 2005 ist vor der Reform 2007

Wie wir schon angesprochen haben, werden diese Schritte in einem langjährigen Reformprozess umzusetzen sein. Schon seit 1975 können wir beobachten, dass Gesundheitsreformen und Wahlzyklen in einer bestimmten Gesetzmäßigkeit zueinander stehen. Gesundheitsreformen erfolgen nämlich stets nach der Wahl, da sie in der Regel dem Wähler wenig Erfreuliches bescheren, und das wiederum am Ende des ersten Nachwahljahres. Wird also z.B. im Herbst 2005 gewählt so ist zum 01.01.2007 die nächste große Gesundheitsreform oder besser der nächste Reformschritt vorprogrammiert. Diese Reihung ergibt sich durch die Lage der

Landtagswahlen und den Prozeduren der Abstimmung im Bundestag und Bundesrat. In der folgenden Abbildung 10 haben wir diese gesetzmäßige Abhängigkeit zwischen Reformprozess und Wahlzyklen abgebildet. Es ist zu erkennen, dass durch die vorgezogene Bundestagswahl 2005 sich an der Gesetzmäßigkeit wenig geändert hat, sondern sich lediglich der Zeitablauf verschoben hat.

V. Ausblick

Die demographische Entwicklung führt in Deutschland dazu, dass die Innovationsbereitschaft und die Reformbereitschaft der Bevölkerung spürbar zurückgehen. Dies wird gerade im Bereich der sozialen Reformen deutlich.

Das heutige Sozialleistungssystem begünstigt die Bevölkerung die 50 Jahre und älter ist, da sie für den Rest ihres Lebens von den staatlichen Einrichtungen einschließlich der Sozialversicherung Nettoauszahlungen zu erwarten haben. So hat etwa ein 70-jähriger noch rund 130.000 € an Auszahlungen vom Staat und der Sozialversicherung zu erwarten, während ein 20-jähriger für den Rest seines Lebens noch etwa 230.000 € an Zahlungen an Staat und Sozialversicherung netto zu leisten hat. Es ist ersichtlich, dass der Jüngere eine Reform des Systems wünschen muss, während der Ältere gerade einer solchen Reform ablehnend gegenübersteht. Nun hat aber letztere Gruppe mit 56 Prozent der Stimmen die Mehrheit im demographischen Abstimmungsprozess.

Es kommt noch hinzu, dass die ältere Bevölkerung in einem höheren Prozentsatz von ihren Wahlrechten Gebrauch macht als die Gruppe der Jüngeren. Damit kann keine größere Partei mehr an dem Wollen der älteren Bevölkerungsgruppe vorbeigehen. Dies führt aber letztlich dazu, dass Deutschland in einer demographisch-demokratischen Reformfalle sitzt. Einerseits müssten Reformen vorangebracht werden, um das Land zukunftsfähig zu machen, andererseits steht diesen die Mehrheit der Wähler skeptisch bzw. abweisend gegenüber. Schon heute können wir feststellen, dass die Politik für die Zukunftssicherung in Form von Investitionen deutlich weniger tut als für den Sozialkonsum, der die ältere Generation begünstigt. An Investitionen standen 2004 in Deutschland insgesamt 31 Mrd. € zur Verfügung, während für den Sozialkonsum 585 Mrd. € verausgabt wurden, das sind aber rund zwanzig mal so viel wie das Investitionsvolumen. Erschwerend kommt hinzu, dass den Investitionen im Jahr 2004 noch 80 Mrd. € Nettoschulden gegenüberstehen, die ebenfalls die jüngere Generation belasten.

Will man aus dieser demographisch-demokratischen Falle entrinnen, so müssen die Stimmengewichte für die jüngere Generation neu justiert werden. Ein Weg hierzu wäre, dass die Stimmen der Kinder auf ihre Eltern übertragen werden. Dies würde, wie die Abbildung 11 auch ausweist, die Stimmenverhältnisse zugunsten der jüngeren Generation umgewichten. Den heute 44 Prozent Wahlberechtigten stünden dann 56 Prozent an Wählerstimmen zur Verfügung. Doch auch diese Stimmenmehrheit wird sich in absehbarer Zeit zu einem Gleichgewicht bzw. zu einer Minderheit wandeln, wenn die Bevölkerung, wie vorhersehbar, weiter schrumpft.

Ein Radikalvorschlag wäre demnach, wenn wir die Wählerstimmen mit ihrer künftigen Lebenserwartung gewichten würden. In Abb. 11 wollen wir diesen Schritt mit der von links oben nach rechts unten verlaufenden Geraden andeuten: unterstellen wir eine Lebenserwartung in Deutschland von 100 Jahren, erhält der 1-jährige das Stimmengewicht 100, während der 100-jährige das Stimmengewicht 1 erhält. Bei einer solchen asymmetrischen, der Lebenserwartung folgenden Stimmverteilung, würde unsere Gesellschaft auf lange Sicht reformfähig bleiben. Nun wissen wir auch, dass ein solcher Vorschlag zwar keine Aussicht auf Umsetzung hat, gleichwohl aber zum Nachdenken anregen kann, wie nach den Regeln der Demokratie unsere Gesellschaft und damit unser Sozialleistungssystem reformfähig gehalten werden könnte.

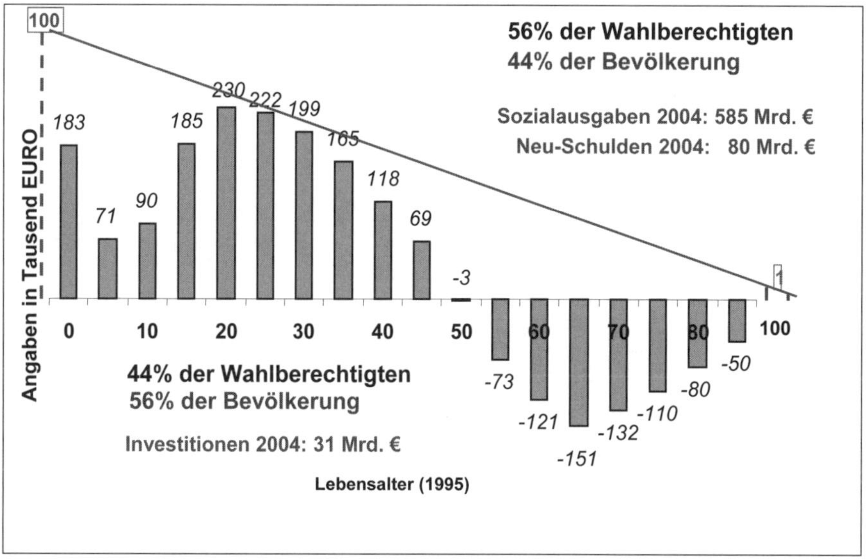

Quelle: Deutsche Bundesbank 1997, 10. koordinierte Bevölkerungsvorausberechnung des Statistischen Bundesamtes 2003, Statistisches Bundesamt 2006

Abb. 11: Deutschland in der demographisch-demokratischen Reformfalle

Literaturverzeichnis

Breyer, F. und *V. Ulrich*, 2000. Gesundheitsausgaben, Alter und medizinischer Fortschritt: eine Regressionsanalyse. Jahrbücher für Nationalökonomie und Statistik 220 (2000), S. 1 – 17.

Bruckenberger, E., 2005, Herzbericht 2004, o.A.O.

Deutsche Bundesbank, 1997, Monatsbericht November 1997, S. 17 – 30.

Neubauer, G., et al., 2007. Marktwandel und Sicherstellung der regionalen Krankenhausversorgung. Erschienen in *J. Klauber* et al, Krankhaus-Report 2006, Stuttgart 2007 Statistisches Bundesamt.

Neubauer, G., 2005. Ökonomische Grundlagen der Medizin – Risiken und Chancen. MedReview, 6. Jg., 09/2005, S. 20 – 21.

Neubauer, G., 2001. DRG Risikomanagement – Eine Strategie zur Risikosenkung und Chancenerhöhung unter einem DRG-Vergütungssystem. Der Chirurg, 40. Jg., Nr. 12/2001, S. 322 – 326.

Neubauer, G., 2000. Kooperation, Fusion, Betreibergesellschaft als Wege in die Zukunft. f&w führen und wirtschaften im Krankenhaus, 17. Jg., 04/2000, S. 382 - 385.

Statistisches Bundesamt, 2006, Statistisches Jahrbuch 2006, Wiesbaden 2006.

Statistisches Bundesamt, 2003, 10. koordinierte Bevölkerungsvorausberechnung, Wiesbaden 2003.

Verband der privaten Krankenversicherung, 2003. Die Private Krankenversicherung – Zahlenbericht 2002/2003, Köln 2003.

Fünftes Kapitel

Wirtschaftsförderung bei Bevölkerungsrückgang

A. Regionen im Wettbewerb um Bevölkerung

Florian W. Bartholomae und *Alina M. Popescu*

I. Einleitung

Schätzungen zufolge wird die Bevölkerung in Deutschland sowie in den am stärksten entwickelten Staaten in den nächsten 40 Jahren mehr oder weniger stark zurückgehen. Die demographischen Probleme sind Folge der niedrigen Geburtenrate, der steigenden Lebenserwartung aber auch der internen Migration. Durch die demographische Entwicklung werden schwerwiegende Probleme in Deutschland verursacht. Niedrige Geburtenraten und eine steigende Lebenserwartung werden zu einer zunehmenden Überalterung der Gesellschaft in Deutschland führen. Dies führt zu einer Reihe ökonomischer, aber auch struktureller Änderungen, denen die deutsche Bevölkerung begegnen muss.

Zusätzlich wird die natürliche demographische Entwicklung durch interne Migration verschärft, die zu großen regionalen Disparitäten in Deutschland führt. Viele junge Menschen, besonders junge Frauen im Alter zwischen 18 und 29 Jahren, migrieren von Ost- nach West-Deutschland. Als Konsequenz kann dort eine nur noch ungenügende Nutzung der Infrastruktur beobachtet werden. Gemeinden im früheren Staatsgebiet der DDR werden bereits heute mit den demographischen Problemen konfrontiert, die in den süd-westlichen Teilen des Landes erst in 20 Jahren zu erwarten sind. Interne Migration verschärft die Lage dadurch, dass sie die demographischen Änderungen in manchen Regionen – den Regionen mit positiver Netto-Migration – verzögert, wodurch dieser Problematik dort nur unzureichend Aufmerksamkeit geschenkt wird. Andererseits werden die demographischen Probleme in Regionen mit negativer Netto-Migration zunehmend verschärft. Die Folge ist ein Wettbewerbszustand zwischen den Gemeinden zur Attraktion von Bevölkerung. Es wird versucht, Einwohner durch verschiedene Maßnahmen und ökonomische Anreize anzulocken oder zumindest zu halten. Schließlich zeichnet sich eine Situation hoher Ausgaben zur Attraktion der Bevölkerung und trotzdem geringer Bevölkerungszahlen ab. Begegnen Regionen dieser Konkurrenzsituation nur unzureichend, führt dies zur Entstehung regionaler Disparitäten.

Ziel dieser Studie ist es, aufzuzeigen, dass es für Regionen, trotz starkem Wettbewerb, optimal sein kann, nicht auf politische Maßnahmen der konkurrierenden Region(en) zu reagieren. Eine Änderung der eigenen politischen Maßnahmen als Reaktion auf politische Änderungen anderer Regionen kann zu einem unvorteilhafteren Ergebnis führen. Ausgehend von zwei nutzenmaximierenden Gemeinden, der Berücksichtigung einer Mindestbevölkerung, die für die effiziente Nutzung der vorhandenen Infrastruktur mindestens erforderlich ist, sowie der Situation regionaler Konkurrenz um zusätzliche Einwohner, wird aufgezeigt, dass unterschiedliche Reaktionsmöglichkeiten bestehen, abhängig von der jeweiligen (relativen) demographischen Situation der betrachteten Regionen.

II. Bevölkerungsstruktur und -politik in Deutschland – Stilisierte Fakten

Die demographischen Änderungen in Deutschland stellen vor allem ein ökonomisches Problem dar. An erster Stelle verursacht die Bevölkerungsalterung eine Strukturänderung der deutschen Gesellschaft durch rückläufige Erwerbsbeteiligung. Im Jahr 2030 wird der Bevölkerungsanteil der über 60-jährigen etwa 35% betragen und damit fast doppelt so hoch sein wie der Anteil der unter 20-jährigen (Lehr 2003; Birg 1987). Folglich sieht sich eine schrumpfende Gruppe Erwerbstätiger, einer stetig wachsenden Anzahl älterer Menschen gegenüber, deren Renten, spezielle Pflege und sonstige Aufwendungen sie finanzieren muss, nicht zuletzt deshalb, da mit zunehmendem Alter der Menschen auch deren Erwerbsbeteiligung sinkt. Weltweit wird erwartet, dass sich die Anzahl der über 60-jährigen bis 2050 verdreifachen wird. Bislang beträgt der Anteil der älteren Menschen an der Gesamtbevölkerung noch 20% in den entwickelten Ländern, jedoch wird ein Anstieg auf 32% im Jahr 2050 angenommen (United Nations 2005). Spätestens im Jahr 2040 wird die Bevölkerung Deutschlands rückläufig, wenn die Mitglieder der „Babyboom"-Generation der 1960er sterben (Börsch-Supan, Ludwig, Sommer 2003). Allen Szenarien gemein ist ein Bevölkerungsrückgang in Deutschland um mindestens 6 Millionen Menschen. Die Bevölkerung von heute knapp 83 Mio. wird auf 77 Mio. Einwohner sinken.

Indikatoren wie die natürliche Bevölkerungsentwicklung (Verhältnis von Geburten und Sterbefällen), die Fertilitätsrate (durchschnittliche Anzahl von Kindern pro Frau), der Frauenanteil (im Verhältnis zu den Männern) und der Anteil der unter 20-jährigen an der Gesamtbevölkerung, ebenso wie die Migration ermöglichen es, die demographische Entwicklung auszuwerten und zu prognostizieren. In der Bundesrepublik Deutschland variieren diese Indikatoren auf regionaler Ebene in erheblichem Umfang. Vor allem die deutsche Wiedervereinigung führte zu massiven Wanderungsbewegungen zwischen den neuen und alten Bundesländern und änderte damit die demographischen Entwicklungen und Perspektiven dieser Regionen.

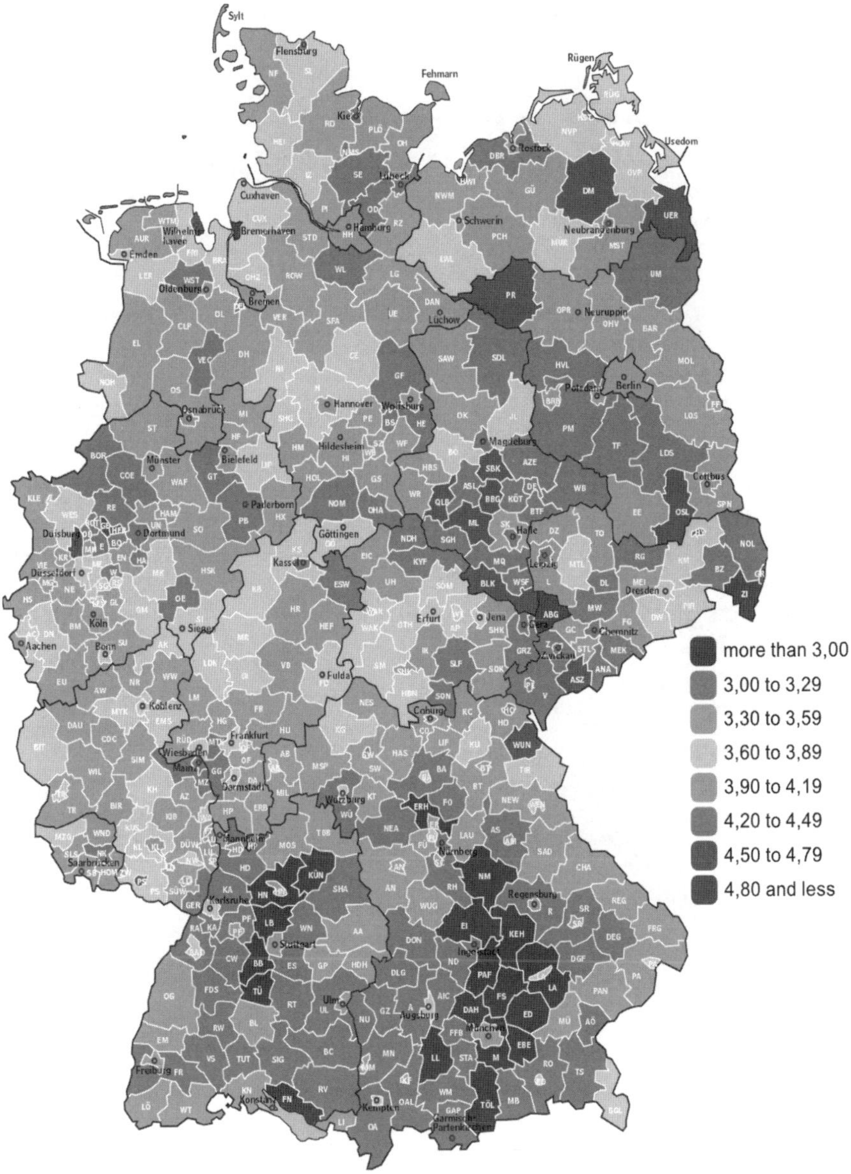

Quelle: Kröhnert, S., Van Olst, N., Klingholz R., 2004

Abb. 1: Untersuchung zur demographischen Situation in allen deutschen Regionen.

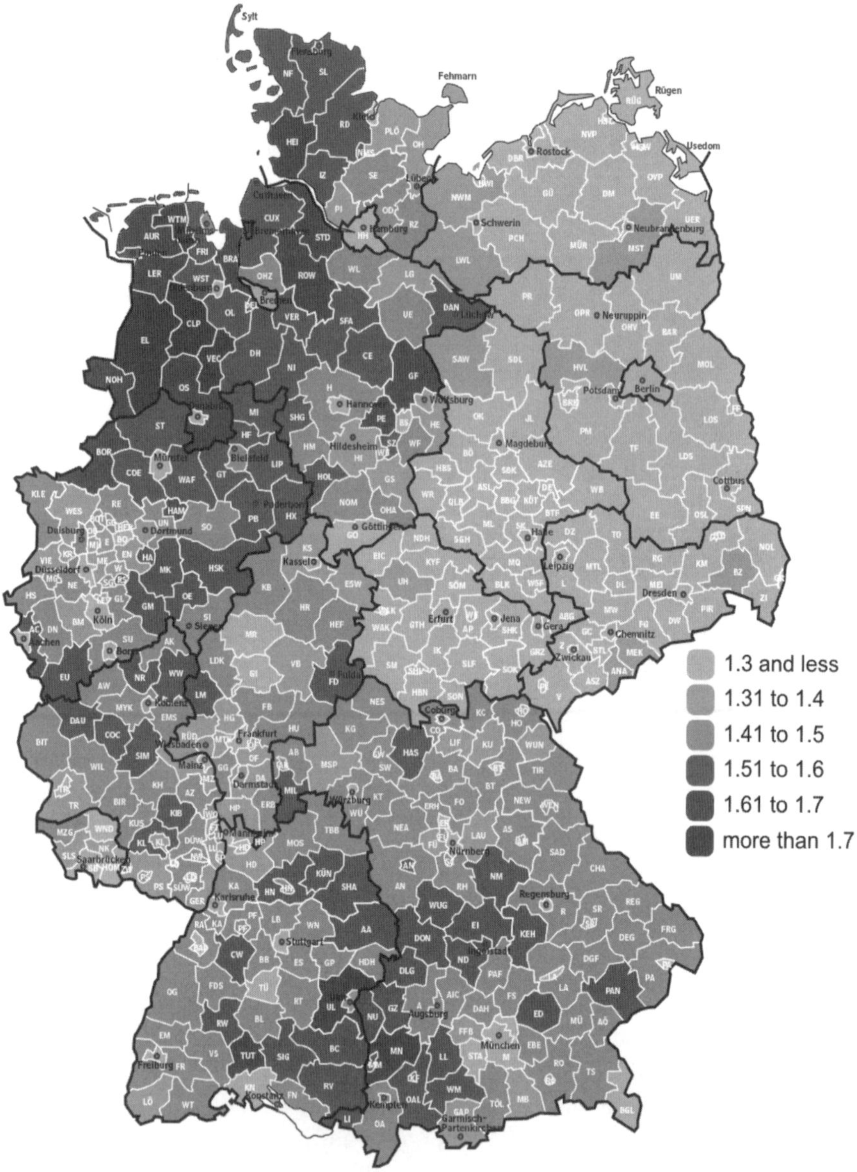

Quelle: Kröhnert, S., Van Olst, N., Klingholz R., 2004

Abb. 2: Fertilitätsraten in Deutschland.

Die demographische Situation in Deutschland wird in Abbildung 1 dargestellt. Die beste Bewertung, die eine Region erzielen kann, ist 1, die schlechteste ist 6. Abgesehen von München und Stuttgart gibt es nur 19 weitere Gemeinden, die eine bessere Bewertung als 3 haben (Kröhnert, van Olst, Klingholz 2004). An der Abbildung ist deutlich der Unterschied zwischen Ost und West sowie Nord und Süd zu erkennen.

Jede dritte Frau in Deutschland bleibt kinderlos. Dadurch ist die Stabilität der Bevölkerungszahl nicht länger sichergestellt (Kröhnert, van Olst, Klingholz 2004). Auch bei den Fertilitätsraten lassen sich regionale Unterschiede erkennen, wie Abbildung 2 zeigt.

Sinkende Fertilitätsraten sind ein Phänomen, das in den meisten entwickelten Ländern zu beobachten ist, wie die durchschnittliche Fertilitätsrate aller OECD Länder im Zeitablauf zeigt. Innerhalb von nur 30 Jahren ist sie auf 1,3 gesunken. 1960 betrug die Fertilitätsrate noch 2,9, während sie am Ende der 1990er bereits auf 1,6 gesunken ist (Adserá 2003). Weltweit beträgt die Fertilitätsrate momentan 2,65 – allerdings auch mit abnehmender Tendenz (United Nations 2005; Birg 2005). Hauptfolge abnehmender Fertilitätsrate und zunehmender Lebenserwartung ist eine Überalterung der Bevölkerung. Dieses Problem verschärft sich für viele Regionen durch die interne Migration junger Menschen zwischen Ost und West. Dabei wird der Bevölkerungsrückgang nicht nur ökonomische Konsequenzen haben, sondern auch soziale und psychologische. Es erstaunt daher wenig, dass die Prognosen für 2030 aus den genannten Gründen – Bevölkerungsrückgang, kontinuierliche Abnahme der Fertilitätsrate, Migration – ein düsteres Bild für Deutschland zeichnen. Es wird zwar erwartet, dass im Zeitraum von 2005 bis 2050 rund 200.000 internationale Migranten im Jahresdurchschnitt nach Deutschland einwandern, aber angesichts der Tatsache, dass diese Migranten ihren Wohnort innerhalb Deutschlands nicht in jenen Regionen wählen, die besonders von der demographischen Entwicklung betroffen sind, werden die beschriebenen Probleme kaum gelöst (United Nations 2005). Wahrscheinlicher ist, dass sie in Regionen wandern, die bereits über eine vitale Gemeinschaft ausländischer Bewohner verfügen und nicht unter starkem Bevölkerungsrückgang leiden (Detig, Feng, Friedrich 2002).

Infolge der abnehmenden Anzahl von Menschen im erwerbsfähigen Alter, verursacht durch die Bevölkerungsalterung, entsteht Arbeitskräfteknappheit. Szenarien, nach denen die Frauenerwerbsquote gleich der Männererwerbsquote ist, das Pensionsalter höher und die Arbeitslosenrate bei 5% liegt, prognostizieren langfristig 8 Mio. weniger Erwerbstätige im Vergleich zum Jahr 2000 trotz der erhöhten Beschäftigungsrate (Börsch-Supan, Ludwig, Sommer 2003). Durch die Verknappung des Faktors Arbeit wird dem Kapital eine gestiegene Bedeutung zukommen. Die Kapitalintensivierung wird einerseits durch das Ersetzen der Arbeit durch Kapital und andererseits durch Auslandskapitalanlagen in Form ausländischer Direktinvestitionen (FDI) erklärt. Das FDI stellt sicher, dass der unveränderte Konsumbedarf durch Importe gedeckt werden kann (Börsch-Supan, Ludwig, Sommer 2003). Allerdings können hohe Kapitalabflüsse in Länder mit großem ökonomischen Potential und einer besseren demographischen Entwicklung nicht vermieden werden (Kinsella, Phillip 2005).

Zugleich ändern sich die Konsumgewohnheiten durch die Alterung der Gesellschaft. Der Bedarf an Gesundheits- und Pflegeleistungen wird zunehmen, während der Bedarf an Bildung oder Kinderbetreuungsangeboten – nicht zuletzt wegen der gesunkenen Fertilitätsraten – abnehmen wird. Bereits heute kann in vielen ostdeutschen Regionen das Phänomen leer stehender Wohnungen beobachtet werden, da viele junge Familien abwandern. Der Bedarf an Verkehrsnetzen, Wohnungen und Schulen wird unvermeidlich mit der Bevölkerung zurückgehen. Der Gesundheits- und Pflegesektor hingegen wird kräftig wachsen.

Da sich die Haushaltlage vieler Gemeinden dadurch bereits geändert hat[1] oder noch ändern wird, wird bereits darüber diskutiert, eine demographische Komponente für eine bessere Berechnung des kommunalen Finanzausgleiches einzuführen um dem, durch rückläufige Bevölkerungszahlen hervorgerufenen, dauerhaften oder steigenden finanziellen Bedarf zu begegnen.

Prinzipiell lassen sich politische Maßnahmen zur Begegnung des demographischen Wandels in zwei Kategorien einordnen: einerseits die Förderung zur Erhöhung der Fertilität (z.B. Unterstützung von Familien mit mehr als 3 Kindern) und andererseits die Attraktion internationaler Migration (z.B. durch Integrationsangebote für Migranten). Um die prognostizierte Überalterung zu bekämpfen, wäre, nach Berechnungen der Vereinten Nationen, bis zum Jahr 2050 eine Zuwanderung von 188 Mio. Menschen nötig (United Nations 2000). Diese große Zahl resultiert daraus, dass die Überalterung nur solange hinausgezögert wird, bis die Zuwanderer selbst älter werden. Die Berechnung geht hierbei von einer Fertilitätsrate der Migranten von 1,9 aus und liegt damit unter der für eine nachhaltige Bevölkerungsverjüngung benötigten Rate von 2,1 Kindern je Frau (Birg 2002). Allerdings muss berücksichtigt werden, dass die internationale Migration auch bestehende Probleme verschärfen kann, da viele Migranten in die Sozialsysteme und nicht in sozialversicherungspflichtige Arbeit wandern. Die Zahl der Einwohner mit Migrationshintergrund hat sich zwischen 1970 und 2002 mehr als verdoppelt. Lebten zu Beginn der 1970er noch 3 Mio. Migranten in Deutschland, so waren es im Jahr 2002 bereits 7,4 Mio. Die Anzahl erwerbstätiger Migranten

1 Siehe hierzu auch die Beiträge von Helmut Jenkis, S. 161, und Helmut Brede, S. 119, in diesem Band.

blieb dabei jedoch fast unverändert: zu Beginn der 1970er waren es 1,8 Mio. verglichen mit 1,9 Mio. im Jahr 2002 (Beckstein 2004).
Maßnahmen zur Steigerung der Fertilitätsrate allein werden aber ebenfalls keine besseren Resultate liefern als die Migrationlösung. Hierzu müsste eine Fertilitätsrate von 3,8 Kinder pro Frau erreicht werden (Birg 2002). Wie eine so hohe Fertilitätsrate angesichts einer zunehmenden Frauenerwerbsquote bei gleichzeitigem Mangel an Kinderbetreuungsangeboten erreicht werden soll, bleibt fraglich. Auch bedarf es dazu tief greifender Strukturänderungen sowohl in der Familie als auch in der Gesellschaft.

III. Regionaler Wettbewerb um Bevölkerung

In Deutschland kann ein starker Wettbewerb um Einwohner zwischen Regionen beobachtet werden. Um Standortvorteile zu generieren, versuchen die Regionen hochqualifiziertes Personal zu rekrutieren. Durch diesen intensiven Wettbewerb kommt es zu großen regionalen Unterschieden, denen nicht alle Regionen adäquat begegnen können. Hohe Migration kann zwischen ländlichen Gebieten und Ballungsräumen beobachtet werden (Bundesministerium für Familie, Senioren, Frauen und Jugend 2005). In den neuen Bundesländern gibt es Regionen, deren Wanderungssaldos pro 1000 Einwohner –15 beträgt, d.h. pro 1000 Einwohner verlassen 15 Einwohner die Region mehr, als zuwandern.
Abbildung 3 stellt den Wanderungssaldo aller Regionen dar. Vor allem die Migration beruflich benachteiligter junger Frauen aus dem Osten kann in armen Regionen beobachtet werden. Wie Abbildung 4 zeigt, weisen diese Regionen einen niedrigen Frauenanteil auf, d.h. die Möglichkeit für eine steigende Geburtenrate sinkt ebenso. In fast allen Regionen Ost-Deutschlands ist ein Frauenanteil von unter 84 zu beobachten, d.h. auf 100 Männer zwischen 18 und 29 Jahren kommen weniger als 84 gleichaltrige Frauen, während im Westen der Republik die Anzahl der Frauen die der Männer deutlich übertrifft (Kröhnert, van Oslt, Klingholz 2004).
Analog lassen sich die gleichen regionalen Unterschiede auch bei der Fertilität beobachten. Im gesamten Bundesgebiet beträgt die durchschnittliche Anzahl von Kindern pro Frau 1,37. Betrachtet man den Osten (1,2) und Westen (1,41) getrennt, so sind beträchtliche Unterschiede zu erkennen, wenngleich beide viel zu niedrig sind.

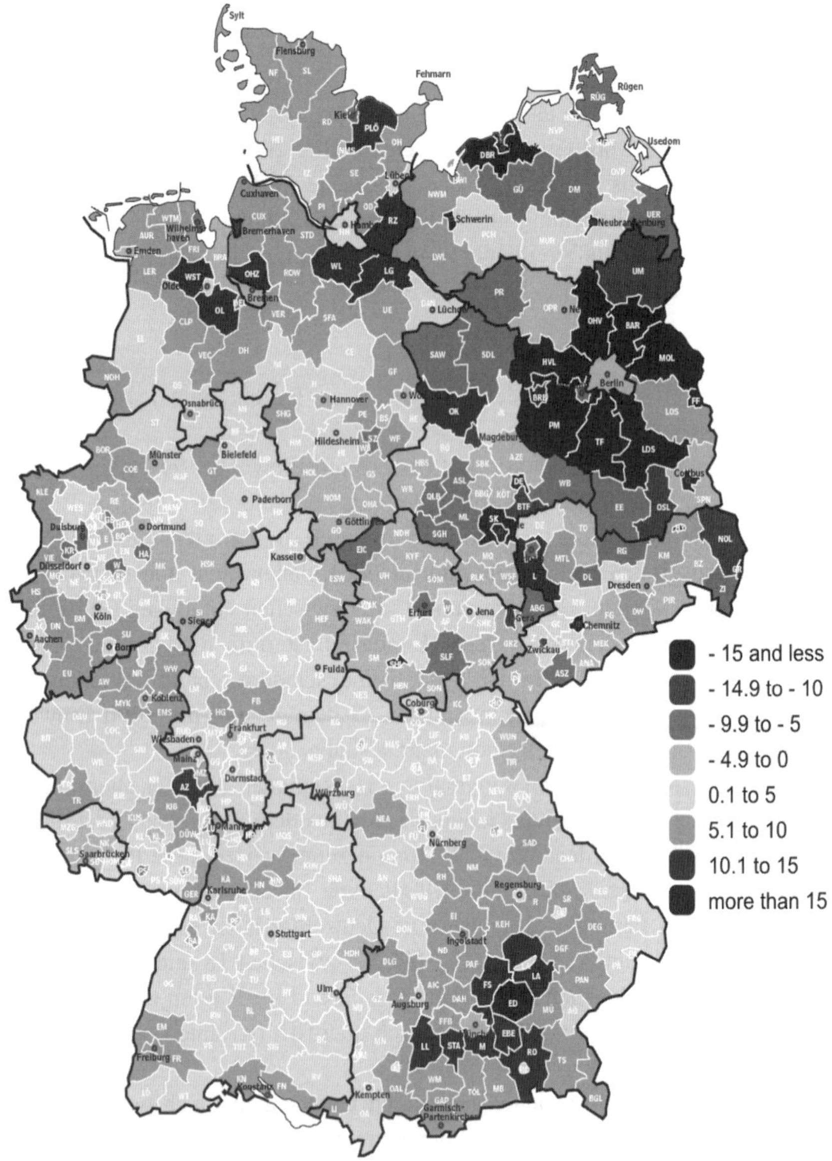

Quelle: Kröhnert, S., Van Olst, N., Klingholz R., 2004

Abb. 3: Wanderungssaldo je 1000 Einwohner.

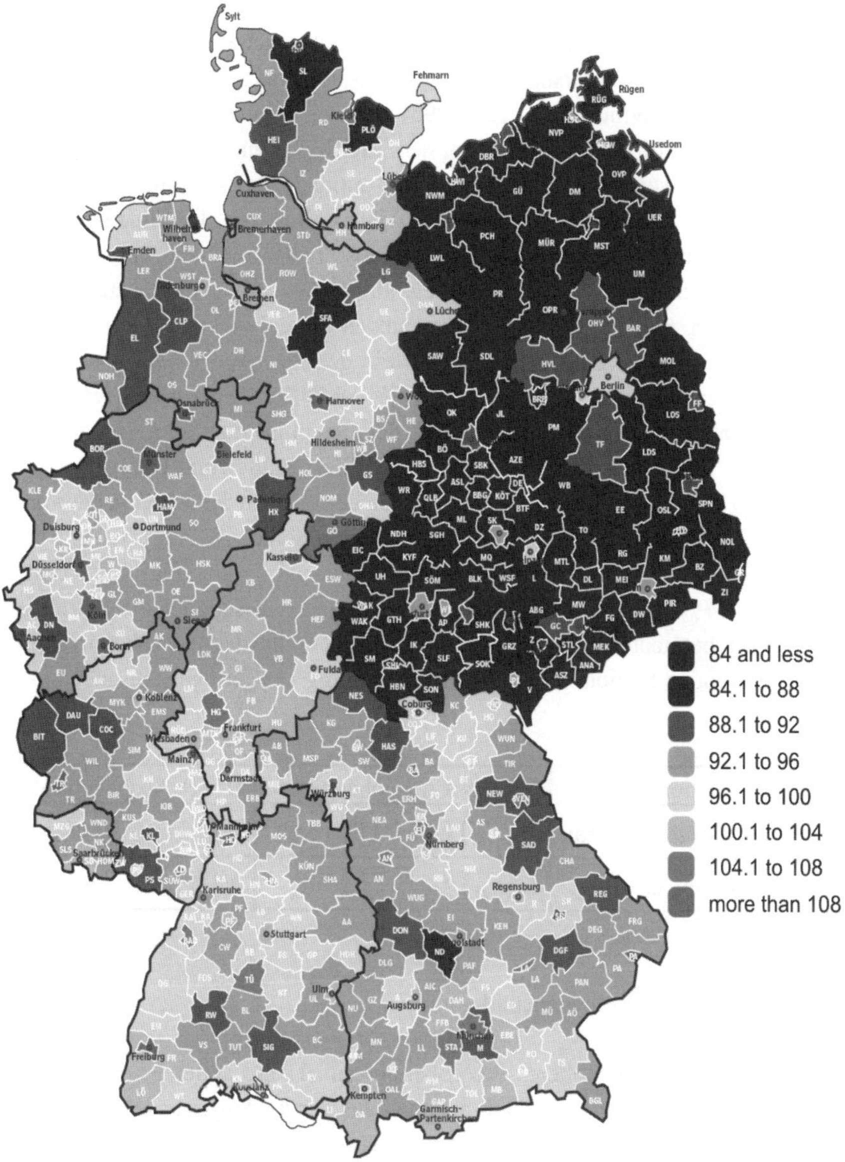

Quelle: Kröhnert, S., Van Olst, N., Klingholz R., 2004

Abb. 4: Frauenanteil der 18 - 29 jährigen im Verhältnis zu Männern der gleichen Alterskohorte.

Nach dieser Darstellung stilisierter Fakten, wird die Problematik der Bevölkerungskonkurrenz, der sich die Regionen gegenüber sehen, anhand eines einfachen Modells näher untersucht. Das bekannte Gefangenendilemma (vgl. hierzu z.B. Mas-Colell, Whinston, Green 1995) stellt einen adäquaten Ausgangspunkt dar, um den Konflikt zu beschreiben, dem die Regionen gegenüberstehen, wenn sie unabhängig voneinander versuchen ihre optimale Bevölkerungspolitik umzusetzen. Die in Abbildung 5 aufgeführte Matrix illustriert die Situation für den Fall zweier symmetrischer Regionen *i* und *j* als Spieler, die unabhängig und nicht beobachtbar voneinander ihre Strategie wählen. Als Strategiealternativen stehen vereinfachend angenommen zwei verschieden hohe Niveaus an Ausgaben zur Verfügung, entweder ein hohes (r_h) oder ein geringes (r_g) Niveau. Die resultierenden Auszahlungen ergeben sich dann aus der Differenz zwischen dem, in monetären Einheiten ausgedrückten, Nutzen der Gemeinde durch ihre (zusätzlichen) Einwohner und den Kosten der Maßnahme. Die resultierende Einwohneranzahl bzw. Auszahlung ist allerdings nicht nur von der eigenen Strategie, sondern auch von der Maßnahme der konkurrierenden Region abhängig. Es erscheint daher plausibel die resultierenden Bevölkerungsanzahl wie folgt zu ordnen: $P_{hg} > P_{gg} = P_{hh} > P_{gh}$. Der erste Buchstabe im Index beschreibt die Politikmaßnahme der betrachteten Region, der zweite beschreibt das Ausgabenniveau der konkurrierenden Region, wobei *h* ein hohes und *g* ein geringes Ausgabenniveau darstellt.

Region i, Region j	Geringes Ausgabenniveau	Hohes Ausgabenniveau
Geringes Ausgabenniveau	$U(P_{gg})-r_g,\ U(P_{gg})-r_g$	$U(P_{gh})-r_g,\ U(P_{hg})-r_h$
Hohes Ausgabenniveau	$U(P_{hg})-r_h,\ U(P_{gh})-r_g$	$U(P_{hh})-r_h,\ U(P_{hh})-r_h$

Quelle: Eigene Darstellung.

Abb. 5: Matrix des Gefangenendilemmas.

Hat eine Region ein höheres Ausgabenniveau als die andere, wird sie mehr Migranten, sowohl von außerhalb als auch aus der konkurrierenden Region, anlocken können. Haben beide das gleiche Ausgabenniveau, verteilen sich die umzugswilligen, nutzenmaximierenden Migranten zu gleichen Teilen auf beide Regionen. Jedoch muss auch der negative Nutzen aus höheren Ausgaben berücksichtigt werden, weshalb es für eine Region vorteilhafter ist, ein niedriges Ausgabenniveau zu haben. Unter den Annahmen, dass im Falle unterschiedlicher Ausgabenniveaus der Regionen der Vorteil, den die Gemeinde mit den höheren Ausgaben aus den zusätzlichen Migranten hat, höher ausfällt als der Nachteil aus den höheren Ausgaben und der Vorteil aus einem geringeren Ausgabenniveau durch den Nachteil aus der geringeren Bevölkerung überkompensiert wird, stellt ein hohes Ausgabenniveau eine dominante Strategie für beide Regionen dar. Wie die spätere Analyse ergeben wird, ist das natürlich von vielen Faktoren abhängig, unter anderem auch der Effektivität der Politikmaßnahmen. In dieser einfachen Betrachtung stellt sich jedoch das klassische Gefangenendilemma ein: obwohl für beide Regionen niedrige Ausgaben besser wären, schließlich wird die gleiche Anzahl an Migranten angelockt, wie bei hohen Kosten, haben beide immer einen Anreiz auf das hohe Ausgabenniveau abzuweichen. Im Verlauf der Analyse wird sich zeigen, dass die Konkurrenzsituation nicht in einem Gefangenendilemma enden muss.

System	Anpassungs-fähigkeit	Betriebstechnische Maßnahmen	Investive Maßnahmen (Anpassung, Stilllegung, Rückbau)
Elektroenergie	+	Veränderung der Schaltzustände	Kabel, Trafostationen
Gas	+ / –	Netzänderung, Druckstufenänderung	Leitungen, Druckregelanlagen
Fernwärme	– –	Änderung der Betriebsweise	Trassen, Wärmeübergabestationen, Reduzierung von 4- auf 2-Leitersystem
Trinkwasser	– –	Netzänderung, Rohrnetzspülung, Druckstufenänderung	Leitungen, Querschnittsreduzierung, Behälter, Druckerhöhungsanlagen
Abwasser	–	Kanalreinigung	Querschnittsreduzierung, Entlastungsbauwerke

Quelle: Herz, R., M. Werner, L. Marschke 2002

Tab. 1: Anpassungsfähigkeit verschiedener Ver- und Entsorgungssysteme an den demographischen Wandel

Grundlegend für die folgende Betrachtung ist die konkrete Spezifizierung der Nutzenfunktion der Region und der darin eingehenden Einflussgrößen. In allgemeiner Form ist die Nutzenfunktion von Region *i* bestimmt durch

$$U_i = U\left(P, P_i^*\right). \qquad (1)$$

Der Nutzen ist positiv abhängig von der aktuellen Einwohnerzahl, *P*, der Region

$$\partial U_i / \partial P > 0.$$

Von besonderer Bedeutung für die Analyse ist das kritische Bevölkerungsniveau, P_i^*. Dieses ist definiert als die, zur Aufrechterhaltung der vorhandenen Infrastruktur, notwendige Mindestbevölkerung. Zur Verdeutlichung der Problematik kann als Beispiel die Wasserversorgung aufgeführt werden: um sicherzustellen, dass die Rohre nicht durch Bakterien verunreinigt werden oder verstopfen, ist ein Mindestwasserdurchfluss erforderlich. Tabelle 1 zeigt auf, dass vor allem die Anpassungsfähigkeit der Wasserversorgung nur sehr eingeschränkt – wenn überhaupt – gegeben ist. Die Aufrechterhaltung der für den Betrieb notwendigen Bevölkerung kann den kostspieligen Umbau der Systeme vermeiden.
Aber auch Theater, Kinos, Museen, öffentliche Bäder, Schulen oder Krankenhäuser erfordern gewisse Besucheranzahlen, zumindest aber ausreichend Personal um überhaupt den Betrieb aufnehmen zu können. P^* stellt folglich einen relevanten Politikentscheidungsparameter dar und muss entsprechend Berücksichtigung bei der Bestimmung des optimalen Ausgabenniveaus finden. Ist die aktuelle Bevölkerungszahl (knapp) unterhalb des kritischen Niveaus wird jeder zusätzliche Einwohner den Nutzen der Gemeinde in beträchtlichem Umfang erhöhen je mehr sich die Gesamtbevölkerung der Mindestbevölkerung nähert, schließlich sind dann keine teuren Anpassungskosten für die Infrastruktur mehr erforderlich. Ist die Bevölkerung nahe null, wird ein zusätzlicher Bürger kaum Nutzen für die Region stiften – sofern ein Migrant sich überhaupt in einer menschenleeren Region niederlässt – daher gilt

$$\partial^2 U_i / \partial P^2 \big|_{P<P_i^*} > 0 .$$

Ist das kritische Niveau jedoch erreicht, so stiftet jeder weitere Bürger zwar immer noch einen zusätzlichen Nutzen für die Region, der (marginale) Beitrag ist jedoch geringer, als der des letzten Zuwanderers, der die Region genau das kritische Niveau erreichen ließ,

$$\partial^2 U_i / \partial P^2 \big|_{P>P_i^*} \leq 0 .$$

Abbildung 6 veranschaulicht diese Situation anhand einer abschnittsweise definierten, geknickten Nutzenfunktion. Steigt die Bevölkerung weiter (über den abgebildeten Bereich), so ist es realistisch anzunehmen, dass der Nutzen nicht endlos steigt, schließlich wird dann der Bau zusätzlicher Infrastruktur erforderlich. Der Verlauf der Nutzenfunktion ist dann abhängig davon, ob der marginale Nutzen des Zuwanderers größer oder kleiner als die marginalen Kosten des Infrastrukturaufbaus ist. Da Infrastruktur nicht in stetigem, sondern nur in diskretem Umfang zur Verfügung gestellt werden kann, ist es vorstellbar, dass der Nettonutzen ab einem bestimmten Bevölkerungsniveau, bei dem die Kapazität der vorhandenen Infrastruktur voll ausgeschöpft ist, zurückgeht und dann wieder ansteigt. In der folgenden Analyse wird der Fall einer zu großen Zuwanderung jedoch nicht untersucht.

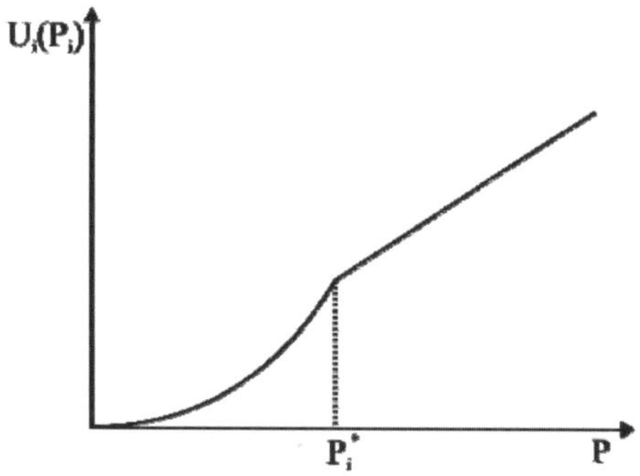

Quelle: Eigene Darstellung

Abb. 6: Nutzenfunktion einer Region in Abhängigkeit von der kritischen Bevölkerungsmasse.

Letztendlich stehen jeder Region damit drei Optionen zur Auswahl, wie sie mit einem Rückgang der Bevölkerung umgehen kann:

(i) Rückbau der vorhandenen Infrastruktur, um damit die notwendige Minimalbevölkerung ebenfalls zu reduzieren

(ii) Einführung oder Erhöhung der bevölkerungspolitischen Ausgaben um zusätzliche Bewohner für die Region zu gewinnen (natürlich sollten dafür nur monetäre Anreize herangezogen werden, wie Steuerbefreiung, Subventionen, Arbeitsvermittlung usw., da Investitionen in Infrastruktur das kritische Niveau wieder erhöhen würden und damit eher kontraproduktiv wirken würden)

(iii) „laissez-faire"

Welche Maßnahme am besten für die Region geeignet ist, ist davon abhängig, wo genau sie sich auf der Nutzenkurve in Abbildung 6 befindet. Werden zwei konkurrierende Regionen betrachtet, lassen sich daher prinzipiell drei Intensitätsstufen des Wettbewerbs unterscheiden. Die folgende Tabelle 2 veranschaulicht diese Überlegung für die beiden Regionen *i* und *j*:

Wettbewerbssituation	**Region *i***	**Region *j***
Starker Wettbewerb	$P_i < P_i^*$	$P_j < P_j^*$
Mittlerer Wettbewerb	$P_i > P_i^*$	$P_j < P_j^*$
Schwacher Wettbewerb	$P_i > P_i^*$	$P_j > P_j^*$

Quelle: Eigene Darstellung

Tab. 2: Arten des Wettbewerbs.

Die Nutzenfunktion aus Gleichung (1) kann jedoch weiter spezifiziert werden, um eine realistischere Betrachtung zu ermöglichen:

$$U_i = U\left[P_i\left(n_i, M_i, S\left(r_i, r_j\right)\right), P_i^*\left(\bar{I}_i, R_i - r_i\right), G\left(R_i\right)\right]. \tag{2}$$

Die Variablen bedeuten im Einzelnen:

P	aktuelle Bevölkerungsanzahl
n	natürliche Wachstumsrate (Differenz zwischen Geburten- und Sterberate); positiv, wenn mehr Menschen geboren werden als sterben
M	Nettozuwanderung (Differenz zwischen Immigration und Emigration); positiv, wenn Zuwanderung höher als Abwanderung
r_i	Ausgaben der Region *i* zur Attraktion von Bevölkerung
r_j	Ausgaben der Konkurrenzregion *j* zur Attraktion von Bevölkerung
R_i	Gesamtausgaben für Bevölkerungspolitik ($R_i - r_i$: Ausgaben zum Rückbau von Infrastruktur)
G	Ausgabenfunktion, die u.a. administrative Kosten berücksichtigt
P^*	kritisches Bevölkerungsniveau, das die Mindestbevölkerung darstellt, die zur Aufrechterhaltung der aktuellen Infrastruktur erforderlich ist
P_i^0	Bevölkerung zum Anfangszeitpunkt $t = 0$
$\bar{I}$	vorhandene Infrastruktur
α	Effektivität der eigenen Bevölkerungspolitik
β	Effektivität der Bevölkerungspolitik der konkurrierenden Region auf die Bevölkerungsentwicklung der eigenen Region (dieser Parameter wird u.a. beeinflusst durch die Entfernung zwischen den Regionen, Präferenzen der Migranten und anderen Standortfaktoren)

Zur Vereinfachung wird Option (i), Rückbau der Infrastruktur, in der folgenden Analyse ausgeschlossen. Der Rückbau stellt bei einer zu geringen Bevölkerungszahl ohnehin die einzige Möglichkeit dar, Ziel der Region ist aber die Bevölkerungsattraktion, daher gilt $r_i = R_i$. Diese Maßnahmen wird sicherlich erforderlich, sollte es zu einer globalen Veränderung der Demographie kommen. Eine derart extreme Entwicklung ist in nächster Zeit (bis fünfzig Jahre) nicht absehbar. (2) kann daher, sofern auch noch von administrativen Kosten abstrahiert wird, vereinfacht werden zu

$$U_i = U\left[P_i^0\left(1 + n_i\right) + M_i, P_i^*\left(\bar{I}_i\right), \alpha r_i, \beta r_j\right]. \tag{3}$$

Es wird angenommen, dass diese Nutzenfunktion die folgenden, plausiblen Eigenschaften erfüllt: Ein Anstieg der Anfangsbevölkerung, der natürlichen Wachstumsrate oder der Nettozuwanderung erhöht die Bevölkerungszahl und damit den Nutzen der Region. Die entsprechenden Bedingungen erster Ordnung lauten damit

$$\partial U_i / \partial P_i^0 > 0,\ \partial U_i / \partial n_i > 0 \text{ und } \partial U_i / \partial M_i > 0 .$$

Erhöht die konkurrierende Region ihre Ausgaben oder ist von einer höheren, vorhanden Infrastruktur in der Region, im Vergleich zu einer anderen, ansonsten identischen Region, auszugehen, sinkt der Nutzen. Dementsprechend ergeben sich

$$\partial U_i / \partial r_j < 0 \text{ und } \partial U_i / \partial \bar{I}_i < 0 .$$

Ein hohes Ausgabenniveau der konkurrierenden Region hat einen direkten Einfluss auf das Verhalten der Migranten und der Bevölkerung, indem es diese stärker attrahiert. Ein höheres vorhandenes Infrastrukturniveau senkt den Nutzen nur indirekt, da es die notwendige Mindestbevölkerungsanzahl erhöht. Die Politikmaßnahmeneffektivitätsparameter α und β haben zweifelsfrei einen entgegen gerichteten Effekt auf das Nutzenniveau,

$$\partial U_i / \partial \alpha > 0 \text{ und } \partial U_i / \partial \beta < 0 .$$

Der Einfluss der strategischen Variablen einer Region, r_i, das Ausgabenniveau für Bevölkerungsattraktion, ist nicht eindeutig. Einerseits liegt ein positiver Effekt vor, schließlich wird durch ein hohes Ausgabenniveau ceteris paribus mehr Bevölkerung angelockt, andererseits jedoch verursachen die Ausgaben auch Kosten, die den Nutzen der Region schmälern. Um das optimale Ausgabeniveau bestimmen zu können, müssen sowohl die Bedingung erster Ordnung, als auch zweiter Ordnung erfüllt sein,

$$\partial U_i / \partial r_i = 0 \text{ und } \partial^2 U_i / \partial r_i^2 < 0 .$$

Auflösen nach r_i unter Beachtung von r_j ergibt die folgende Reaktionsfunktion

$$r_i(r_j) = f\left[P_i^0(1+n_i), M_i, \beta r_j, P_i^*(\bar{I}_i)\right], \tag{4}$$

für $i, j = 1, 2$ und $i \neq j$. Bevor mit der graphischen Analyse begonnen wird, sollen hier nur kurz die zugrunde liegenden Annahmen dargestellt werden, um das Verständnis zu erleichtern. Trivialerweise sind beide Regionen für potentielle Zuwanderer eindeutig zu unterscheiden. Aus Sicht des Migranten bieten die beiden betrachteten Regionen sozusagen eine Art differenziertes Gut an. Beide Regionen verfolgen das Ziel der Ausgabenminimierung, schließlich müssen die politischen Entscheidungsträger spätestens bei den nächsten Wahlen darüber Rechenschaft ablegen. Die Nutzenfunktionen sind hinreichend spezifiziert. Dabei sind für jede Region, d.h. für jeden Spieler die Spielstruktur, die Spielregeln, die Auszahlungen sowie die zur Verfügung stehenden Strategien gemeinsames Wissen. Die Struktur des Spiels impliziert dabei imperfekte Information, da beide simultan bzw. voneinander unbeobachtbar entscheiden. Im letzten Teil der Analyse wird die Annahme der vollständigen Information gelockert. Der hier vorgestellte

Ansatz basiert größtenteils auf dem von Krelle (1961) und Ott (1972) entwickelten Oligopolmodell (vgl. hierzu auch Krelle 1963).

IV. Optimale Bevölkerungspolitik

Abbildung 7 zeigt die durch Gleichung (4) beschriebene Reaktionsfunktion von Region 2, $r_2(r_1)$. Die optimale Reaktion von Region 2 ist es, immer einen Punkt auf ihrer Reaktionsfunktion zu wählen. Zunächst werden die Auswirkungen eines Rückgangs der Ausgaben von Region 1 auf die Entscheidung von Region 2 untersucht. Ist die ursprüngliche Ausgabenkombination ein beliebig gewählter Punkt links von der Reaktionsfunktion z.B. A, so führt eine Ausgabensenkung von Region 1 zu einer Ausgabenerhöhung von Region 2, wohingegen eine Ausgabenkombination rechts von der Reaktionsfunktion, Punkt B, eine Ausgabenkürzung von Region 2 nach sich zieht. Bei einer Ausgabenerhöhung der Region 1 ist es die optimale Reaktion von Region 2 bei einer Ausgangsausgabenkombination links von $r_2(r_1)$, Punkt C, ebenfalls eine Ausgabenerhöhung durchzuführen, wohingegen sie dieser rechts von den Reaktionsfunktion, Punkt D, mit einer Ausgabenkürzung begegnen wird. Es zeigt sich aus dieser einfachen Analyse, dass unabhängig davon, ob Region 1 eine Ausgabenerhöhung oder -senkung durchführt, Region 1 bei einer anfänglichen Anfangsausgabenkombination links von der Reaktionsfunktion immer ihre Ausgaben erhöht und rechts davon immer senkt.

Diese Überlegung legt nahe, dass ein spezieller Punkt oder auch ein bestimmtes Gebiet von Ausgabenausgangskombinationen existiert, der/das die Eigenschaft aufweist, dass Region 1 kein Interesse daran hat, sein Ausgabenniveau zu ändern, immer unter Berücksichtigung der Reaktion von Region 2. Eine Ausgabenkombination erfüllt diese Anforderung mit Sicherheit: der Schnittpunkt zwischen den Reaktionsfunktionen von Region 1 und Region 2, das Cournot-Nash-Gleichgewicht. Die folgende Analyse zeigt jedoch, dass ein kleiner Bereich existiert, der ebenfalls Gleichgewichtskombinationen enthält. Auch dort hat keine Region einen Anreiz, ihre Ausgabenpolitik zu ändern.

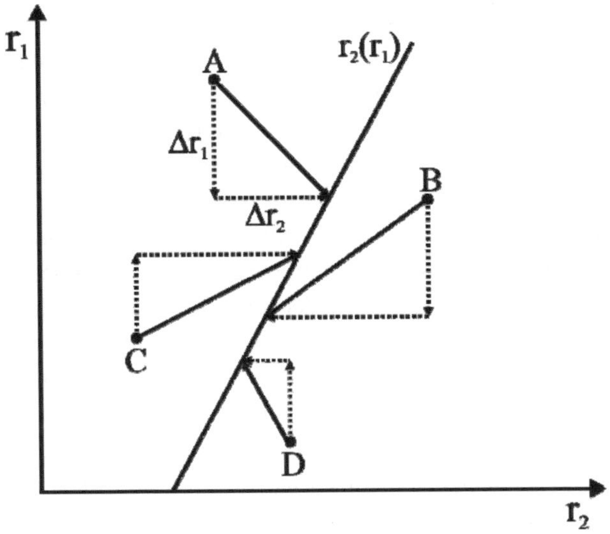

Quelle: in Anlehnung an Ott (1972)

Abb. 7: Reaktionen von Region 2 auf Abweichungen der Region 1 bei verschiedenen r_1r_2-Ausgangskombinationen.

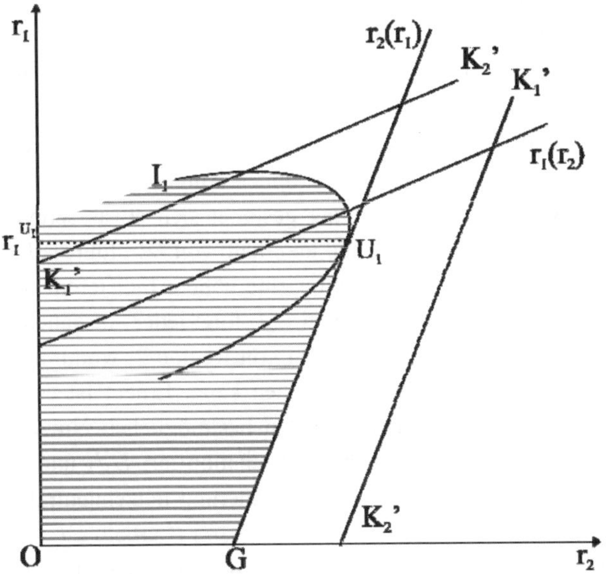

Quelle: in Anlehnung an Ott (1972)

Abb. 8: Gleichgewichtsgebiet von Region 1 bei Ausgabensenkungen.

Abbildung 8 stellt das Gleichgewichtsgebiet, OGU_1I_1, von Region 1 dar, bei der sie keinen Anreiz hat, ihre Ausgaben zu senken. Es ist relativ einfach, diese These zu beweisen. Rechts von $r_2(r_1)$ und oberhalb von U_1I_1 kann sich Region 1 durch eine Ausgabensenkung besser stellen, sofern Region 2 sich rational verhält (wovon auszugehen ist) und ebenfalls ihre Ausgaben kürzt. Die bestenfalls zu erreichende Indifferenzkurve für Region 1 stellt I_1 dar. Annahmegemäß führen niedrigere Ausgaben zu einem höheren Nutzen für die Gemeinde, daher stellen alle Indifferenzkurven, die sich näher am Ursprung der Reaktionsfunktion befinden, ein höheres Nutzenniveau dar. Links von $r_2(r_1)$ und unterhalb von U_1I_1 folgt jeder Ausgabenkürzung der Region 1 eine Ausgabenerhöhung der konkurrierenden Region 2. Region 1 kann dann nur noch eine weiter außen liegende Indifferenzkurve und damit ein geringeres Nutzenniveau erreichen. Sollte die Ausgabenkombination auf I_1 liegen und wird eine Ausgabensenkung exakt auf r_1U_1 durchgeführt, so befindet sich Region 1 nach wie vor auf I_1 und damit dem gleichen Nutzenniveau wie zuvor. Außerhalb des gekennzeichneten Gebiets, z.B. rechts von $r_2(r_1)$, führt jede Ausgabensenkung zu einem höheren Nutzenniveau für Region 1 und sollte daher durchgeführt werden. In dieser und den folgenden Abbildungen sind zusätzliche Aspekte eingezeichnet, die für die kommende Analyse von Bedeutung sind. Auf der Kurve $K_i'K_i'$, wobei $i = 1, 2$, liegen alle maximal erreichbaren Indifferenzkurven bei einem gegebenen Wert von r_j. Alle Indifferenzkurven biegen sich daher vom Schnittpunkt mit $K_i'K_i'$ weg. Der Tangentialpunkt U_1 ist der Stackelbergsche Asymmetrielösungspunkt (Stackelberg 1948). Region 1 befindet sich dabei in der unabhängigen und Region 2 in der abhängigen Position.

Abbildung 9 stellt das Gleichgewichtsgebiet, die gekennzeichnete Fläche I_1U_1DL', von Region 1 dar, bei der sie keinen Anreiz hat, ihre Ausgaben zu erhöhen. Der Beweis dieser Behauptung gestaltet sich etwas schwieriger als im vorherigen Fall. Rechts von $r_2(r_1)$ und unterhalb von DL' führt jeder Anstieg des Ausgabenniveaus dazu, dass die Region eine höhere Indifferenzkurve erreichen kann. Links von $r_2(r_1)$ und oberhalb von U_1I_1 folgt jeder Ausgabenerhöhung von Region 1 eine Ausweitung der Ausgaben von Region 2, wodurch Region 1 nur noch ein geringeres Nutzenniveau erreichen kann. Erneut ist es möglich, eine Ausgabenänderung durchzuführen, die den bestmöglichen Nutzen unverändert lässt: Liegt die anfängliche Ausgabenkombination auf U_1I_1 und die Ausgaben werden exakt auf r_1U_1 erhöht, so ist die Änderung nutzenneutral. Eine Ausgabenerhöhung aus dem Gebiet rechts von $r_2(r_1)$ und oberhalb DL' senkt den Nutzen von Region 1. In Abbildung 10 wird verdeutlicht, wie die für die Analyse wichtige Kurve LL' konstruiert wurde.

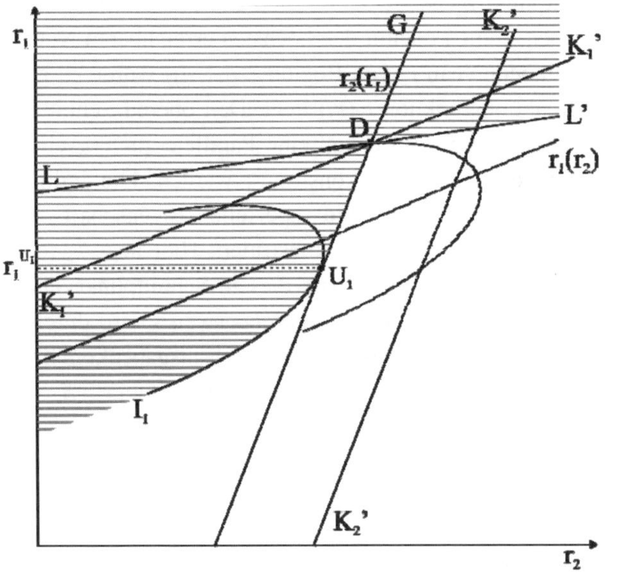

Quelle: in Anlehnung an Ott (1972)

Abb. 9: Gleichgewichtsgebiet von Region 1 bei Ausgabenerhöhungen.

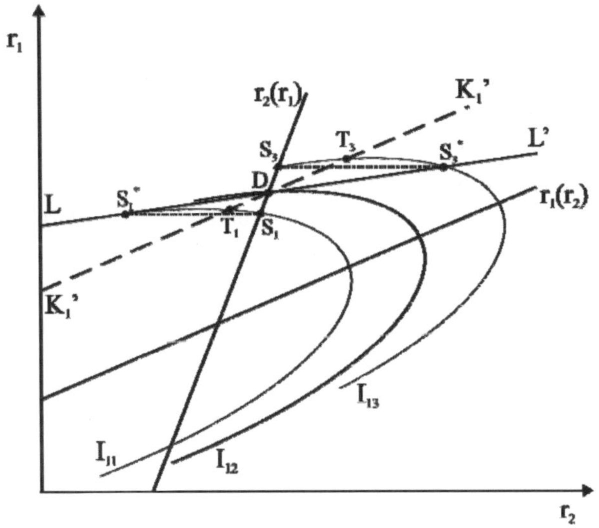

Quelle: in Anlehnung an Ott (1972)

Abb. 10: Konstruktion von LL'.

T_1 ist der Schnittpunkt zwischen $K_1'K_1'$ und der Indifferenzkurve I_{11}. Wie oben bereits beschrieben, stellt T_1 damit den höchsten erreichbaren Nutzen für das entsprechende Ausgabenniveau r_2 von Region 2 dar. I_{11} wurde so gewählt, dass T_1 links von der Reaktionsfunktion $r_2(r_1)$ liegt. Den oberen Schnittpunkt zwischen I_{11} mit $r_2(r_1)$ bezeichnet S_1. Wird nun eine Parallele zur r_2-Achse durch S_1 gezeichnet, so kann der Punkt S_1* konstruiert werden. Die Indifferenzkurve I_{12} wurde so gewählt, dass sie die spezielle Eigenschaft aufweist, dass $T_2 = S_2 = S_2* = D$. Analog wurde I_{13} konstruiert. Hier liegt T_3 rechts von $r_2(r_1)$. S_3 liegt links von T_3 und S_3* rechts von diesem Schnittpunkt. Die ökonomische Intuition hinter dieser geometrischen Vorgehensweise wird durch die folgenden Erläuterungen klar. Angenommen, die Ausgangsausgabenkombination liegt auf der Indifferenzkurve I_{11} zwischen S_1* und S_1, im Punkt $T_2 = S_2 = S_2* = D$, oder auf I_{12} zwischen S_3 und S_3*. Erhöht Region 1 seine Ausgaben und Region 2 reagiert optimal entsprechend ihrer Reaktionsfunktion, so stellt sich Region 1 immer schlechter. Die Kurve *LDL'*, die Verbindungslinie aller $S*$, beschreibt somit die untere Grenze für das Gebiet oberhalb *DL'*.

In Abbildung 11 werden alle Resultate der vorangegangenen Analyse zusammengefasst. Zum einen dargestellt ist das Gleichgewichtsgebiet von Region 1 (horizontal gestreifte Fläche, die durch I_1 begrenzt ist), das alle Ausgabenkombinationen umfasst, bei denen Region 1 weder einen Anreiz hat ihre Ausgaben zu erhöhen, noch zu senken. Analog kann ein Gleichgewichtsgebiet für Region 2 konstruiert werden (vertikal gestreifte Fläche, die durch I_2 begrenzt ist). In der Schnittmenge der beiden Gleichgewichtsgebiete, VU_1CU_2, hat keine der beiden Regionen einen Anreiz ihr Ausgabenniveau zu ändern, da die jeweils konkurrierende Region durch ihre Reaktion eine Ausgabenkombination herbeiführen kann, die für die Region im Vergleich zur Ausgangslage schlechter ist. Als optimale Handlungsoption für Regionen, deren Ausgabenkombination sich in diesem Gebiet befindet – sei es aus Zufall oder aufgrund historischer Gründe, die Ursachen werden an dieser Stelle nicht näher untersucht – empfiehlt sich daher die Alternative (iii), also „Nichtstun". Es besteht vor allem kein Anreiz, das Cournot-Nash-Gleichgewicht zu erreichen, um damit die scheinbar dominante Strategie zu wählen.

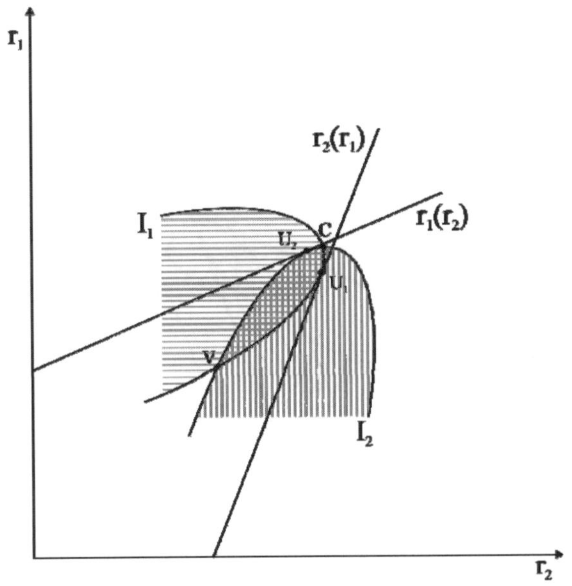

Quelle: in Anlehnung an Ott (1972)

Abb. 11: Gemeinsames Gleichgewichtsgebiet beider Regionen bei Ausgabenerhöhung und -senkung.

Bislang ging die Analyse von vollständiger Information aus. Realistischer ist es, anzunehmen, dass beispielsweise Region 1 kaum Kenntnisse über bestimmte Eigenschaften von Region 2 hat, etwa über die genaue Infrastruktur, die Nettozuwanderung oder die (prognostizierte) Bevölkerungsentwicklung, im Terminus der Spieltheorie also den Typen von Region 2 nicht kennt und damit die genaue Lage der Reaktionsfunktion im r_1r_2-Diagramm. Zur Vereinfachung werden nur zwei mögliche Typen von Region 2 angenommen, die auch als extremste Ausprägungen einer Gleichverteilung von Typen interpretiert werden können. Region 2 kann entweder eine Region mit „normalen" oder „hohen" Ausgaben sein. „Hohe" Ausgaben bedeuten, dass diese Region bei jedem beliebigen Niveau von r_1 höhere Ausgaben aufweist als der normale Typ. Abbildung 12 veranschaulicht diese Situation graphisch.

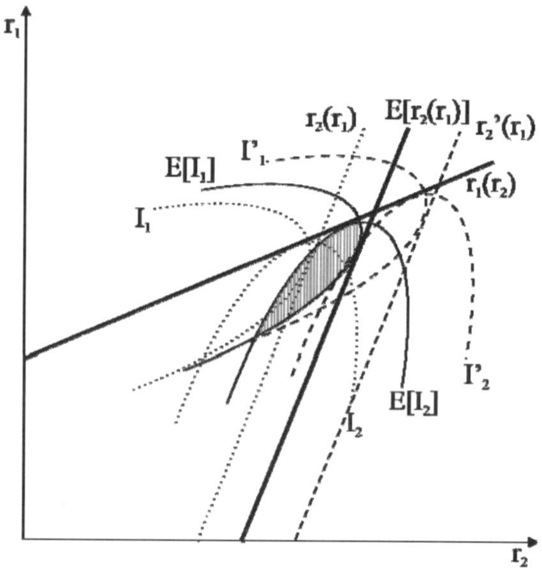

Quelle: Eigene Darstellung

Abb. 12: Unvollständige Information über Region 2.

Region 1 hat keine Informationen über die genaue Ausgabenstruktur von Region 2, daher wird sie sich an der erwarteten Lage der Reaktionsfunktion $E[r_2(r_1)]$ von Region 2 orientieren. Das sich ergebende Gleichgewichtsgebiet ist in Abbildung 12 entsprechend gekennzeichnet. Einerseits ist ganz klar festzustellen, dass im Falle einer „normalen" Region die resultierenden Gleichgewichtsausgaben tendenziell zu hoch ausfallen (wobei allerdings ein kleines Gebiet existieren kann, bei dem sich die Gleichgewichtsgebiete der „hohen" und „normalen" Regionen überlappen). Andererseits, wenn es sich um eine Hochausgaben-Region handelt, sind die resultierenden Ausgaben eher zu gering, jeweils im Vergleich zwischen der Reaktion auf die erwartete Lage der Reaktionsfunktion und der tatsächlichen Lage. Würde Region 1 einen der beiden Typen als sicher annehmen und sich dementsprechend verhalten, besteht natürlich die Gefahr dass sie falsch liegt. Je unwahrscheinlicher das Auftreten einer der beiden Typen von Region 2 ist oder je ähnlicher sie sind, desto größer ist die Schnittmenge zwischen dem erwarteten und dem tatsächlichen Gleichgewichtsgebiet. Allerdings ist Region 2 bekannt, dass Region 1 ihren tatsächlichen Typen nicht kennt. Sie wird dies in ihrem Kalkül berücksichtigen, daher ist das erwartete Gleichgewichtsgebiet stabil.

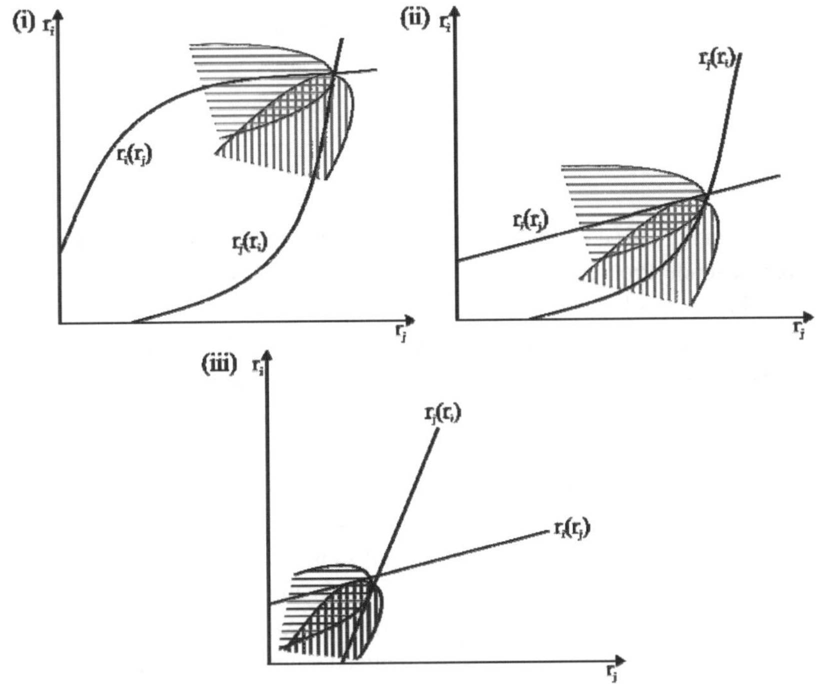

Quelle: Eigene Darstellung

Abb. 13: Drei Fälle: (i) starker Wettbewerb, (ii) mittlerer Wettbewerb und (iii) schwacher Wettbewerb.

Abbildung 13 stellt die drei möglichen Fälle dar, wie sie in Tabelle 2 beschrieben wurden. Fall (i) veranschaulicht die Situation wenn beide Regionen in starkem Wettbewerb zueinander stehen und zusätzliche Bevölkerung benötigen, um das kritische Bevölkerungsniveau P^* zu erreichen. Sie werden hohe Ausgaben aufbringen bis die notwendigen Migranten attrahiert sind. Ab dann werden sie passiver und reduzieren ihre Grenzausgaben, wenn sich beide Regionen in einem Gleichgewichtsgebiet hoher Ausgaben befinden. Fall (ii) beschreibt eine mittlere Wettbewerbssituation, bei der die Anfangsbevölkerung einer Region i bereits über dem kritischen Niveau liegt und sie nur einen geringen Anreiz hat, weitere Migranten zu attrahieren. Die konkurrierende Region j befindet sich noch nicht in dieser glückliche Lage und wendet hohe Ausgaben auf, um die kritische Bevölkerungsmasse zu erreichen. Fall (iii) stellt schließlich eine schwache Wettbewerbssituation dar, da beide nicht notwendigerweise mehr Bevölkerung benötigen. Die Ausgabenniveaus in den Fällen (i) und (iii) sind symmetrisch, d.h. beide Regionen haben entweder hohe oder niedrige Ausgaben, da beide entweder zusätzliche Bevölkerung benötigen oder nicht. In (ii) sind die Ausgabenniveaus unterschiedlich, im Gleichgewichtsgebiet gibt Region *j* immer mehr aus als Region *i*.

V. Fazit

Der Rückgang und die Alterung der Bevölkerung werden Deutschland vor schwerwiegende Probleme stellen. Viele ökonomische, soziale und psychologische Probleme werden zu bewältigen sein. Vor allem die Sozialsysteme werden von den Auswirkungen schwer betroffen sein. Im umlagefinanzierten Rentensystem stehen bereits heute immer weniger Beitragszahler immer mehr Rentenempfängern gegenüber, die die Pensions- und Rentenansprüche aufbringen müssen. Die kürzlich verabschiedete Erhöhung des gesetzlichen Renteneintrittsalters ist nur einer von zahlreichen Versuchen, die angespannte Situation zu entschärfen. Der medizinische Fortschritt ermöglicht ein immer längeres und leistungsfähigeres Leben, führt aber auch zu immer weiter steigenden Ausgaben der Gesundheitssysteme. Durch den prognostizierten Rückgang der Erwerbsbevölkerung wird das Wirtschaftswachstum direkt beeinflusst. Als Abhilfe bieten sich zwei Ansätze in der Bevölkerungspolitik an: entweder fertilitätserhöhende Maßnahmen oder Zuwanderung aus anderen Ländern. Diese Lösungsansätze können aber Probleme auf anderer Ebene verursachen, z.B. durch Migration in die Sozialsysteme. Es ist nur wenig überraschend, dass dieses deutschlandweite Problem auch auf regionaler Ebene eine Rolle spielt und zu Wettbewerb zwischen Gemeinden führt. Vor allem in den östlichen Bundesländern ist das Problem stark ausgeprägt, da viele junge Menschen in den Westen abwandern.

Das hier vorgestellte Modell betrachtete den Bedarf der Regionen an einer kritischen Bevölkerungsmasse, um die vorhandene Infrastruktur aufrechterhalten zu können. Abhängig davon, wie sich die Bevölkerungsgrößen der Regionen in Bezug auf das kritische Niveau zueinander verhalten, können drei Wettbewerbssituationen unterschieden werden. Jeder Region stehen prinzipiell drei mögliche Strategien zur Verfügung, wie sie dem demographischen Problem begegnen können: Rückbau der vorhandenen Infrastruktur, Erhöhung der Ausgaben zur Bevölkerungsattraktion oder laissez-faire. Die Analyse zeigte, dass ein Gleichgewichtsgebiet existiert, in dem keine Region einen Anreiz hat ihr Ausgabenniveau zu ändern. Abhängig von der Art der Wettbewerbsituation ist dieses Gebiet symmetrisch oder asymmetrisch.

Literaturverzeichnis

Adserá, A., Changing Fertility Rates in Developed Countries. The Impact of Labor Market Institutions, in: Journal of Population Economics, 17, 2004, S. 17-43.

Beckstein, G., Die demografische Entwicklung – eine Herausforderung für Staat und Kommunen, in: Politische Studien, 399, 2005, S. 15-24.

Birg, H., H. Koch, Der Bevölkerungsrückgang in der Bundesrepublik Deutschland, Frankfurt am Main: Forschungsbericht des IBS, Bd. 13, 1987.

Birg, H., Perspektiven der Bevölkerungsentwicklung in Deutschland und Europa – Konsequenzen für die sozialen Sicherungssysteme. Gutachten für das Bundesverfassungsgericht, in: Materialien des Instituts für Bevölkerungsforschung und Sozialpolitik, 48, Bielefeld 2002.

Birg, H., Dynamik der demographischen Alterung, Bevölkerungsschrumpfung und Zuwanderung in Deutschland, in: Aus Politik und Zeitgeschichte, 20, 2003, S. 6-17.

Birg, H., Dynamik der demographischen Alterung und Bevölkerungsschrumpfung. Wirtschaftliche und gesellschaftliche Auswirkungen in Deutschland, in: Politische Studien, 399, 2005, S. 24-36.

Börsch-Supan, A., Germany: A Social Security System on the Verge of Collapse, in: Redesigning Social Security, hrsg. von H. Siebert, Tübingen 1997, S. 129-159.

Börsch-Supan, A., A. Ludwig, M. Sommer, Demographie und Kapitalmärkte. Die Auswirkungen der Bevölkerungsalterung auf Aktien-, Renten- und Immobilienvermögen, Köln 2003.

Bryant, R. C., 'Demographic Pressures on Public Pension Systems and Government Budgets in Open Economies', Brookings Discussion Paper in International Economics No 164, 2004.

Bundesministerium für Familie, Senioren, Frauen und Jugend, Die Zeit, Prognos, Familienatlas 2005, Berlin 2005.

Detig, S, X. Feng, P. Friedrich, FOCJ als Grundlage für Förderinstitutionen „Aufbau-Ost und Bevölkerung-Ost" in: P. Friedrich (Edt.), Öffentliche Unternehmen im Standortwettbewerb für den Aufbau Ost, Discussion Paper Nr. 41, Lehrstuhl für Finanzwissenschaft, Universität der Bundeswehr München, Neubiberg 2002, S. 82-115.

Herz, R., M. Werner, L. Marschke, Abschlussbericht Unterirdischer Städtebau „Erfordernisse und Finanzierung der Anpassung der stadttechnischen Infrastruktur im Zuge des Stadtumbaus", TU Dresden Juni 2002.

Kinsella, K., D. R. Phillips, Global Aging: The Challenge of Success, in: Population Bulletin, Vol. 60, Nr. 1, 2005, S. 3-42.

Krelle, W., Preistheorie, Tübingen 1961.

Krelle, W., Unbestimmtheitsbereiche beim Dyopol, Jahrbücher für Nationalökonomie und Statistik, Bd. 175, 1963, S. 232-236.

Kröhnert, S., N. Van Olst, R. Klingholz, Deutschland 2020. Die demographische Zukunft der Nation, Berlin 2004.

Lehr, U., Die Jugend von gestern – und die Senioren von morgen, in: Aus Politik und Zeitgeschichte, 20, 2003, S. 3-5.

Mas-Colell, A., M. D. Whinston and J. R. Green, Microeconomic Theory, Oxford 1995.

Ministerium für Gesundheit und Soziales NRW, Gesundheitsreport 1994, Bielefeld 1995.

Ott, A. E., Grundzüge der Preistheorie, Göttingen 1972.

Stackelberg, H. v., Grundlagen der theoretischen Volkswirtschaftslehre, Bern 1984.

United Nations, Replacement Migration, New York 2000.

United Nations, World Population Prospects. The 2004 Revision, New York 2005.

B. Einwohnerkonkurrenz bis zum Ruin? – Folgen der Suburbanisierung am Beispiel der Region Bremen

Ernst Mönnich

I. Wirtschaftliche Entwicklung durch Anwerbung von Einwohnern – kein neues Phänomen

Demographie ist in Mode und vor dem Hintergrund der Angst um die sozialen Sicherungssysteme geeignet für Bestseller. Mindestens ebenso dramatisch wie die Auswirkungen auf Rente und Krankenversicherung sind die Wirkungen der Bevölkerungsentwicklung und -verteilung auf Städte, Regionen und die Kosten der Infrastruktur. Wie aktuelle Beispiele zeigen, bemühen sich Städte und Gemeinden heute in Deutschland um die Gewinnung von Einwohnern. Universitätsstädte ködern die Studenten mit Prämien zur Verlegung des ersten Wohnsitzes in ihre Stadt. Umlandgemeinden betreiben Fernsehwerbung, um auf Grundstücke zum Bau eines freistehenden Eigenheimes aufmerksam zu machen. Diese öffentliche Einwohnerwerbung mit Marketinginstrumenten ist neu und sie kennzeichnet ein Wettbewerbsverhalten als Reaktion auf aktuell oder potenziell sinkende Einwohnerzahlen. Sie spiegelt zudem wider, dass Gebietskörperschaften den Stellenwert der Einwohnerkonkurrenz für die finanzielle Lage eines Gemeinwesens zumindest für die innerregionale Konkurrenz begriffen haben (Schlömer, Bucher 2001, S. 33ff.).[1] Die Fokussierung auf diese Form kommunalen Wettbewerbs findet somit ihre Begründung auch darin, dass die bisher vorherrschende Bürgermeisterkonkurrenz um gewerbliche Investoren für die kommunale Steuerkraft an Bedeutung verloren hat. In diesem Beitrag wird das Phänomen des Einwohnerwettbewerbs (Mönnich 2005, S. 32ff.):[2]

- im Lichte empirischer Informationen etwas näher beleuchtet und
- als potenziell ruinöser Wettbewerb vor dem Hintergrund des demographischen Wandels charakterisiert.
- Die Instrumente des Finanzausgleichs werden als wesentliche Antriebskraft der Wettbewerbsprozesse aus kommunaler Sicht eingestuft und
- Lösungsansätze zur Eliminierung von Fehlsteuerungseffekten auf der Ebene öffentlicher Organisationsstrukturen diskutiert.

---

1 Für die Erklärung überregionaler Wanderungsströme lässt sich dagegen mit gutem Grund auf die Bedeutung von Arbeitsmarktbedingungen hinweisen. Dieses ist allerdings nicht der einzige Bestimmungsgrund und vor allem sind es nicht nur die neoklassischen Lohndifferenzen, die das Wanderungsverhalten prägen.

2 Die vorliegende Fassung aktualisiert einen Aufsatz aus 2005.

Hierbei muss man sich darüber im Klaren sein, dass Wettbewerbsprozesse zur Gewinnung von Einwohnern als Mittel wirtschaftlicher Entwicklung kein historisch völlig neues Ereignis ist. Ferner soll es natürlich auch nicht darum gehen, jeden Wettbewerb von Gebietskörperschaften, sei es um Investoren oder um Einwohner, als ruinös zu diffamieren.

Betrachten wir kurz historische Beispiele von Einwohnerkonkurrenz, so ergeben sich zwei Typen, wie die Einwohnerwerbung in einem zirkulären Prozess von Wertschöpfungs- Arbeitsplatz- und Einwohnerwachstum wirken kann. Zunächst lassen sich – vor allem während der Industrialisierung im 19. und im beginnenden 20. Jahrhundert – Formen der **Einwohnerwerbung als induzierte Aktivität** identifizieren. Wachsende Wertschöpfung und industrielle Arbeitsplätze in den dynamischen Regionen und den rasch wachsenden Städten lockten überschüssige Arbeitskräfte und ihre Familien aus ländlichen Regionen und dem ländlichen Umland an (Kocka 1990, S. 37ff.). Reichte die Sogkraft der besseren Einkommenschancen in den dynamischen Regionen allein nicht aus, so übernahm vor allem die Industrie selbst die Anwerbung von Arbeitskräften um Entwicklungsengpässe zu vermeiden (Mönnich 1971, S. 157ff.).

Die zweite historische Form der **Einwohnerwerbung kann demgegenüber als eine die Entwicklung antreibende Aktivität** eingestuft werden. Sie ist zudem historisch älter. Feudale Landesherren lockten Siedler und unternehmerisch begabte religiöse Minderheiten, um die wirtschaftliche Entwicklung ihres Einflussbereiches zu stimulieren (Landgrebe 1977, S. 251ff.).

Auch nach diesen historischen Schlaglichtern bleibt die Frage somit offen, ob der Wettbewerb um Einwohner Folge oder Ursache regionaler und/oder lokaler wirtschaftlicher Entwicklung ist. In diesem Beitrag wird geprüft, ob unter den erkennbaren demographischen Rahmenbedingungen Einwohnerwerbung als entwicklungsstimulierende Aktivität zu sinnvollen Ergebnissen führen kann. Aus theoretischer Sicht ist es ein Beitrag zu der Frage, ob eine Abflachung der Rang-Größen-Verteilung von Einwohnern als Verstoß gegen Auerbachs Gesetz der Bevölkerungskonzentration eingestuft werden kann. Hierfür sprechen einige Argumente. Da wir allerdings aus der Vergangenheit wissen, dass es nationale Unterschiede stärker zentraler oder dezentralisierter Städtesysteme gibt (Böventer 1979, S. 38ff. und 247)[3] und Infrastrukturen mit Grenzen hieran angepasst werden können, soll nicht unterstellt werden, es gäbe nur eine wirtschaftlich vertretbare Form der Bevölkerungsverteilung.

3 Hierzu und zum Auerbachschen Gesetz allgemein.

Aktivitäten der Wirtschaftsförderung als elementarer Teil der kommunalen Selbstverwaltung sind ebenfalls keine neue Erscheinung. Diese Aktivitäten zielten allerdings in der Vergangenheit primär auf die Gewinnung mobiler Investoren. Die begrenzte Wirksamkeit dieser exogenen Entwicklungsstrategie wurde über Jahrzehnte beklagt.[4] Die mangelnde Effektivität und Effizienz der Bürgermeisterkonkurrenz um Gewerbeansiedlungen hat sich mit vielen Fehlinvestitionen in Infrastrukturvorleistungen bei der Wirtschaftsförderung in den neuen Bundesländern erneut bestätigt.

Ein relativ neues Phänomen kommunaler Entwicklungskonkurrenz ist demgegenüber der aktive **Wettbewerb um Einwohner** ohne den Umweg der Investitions- und Arbeitsförderung. Einzelne Städte und Gemeinden versuchen durch Werbung oder gezielte Flächenplanung ihre Einwohnerzahl vor allem bei finanzkräftigen Bevölkerungsschichten zu steigern oder zu halten. Im Erfolgsfall ergeben sich Wirtschaftswachstum und Arbeitsplätze am neuen Wohnort als Folgewirkung. Auch wenn die neuen Einwohner nur ihren Wohnsitz innerhalb der Region verlegen profitiert der Wohnstandort. Durch diese aktive Einwohnerwerbung ergibt sich eine Reihe von Fragen, die im Folgenden etwas näher geprüft werden sollen.

Lässt sich die Vermutung aktiver Einwohnerkonkurrenz bei Analyse von Daten zur Flächennutzung für Wohnzwecke bestätigen?

Die Gewinnung von Einwohnern gelingt durch Aktivitäten, die eine Gemeinde für die Wahl als Wohnstandort attraktiv machen. Zunächst haben für die Wahl des Wohnstandortes die relative Lagegunst und natürliche Standortgegebenheiten Bedeutung. Von Interesse ist hier allerdings nur der aktiv gestaltbare Bereich. Dabei handelt es sich neben der verkehrsmäßigen Erschließung vor allem um Einrichtungen der sozialen Infrastruktur. Einrichtungen wie Kindergärten, Schulen usw. werden allerdings im günstigsten Fall mit neuen Wohngebieten geplant und realisiert.

Als **vorrangiges Instrument der Einwohnergewinnung** kann daher die **Ausweisung und Realisierung von Wohngebieten in kommunalen Flächennutzungs- bzw. Bebauungsplänen** eingestuft werden. Betrachtet man hierzu die generelle Entwicklung der Flächeninanspruchnahme in der BRD in den Jahren seit 1989, so ergibt sich eine stetige Steigerung der Ansprüche für die Funktion

4 Aus der Vielfalt einschlägiger Wertungen in der Literatur sei nur verwiesen auf Ewers u.a. (1980, S. 13f.). Eine plastische Undercover-Analyse der Auswüchse von Bürgermeisterkonkurrenz in der Wirtschaftsförderung bietet Heimbrecht (1984). Zu aktuellen Bilanzen vgl. Hollbach-Grömig (2001) und Mönnich (2004).

Wohnen und Verkehr (Dosch 2002, S. 33). Diese Entwicklung wird hier am Beispiel des Oberzentrums Bremen im Vergleich zur Entwicklung im Umland betrachtet.

Wertet man die Entwicklung der tatsächlichen Flächennutzung in Bremen-Stadt und im Bremer Umland (vgl. Abb. 1) nach einer Abgrenzung des Senators für Finanzen aus (Holzschneider, Müller 1999), so ergibt sich eine Bestätigung für die Ausgangsvermutung. **Die Entwicklung der tatsächlich für Wohnzwecke in Anspruch genommenen Flächen verlief in allen betrachteten Teilräumen expansiv.** Sie ging z.B. im Umland deutlich über die Einwohnerexpansion im Zuge des Suburbanisationsprozesses hinaus und verlief dort expansiver als in der Kernstadt (vgl. Abb. 2 und 3 sowie Tab. 1). Festzustellen ist auch, dass insbesondere die Umlandgemeinden außerhalb des unmittelbaren „Speckgürtels“ (Umland II) eine Flächenpolitik mit Sogwirkung betrieben haben. Diese Beobachtungen in meiner Beispielregion decken sich mit den allgemeinen Trends der Flächeninanspruchnahme für Siedlungs- und Verkehrsflächen (Dosch 2002, S. 35). Auch die Kernstadt weitet bei geringem Einwohnerrückgang im gesamten Analysezeitraum die Wohnflächen kräftig aus. Der Versuch, über Flächenausweisung Einwohner zu halten, ist in einer summarischen Betrachtung allerdings gescheitert.

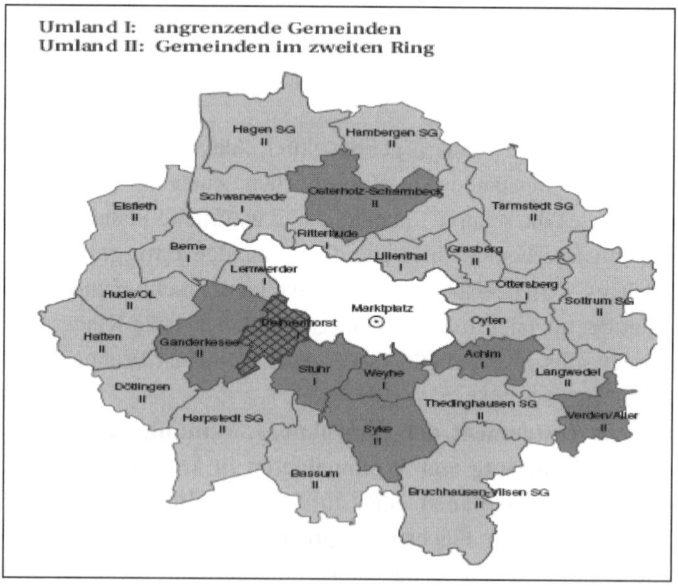

Quelle: Mönnich 2005, S. 34

Abb. 1: Bremen und sein Umland

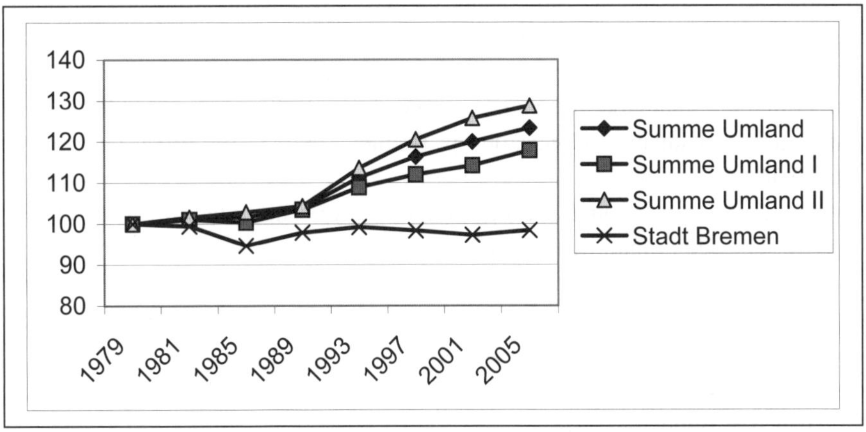

Quelle: eigene Darstellung

Abb. 2: Einwohnerentwicklung von 1979 bis 2005 (in % zum Basisjahr)

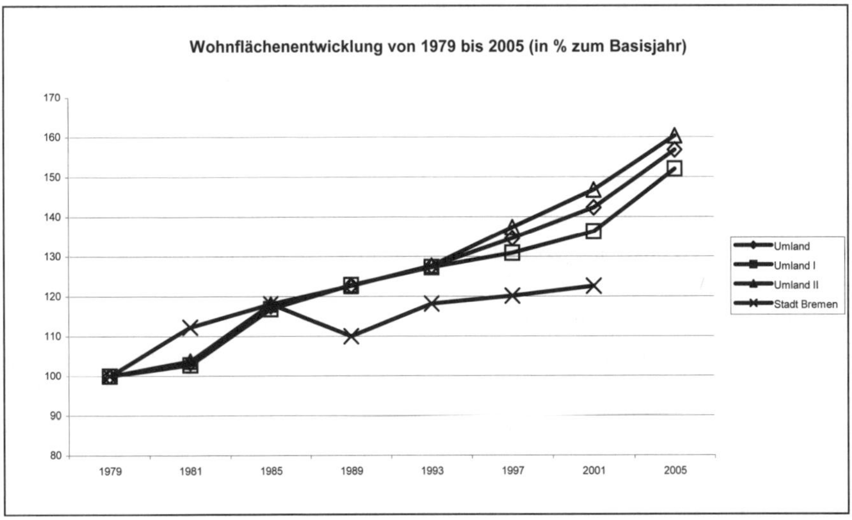

Quelle: eigene Darstellung

Abb. 3: Wohnflächenentwicklung von 1979 bis 2005 (in % zum Basisjahr)

Betrachtet man die Flächen- und Wohnungspolitik der Stadt Bremen für das letzte Jahrzehnt, so fällt auf, dass spätestens mit dem Beginn der Sanierungsphase[5], also ab 1993, eine noch expansiver ausgerichtete Einwohnerwerbung begann. Die rückläufige Bevölkerungsentwicklung seit Mitte der 70er Jahre war mit der

5 Bremen ist – wie das Saarland – seit 1993, als Folge einer Entscheidung des Bundesverfassungsgerichtes, ein Bundesland, dem eine extreme Haushaltsnotlage bescheinigt wurde.

Migrationswelle Ende der 80er Jahre partiell ausgeglichen worden. Der anhaltende Suburbanisierungstrend lockte insbesondere jüngere Besserverdiener aus der Stadt. Für das Erreichen der Sanierungsziele wurde ein Trendbruch angestrebt und als Zielmarke die Steigerung der Einwohnerzahl um 44.000 bis 2010 ausgegeben (Stadtentwicklungskonzept Bremen 1999, S. 10, 59ff.). Instrumente zur Zielerreichung waren:

- die Ausweisung von Baugebieten für die typischen Stadtflüchten, d.h. für freistehende Einfamilienhäuser;
- die Ausweisung von Baugebieten für stadttypische Wohnformen mittlerer und höherer Einkommensschichten (Eigentumswohnungen in verdichteter Bauweise in exponierten Lagen);
- die Subventionierung von Baugrundstücken mit dem Programm „Bremer bauen in Bremen";
- die Einführung einer Zweitwohnsitzsteuer mit dem Ziel, Bremer, die nicht mit erstem Wohnsitz in der Stadt gemeldet sind, zur Verlagerung des ersten Wohnsitzes zu bewegen.

Diese Maßnahmen hatten bis zum Jahre 2000 nicht den erhofften Erfolg. Die Abwanderung ins Umland wurde allenfalls gebremst. Die **Reaktion** war einerseits ein Verzicht auf utopische Ziele, andererseits jedoch **verstärkte Bemühungen in der Einwohnerkonkurrenz** wie die Gründung einer **Neubürgeragentur** mit speziellem Werbeauftrag.[6] In den letzten fünf Jahren ist eine Stagnation bzw. ein leichter Wiederanstieg der Einwohnerzahlen zu verzeichnen.[7] Diese Entwicklung wird vom Senat als Erfolg gewertet. Fraglich ist allerdings, ob tatsächlich eine Trendwende vorliegt oder nur eine Atempause im Schrumpfungsprozess. M.E. spricht viel für die zweite Hypothese, denn die derzeit leichte Erhöhung der Einwohnerzahl ist wohl vor allem auf die Mobilisierung ohnehin vorhandener Einwohner in der offiziellen Statistik[8] und auf konjunkturell bedingte Schwächen im Wohnungsbausektor zurückzuführen. Wie sich der Abbau steuerlicher Wohnungsbausubventionen und die Kürzung von Pendlerpauschalen auf die Stadt-Umland-Wanderung auswirken werden, lässt sich derzeit schwer prog-

6 Vgl. Bremische Bürgerschaft: Drs. 16/102, bremen_service, die Neubürgeragentur, vom 16.12.2003. Zum Echo in der Literatur vgl. Wehling u.a. 2002.

7 So stieg die Bevölkerung der Stadt Bremen gegenüber dem Tiefstand im Jahre 2000 (539.403 Einwohner) um 6529 Einwohner an. Diese positive Einwohnerentwicklung ist allerdings zu 64,3% oder 4201 auf zusätzliche ausländische Mitbürger zurückzuführen. Einen positiven Wanderungssaldo gibt es auch für die Binnenfernwanderung. Hier liegt die Hauptursache in den anhaltenden Bevölkerungsverlusten der neuen Bundesländer. Einwohnerverluste durch Stadt-Umland-Wanderung werden zurzeit durch Zuzüge jüngerer Jahrgänge (Studenten, Auszubildende) ausgeglichen. Durch Wanderungsgewinne muss ein negativer natürlicher Bevölkerungssaldo von ca. 1500 Einwohnern pro Jahr ausgeglichen werden. Vgl. Statistisches Jahrbuch 2005, S. 7ff.

8 So verlegen Studenten verstärkt ihren 1. Wohnsitz nach Bremen um das Begrüßungsgeld von 150 Euro zu vereinnahmen. Dieser Effekt soll mit der Einführung von Studiengebühren verstärkt werden, die nur für „Landeskinder" erlassen werden. Ob diese Regelung nach der Hamburger Erfahrung rechtlich Bestand haben kann, ist allerdings zu bezweifeln.

nostizieren. Preisrückgänge im Immobiliensektor sowohl in der Kernstadt als auch im Umland sind allerdings realistisch. Dauerhaft wird eine reine Preiskonkurrenz und Anreizpolitik den Suburbanisierungstrend nicht brechen können, zumal die Umlandgemeinden bei diesen Einflussgrößen eine bessere Position besitzen.[9] Als Zwischenergebnis der Erfahrungen im Fallbeispiel lässt sich formulieren, dass erfolgreiche Einwohnerwerbung für eine Kernstadt über das bisher genutzte Instrumentarium von Flächenausweisungen und materiellen Anreizen hinausgehen muss.

Ist die aktive Gewinnung von Einwohnern im Erfolgsfalle für die Gemeinde vorteilhaft?

Betrachtet man die **Entwicklung der Einnahmen** von Gebietskörperschaften im Bremer Umland im Vergleich zur Einnahmenentwicklung in der Kernstadt, so lässt sich die **aktive Einwohnergewinnung** als eine **lohnenswerte Investition** einstufen. **Die Umlandgemeinden konnten ihre Einnahmen im Vergleich zur Kernstadt sowohl absolut, als auch bezogen auf die Einwohnerzahl deutlich steigern.** Zu diesem Ergebnis kam zum einen die Vergleichsstudie des Senators für Finanzen mit einem Zeithorizont von 1983 bis 1998, zum anderen auch die regionalstatistische Auswertung der Statistischen Landesämter mit einem Zeithorizont bis 1999 (Holzschneider, Müller 1999, S. 9; Statistisches Landesamt Bremen, Niedersächsisches Statistisches Landesamt 2001, S.61f.). Da sich dieses überproportionale Einnahmewachstum sowohl aus der Entwicklung aller Steuereinnahmen pro Einwohner ergibt, als auch aus der Entwicklung des Gemeindeanteils an der Einkommenssteuer als wichtige kommunale Einnahmequelle, lässt sich ein ursächlicher Zusammenhang zwischen der Gewinnung vor allem einkommensstärkerer Einwohner und erhöhten Steuereinnahmen mit gutem Grund annehmen.

Allerdings ist eine Betrachtung finanzieller Vorteile durch zusätzliche Einwohner noch unvollständig, wenn hierbei nur die Einnahmeseite des Haushaltes betrachtet wird. Für die Einwohnergewinnung sind zunächst Investitionen für dic Erschließung von Wohngebieten erforderlich, die allerdings zu erheblichen Anteilen über die Beitragserhebung refinanziert werden oder über die Gebührenerhebung als rentierliche Investitionen einzustufen sind. Problematisch sind demge-

9 Immobilienpreisspiegel der Bausparkassen für die Bremer Region zeigen bereits eine deutliche Nivellierung von Preisunterschieden. Ungeachtet solcher Warnsignale geht der Senat in seiner Bevölkerungsprognose davon aus, bei Realisierung des Investitionssonderprogramms sowie des Anschlussinvestitionsprogramms bis 2020 die Bevölkerungszahlen vor allem durch positive Salden der Binnenfernwanderungen und Auslandswanderungen stabilisieren zu können. Vgl. Senat der Freien Hansestadt Bremen: Langfristige Gesamtplanung – www.rathaus-bremen.de – 24.3.2004. Die Investitionsplanung muss gekürzt werden. Daher wäre eigentlich bis 2020 ein Bevölkerungsverlust von 12.000 Einwohnern zu erwarten. Diese Möglichkeit wird in den jüngsten Prognosen allerdings verdrängt.

genüber dauerhafte Ausgabelasten aus der Infrastrukturbereitstellung für Straßen, Schulen, Kultur- und Freizeiteinrichtungen usw., denen keine laufenden Einnahmen gegenüberstehen. Ein annähernd aussagekräftiger **Indikator für finanzwirtschaftliche Nettoeffekte**, für den auch Daten auf Gemeindeebene für den längerfristigen Vergleich zur Verfügung stehen, ist die Entwicklung der **Gesamtverschuldung pro Kopf** (vgl. Abb. 4 und Tab. 2). Dieser Indikator soll als Indiz für die finanzwirtschaftlichen Nettoeffekte von Bevölkerungsveränderungen herangezogen werden. Hier dürften für die einzelne Gemeinde natürlich auch andere Einflussfaktoren von Bedeutung sein. Wenn aber unserer System der Steuerverteilung bei wichtigen Steuerarten auf Einwohner abstellt und auch die kommunalen Ausgaben von der Einwohnerzahl (mit einer Steigerung nach Zentralität) abhängen, so ist die Verschuldungsentwicklung in einer vergleichenden Betrachtung von einiger Aussagekraft.

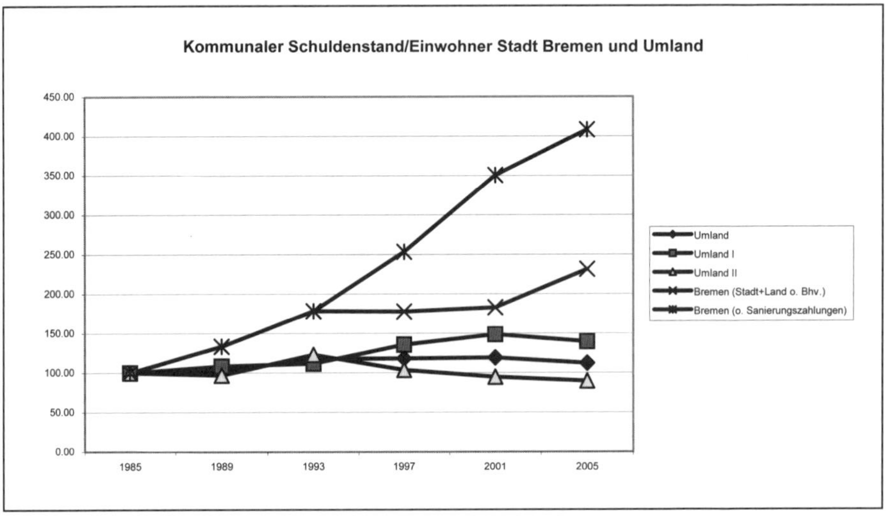

Quelle: eigene Darstellung

Abb. 4: Entwicklung der Verschuldung – Stadt Bremen und Umland von 1985 bis 2005 (in % zum Basisjahr)

Betrachtet man hier die Entwicklung seit 1985, so lässt sich feststellen, dass ohne Zweifel das Umland im Vergleich zur Kernstadt finanzieller Gewinner ist. Während die Pro-Kopf-Verschuldung in Bremen bis 2005 um ca. 130% oder – bei Ausklammerung der Sanierungszahlungen – um mehr als 300% steigt,[10] nimmt

10 Da die Entwicklung der Pro-Kopf-Verschuldung für die Stadt Bremen wegen der Vermischung von städtischen und Landesaufgaben wenig aussagekräftig ist, wenn man allein den Haushalt der Stadtgemeinde betrachtet, führt Anl. 2 die Entwicklung der Schulden pro Kopf ohne Bremerhaven auf. Hierbei zeigt die erste Zeitreihe die Verschuldungsentwicklung in realen Daten, d.h. unter Einbezug

dieser Indikator für das Umland in einer Durchschnittsbetrachtung nur um 12% zu. Allerdings verschieben sich hier die Relationen etwas, wenn der Kreis der engeren und weiteren Umlandgemeinden differenziert betrachtet werden. **Während im häufig als Speckgürtel bezeichneten engeren Ring der Umlandgemeinden die Verschuldung pro Kopf im betrachteten Zeitraum um ca. 40% ansteigt, sinkt die Verschuldung im zweiten Umlandring nach einem zwischenzeitlichen Anstieg deutlich unter das Ausgangsniveau.** Materialkritisch ist hier anzumerken, dass inzwischen auch mittlere Städte dazu übergehen, Gemeindeschulden in Sondervermögen auszulagern (Niedersächsisches Landesamt für Statistik 2005). Eine Berücksichtigung dieser Vorgänge würde das Verschuldungsbild noch realistischer zeigen. Die Ergebnisse der Auswertungen erfordern somit eine differenzierte Antwort.

Als Ursachen für finanzielle Vorteile durch den Anstieg der Einwohnerzahlen auf der Einnahmeseite öffentlicher Haushalte lassen sich zwei bekannte Argumente anführen:

1. Seit den Änderungen der Steuerverteilungsregeln Ende der 60er Jahre erfolgt die Verteilung von Steuereinnahmen in der BRD zu erheblichen Anteilen einwohnerbezogen. Hieraus ergibt sich ein Vorteil aus einer reinen Einwohnersteigerung ohne Betrachtung der Wertschöpfungsentwicklung.[11]
2. Allerdings lässt sich mit diesem Argument noch nicht erklären, weshalb auch ein überproportionaler Anstieg der Pro-Kopf-Steuereinnahmen zu verzeichnen war. Die Erklärung hierfür ist die Abwanderung relativ einkommensstarker Bevölkerungsgruppen im Zuge der Suburbanisierung (Holzschneider, Müller 1999, S. 9; Pohl, Haller o.J.). Da die Lohn- und Einkommenssteuer wohnortbezogen zerlegt wird, profitieren die Umlandgemeinden von zusätzlichen Einwohnern, die über einen Arbeitsplatz und überdurchschnittliches Einkommen verfügen. Die im Zeitablauf wachsende Differenz von BIP und BSP für Bremen (Holzschneider, Müller 1999, S. 5) wirkt sich so aus, dass durch zusätzliche Wertschöpfung erzielbare Steuermehreinnahmen vorwiegend im Umland anfallen.[12]

Die Entwicklung finanzieller Vor- und Nachteile im Spiegel der Verschuldungsentwicklung hat demgegenüber bisher nur den zweiten Umlandring als eigentlichen Gewinner.

---

der relativen Verschuldungsstagnation in Folge der Sanierungszahlungen. Die zweite Zeitreihe zeigt die fiktive Verschuldungsentwicklung, die ohne Sanierungszahlungen hätte eintreten können. Hierzu vgl. Der Senator für Finanzen der Freien Hansestadt Bremen (2003, S. 32f.).

11 Vgl. Klusewitz 1997, S. 2f.. Zur aktuellen Diskussion alternativer Zerlegungsmaßstäbe vgl. Kitterer u.a. 2004.

12 Vgl. Der Senator für Finanzen, Jahresbericht 2002, a.a.O., S. 44f. In der Grafik auf S. 45, die den überwiegenden Anteil aller ISP-bedingten zu erwartenden Steuermehreinnahmen dem Bund und den anderen Ländern zuweist, würde man sich allerdings eine Differenzierung nach Gewinnen für Niedersachsen durch versteuerte Pendlereinkünfte und den Vorteilen für die anderen Bundesländer wünschen.

3. Die Kernstadt selbst verliert, da sie laufende Ausgaben für die Unterhaltung von Infrastrukturen nicht so rasch abbauen kann, wie sie Einwohner verliert. Investitionen im Wettbewerb um einkommensstarke Einwohner bewirken ihrerseits wieder künftige Ausgaben für den Infrastrukturerhalt und -betrieb.
4. Der erste Umlandring gewinnt deutlich an Einnahmen pro Kopf, aber er bezahlt diesen Vorteil mit wachsenden Ansprüchen der neuen Einwohner an eine Infrastrukturversorgung auf städtischem Niveau. Die Verschuldung pro Einwohner steigt geringer als in der Kernstadt, aber dennoch deutlich.
5. Als Folge einer expansiven Wohnflächenausweisung steigt die Einwohnerzahl im zweiten Umlandring überproportional an. Dieser Einwohnergewinn schlägt sich offensichtlich nicht nur in steigenden Steuereinnahmen nieder, sondern bisher auch noch in nicht überproportional anwachsenden Ausgabelasten. Einmalige Investitionen der Erschließung amortisieren sich noch. Die Verschuldung pro Kopf kann im betrachteten Zeitraum sogar zurückgeführt werden.[13]

Fraglich ist allerdings, ob diese Situation so bleibt oder ob der Einwohnerwettbewerb bei Berücksichtigung der erkennbaren demographischen Entwicklung am Ende nur noch Verlierer (allerdings mit unterschiedlicher Verlustintensität) übrig lässt.

III. Demographischer Wandel – Auswirkungen des Bevölkerungsrückgangs auf Städte und Regionen

Was macht die Einwohnerkonkurrenz zum potentiell ruinösen Wettbewerb?
Der Wettbewerb der Gemeinden um Einwohner müsste zunächst keine negative Entwicklung sein. Er würde im politischen System eine erhöhte Aufmerksamkeit für die Interessen der Bürger auslösen können. **Als ruinös lässt sich ein Wettbewerbsprozess** jedoch **dann einstufen, wenn** z.B.:

- ein Marktaustritt für die Wettbewerber nicht oder nur mit hohen Verlusten möglich ist,
- wegen der Schrumpfung des Marktes nicht alle Wettbewerber am Markt überleben können,
- wegen der hohen Bedeutung von Fixkosten bzw. economies of scale eine starke Preiskonkurrenz die Marktbedingungen bestimmt.

13 Über die Ursachen lässt sich nur spekulieren. Auf der Einnahmeseite spielt sicher die Zuwanderung einkommensstarker Steuerzahler eine Rolle, die hier noch großzügig bauen können. Allerdings ist weder das Niveau der Steuereinnahmen pro Einwohner noch die Entwicklung der Steuereinnahmen pro Einwohner besser als im ersten Umlandring (Statistisches Landesamt Bremen, Niedersächsisches Statistisches Landesamt 2005). Plausibler ist daher die Annahme, dass sich im zweiten Umlandring bisher weniger in dauerhaft erhöhten Ausgaben für die Unterhaltung stadtadäquater Infrastrukturen niederschlägt.

Im Folgenden ist zu prüfen, ob derartige Bedingungen den kommunalen Wettbewerb um Einwohner bestimmen bzw. in absehbarer Zukunft bestimmen werden:

1. Hinsichtlich der ersten Bedingung kann festgestellt werden, dass Gemeinden nicht gezwungen sind, aktiv am Wettbewerb um Einwohner teilzunehmen. Bei Schrumpfung ist eine Auflösung oder eher eine Integration in umliegende Gemeinden denkbar. Allerdings ist es realistisch, einen Widerstand gegen einen derartigen Prozess von Schrumpfung zu erwarten, da verbleibende Bewohner durch den Einwohnerschwund Nachteile hinsichtlich ihrer Versorgungsqualität mit öffentlichen und privaten Gütern zu erwarten haben. Schon vorher hat das Auftreten von Kostenremanenzeffekten für das Verhalten öffentlicher Entscheidungsträger Bedeutung. Der Ausstieg aus der Einwohnerkonkurrenz ist daher schwierig.

2. Bezogen auf die zweite Bedingung ruinöser Einwohnerkonkurrenz ist die demographische Entwicklung zu prüfen. Wir können grob drei Phasen unterscheiden. In der ersten Phase seit Beginn der Industrialisierung gab es über ca. 150 Jahre ein dynamisches Städtewachstum. Dieses vollzog sich durch eigenes Bevölkerungswachstum der Städte und stärker durch eine Sogwirkung auf den Bevölkerungs- und Arbeitskräfteüberschuss im ländlichen Raum. Die Umverteilung der Bevölkerung war wegen der generell wachsenden Bevölkerung nicht zwingend mit Schrumpfung der Bevölkerung in ländlichen Gebieten verbunden.

Die zweite Phase der demographischen Entwicklung lässt sich auf den Beginn der 70er Jahre des 20. Jahrhunderts terminieren. Suburbanisierungsprozesse lösten das Städtewachstum ab. Die Mehrzahl aller Großstädte verzeichnete seit Mitte der siebziger Jahre entgegen vorheriger Prognosen Bevölkerungsverluste. Suburbanisierungsprozesse halten an. Sie sind allerdings bisher wegen der Zuwanderung aus dem Ausland oder großräumigen Bevölkerungsverlagerungen in Deutschland in der Mehrzahl der Regionen noch mit Bevölkerungszuwachs verbunden. Insbesondere Ende der 80er und Anfang der 90er Jahre konnten die schrumpfenden Großstädte ihre Bevölkerungsverluste durch Zuwanderung aus dem Ausland zu einem erheblichen Teil kompensieren.

Als dritte Phase der Bevölkerungsentwicklung ist nun eine schrumpfende Bevölkerungszahl in der Mehrzahl aller deutschen Regionen zu erwarten.[14] Bei anhaltender Suburbanisierung steht den städtischen Zentren ein drastischer Bevölkerungsverlust ins Haus. Die Einzelkomponenten dieser Entwicklung bestehen in einer fortschreitenden Überalterung der städtischen Bevölkerung und, damit einhergehend, sinkenden Geburten- und steigenden Sterberaten. Ohne deutliche

14 Vgl. Müller 2003, S. 28-42 und für die generelle Prognose der Bevölkerungsentwicklung im langfristigen Zeitraum Bundesministerium des Innern: Modellrechnungen zur Bevölkerungsentwicklung in der Bundesrepublik Deutschland bis zum Jahre 2050, Stand Juni 2000. Zu den aktuellsten regionalisierten Bevölkerungsprognosen vgl. Bundesamt für Bauwesen und Raumordnung 2006.

Zuwanderung ist daher der Bevölkerungsverlust programmiert. Einwohnerkonkurrenz müsste daher den Suburbanisierungstrend brechen. Partielle Bevölkerungsgewinne können die Großstädte ansonsten allenfalls durch Migranten und Studenten erzielen. Diese Perspektive führt dazu, dass der deutsche Städtetag bis 2015 für die Mehrzahl aller deutschen Großstädte deutliche Bevölkerungsverluste erwartet (Deutscher Städtetag o.J.).
Diese Erwartung von Bevölkerungsverlusten wird auch durch Prognosen der Bertelsmann Stiftung für den Zeitraum bis 2020 bestätigt.

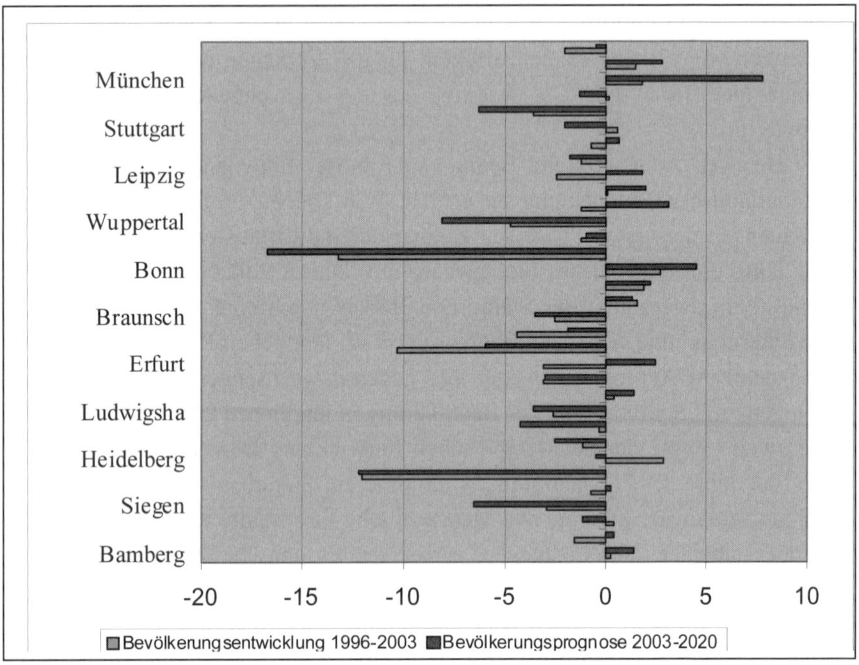

Quelle: eigene Darstellung nach Daten der Aktion demographischer Wandel/Bertelsmann Stiftung (www.aktion2050.de)

Abb. 5: Veränderung der Bevölkerung in ausgewählten Großstädten bis 2020

3. Bezogen auf die dritte Bedingung für das Auftreten ruinöser Konkurrenz kann darauf verwiesen werden, dass ein erheblicher Anteil städtischer Infrastrukturen überproportionale Fixkostenanteile aufweist. Dieses gilt für die Verkehrsinfrastruktur ebenso wie für Einrichtungen der leitungsgebundenen Ver- und Entsorgung. Eine Ausdünnung der Einwohnerzahl in alten Wohngebieten lässt die

Stückkosten der Versorgung sprunghaft ansteigen.[15] Die Ausweisung neuer Wohngebiete ist mit Erschließungskosten und folglich einem Anstieg des Fixkostenblocks verbunden. Diese Kostenstruktur lässt eine Anfälligkeit für einen Wettbewerb mit Dumpingpreisen erwarten.

Wie reagieren die Städte auf die verschärfte Wettbewerbssituation?

Seitens der bisherigen Gewinner im Suburbanisationsprozess, der Städte und Gemeinden im Umland der Kernstädte, wird eine Fortdauer der positiven Einwohnerentwicklung erwartet und betrieben. Planend einschränkende Eingriffe übergeordneter Instanzen sind erwünscht, aber nur schwer durchzusetzen.[16] Allerdings kann sich die bisherige Bevölkerungsexpansion bei deutlich sinkenden Zahlen für die Gesamtbevölkerung und die Mehrzahl aller Regionen nicht im fortgeschriebenen Trend entwickeln. Nachfragermärkte und ein Preisverfall für Bauland sind plausibel. Eine mildernde Wirkung hat hier nur die kontinuierliche Steigerung der pro Kopf beanspruchten Wohnflächen.

Die Kernstädte als erste Verlierer des Wettbewerbs verstärken ihre Anstrengungen, um Einwohner zu halten oder Einwohner in Bevölkerungssegmenten, für die die städtische Umgebung attraktiv ist, neu zu gewinnen. Dieses bewirkt entsprechend dem Bremer Beispiel eine Baulandausweisung ohne dauerhaft erkennbaren Bedarf. Ferner wird die Diskussion davon geprägt, die städtische Attraktivität zu erhalten und nicht durch Schließung öffentlicher Einrichtungen, durch Ausdünnung des kulturellen und sozialen Angebots in eine Abwärtsspirale der Entwicklung zu gelangen.

Die **Risiken dieser Entwicklung** sind bereits heute erkennbar (Gatzweiler u.a. 2003, S 557ff.) und an Beispielen zu bewerten:

- Es tritt eine weitere **Ausdünnung verdichteter städtischer Wohngebiete** ein. Entwicklungsalternativen sind die subventionierte Sanierung, die Versäumung und der Abriss. Dieses wird dann euphemistisch als **„Rückbau"** einer öffentlichen Förderung zugänglich.[17]
- Wegen der Ausweisung neuer Baugebiete ergeben sich für die Städte, die Einwohner verlieren, **erweiterte Infrastrukturen bei verminderten Finanzen**. Die ohnehin prekäre Finanzlage vieler Städte wird sich verschärfen.

---

15 Erste exakte Berechnungen dieser Kostenremanenzeffekte auf der Basis der Erfahrungen des Bevölkerungsrückganges der Kernstädte in den neuen Bundesländern finden sich bei Schiller und Siedentop (2005, S. 83ff.).

16 So wird auch in der Literatur darauf verwiesen, sinnvollen räumlichen Konzepten müsste wieder praktische Bedeutung verschafft werden (vgl. Aring 1999, S. 646). Allerdings plädiert der gleiche Autor gegen eine restriktive Flächenpolitik im Zeitraum bis 2010 (vgl. ebenda, S. 648ff.).

17 Bezeichnenderweise ist der Stadtteil Osterholz-Tenever in Bremen, ein städtebauliches Modellvorhaben aus der kernstädtischen Expansionsphase zu Beginn der 70er Jahre, nun ein Modellvorhaben für den Stadtumbau-West, mit dem die wachsenden Leerstände in den Großwohnsiedlungen bekämpft werden sollen.

- Eine erneute **Auffüllung der Leerstände in den Kernstädten durch Migranten** oder einkommensschwache Bevölkerungsschichten ist nicht auszuschließen.[18] Dieses könnte Suburbanisierungsprozesse verstärken, anstatt sie wegen des geringeren Preisgefälles für Boden und Wohnraum zu vermindern.

Die Konsequenzen wären für alle Städte als Konkurrenten im Einwohnerwettbewerb problematisch. Von einer nachhaltigen Entwicklungsplanung kann nicht die Rede sein. Finanziell würde sich eine Situation ergeben, in der die bisherigen Verlierer in eine **ruinöse Abwärtsentwicklung** geraten.

Auch die bisherigen Gewinner können zu Verlierern werden. Dieses ist für den ersten Umlandkreis von Gemeinden, gemessen an der Pro-Kopf-Verschuldung, bereits jetzt der Fall. Eine insgesamt rückläufige Einwohnerzahl wird diesen Trend verstärken. Ob auch der zweite Kreis von Umlandgemeinden auf die Verliererstraße gerät, hängt – neben der relativen Wettbewerbsstärke im Minus-Summen-Spiel – auch davon ab, in welchem Ausmaß neu gewonnene Einwohner Ansprüche an eine Infrastrukturausstattung nach städtischen Maßstäben erheben. Spätestens hier würde sich eine stark abgeflachte Rang-Größen-Verteilung der Einwohner als insgesamt unwirtschaftliche Lösung erweisen. Die beschriebenen Szenarien sind natürlich partiell spekulativ. Insbesondere Trends der Außenwanderung und Wirkungen zentralstaatlicher Instrumente (wie Abbau von Steuerentlastungen für Pendler oder Eigenheimsubventionen) sind nur begrenzt prognostizierbar.

IV. Bevölkerung und Finanzausgleich

Ist eine Kompensation durch den Finanzausgleich eine Lösung für die Kernstädte?

Wie dargestellt, sind vor allem die Kernstädte die Verlierer des demographischen Wandels. Eine weitere nachhaltige Abflachung der Rang-Größen-Verteilung der Einwohner wird mit Problemen der Infrastrukturplanung und massiven Finanzierungsschwierigkeiten einhergehen. Die Instrumente zur Bewältigung derartiger Anpassungskrisen im deutschen föderalen System sind traditionell der Finanzausgleich und seit Anfang der 70er Jahre die Raumplanung. Während der Raumplanung als hierarchisches Koordinationsinstrument eine sehr eingeschränkte

18 Wie oben dargestellt, entfällt der größte Teil aktueller Wanderungsgewinne auf die Auslandswanderung. Hierbei besteht nur partiell die Chance zum „brain gain“, die mit der Zuwanderung ausländischer Studenten und Wissenschaftler verbunden ist. Die Mehrzahl der Migranten verschärft soziale Gegensätze und innerstädtische Ghettobildung. Die Bevölkerungsstatistik verschleiert diese Probleme z.T., da Aussiedler aus den osteuropäischen Staaten sofort eingebürgert werden.

Steuerungsfähigkeit zugebilligt wird,[19] hat sich der Finanzausgleich bisher als wirksames Instrument zur Gewährleistung der kommunalen Handlungsfähigkeit erwiesen.[20] Sowohl durch den Länderfinanzausgleich im Falle der Stadtstaaten als auch durch den kommunalen Finanzausgleich in den Flächenländern wurden die Finanzprobleme der Kernstädte deutlich gemildert. Ausgelöst wurden diese Probleme durch eine Steuerverteilung nach dem Einwohnerkriterium bei den wichtigsten Steuerarten. Sie wurden verstärkt durch die Stadt-Umland-Wanderung und die in den Kernstädten überproportional auftretenden Lasten der hohen Arbeitslosigkeit und Alterung der Bevölkerung. **Ausgleichsinstrumente in den Finanzausgleichssystemen** sind z.B. **Indikatoren für die Belastung des Sozialsystems** (Arbeitslosenquote, Sozialhilfeausgaben/Einwohner) und **Einwohnermultiplikatoren** als Ausgleich für die Bereitstellung überörtlicher Infrastrukturen.[21] Die Wirkung dieser Systemkorrekturen ist allerdings mit einigen Problemen verbunden:

- Einwohnermultiplikatoren im Finanzausgleich erzeugen eine Vervielfachung der finanziellen Verluste (der Kernstädte) bei Suburbanisierung. Der Stadtstaatenbonus im Länderfinanzausgleich bewirkt einen Einnahmeverlust von ca. 3000 €/J. pro abwanderndem Einwohner (Der Senator für Finanzen der Freien Hansestadt Bremen 1997). Die Einnahmeverluste durch Abwanderung aus Großstädten im kommunalen Finanzausgleich der Flächenländer haben ebenfalls erhebliche finanzielle Bedeutung. Für Ruhrgebietsstädte wird allein für jährliche Verluste bei Schlüsselzuweisungen und Investitionspauschalen mit bis zu 700 €/Einwohner gerechnet. Dieser Wert erhöht sich durch Verluste bei Bedarfszuweisungen und zweckgebundenen Zuweisungen noch (von Loeffelholz, Rappen 2002, S. 34ff.). Ein Ausstieg aus der ruinösen Einwohnerkonkurrenz wird hierdurch unwahrscheinlicher.
- Die wirtschaftliche Logik der in internationalen Vergleichen immer wieder bestätigten „rank size rule“[22] findet sich im Zentrale Orte-Modell-Christallers

19 So spricht Aring zu Recht von einer Kluft zwischen anerkannten Leitbildern der Regionalplanung und realer Planung und Entwicklung. Vgl. Aring 1999, S. 646.

20 Eine Überblicksdarstellung des ab 2005 geltenden Finanzausgleichssystems findet sich bei Dönnebrink (2003, S. 259ff.). Im gleichen Schwerpunktheft der IzR wird dankenswerterweise der Versuch unternommen, auch die regionalen Ausgleichswirkungen von sozialen Sicherungssystemen und Staatsausgaben stärker zu beleuchten. Zur Bewertung der bisherigen Komplexität des bundesstaatlichen Finanzausgleichs sei ein Blick auf die Regelungen im kommunalen Finanzausgleich der Flächenländer empfohlen. Als Beispiel vgl. Gesetz zur Regelung der Zuweisungen des Landes Nordrhein-Westfalen an die Gemeinden, www.im.nrw.de/gfg/GFG2003.htm. Hier finden sich neben Einwohnermultiplikatoren (max. 157%) auch Verteilungskriterien wie die Schülerzahl, die Sozialhilfeausgaben und die Zahl der Arbeitslosen (mit der Dauer der Arbeitslosigkeit gewichtet). Vgl. ebenda § 8.

21 Vgl. Gesetz zur Regelung der Zuweisungen des Landes Nordrhein-Westfalen an die Gemeinden, www.im.nrw.de/gfg/GFG2003.htm insb. § 8.

22 Die Annahme einer stabilen Aufteilung der Bevölkerung eines Landes auf die (große) Hauptstadt und die kleineren Städte in der Städtehierarchie wird seit Auerbachs Überlegungen zu einem Gesetz der Bevölkerungskonzentration von 1919 immer wieder untersucht und in internationalen Verglei-

(1933). Zwar lassen sich Leistungsstrukturen für zentrale Güter partiell der räumlichen Einwohnerverteilung anpassen. Dennoch bewirkt eine nachhaltig abgeflachte Einwohner-Größen-Verteilung eine Tendenz zu Doppelstrukturen und ein insgesamt unwirtschaftliches Infrastrukturangebot.
- Aus Sicht des politischen Systems gibt es Grenzen des finanziellen Ausgleichs bei einer Wählermehrheit für Nicht-Kernstädte.[23] Diese Situation ist in der Mehrzahl aller Länder bereits erreicht. Ließen sich Einwohnerverluste weiterhin durch Indikatorenkorrektur kompensieren, so täuscht dieser Ausgleich zudem über die Existenz eines Null-Summen-Spiels hinweg oder erfordert Steuererhöhungen.

Als **Zwischenfazit** lässt sich feststellen, dass die in der Literatur diskutierten **Kriterien einer bedarfsgerechten Steuerverteilung** nur eine **begrenzte Rationalität** aufweisen. Das insbesondere vom Bundesverfassungsgericht hervorgehobene Einwohnerkriterium als Bedarfsgrundlage (Bundesverfassungsgericht 11.11.1999, www.bverfg.de) bietet kaum Anreize für Wirtschaftsförderung und Schaffung von Arbeitsplätzen.[24] Das früher genutzte Betriebsstätten- und/oder Unternehmenssitzkriterium für die Steuerverteilung bewirkte ebenfalls Ungerechtigkeiten. Auch das praktizierte System mit gewichteten Einwohnerwerten ist nur in grober Näherung imstande, eine Identität von Leistungsempfängern und finanziers öffentlicher Güter zu bewirken. Es erzeugt zudem die oben beklagten Fehlsteuerungseffekte.

V. Anpassung öffentlicher Organisationsstrukturen an die Regionalisierung des Lebens

Kann ruinöser Einwohnerwettbewerb zwischen Gebietskörperschaften durch eine Anpassung öffentlicher Organisationsstrukturen vermieden werden?

Wie oben angedeutet, ist die Reaktion städtischer Zentren mit einem Vorlauf im Einwohnerschwund – dieses gilt insbesondere für die Nicht-Leuchtturmstädte der neuen Länder – der subventionierte Rückbau. Die Mehrzahl aller vom Einwohnerschwund bedrohten Städte favorisiert allerdings eine Strategie der aktiven Einwohnerwerbung (Deutscher Städtetag, a.a.O., S. 8ff.). Diese Haltung ist, wie Abschnitt IV gezeigt hat, systemimmanent konsequent. Die hier abschließend zu

chen auch bestätigt. Vgl. z.B. Reed (2002, S. 1ff.). Zur näheren Diskussion vgl. Böventer (1979, S. 38ff.).

23 Die Großstädte haben 2001 noch einen Bevölkerungsanteil von 27,6% im Bundesdurchschnitt (Westdeutschland 25,6%, Ostdeutschland 35,3%). Vgl. Gatzweiler u.a. 2003, S. 559.

24 Zur Rechtfertigung einer Besserstellung wertschöpfungsstarker Agglomerationen im Finanzausgleich z.B. über Einwohnermultiplikatoren vgl. z.B. Zimmermann 2001, S. 222ff.

beantwortende Frage bemüht den alten Gestaltergrundsatz, dass die Form der Funktion zu folgen habe. Durch das Städtewachstum und den folgenden Suburbanisierungsprozess hat sich zweifellos das räumliche Muster von Lebensfunktionen in den Bereichen Wohnen, Arbeiten, Einkaufen und Freizeitgestaltung drastisch geändert. Wir sind nicht mehr eindeutige Städter oder Landbewohner. Lebensvollzüge haben sich regionalisiert, sie entwickeln sich innerhalb der Einstundenpendelobergrenze.[25]

Die **traditionelle organisatorische Antwort** der Städte auf das Städtewachstum am äußeren Rand ist die **Eingemeindung**. Dieses ist für Bremen kontinuierlich bis zum Kriegsende 1945 nachweisbar. In den Flächenstaaten Westdeutschlands vollzog sich die letzte Eingemeindungswelle, mit der Stadtflüchten wieder zur Finanzierung städtischer Infrastrukturlasten herangezogen wurden, bekanntlich Mitte der 70er Jahre. Die Nutzung des organisatorischen Instruments der Eingemeindung ist heute unrealistisch geworden.[26] Dieses hat zwei Gründe: Erstens ist der früher bestehende finanzielle Anreiz für das Umland, sich in das Stadtgebiet einzugliedern, mit der Änderung der Steuerverteilungskriterien entfallen. Zweitens finden sich in den Landtagen keine politischen Mehrheiten für die Integration in die großen Städte. Im Sonderfall Bremens ist die Eingemeindung zudem wegen der Stadtstaatenlösung von speziellen historischen Bedingungen abhängig und damit besonders unrealistisch.

Als **zweite organisatorische Antwort** auf das beschriebene Dilemma könnte auf das Mittel **hierarchischer Koordination im Rahmen der Landesentwicklungsplanung**, d.h. hier insbesondere die restriktive Genehmigung kommunaler Flächennutzungspläne zurückgegriffen werden. Alternative Instrumente mit gleicher Wirkungsrichtung werden z.B. in Form einer Baulandausweisungsumlage diskutiert (Krumm 2003, S. 409ff.).

Schon diese Diskussion über finanzielle Strafen für die Baulandausweisung zeigt jedoch, dass die hierarchisch-planende Koordination offensichtlich in der Vergangenheit wenig wirksam war. Dieses dürfte sich für mein regionales Beispiel, das Bremer Umland, mit der Auflösung der Regierungsbezirke in Niedersachsen und der Verlagerung der Raumordnungskompetenz auf die Landkreise noch verschlimmern. Auch wenn man die einschlägigen Bemühungen der für die Raumordnung Verantwortlichen als richtigen Weg nachhaltiger Ressourcenbewirt-

25 Diese Einschätzung schließt nicht aus, dass ein Wohnsitz innerhalb oder außerhalb der Kernstadt in verschiedenen Altersgruppen, sozialen Schichten oder Familientypen auch unterschiedlich attraktiv sein kann. Hierzu vgl. Bähr (2003, S. 4ff.) und Heitkamp (a.a.O., S. 166ff.). Diese für die Erfolgschancen im Einwohnerwettbewerb wichtigen Differenzierungen verdecken jedoch die Erkenntnis, dass alle unterscheidbaren Gruppen mit wachsender Mobilität unabhängig vom Wohnsitz Infrastrukturleistungen in der gesamten Region in Anspruch nehmen.

26 Diese Aussage spricht nicht gegen den „theoretischen Charme" dieses Lösungsansatzes angesichts ineffizienter raumordnungspolitischer Koordination, vgl. Elsner (2002).

schaftung begrüßt (Bundesministerium für Verkehr, Bau- und Wohnungswesen 2005a), muss man bezüglich der Umsetzbarkeit skeptisch bleiben.

Die **dritte** in der Öffentlichkeit angebotene **organisatorische Lösung** ist die **regionale Kooperation in freiwilliger Form**. Nun ist freiwillige Kooperation ein prinzipiell sinnvolles Mittel. Die Erfahrung zeigt jedoch, dass sie sich nur für win-win Situationen eignet. Es mag daher dem Kommunalverbund Bremen Niedersachsen noch gelungen sein, gemeinsam Mittel für das „Intra-Projekt" zum Flächenmonitoring einzuwerben (Regionale Arbeitsgemeinschaft Bremen/ Niedersachsen, Kommunalverbund Niedersachsen/Bremen e.V. 2004). Eine Umsetzung von Planungsrestriktionen in einer Situation ruinöser Konkurrenz wird in freiwillig kooperativer Form in aller Regel scheitern.[27] Der aktuelle Diskussionsstand im Kommunalverbund Niedersachsen/Bremen e.V. und in der Regionalen Arbeitsgemeinschaft als Nachfolgeorganisation der Gemeinsamen Landesplanung Bremen/Niedersachsen sieht daher auch keine Verbindlichkeit für kommunale Planungen vor.

Die **organisatorische Lösung der Wahl** ist in dieser Situation eine **regionale Kooperation in verbindlicher Form**.[28] Hierbei können für einzelne infrastrukturelle Aufgaben **Zweckverbände** gegründet werden, die für Defizitgeschäfte, wie den öffentlichen Nahverkehr, eine Identität von Nutzern, Entscheidern und Finanziers herstellen. Will man jedoch auch die ruinöse Konkurrenz um Einwohner ausschalten und auf ein normales Maß reduzieren, so bietet sich der **regionale Planungsverband** mit ausgelagerten Kontrollkompetenzen an (Fürst u.a. 1994, S. 234). Sollen beide Aspekte integriert werden, so ergibt sich die bereits von Hoffmann skizzierte **regionale Gebietskörperschaft** (Hoffmann 2000), die **regionale Planungskompetenz** mit **demokratischen Entscheidungsstrukturen** und der Möglichkeit einer **Trägerschaft für regional genutzte Infrastrukturen** verbindet. Diese Lösung ist modellhaft in Niedersachsen mit der Region Hannover realisiert[29] und erfordert auch von der Kernstadt die Abgabe von Kompetenzen, die mit dem Status der Kreisfreiheit verbunden sind. Solche Kompetenzen betreffen nach dem Modell Region Hannover z.B.:

– Trägerschaft für die Regionalplanung,
– regionale Wirtschafts- und Beschäftigungsförderung,

27 Eine völlig andere Frage besteht darin, welche Funktion freiwillige Kooperation in regionalen Netzwerken innerhalb einer Gesamtkonzeption von „Regional Governance" haben kann. Dieses neue Forschungsfeld wirft aber z.Zt. mehr Fragen auf, als sie mit einer vagen neuen Begrifflichkeit bereits beantwortet werden können. Vgl. Fürst 2001, S. 370ff.

28 Zur Bewertung alternativer Organisationsformen und zu detaillierten Vorschlägen für die Bremer Region vgl. Fürst u.a. 1994.

29 Zur Konzeption vgl. Priebs 1999, S. 617ff. Für eine Bewertung der Effizienz dieser Organisationsform ist es natürlich kurz nach der Gründung der Region Hannover noch zu früh. Allerdings macht der Umstand durchaus Mut, dass im Südosten Niedersachsens unverändert eine eher am Nachhaltigkeitskriterium orientierte restriktive Ausweisung von Wohnbauflächen festzustellen ist als in unserer Beispielregion. Vgl. Schleifnecker 2003, S. 77ff.

- örtliche Trägerschaft von Sozial- und Jugendhilfe,
- Trägerschaft für berufsbildende Schulen,
- Funktion als öffentlich-rechtlicher Entsorgungsträger.[30]

Der besondere Charme dieser Lösung ist in finanzwirtschaftlicher Hinsicht eine Regionalisierung vielfältiger Ausgabe- und Infrastrukturlasten, die derzeit verstärkt die Kernstädte treffen. Eine Übertragung des Modells auf unsere Beispielregion, Bremen und sein Umland, ist natürlich besonders schwierig und langwierig. Dieses ist eine Folge der Stadtstaatenproblematik und der Regelungen des Länderfinanzausgleichs, von denen vor allem Niedersachsen und das Umland profitieren, solange Bremen nicht der ruinösen Konkurrenz erlegen ist.

Regionale Kooperation in verbindlicher Form funktioniert im behandelten Beispiel bereits im regionalen Verkehrsverbund Bremen Niedersachsen. Für weitere Schritte der freiwilligen Integration in einen Planungsverband oder eine regionale Gebietskörperschaft fehlt vor allem im Umland noch die Einsicht in die Notwendigkeit. Der Änderungsdruck im regionalen Zentrum wächst mit der nach Auslaufen der Bundeshilfen grassierenden Haushaltskrise und dem Zwang, öffentliche Leistungen zu streichen. Vor dem ersatzlosen Verlust der nur im Oberzentrum zu erbringenden Leistungen könnte auch im Umland die Bereitschaft zu kooperativen Lösungen wachsen. Die Chance für weitere Schritte in die hier für richtig eingestufte Richtung ist jedenfalls größer, als eine wirksame Lösung über die skizzierten organisatorischen Alternativen.

Literaturverzeichnis:

Aring, J., Modernisierung der Regionalplanung, in: Informationen zur Raumentwicklung, Heft 9/10, 1999, S. 645-660.

Bähr, J., Binnenwanderungen: Konzepte, Typen, Erklärungsansätze, in: Geographische Rundschau, 55. Jg., Heft 6, 2003, S. 4-8.

Böventer, E. von, Standortentscheidung und Raumstruktur, Hannover 1979.

Bundesamt für Bauwesen und Raumordnung (Hrsg.), Raumordnungsprognose 2020/2050, Berichte Bd. 23, Bonn 2006.

Bundesministerium für Verkehr, Bau- und Wohnungswesen (Hrsg.), Öffentliche Daseinsvorsorge und demographischer Wandel, Berlin und Bonn 2005.

Christaller, W., Die Zentralen Orte in Süddeutschland, Jena 1933.

Der Senator für Finanzen der Freien Hansestadt Bremen (Hrsg.), Steuerliche Effekte von Arbeitsplätzen und Einwohnern, in: Finanzbericht Bremen, Heft 1, 1997.

Der Senator für Finanzen der Freien Hansestadt Bremen (Hrsg.), Sanierung der bremischen Haushalte – Jahresbericht 2002 – , Bremen 2003, S. 32-33.

Deutscher Städtetag, Auswirkungen des Bevölkerungsrückgangs auf die Stadtentwicklung, Arbeitspapier der Fachkommission Stadtentwicklungsplanung des Dt. Städtetages, o.O., o.J.

Dönnebrink, E., Verteilungsschlüssel im Finanzausgleich vor dem Hintergrund der Neuordnung zum Jahr 2005, in: Informationen zur Raumentwicklung, Heft 5, 2003, S. 259-270.

Dosch, F., Auf dem Weg zu einer nachhaltigeren Flächennutzung? in: Informationen zur Raumentwicklung, Heft 1/2, 2002, S. 31-45.

30 Vgl. den vollständigen Aufgabenkatalog der Region Hannover in den §§ 7-12 des Gesetzes über die Region Hannover vom 5. Juni 2001, Nds. GVBl. S. 348.

Elsner, W., Länder-Neugliederung, Betriebsstätten-Prinzip und Einwohnerwertung: Das Verfassungsgebot leistungsfähiger Bundesländer ernstnehmen, Ländervielfalt bewahren, Länderfinanzausgleich entlasten – Eine Einführung am Beispiel des Stadtstaates Bremen, in: Neue Alternativen des Länderfinanzausgleichs, Hrgs. von ders., Frankfurt a.M. u.a. 2002.
Ewers, H.-J. u.a., Innovationsorientierte Regionalpolitik, Bonn 1980.
Fürst, D., B. Müller und *D. Schefold*, Weiterentwicklung der Gemeinsamen Landesplanung Bremen/Niedersachsen, Baden-Baden 1994.
Fürst, D., Regional governance – ein neues Paradigma der Regionalwissenschaften? in: Raumforschung und Raumordnung, Heft 5/6, 2001, S. 370-380.
Gatzweiler, H.-P., K. Meyer und *A. Milbert*, Schrumpfende Städte in Deutschland? Fakten und Trends, in: Informationen zur Raumentwicklung, Heft 10/11, 2003, S. 557-574.
Heimbrecht, J., Das Milliardending, Köln 1984.
Heitkamp, Th., a.a.O., S. 166ff.
Hoffmann, R., Regionalkörperschaft Bremen-Unterweser, Diskussionspapier der Senatskanzlei, Bremen 2000.
Hollbach-Grömig, B., Kommunale Wirtschaftsförderung in der Bundesrepublik Deutschland, ausgewählte Ergebnisse einer Umfrage im Jahre 2000, Deutsches Institut für Urbanistik, Berlin 2001.
Holzschneider, M. und *M. Müller*, Stadtregion Bremen, Die Stadt Bremen und ihr Umland, in: Finanzbericht Bremen, Heft 4, 1999.
Klusewitz, S., Steuerliche Effekte von Arbeitsplätzen und Einwohnern, in: Finanzbericht 1, 1997, S. 2-3.
Kitterer, W., T. Burckardt und *H. Löwer*, Die Einbeziehung der Stadtstaaten in das bundesdeutsche Finanzverteilungssystem, in: Stadtstaaten und Finanzausgleich, hrsg. Von Haller, F. und M. Schönert, Bremen 2004.
Kocka, J., Arbeitsverhältnisse und Arbeiterexistenzen, Grundlagen der Klassenbildung im 19. Jahrhundert, Bonn 1990.
Krumm, R., Die Baulandausweisungsumlage als flächenpolitisches Steuerungsinstrument, in: Wirtschaftsdienst, Heft 6, 2003, S. 409-416.
Landgrebe, P., Minoritätengruppe und wirtschaftliche Bedeutung: Zum Einfluss der Hugenotten auf die deutsche Wirtschaftsentwicklung, Sickte 1977.
Mönnich, E., Erklärungsansätze regionaler Entwicklung und politisches Handeln, Frankfurt a.M. u.a. 2004.
Mönnich, E., Ruinöse Einwohnerkonkurrenz, in: Raumforschung und Raumordnung, Heft 1, 2005, S. 32-46.
Mönnich, H., Aufbruch ins Revier, Aufbruch nach Europa, München 1971.
Müller, B., Regionalentwicklung unter Schrumpfungsbedingungen, in: Raumforschung und Raumordnung, Heft 1/2, 2003, S. 28-42.
Niedersächsisches Landesamt für Statistik, Statistische Berichte Niedersachsen, Schulden des Landes, der Gemeinden, Samtgemeinden und Landkreise sowie der öffentlich bestimmten Fonds, Einrichtungen und wirtschaftlichen Unternehmen am 31. Dezember 2004, Hannover 2005.
Pohl, M. und *F. Haller*, Zur Standortbindung einkommensstarker Haushalte in Bremen, Bremen 2001.
Priebs, A., Die Region ist die Stadt! Ein Plädoyer für dauerhafte und verbindliche Organisationsstrukturen für die Stadtregion, in: Informationen zur Raumentwicklung, Heft 9/10, 1999, S. 617-628.
Reed, W.J., On the rank-size distribution for human settlements, in: Journal of Regional Science, Vol. 42, No. 1, 2002, S. 1-17.
Regionale Arbeitsgemeinschaft Bremen/Niedersachsen; Kommunalverbund Niedersachsen Bremen e.V. (Hrsg.), Interkommunales Raumstrukturkonzept Region Bremen, Endbericht Delmenhorst, Syke 2004.
Schiller, G. und *S. Siedentop*, Infrastrukturfolgekosten der Siedlungsentwicklung unter Schrumpfungsbedingungen, in: DISP 160, 2005, S. 83-93.
Schleifnecker, T., Zehn Jahre Bauland-Monitoring in Niedersachsen, in: Neues Archiv, Heft 1, 2003, S. 77-85.
Schlömer, C. und *H. Bucher*, Arbeitslosigkeit und Binnenwanderungen, in: Informationen zur Raumentwicklung, Heft 1, 2001, S. 33-47.
Stadtentwicklungskonzept Bremen, Der Senator für Bau, Verkehr und Stadtentwicklung, Bremen 1999.
Statistisches Landesamt Bremen (Hrsg.), Statistisches Jahrbuch 2005, Bremen 2005.
Statistisches Landesamt Bremen(Hrsg.), Niedersächsisches Statistisches Landesamt, Gemeinsame Landesplanung Bremen/Niedersachsen, Regionalstatistische Grundlagen, in: Statistische Mitteilungen des Statistischen Landesamtes Bremen, Heft 104, Oktober 2001, S. 61-62.
Loeffelholz, H. D. von und *H. Rappen*, Bevölkerungsentwicklung und Kommunalfinanzen im Ruhrgebiet – Ein Problemaufriss, Essen 2002.

Wehling, W., J. Peters und *S. Wiebe*, Arbeitsplätze schaffen – Einwohner gewinnen, in: BAW-Monatsbericht, Heft 10, 2002.
Zimmermann, H., Haben Ballungsgebiete einen höheren Finanzbedarf? In: Wirtschaftsdienst, Heft 4, 2001, S. 222-226.

Anlage 1: Kommunaler Schuldenstand/Einwohner Stadt Bremen und Umland

Gemeinde		1985	1989	1993	1997	2001	2005
Summe Umland	S i. 1000E	303043	317000	391123	410338	426276	412864
	Einwohner	470102	480447	514579	537950	554880	570377
	Schulden/E	644.63	659.80	760.08	762.78	768.23	723.84
		100.00	102.35	117.91	118.33	119.17	112.29
Summe Umland I	S i. 1000E	141576	158062	172055	214518	239318	231995
	Einwohner	229412	236447	248917	255999	260908	269330
	Schulden/E.	617.13	668.49	691.21	837.96	917.25	861.38
		100.00	108.32	112.01	135.79	148.63	139.58
Summe Umland II	S i. 1000E	161467	158938	219068	195820	186958	180869
	Einwohner	240690	244000	265662	281951	293972	301047
	Schulden/E.	670.85	651.39	824.61	694.52	635.97	600.8
		100.00	97.10	122.92	103.53	94.80	89.56
Schuldenentwicklung Bremen (Stadt + Land o. Bhv.):							
	S i. 1000E	4676900	6460100	8740100	8636100	8792600	11244500
	Einwohner	526377	544327	551604	546968	540950	547275
	Schulden/E.	8,885.08	11,868.05	15,844.88	15,789.04	16,254.00	20,546.34
		100.00	133.57	178.33	177.70	182.94	231.25
Schuldenentwicklung Bremen ohne Sanierungszahlungen:							
	S i. 1000E	4676900	6460100	8740100	12317400	15848500	19851500
	Einwohner	526377	544327	551604	546968	540950	547275
	Schulden/E.	8,885.08	11,868.05	15,844.88	22,519.42	29,297.53	36,273.35
		100.00	133.57	178.33	253.45	329.74	408.25

Quelle: Senator für Finanzen HB, Niedersächsisches Landesamt für Statistik, eig. Berechnungen
Schulden/E. in €

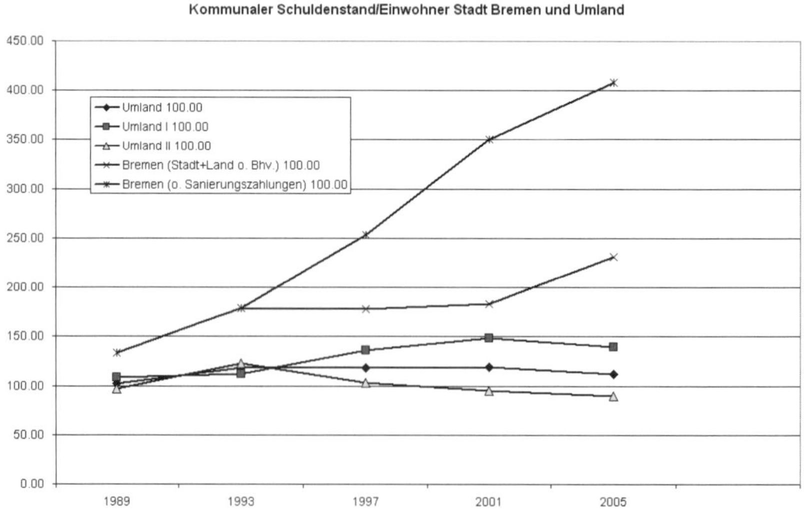

Anlage 2: Kommunaler Schuldenstand/Einwohner Stadt Bremen und Umland

	1985	1989	1993	1997	2001	2005
Umland	100.00	102.35	117.91	118.33	119.17	112.29
Umland I	100.00	108.32	112.01	135.79	148.63	139.58
Umland II	100.00	97.10	122.92	103.53	94.80	89.56
Bremen (Stadt+Land o. Bhv.)	100.00	133.57	178.33	177.70	182.94	231.25
Bremen (o. Sanierungszahlungen)	100.00	133.57	178.33	253.45	350.50	408.25

Quelle: Senator für Finanzen HB, Niedersächsisches Landesamt für Statistik, eig. Berechnungen

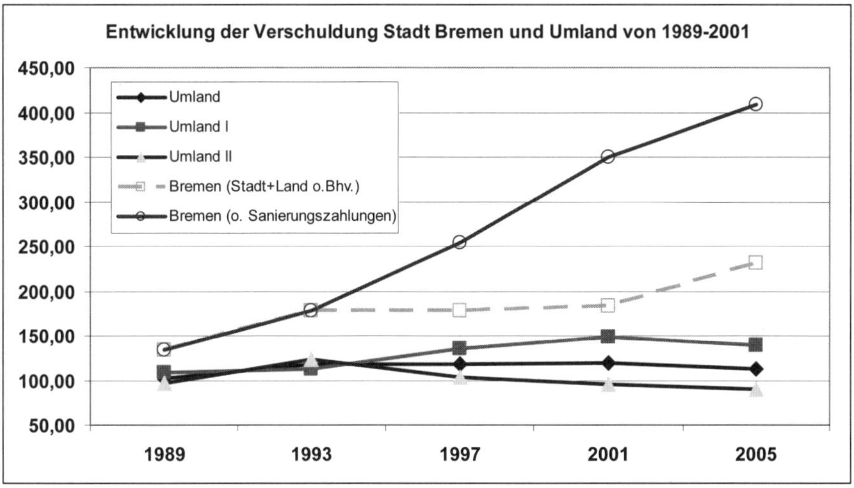

C. Demographischer Wandel in der Wirtschaftsregion München – Perspektiven aus Sicht der Wirtschaft

Robert W. Obermeier

I. Vorbemerkung

Die zu erwartenden Probleme des demographischen Wandels in der Bundesrepublik Deutschland sind in aller Munde. Teilweise wird jedoch mit dem falschen Vokabular gearbeitet. So ist z.B. von der „demographischen Zeitbombe" die Rede. Der vor uns liegende Prozess ähnelt jedoch mehr der Veränderung an einem Gletscher über viele Jahrzehnte hinweg.
Die in den nächsten 20 bis 30 Jahren eintretenden demographischen Veränderungen in Deutschland werden sich auch nachteilig auf die wirtschaftlichen Möglichkeiten auswirken. Die erfolgreiche Wirtschaftsregion München hat dabei den Vorteil, dass die Entwicklungen zunächst nur in abgemilderter Form auftreten werden. Der vorliegende Beitrag versucht aus der Sicht des Praktikers einige wirtschaftliche Konsequenzen für den Raum München aufzuzeigen.

1. Wo steht die Wirtschaftsregion heute?

Die Wirtschaftsregion München hat sich in den vergangenen Jahrzehnten zu einem wissenschaftlich-technischen Zentrum von internationalem Rang entwickelt und gilt heute als Synonym für Wachstum und Wohlstand. Aktuelle Städte- und Regionen-Rankings bescheinigen dem Wirtschaftsraum immer wieder eine Spitzenposition. Die Wirtschaftsregion im engeren Sinne besteht heute aus der Planungsregion München, d.h. aus der Landeshauptstadt München und den acht umliegenden Landkreisen.
Versucht man die Wirtschaftsregion München nach der derzeit gängigen Diskussion um die „Metropolregionen" abzugrenzen, so dürften darüber hinaus auch die Räume Ingolstadt, Rosenheim, Augsburg und Landshut mit zur Wirtschaftsregion zählen.
Der Wirtschaftsstandort München heute ist

- die drittgrößte Stadt Deutschlands,
- der zweitgrößte Beschäftigungsstandort Deutschlands,
- Deutschlands führender Standort der Informations- und Kommunikationstechnologie, der Medienwirtschaft und der Life Sciences und

– laut einer Untersuchung der Zeitschrift „Wirtschaftswoche" auch der heimliche Bankenplatz Nr. 1.

Abb. 1: Region München

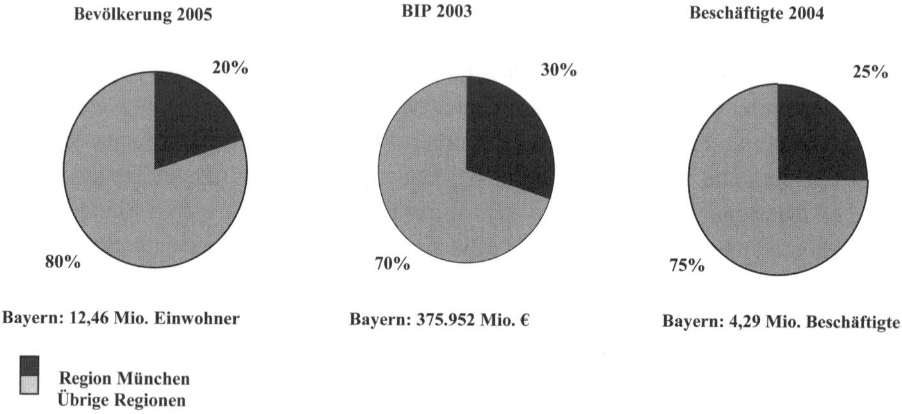

Abb. 2: Anteile der Region München an Bayern

Die Region in der Definition der Planungsregion repräsentiert
- 20% der bayerischen Bevölkerung,
- 30% des bayerischen Bruttoinlandsprodukts und
- 25% der insgesamt in Bayern Beschäftigten.

Im Zeitraum 2000 bis 2005 wies die Region München mit +4,8% ein über dem Landesdurchschnitt (-2,2%) liegendes Bevölkerungswachstum auf.

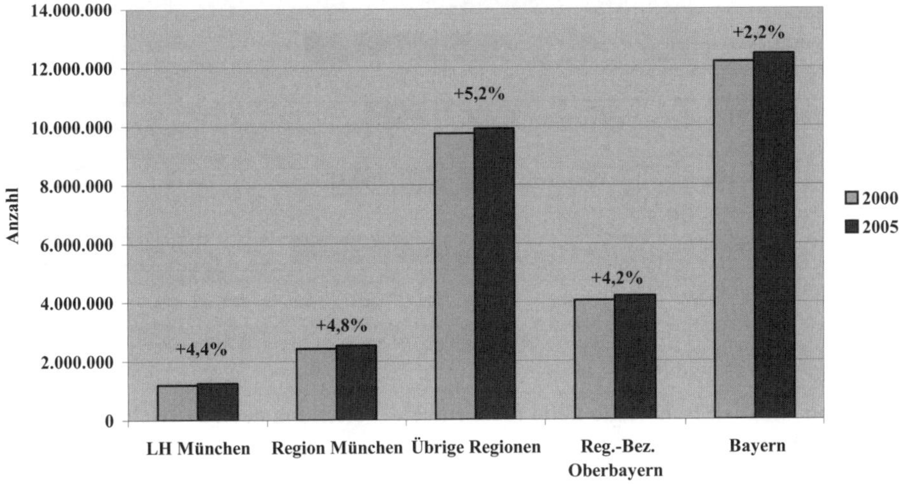

Quelle: Bayerisches Landesamt für Statistik und Datenverarbeitung, Beitragsheft: Regionalisierte Bevölkerungsvorausberechnung für Bayern: Ergebnisse für kreisfreie Städte und Landkreise bis 2023, München 2006

Abb. 3: Bevölkerungsentwicklung 2000/2005

Die Zahl der sozialversicherungspflichtig Beschäftigten im Zeitraum 2000/2004 hat sich in der Region München insgesamt um -0,1% reduziert. Dahinter steckt jedoch ein Beschäftigungszuwachs von 2,7% im Umland der Region und eine Abnahme der Beschäftigtenzahl um -1,8% in der Landeshauptstadt. Das Land Bayern weist im Vergleich dazu einen deutlich höheren Beschäftigungsrückgang auf (-1,7%). Interessant ist die räumliche Verteilung der Beschäftigungsveränderung im Raum München. Während die im Norden, Nordosten und Osten gelegenen Landkreise zum Teil Beschäftigungsgewinne verbuchen konnten, ging die Beschäftigung in den Landkreisen Fürstenfeldbruck und Starnberg – ebenso wie in der Stadt München – zurück. Rund 50% der Beschäftigten in der Region München sind im Sektor „Sonstige Dienstleistungen" tätig, rund 24% im Bereich „Handel, Gastgewerbe und Verkehr" und lediglich nur noch rund 25% im Produzierenden Gewerbe. In Bayern liegt der Anteil der Beschäftigten im Produzierenden Gewerbe mit knapp 38% noch deutlich höher.

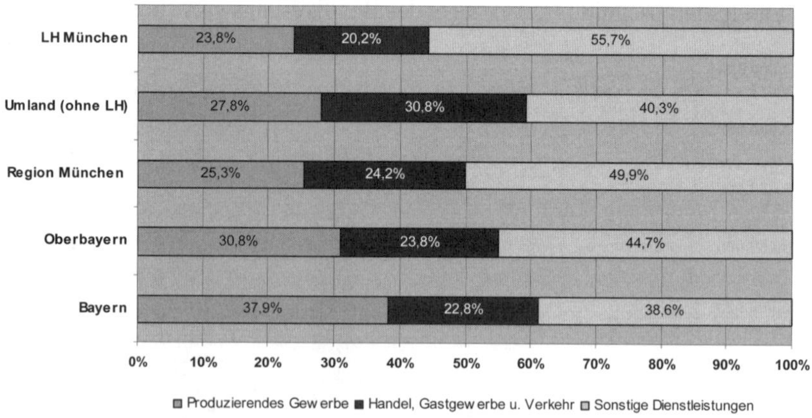

Abb. 4: SV-Beschäftigte 2004 (Prozentuale Verteilung nach Wirtschaftsbereichen)

Für die Wirtschaft im Raum München spielt der Export eine herausragende Rolle. Über 57% der in der Region München produzierten Erzeugnisse werden ins nahe oder entfernte Ausland exportiert. Neben den traditionellen Absatzmärkten in der Europäischen Union haben sich in den vergangenen Jahren gerade Wirtschaftsbeziehungen nach Osteuropa und Russland besonders dynamisch entwickelt. Den Schwerpunkt der Ausfuhren bilden technisch hochwertige Investitionsgüter, wie Fahrzeuge, Maschinen und Erzeugnisse der Elektrotechnik. Aufgrund dieser starken Exportorientierung hat die Wirtschaft auch in den vergangenen Jahren ein vergleichsweise günstigeres Konjunkturbild entwickelt.

Ein weiterer Grund für die relativ wirtschaftliche Stabilität in der Region ist die Tatsache, dass die Chancen neuer Technologien auf breiter Front genutzt werden. Der Raum München verfügt über eine ausgezeichnete Forschungs- und Hochschulinfrastruktur und hat sich zu einem der bedeutendsten Forschungsstandorte in Europa entwickelt. Über 50% aller Firmen des Industriesektors sind in den Hightech-Sektoren Kraftfahrzeugbau, Luft- und Raumfahrt, Elektrotechnik und Maschinenbau angesiedelt. Hinzukommt ein hoch entwickelter und diversifizierter Dienstleistungssektor mit einem bedeutenden globalen Finanzdienstleistungsplatz und der größten Ballung an Versicherungsgesellschaften.

Eine dritte Säule für die wirtschaftliche Stabilität ist der moderne Branchenmix mit Start Up-Firmen und Global Players in allen Industriezweigen. München ist ein Zentrum für Venture Capital in Deutschland mit mehr als 30 entsprechenden Firmen, ein Top-Medienstandort und einem wachsenden neuen Cluster für Biotechnologiefirmen. Schließlich verfügt der Raum über einen leistungsfähigen Arbeitsmarkt. Die Arbeitslosenquote ist im deutschen Vergleich sehr niedrig, die Akademikerquote ist in keiner Region Deutschlands so hoch wie im südlichen Bayern. Auch die Qualifikation der Fachkräfte gilt als Standortvorteil schlechthin. Durch gezielte Investitionen in die Aus- und Fortbildung wird ein unverzichtbarer Wettbewerbsvorteil geschaffen.

II. Wie sehen die wesentlichen demographischen Trends aus?

Der demographische Wandel in der Bundesrepublik Deutschland findet schon seit langem statt. Dieser Prozess verläuft jedoch nicht nur in Deutschland, sondern läuft global und langfristig ab. In Europa begann er bereits in der zweiten Hälfte des 19. Jahrhunderts und wird im Verlauf des aktuellen Jahrhunderts alle Länder dieser Welt im unterschiedlichen Ausmaß betreffen. Die diskutierten Effekte setzen sich aus zwei Komponenten zusammen:

- aus dem Absinken der Geburtenrate in den siebziger Jahren des vergangenen Jahrhunderts und
- in einer steigenden Lebenserwartung der Bevölkerung.

Wenn die Geburtenhäufigkeit unter das Ersatzniveau der älteren Generation fällt, fängt der Alterungsprozess einer Gesellschaft an. Im heutigen Altersaufbau der Bevölkerung ist das Altern auch ohne die zukünftig zu erwartende Geburtenhäufigkeit und hohe Lebenserwartung aufgrund unserer demographischen Vergangenheit bereits vorherbestimmt.

Die Familienplanung beginnt in Deutschland immer später. Bei der Geburt des ersten Kindes nähert sich das Durchschnittsalter dem 30. Lebensjahr an. Damit haben sich die Altersmuster bei der Erstheirat und der Geburt der Kinder komplett gewandelt. Noch in den siebziger Jahren des vergangenen Jahrhunderts erfolgten die Familiengründungen etwa fünf Jahre früher.

Hinzukommt ein stetiger Anstieg der Lebenserwartung bei der Geburt seit Beginn der siebziger Jahre in den alten Bundesländern und auch eine beständige Zunahme in den neuen Bundesländern seit Beginn der neunziger Jahre. Bei Männern ist die Lebenserwartung in den vergangenen 35 Jahren von 67,6 auf 75,1 Jahre gestiegen, bei den Frauen von 73,5 auf 80,9 (alte Bundesländer).

Als Fazit der bundesweiten Entwicklung lässt sich festhalten, dass sich der Alterungsprozess unserer Gesellschaft nicht aufhalten lässt. Niedrige Geburtenhäufigkeit, hohe Lebenserwartung haben unauslöschbare Spuren hinterlassen. Ein Wiederanstieg der Kinderzahl erscheint eher unwahrscheinlich – dieser müsste ohnehin langfristig stabil sein, um zu Effekten zu führen. Auch Zuwanderung ist keine Alternative. Wenn sie wirksam wäre, würde sie zu einer Verstädterung des Landes führen. Der Alterungsprozess kann zwar verlangsamt, aber nicht zum Stillstand gebracht werden. Die Politik muss Antworten finden, um die entsprechenden Probleme in den sozialen Sicherungssystemen zu lösen und sie muss Änderungen in der Bildungs-, Familien- und Zuwanderungspolitik formulieren.

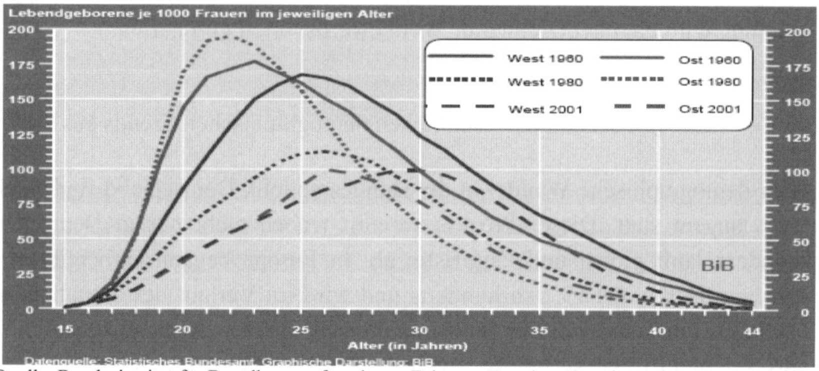

Quelle: Bundesinstitut für Bevölkerungsforschung, Fakten – Trends – Ursachen – Erwartungen – Die wichtigsten Fragen, Wiesbaden 2004, S. 30

Abb. 5: Altersspezifische Geburtenziffern 1960-2001

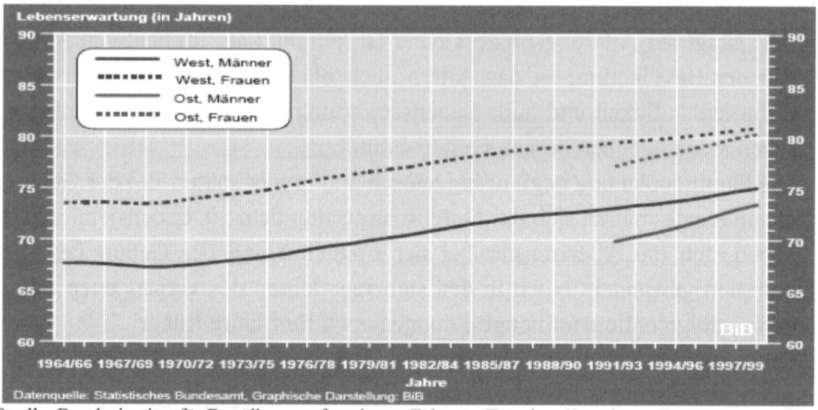

Quelle: Bundesinstitut für Bevölkerungsforschung, Fakten – Trends – Ursachen – Erwartungen – Die wichtigsten Fragen, Wiesbaden 2004, S. 41

Abb. 6: Lebenserwartung bei der Geburt 1964-1998

Die bundesweiten Bevölkerungsprognosen bis 2050 variieren von einem Absinken der Bevölkerung auf knapp über 80 Mio. bis zu einem deutlichen Absinken auf etwa 67 Mio. Einwohnern. Dabei wird stets die gleiche Geburtenrate (1,4) unterstellt, variabel sind die Parameter „Lebenserwartung" und „Zuwanderungssaldo". Bei der Zuwanderung schwanken die Prognosen zwischen einer jährlichen Zuwanderung von 100.000 bis 300.000 Personen.

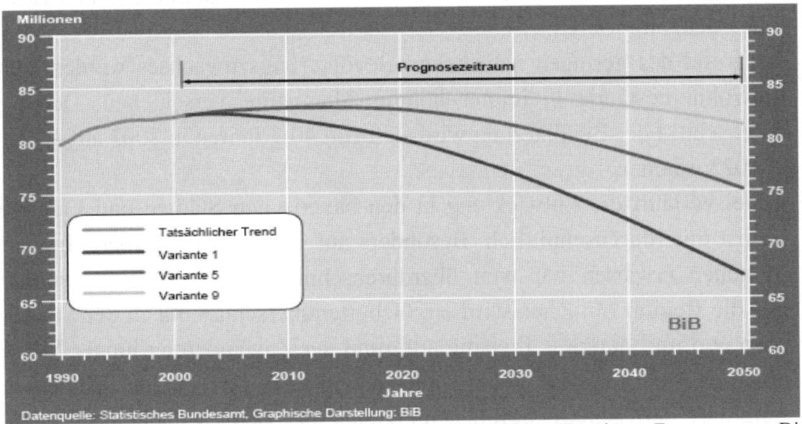

Quelle: Bundesinstitut für Bevölkerungsforschung, Fakten – Trends – Ursachen – Erwartungen – Die wichtigsten Fragen, Wiesbaden 2004, S. 63

Abb. 7: Bevölkerungsprognosen bis 2050

Die ökonomischen sozialen Auswirkungen des Alterns lassen sich wie folgt zusammenfassen:

- Die Arbeitskräfte werden knapper und älter. Dies muss zu einer Weiterbeschäftigung oder Wiedereingliederung älterer Arbeitnehmer führen und gleichzeitig zu einer stärkeren Erwerbsbeteiligung von Frauen.
- Ebenfalls sind rückläufige Schülerzahlen und Alterung der Lehrer zu erwarten. Mittelfristig besteht ein Bedarf an der zusätzlichen Einstellung von Lehrern.
- Auch die Siedlungsstruktur dürfte von den flächendeckenden Auswirkungen nicht unberührt bleiben; wahrscheinlich sind insbesondere sogenannte Ruhesitzwanderungen.
- In den Bereichen Gesundheit und Pflege dürften wirtschaftlich bedeutende Wirkungen auftreten.
- Die Sicherung der Rentenansprüche ist ebenfalls eine Gestaltungsaufgabe für die Politik.

III. Welche Auswirkungen erwartet der Wirtschaftsraum?

Die vom Bayerischen Landesamt für Statistik und Datenverarbeitung im vergangenen Jahr veröffentlichten regionalisierten Bevölkerungsvorausberechnungen für Bayern bis 2023 machen deutlich, dass die Zahl der Bürger in

Bayern stark von der Zahl der Zuwanderer abhängt. Die Zahl der Gestorbenen übersteigt in fast allen Landkreisen die Zahl der Geborenen. Damit würde die natürliche Bevölkerungsbewegung allein zu einem kontinuierlichen Bevölkerungsrückgang führen.
Aufgrund des geringen natürlichen Bevölkerungszuwachses werden sich die Einwohnerbestände in immer höhere Altersjahre verschieben. Der Altersdurchschnitt der Bevölkerung wird sich von 40,7 Jahren in 2003 auf 44,1 Jahre in 2023 erhöhen.
Dabei verläuft die Entwicklung in den bayerischen Städten und Landkreisen höchst unterdurchschnittlich. Besonders auf der Achse Nürnberg–Ingolstadt–München erwarten wir weit überdurchschnittliche Bevölkerungszunahmen. Für die Region München wird ein Geburtenüberschuss nur in der Stadt München und im Landkreis Freising aufgrund der Zuwanderung junger Menschen erwartet. Den höchsten Wanderungsgewinn in Bayern aus der Binnenwanderung wird der Landkreis München erzielen. Die Stadt München hingegen profitiert insbesondere von der Außenwanderung.

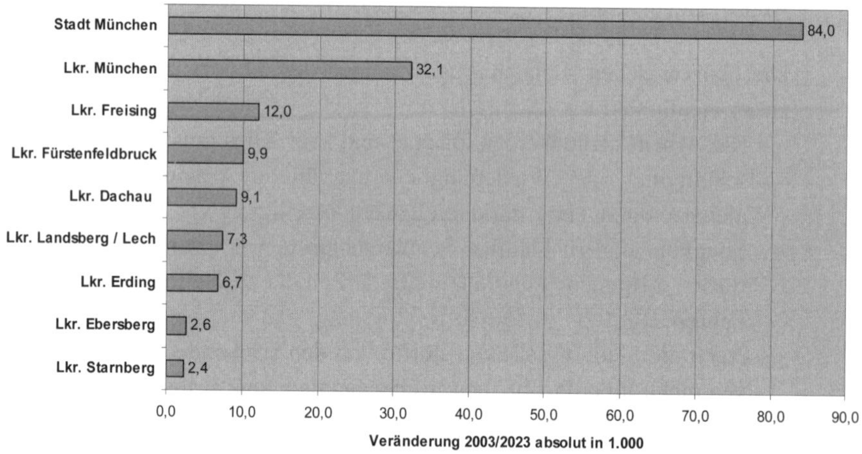

Quelle: Bayerisches Landesamt für Statistik und Datenverarbeitung, Beitragsheft: Regionalisierte Bevölkerungsvorausberechnung für Bayern: Ergebnisse für kreisfreie Städte und Landkreise bis 2023, München 2006

Abb. 8: Bevölkerungsveränderung absolut 2003/2023 Variante 4b1

Nach der von den Gutachtern als wahrscheinlichster Fall berechneten Variante 4b1 wird die Bevölkerung in der Stadt München im Zeitraum 2003/2023 um 84.000 Einwohner zunehmen. Im Landkreis München beträgt der Zuwachs 32.000 Einwohner, im Landkreis Freising 12.000. Den niedrigsten Zuwachs erwartet der Landkreis Starnberg mit 2.400 Einwohnern.

Nach einer Bevölkerungsprognose der Bertelsmann-Stiftung steht auch ebenfalls die Stadt München (im Zeitraum 2003/2020) mit einem Zuwachs von 97.000 Personen an der Spitze, gefolgt vom Landkreis Landsberg am Lech mit 30.000 und dem Landkreis München mit knapp 19.000 Einwohnern (Esche u.a. 2006). Prozentual betrachtet hat damit die Stadt München ein Bevölkerungswachstum von mehr als 10% zu erwarten, bei den meisten Landkreisen in der Region sind es zwischen 5% und 7%. In der optimistischeren Variante 5a1 beträgt der Zuwachs hingegen für die Stadt 15,5% und die meisten Landkreise zwischen 8% und 12%.

Gespeist wird die Bevölkerungszunahme insbesondere von den Zuwanderungen: Sie beträgt in der Variante 4b1 für die Stadt München knapp 79.000 Personen, für den Landkreis München knapp 48.000 Personen. Hier ist zu bemerken, dass der Landkreis München mit -13.000 Personen den höchsten negativen Geburtensaldo haben wird.

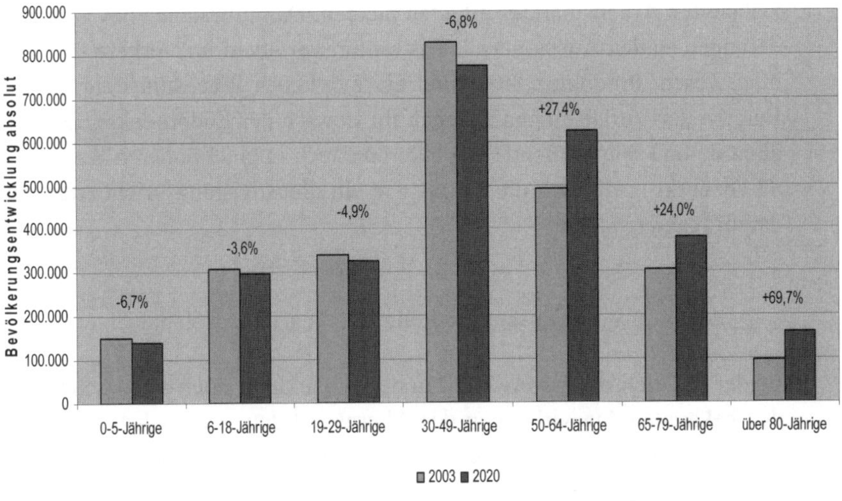

Quelle: Esche u.a. 2006

Abb. 9: Entwicklung der Altersstruktur 2003/2020 München – Variante Bertelsmann Stiftung

Besonderes interessant ist der Vergleich der Entwicklung der Altersstruktur zwischen 2003 und 2020 in der Region München mit Gesamtbayern. Aus den Berechnungen der Bertelsmann-Stiftung wird deutlich, dass die Veränderungen der Bevölkerung im erwerbsfähigen Alter im bayerischen Durchschnitt wesentlich dramatischer ausfallen werden als in der Region München. So beträgt z.B. der Rückgang bei 30- bis 49-Jährigen bayernweit knapp 17%, in

München sind es nur knapp 7%. Die Gruppe der 50- bis 64-Jährigen steigt in Bayern um 35%, in der Region München hingegen nur um 27%.

IV. Welche ökonomischen Konsequenzen erwarten wir?

Aus den Ergebnissen in Kapitel 3 wird deutlich, dass sich das Thema „Bevölkerungsrückgang" für die Region München noch nicht stellt. Vielmehr ist bis ca. 2020 für die Region sogar zuwanderungsbedingt mit einer Bevölkerungszunahme zu rechnen. Damit besteht für die Region eine einmalige Situation, nämlich ein Zeitgewinn, um jetzt schon Strategien zur Bewältigung des Wandels zu entwickeln.

Wichtigste Maßnahme muss eine Anpassung der Produkte und Produktionsfaktoren an die ablaufenden Prozesse sein. Die Bereitstellung eines quantitativ wie qualitativ ausreichenden Arbeitsangebots ist die conditio sine qua non für die Region. In räumlicher Hinsicht müssen die Bedingungen eines großen spezialisierten Arbeitsmarktes erhalten bleiben. Damit bestehen besondere Anforderungen an den Ausbau der Infrastruktur, vor allem im Verkehr und im Siedlungswesen. Produkte „50+" sind ein mögliches Wachstumsfeld, sowohl im Bereich der Vorleistungen als auch im Bereich der Endprodukte. Da sich eine alternde und schrumpfende Bevölkerung auch in einer höheren Kapitalintensität auswirkt, stellt sich die Frage, wie ein dienstleistungsorientierter Standort darauf reagieren kann.

V. Was sagt die Raumordnung/Landesplanung?

Leider hat sich die bayerische Landesentwicklung noch nicht sehr detailliert den bekannten Auswirkungen des Alterns auf den bayerischen Raum befasst. Im neuen Entwurf des Landesentwicklungsprogramms finden sich hierzu nur wenige Aussagen, so z.B.:

- im Ziel A I 2 (G), in dem eine räumlich ausgewogene Bevölkerungsentwicklung des Landes und seiner Teilräume angestrebt wird oder
- im Ziel A I 3.1.2 (G), wo Missverhältnissen bei Entwicklung der Bevölkerungs- und Arbeitsplatzstrukturen (in den Verdichtungsräumen) entgegengewirkt werden soll oder
- im Ziel A I 4.1.2 (Z), wo das Vorhalteprinzip der Infrastruktureinrichtungen im Ländlichen Raum unter Beachtung der Bevölkerungsentwicklung und Altersstruktur gefordert wird.

In der Begründung zum Ziel A I 2.2 wird immerhin ausgeführt, dass Verschiebungen in der Alterspyramide unmittelbar bevorstehen, mit erheblichen

Auswirkungen auf die Infrastrukturen. Die Fachverwaltungen in den Bereichen Bildung, Kultur, Soziales, Gesundheit, Verkehr usw. sollen entsprechende Gewichtungen in ihren Planungen vornehmen, um die negativen Folgen auszugleichen.
Für die Metropolregion München gibt es – wenn überhaupt – nur ganz allgemeine Aussagen zum Thema „Demographischer Wandel".

VI. Handlungsmöglichkeiten aus Sicht der Wirtschaft

Die wichtigste Maßnahme aus Sicht der Wirtschaft stellt die Integration älterer Arbeitnehmer in den Arbeitsmarkt dar. In Deutschland sind weniger als 40% der älteren Erwerbspersonen zwischen 55 und 64 Jahren beschäftigt. In Schweden und Norwegen sind es jeweils 69%, in der Schweiz 66%. Hinzu kommt, dass fast 25% der registrierten Arbeitslosen, damit rund 1,3 Mio. Personen, älter als 50 Jahre sind. Die Auswirkungen dieser Situation sind bekannt:

- Die sozialen Sicherungssysteme werden überlastet und
- für die Volkswirtschaft droht ein Verlust von wichtigem Know-how.

Die Integration älterer Arbeitnehmer in den Arbeitsmarkt ist daher ein Schwerpunktthema 2006 der IHK-Organisation. Die IHK für München und Oberbayern ist hier auf drei Handlungsfeldern aktiv. Zum einen informieren wir unsere Mitgliedsunternehmen über die Potenziale von älteren Arbeitnehmern, zum anderen versuchen wir Einflussnahme auf die wirtschaftspolitischen Rahmenbedingungen zu nehmen, d.h. wir wenden uns z.B. gegen alle Frühverrentungsansätze usw. Schließlich besteht das Ziel, die IHK-Weiterbildungsangebote speziell für diesen Personenkreis auszubauen.
Eine weitere Strategie besteht in der Erhöhung der Frauenerwerbsbeschäftigung. 70% der Frauen ohne Beschäftigung und mit Kindern unter 12 Jahren würden gerne arbeiten. Hinzu kommt, dass Frauen mittlerweile genauso gut ausgebildet sind wie Männer. Die Voraussetzung für die Umsetzung dieser Bedarfe ist jedoch eine bessere Vereinbarkeit von Familie und Beruf. Dies bezieht sich zum einen auf ein bedarfsgerechtes Kinderbetreuungsangebot für Kinder ab 0 Jahren und zum anderen auf familienfreundliche Arbeitsbedingungen in den Unternehmen.
Die IHK initiiert z.Z. ein „Münchner Bündnis für Familien", da wegen der hohen Mieten und Lebenshaltungskosten und einem vielfach kinderunfreundlichen Umfeld die Kinderbetreuung in München nicht bedarfsdeckend ist. Die Bündnisidee besteht darin, Vertreter der Stadt München, Unternehmen, Kirchen und andere gesellschaftliche Akteure zusammenzuführen und sich ge-

meinsam für familienfreundlichere Lebens- und Arbeitsbedingungen einzusetzen.

Für die Wirtschaft gibt es hier ganz konkrete Handlungsfelder:

- Der Ausbau der betriebsnahen Kinderbetreuung,
- eine familienorientierte Personalpolitik,
- ein stadtteilbezogenes Engagement der Unternehmen und
- die Verbesserung des Kontakts zwischen Schule und Wirtschaft.

Als weitere Strategie müssen die Felder „Wohnungspolitik“, „Regional- und Flächenentwicklung“ angegangen werden. Für München ist zu erwarten, dass die Zahl der Haushalte steigen wird, da die Zahl der kleinen Haushalte wächst: In München gibt es künftig mehr Rentner, mehr Singles und weniger Familien mit Kindern. Die Verlagerung der Familien mit Kindern in die Region wird anhalten. Außerdem ist von einem weiter wachsenden Wohnflächenbedarf pro Kopf auszugehen. Damit ist durch den demographischen Wandel keine Entspannung auf dem Münchner Wohnungsmarkt zu erwarten: Die Schere bei den verschiedenen Marktsegmenten wird sich weiter öffnen.

VII. Abschließende Thesen

Die Entwicklung in der Wirtschaftsregion München soll anhand von drei abschließenden Thesen nochmals skizziert werden:

These 1:

Die Wirtschaft in der Region München ist ein sehr servoindustrieller Komplex, d.h. Produktion mit hohem Technologieerhalt wird von wissensbasierten Dienstleistungen flankiert. Sie bilden auch weiterhin das ökonomische Rückgrat der Region. Eine reine Dienstleistungsorientierung ist aufgrund der vorhandenen Spezialisierung nicht zielführend und würde auch aufgrund der zu erwartenden Kapitalintensität (Demographie) zu Problemen führen.

These 2:

Für die nicht produktionsorientierten Dienstleistungen bestehen in der Region München – neben den vorhandenen Produktionsclustern – noch Entwicklungspotenziale.

These 3:

Die drei wichtigsten Themen für München beziehen sich auf den Produktionsfaktor „Arbeit“:

- Ältere Arbeitnehmer
- Familie und Beruf
- Qualifikation

Insbesondere für die Aufrechterhaltung der älteren Arbeitnehmer besteht künftig ein Marktpotenzial.

Literaturverzeichnis:

Bayerische Staatsregierung, Landesentwicklungsprogramm Bayern, Entwurf vom 12. Juli 2005.

Bayerisches Landesamt für Statistik und Datenverarbeitung, Beitragsheft: Regionalisierte Bevölkerungsvorausberechnung für Bayern: Ergebnisse für kreisfreie Städte und Landkreise bis 2023, München 2006.

Bundesinstitut für Bevölkerungsforschung, Fakten – Trends – Ursachen – Erwartungen – Die wichtigsten Fragen, Wiesbaden 2004.

Esche, A., C. G. Starmann und *K. Schmidt* (Hrsg.), Wegweiser Demographischer Wandel 2020, Analysen und Handlungskonzepte für Städte und Gemeinden, 2006.

D. The Dynamics and Territorial Distribution of Human Resources and Infrastructure-Related Issues in Romania

Zizi Goschin, Daniela L. Constantin und *Cornelia Parlog*

I. Introduction

The evolution of a country's human potential is closely related to the general economic development level, the volume and the quality of social services and the demographic policy co-ordinates. Human resources are a basic factor of any economic development strategy and subject of important influences coming from the economic and social environment and corresponding infrastructure the same time.

In the last 16 years Romania's population has recorded a downwards dynamics, strongly correlated with the general economic decline for many years since 1990. The main causes refer to the production decrease (especially the industrial one) as a result of the internal market tightening and the losing of important segments of the external market, failures in macro stabilization and privatization delays, low investment level (including foreign direct investment), low occupational mobility of labor force, constraints generated by the international situation.

At the same time the population decrease has been influenced by the new legislation regarding the birth regime (abortion liberalization) and the major increase in out-migration flows (especially in 1990-1992 period) as well.

The overall economic decline has been reflected by the weak endowment and bad state of infrastructure in all its components: transportation, communications, energy supply, water supply, environment, health, education, urban amenities, sports and tourist facilities, social and cultural amenities. There are not only significant territorial disparities in this respect but also a much lower national level compared to the European average. Many difficulties can be still noticed with regard to economic infrastructure modernization – at both sectorial and regional level, as well as the improvement of social services quality.

This paper proposes an analysis of the demographic potential and human resources dynamics in Romania since 1990 in relation with the economic and social infrastructure evolution at both national and regional level. Possible influences of infrastructure state upon population dynamics will be also envisaged.

The analysis begins with a brief characterization of the general economic and social situation and population dynamics at national level, followed by an insight into specific evolutions of regional structures. Then, synthetic indices for human resources and infrastructure calculated by means of a specific methodology highlight the regional hierarchies established over time and also serve for measuring the correlation between human resources and infrastructure dynamics at regional level. They can be further employed in order to conceive and implement regional policies differentiated in accordance with each region's position in the national context.

II. Brief characterization of the General Economic Situation and Human Resources Dynamics in Romania Since 1990

Romania's transition to the market economy determined a long and painful process of transforming the economic mechanisms in accordance with the new economic and social principles. The overall economic decline during the 90's has had an important negative impact on both demographic potential and employment, the relative decrease in employment exceeding the decrease in GDP. All these phenomena are reflected by the evolution of the key performance indicators between 1990 and 2004 (Tab. 1).

Year	GDP Change (compared to the previous year) (%)	Population (million people)	Employment dynamics (%)	Unemployment rate (%)	Inflation rate (%)
1990	-5.6	23.2	100.0	0.4	5.1
1991	-12.9	22.8	99.5	3.0	170.2
1992	-8.8	22.7	96.5	8.2	210.4
1993	1.5	22.6	92.8	10.4	256.1
1994	3.9	22.6	92.3	10.9	136.8
1995	7.1	22.6	87.5	9.5	32.3
1996	4.0	22.6	86.7	6.6	38.8
1997	-6.1	22.5	83.2	8.9	151.4
1998	-4.8	22.5	81.5	10.4	40.6
1999	-1.2	22.4	77.7	11.8	45.8
2000	1.6	21.7	79.6	10.5	45.7
2001	5.7	21.8	78.97	8.8	34.5
2002	5.1	21.8	85.1	8.4	22.5
2003	5.2	21.8	85.1	7.4	15.3
2004	8.4	21.7	84.5	6.3	9.5

Source: Calculation using data from Statistical Yearbook of Romania, 1999-2005

Tab. 1: Key Economic Performance Indicators in Romania between 1990 and 2004

Four sub-periods can be identified, namely: 1990-1992 (the beginning of transition), when the GDP recorded a serious drop; 1993-1996, when a macro stabilization programme was applied, with positive consequences upon economic growth, unemployment and inflation rate; 1997-2000, when the economic decline (until 1999) represented the first result of the massive restructuring and privatization process (too much delayed in Romania) undertaken in this period, being followed by a slow recovery in the first few years after 2000 and a more important one at present (Mitrut, Constantin 2006, p. 3).

Within this general context the evolution of population and labor resources expresses a variety of demographic and social-economic conditions and causes, closely interrelated. The demographic changes mainly refer to: accelerated fertility decrease, high level of mortality, important increase in out-migration, high share of the aged population (60 years and over), high level of demographic dependency ratio, particularly in rural areas. The social-economic causes concentrate on the decrease in the standard of living and quality of medical services, etc. (Constantin et al. 2005, p. 42).

As a result of the negative natural increase as well as negative net external migration Romania's population diminished by 1.5 million people between 1990 and 2004. During this period the fertility rate dropped from 56.2 live births per 1000 women between 15-49 years of age in 1990 to 38.4‰ in 2004 whereas the death rate raised from 10.6 per 1000 inhabitants in 1990 to 11.9‰ in 2004.

Between 1990 and 2004 total employment diminished by 1.6 million people (from 10.8 to 9.2 million people). As regards unemployment – very low and hidden before 1990 – it recorded significant levels starting with 1990. Despite some oscillatory variations it displays an upward trend in long run. Thus, in the first phase (1991-1994) it grew continuously, reaching the highest level in March 1994 (11.2%), as a result of the serious economic decline (mainly in industry). The short term recovery thereafter entailed a decrease in the unemployment rate between 1995 and 1996. Since 1997, when the massive restructuring (especially in mining industry and manufacturing) began, at the same time with applying permissive laying off regulations, unemployment re-started to grow until the year 2000 (the beginning of a new economic growth phase).

These evolutions are specifically reflected by the activity rate (active population/ total population): between 1990 and 1997 it raised from 47.2% to 52.2%, then diminished continuously until 2004 (45.9%).

There are also important differences between regions, as described in the next section.

III. Regional Differences in Human Resources and Their Use

For grasping the facts revealed by the data that are to be analyzed below, it should be mentioned that Romania's administrative-territorial structure comprises one regional level – the counties, named "judete", corresponding to

NUTS3 level of the EUROSTAT (there are 41 counties plus Bucharest municipality) and one local level (cities, towns, communes). Also, according to the Regional Development Act 151/1998 eight development regions, corresponding to NUTS2 level have been established on a voluntary basis (without being administrative units) in order to ensure the regional development policy elaboration and implementation framework. Each region comprises between 4 and 7 counties (excepting Bucharest-Ilfov region), as presented in Annex 3 (this regional structure is maintained in the new Regional Development Act, No. 315/2004).

The key aspects of current regional disparities refer to the major imbalance between Bucuresti-Ilfov region and the other regions, an important imbalance between East (lagging behind) and West (well developed) of Romania, the severe underdevelopment of North-East (at the border with the Republic of Moldova) and South (alongside of Danube river), intra-regional imbalances more important than the interregional ones (big variations between counties within the same region), the economic decline recorder by small and medium sized towns, severe negative impact of economic restructuring upon mono-industrial areas (Constantin 2006, p. 11).

As regards the human potential, it has **an uneven territorial distribution**. Thus, the North-East region (including Bacau, Botosani, Iasi, Neamt, Suceava and Vaslui county) has the biggest population and the negative natural growth is a relatively recent phenomenon, whereas the West region (including Arad, Caras-Severin, Hunedoara and Timis county) is characterized by a low number of population and a chronicle negative natural growth.

Significant differences in labor aged population number and dynamics can be noticed not only between regions but also between counties. The highest level of labor resources is recorded in Iasi, Prahova, Constanta, Cluj, Timis, Suceava, Bacau and Dolj county and the lowest in Salaj, Covasna, Tulcea, Ilfov, Ialomita, Giurgiu, Calarasi, Mehedinti and Bistrita-Nasaud county; in general, there is a positive correlation between the economic development level and the level of labor resources.

In almost all regions labor resources are predominant in urban areas excepting for North-East and South region, which include some of the poorest counties. North-East, South-West and South also record the highest level of the dependency ratio (number of labor aged persons per 1000 persons out of labor age).

In the first ten years transition determined a generalized diminishing of the use of human capital (the relative decrease in employment was greater than the rate of GDP decrease), significantly differentiated by regional economic structure.

The rate of employment decrease was above the national average in both longstanding industrial traditional zones (e.g. Banat, Transilvania) and zones of industrial structures created in the centralized economy period (Oltenia, Moldova).

In other zones, such as Muntenia, Dobrogea and Lower Danube the rate of employment decrease was slower than the average owing to a compensating flow of employment increase in agriculture (more intense than in other zones) on the one hand and the investment attraction exerted by the two big urban areas that dominate these zones, namely Bucharest and Constanta. They have complex, diversified economic structures, with relatively well developed infrastructure and large business opportunities, enabling then to adjust with good results to changing economic circumstances.

In 2004 the unemployment rate was above the national average of 6.3% in counties like Vaslui (11%) in North-East region and Hunedoara (10.8%) – a monoindustrial county in West region. The lowest unemployment rates were recorded by Satu Mare (2%) and Bihor (2.1%), both of them belonging to North-West region. The territorial distribution of unemployment reflects a tendency of concentration in monoindustrial, poor zones, with an important number of active population at the same time.

An overall image of the interregional imbalances is offered by Table 2, which depicts the regions' ranking at national level taking into consideration some of the main economic and social indicators.

Region	GDP per capita	Employment rate	Share of employment in agriculture in total employment	Average net nominal monthly earnings
North-East	8	1	1	8
South-East	5	7	4	4
South	7	4	3	5
South-West	6	2	2	2
West	2	5	6	3
North-West	4	6	5	6
Centre	3	8	7	7
Bucharest-Ilfov	1	3	8	1

Source: Authors' calculations based on data from Statistical Yearbook of Romania, 2005
Note: In the ranking above 1 represents the highest value of the corresponding indicator.

Tab. 2: Regional Hierarchy by Main Economic and Social Indicator in 2004

Interregional economic and social differences are closely related to labor force migration phenomenon. Over the centralized economy years was recorded a long-term tendency of migration towards industrialized or industrializing zones, whereas the industrial activity decline in the 90's gradually reduced this process.

In the first few years after 1989 the urban-rural migration flows became predominant. These flows contributed in reducing unemployment rate in the origin zones and its increase in the destination ones (Constantin et. al. 2003, p. 12).

Territorial imbalances might deeper in the future as a result of the action of market-based mechanisms. Other countries experience proves the higher investment attractiveness of the developed regions, of long industrial traditions and good infrastructure compared to the disadvantaged zones, with reducing development perspectives. In this context the next section concentrates on a synthetic evaluation of the relationship between human resources and infrastructure on Romania's territory.

IV. The Correlation Between Human Resources and Infrastructure at Regional Level

1. Methodology

In order to highlight the territorial relations between human resources and infrastructure and to quantify their intensity a complex sequence of steps has been followed, as described below.

The first step consisted in **the identification of potential indicators** considered to be important for the two fields of interest envisaged, namely human resources and infrastructure. Based on relevant criteria and data availability at regional level the following indicators have been selected:

- indicators relevant for **human resources**: population, natural increase rate, unemployment rate;
- indicators relevant for **infrastructure**: public roads length, railroads length, the length of sewage pipes, number of phone subscriptions, number of volumes in public libraries, number of hospital beds.

The second step involved the **computation of some derived indicators** aiming to ensure a higher level of interregional comparability. Considering the significant differences of surface and population between the 8 development regions in Romania, we considered necessary the transformation of some of the previous indicators with reference to the surface or to the population of the region. Therefore, the population, the length of public roads and that of railroads, as well as the length of sewage pipes have been divided by the surface, while the number of hospital beds, number of volumes in public libraries and the number of phone subscriptions have been divided by the population (the list of final indicators and their values by region is presented in Annexes 1 and 2).

The third step was the **standardization of primary data.** The primary indicators are expressed in different measuring unit (for instance percentage, values per 100 km or per 1000 persons) that does not allow their comparison or direct aggregation. The method used to find a common measuring unit for the primary indicators was the method of minimum-maximum standardization, applied differently according to the type of the indicator as follows:

- in the case of indicators expressing a situation where the more favorable the greater values (such as the number of volumes in the library/100 inhabitants, density of public roads/1000 inhabitants and so on) – the standardized value (comprised between 0 and 1) of each primary indicator is determined by the formula:

$$y_{ij} = \frac{x_{ij} - \min(x_j)}{\max(x_j) - \min(x_j)}, \text{ where:}$$

y_{ij} – the standardized value of the indicator j for region i; i = $\overline{1,8}$, j = $\overline{1,9}$

x_{ij} - primary value of indicator j for region i

– for the indicators expressing a situation where the better the smaller values (for example the unemployment rate) the following formula was applied:

$$y_{ij} = \frac{\max(x_j) - x_{ij}}{\max(x_j) - \min(x_j)}.$$

This method ensures a unitary evaluation, independent of the nature of partial indicators and their real measuring units. The maximum territorial performance for a certain indicator will receive value 1, while the region with the worst result will record the standardized value 0.

The fourth step of the analysis was **the integration of potential indicators** (their standardized values) in a general index of human resources (IHR) and a general index of the infrastructure (IIS). It is much easier to analyze the variation of a synthetic indicator than to look for common tendencies of evolution of the partial indicators. The synthetic indicators are useful for establishing the hierarchy of the regions, for emphasizing the disparities and for measuring the intensity of the correlation between the human resources and infrastructure.

The computation of the two synthetic indices (IHR, IIS) was performed at the level of each region i. The standardized values of the indicators are comprised in each index by means of the simple arithmetic mean:

$$\text{IHR}_i = \left(\sum_{j-1}^{3} y_{ij}\right)/3$$

$$\text{IIS}i = \left(\sum_{j=1}^{6} y_{ij}\right)/6, \quad \text{i} = \overline{1,8}$$

The last step consisted in the determination of **the correlation coefficient** between human resources and infrastructure, using the following mathematic expression:

$$R_{IS/HR} = \frac{8\sum_{i=1}^{8} IHR_i \cdot IIS_i - \sum_{i=1}^{8} IHR_i \cdot \sum_{i=1}^{8} IIS_i}{\sqrt{\left[8\sum_{i=1}^{8} IHR_i^2 - \left(\sum_{i=1}^{8} IHR_i\right)^2\right] \cdot \left[8\sum_{i=1}^{8} IIS_i^2 - \left(\sum_{i=1}^{8} IIS_i\right)^2\right]}}$$

2. Results

The above mentioned method was applied for the 8 Romanian development regions, for years 1995, 2000 and 2004. The results are presented in Table 3.

Region	**1995**		**2000**		**2004**	
	IHR	**IIS**	**IHR**	**IIS**	**IHR**	**IIS**
North-East	0.3436	0.2177	0.3445	0.1673	0.3452	0.1392
South-East	0.3961	0.1628	0.241	0.0789	0.1976	0.0683
South	0.2664	0.0841	0.1841	0.0798	0.0772	0.0748
South-West	0.2370	0.0216	0.1368	0.0893	0.0254	0.1028
West	0.2667	0.2798	0.138	0.2062	0.1733	0.2174
North-West	0.3033	0.2721	0.3243	0.2419	0.3806	0.2207
Centre	0.3301	0.2408	0.313	0.1934	0.2307	0.1743
Bucharest-Ilfov	0.6667	1	0.6667	1	0.8133	1

Tab. 3: Synthetic Indices of Human Resources (IHR) and Infrastructure (IIS)

According to the values indicated by the coefficient of correlation, the intensity of the relations between human resources and infrastructure is very strong: 0.927 in year 1995, 0.905 in 2000 and 0.91 in 2004. The relations tend to deepen over time.

There are considerable differences between the hierarchy of the regions according to the human resources and the hierarchy drawn up from the perspective of the infrastructure: even though the human resources have proven to be the determinant factor with respect to the territorial variations of the infrastructure, there are numerous other important factors of influence such as: the variations in economic development and geographical location, the entrepreneurial culture, the community education and culture.

As far as the territorial hierarchy is concerned, Bucharest-Ilfov region has a strong dominance, in all the years with respect to both human resources and infrastructure.

The territorial disparities are significant and have the tendency to enlarge for the synthetic index of human resources, but they are diminishing for the infrastructure index, as showed by Figures 1 to 3.

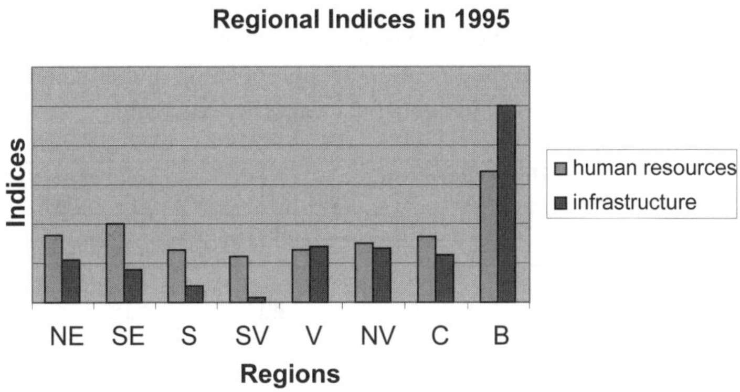

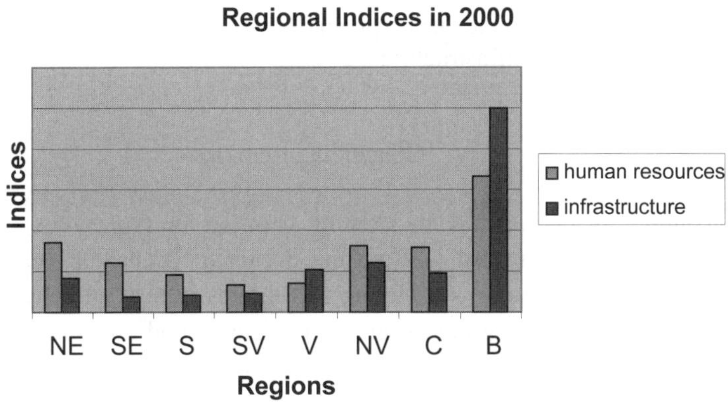

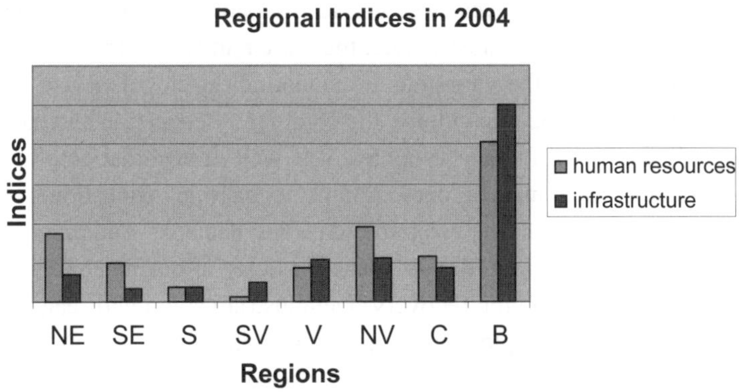

Fig. 1 to 3: Human Resources and Infrastructure

The assessment of hierarchies for the development regions in Romania according to the two synthetic indices (Tab. 4) recorded small changes during the period analyzed. Thus, some of the regions such as Bucharest-Ilfov, Centre, and North-West have a slight or no modification of their position in the hierarchy. Also for the other regions, their position generally varies by one rank.

Region	**Human Resources**			**Infrastructure**		
	1995	**2000**	**2004**	**1995**	**2000**	**2004**
North-East	3	2	3	5	5	5
South-East	2	5	5	6	8	7
South	7	6	7	7	7	6
South-West	8	8	8	8	6	8
West	6	7	6	2	3	3
North-West	5	3	2	3	2	2
Centre	4	4	4	4	4	4
Bucharest-Ilfov	1	1	1	1	1	1

Tab. 4: The Hierarchy of the Development Regions by Synthetic Index of Human Resources and Infrastructure

V. Concluding Remarks

The economic disparities already existing between the prosperous and the lagging regions have increased in Romania during the transition years and they might deepen in the future considering that the investment attractiveness of the developed regions, of long industrial traditions and good infrastructure is higher than that of the disadvantaged zones, with reducing development perspectives.

The analysis undertaken in this paper indicates a strong correlation between human resources and infrastructure at regional level. Nevertheless, even though the human resources have proven to be the determinant factor with respect to the territorial variations of the infrastructure, there are numerous other important factors of influence such as: the variations in economic development and geographical location, the entrepreneurial culture, the community education and culture.

As regards the use of human resources, it is well known that employment question is related to a mix of demographic, economic, educational and social-political factors: though, the economic ones are decisive. The main cause of the chronicle unemployment in the 90's was the delay in macroeconomic restructuring and sustained economic recovery. Deindustrialization and reagrarization had a negative impact on employment opportunities in all regions; on the other hand, the service sector still remains underdeveloped, unable to create an important number of jobs.

Though, some favorable evolutions can be noticed: the employment increase in the private sector, professional structure diversification. Also, within the European labor market Romania holds some comparative advantages, in terms of quality-cost relationship and young labor force potential.

References

Armstrong, H. and *J. Taylor*, Regional Economics and Policy, Blackwell 2000.

Bruinsma, F., P. Nijkamp and *P. Rietveld*, Employment Impacts of Infrastructure Investment, in: Infrastructure and the Space-Economy. Essays in Honour of Rolf Funck, ed. by K. Peschel, O.o 1990, p. 209-226.

Constantin, D.L., Z. Goschin and *C. Parlog*, Territorial Mobility of Labour Force in Romania During the 1990s, paper presented at the 43rd Congress of the European Regional Science Association, Jyväskyla, Finland 2003.

Constantin, D.L., Z. Goschin and *C. Parlog*, Interregional Migration in Romania After 1990, in: Romanian Journal of Economic Forecasting, No. 2, 2005, P. 38-57.

Constantin, D.L., Institutional Challenges to Romania's Regional Policy in the Perspective of Accession to the European Union, paper presented at the Regional Studies Association Conference "Reshaping EU Regional Policy", Leuven 2006.

Horwitz, L. and *L. Ferleger*, Statistics for Social Change, Boston 1980.

McCann, P., Urban and regional economics, Oxford 2001.

Mitrut, C. and *Constantin, D.L.*, Regional Policy and SMEs in Romania. Challenges in the Context of European Integration, paper presented at the 3rd Conference of the Association of South-East European Universities, Sofia 2006.

Nica, N.A., Romania's Labour Market Between European Integration and National Planning (in Romanian), in: Regional Development and European Integration, ed. by C. Parlog and D.L. Constantin, Bucharest 2003, P. 315-324.

Nijkamp, P., Infrastructure and Regional Development: A Multidimensional Policy Analysis, in: Empirical Economics, Nr. 11, 1986, P. 1-21.

Partenie, C., D. Jula, D. L. Constantin, C. Pârlog and *E. Dinga*, Institutions and Regional Labour Markets in Romania, in: Institutions and Regional Labour Markets in Europe, ed. by van der Laan, L., Ruesga, S., Avebury – Aldershot, 1998, P. 223-253.

Pascariu, G., M. Stanculescu, D. Jula and *M. Lutas*, EU Cohesion Policy and Romania's Regional and Social Development, Pre-Accession Impact Studies, Bucharest 2002.

Annex 1. Human Resources Indicators

Region	Population density (inhabitants/km^2)			Natural increase rate (per 1000 inhabitants)			Unemployment rate (%)		
	1995	2000	2004	1995	2000	2004	1995	2000	2004
North-East	102.7	103.75	101.5	2.2	2.5	0.8	13.7	13.2	7.8
South-East	82.62	82.05	79.7	-0.8	-0.5	-1.5	10.6	11.4	6.9
South	102.31	100.58	97.0	-2.7	-2.3	-3.6	9.0	10.4	7.4
South-West	83.43	82.15	79.3	-2.5	-2.1	-4.2	9.9	11.6	7.5
West	65.10	63.72	60.5	-3.6	-2.9	-3.6	7.5	10.4	5.8
North-West	84.41	83.26	85.5	-1.7	-1.3	-2.2	8.6	8.5	4.2
Centre	78.54	77.48	74.5	-1.3	-0.1	-0.8	9.1	10.3	7.8
Bucharest-Ilfov	1280.96	1254.63	1212.3	-4.1	-3.1	-2.0	5.1	5.8	2.8
Romania	95.14	94.51	90.9	-1.5	-0.9	-1.9	9.5	10.5	6.3

Annex 2. Infrastructure Indicators

Region	Public roads density (km/100 km^2)			Railways density (km/1000 km^2)			Sewage pipes density (km/100 km^2)		
	1995	2000	2004	1995	2000	2004	1995	2000	2004
North-East	34.5	36,2	36.3	40.9	40.9	40.7	5.98	6.64	6,81
South-East	27.9	29,6	29.5	36.7	37.2	37.9	6.39	6.59	6,85
South	32.2	34.3	34.8	48.5	49.3	49.4	5.34	5.75	6,26
South-West	34.0	34.8	35.9	33.7	34.3	33.9	4.38	4.59	5,02
West	27.3	31.8	31.9	62.8	62.8	62.7	5.75	6.26	6,83
North-West	31.3	33.9	34.7	52.8	48.2	48.0	5.70	6.38	6,56
Centre	26.1	29.4	29.7	61.2	43.1	44.5	6.04	6.35	6,99
Bucharest-Ilfov	43.4	45.2	47.9	176.8	194.4	188.4	95.61	102.86	116,34
Romania	30.6	32.9	33.3	47.7	46.2	46.4	6.37	6.86	7,35
North-East	101.8	129.8	150.5	7.46	6.79	5.76	6.87	7.02	8.03
South-East	218.8	173.7	198.5	6.32	6.29	5.53	5.22	5.21	5.44
South	161.9	132.03	161.3	5.99	5.69	4.85	4.56	4.80	5.13
South-West	86.3	118.04	153.3	6.88	6.67	5.85	5.15	5.44	6.05
West	124.2	175.95	218.5	9.48	8.91	7.37	6.39	6.88	7.62
North-West	120.4	156.35	191.5	8.27	8.25	7.33	7.83	8.15	8.77
Centre	133.9	184.44	217.5	8.51	8.20	7.13	7.05	7.24	7.92
Bucharest-Ilfov	286.6	339.64	368.8	9.48	10.28	10.43	13.64	14.92	17.09
Romania	129.4	169.98	200.1	7.64	7.44	6.58	6.91	7.23	8.0

Annex 3. Counties grouping by development region

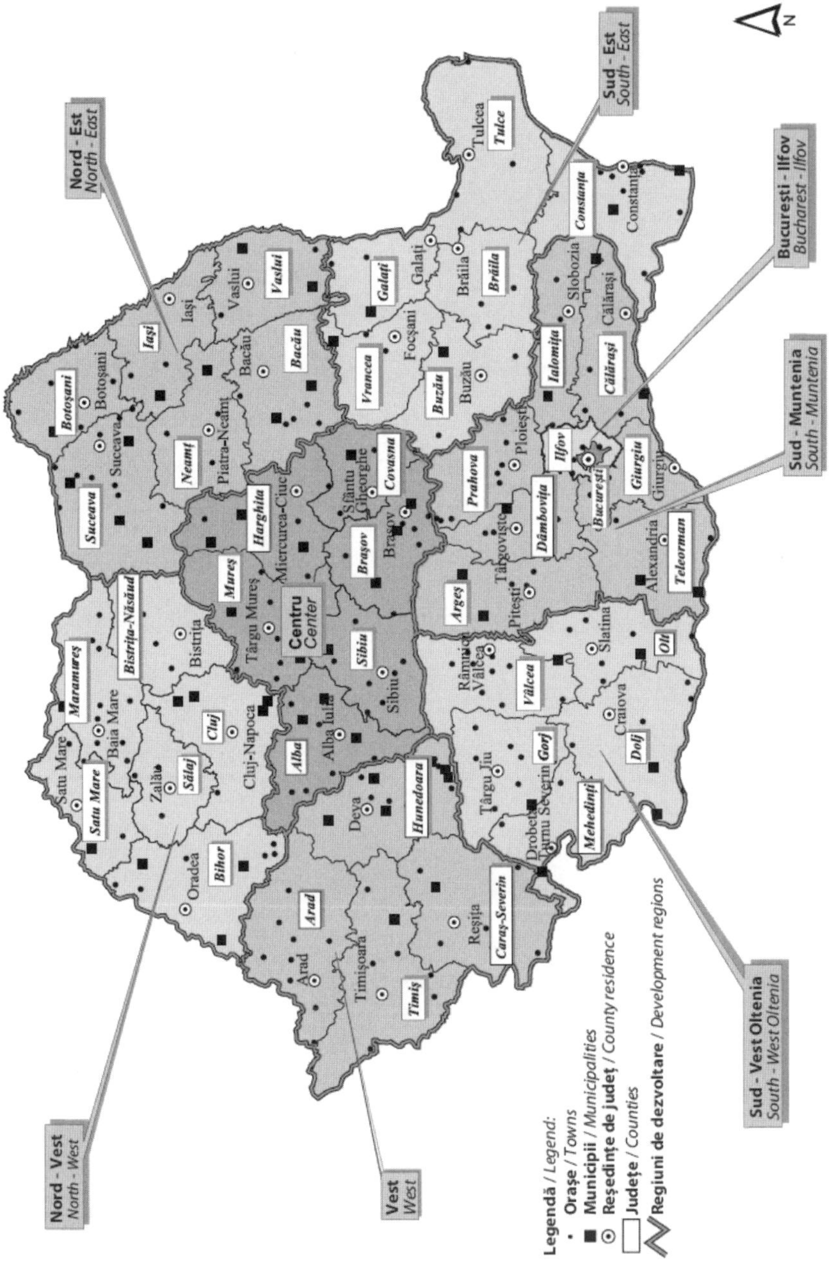

Sechstes Kapital

Arbeitsmarkt und Bevölkerungsrückgang

A. Arbeitslosigkeit und Migrationsprobleme in Polen

Zenon Wiśniewski

I. Die Arbeitsmarktsituation

Polen verfügt über einen großen Arbeitsmarkt und verhältnismäßig hochqualifizierte Arbeitskräfte. Die erwerbsfähige Bevölkerung umfasst 24,2 Mio. Personen. Die Gesamtzahl der in der polnischen Volkswirtschaft Beschäftigten ist jedoch im Transformationsprozess von 17,6 Mio. bis auf 13,6 Mio. Personen gesunken. Deshalb ist die Beschäftigungsrate sehr niedrig und beträgt nur 52,4%, während diese in der Europäischen Union 67,7% beträgt.

Die Arbeitslosigkeit stieg in Polen von einem offiziell ausgewiesenen Niveau nahe Null am Ende der achtziger Jahre auf 16,4% im Jahre 1993. Danach sank die Arbeitslosenquote bis zum Jahre 1997 auf ein Niveau von 10,3% und seit dem Jahr 1998 ist diese wieder gewachsen. Seit dem Jahr 2004 schrumpft die Arbeitslosenquote wieder und beträgt heute 18,0%.

Zu den charakteristischen Merkmalen der Arbeitslosigkeit in Polen gehören:

- Nur 18% der Arbeitslosen haben den Anspruch auf Arbeitslosengeld.
- Jugendliche sind überproportional von Arbeitslosigkeit betroffen. Der Anteil der Jugendlichen an der Gesamtzahl der Arbeitslosen beträgt mehr als 35%.
- Es existiert eine langfristige strukturelle Arbeitslosigkeit (50%) in verschiedenen Regionen mit der Konsequenz wachsender Verarmung der Bevölkerung.
- Die Arbeitslosen verfügen über eine schlechte Ausbildung. Mehr als 60% verfügen nur über eine achtjährige Grundausbildung oder Berufsgrundschulausbildung.

Als besonders schwierig muss die Arbeitsmarktsituation in den ländlichen Gebieten betrachtet werden. Die notwendige Arbeitskraftumschichtung in den durch die Landwirtschaft dominierten Regionen ist außerordentlich hoch: Um das EU-Beschäftigungsmuster zu erreichen, wären 2,5 Mio. Menschen in der polnischen Landwirtschaft vom Beschäftigungsabbau bzw. -umbau betroffen (Karpiński, Paradysz 1996, S. 28).

In Polen existiert keine auf Arbeitnehmerbeiträge gestützte Arbeitslosenversicherung, sondern ein quasi Arbeitslosenversicherungssystem, bei dem nur die Arbeitgeberseite einen Beitrag in der Höhe von 2,45% des Arbeitnehmerlohns an den sog. Arbeitsfonds entrichtet. Dieser Fonds erhält außerdem Dotationen aus dem Staatshaushalt. Aus diesem Fonds werden die passiven und aktiven arbeitsmarktpolitischen Maßnahmen finanziert.

Der Bericht über „Vor- und Nachteile des Beitritts Polens in die EU – eine Bilanz" lässt schlussfolgern, dass die ersten Jahre unserer EU-Mitgliedschaft keine sofortige und bedeutsame Verbesserung auf dem polnischen Arbeitsmarkt herbeigeführt haben. Erst in den Jahren 2007-2014 erhofft man sich eine langsame Abnahme der Arbeitslosigkeit. Es wird angenommen, dass im Jahre 2014 die Arbeitslosenquote in Polen etwa 12% betragen wird. Eine Prognose zur Arbeitslosigkeitsentwicklung wird in der Tabelle 1 dargestellt, die dem Nationalen Entwicklungsplan für Polen 2005-2020 entnommen wurde und eindeutig auf ein langsames Tempo der Abnahme der Arbeitslosigkeit hinweist.

	2005-2006	2007-2013	2014-2020
Arbeitslose in 1.000	2969	2455	2035
Arbeitslosenquote	17,5	14,4	11,9
Veränderung des BIP in Prozent	4,9	5,5	5,0

Quelle: Narodowy Plan Rozwoju. Projekt wstępny 2007-20013, Warszawa 2005, S. 18

Tab. 1: Arbeitslosigkeitsprognose in Polen, 2005-2020

An dieser Stelle muss man einige Ergebnisse von Untersuchungen aus dem Jahre 1998 darstellen, die darauf hinweisen, dass bei einem jährlichen Wirtschaftswachstum von etwa 6% bis 7% die polnische Wirtschaft die Distanz zu den schwächsten EU-Ländern, wie etwa Griechenland oder Portugal, in etwa 18 bis 20 Jahren aufholen wird. In etwa 30 Jahren erreicht sie dagegen ein durchschnittliches Niveau der wirtschaftlichen Entwicklung (BIP pro Kopf) der alten 15 EU-Länder.

Laut den Angaben von Eurostaat vom Januar 2006 beträgt das polnische BIP etwa 50,1% des durchschnittlichen BIP der EU 25. Die polnische Wirtschaft muss somit deutlich wachsen, um die existierende Differenz zu den hoch entwickelten EU-Ländern zu reduzieren.

II. Der Regulierungsgrad des Arbeitsmarktes in Polen und den EU-Ländern

Die heutigen Arbeitsmärkte werden durch den Globalisierungsprozess beeinflusst, der als Erschaffung eines einheitlichen Wirtschaftsraumes durch Auflösung der Barrieren, welche die jeweiligen Märkte teilen, verstanden wird. In den Überlegungen zu Einwirkungsrichtungen und -ausmaß des Prozesses überwiegen pessimistische Ansichten, besonders bei den Arbeitnehmern. Es wird allgemein auf die Notwendigkeit der Erhöhung der Arbeitsmarktflexibilität durch dessen Deregulierung hingewiesen, was zur größeren Freiheit der Arbeitsmarktakteure führen soll, sowie zur Verringerung des Ausmaßes der staatlichen Regulierung im Bereich der allgemeinen Arbeitsverhältnisse. Die Befürworter der Deregulierung betonen, dass starre Institutionen und Arbeitsmarktregulierungen die dynamische Wirtschaftsentwicklung verhindern, weil sie das Anpassungspotential der Arbeitsmarktakteure sowie des Arbeitsmarktes allgemein einschränken (Siebert 1995, S. 24ff.).

Betont wird bei dieser Kritik, dass in einem marktwirtschaftlichen System die alle Arbeitnehmer betreffenden Schutzregulierungen mit den Rentabilitätsgesichtspunkten der Firmen nicht vereinbar sind, und dass Unternehmen nicht mehr ganz frei über den produktiven Einsatz ihrer Arbeitskräfte entscheiden können. Starre Regulierung der Arbeitsverhältnisse erschwert die Umstrukturierung der Volkswirtschaft, weil die mangelnde Arbeitsmarktflexibilität in den Zeiten der schnellen strukturellen Umwandlungen die notwendigen Veränderungen bremst und damit Wachstumsverluste verursacht. Durch die Erhöhung der Flexibilität des Beschäftigungssystems wird versucht, den neuen Anforderungen der Informationsgesellschaft und Globalwirtschaft gerecht zu werden.

Die Bestimmung des Regulierungsgrades des Arbeitsmarktes ist schwierig, weil objektive und messbare Kriterien fehlen. Dennoch wird versucht, solche Messungen auf Grund von synthetischen Maßstäben vorzunehmen, die einige qualitative Eigenschaften berücksichtigen. Solche Methoden werden von OECD-Experten erarbeitet und für internationale Vergleiche angewendet (OECD 1994, 1999). Auch die Experten der Weltbank unternehmen den Versuch, den Grad der Arbeitsmarktregulierung zu bestimmen. Bei der Bestimmung des Arbeitsmarktregulierungsgrades werden von ihnen folgende Maßstäbe angewandt:

- Gewerkschaftsgradindex und prozentualer Anteil der Beschäftigten, die durch Kollektivtarifverträge (**coverage**) abgedeckt sind,
- Index der Flexibilität des Rechtsschutzes des Arbeitsverhältnisses (EPL),
- Index der steuerlichen Belastung der Arbeitskosten,
- Ausmaß und Effektivität der Ausgaben für die Bekämpfung der Arbeitslosigkeit und
- Mindestlohn-Gesetzgebung.

In den neunziger Jahren wurde der Bedarf nach Liberalisierung des Arbeitsmarktes und Veränderungen in der Wirtschaftspolitik immer deutlicher gesehen (Wiśniewski 1999, S. 37ff.). In den meisten Ländern wurden aber aufgrund der Hindernisse struktureller und politischer Natur keine entscheidenden Reformen durchgeführt. Radikale Reformen wurden nur in Großbritannien ausgeführt. Das Gegenteil fand in Frankreich statt, wo man versucht hat, starre Sicherheitsregulierungen bezüglich der Arbeitsverhältnisse, Arbeitszeiten und Löhne zu erhalten. In anderen Ländern hat man versucht, einen dritten Weg zwischen voller Deregulierung (das amerikanische Modell) und der Arbeitsmarktregulierung zu finden.

Eine radikale Arbeitsmarktderegulierung wurde aus sozialer Hinsicht und durch bisherige Praktika eingeschränkt. Es wird betont, dass eine starke soziale und politische Position der Arbeitsnehmer größere Veränderungen unmöglich macht. So kam es in Frankreich aufgrund sozialer Gerechtigkeit zu keiner Mindestlohnreduzierung bei den Jugendlichen, in Schweden gelang es nicht, das Unterstützungsgeld für Arbeitslose zu verringern, und in Ostdeutschland führten Lohnverhandlungen unter anderem zur Auflösung vieler Arbeitsplätze. Da der Bedarf nach Erhaltung sozialen Friedens dominierte, wurde die Arbeitsmarktderegulierung selektiv ausgeführt. Nur in Großbritannien, das den Vereinigten Staaten Nordamerikas ähnelt, wurden konsequent Maßnahmen in Richtung größerer Deregulierung des Arbeitsmarktes unternommen. Deutschlands Beispiel zeigt, dass die sich verschlechternde Arbeitsmarktsituation Veränderungen in der Einstellung dazu erfordert, und erst jetzt wird das schwierige Reformprogramm „Agenda 2010“ realisiert.

Die Erfahrungen in den 90er Jahren haben gezeigt, dass:

- in den EU-Ländern, die imstande waren die Arbeitslosigkeit zu reduzieren, die Arbeitsmärkte liberalisiert wurden,
- in keinem der Länder, wo es nicht zur Liberalisierung kam (Frankreich, Deutschland, Italien), die Arbeitslosenquote gesenkt wurde,
- kleinere Länder eine bessere Beschäftigungssituation haben und weniger von schwierigen Reformen, die unternommen werden müssen, bedroht sind als die großen,
- zwar viele Maßnahmen unternommen wurden, die der Arbeitslosigkeit entgegenwirken sollten, jedoch waren diese uneffektiv oder haben nach politischen Korrekturen das Gegenteil bewirkt.

Zum Schluss muss noch erwähnt werden, dass zahlreiche Untersuchungen auf die wichtige Rolle des Flexibilitätsmangels des Arbeitsmarktes und besonders auf die Tarifverhandlungen beim Erklären von Differenzen in der Arbeitslosenquote zwischen den Vereinigten Staaten und einer typischen EU-Wirtschaft hinweisen. Diese Analysen unterstützen Krugmans Hypothese, dass negative Nachfrageschocks zu größeren Disproportionen bei den Reallöhnen zwischen unqualifizierten und hoch qualifizierten Arbeitnehmern in den USA führen und in Kontinentaleuropa die Arbeitslosigkeit bei den wenig qualifizierten Personen erhöhen. Es seien laut Krugman „zwei Seiten der Medaille“ (Krugman 1994, S. 14ff.).

Land	Individueller Schutz gegen Entlassungen	Zusätzliche Regulierung bei Massen-Entlassungen	Regulierung von Teilzeitarbeit	Gesamt-indikator (gewichteter Durchschnitt)	Arbeitslosen-quote 1998 (%)
Großbritannien	0,8	2,9	0,3	0,9	6,3
Irland	1,6	2,1	0,3	1,1	7,8
Dänemark	1,6	3,1	0,9	1,5	5,1
Finnland	2,1	2,4	1,9	2,1	11,4
Niederlande	3,1	2,8	1,2	2,2	4,0
Österreich	2,6	3,3	1,8	2,3	4,7
Belgien	1,5	4,1	2,8	2,5	9,5
Schweden	2,8	4,5	1,6	2,6	8,3
Deutschland	2,8	3,1	2,3	2,6	9,4
Frankreich	2,3	2,1	3,6	2,8	11,7
Spanien	2,6	3,1	3,5	3,1	18,7
Italien	2,8	4,1	3,8	3,4	12,2
Griechenland	2,4	3,3	4,8	3,5	10,7
Portugal	4,3	3,6	3,0	3,7	5,1
Tschechien	2,8	4,3	0,5	2,1	6,5
Polen	2,2	3,9	1,0	2,0	10,6
Ungarn	2,1	3,4	0,6	1,7	7,8

Quelle: OECD, *Employment Outlook*, Paris 1999, S. 57.
Ein niedrigerer Indikator signalisiert mehr Flexibilität.

Tab. 2: Flexibilität der Arbeitsmärkte in den EU-Ländern im Jahre 1998

Die institutionellen Arbeitsmarktbedingungen sind in Polen und auch in den meisten anderen mittel- und osteuropäischen Ländern mit denen in Kontinentaleuropa vergleichbar (Tabelle 2). Insbesondere Abfindungsentschädigungen und Kündigungsschutzregelungen folgen dem kontinentaleuropäischen Muster. Eine Untersuchung der OECD hat gezeigt, dass Polen, Ungarn und Tschechien einen deutlich niedrigeren Gesamtindikator erreichen, da sie sehr liberale Regelungen besitzen und ihr Arbeitsmarkt deshalb relativ flexibler ist.
In Polen ist der Einfluss der kollektiven Arbeitsverhältnisse sehr komplex. Das Arbeitsgesetzbuch garantiert einen relativ guten Arbeitsschutz, doch gibt es viele private Unternehmen, die in die kollektiven Arbeitsverhältnisse nicht eingebunden sind. Manchmal wird sogar gegen das geltende Arbeitsrecht verstoßen. Andererseits, besonders in niedergehenden und/oder uneffektiven Sektoren, bleiben starke Gewerkschaften und überbetriebliche Tarifabkommen erhalten, die den Arbeitnehmern besseren Arbeitsschutz als das Arbeitsgesetzbuch sichern. Dennoch, in Zeiten der massiven Arbeitslosigkeit neigen die Arbeitnehmer, in der Hoffnung auf eine Situationsverbesserung, sogar dazu, einen totalen oder teilweisen Aufschub der Gehaltsauszahlung oder Lohnherabsetzungen für den Erhalt der Arbeitsplätze und der Firma zu akzeptieren. Aus den gleichen Gründen neigen sie dazu, sich in flexibler Form einstellen zu lassen. Diese letzte Neigung betrifft vor allem die Firmen, bei denen es gar keine Gewerkschaften gibt bzw.

diese sehr schwach sind und es keine überbetrieblichen Tarifabkommen gibt. Charakteristisch für kollektive Arbeitsverhältnisse in Polen sind: große Politisierung der Gewerkschaftszentralen und Schwäche der miteinander konkurrierenden Arbeitgeberverbände. Demgemäß ist der Einfluss der kollektiven Arbeitsverhältnisse auf die Deregulierung des Arbeitsmarktes als Resultat dieser verschiedenen Faktoren zu sehen.

Polen stellt allerdings im Hinblick auf die empirische Evidenz eines Zusammenhangs von Arbeitsmarktflexibilität und Umsetzungen am Arbeitsmarkt eine Ausnahme dar: Trotz eines relativ moderaten Indexwertes ist in Polen die Zahl der Neueinstellungen und Entlassungen sehr gering und der Verbleib eines Arbeitnehmers bei ein und demselben Arbeitgeber sehr lang.

III. Analyse von Korrelationen zwischen Migrationen aus den Ostmitteleuropa-Ländern in die EU

Zu potenziellen Faktoren, die einen Einfluss auf Migrationen ausüben, gehören ökonomische und außerökonomische Variablen. Empirische Untersuchungen bezüglich der internationalen Migrationen weisen auf eine wesentliche Bedeutung der Einkommensdifferenzen und Arbeitsmarktlagen zwischen Ein- und Ausreiseländern hin. Bezüglich der Einkommensunterschiede wird eine positive Korrelation gegenüber dem Migrationsniveau erwartet, dagegen bezüglich der Arbeitslosenquote im Einreiseland entsprechend eine negative Korrelation (höhere Arbeitslosigkeit im Einwanderungsland bedeutet eine niedrigere Anforderung ausländischer Arbeitskräfte, die von einheimischen Arbeitsgebern und niedrigerer Einwanderung angemeldet werden).

Zum Zwecke der Feststellung von Faktoren, die mit dem Migrationlevel aus den OME-Ländern in die EU der 15 zu tun haben, wurde eine Analyse über bilaterale Migration in den 90er Jahren zwischen ausgewählten Staaten Ost- und Westeuropas durchgeführt. Als Variablen wurden kumulierte Größen bezüglich der Einwanderung von Migranten aus: Polen, Tschechien, Slowakei, Slowenien, Ungarn, Bulgarien, Rumänien und den Baltikumstaaten nach: Deutschland, Österreich, Dänemark, Holland und Frankreich aus der Zeit 1990-1999, geteilt durch die durchschnittliche Einwohnerzahl der Ausreiseländer, angenommen. Die beschriebenen Angaben stammen aus der Datenbank von „International Migration from Countries with Economies in Transition 1980-2000". Zusätzlich wurden Einwirkungen analysiert, die aus der Intensivität der Transformationsprozesse in den OME-Ländern resultieren und sich auf das Migrationsniveau auswirken. Unter außerökonomischen Faktoren wurden diejenigen getestet, die aus der geographischen Entfernung und der politischen Stabilität resultieren.

Insbesondere wurde die Relevanz von korrelativen Beziehungen zwischen einer kumulierten Auswanderungsquote und folgenden Faktoren geprüft:

Variablen	Pearsons Korrelationskoeffizient	t-Statistik
Gemeinsamer Grenze	0,217	1,505
EU-Kandidaten für die erste Erweiterung	0,014	0,096
BIP pro Kopf-Differenzen	-0,018	-0,123
Lohndifferenzen	0,269	1.892
Transformationskoeffizient	-0014,	-0,097
Arbeitslosenquote im Einwanderungsland	-0,164	-1,129
Arbeitslosenquote im Auswanderungsland	0,004	0,027
Quotient von Arbeitslosenquoten	0,033	0,224

Quelle: eigene Berechnungen

Tab. 3: Korrelationskoeffiziente zwischen der kumulierten Migration aus den OME-Ländern in die EU der 15 und ausgewählten Variablen

- eine null- eins Variable bezüglich Staatenpaaren mit gemeinsamer Grenze,
- eine null- eins Variable bezüglich Staaten, die in den 90er Jahren des letzten Jahrhunderts als EU-Kandidaten für die erste Erweiterung anerkannt wurden,
- BIP pro Kopf – Differenzen zwischen westlichen und östlichen Staatenpaaren im Jahre 1996,
- Differenzen im Lohnniveau im Jahre 1996,
- Transformationskoeffizient – eine Variable, die den Fortschritt vom Transformationsprozess der ostmitteleuropäischen Wirtschaften beschreibt und deren Werte einen Durchschnitt von Koeffizienten aus dem Transformationsfortschritt, die durch die Europäische Bank für Wiederaufbau und Entwicklung genutzt werden, darstellen,
- Arbeitslosenquote im Einwanderungsland im Jahre 1995,
- Arbeitslosenquote im Auswanderungsland im Jahre 1995,
- Quotient von Arbeitslosenquoten im Aus- und Einwanderungsland.

Die Vorzeichen der meisten Koeffizienten stimmen mit den Erwartungen, die aufgrund der Theorie und der früheren Analysen von Auswirkungen auf Migrationen formuliert wurden, überein. Jedoch korrelieren unter allen in dieser Analyse berücksichtigten Variablen lediglich die Differenzen im Lohnniveau mit dem Migrationsniveau, und zwar knapp auf einem 10%-Niveau. Dieses Ergebnis verstärkt lediglich Schlussfolgerungen aus anderen Bearbeitungen, in denen behauptet wurde, dass die Zahl bzw. Größe von Migrationstransfers zwischen einer relativ armen und wohlhabenden Region von der Differenz im Lohnniveau abhängig ist. Je größer die Einkommensunterschiede, desto größer die Motivation von niedrig bezahlten Arbeitskräften aus Ostmitteleuropa, im alten EU-Ausland eine besser vergütete Arbeit zu suchen.

Die Perspektive einer schnellen Mitgliedschaft und die Intensität vom marktwirtschaftlichen Wandel scheinen keinen Einfluss auf das Migrationsiveau auszuüben. Es wurde keine Korrelation zwischen der Migration und der Arbeitslosenquote in einem Ausreiseland festgestellt. Daraus resultiert – abgesehen von der Tatsache, dass die Arbeitslosenquote als ein die Migration verstärkender Faktor gesehen wird, dass die Arbeitslosenquote im untersuchten Zeitraum die Entscheidungen von Migranten wegen einer restriktiven EU-Beschäftigungspolitik in Bezug auf die Ausländer nicht beeinflussen konnte. Damals waren die westlichen Arbeitsmärkte für die Arbeitskräfte aus Ostmitteleuropa praktisch völlig geschlossen.

Bei sieben irrelevanten Variablen wurden höchste Statistikwerte im Falle des angrenzenden Länderpaares (1,505) und im Falle der Arbeitslosenquote im Einwanderungs- bzw. Zielland (-1,129) festgestellt. Interessant erscheint der Vergleich zwischen der Abhängigkeitskraft von Arbeitslosigkeitsraten im Aus- und Einreiseland. Eine ungünstige Arbeitsmarktlage im Ausland und daraus folgende Schwierigkeiten bei der Arbeitsaufnahme scheinen die Arbeitsmigration wesentlich stärker zu beschränken, als die Arbeitslosenquote im Ausreiseland, die den Migrationsdruck erhöht. Diese Regel, obwohl auf statistisch irrelevanten Werten basierend, scheint bis zum gewissen Grade die sehr wichtige Rolle der Arbeitsnachfrage zu bestätigen, welche die Arbeitgeber im Zielland artikulieren.

Als Ursache für eine fehlende statistische Relevanz der meisten Beziehungen gilt wahrscheinlich ein hoher Abhängigkeitsgrad der Migration von Einreisevorschriften in allen westlichen Ländern mit relativ frei gestalteten Einwanderungspolitiken. Die in einzelnen Ländern unterschiedlichen Einschränkungen bezogen auf einzelne Migrantengruppen – Arbeitsemigranten, Migranten aus Familienzusammenführung sowie Asylanten – tragen dazu bei, dass das allgemeine Einreiseniveau wesentlich von rechtlichen Regelungen abhängt. Im untersuchten Zeitraum hatten lediglich ein Teil der wohlhabenden Länder eine selektive Aufnahmepolitik bezüglich ausländischer Arbeitskräfte aufgrund von bilateralen Abkommen und vom festgesetzten Betrag betrieben. Die Durchführung einer detaillierten Analyse wurde durch das Fehlen von vergleichbaren Angaben zur Migration in den besprochenen Hauptkategorien unmöglich.

IV. Arbeitsmigration nach Polens EU-Beitritt

Die Erfahrungen aus den letzten EU-Erweiterungen deuten darauf hin, dass die Arbeitsmigrationen abnehmen, je größer der Wohlstand in den jeweils neuen EU-Ländern geworden war. Am Beispiel Spaniens sehen wir, dass die Migration Anfang der 70er Jahre etwa 200.000 Personen pro Jahr betrug, dagegen in den 80er Jahren lediglich 120.000 und in den 90ern knapp 2 bis 3.000 Personen jährlich.

Nach dem 1. Mai 2004 dürfen die polnischen Bürger ihren Arbeitsplatz nur in Irland, Großbritannien und Schweden frei wählen. Laut des publizierten Berichts von European Citizen Action Service waren unter anderem die deutschen Voraussagen, die vor einer 4 Mio. starken Migrantenwelle aus den Ländern Ostmitteleuropas gewarnt haben, weitgehend übertrieben (Rzeczpospolita 2005). Es hatte sich herausgestellt, dass die ersten offenen Arbeitsmärkte der sogenannten alten EU nach dem ersten Mitgliedschaftsjahr 10 neuer EU-Staaten etwa 200.000 Personen empfangen haben. Die Ängste der übrigen EU-Länder vor einer Überschwemmung ihrer Märkte durch Polen sind unbegründet, was selbst die Botschafter dieser Staaten am 17.11.2004 in Warschau vor einem polnischen Parlamentsausschuss für EU-Angelegenheiten zugegeben haben.
Die älteren EU-Gesellschaften müssen innerhalb von den nächsten 20 Jahren mindestens etwa 50 Mio. neue Migranten aufnehmen, um das heutige Wirtschaftswachstum aufrechtzuerhalten. Zum Beispiel die Bundesrepublik Deutschland müsste bis zum Jahre 2025 etwa 12 Mio. neue Migranten und Italien etwa 7,5 Mio. aufnehmen. In dieser Lage wäre eine Blockade des EU-Arbeitsmarktes für Arbeitsmigrationen wenigstens als unvernünftig zu sehen.
Während der letzten, umfangreicheren EU-Erweiterung sind natürlich ärmere Länder als damals Spanien EU-Mitglieder geworden. Somit werden die Ausgleichsprozesse bezüglich Einkommensdifferenzen länger andauern. Dagegen sind die Migrationsziele von der Reihenfolge der weiteren Arbeitsmarktöffnungen durch die übrigen alten EU-Länder abhängig.
Das polnische Ministerium für Wirtschaft und Arbeit hatte für das Jahr 2005 eingeschätzt, dass etwa 500.000 Personen in Deutschland eine Arbeit, vor allem saisonal in der Landwirtschaft, angenommen haben. Auf dem zweiten Platz befand sich das Vereinigte Königreich, wo 190.000 Polen einen Job bekommen haben. Man muss hinzufügen, dass in diesem Land nach Polens Eintritt in die EU mehr als 400.000 Personen eine Arbeit gefunden haben. An der dritten Stelle war Irland mit 80.000 Migranten aus Polen.
In jedem Jahr brechen etwa 5% aller Hochschulabsolventen in die EU-Länder auf, um dort eine Arbeit und ein besseres Leben zu finden. Laut den Untersuchungen von European Citizen Action Service (Lobbyverein mit Sitz in Brüssel) lässt sich etwa die Hälfte von ihnen dort nieder. Die Arbeitsemigranten können in zwei unterschiedliche Gruppen eingeteilt werden. Zum einen sind es qualifizierte Spezialisten, die selbst von westlichen Konzernen eingeladen werden, zum zweiten sind es körperliche Arbeitskräfte, die abgesehen von ihren nicht selten hohen Qualifikationen, sich doch für ein besseres EU-Einkommen als in Polen entscheiden.
Der Beitritt Polens in die EU hatte keinen wesentlichen Wandel in den Charakterzügen polnischer Arbeitsmigrationen mit sich gebracht. Weiterhin arbeiten die

meisten Migranten saisonal in der Landwirtschaft, Gastronomie und im Obstbau-, Forst-, Hotel- und Bauwesen. Sichtbar ist eine stetige Beschäftigungszunahme unserer Bürger in den EU-Ländern (Wiśniewski, Oczki 2005, S. 29ff.). Historisch gesehen muss festgestellt werden, dass Polen bezüglich der Arbeitsmigrationen immer ein Exilland gewesen war. Es wird zum Beispiel geschätzt, dass in der Zeit nach dem Kriegsrecht in Polen bis zum Jahre 1989 etwa 700.000 Personen Polen verlassen haben. Daher kann angenommen werden, dass in den Jahren 1990-2004 etwa 200 bis 300.000 Polen ins ständige Exil gegangen sind. Somit verließen Polen seit dem Kriegsrecht 1981 bis 2004 etwa 1 Mio. Bürger.

Land	Migration in 1.000
Bundesrepublik Deutschland	500
Großbritannien	190
Irland	70-80
Italien	40
Niederlande	33
Norwegen	15
Spanien	17
Schweden	4

Quelle: Ministerstwo Gospodarki i Pracy, Warszawa

Tab. 4: Arbeitsmigration aus Polen nach Ländern im Jahre 2005

Im Mai 2004 wurde nach dem Beitritt Polens in die EU eine Umfrage unter über 2.000 Studenten an den 10 größten polnischen Hochschulen durch die Agentur Student News durchgeführt. Aus der Untersuchung folgt, dass etwa 66% aller Studenten vorhaben, im Ausland zu arbeiten. Der Wille zur Aufnahme eines solchen Auslandsjobs sinkt, wenn die Forscher fragen, ob die Studenten etwas in dieser Richtung bereits getan haben, wie etwa, ob sie wissen, wie viel Geld am Beginn eines „solchen Unternehmens“ investiert werden muss bzw., ob sie jemand im Ausland diesbezüglich kennen. Es stellte sich heraus, dass etwa 15% aller Befragten wirklich an einem Auslandsjob interessiert sind, 20% davon möchten etwa über ein Jahr im Ausland verbringen, 19% denken an einen Saisonjob und lediglich 18% an Exil.

Was müsste geschehen, damit die Studenten die Idee, im Ausland ihr Geld zu verdienen, aufgeben? Auf diese Frage haben drei Viertel aller Befragten erwidert – feste Einstellung zu Hause. Somit werden die Hauptargumente für Arbeitsmigration auf das niedrige Lohnniveau und die schlechte Lage auf dem polnischen Arbeitsmarkt reduziert. Man kann feststellen, dass die Arbeitsmigrationen solange unternommen werden, bis sich die Arbeitsmarktlage in Polen wesentlich verbessert hat und die Arbeitslosigkeit stark abnimmt.

V. Schlussbemerkung

Die in diesem Beitrag dargestellten Überlegungen weisen darauf hin, dass Polens Eintritt in die EU eine Reihe von gegensätzlichen Konsequenzen für das Wirtschaftswachstum und die Situation auf dem Arbeitsmarkt haben kann. Einerseits kann langfristig ein beschleunigtes Wirtschaftswachstum und eine Wohlstandserhöhung erwartet werden, sofern die polnische Wirtschaftspolitik rechtzeitig die in einigen Bereichen dringend erforderlichen Verbesserungen anstößt (Oczki 2005, S. 109 ff.). Auf der anderen Seite muss mit ungünstigen Auswirkungen gerechnet werden und zwar im Zusammenhang mit einem vorübergehenden Handelsbilanzdefizit, mit der Steigerung der strukturellen Arbeitslosigkeit, insbesondere auf dem Lande, sowie mit Arbeitslosigkeit, die durch die Modernisierung und Restrukturierung bestehender Unternehmen entsteht. Das besondere Augenmerk bei der Bekämpfung der Arbeitslosigkeit wird daher auf der Nutzung aller einschlägigen arbeitsmarktrelevanten Programme der EU liegen müssen. Das Ausmaß der negativen Phänomene wird vor allem davon abhängen, in welchem Grade die polnische Wirtschaft nach dem EU-Beitritt umstrukturiert wird und welche Konkurrenzvorteile polnische Produkte auf dem EG-Binnenmarkt erlangen können. Der Eintritt Polens in die EU ist eine große Chance, aber zugleich auch eine große Herausforderung.

Schlussfolgernd kann man die Forschungsergebnisse des Instituts für Meinungsumfragen Pentor nach einem Jahr der EU-Mitgliedschaft Polens bezüglich der polnischen Hoffnungen der EU gegenüber darstellen (o.V. 2005). Es lässt sich folgendes Bild zusammenstellen:

Zum Ersten, etwa 70% aller Befragten behaupten, dass die EU-Mitgliedschaft für Polen eine Entwicklungschance bedeutet.

Zum Zweiten behaupten etwa 51%, dass die EU uns bei der Angleichung der Lebensverhältnisse behilflich sein wird und Polen eine schnelle Anpassung an den Wohlstand Deutschlands und Frankreichs ermöglicht.

Zum Dritten glauben etwa 43% aller Befragten, dass die EU eine Garantie für Frieden und Sicherheit in Europa darstellt und einen wirksamen Kampf gegen Terrorismus zusichert.

Zum Vierten erhoffen etwa 43%, dass polnische Staatsbürger ihren Arbeitsplatz bald in allen EU-Ländern frei wählen dürfen.

Zum Letzten behaupten etwa 39%, dass die EU-Mitgliedschaft für Polen bessere Ausbildungschancen eröffnet und (bis 89%), dass die polnischen Hochschulabschlüsse überall in der EU anerkannt werden.

Literaturverzeichnis

Borkowska, S. (Hrsg.), Rynek pracy wobec integracji europejskiej, IPiSS, Warszawa 2003.

Carstensen, K. und *F. Toubal*, Foreign Direct Investment in Central and Eastern European Countries: a Dynamic Panel Analysis, in: Journal of Comparative Esconomics, Vol. 32, 2004, S. 3-22.

Esping-Andersen, G. und *M. Regini* (Hrsg.), Why Deregulate Labour Markets, Oxford 2000.

Eurostat, Statistical Yearbook on Candidate and South-East European Countries, Data 1996-2000, European Communities 2002.

Karpiński, A. und *S.*, *Paradysz,* Studia nad możliwymi kierunkami zmian w poziomie i strukturze zatrudnienia w Polsce w perspektywie roku 2010, Warszawa 1996.

Krugman, P., Past and Prospective Causes of High Unemployment, in: Economic Review, 4th Quarter, 1994, Federal Reserve Bank of Kansas City, S. 23-43.

Oczki, J., Integracja Polski z Unią Europejską a zachodnie rynki pracy, Wydawnictwo Uniwersytetu Mikołaja Kopernika, Toruń 2005.

OECD, Jobs Study, Paris 1994.

OECD, Employment Outlook, Paris 1999.

OECD, Employment Outlook, Paris 2001.

o.V., European Citizen Action Service, in: Rzeczposplita, 7. September 2005.

o.V., Euro-entuzjaści znad Wisły, in: „Metro“, 15-17. Juli 2005.

Rada Ministrów, Narodowy Plan Rozwoju. Projekt wstępny 2007-2013, Warszawa 2005.

Siebert, H., Hundert Punkte für mehr Beschäftigung, Kieler Diskussionsbeiträge 264, Kiel 1995.

Wiśniewski, Z., Kierunki i skutki deregulacji rynku pracy w krajach Unii Europejskiej, UMK, Toruń 1999.

Wiśniewski, Z., Unemployment, Migration and the Effects of the EU Membership on the Polish Labour Market, in: North European and Baltic Sea Integration (NEBI) Yearbook 2000, hrsg. von L. Hedegaard and B. Lindström, Berlin, Heidelberg und New York 2000, S. 49-62.

Wiśniewski, Z., Polish Labor Market in the Context of the EU Membership, in: Central and Eastern Europe in Transition, hrsg. von F. Columbus, Huntington und New York 2001, S. 95-108.

Wiśniewski, Z. und *J. Oczki*, Migration Effects of Poland's EU Membership, in: Intereconomics. Review of European Economic Policy, 2001, Nr. 4, S. 174-178.

Wiśniewski, Z. und J. Oczki, Polish Labour Market and Migration Potential, Diskussionspapier des Lehrstuhls für Finanzwissenschaft der Universität der Bundeswehr München, Nr. 49, München 2005.

B. Mikroökonometrische Analyse der Arbeitslosigkeitsdauer in Deutschland und in Polen

Joanna Małgorzata Landmesser

I. Einleitung

Ziel der Arbeit ist eine Untersuchung der Arbeitslosigkeitsdauer mit Hilfe der Ereignisanalyse. Durch das Einbeziehen von erklärenden Variablen wird der Effekt von bestimmten Merkmalen, wie Alter, Geschlecht, Ausbildungsniveau und Nationalität, auf die Arbeitslosigkeitsdauer quantifiziert.

In einer alternden Gesellschaft werden teilweise die absolute Anzahl alter Menschen und der Anteil der alten Menschen in der Bevölkerung zunehmen. Wird diese Entwicklung die der Arbeitslosigkeit erhöhen oder senken? Dies wird für ein Land, in welchem schon eine beträchtliche Alterung der Bevölkerung eingetreten ist, nämlich Deutschland und für Polen untersucht, das erst am Anfang dieser Entwicklung steht.

Als Datengrundlage werden die Informationen aus dem Sozio-ökonomischen Panel (SOEP) für Deutschland und dem Labour Force Survey (BAEL) für Polen verwendet.

Die abhängige Variable ist die Wahrscheinlichkeit des Übergangs von der Arbeitslosigkeit in die Erwerbstätigkeit. Der Einfluss verschiedener Faktoren auf diese Variable wurde von Uhlendorff (2003) und Hujer, Schneider (1996) durchgeführt. Wir formulieren folgende Hypothesen, die in dieser Arbeit empirisch untersucht werden:

- Je älter die Arbeitslosen sind, desto geringer ist die Wahrscheinlichkeit der Aufnahme einer Erwerbstätigkeit.
- Arbeitslose Frauen nehmen mit einer geringeren Wahrscheinlichkeit eine Erwerbstätigkeit auf als arbeitslose Männer.
- Je länger die Ausbildungsdauer einer arbeitslosen Person ist, desto größer ist die Wahrscheinlichkeit der Aufnahme einer Erwerbstätigkeit.
- Ausländische Arbeitslose nehmen mit einer geringeren Wahrscheinlichkeit eine Erwerbstätigkeit auf.

II. Auswahl und Grundlagen eines geeigneten Analyseinstrumentes

Empirische Dauerdaten können ausschließlich positive Werte annehmen – negative Zeitdauern existieren nicht! Außerdem können Zeitdauern nur teilweise beobachtet und gemessen werden (censoring problem). Aufgrund dieses besonderen

Charakters der empirischen Daten ist die Anwendung klassischer Regressionsmodelle ausgeschlossen. Dies alles hat zur Entwicklung der so genannten Überlebenszeitanalyse (**Survival Analysis**) geführt. [1]

Das Ziel von Survival Analysen besteht darin, die beobachtete Verteilung von Dauern – des Andauerns von Zuständen in Zeiträumen – mit Hilfe von so genannten Hazard-Funktionen abzubilden.

Survival Analysis findet in verschiedenen technischen und gesellschaftlichen Forschungen ihre Anwendung. Hazard Modelle werden dort eingesetzt, wo der Zeitpunkt des Eintritts eines bestimmten Ereignisses prognostiziert werden soll. Beispiele sind:

- die Prognose des Zeitpunktes, zu dem jemand nach einer Operation stirbt,
- die Prognose des Zeitpunktes, zu dem eine Maschine versagt,
- die Prognose des Zeitraums bis zur Marktdurchdringung eines neuen Produktes,
- die Prognose der Dauer eines Arbeitskampfes bis zu dessen Schlichtung.

Eine Prognose der Arbeitslosigkeitsdauer bis zur Wiederaufnahme einer Beschäftigung gilt als typischer Anwendungsfall (Devine, Kiefer 1991; Lancaster 1979).

Innerhalb der Survival Analysis wurden Modelle entwickelt, die sich durch die Verteilungsannahmen zur individuellen Ereigniszeit T unterscheiden.

T ist eine nicht-negative Zufallsvariable und beschreibt die Zeit bis zum Eintritt eines Ereignisses, mit Dichte $f(t)$ und Verteilung $F(t)$. Es sind folgende alternative Darstellungsformen der Wahrscheinlichkeitsverteilungen von T möglich.

Die **kumulative Verteilungsfunktion** $F(t)$ liefert die Wahrscheinlichkeit dafür, dass der Zeitpunkt des Ereigniseintritts vor oder genau an einem gewählten Zeitpunkt t liegt.

$$F(t) = Pr[T \leq t]$$

In den Anwendungen der Survival Analysis steht das Überleben von Prozessen über den gewählten Zeitpunkt im Mittelpunkt. Die **Survival Funktion** $S(t)$ drückt die Wahrscheinlichkeit des Überlebens über einen Zeitpunkt t hinaus aus.

$$S(t) = Pr[T > t] = 1 - F(t)$$

Die Funktion kann Werte zwischen 0 und 1 annehmen $S(0)=1$. Sie ist eine monoton abnehmende Funktion der Zeit.

Die **Dichtefunktion** bzw. Probability Density Function $f(t)$

$$f(t) = \frac{dF(t)}{dt} = \frac{dS(t)}{dt} = \lim_{dt \to 0} \frac{Pr[t < T < t + dt]}{dt}$$

1 Zu diesem Thema vgl.: Kalbfleisch, Prentice (1980); Cox, Oakes (1984); Heckman, Singer (1984); Blossfeld u. a. (1986); Kiefer (1988); Lancaster (1990); Green (2000).

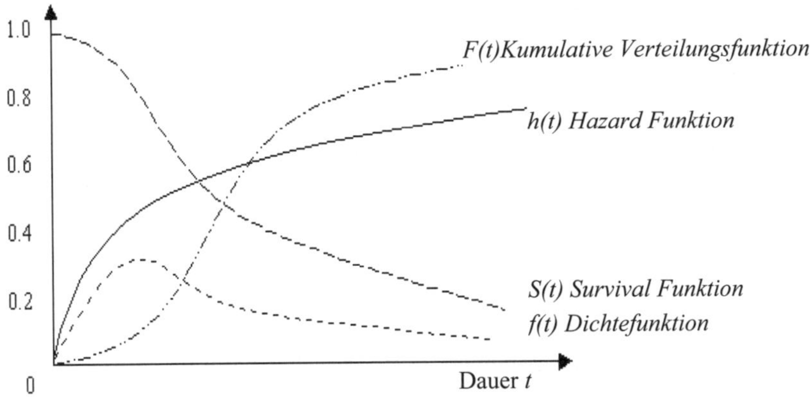

Abb. 1: Alternative Darstellungsformen der Wahrscheinlichkeitsverteilungen von T

Die häufigste Darstellungsform der Wahrscheinlichkeitsverteilung von T ist jedoch die **Hazard-Funktion** $h(t)$. Die Hazard-Funktion $h(t)$ (conditional failure function, hazard function) schätzt die „Wahrscheinlichkeit“ bzw. das unmittelbare Risiko, dass der Eintritt eines Ereignisses in einer kleinen Zeitspanne zwischen t und $t+dt$ zu erwarten ist – vorausgesetzt das Ereignis ist bis zum Zeitpunkt t nicht eingetreten.

$$h(t) = \frac{f(t)}{S(t)} = \lim_{dt \to 0} \frac{Pr\left[t < T < t + dt \mid T > t\right]}{dt}$$

Hazardraten sind keine Wahrscheinlichkeiten im eigentlichen Sinne, sondern latente Variablen, die als Intensität des Übergangs von einem Zustand in einen weiteren aufgefasst werden können. Je höher der Funktionswert ($\in[0,\infty]$), desto schneller findet im Durchschnitt der Übergang von Zustand A nach B statt.

III. Hazardmodelle

Eine Reihe von Modellen wird in der Klasse Hazardmodelle zusammengefasst. Man unterscheidet:

1. nicht-parametrische Hazardmodelle (z.B. Kaplan-Meier-Schätzer),
2. parametrische Hazardmodelle (parametric hazard models):
   a) proportional hazard models PH
      (z.B. Exponentiell, Weibull, Gompertz),
   b) accelerated failure-time models AFT
      (z.B. Exponentiell, Weibull, Log-logistisch, Lognormal),
3. semi-parametrische (z.B. Cox Regression).

Im Fall vom **Kaplan-Meier-Schätzer** wird keinerlei Annahme über die Verteilung der Überlebensfunktion und den Einfluss von Kovarianten getroffen. Der KM-Schätzer ist ein Schätzer der Survival Funktion.

Aber Hazardmodelle berücksichtigen im Allgemeinen nicht nur die aktuelle Dauer für den Eintritt von Ereignissen, sondern auch weitere Bestimmungsgrößen. In **Proportional Hazard Modellen** werden die zusätzlichen erklärenden Variablen als Funktion eines multi-dimensionalen Vektors definiert (*X*), die multiplikatorisch auf die zugrundeliegende Hazard-Funktion (baseline hazard) wirkt.

$$h(t|X) = h_0(t)g_0(X) = h_0(t)exp(X\beta)$$

Dabei finden folgende Bezeichnungen Verwendung: X – Vektor der Kovariablen, β – Vektor der Schätzparameter, $h_0(t)$ – baseline hazard.

Die vorherige Gleichung logarithmiert ergibt:

$$log\ h(t|X) = \alpha(t) + \beta_1 x_1 + \ldots + \beta_k x_k$$

Die Eigenschaften der Hazard-Funktionen ändern sich proportional zur Ausprägung der Kovariablen.

Die Gestalt von Hazard-Funktionen kann aufgrund unterschiedlicher Verteilungsannahmen zur baseline hazard, verschiedene Formen annehmen:

- konstante Ausprägung (Prozesse, bei denen kein erkennbarer Zusammenhang zwischen dem Andauern und dem Abbruch des Vorgangs besteht),
- monoton steigende (Prozesse, deren Beendigung immer wahrscheinlicher wird, je länger sie dauern; z.B. Entscheidungsfindungen),
- monoton fallende (Prozesse, deren Beendigung mit fortschreitender Dauer unwahrscheinlicher wird),
- U-förmige.

Zur Parametrisierung des Effekts der Verweildauer auf die Hazardrate können verschiedene funktionale Formen unterstellt werden (siehe Abb. 2 und Tab. 1).

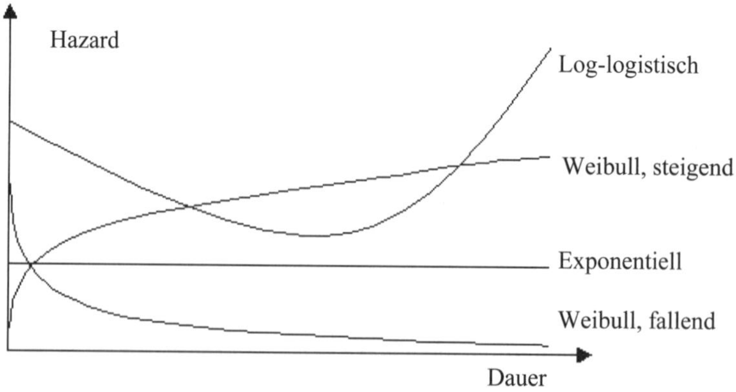

Abb. 2: Mögliche Ausprägungen von Hazardfunktionen

In der Ökonomie werden vorwiegend PH Modelle verwendet, in der Technik eher **accelerated failure-time Modelle** (AFT). Es wird eine Parametrisierung für $\tau_i = t_i exp(-X\beta)$ angenommen. $exp(-X\beta)$ ist der „Beschleunigungsparameter“ (acceleration parameter). Wenn $exp(-X\beta)=1$, dann ist $\tau_i = t_i$ und die Zeit vergeht „normal“. Wenn $exp(-X\beta)>1$, dann ist die Zeit „beschleunigt“ und das Ereignis tritt für diese Beobachtung eher ein. Wenn $exp(-X\beta)<1$,dann ist die Zeit „verlangsamt“. In AFT Modellen besteht Interesse an $t_i = exp(X\beta)\tau_i$, d.h. $E[ln(t_i)|x_i]$ für unterschiedliche x_i.

Verteilung	Survival Funktion $S(t)$	Hazard Funktion $h(t)$	baseline hazard $h_0(t)$	Parameter	Eigenschaften
Exponential	$\exp(-\lambda t)$	λ	1	$\lambda, \lambda = \exp(X\beta)$	Konstanter Hazard
Weibull	$\exp(-\lambda t^{p})$	$pt^{p-1}\lambda$	pt^{p-1}	$p, \lambda, \lambda = \exp(X\beta)$	Hazard monoton
Gompertz	$\exp(-\lambda\gamma^{-1}(\exp(\lambda t)-1))$	$\exp(\gamma t)\lambda$	$\exp(\gamma t)$	$\gamma, \lambda, \lambda = \exp(X\beta)$	Hazard monoton

Verteilung	Survival Funktion $S(t)$	Dichtefunktion $f(t)$	Parameter	Eigenschaften
Log-logistisch	$\frac{1}{1+(\lambda t)^{1/\gamma}}$	$\frac{\lambda^{1/\gamma} t^{1/\gamma - 1}}{\gamma(1+(\lambda t)^{1/\gamma})^2}$	$\gamma, \lambda,$ $\lambda = \exp(-X\beta)$	Hazard nicht-monoton
Lognormal	$1-\Phi\left\{\frac{\ln(t)-\mu}{\sigma}\right\}$	$\frac{1}{t\sigma\sqrt{2\pi}}\exp\left[\frac{-1}{2\sigma^2}\{\ln(t)-\mu\}^2\right]$	$\sigma, \mu, \mu = X\beta$	Hazard nicht-monoton

Quelle: In Anlehnung an Green (2000)

Tab. 1: Übliche Parametrisierungen in Verweildauermodellen

Im **Cox-Regression-Modell** werden keine expliziten Verteilungsannahmen zur baseline hazard getroffen. Der Verzicht auf Verteilungsannahmen schützt davor, falsche Schlüsse aufgrund eines unpassenden Modells zur baseline hazard zu ziehen. Die Schätzung des Kovariantenparameters β steht im Mittelpunkt des Interesses. Ihr Nachteil besteht darin, dass heterogeneity effects nicht berücksichtigt werden.

IV. Die Datengrundlage

Als I. Datenbasis für unsere Untersuchung dient das Sozio-ökonomische Panel (**GSOEP – The German Socio Economic Panel Study**) für Deutschland. Das SOEP ist eine Haushalts- und Personenstichprobe mit Panelcharakter. Diese repräsentative Wiederholungsbefragung privater Haushalte wird im jährlichen Rhythmus seit 1984 bei denselben Personen und Familien in der BRD (4528

Haushalte) durchgeführt. Im Juni 1990 wurde die Studie auf das Gebiet der ehemaligen DDR (2179 Haushalte) ausgeweitet. Für unsere Analyse wurden 7 Wellen des SOEP von I.1996 bis XII.2000 genutzt (monatliche Daten).

In der Befragung werden Informationen zur Erwerbssituation der Personen und ihrem persönlichen Hintergrund ermittelt. In dem Erwerbskalendarium sind Informationen über verschiedene Erwerbszustände, beispielsweise Vollzeit-Beschäftigung, Teilzeit-Beschäftigung, berufliche Weiterbildung, Arbeitslosigkeit, usw. in monatlicher Differenzierung verfügbar.

Die verwendete Stichprobe umfasst Personen im Alter von 16 bis 59 Jahren, die während des Beobachtungszeitraums mindestens eine Arbeitslosigkeitsepisode hatten. Arbeitslosigkeitsepisoden werden als vollständig definiert, wenn ein Übergang in Beschäftigung, Weiterbildung oder Pension zu beobachten ist. Andernfalls werden sie als rechtszensiert behandelt (right censored). Linkszensierte Episoden (left censored) werden aus methodischen Gründen von der Analyse ausgeschlossen.

Aufgrund der Selektionskriterien hat sich eine Stichprobe von 1455 Individuen ergeben. Als Ergebnisvariable dient die individuelle Arbeitslosigkeitsdauer in Monaten (*Y*). Im Untersuchungszeitraum betrug die durchschnittliche Dauer einer Arbeitslosigkeitsperiode in Deutschland 10,91753 Monate.

Folgende Einflussvariablen werden berücksichtigt:

- gebjahr – Geburtsjahr,
- sex – Geschlecht (1=Mann, 0=Frau),
- bildzeit – Dauer der Ausbildung, in Jahren,
- nat – Nationalität (1 = Deutscher, 0 = Ausländer).

1999				2000				2001			
1	2	3	4	1	2	3	4	1	2	3	4
X	–	–	X	X							
X	X	–	–	X	X						
	X	X	–	–	X	X					
		X	X	–	–	X	X				
			X	X	–	–	X	X			
				X	X	–	–	X	X		
					X	X	–	–	X	X	
						X	X	–	–	X	X
							X	X	–	–	X

Quelle: GUS, Aktywność ekonomiczna ludności Polski. III kwartał 2004, Warszawa 2005, S. XXII

Tab. 2: Die Struktur des BAEL-Panels

Als 2. Datenbasis für meine Untersuchung dient das Labour Force Survey (**BAEL – Badanie Aktywności Ekonomicznej Ludności**) für Polen vom IV. Quartal 2000. Das BAEL ist eine Haushaltsstichprobe, die seit dem II. Quartal 1993 erhoben wird. Den Personen werden u.a. retrospektive Fragen gestellt, die ihre berufliche Vergangenheit betreffen.

Die Probe BAEL ist ein Rotationspanel mit folgender Struktur:

Ein Haushalt wird viermal befragt, z.B.: im 1. und 2. Quartal der Untersuchung und dann im ersten und zweiten Quartal des nächsten Jahres. Bei jeder neuen Untersuchung wird ein Viertel der Probe neu ausgewählt. Deswegen beruht meine Analyse auf den retrospektiven Fragen.

Die verwendete Stichprobe umfasst Personen im Alter von 16 bis 59 Jahren, die in der Woiwodschaft Mazowieckie in Polen wohnhaft sind und die während des Beobachtungszeitraums mindestens eine Arbeitslosigkeitsepisode aufweisen.

Aufgrund der Selektionskriterien hat sich eine Stichprobe von 363 Individuen ergeben. 170 von ihnen waren bereits arbeitslos (rechtszensierte Daten) und 193 waren in der Vergangenheit arbeitslos.

Als Ergebnisvariable dient die individuelle Arbeitslosigkeitsdauer in Monaten (Y). Die durchschnittliche Dauer einer Arbeitslosigkeitsperiode in Polen betrug 13,017 Monate.

Folgende Einflussvariablen werden berücksichtigt:

- alter – Alter in Jahren,
- sex – Geschlecht (1=Mann, 0=Frau),
- bildniv – Niveau der Ausbildung
  (1=Universität, 2=Fachhochschule, 3=Berufsausbildung mit Abitur, 4=Abitur, 5= Berufsschule, 6=Hauptschule, 7=kein Schulabschluss).

V. Schätzung von Hazardmodellen

Bei der Analyse von Dauerdaten ist die Verwendung der Kleinst Quadrate-Schätzung aufgrund von Annahmen zu den Modellergebnissen und aufgrund des besonderen Charakters der empirischen Daten problematisch.

Empirische Dauerdaten und somit auch Ergebnisse von Schätzungen können ausschließlich positive Werte annehmen. Zeitdauern können oft nur teilweise beobachtet werden (censoring problem). Wenn Prozesse zum Teil schon vor dem Beginn der Untersuchungen eingesetzt haben, spricht man von linkszensierten Daten. In solchen Fällen wird der wahre Beginn einer Dauer ignoriert. Als Anfangszeitpunkt wird der Start des Beobachtungszeitraums definiert (zensiert). Mit rechtszensierten Daten hat man zu tun, wenn der in Wirklichkeit abgelaufene Prozess länger als der beobachtete Prozess innerhalb der Untersuchung ist.

Die unbekannten Regressionsparameter werden mit der **Maximum-Likelihood-Methode** geschätzt. Diese Methode ermöglicht, rechtzensierte Daten im Schätzvorgang zu berücksichtigen. Standardmäßig wird für die Konstruktion der Likelihood-Funktion ein bedingt unabhängiger Zensierungsmechanismus vorausgesetzt.

Sei *[0,T]* – der Beobachtungszeitraum, t_i – die Dauer der Episode und X_i – der Vektor der Kovariablen. Rechtszensierte Daten werden in Hazardmodellen durch den Zensierungsindikator C_i explizit berücksichtigt ($C_i = 1$, wenn $ti \leq T$, d.h. die Beobachtung ist nicht zensiert; $C_i = 0$, wenn $ti > T$, d.h. die Beobachtung ist zensiert). Die **Likelihood-Funktion** lautet:

$$L = \prod_{i=1}^{I} f_i(t_i/X_i)^{C_i} \prod_{i=1}^{I} S(T/X_i)^{1-C_i} = \prod_{i=1}^{I} h_i(t_i/X_i)^{C_i} S(T/X_i)$$
$$= \prod_{i=1}^{I} h_i(t_i/X_i)^{C_i} \exp(-\int_0^T h_i(u/X_i)du) \quad ,$$

wobei der Term $h_i(t_i/X_i)^{C_i}$ die Abgangsrate zeigt, und sich in $\exp(-\int_0^T h_i(u/X_i)du)$ die Überlebensfunktion niederschlägt.

Die folgende Log-Likelihood-Funktion wird in Abhängigkeit von einem Parametervektor θ, der insbesondere die Regressionskoeffizienten βj enthält, maximiert:

$$\ln L(\theta, X_i) = \sum_{i=1}^{I} \left(C_i \ln h_i(t_i / X_i, \theta) - \int_0^T h_i(u / X_i, \theta) du \right)$$

Die Anpassung der Hazardmodelle an die empirischen Daten kann mit Hilfe statistischer Methoden geprüft werden. Die Analyse der Loglikelihood-Werte (je kleiner *-2lnL*, desto besser), der Likelihood-Ratio-Test mit Test-Statistik $2(\ln L_1 - \ln L_0)$, die χ^2- verteilt wird (L_0 – Likelihood-Wert des endgültigen Modells, L_1 – Likelihood-Wert des Nullmodells), die Informationskriterien (AIC, BIC) und die Prüfung der Signifikanz der Parameter ermöglichen Aussagen über die Anpassungsgüte. Die Schätzungen wurden im Programm STATA durchgeführt.

1. Das Weibullmodell PH

Ein mögliches Modell für die Dauer von Arbeitslosigkeit wäre die Annahme eines Weibullmodells. Eine Zufallsvariable heißt weibullverteilt mit Parameter $p>0$ (shape parameter), falls ihre survival function folgende Gestalt hat:

$$S(t) = exp(-exp(X\beta)t^p).$$

Die Hazard Funktion und baseline hazard lauten:

$$h(t) = pt^{p-1} exp(X\beta) \quad \text{und} \quad h_0(t) = pt^{p-1}.$$

Im Rahmen eines Weibullmodells kann man Fragen von politischem Interesse erörtern, nämlich wie wirkt sich die Wahl des Parameters p auf die Dauer der Arbeitslosigkeit aus. Falls $p=1$ gilt, wäre die Hazardrate konstant (Modell mit Exponentialverteilung); dies hieße, dass die Dauer der bisherigen Arbeitslosig-

keit keine Rolle für den nächsten Zustand (arbeitslos oder nicht) spielt. Bei *p<1* sinkt die Hazardrate; dies bedeutet, dass die Chance Arbeit zu finden sinkt, je länger man arbeitslos ist. Falls man *p>1* annimmt, steigt die Hazardrate; dies könnte dahingehend interpretiert werden, dass Arbeitslose eher geneigt sind, sich einen Job zu suchen, wenn die staatlichen Unterstützungen auslaufen.
Im Weibullmodell können wir nicht nur die Dauer für den Ereignisseintritt (Ende der Arbeitslosigkeit), sondern auch weitere Bestimmungsgrößen (wie Geburtsjahr, Geschlecht, Dauer der Ausbildung, Nationalität) berücksichtigen. *X* = (gebjahr, sex, bildzeit, nat) bezeichnet den Vektor von Einflussvariablen.
Schätzergebnisse für das Weibullmodell für Deutschland sind folgender Tabelle zu entnehmen.

Number of obs = 1455 Log likelihood = -1940.7108			LR chi2(4) = 347.52 Prob > chi2 = 0.0000		
t	Coef.	Std.Err.	z	P>z	[95% Conf. Interval]
Gebjahr	0.03887	0.00248	15.67	0.000	0.03401 0.04373
Sex	0.12867	0.06141	2.10	0.036	0.00831 0.24903
bildzeit	0.12220	0.01274	9.59	0.000	0.09724 0.14717
Nat	0.28203	0.09681	2.91	0.004	0.09228 0.47177
cons	-80.64718	4.90190	-16.45	0.000	-90.25472 -71.03964
P	1.05964	0.02432			1.01303 1.10838

Quelle: Eigene Berechnungen

Tab. 3: Schätzergebnisse für das Weibullmodell für Deutschland

Die Parameterschätzer können wie folgt interpretiert werden:

- gebjahr (Geburtsjahr): eine Erhöhung des Alters um 1 Jahr führt zu einer 4% Senkung der Chance eine neue Arbeit zu finden (exp(0,039)=1,04),
- sex (Geschlecht): Männer haben Frauen gegenüber eine um 13,7% größere Chance eine Arbeit zu finden (exp(0,129)=1,137),
- bildzeit (Ausbildungsdauer): eine Erhöhung der Ausbildungsdauer um 1 Jahr führt zu einer 13% Erhöhung der Chance eine Arbeit zu bekommen (exp(0,122)=1,13),
- nat (1 = Deutscher, 0 = Ausländer): Deutsche haben eine um 32,6% höhere Chance eine Arbeit zu finden als Ausländer (exp(0,282)=1,326).

Der Parameter *p*=1.059636>1 deutet auf die positive Dauerabhängigkeit (die Hazardrate steigt) hin. Arbeitslose sind eher geneigt, sich einen Job zu suchen, wenn die staatlichen Unterstützungen auslaufen.

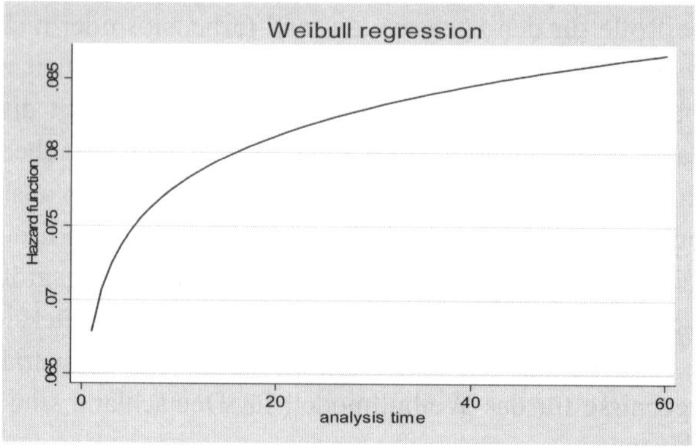

Abb. 3: Hazardfunktion für das Lognormalmodell für Deutschland

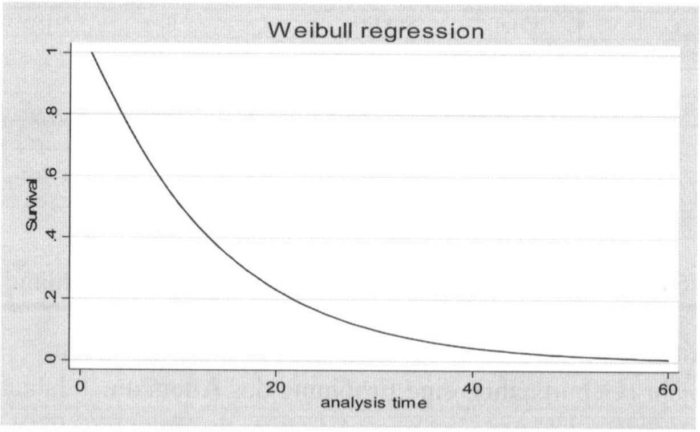

Abb. 4: **Survival function** für das Lognormalmodell für Deutschland

Unter Verwendung der polnischen BAEL-Daten resultieren die in der Tabelle 4 angegebenen Schätzergebnisse für das Weibullmodell.

Number of obs = 363 Log likelihood = -369.03173			LR chi2(4) = 27.75 Prob > chi2 = 0.0000			
t	Coef.	Std.Err.	z	P>z	[95% Conf. Interval]	
alter	-0.02362	0.00768	-3.08	0.002	-0.03866	-0.00858
sex	0.51011	0.15061	3.39	0.001	0.21491	0.80531
bildniv	-0.11741	0.05520	-2.13	0.033	-0.22559	-0.00926
cons	-3.09608	0.35231	-8.79	0.000	-3.78660	-2.40556
p	1.31718	0.07320			1.18124	1.46876

Quelle: Eigene Berechnungen

Tab. 4: Schätzergebnisse für das Weibullmodell für Polen

Die Parameterschätzer können wie folgt interpretiert werden:

- alter (Alter): eine Erhöhung des Alters um 1 Jahr führt zu einer 2,4% Senkung der Chance eine neue Arbeit zu finden (exp(-0,024)=0,976=1-0,024),
- sex (Geschlecht): Männer haben um 66,6% größere Chance eine Arbeit zu finden als Frauen (exp(0,51)=1,666),
- bildniv (Ausbildungsniveau): eine höhere Ausbildung führt zu einer 11,1% Erhöhung der Wahrscheinlichkeit eine Arbeit zu bekommen (exp(-0,117)=0,889).

2. Das Lognormalmodell AFT

Charakteristisch ist, dass der Logarithmus für die Verweildauer $ln t_i = X\beta + ln \tau_i$ normalverteilt ist. Die Survival-Funktion ist die folgende:

$$S(t) = 1 - \Phi\left\{\frac{ln(t) - X\beta}{\sigma}\right\}$$

mit Φ – Verteilungsfunktion der Standardnormalverteilung. Die Dichtefunktion:

$$f(t) = \frac{1}{t\sigma\sqrt{2\pi}} exp\left[\frac{-1}{2\sigma^2}\{ln(t) - X\beta\}^2\right]$$

Schätzergebnisse für das Lognormalmodell für Deutschland sind folgender Tabelle zu entnehmen.

Number of obs = 1455 Log likelihood = -1887.6586		LR chi2(4) = 328.55 Prob > chi2 = 0.0000			
t	Coef.	Std.Err.	z	P>z	[95% Conf. Interval]
gebjahr	-0.03786	0.00241	-15.68	0.000	-0.04259 -0.03313
sex	-0.15447	0.06157	-2.51	0.012	-0.27515 -0.03379
bildzeit	-0.11020	0.01320	-8.35	0.000	-0.13608 -0.08433
nat	-0.33841	0.09703	-3.49	0.000	-0.52859 -0.14823
cons	77.94248	4.72727	16.49	0.000	68.67720 87.20775
sigma	1.10115	0.02401			1.05509 1.14922

Quelle: Eigene Berechnungen

Tab. 5: Schätzergebnisse für das Lognormalmodell für Deutschland

Die negativen Schätzwerte bedeuten, dass die Zeit ein „Beschleunigungsparameter“ ist. Wenn eine erklärende Variable wächst, dann beschleunigt das den Eintritt des Ereignisses „Ende der Arbeitslosigkeit“.

Die log-normale Verteilung findet Anwendung, wenn die Daten nicht-monotone Hazardraten aufweisen, insbesondere zuerst wachsende, dann sinkende.

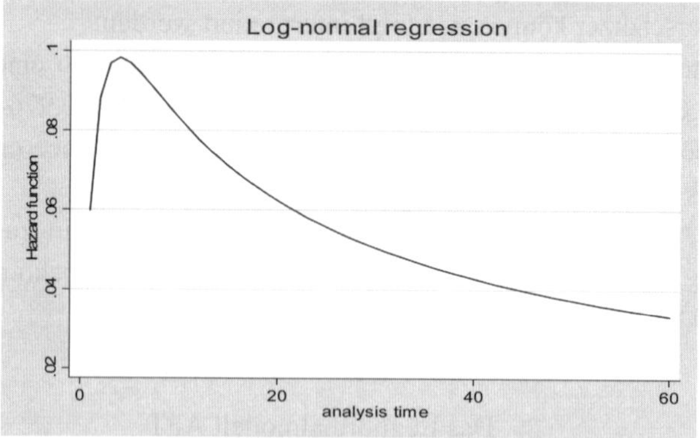

Abb. 5: Hazardfunktion für das Lognormalmodell für Deutschland

Unsere Ergebnisse zeigen, dass die Wahrscheinlichkeit der Wiederbeschäftigung eines Arbeitslosen kurz nach dem Verlust des Arbeitsplatzes am größten ist. Die Wiederbeschäftigungschancen sinken jedoch im Zeitablauf („lagged duration dependence" Heckman, Borjas 1980, S. 247 ff.).
Ein jüngeres Alter, männliches Geschlecht und ein höheres Bildungsniveau senken auch in Polen die Länge der Arbeitslosigkeitsdauer.

Number of obs = 363 Log likelihood = -364.71719			LR chi2(4) = 16.44 Prob > chi2 = 0.0009			
t	Coef.	Std.Err.	z	P>z	[95% Conf. Interval]	
Alter	0.01457	0.00578	2.52	0.012	0.00324	0.02590
Sex	-0.24956	0.12324	-2.03	0.043	-0.49111	-0.00802
bildniv	0.11161	0.04754	2.35	0.019	0.01843	0.20479
cons	1.93517	0.26095	7.42	0.000	1.42371	2.44663
sigma	1.00823	0.05248			0.91044	1.11652

Quelle: Eigene Berechnungen

Tab. 6: Schätzergebnisse für das Lognormalmodell für Polen

VI. Resümee

Ziel der Studie war es, die Arbeitslosigkeitsdauer mit Hilfe von Methoden der Ereignisanalyse zu untersuchen. In der Studie wird eine empirische Analyse der Effekte von bestimmten Merkmalen auf die individuelle Arbeitslosigkeitsdauer durchgeführt. Die Ergebnisse zeigen, dass Alter, Geschlecht, Ausbildungsniveau und Nationalität die individuelle Arbeitslosigkeitsdauer und die Wahrscheinlichkeit einer Zustandsveränderung bestimmen.
Ein jüngeres Alter senkt in Deutschland die Dauer der Arbeitslosigkeit in stärkerem Maße als in Polen. Männer haben sowohl in Deutschland als auch in Polen

eine bessere Chance, Arbeit zu finden, wobei dieser Effekt in Polen stärker ist. Es hat sich ergeben, dass ein höheres Bildungsniveau die Lage der Arbeiter in beiden Ländern verbessert.

Die Resultate der durchgeführten Untersuchung deuten darauf hin, dass Hazardmodelle ein geeignetes Mittel für die Analyse der Arbeitslosigkeitsdauer bieten. Mit welchen Folgen für Arbeitsmärkte muss aufgrund der Zunahme der Gesellschaftsalterung gerechnet werden? Nachdem wir den Altersfaktor in unseren Modellen analysiert haben, lassen sich folgende Effekte der Alterung eruieren. Gemäß unseren Ergebnissen ist zu vermuten, dass die Dauer der durchschnittlichen Arbeitslosigkeitsperiode größer wird. Dies zeigt auch die stärkere Ausprägung unserer Ergebnisse für Deutschland mit seinem fortgeschritteneren Alterungsprozess der Bevölkerung. Für den Arbeitgeber wird es immer schwieriger, gut qualifizierte Arbeitskräfte, die über moderne, zeitgemäße Berufsausbildung verfügen, zu finden. Ferner kann die Zahl der Arbeitsplätze abnehmen. Die alternden Menschen werden immer weniger berufstätig. Eine bessere Ausbildung könnte die Arbeitslosigkeitsdauer älterer Menschen mindern. Auch eine Flucht der älteren Arbeitskräfte ins Ausland wird keine Verbesserung ihrer Situation bringen, da für ältere Immigranten im Aufnahmeland wiederum schlechtere Beschäftigungschancen bestehen. Das Beispiel Deutschland weist darauf hin, dass sich im Alterungsprozess die Beschäftigungschancen älterer Beschäftigter nicht erhöhen. Allerdings kann eine auf Vergangenheits- und Gegenwartsdaten basierende Analyse nicht die Folgen künftiger möglicher sektoraler Anpassungen, der Beschäftigung älterer Menschen im Schattensektor (Friedrich, Wimmert 2006), usw. einbeziehen.

Literaturverzeichnis

Blossfeld, H.-P., A. Hamerle und *K. Mayer*, Ereignisanalyse, Statistische Theorie und Anwendung in den Wirtschafts- und Sozialwissenschaften, Frankfurt/Main 1986.

Cox, D. und *D. Oakes*, Analysis of Survival Data, London 1984.

Devine, T. und *N. Kiefer*, Empirical Labor Economics, New York und Oxford 1991.

Friedrich P. und W. Wimmert, Aspects of Regional Population Development, in: New Members – New Challenges for the European Regional Development Policy, hrsg. von T. Markowski und M. Turala, Warschau 2006, S. 72–85.

Green, W., Econometric Analysis, New York 2000.

GUS, Aktywność ekonomiczna ludności Polski. III kwartał 2004, Warszawa 2005.

Heckman, J. und *G. Borjas*, Does Unemployment Cause Future Unemployment? Definitions, Questions and Answers from a Continuous Time Model of Heterogenity and State Dependence, in: Economica, Vol. 47, 1980, S. 247-283.

Heckman, J. und *B. Singer*, Econometric duration analysis, in: Journal of Econometrics, Vol. 24, 1984, S. 63-132.

Hujer, R. und *H. Schneider*, Institutionelle und strukturelle Determinanten der Arbeitslosigkeit in Westdeutschland. Eine mikroökonometrische Analyse mit Paneldaten, in: Arbeitslosigkeit und Möglichkeiten ihrer Überwindung, hrsg. von B. Gahlen, H. Hesse und H. Ramser, Tübingen 1996, S. 53-76.

Kalbfleisch, J. und *R. Prentice*, The Statistical Analysis of Failure Time Data, New York 1980.

Kiefer, N., Economic Duration Data and Hazard Functions, in: Journal of Economic Literature, Vol. 26, 1988, S. 646-679.

Lancaster, T., Econometric Methods for the Duration of Unemployment, in: Econometrica, Vol. 47, 1979, S. 939-956.

Lancaster, T., The Econometric Analysis of Transition Data, Cambridge, New York und Melbourne 1990.

Uhlendorff, A., Der Einfluss von Persönlichkeitseigenschaften und sozialen Ressourcen auf die Arbeitslosigkeitsdauer, Berlin 2003.

Namenverzeichnis

Sachverzeichnis

Schriftenverzeichnis von Prof. Dr. Dr. h.c. Peter Friedrich

I. Bücher, Beiträge in Sammelwerken, Zeitschriftenaufsätze

Volkswirtschaftliche Investitionskriterien für Gemeindeunternehmen, Schriften zur angewandten Wirtschaftsforschung, Bd. 22, Hrsg.: Walther G. Hoffmann, Tübingen 1969.

Cost-Benefit-Analyse und Koordinierung kommunaler Ausgaben, Archiv für Kommunalwissenschaften, Jg. 9 (1970), S. 64-91.

Untersuchungen über den Nutzen kommunaler Wirtschaftsfördermaßnahmen, Untersuchungen über das Spar-, Giro- und Kreditwesen, Bd. 49, Hrsg.: Fritz Voigt, Berlin 1970, zusammen mit Peter Eichhorn.

Diskussionsbeitrag zum Referat: Möglichkeiten und Grenzen der Methode der Nutzen-Kosten-Analyse von Horst C. Recktenwald, in: Grundfragen der Infrastrukturplanung für wachsende Wirtschaften, Schriften des Vereins für Socialpolitik, N.F., Bd. 58, Hrsg. Helmut Arndt, Dieter Swatek, Berlin 1971, S. 263-269.

Die Nutzen-Kosten-Analyse als Entscheidungshilfe für Industrieansiedlungen aus der Sicht der Maximierung der isolierten Wohlfahrt, in: Nutzen-Kosten-Analysen bei öffentlichen Investitionen, Beiträge und Untersuchungen des Instituts für Siedlungs- und Wohnungswesen der Universität Münster, Hrsg.: Hans K. Schneider, Bd. 76, Münster 1971, S. 163-224.

Die Nutzen-Kosten-Analyse als Entscheidungshilfe für Industrieansiedlungen aus der Sicht der Maximierung der Gesamtwohlfahrt, in: Nutzen-Kosten-Analysen bei öffentlichen Investitionen, Beiträge und Untersuchungen des Instituts für Siedlungs- und Wohnungswesen der Universität Münster, Hrsg.: Hans Karl Schneider, Bd. 76, Münster 1971, S. 89-162, zusammen mit Peter Eichhorn.

Sind Investitionskriterien Leerformeln?, Archiv für öffentliche und freigemeinnützige Unternehmen, Bd. 9 (1972), S. 349-354.

Entwicklung einer gemeindespezifischen Produktionsfunktion, Environment and Planning, Vol. 4 (1972), S. 273-321, zusammen mit Herbert Biermann.

Modelle des kommunalen Industrieansiedlungswettbewerbs unter Berücksichtigung spieltheoretischer Ansätze, in: Tagungsbericht der Tagung der Universität Dortmund zur Theorie und Praxis der planerischen Entscheidung, Bd. 2, Dortmund 1974, S. 37-76.

Regionalpolitik und Beschaffungsmaßnahmen öffentlicher Unternehmen, in: Der öffentliche Haushalt, Jg. 16 (1975), S. 14-26.

Standorttheorie für öffentliche Verwaltungen, Schriften zur öffentlichen Verwaltung und öffentlichen Wirtschaft, Hrsg.: Peter Eichhorn, Peter Friedrich, Bd. 5, Baden-Baden 1976.

Verwaltungsökonomie, Schriften zur öffentlichen Verwaltung und öffentlichen Wirtschaft, Hrsg.: Peter Eichhorn, Peter Friedrich, Bd. 1, Teil I., Baden-Baden 1976, zusammen mit Peter Eichhorn.

Die Konzepte eines konjunkturneutralen Haushalts für die öffentlichen Unternehmen, in: Öffentliche Unternehmen in Rezession und Aufschwung, Schriftenreihe der Gesellschaft für öffentliche Wirtschaft und Gemeinwirtschaft e. V., Heft 14, Berlin 1977, S. 103-127.

Modelle kommunalen Industrieansiedlungswettbewerbs, in: Über Wachstum und Wachstumslenkung, Karlsruher Beiträge zur Wirtschaftspolitik und Wirtschaftsforschung, Heft 6, Karlsruhe 1977, S. 19-90.

Die öffentlichen Haushalte in der Finanzierungsrechnung, in: Sparkasse, Jg. 94 (1977), S. 28-34.

Strukturpolitische Auswirkungen der Standortentscheidungen öffentlicher Verwaltungen, in: Funktionalreform in Nordrhein-Westfalen, Hrsg.: Deutsches Institut für Urbanistik, Berlin 1977, S. 113-141.

Die Operationalisierung der Unternehmensziele, in: Auftrag und Führung öffentlicher Unternehmen, Schriftenreihe der Hochschule für Verwaltungswissenschaften Speyer, Bd. 68, Berlin 1977, S. 107-127.

Abgabegrenzen konkurrierender Verwaltungen, Konkurrenz zwischen kleinen Regionen, Competition among Small Regions, Hrsg.: Walter Buhr, Peter Friedrich, Schriften zur öffentlichen Verwaltung und öffentlichen Wirtschaft, Hrsg.: Peter Eichhorn, Peter Friedrich, Bd. 23, Baden-Baden 1978, S. 171-208.

Wichtige Aspekte der Konkurrenz zwischen kleinen Regionen, in: Konkurrenz zwischen kleinen Regionen, Competition among Small Regions, Hrsg.: Walter Buhr, Peter Friedrich, Schriften zur öffentlichen Verwaltung und öffentlichen Wirtschaft, Hrsg.: Peter Eichhorn, Peter Friedrich, Bd. 23, Baden-Baden 1978, S. 11-39, zusammen mit Walter Buhr.

Zeitersparnisse als Leistungskriterien gemeinwirtschaftlicher Unternehmen, Schriftenreihe Gemeinwirtschaft, Heft 31, Frankfurt 1978.

Ausrichtung der Preisbildung öffentlicher Unternehmen am Grenzkostenpreisprinzip bei differierenden Marktformen, in: Grenzkostenpreisbildung öffentlicher Unternehmen, Schriftenreihe der Gesellschaft für öffentliche Wirtschaft und Gemeinwirtschaft, Heft 16, Berlin 1978, S. 90-129.

Die Besteuerung öffentlicher Unternehmen, in: Öffentliche Wirtschaft und Gemeinwirtschaft, Jg. 29 (1979), S. 70-73.

Das Sunset-Konzept als Managementkonzeption für öffentliche Verwaltungen in Deutschland, in: Die Fortbildung, Jg. 1979, S.12-15.

Zur mikroökonomischen Steuerüberwälzung bei öffentlichen Unternehmen, in: Zeitschrift für öffentliche und gemeinwirtschaftliche Unternehmen, Bd. 2, 1979, S. 365-400.

Steuerliche Gleichbehandlung öffentlicher und privater Unternehmen, in: Wirtschaftsdienst, Jg. 59 (1979), S. 623-630, zusammen mit Peter Kupsch.

Steuerüberwälzung bei oligopolistischem Wettbewerb öffentlicher Unternehmen, in: Besteuerung öffentlicher Unternehmen, Hrsg: Peter Friedrich, Peter Kupsch, Schriften zur öffentlichen Verwaltung und öffentlichen Wirtschaft, Hrsg.: Peter Eichhorn, Peter Friedrich, Bd. 57, Baden-Baden 1981, S. 221-251.

Betriebswirtschaftliche und finanzwissenschaftliche Aspekte der Besteuerung öffentlicher Unternehmen, in: Besteuerung öffentlicher Unternehmen, Hrsg.: Peter Kupsch, Peter Friedrich, Schriften zur öffentlichen Verwaltung und öffentlichen Wirtschaft, Hrsg.: Peter Eichhorn, Peter Friedrich, Bd. 57, Baden-Baden 1981, S. 13–55, zusammen mit Peter Kupsch.

Manual for Identifying the Effects of the Settlement of a Public Office, in: Locational Developments and Urban Planning, Hrsg.: Peter Nijkamp, Wal F.J. van Lierop, Amsterdam 1981, S. 347-388, zusammen mit Heinrich Günter Wonnemann.

Öffentliche Unternehmen in der Staatsquote, in: Öffentliche Wirtschaft und Gemeinwirtschaft, Jg. 30 (1981), S. 124-127.

Das Sunset-Konzept als Managementkonzeption der Kontrolle für öffentliche Unternehmen, in: Kontrolle öffentlicher Unternehmen, Bd. 2, Schriftenreihe der Gesellschaft für öffentliche Wirtschaft und Gemeinwirtschaft, Heft 20, Baden-Baden 1982, S. 135-152.

Analyse des Averch-Johnson-Effekts bei öffentlichen Unternehmen, in: Öffentliche Bindung von Unternehmen, Schriftenreihe der Gesellschaft für öffentliche Wirtschaft und Gemeinwirtschaft, Heft 22, Baden-Baden 1982, S. 139-173.

Public X-Inefficiency, Informal and Institutional Constraints, Comment, in: Anatomy of Government Deficiencies, Hrsg.: Horst Hanusch, Berlin, Heidelberg, New York, Tokio 1983, S. 138-1945.

Falldokumentation zur Standortproblematik bei neugegründeten und verlagerten Behörden, Forschungsprojekt BMBau RS II 1-70 4102 – 78.215, Hrsg.: Bundesminister für Raumordnung, Bauwesen und Städtebau, Bonn 1983, zusammen mit ARP Berlin und Heinrich Günter Wonnemann.

Regional Aspects of X-Inefficiency in the Public Sector, in: Konzeptionelle Probleme öffentlicher Planung, Hrsg.: Eberhard Wille, Bern 1983, S. 189-244.

Volkswirtschaftliche Effekte der Fernwärmeversorgung in einer Stadt, in: Kommunalwirtschaft, Jg. 1983, zusammen mit Dimitrios Tsimopoulos.

Eine Analyse der Vor- und Nachteile der Fernwärmeauskopplung aus dem Großkraftwerk Franken II, in: Versorgungskonzepte, Hrsg. Norbert Eickhof, Schriftenreihe des Arbeitskreises für Wirtschaft und Verwaltung an der Universität Bamberg e.V., Bd. 6, Bamberg 1983, S. 194-203, zusammen mit Dimitrios Tsimopoulos.

Aufgabenwandel bei öffentlichen Wirtschaftsförderungsinstitutionen, in: Aufgabenwandel öffentlicher Unternehmen, Schriftenreihe der Gesellschaft für öffentliche Wirtschaft und Gemeinwirtschaft, Heft 24, Baden-Baden 1983, S.207-228.

Volkswirtschaftslehre der öffentlichen Verwaltung, in: Handbuch für die öffentliche Verwaltung, Bd. 1, Hrsg.: Albert von Mutius, Neuwied, Darmstadt 1984, S. 945-1035.

Zu einer angebotsorientierten Betrachtung öffentlicher Güter, in: Öffentliche Güter und öffentliche Unternehmen, Schriftenreihe der Gesellschaft für öffentliche Wirtschaft und Gemeinwirtschaft, Heft 25, Baden-Baden 1984, S. 103-113.

Ein verwaltungsökonomisches Simulationsmodell, in: Angewandte Wirtschafts- und Sozialkybernetik, Hrsg.: Bernd Schiemenz, Adolf Wagner, Berlin 1984, S. 277-303, zusammen mit Arne Pfeilsticker.

Messen, Ausstellungen und Mehrzweckhallen, in: Handbuch der kommunalen Wissenschaft und Praxis, Bd. 5, Hrsg.: Günter Püttner, Berlin, Heidelberg, New York, Tokio 1984, S. 535-564, zusammen mit Günter Valjak.

Erfahrungsbericht über Behördenverlagerung, vorwiegend in europäischen Ländern, unter Berücksichtigung der für den Freistaat Bayern verwertbaren Erkenntnisse, Bayerisches Staatsministerium für Landesplanung und Umweltfragen, Materialien, Heft 30, München 1984 zusammen mit Hermann Liebel und Edith Buckl.

Evaluierung eines Versorgungskonzeptes: Vorgehen und Ergebnisse, in: Zeitschrift für öffentliche und gemeinwirtschaftliche Unternehmen, Bd. 7 (1984), S. 163-189, zusammen mit Dimitrios Tsimopoulos.

Bestimmung der Zahl öffentlich Bediensteter, Stellenkegelwirkungen dargestellt im Rahmen eines Simulationsmodells der Verwaltungskoordination, in: Produktivitätsentwicklung staatlicher Leistungen, Hrsg.: Karl Häuser, Schriften des Vereins für Socialpolitik, N.F., Bd. 145, Berlin 1985, S. 199-286.

Allokation, in: Verwaltungslexikon, Hrsg.: Peter Eichhorn et. al.,1. Aufl., Baden-Baden 1985, S. 16-18.

Finanzwissenschaft, in: Verwaltungslexikon, Hrsg,: Peter Eichhorn et. al., 1. Aufl., Baden-Baden 1985, S. 324-328.

Financial Effects of Localization of Public Enterprises, in: Papers and Proceedings of the Regional Science Association, Vol. 53 (1985), S. 229-247, zusammen mit Heinrich Günter Wonnemann.

Fiscal Effects of Transportation Investment, in: Proceedings of the Korea-US Joint Seminar on Urban/Regional/Transportation Development, Planning, and Environmental Management, Seoul 1985, S. 175-218.

Zur Umwegrentabilität von Konzert- und Kongreßhallen, in: Kultur-, Kongreß- und Mehrzweckhallen als Wirtschaftsförderungsinstrument, Nr. 2, München 1991.

Behördenverlagerung in europäischen Ländern (I), Perspektiven und Behördendezentralisierung, in: Verwaltungspraxis, Jg.8 (1986), S. 143-149, zusammen mit Edith Buckl.

Regional Competition under Stagnation, in: Fiscal Decentralization, Hrsg.: Peter Friedrich, Paul van Rompuy, Schriften zur öffentlichen Verwaltung und öffentlichen Wirtschaft, Hrsg.: Peter Eichhorn, Peter Friedrich, Bd. 93, Baden-Baden 1986, S. 85-133.

Simulation staatlichen Bürokratieverhalten, in: Konkrete Probleme öffentlicher Planung, Hrsg.: Eberhard Wille, Frankfurt, Bern, New York 1986, S. 99-142, zusammen mit Arne Pfeilsticker.

Wirtschaftliche Effekte der Behördenverlagerung anhand von Beispielen aus der Bundesrepublik Deutschland, in: Dezentralisierung von Behörden und hochrangigen kulturellen und wirtschaftlichen Einrichtungen, Wien 1986, S. 189-192.

Aspekte der Finanzierung kommunaler Investitionen über geschlossene Immobilienfonds, in: Finanzierung kommunaler Investitionen über geschlossene Immobilienfonds, Hrsg.: Peter Friedrich, Schriften zur öffentlichen Verwaltung und öffentlichen Wirtschaft, Hrsg.: Peter Eichhorn, Peter Friedrich, Bd. 91, Baden-Baden 1987, S. 11-25, zusammen mit Johannes Reich.

Ordnungspolitische Aspekte öffentlicher Unternehmen, in: Theorie öffentlicher Unternehmen, Hrsg.: Theo Thiemeyer, Schriften der Gesellschaft für öffentliche Wirtschaft und Gemeinwirtschaft, Baden-Baden 1987, S. 15-51.

Regional Effects of the Establishment of Public Offices, in: Urban and Regional Policy in Korea and International Experiences, Hrsg.: Harry W. Richardson, Myong-Chan Hwang, Seoul 1987, S. 325-350.

X-Ineffizienz ein ausschlaggebendes Privatisierungsargument?, in: Probleme der Privatisierung, Hrsg.: Helmut Brede, Schriften der Gesellschaft für öffentliche Wirtschaft und Gemeinwirtschaft, Baden-Baden 1988, S. 235-256.

Technologietransfer mit Hilfe von Joint-Ventures in Polen: Möglichkeiten, Chancen und Probleme, in: Wissenschaftlich-technische Zusammenarbeit in den gegenwärtigen Ost-West-Beziehungen, Hrsg.: Clemens Burrichter, Zbigniew M. Klepacki, Erlangen 1988, S. 81-158.

Transfer technologii w Polsce za pomoca Joint-Ventures, in: Wspolpraca naukowo-techniczna na obecnym etapie stosunkow Wschod-Zachod, Instytut Krajow Socjalistycznych PAN, Warschau 1988, S. 58-99 und in: Biuletyn Informacyjny, no 4, 83, rok 22, Instytut Krajow Socjalistycznych PAN, Warschau 1989, S. 58-99.

Volkwirtschaftslehre öffentlicher Institutionen, in: Handwörterbuch der öffentlichen Betriebswirtschaft, Hrsg.: Klaus Chmielewicz, Peter Eichhorn, Stuttgart 1989, S. 1767-1777.

Nuovi sviluppi nella cooperazione fra comunit e impresa privata in Germania, in: publico e privato, cooperazione finanziarria ed organizzativa fra privati ed enti locali nelle aree urbane, Hrsg. Emilio Samek Lodovici, Gian Maria Bernareggi, Mailand 1990, S. 247-284.

Kriterien zur Beurteilung eines Joint-Ventures aus der Sicht des Deutschen Investors und der polnischen Mitwirkenden, in: Joint-Ventures in Polen, ICC (Hrsg.), Bonn, Bad Godesberg 1990, S. 1-23.

Prinzipien der Besteuerung für duale sozialistische Wirtschaftsordnungen unter Berücksichtigung von Joint-Ventures, Jahrbuch für Sozialwissenschaft, Bd. 41 (1991), S. 312-342.

Volkswirtschaftliche Aspekte einer Arbeitszeitverlängerung, in: Arbeitszeitveränderung in wirtschaftlicher, gesellschaftlicher und ethischer Sicht, Hrsg.: Peter Friedrich, Peter Gross, Schriften zur öffentlichen Verwaltung und öffentlichen Wirtschaft, Bd. 118, Baden-Baden 1991, S. 266-289.

Problematik des Kontenrahmens eines gesellschaftsbezogenen Rechnungswesens, in: Dienstprinzip und Erwerbsprinzip – Fragen der Grundorientierung in Verkehr und öffentlicher Wirtschaft, Hrsg.: Peter Faller, Dieter Witt, Schriften zur öffentlichen Verwaltung und öffentlichen Wirtschaft, Bd. 128, Baden-Baden 1991, S. 193-235.

Zasady opodatkowania joint ventures, in: Opodatkowanie przedsiebiorstw z udzialem kapitalu zagranicznego, Hrsg: Jan Gluchowski, Thorn 1991, S. 7-65.

Die deutsche Treuhandanstalt als Wirtschaftsförderungsinstrument, in: Reformen in Osteuropa II, Gemeinwirtschaft, o. Jg.(1991), S. 77-116.

Comparative approaches to local government finance, a review article, Town Planning Review, Vol. 62 (1991), S. 481-488.

Die umweltpolitischen Konsequenzen eigenwirtschaftlicher Preisbildung, in: Beiträge zur Theorie öffentlicher Unternehmen, Hrsg.: Peter Friedrich, Beiheft der Zeitschrift für öffentliche und gemeinwirtschaftliche Unternehmen, Nr. 14, 1992, S. 208–214, zusammen mit Hans Putnoki

70) Der vertikale Wettbewerb im Prinzipal-Agent-Verhältnis: Ein Ansatz zur Weiterentwicklung der Theorie der öffentlichen Unternehmen, in: Beiträge zur Theorie öffentlicher Unternehmen, Beiheft der Zeitschrift für öffentliche und gemeinwirtschaftliche Unternehmen, Nr. 14, 1992, S. 178-207.

From Centrally Planned to Market Orientated Economies: Problems of Transition in East Germany and Eastern Europe, in: Towards a New South African Economy: Comparative Perspectives, Hrsg.: Heribert Weiland, Matthew Braham, Freiburg 1992, S. 62-73.

Pluspunkt im Standortwettbewerb, in: Wirtschaftsinformation – IHK – Industrie- und Handelskammer Erfurt, Jg.3 (1992), S. 64-65.

Prywatyzacja a rynek pracy we wschodniej czesci RFN, in: Polityka Spoleczna, Nr. 11/12, Jg. 19 (1992), S. 22-24.

Ein gesellschaftsbezogenes Rechnungswesen am Beispiel der Stadthalle Osnabrück, in: Zeitschrift für öffentliche und gemeinwirtschaftliche Unternehmen, Bd. 16 (1993), S. 245-274, zusammen mit Günter Valjak, Heinrich-Günter Wonnemann und Klaus Jahn.

Katalog der Zulieferindustrie, Opole – Oppeln/ Polen, Internationales Institut für Kommunal- und Freizeitwirtschaft, Dr. Rödl & Partner GmbH, Nürnberg, München 1993.

Ansätze einer Theorie des Verkaufs von Treuhandvermögen an Kommunen, in: Jahrbuch für Sozialwissenschaft, Bd. 44 (1993), S. 233- 277, zusammen mit Xiao Feng.

Economic Aspects of German Unification: Privatisation and Structural Changes in the Eastern Part of Germany, in: The Disintegration of the Soviet Union and Its Impact on Korea and Germany, East and West Studies Series 27, Yonsei University, Seoul 1993, S. 109-137.

Summary Outline of an Approach on the Prospective Tasks and Aims of the Treuhandanstalt and Institutional Perspectives of their Execution with the Aid of Public Enterprises, in: Economic Problems, The Research Institute for National Unification, Seoul 1993, S. 85-106.

Die Treuhandanstalt ein Instrument zum Aufbau des Föderalismus?, in: Finanzierungsprobleme der deutschen Einheit I, Berlin 1993, S. 77-174, zusammen mit Steffen Lindemann.

Zarys perspektywicznych zadan i celow Urzedu Powierniczego oraz instytucjonalne podstawy ich realizacji, Przedsiebiorstwo w procesie transformacji rynkowej, Uniwersytet Mikolaja Kopernika, Wydzial Nauk Ekonomicznych i Zarzadzania, Thorn 1993, S. 106-122.

Zukünftige Ziele und Aufgaben der Treuhandanstalt, in: Zeitschrift für öffentliche und gemeinwirtschaftliche Unternehmen, Bd. 17 (1994), S. 1-23.

Strategia transformacji systemowej i polityka rynku pracy w Niemczech Wschodnich, ACTA Universitatis Nicolai Copernici, Ekonomia, Vol. XXIII, 1994, S. 45–59.

Welfaretheoretische Kriterien für die Zuordnung von Treuhandvermögen, in: Standortbestimmung öffentlicher Unternehmen in der Sozialen Marktwirtschaft, Hrsg.: Peter Eichhorn, Werner Wilhelm Engelhardt, Schriftenreihe der Gesellschaft für öffentliche Wirtschaft, Bd. 35, Baden-Baden 1994, S. 171-195.

Prospective Tasks and Aims of the Treuhandanstalt and Institutional Perspectives of their Execution with the Help of Public Enterprises, in: Economic Problems and National Unification, Hrsg.: Wolfgang Gerstenberger, Rigmar Osterkamp, ifo Studien zur Ostforschung, München 1994, S. 74-95.

Thesen zur zukünftigen Gestaltung der Treuhandanstalt, in: Zeitschrift für öffentliche und gemeinnützige Unternehmen, Bd. 18, Heft 1 (1994), S. 75-84, zusammen mit Helmut Brede, Hans Hirsch, Karl Oettle.

Die Politik der Treuhandanstalt – Erfolge und unbewältigte Probleme, in: Probleme der deutschen Vereinigung, in: Die Wettbewerbsfähigkeit der ostdeutschen Wirtschaft, Hrsg.: Gernot Gutmann, Schriften des Vereins für Socialpolitik, Bd. 239, Berlin 1995, S.95-165.

Ansätze zu einer Theorie des Vertragsmanagements, in: Zeitschrift für öffentliche und gemeinnützige Unternehmen, Bd. 18, Heft 3, 1995, S. 277-297, zusammen mit Xiao Feng.

The Role of Treuhand in Interregional Competition for the New German States, in: Politische Steuerung moderner Industrie-Gesellschaften des Instituts für Staatswissenschaften der Universität der Bundeswehr München, Heft 8, München 1995, zusammen mit Steffen Lindemann.

Towards a Theory of Contract Management, in: Privatisation in Poland and Germany, Working Paper, Osteuropa Institut München, München 1995, S.116-143, zusammen mit Xiao Feng.

Ein Zulieferkatalog als Instrument der Wirtschaftsförderung für die Wojewodschaft Oppeln, in: Auslandsinvestitionen in Polen, Hrsg.: Peter Friedrich, Jan Tkaczynski, Berlin 1995, S. 177-195.

Wirkungen des Eintritts Polens in die Europäische Union, in: Peter Friedrich, Wydawnictwo Uniwersytetu Mikolaja Kopernika, Hrsg.: Andrzej Jamiolkowski, Thorn 1996, S. 41-50.

Nastepstwa przystapienia Polski do Unii Europejskiej, in: Acta Universitatis Nicolai Copernici, Economia, Bd. 27, Hrsg.: Zenon Wisniewski, Thorn 1996, S. 5-11.

Regional Aspects of Treuhand Contract Management, in: Border Regions, Hrsg.: Knut Ignar Western, Steinkjer 1998, S. 471-507, zusammen mit Xiao Feng.

Cluster Formation in the Framework of the Treuhand Approach: From Socialist to Market-oriented Clusters, in: Clusters and Regional Specialisation, Hrsg.: Michael Steiner, London 1998, S. 129-180, zusammen mit Xiao Feng.

Gebührensteuerung mittels geeigneter Kostenrechnung, in: Preise und Gebühren in der Entsorgungswirtschaft, Hrsg.: Helmut Brede, Schriftenreihe der Gesellschaft für öffentliche Wirtschaft, Bd. 43, Baden-Baden 1998, S. 181-220.

Ein Modell zur Analyse des Vertragsmanagements der Bundesanstalt für vereinigungsbedingte Sonderaufgaben, in: Anwendungen der Spieltheorie, Institut für angewandte Systemforschung und Informatik, Universität der Bundeswehr München, S 97-103, Neubiberg 1997.

Die Rolle öffentlicher Unternehmen bei der Konkurrenz zwischen Regionen, in: Stand und Perspektiven der Öffentlichen Betriebswirtschaftslehre, Hrsg.: Dietmar Bräuning, Dorothea Greiling, Berlin 1999, S. 254-267.

The Treuhandanstalt in Interregional Competition, in: European Spatial Research and Policy, Vol.6 (1999), S. 5-30, zusammen mit Steffen Lindemann.

Economic Effects of Localisation of Tourist Facilities, in: Tourism Sustainability and Territorial Organisation, Hrsg.: ADPR, Coimbra 2000, S.143-174, zusammen mit Xiao Feng, Günter Wonnemann, Klaus Jahn, Günter Valjak.

A Two-levelled Approach to Municipal Competition in Business Promotion, in: Competition and Coexistance in the Process of European Integration, Hrsg.: Ewa Bojar, Warschau 2000, S. 99-126, zusammen mit Steffen Lindemann.

The Role of Public Enterprises in Regional Competition, in: Regional Competition, Hrsg.: Peter Batey, Peter Friedrich, Heidelberg 2000, S. 186-202, zusammen mit Xiao Feng.

Aspects of Regional Competition, in: Regional Competition, Hrsg.: Peter Batey, Peter Friedrich, Heidelberg 2000, S. 3-33, zusammen mit Peter Batey.

Aspects of Policies of Regional Competition, in: Policies of Regional Competition, Hrsg.: Peter Friedrich, Sakari Jutila, Schriften zur öffentichen Verwaltung und öffentlichen Wirtschaft, Bd. 161, Baden-Baden 2001, S. 13-61, zusammen mit Sakari Jutila.

The Role of Public Institutions in Regional Competition in: G. Atalik, M. Fisher, Hrsg.: Regional Development Reconsidered, Berlin, Heidelberg et.al. 2002, S. 79-113, zusammen mit Xiao Feng

FOCJ als Grundlage für Förderinstitutionen "Aufbau-Ost" und "Bevölkerung-Ost", in: Öffentliche Unternehmen im Standortwettbewerb für den Aufbau-Ost, Hrsg.: Peter Friedrich, München 2002, S. 82–115, zusammen mit Stefan Detig und Xiao Feng.

Functional, Overlapping, Competing, Jurisdictions-FOCJ – An Instrument of Regional Competition, in: Urban Regions: Governing Interacting Economic, Housing, and Transport Systems Development, Hrsg.: Jouke van Dijk, Paul Elhorst, Jan Oosterhaven, Egbert Wever, Nederlandse Geografische Studies, Nr. 303, Utrecht 2002, S. 237-263.

Regionaler Wettbewerb im Rahmen der Erweiterung der EU mit Hilfe öffentlicher Unternehmen, in: Wettbewerb und öffentliche Unternehmen, Schriftenreihe des Europakollegs Hamburg zur Integrationsforschung, 42, Hrsg.: Rolf H.Hasse, Karl-Ernst Schenk, Andreas Graf Wass von Czege, Baden-Baden 2004, S. 76-104, zusammen mit Janusz A. Kosiński.

Effects of Taxation on Public Administration, in: Regional Public Finance, Hrsg.: J. Moennesland, London 2003, S. 132–151, zusammen mit Xiao Feng.

Ein Steuerüberwälzungsmodell für Verwaltungen, in: Öffentliche Wirtschaft, Sozialwirtschaft und Daseinsvorsorge im Wandel, Zum Spannungsfeld von Europäischer Wettbewerbsordnung und Allgemeininteresse, Hrsg.: Ulrich Kirchhoff, Gerhard Trilling, Regensburg 2003, S. 81-116, zusammen mit Xiao Feng.

Rola przedsiebiorstw sektora publicznych w ksztaltowaniu konkurencyjnosci regionow europejskich, in: Przeglad Europy Srodkowej i Wschodniej, tom 1 (2003), S. 211-131, zusammen mit Xiao Feng, Janusz A. Kosinski und Joanna Gwiazda.

Ermittlung der Effekte von Sportstadien im europäischen Wettbewerb der Regionen, in: The Polish Economy on the Road to European Union, Hrsg.: Zenon Wisniewski, Thorn 2003, S.154-189, zusammen mit Xiao Feng, Janusz A. Kosinski und Heinrich Günter Wonnemann.

A Standard Chart of Social Accounts for Ecological Banks, in: Finance and Natural Environment, Hrsg.:Leszek Dziawgo, Danuta Dziawgo, Thorn 2003, S.279-322, zusammen mit Janusz A. Kosinski und Ingrid Türk.

Thuringia, Saxony-Anhalt and Saxony as Cases of Transition, in: From Old Industries to New Regions, Hrsg.: Michael Steiner, Graz 2003, S. 215–239

Prinzipal-Agent-Modelle, in: Verwaltungslexikon, Hrsg.: Peter Eichhorn et. al., 3. Aufl., Baden-Baden 2003, S. 835-836.

Public Choice, in: Verwaltungslexikon, Hrsg,: Peter Eichhorn et. al., 3. Aufl., Baden-Baden 2003, S. 856-857.

Transformation der öffentlichen Verwaltung und öffentlichen Wirtschaft, in: Verwaltungslexikon, Hrsg.: Peter Eichhorn et. al., 3. Aufl., Baden-Baden 2003, S. 1049-1051.: Peter Eichhorn et. al., Baden-Baden 2003, S. 1049-1051.

Regionale Konkurrenz, in: Verwaltungslexikon, Hrsg.: Peter Eichhorn et. al., 3. Aufl., Baden-Baden 2003, S. 894-895.

Housing Development in Munich, Housing in European Agglomerations, zusammen mit Piesch (in Druck).

Behördenansiedlung ein erfolgversprechendes Wirtschaftsförderungsinstrument?, in: Business Promotion Activities in Poland and Germany, Wirtschaftsförderung in Polen und Deutschland, Hrsg. Peter Friedrich, Jan Wiktor Tkaczynski, Thorn 2003, S. 115–132.

Local Public Finance in Europe, CESifo working paper, No. 1107, München 2003, zusammen mit Joanna Gwiazda, Chang Won Nam.

Wskaniki konkurencyjnosci i ich rola w badaniu konkurencji regionalnej, in: Miedzynarowodowe uwarunkowiana konkurencynosci regionu, Hrsg.: Wojciech Kosedowskiego,Wloclawek 2004, S.223-253, zusammen mit Joanna Gwiazda, Janusz A. Kosinski und Maciej Lipinski.

Strengthening Municipal Fiscal Autonomy Through Intergovernmental Transfers, in:Urban Dynamics and Growth, Advances in Urban Economics, Hrsg. Peter Nijkamp, Roberta Capello, Amsterdam 2004, S. 691–728, zusammen mit Joanna Gwiazda, Chang-Won Nam.

Überörtliche Sozialhilfe im Freistaat Sachsen und Alternativen zur gegenwärtigen Verteilung von Aufgaben und Kostenträgerschaft für überörtliche Sozialleistungen, ifo-Forschungsberichte, Heft 21, München 2004, zusammen mit Jochen Hammerschick, Helmut Hartmann und Rüdiger Parsche.

Die Besteuerung gemeinnütziger Organisationen im internationalen Vergleich, Ifo Forschungsberichte, Bd. 24, München 2005, zusammen mit Anita Kaltschütz, Chang Woon Nam, Rüdiger Parsche, Dietmar Wellisch.

Aspects of Regional Population Development, in: New Members – New Challenges for the European Regional Development Policy, Hrsg. Tadeusz Markowski, Maciej Turala, Warschau 2006, S. 72–85, zusammen mir Werner Wimmert.

FOCJ as Institution of Population Policy, in: New Members – New Challenges for the European Regional Development Policy, Hrsg. Tadeusz Markowski, Maciej Turala, Warschau 2006, S. 228–242, zusammen mit Alina Popescu

Berücksichtigung von volkswirtschaftlichen Auswirkungen bei den Entscheidungen über die Einbindung privater Unternehmen in PPP, in: Die XIV. Wirtschaftspolitische Konferenz, Berlin, Tallin 2006, S. 263-290.

Assets of Estonian Central Bank after Starting Using EURO, in: Finanse I Rachunowosc Wobec Wyzwan Procesow Globalizacyjnych, Hrsg. Jan Gluchowski, Torun 2007, S. 57-73, zusammen mit Janno Reiljan.

Ein verwaltungsökonomisches Standortmodell, in: Stand und Perspektiven der Öffentlichen Betriebswirtschaftslehre II, Hrsg. Dietmar Bräuning, Dorothea Greiling, Berlin 2007, S. 257-271, zusammen mit Xiao Feng

Öffentliche Unternehmen in Estland, in: Zeitschrift für öffentliche und gemeinnützige Unternehmen, Bd. 30 (2007) , S. 89-106, zusammen mit Kairi Ramcke.

II. Forschungsberichte, Diskussionspapiere

Ansätze zu einer Wachstumstheorie für einzelne Verwaltungen, Diskussionspapier Nr. 2, Lehrstuhl für Finanzwissenschaft, Universität Bamberg, Bamberg 1980.

Auswirkungen von Standortentscheidungen für Dienststellen des Bundes und des Landes auf die Standortgemeinde und das Umland, Abschlußbericht eines Forschungsprojektes für das Land Nordrhein-Westfalen, Bamberg 1981, zusammen mit Heinrich Günter Wonnemann.

Forschungsberichte über volkswirtschaftliche und haushaltsmäßige Effekte von Stadthallen, Kultur- und Kongresshallen und kulturellen Einrichtungen: Bamberg 1983, Freiburg 1985, Regensburg 1986, Itzehoe 1987, Osnabrück 1992, Dresden 1992, zusammen mit Georg Crezelius, Hans-Ulrich Derlien, Günter Valjak und Heinrich Günter Wonnemann.

Forschungsberichte über volkswirtschaftliche und haushaltsmäßige Effekte einer Fernwärmeversorgung und deren Bewertung: Erlangen 1981 zusammen mit Gerhard Schoolmann, Dimitrios Tsimopoulos, Heinrich Günter Wonnemann für das Bundesministerium für Raumordnung, Bauwesen und Städtebau.

Forschungsberichte über volkswirtschaftliche und haushaltsmäßige Effekte von Bildungseinrichtungen und Forschungsinstituten: Geophysikalisches Institut, Bamberg 1983, Akademie für moderne Ernährung, Kulmbach 1983, Führungsakademie einer Bundesanstalt, Bamberg 1984, Universität Bamberg , Bamberg 1984, zusammen mit Edith Buckl und Heinrich Günter Wonnemann.

Forschungsberichte über Verlagerungen von Landesverwaltungen, Oberfranken 1984, zusammen mit Edith Buckl und Heinrich Günter Wonnemann.

Forschungsbericht über die ökonomischen, haushaltsmäßigen und sozialpsychologischen Wirkungen einer Zusammenführung städtischer Behörden und ihrer Bewertung, Weissenburg 1985, zusammen mit Hermann Liebel.

Forschungsbericht über die ökonomischen und haushaltsmäßigen Effekte von Einzelhandelsansiedlungen, Kulmbach 1986, zusammen mit Werner Wimmert, Heinrich Günter Wonnemann.

Forschungsberichte über Wirkungen des Straßenbaues in Siegen, Bamberg 1987, ein Konzept für den innerstädtischen Verkehr in Kulmbach, Kulmbach 1988, zusammen mit Werner Wimmert und Analyse der Hotelsituation in einer Mittelstadt, Bamberg 1988.

Forschungsbericht über die volkswirtschaftlichen und fiskalischen Effekte des "World Tourist Center Oberhausen", Oberhausen 1989 zusammen mit Sylvia Golder, Stefan Rohrwasser und Günter Wonnemann.

Forschungsbericht über die Umwidmung von Schulen im Freistaat Bayern, Bamberg 1989 zusammen mit Peter Buba und Peter Gross.

Forschungsbericht zu Vorschlägen zur Gestaltung der Investitionspolitik in Polen, München 1990 zusammen mit Sylvia Golder, Zenon Wisniewski, Janusz Czarnek und Jerzy Tomala.

Forschungsbericht über die Besteuerung der Treuhandanstalt, München 1991 zusammen mit Joachim Göldner.

Forschungsbericht über die Probleme der Zuliefererindustrie in Polen, München 1992, zusammen mit Sylvia Golder, Barbara Perner und Zenon Wisniewski.

Forschungsbericht über "Ein Kontenrahmen für das gesellschaftsbezogene Rechnungswesen der Stadthalle Osnabrück", München 1992, zusammen mit Günter Valjak und Klaus Jahn.

Forschungsbericht über "Effekte des Veranstaltungsverbundes Dresden", Osnabrück, München, 1993, zusammen mit Günter Valjak und Heinrich-Günter Wonnemann

Forschungsbericht über "Effekte des Neubrandenburger Verbundes für Veranstaltungen", Osnabrück, München, 1994, zusammen mit Peter Börner, Günter Valjak und Heinrich Günter Wonnemann.

Forschungsbericht über "Eine Treuhandanstalt für die Volksrepublik China", München 1995 zusammen mit Xiao Feng
Forschungsbericht über "Volkswirtschaftliche Effekte des CENTRIC – Center for Information and Communication", Regensdorf / Zürich, München 1996.

Forschungsbericht: Adäquate Standortpolitik für die Volksrepublik China, zusammen mit Xiao Feng, München 2000.

Forschungsbericht: Erkenntnisse zur Transformation von Industrien in Sachsen-Anhalt und Thüringen, München 2001.

Forschungsbericht: Effekte des neuen Fußballstadions München, Industrie- und Handelskammer für München und Oberbayern, München 2001, zusammen mit Xiao Feng, Janusz A. Kosiński und Heinrich Günter Wonnemann.

Berichte zur überörtlichen Sozialhilfe im Freistaat Sachsen für das Ifoinstitut, München 2003, zusammen mit Alina Popescu.

Forschungsbericht: Effekte der Spiele der Fußballweltmeisterschaft 2006 in München, Industrie- und Handelskammer für München und Oberbayern, München 2005, zusammen mit Alina Popescu und Heinrich Günter Wonnemann.

Regional Competition under Transformation Conditions, Lehrstuhl für Finanzwissenschaft, Universität der Bundeswehr München, München 2005.

Forschungsbericht: Volkswirtschaftliche und Fiskalische Effekte der Magnetbahnverbindung vom Hauptbahnhof der Landeshauptstadt zum Franz-Josef-Strauß Flughafen in München, München 2006, zusammen mit Alina Popescu und Heinrich Günter Wonnemann.

III. Sonstige Publikationstätigkeiten

Herausgeberschaften: Schriften zur öffentlichen Verwaltung und öffentlichen Wirtschaft beimm Nomos-Verlag, Baden-Baden und dem Berliner Wissenschaftsverlag, Berlin, bis Ende des Jahres 2006 , zusammen mit Peter Eichhorn.

Weitere Publikationen betreffen die Herausgebertätigkeit bei einzelnen Sammelwerken sowie von Sammelwerken, die Mitherausgeberschaft des Verwalungslexikons, Baden-Baden, die Mitarbeit an Stellungnahmen, insbesondere des Wissenschaftlichen Beirates der Gesellschaft für öffentliche Wirtschaft, Berlin, und etliche Zeitungsartikel.

Lebensdaten von
Prof. Dr. Dr. h.c. Peter Friedrich

Studium der Volkswirtschaftslehre an der Westfälischen Wilhelms-Universität Münster, Diplomexamen 1964 als Volkswirt an der Universität Münster, 1964 wissenschaftlicher Assistent und Akademischer Rat an der Universität Münster, Habilitation 1974 an der Universität Münster, 1974 Dozent an der Universität Münster, 1974-1978 Übernahme des Lehrstuhls für Finanzwissenschaft an der Universität Siegen, 1978-1988 Lehrstuhl für Finanzwissenschaft an der Otto-Friedrich-Universität Bamberg, ab 1988 Lehrstuhl für Finanzwissenschaft an der Universität der Bundeswehr München, Ehrenpromotion der Nikolaus-Kopernikus-Universität Thorn/Toruń 1996, Mitwirkung in der Lehre in der Volkswirtschaftlichen Fakultät der Ludwig-Maximilians-Universität München, an der Hochschule für Politik München und in Verwaltungs- und Wirtschafts-akademien, Beteiligung an den Arbeiten im Internationalen Institut für Kommunal- und Freizeitwirtschaft München, sowie in der Gesellschaft zur Förderung der regionalen und urbanen Strukturforschung-GFS-e.V., Wyzsza Szkota Bankowa Toruń Polen, Extraordinariat für Finanzwissenschaft an der Universität Tartu, Estland.

SCHRIFTEN zur öffentlichen Verwaltung und öffentlichen Wirtschaft

Herausgegeben von:

Prof. Dr. Dr. h. c. mult. Peter Eichhorn
Universität Mannheim

Prof. Dr. Dr. h. c. Peter Friedrich
Universität der Bundeswehr München

188 Dominik Böllhoff
The Regulatory Capacity of Agencies
A Comparative Study of Telecoms Regulatory Agencies in Britain and Germany
2005, 283 S., geb., engl., 58,– Euro, ISBN 978-3-8305-0845-8

189 Gabriele Roth
IuK-gestützte Prozesskostenrechnung für Netzwerke von Krankenhäusern
2004, 434 S., geb., 79,– Euro, ISBN 978-3-8305-0839-7

190 Kai Gregor Klinger
Kapitalmarktorientierte Beteiligungsfinanzierung für stationäre Gesundheitsunternehmen
2005, 282 S., geb., 58,– Euro, ISBN 978-3-8305-1052-7

191 Elisabeth Maria Leonhard
Abgrenzung von klinischer Forschung, Lehre und Krankenhausversorgung
Auswirkungen auf Finanzierung und Organisation von Universitätsklinika
2005, 236 S., geb., 32 s/w Abb., 44,– Euro, ISBN 978-3-8305-1051-9

192 Jörg Meinen
Konzernrecht im kommunalen Bereich
2006, 357 S., geb., 69,– Euro, ISBN 978-3-8305-1125-0

193 Andrej Teterin
Unternehmensbewertung von Nonprofit-Unternehmen
Nutzenorientierte Beteiligungsbewertung am Beispiel von Krankenhäusern
2006, 253 S., geb., 59,– Euro, ISBN 978-3-8305-1231-8